Offshore Tax Planning

Offshore Tax Planning

Giles Clarke
MA (Cantab), PhD, FTII, Barrister

Thirteenth Edition

LexisNexis®
Tolley

Members of the LexisNexis Group worldwide

United Kingdom	LexisNexis Butterworths, a Division of Reed Elsevier (UK) Ltd, RSH, 1–3 Baxter's Place, Leith Walk, EDINBURGH EH1 3AF and Halsbury House, 35 Chancery Lane, LONDON WC2A 1EL
Argentina	LexisNexis Argentina, Buenos Aires
Australia	LexisNexis Butterworths, Chatswood, New South Wales
Austria	LexisNexis Verlag ARD Orac GmbH & Co KG, Vienna
Benelux	LexisNexis Benelux, Amsterdam
Canada	LexisNexis Canada, Markham, Ontario
Chile	LexisNexis Chile Ltda, Santiago
China	LexisNexis China, Beijing and Shanghai
France	LexisNexis SA, Paris
Germany	LexisNexis Deutschland GmbH, Munster
Hong Kong	LexisNexis Hong Kong, Hong Kong
India	LexisNexis India, New Delhi
Italy	Giuffrè Editore, Milan
Japan	LexisNexis Japan, Tokyo
Malaysia	Malayan Law Journal Sdn Bhd, Kuala Lumpur
Mexico	LexisNexis Mexico, Mexico
New Zealand	LexisNexis NZ Ltd, Wellington
Poland	Wydawnictwo Prawnicze LexisNexis Sp, Warsaw
Singapore	LexisNexis Singapore, Singapore
South Africa	LexisNexis Butterworths, Durban
USA	LexisNexis, Dayton, Ohio

Published by LexisNexis Butterworths

A CIP Catalogue record for this book is available from the British Library.

1st edition 1986	6th edition 1999	13th edition 2006
2nd edition 1990	7th edition 2000	
3rd edition 1994	8th edition 2001	
Reprinted 1995	9th edition 2002	
4th edition 1996	10th edition 2003	
Special edition 1997	11th edition 2004	
5th edition 1998	12th edition 2005	

ISBN 1 405 71113 2

Typeset by Columns Design Ltd, Reading, England

Printed and bound in Great Britain by CPI Bath Press, Bath

Visit LexisNexis Butterworths at: www.lexisnexis.co.uk

Preface

I have expanded this edition to take account of the many changes which have occurred during the past year. The most important are the Finance Act provisions dealing with trusts, the Court of Appeal decision in *Wood v Holden*, and the judgment of the European Court of Justice in *Cadbury Schweppes plc v CIR*.

The law is stated as at 31 August 2006, although I have included the decision in *Cadbury Schweppes* and one or two other later developments.

As always I am indebted to the many colleagues and readers who have discussed or commented on different aspects of the book. But responsibility for errors remains mine alone.

Giles Clarke
1 October 2006

Contents

Table of Statutes

Table of Statutory Instruments

Table of Cases

A

B

C

D

E

F

G

H

I

J

K

L

M

N

O

P

Q

R

S

T

U

V

W

X

Y

Decisions of the European Court of Justice are listed below numerically. These decisions are also included in the preceding alphabetical list.

Part A

Planning

Section I

Introduction

Chapter 1

Introduction

What is offshore tax planning?

1.1 Offshore tax planning may be defined as arrangements which use the territorial limits of the UK tax code to minimise UK tax without incurring significant tax liabilities in other jurisdictions. In general the ultimate owner or beneficiary is able to continue living in the UK but in some scenarios emigration may be contemplated.

Private clients

1.2 In relation to private clients offshore tax planning has two principal applications. The first is the sheltering of income and gains which may be achieved for UK domiciliaries through entities resident abroad. The most effective vehicle is the offshore trust, but offshore companies, mutual funds, and even life policies figure as well. Offshore tax planning of this kind is described in Section II of this Part.

The second application is the use of the various reliefs available to non-domiciliaries to shelter their assets and income from UK tax. Such sheltering relies on the remittance basis for income tax and capital gains tax and on the excluded property concept under inheritance tax. Offshore entities also figure prominently, specifically the excluded property settlement. Tax planning for non-domiciliaries is discussed in Section V of this Part.

At the time of writing a question hangs over the favourable tax regime for non-domiciliaries, for the government is reviewing the rules relating to residence and domicile. A background paper was published in April 2003 and the government is continuing to consider whether and if so what reform is required.

Business

1.3 International groups make widespread use of offshore jurisdictions and of high-tax jurisdictions which offer incentives to attract inward investment. In the main such activity may be characterised as international tax planning rather than purely offshore tax planning. In general it is designed to minimise tax on income flows and overall tax on global profits. An analysis of how offshore structures may be used in a business context is given in Section VI of this Part, and the two key anti-avoidance codes, the CFC legislation and that relating to transfer pricing, are explained in Chapters 67 and 68.

Offshore jurisdictions

1.4 In order to avoid tax outside the UK the entities used in these various kinds of tax planning need to be based in offshore jurisdictions. In such jurisdictions, nil or nominal direct taxes are payable either generally or at least by certain categories of taxpayer such as companies or trusts owned or settled by foreigners. For many years the core offshore jurisdictions have been islands in Europe and the Caribbean and this is why the term offshore is used even as respects jurisdictions which are totally landlocked.

Most of the main offshore jurisdictions are British in the sense that they are Crown Dependencies, Overseas Territories, or former colonies. During the latter part of the twentieth century, development of their financial sectors was in many cases encouraged by the British authorities. For the UK practitioner, the great advantage of these jurisdictions is that their trust and company laws mostly follow English law and thus are familiar. This work does not include any review of offshore jurisdictions, but such may be found in *Spitz and Clarke: Offshore Service* (LexisNexis Butterworths looseleaf). That publication also contains the trust and company legislation of the key jurisdictions and reports of cases decided offshore.

Official response

1.5 Offshore tax planning and the use of offshore jurisdictions deny the UK tax authorities of revenue which they might otherwise secure. It is tempting to conclude that as a result offshore tax planning is per se undesirable, but this would be a mistake. Often it is simply a means of enabling those affected by otherwise unreasonable tax rules to minimise the economic damage those rules can cause. A prime example is capital gains tax on trading company shares, which was widely avoided in the 1980s by means of offshore trusts. Now the economic drawbacks of such tax have been recognised by taper relief which delivers onshore much of what previously had to be achieved offshore.

National anti-avoidance rules

1.6 Nonetheless, as a general rule the UK tax authorities have sought to counter offshore tax planning. Since the 1930s, successive Finance Acts have deployed a powerful body of anti-avoidance legislation, all of which is analysed in Part B of this work. In the 1990s legislation was enacted which focuses on CGT avoidance and as a result many offshore trusts which were set up before then now have to be operated in an altogether harsher fiscal climate. Planning strategies for these trusts are discussed in Section III of this Part.

An issue of growing interest is the extent to which UK anti-avoidance legislation infringes European law and thus is inoperative. This subject is discussed in Chapters 48 and 49 and is cross-referenced at appropriate points elsewhere.

International initiatives

1.7 In recent years, the official response to offshore jurisdictions has moved to an international level, a move which gained impetus after the first election of the UK's present Labour government in 1997.

Both the OECD and the European Union have attacked what they call harmful tax competition. Thus in 1998, the OECD published its seminal paper, 'Harmful Tax Competition: An Emerging Global Issue'. So too, on 1 December 1997, the EU adopted a Tax Package which led, inter alia, to the Savings Directive discussed in Chapter 50. The global assault on money laundering has also caught tax within its purview in that many jurisdictions, both onshore and offshore, now consider that tax evasion is a crime whose proceeds are caught by money laundering law.

But what is to be stressed about all the attacks is that their thrust is directed at evasion, lack of transparency, and discrimination. Thus money-laundering only comes into issue if tax has been evaded somewhere. So too, after some hesitation, the OECD and the European Union have accepted that offshore jurisdictions can levy no or nil tax provided they do so in a non-discriminatory manner and implement robust regulatory frameworks and information exchange. In short, legitimate tax planning is unaffected.

Planning and evasion

1.8 It is to be stressed that it is lawful tax planning which is the subject of this book. The planning strategies described in the following chapters presuppose that all tax liabilities are properly returned and that full disclosure of the relevant facts is made to the UK tax authorities, so that the efficacy or otherwise of what is set up can be determined in a proper and open manner.

It cannot be emphasised too strongly that full disclosure is essential. This is not only because such is the law under which the ultimate sanction for non-compliance is criminal prosecution. It is also because once full disclosure is made, penalties should be precluded and HMRC have only the one-year period allowed under the self-assessment system within which to raise an enquiry (TMA 1970, ss 9A and 29(3)).

Section II

UK Domiciliaries

Chapter 2

Offshore trusts

Introduction

2.1 This chapter considers the extent to which offshore trusts created now serve as a tax shelter. It presupposes that the setllor is both resident and domiciled in the UK. The taxes it focuses on are income tax, capital gains tax, and inheritance tax and the trusts it considers are traditional, private family trusts.

Income tax

2.2 An offshore trust can shelter income if the following conditions are met:

(1) All the trustees are non-resident.
(2) The trust is discretionary in form.
(3) The income is foreign source.
(4) The settlor and his spouse are wholly excluded and neither receives any benefit.

Residency of the trustees

2.3 The reason why all the trustees must be non-resident is that a settlement created or funded by a UK resident is only non-resident if all the trustees are non-resident. This is as described in Chapter 37.

Form of trust

2.4 The trust must be discretionary in form because, for income tax purposes, a trust is fiscally transparent if it is subject to a life interest or to some other interest conferring the income on a beneficiary as of right. In such a case, the income is deemed to be that of the interest-holder as it arises and so, assuming the interest-holder is UK resident, UK tax is payable. This result is however avoided if the terms of the trust give the trustees discretion over the income. Any distributions in such a case are a new source of income, taxable only to the extent of what is distributed. This is explained further in Chapter 12.

Nature of the income

2.5 The reason why the income must be foreign source is that the UK income of non-resident trusts is taxable at the rate applicable to trusts (FA 1995, s 128(5)). As is explained in Chapter 34, this applies to all forms of UK income, including dividends and interest. The latter are only exempt from tax in the hands of non-resident trustees if none of the beneficiaries is UK resident (see para 34.14).

In many instances, this need to avoid UK source income can be circumvented by holding UK investments through an offshore holding company. The result of such a company is that any income received by the trust is foreign-source dividends paid by the company rather than the underlying UK income. The company itself attracts the general exemption enjoyed by non-residents on dividend and interest income and tax on other classes of income (e g rents) is restricted to the basic rate.

The use of offshore holding companies is discussed further in Chapter 9. There can be countervailing disadvantages.

Exclusion of the settlor and his spouse

2.6 The reason why the settlor and his spouse must be excluded is that without such exclusion the settlement is ineffective for income tax purposes. This is because the income of an offshore trust is assessable as the settlor's if the actual or potential beneficiaries include him or his spouse, if either of them receives a benefit, or if either of them has ever received a capital sum. This is achieved by two sets of provisions, namely TA 1988, s 739 and ITTOIA 2005, Part 5, Chapter 5. The first of these codes deals with the transfer of assets abroad, whether or not involving settlements, and the second is concerned with settlements, whether resident or non-resident.

The settlement code is analysed in Chapter 59. The principal section, ITTOIA 2005, s 624, attributes the income of the settlement to the settlor unless the income is from property in which he has no interest. A settlor has no interest in property only if neither the property nor its income nor any property derived from them are payable or applicable to or for his or his spouse's benefit in any circumstances whatsoever. Income can also be attributed to the settlor if it is paid to his minor children (ITTOIA 2005, s 629) or if he or his spouse receives a capital sum, which includes receiving a loan or being repaid a loan (ITTOIA 2005, s 633).

Section 739 is analysed in Chapters 54 and 55. Unlike the settlement code it extends to all types of offshore arrangement, whether or not involving settlements or bounty. It is, however, subject to a motive test. It applies if the person responsible for setting up the offshore arrangements, the transferor, has what is called power to enjoy, or if he receives or has ever received a capital sum. Power to enjoy is exhaustively defined, but basically a transferor has power to enjoy if he or his spouse benefits, or could in any circumstances benefit, from the offshore arrangements or if they have non-fiduciary powers of control. If any of these conditions is satisfied, the entirety of the offshore income is taxed as that of the transferor.

As will be apparent, there is a wide area of overlap between the settlement code and s 739. In cases of overlap HMRC tend to invoke the settlement code. In tax planning terms four points may be made about s 739. First, the term 'transferor' may extend to persons associated with the setting up of the offshore arrangements as well as to the transferor proper (see para 55.24). Second, receipt of a capital sum occurs if a loan is made to the settlor or a loan made by the settlor is repaid. Third, once a capital sum has been received by the settlor or his spouse s 739 applies not merely in the tax year in which the sum is received but in subsequent years even if the settlor and his spouse are then wholly excluded and do not receive benefit. Fourth, power to enjoy is widely construed. A transferor could, for example, have power to enjoy if the offshore transferee meets his moral obligations or even purchases properties from him in adverse market conditions (cf para 55.5 and *IRC v Brackett* [1986] STC 521).

As references to spouses are now extended to include civil partners, the terms of the settlement must also ensure no civil partner of the settlor could benefit. This is so even if the settlor has no intention whatsoever of ever entering into a civil partnership (see para 55.28).

Deferral or shelter

2.7 Assuming the above conditions are met, the income of the trust is sheltered from UK tax as it arises. Strictly the shelter is merely a deferral, for UK tax has to be faced if income or capital is distributed to UK resident beneficiaries. As is described in Chapters 12 and 13, income distributions are taxed as a new source, and capital is taxed under TA 1988, s 740 to the extent that income has been or is retained in the structure. In contrast to CGT (see below), the tax on capital distributions is not inflated by notional interest to reflect the element of deferment. But to some extent this is counterbalanced by the fact that tax under s 740 does not give credit for any withholding tax suffered by the trustees when the income matched with the benefit arose (see para 56.8).

In reality, however, deferral often turns out to be a complete shelter. Such follows if capital is distributed to a beneficiary who has emigrated, for then, provided the beneficiary is non-resident throughout the tax year of the distribution, no tax is chargeable under s 740. There is no requirement for him to be non-resident for at least five tax years, such as characterises CGT (cf para 27.7).

Equally cogently, there may come a time when beneficiaries look for not the accumulated capital but merely income. Such is taxable as income when distributed, but the income available is enhanced, like a pension fund, by the prior gross accumulation of income within the trust. Further the rate of tax on such distributions may be reduced either by spreading them around low income beneficiaries (so as to use personal allowances and basic rate bands) or by appointing life interests to one or more beneficiaries. As explained in Chapters 43 and 44, such appointments are now without IHT consequences and enable the income to attract the dividend rates in the hands of the beneficiaries (see para 12.2). It should however be noted that if a strategy of distribution is adopted, the recipients cannot include minor children of the settlor, as any distributions to them are taxable as his income (para 59.8).

Capital gains tax

2.8 An offshore trust shelters capital gains if the following conditions are met:

(1) The trustees are all non-resident.
(2) None of the assets settled is pregnant with gain when transferred to the trust.
(3) The settlor, his children, his grandchildren, and their respective spouses are all excluded.

Residency of the trust

2.9 All the trustees must be non-resident as, with effect from 6 April 2007, the trust residency rules applicable to CGT will be the same as those described above in relation to income tax. In addition the general administration of the trusts must be carried on abroad. This is a requirement of the CGT residency rules until 5 April 2007 (see para 37.4).

Once it is established that the trust is non-resident, it does not matter what form the trust takes, as all settlements (other than nominee property) are opaque for CGT purposes (TCGA 1992, s 69(1)). So too it does not matter where the trust assets are situate, for CGT is chargeable only on UK residents (see para 30.5). One exception arises if the non-resident trust is trading in the UK through a branch or agency. In this event the UK branch or agency assets are subject to CGT (TCGA 1992, s 10). This is not of great practical importance but can be material if, for example, the trust owns in-hand UK farmland.

Assets settled

2.10 The reason why none of the assets settled should be pregnant with gain is that the transfer of the assets to the settlement is a disposal for CGT purposes. As the settlor is treated as connected with the settlement, the disposal takes place at the market value of the assets concerned (TCGA 1992, ss 18 and 286). This means that if the assets are showing a gain, liability to CGT results. The gain can be offset by losses, but only by losses realised on other disposals to the same settlement (TCGA 1992, s 18(3)).

The practical result of this is that the assets settled should normally be cash or assets not showing an overall net gain. Further the cash should be sterling unless the foreign currency concerned has depreciated against sterling over the period during which the settlor has held it. This is because foreign currency is a chargeable asset for CGT purposes (TCGA 1992, s 21(1)(b)).

Under UK domestic law, no form of hold-over relief is available on the transfer of the assets to the settlement as the trustees are non-resident (TCGA 1992, ss 166 and 261). It is possible that this limitation on hold-over relief will, in certain cases, be held to breach European law, but it would be unwise to plan in reliance on this happening (see further para 49.14).

At one time taxpayers could have their cake and eat it. This was possible if the circumstances were such that hold-over relief was available on a gift into a resident trust. Where this was so, the assets were transferred into what was called a 'freezer trust', a settlement which was initially resident and which qualified for hold-over relief. The gain was held over and then, in the year of assessment before the assets were sold, the trust migrated. The migration triggered a charge on the held-over gain (FA 1981, s 79), but the subsequent gain was relieved for, by the time it was realised, the trust was non-resident.

Unfortunately, proceeding in this way is not attractive now, for migration occasions a deemed disposal of all the trust assets at market value. As is described in para 28.7, any gain is taxed as the settlor's if he or his spouse are beneficiaries, and otherwise at the trust rate of 40%. It may be that this restriction could in some cases be held to be in breach of EU law but here too it would be unwise to plan in reliance on this point (see para 49.16).

Exclusion of the settlor and his family

2.11 The reason why the settlor's family as well as the settlor have to be excluded is that the net gains of a non-resident settlement are assessable as the settlor's in the tax year in which they arise if what is called a defined person is an actual or potential beneficiary or receives a benefit. The term 'defined person' means not only merely the settlor and his spouse, but also his children and grandchildren and their respective spouses, and companies controlled by all or any of the individual defined persons. These rules are laid down by TCGA 1992, s 86 and Sch 5, and are considered in detail in Chapter 60.

The extended definition of defined person means TCGA 1992, s 86 is the most far-reaching anti-avoidance legislation directed at trusts, whether resident or non-resident. All other anti-avoidance legislation applies only if the settlor or his spouse can or do benefit. The result of s 86 is that gains in an offshore settlement can be attributed to the settlor in many cases where the income is not so attributable.

It may be that in some cases the extension of s 86 to children's and grandchildren's settlements from which the settlor is wholly excluded will be held to be in breach of European law. But as is explained in paras 49.9 and 49.10, significant conceptual hurdles would have to be overcome before this could happen.

Should the settlement be one in which all the settlor's family are excluded, such exclusion, to be effective, must extend to civil partners and any future civil partners as well. As is explained in para 60.9, this is so even if none of the individuals concerned has any intention of ever entering into such a relationship.

Deferral or shelter

2.12 It might be felt that the rules in TCGA 1992, s 86 mean offshore trusts rarely operate as a CGT shelter for UK domiciliaries. In fact this is not so, as self-evidently those rules do not apply when the settlor is dead. Nor do they apply should he decide to emigrate (although, as is explained in para 27.7, non-residence for at least five complete tax years is necessary).

Strictly speaking, the CGT sheltering in such cases operates only as a deferral, on account of the capital payments rules considered in Chapters 63 and 64. They subject capital distributions and other benefits to CGT if the recipient is resident and domiciled in the UK and insufficiency of income means the distribution or benefit is not taxed under TA 1988, s 740. A capital distribution or benefit is only so taxed to the extent that capital gains have been or are in the future realised in the trust or any underlying company. But should the distribution be matched with old gains, the rate of tax is increased by notional interest, the top rate being 64% should the gains be six or more years old (see para 63.29).

The notional interest element in these rules to a large extent counteracts the advantage of the deferral. But even so, the impact of the rules should not be overstated. First, they do not impose tax where the recipient of the capital distribution has emigrated, provided he is non-resident for at least five complete tax years (see paras 63.22 and 63.23). Indeed, in such cases gains are still carried out from the trust pool to the distribution, raising the possibility that subsequent distributions to UK residents can be tax-free (see Chapter 14). Second, if capital is not distributed at all, but income is paid out as current income as per para 13.7, the tax on capital payments does not come into issue, the trust gains simply representing a further tax-free augmentation of the fund generating the income.

Inheritance tax

2.13 Assuming the settlor is UK domiciled, the IHT regime applicable to a trust is the same whether the trust is onshore or offshore. This is because the determinant of IHT liability is the domicile of the settlor rather than the residence of the trustees (see Chapter 45). The regime as it now exists following FA 2006 is explained in Chapters 43 and 44. In summary, the position is as follows:

(1) A gift into trust is immediately chargeable, regardless of whether the trust is discretionary or fixed-interest. Once the settlor's nil-rate band is

exceeded the rate of tax is 20%. The nil rate band is £285,000 in 2006–07 and will be £300,000 in 2007–08 (FA 2005, s 98).

(2) A charge on the entire value of the trust is made every ten years. This too is made regardless of the form of the trust. As is explained in Chapter 43, the maximum rate is 6% and in practice it may be less.

(3) IHT is also charged when property is distributed from the trust. This, the exit charge, is levied at a rate depending on how long has elapsed since the last 10-yearly charge. But as with that charge, the rate can never exceed 6%.

Far and away the most significant of these charges is the entry charge, being at 20% rather than 6%. Indeed, the rate of 20% rises to 40% if the settlor dies within three years, to 32% if he dies in the fourth year, and 24% if he dies in the fifth year.

Tax at this level does, if in fact payable, operate as a deterrent. This is particularly so as outright gifts to other individuals qualify as potentially exempt transfers. In other words, no tax is payable provided the donor survives seven years (IHTA 1984, s 3A). Given this, IHT may be thought to be a powerful argument against offshore trusts, outweighing any advantages of the kind described earlier in this chapter.

In reality, however, this is not so, as there are at least three scenarios on which the entry charge is avoided. The first and most obvious is the nil-rate band. Provided a putative settlor has made no chargeable transfers in the previous seven years, he can give an amount equal to the nil-rate band into a trust without charge to IHT. If he then waits a further seven years without making any other chargeable transfers, he can repeat the exercise, up to whatever limit the nil-rate band then stands at.

The values thus able to be settled may not be great, but they are significant and can be enhanced by two factors. The first is that, in a marriage, the spouses each enjoy a nil-rate band, thereby enabling the tax-free amount to be doubled up. Second, once value is settled into a trust, any growth in value is in the trust and outside the settlor's estate. Thus if growth assets are acquired in the trust, the value in the trust after a few years may be much greater than the nil-rate band. This is particularly in point where shares in young or newly formed private companies are acquired.

The second scenario in which the entry charge is avoided is if the gift into settlement qualifies as normal expenditure out of income. Under IHTA 1984, s 21, a transfer is exempt if it is part of the donor's normal expenditure and is made out of his income, leaving him with sufficient income to maintain his normal standard of living. It is necessary to establish a pattern of regular annual transfers, either retrospectively by what has happened over a number of years, or by prior commitment (see *Bennett v IRC* [1995] STC 54). But once these conditions are met, the gifts are free of IHT and this is so whether the donee is an individual or a trust.

These days many wealthy individuals have substantial incomes way in excess of what is needed to maintain a normal standard of living. With careful planning the surplus can be passed into trust.

The third scenario is where the property settled qualifies for business property relief. This important relief normally comes into issue where unquoted shares in a trading company or group are settled (IHTA 1984, ss 104 and 105(1)(bb)). The important point to remember is that the settlor must have owned the property concerned for at least two years prior to the gift. Further, the business assets must be retained by the trustees for seven years thereafter if the gift is to be free of the IHT charge made should the settlor die within seven years (IHTA 1984, s 113A).

These three scenarios mean that, with careful planning, substantial value can be vested in an offshore trust without IHT charge. A point to stress is that these scenarios do need to be taken advantage of, for IHT is perceived to be a tax of growing severity. It is true that as noted above it is avoided by outright gifts more than seven years before death. But many families do not want to make outright gifts either because the intended recipients are too young or because, even if not too young, they may inevitably at some stage be exposed to commercial risks or the capriciousness of the English divorce courts.

Factors such as this mean that, with careful planning, IHT is an argument in favour of creating trusts rather than the reverse. It is true that once in the trust the assets may attract the charge of 6% every ten years. But to many this is an acceptable price to pay. This is particularly so now that all assets in newly created trusts are outside the estates of the beneficiaries and thus free of IHT even if untimely death means tax on the beneficiary's free estate has not been avoided by potentially exempt transfers. Further, the 6% every ten years may be avoided or reduced by two of the scenarios described above, namely the nil-rate band and business property relief. Property attracting 100% business property relief is not subject to the 10-yearly or exit charges (IHTA 1984, s 103(1)), and, even if that relief is not in point, those charges normally allow a nil-rate band (see paras 43.3 and 43.6).

For all these reasons, settlements represent an attractive IHT planning opportunity. A final point to make is that, as with income tax and CGT, the settlor should not be a beneficiary or able to benefit. If this condition is breached, the settled property is likely to be treated as remaining his for IHT purposes under the gift with reservation rules (see Chapter 47).

Sheltering now possible

2.14 The above discussion shows that an appropriately structured offshore trust created by a UK domiciliary can still operate as a shelter for income and gains. There are three main contexts where this is possible:

(a) Settlements where the settlor is dead.

(b) Settlements where all defined persons within the meaning of TCGA 1992, s 86 are excluded.

(c) Children's and grandchildren's settlements designed as an income shelter.

Settlements where the settlor is dead

2.15 It is self-evident that the rules attributing income and gains to the settlor cannot apply if he is dead. Indeed, gains realised at any time in the tax year of death cannot be attributed to him either (TCGA 1992, Sch 5 para 3).

A settlement is in the position of having a dead settlor if it is an inter vivos settlement whose settlor has died or if it is a testamentary settlement. One advantage of a testamentary settlement is that the assets secure a tax-free updated base cost by reason of the settlor's death (TCGA 1992, s 62). The CGT advantages of an offshore settlement do not obtain during administration, for personal representatives have the deceased's residence and domicile (TCGA 1992, s 62(3)), but the vesting of the property in the trustees is not a CGT disposal (ibid, s 62(4)).

To be effective for CGT and income tax purposes, a will trust needs to be constituted by the will rather than by any variation made by the beneficiaries. This is because, for income tax and CGT purposes, the settlor under a variation is those who are entitled under the will, unless what is being varied is itself a will trust (TA 1988 s 685D; TCGA 1992, s 68C).

A testamentary settlement does not, of course, escape the IHT entry charge, and indeed that charge is at the death rate of 40% rather than the lower inter vivos rate. But unless the legatee is the testator's spouse, this tax is exigeable in any event and in no way increased by the fact the assets are settled by the will. In that sense, therefore, a testamentary offshore settlement is without IHT cost.

Trusts with all defined persons excluded

2.16 Settlements where defined persons are all excluded are difficult to achieve now that the gains of children's and grandchildren's settlements can be attributed to the settlor. But settlements are sometimes made by remote relations or friends of the beneficiaries, and these still operate as a shelter of gains as well as income.

An important context in which such a settlement may be considered is to hold shares in newly-formed private companies. The sum required for the settlement may be modest and the promoter of the company may be able to persuade a friend or distant relative to contribute the necessary funds.

Where the friend or relative genuinely makes the settlement out of his own resources, he is the sole settlor for income tax and CGT purposes and sole transferor for the purposes of TA 1988, s 739. However, it should be stressed that where this is not so, the promoter will normally fall to be treated as a settlor or transferor. Thus a person is treated as the transferor for the purposes of s 739 if he procured the transfer (*IRC v Pratt* [1982] STC 756). A person is deemed to be a settlor under the settlement code if he made or entered into the settlement directly or indirectly, if he directly or indirectly provided funds, or if he made reciprocal arrangements for another person to make the settlement (ITTOIA 2005, s 620; see further para 59.18).

A difficulty is often that the promoter is working for the company and building it up. It is feared that this makes him settlor, as happened in *Butler v Wildin* [1989] STC 22. However, there will be good arguments that the promoter is not a settlor if he is remunerated on a proper commercial basis and the risk and cost of financing the company is borne by the company or the trustees, (cf paras 59.16 and 59.22). It is to be noted that in *IRC v Mills* [1974] STC 130, Viscount Dilhorne said it is not the provision of services but of funds which makes a person settlor. So too in *Jones v Garnett* [2005] EWHC 849 (Ch) (at para 48), Park J said it would be far harder for HMRC to establish there is a settlement if the alleged settlor is 'paid the going rate for employees carrying out the sort of work he does'.

Settlements made by friends or distant relatives achieve the ultimate in sheltering if the friend or relative making the settlement has neither an actual nor a deemed domicile for IHT purposes. In this event, the settlement is excluded property, and so free of IHT (see Chapter 45). But here too, whatever is settled must be genuinely provided out of the resources of the non-domiciliary, for if it is not, and there is some reciprocal or indirect arrangement with a UK domiciliary, the latter will be treated as settlor and the settlement will not be excluded property. This result follows because the IHT definition of settlor is similar to that in the income tax settlement code, and thus includes providers of funds and indirect settlors (IHTA 1984, s 44).

Children's settlements

2.17 As explained at the beginning of this chapter, a children's or grandchildren's offshore settlement is still a perfectly effective shelter of foreign income. In some cases a trust of this sort may come to operate as a CGT shelter as well, notably should the settlor die or emigrate. It may also happen if at some stage the capital is appointed away from the children and grandchildren.

Pending such developments, such a trust could hold either shares in a non-resident trading company or an appropriately structured investment portfolio. As is explained in Chapter 8, it is now possible to construct a portfolio which satisfies all normal investment aspirations where none of the return is taxed as capital gain. The vehicle for achieving this is the non-distributor offshore fund, for here the return on redemption is deemed to be income regardless of the fund's underlying investments (see Chapter 71).

A further and very cogent reason for structuring the portfolio in this way is that it avoids the notional interest on tax should capital be distributed to UK beneficiaries. In other words the cost-free element of deferral described in para 2.12 is secured, again regardless of whether the underlying growth in the fund is income or capital.

The attraction of offshore trusts of this sort has been greatly enhanced by the 2006 changes to IHT. Superficially those changes place an obstacle in the way of such trusts in view of the 20% entry charge. But in fact that charge is an argument in its favour, for if circumvented the result is that the value concerned and any future growth in value has left the settlor's estate without charge to IHT. As is explained above, the 20% entry charge can be avoided by timely use of the nil-rate band and, in the case of high-earners, by judicious use of the normal expenditure out of income relief. Over time those two reliefs can enable significant value to be built up offshore. Once there, the return is gross unless distributed, and the only unavoidable tax cost is the IHT every ten years at 6% or less.

Compliance

2.18 It is fundamental to offshore trusts that the settlor and beneficiaries disclose all relevant liabilities on their tax returns and that all reasonable information requested by HMRC is supplied. It should not be forgotten that HMRC have wide information gathering powers, notably TA 1988, s 745 (where liability under TA 1988, ss 739 and 740 is suspected) and TCGA 1992, s 98, and Sch 5 para 10 (which relate to CGT).

Compliance obligations arise when an offshore trust is set up. Thus a person making a non-resident settlement must, if he is resident and domiciled in the UK, make a return to HMRC within three months giving details of the trustees and the date on which the settlement was made (TCGA 1992, Sch 5A para 3). If assets are settled, a CGT disposal may have to be notified, and if the value transferred to a discretionary settlement involves a chargeable transfer of more than £10,000 an account has to be delivered to the Capital Taxes Office (IHTA 1984, s 216; Inheritance Tax (Delivery of Accounts) (Excepted Transfers and Excepted Terminations) Regulations 2002 (SI 2002/1731)).

A duty often overlooked is that imposed on professionals by IHTA 1984, s 218. Section 218 applies to any person who in the course of a trade or profession is concerned with the making of a settlement. He must within three months make a return to HMRC if he believes the settlor is UK domiciled and the trustees are non-resident. Non-compliance carries a penalty of up to £300 (IHTA 1984, s 245A(1)). Section 218 is not breached if the settlor has returned the settlement to HMRC, or some other person has made a s 218 return.

Section 218 is normally thought of as applying to UK lawyers and other professionals and it does certainly apply where such persons advise or draft in connection with offshore trusts created by UK domiciliaries. Recently HMRC have been arguing that s 218 catches the offshore trustees themselves. It may be doubted whether s 218 is extra-territorial in this way as it is a reasonable inference that its purpose was to secure information from UK professionals which would not readily be forthcoming from foreign trustees. But there is little to be gained by not making s 218 returns and prudent offshore trust providers no doubt now do so whenever the settlor has an actual or deemed UK domicile.

Chapter 3

Offshore companies

Introduction

3.1 In principle, an offshore company is an effective shelter of income and gains. As is described in para 35.2, foreign companies are recognised as separate fiscal entities in the same way as UK companies are. Accordingly their basic treatment is as follows:

(1) Foreign income is not subject to UK tax.
(2) UK source income is at most subject to basic rate tax (see Chapter 34). In the case of dividends and interest, the tax is restricted to tax withheld.
(3) Capital gains are not taxed (see para 30.6).

But for most of the second half of the twentieth century, offshore companies in the direct ownership of UK residents were not widely used in offshore tax planning. Recent developments, however, may result in directly owned offshore companies becoming more popular.

Company residence

3.2 The law relating to company residence is perhaps the main reason why directly-owned companies have been unpopular. As a result of the House of Lords decision in *Unit Construction Co Ltd v Bullock* [1960] AC 351 there was great uncertainty as to whether, and if so how, an offshore company owned by UK resident individuals or trustees could be certain of being non-resident. Indeed the risks in this area were not just financial. In *R v Allen* [2001] UKHL 45, [2001] STC 1537 and *R v Dimsey* [2001] UKHL 46, [2001] STC 1520, HMRC brought criminal prosecutions inter alia on the basis that certain individuals had cheated the Crown of tax on the profits of directly-owned companies. The defendants considered the companies were non-resident and so the companies had not made returns for corporation tax. HMRC took a different view and persuaded the jury that the companies were centrally controlled and managed in the UK. The defendants were convicted and sentenced to terms of imprisonment.

But now the case of *Wood v Holden* [2006] EWCA Civ 26, [2006] STC 443 has brought welcome certainty. That case, and others approved in it, concerned facts recognisable to any offshore practitioner and, perhaps more importantly, entailed the High Court and then the Court of Appeal overturning the decision of the Special Commissioners. HMRC sought permission to appeal further to the House of Lords, but were refused.

What *Wood v Holden* establishes beyond peradventure is that an offshore company is resident where its board meet if the board meets regularly and gives genuine and properly informed consideration to whatever business the company transacts. Provided these conditions are met it does not matter if most if not all of what the company does is pursuant to requests from its controlling shareholder(s). *Wood v Holden* indicates that residence is not jeopardised even if the directors have insufficient understanding to properly discharge their duties as a matter of company law. But relying on the decision in that respect is unwise, both because of the company law implications and because of the importance, in a tax context, of avoiding risk.

Accordingly the upshot of the case is that, provided the board meets and properly discharges its duties under the applicable company law, the company resides where it meets. The risks referred to above still remain if those conditions are not met, but proper corporate disciplines ensure they are avoided. It goes without saying that proper minutes and record-keeping are essential, so that if HMRC require satisfaction as to where the company resides, they can be given it.

Attribution of income and gains

3.3 A second reason why offshore companies have been unpopular is that anti-avoidance legislation attributes the income and gains of non-resident companies to UK resident and domiciled shareholders on an arising basis. But here the bite of the legislation may increasingly prove less severe than its bite.

Income

3.4 The basic rule is that if the UK resident owner of a non-resident company has been responsible for setting it up, the income of the company is taxed as his under TA 1988, s 739. As is explained in Chapters 54 and 55, that section applies as much to companies as to trusts and indeed transfers of assets to offshore companies in return for shares or loan-stock were originally its prime target.

Section 739 is, however, at risk of being truncated by developments in European law. As is explained in para 49.3, there are grounds to argue that that freedom precludes the s 739 charge insofar as the company cannot be characterised as a wholly artificial arrangement and is based in the European Union or the European Economic Area. This may prove to be increasingly significant in offshore tax planning, for those two supranational entities include such jurisdictions as Cyprus, Malta, Liechtenstein and several Eastern European states with flat tax.

Freedom of establishment does not extend outside the EU and the EEA. But a further freedom, freedom of movement of capital, does. It is as yet unresolved as to how far this freedom is in point in relation to companies resident outside the EU and the EEA (see para 49.5).

An issue which is also raised with s 739 is how far it is precluded by any applicable Double Tax Treaty. This, of course, is only in point insofar as the company is resident in a jurisdiction with which the UK has concluded a double tax treaty. The effect on s 739 of any such treaty is discussed in para 55.17 and, at this stage, the only fair conclusion is that the issue is unresolved.

Quite apart from these international points, s 739 has always been subject to a motive or purpose defence (TA 1988, s 741). Recent cases such as *Willoughby v IRC* [1997] STC 995 have established that the scope of that defence is wider than was once thought. It has been tightened up with effect from 5 December 2005 by TA 1988, s 741A but that new section has preserved the distinction, fundamental to *Willoughby*, between tax avoidance and tax mitigation. As is described in Chapter 58, that distinction is still being worked out by the courts, but on one view much ordinary tax planning is mitigation. How far HMRC would accept this is a matter for debate, but as paras 58.19 to 58.25 show, their track record in recent cases has not been good.

The practical result of the motive defence is that in many cases involving directly-owned offshore companies, it may be at least arguable that what is involved is mitigation and thus that s 739 is precluded. Arguments on those lines are clearly much stronger if the company has a genuine economic function and those running it are skilled in its business. Unlike the freedom of establishment or double tax treaties, the motive defence is not territorially limited.

Capital gains

3.5 As is described in Chapter 66, TCGA 1992, s 13 requires gains realised by any non-resident close company to be apportioned among the participators. An exception is made for assets used in a trade carried on by the company but otherwise CGT is charged on such of its gains as are apportioned to participators who are resident and, in the case of individuals, domiciled in the UK.

Except where the limited distribution relief described in para 66.17 applies, s 13 increases tax for, although the corporate gain is apportioned to the shareholders, its value remains reflected in the company's shares. Accordingly, it increases the potential gain on those shares, and while in computing that gain any tax paid under s 13 may be deducted (s 13(7)), this relief is far from complete. It is a deduction of tax from gain and not a deduction of gain from gain.

But, despite the potential difficulties, s 13 is, like s 739, potentially capable of circumvention. The most widely recognised point arises if the company is resident in a country with which the UK has concluded a double tax treaty giving the other country sole taxing rights over gains accruing to its residents. As is described in para 66.21, this precludes a s 13 charge. Some treaties have been renegotiated to remove the protection from s 13 but such renegotiation is still far from general. A further point which some might make is that TCGA

1992, s 79B overrides treaty protection. But this section applies only insofar as trustees are participators in the non-resident company or in any UK company which owns it (para 66.23). It does not catch UK individual participators.

Also significant to s 13 is the potential impact of European law. As is described in para 49.3, freedom of establishment should apply equally to capital gains and if so will disapply s 13 in relation to any company which cannot be characterised as a wholly artificial arrangement and is based in the European Union or the European Economic Area. Whether protection can be achieved for companies based in other jurisdictions turns on how far the freedom of movement of capital may be applicable.

What is possible?

3.6 In the light of the factors described above, it may be concluded that the income and gains of a directly-owned non-resident company stand a good chance of being protected from UK tax if the following conditions are met:

(1) The company's board meet where it is resident and give genuine consideration to decisions required of them.
(2) The company carries on its business where it is based, any work required being done locally by suitably qualified personnel.
(3) The country where the company is resident is in the European Union or the Economic Area, or is one with which the UK has concluded a suitable double tax treaty.

A particular role for directly owned offshore companies arises where a UK domiciliary already carries on business abroad and there are good commercial reasons for carrying on that business through a foreign company. Such reasons may be the existence of other, non-UK, participators or factors such as profile, as was the case in *Carvill v IRC* [2000] STC (SCD) 143 (cf para 58.24). A company formed in this context may be a parallel company of the kind discussed in Chapter 25.

As with trusts, any sheltering in an offshore company strictly represents deferral rather than avoidance. This is because any profits can only reach the UK resident owner as dividend or by way of capital gain on a sale or liquidation. But deferral of itself has value and, as in other areas, may be converted to a complete shelter by migration (see Chapter 27). The deferral may also become a complete shelter where an individual holds shares until death, for then tax-free rebasing is achieved for CGT purposes (TCGA 1992, s 62).

Other issues

3.7 Those considering using a non-resident company should remember that it may have other implications. Three may be mentioned in particular.

Benefits in kind

3.8 Should a UK resident be a director of the company he is taxable not merely on salary but on any benefits in kind (see Chapter 69). In practice concerns over company residence may mean he is not a director, but the benefits code applies if, on the facts, he is a shadow director.

At one time many advisers took the view that benefits were not taxable unless the shadow director was in fact an employee of the company, but in *R v Allen* [2001] UKHL 45, [2001] STC 1537 the House of Lords held that it did. A recent case has given the term 'shadow director' a wider meaning than was once thought. This subject is discussed further in Chapter 53.

Section 703

3.9 TA 1988, s 703 is a wide-ranging section enabling HMRC to counter tax avoidance involving shares and securities. It is not restricted to UK companies and so should be kept in mind if complex transactions involving non-resident companies are in contemplation. It does not apply unless HMRC serve a notice and there is a clearance procedure.

Local tax

3.10 The jurisdiction where a non-resident company is based may itself levy significant tax on the company's profits. Such a result may, indeed, be more likely in jurisdictions which carry greater credibility in terms of the s 739 motive defence and the freedom of establishment under EU law. It will be a matter of judgement whether the local tax outweighs the UK tax advantages achieved by the company.

Offshore companies owned by offshore trusts

3.11 Offshore companies have always had an important role in offshore tax planning when owned in an offshore trust. The subject is discussed in Chapter 9.

Chapter 4

Offshore funds

Introduction

4.1 This chapter explores the sheltering potential of offshore funds. It focuses on material interests in offshore funds in the sense that those terms are defined in the UK anti-avoidance code (TA 1988, ss 757–764).

This legislation in its present form is analysed in Chapter 71. As is there explained, the definition of 'offshore fund' has three main elements:

(1) The fund must be a collective investment scheme within the meaning of the Financial Services and Markets Act 2000.
(2) It must take the form of a non-resident company, a non-resident unit trust or other arrangements governed by foreign law and creating rights in the nature of co-ownership.
(3) The investor must have a reasonable expectation of realising the net asset value of his interest when he sells. In other words, there should be no discount for minority ownership, a provision which restricts funds in corporate form to open-ended companies.

It will be apparent that this definition comprehends most, if not all, forms of mutual fund managed offshore. As such the subject is extremely important, for an increasing proportion of investment is through mutual funds based outside the UK.

Basic tax treatment

Companies

4.2 If an offshore fund is corporate in form, it is so treated for all UK tax purposes.

Unit trusts

4.3 Offshore unit trusts are by definition not authorised and so are not deemed to be companies for income tax purposes (cf TA 1988, s 468). So too TA 1988, s 469 does not deem the unit trust to be a separate fiscal entity as that section applies only to resident unit trusts. The result is that the income tax treatment of unit trusts has to be inferred from general principles. The matter is discussed in para 33.21 and the conclusion there reached is that, in general, offshore unit trusts are likely to be opaque for tax purposes. This means the income of the fund is attributed to investors only insofar as distributed.

For CGT purposes the position is simpler, in that any non-resident unit trust is deemed to be a company and the units shares (TCGA 1992, s 99(1)).

As regards IHT, the issue is whether, for the purposes of that tax, the investor's asset is the unit or an aliquot share in the underlying assets. This issue is discussed in para 31.13 and, as with income tax, the conclusion is reached that offshore unit trusts should, in general, fall to be treated as opaque.

Many advisers are of the view that if it is desired to have certainty as to the IHT and income tax treatment, an offshore fund in corporate form is preferable. This is particularly so where it is important not to receive UK source income or hold UK assets.

Other arrangements

4.4 In civil law jurisdictions, non-corporate mutual funds can be contractual in form. It is unclear how such arrangements should be characterised in UK tax, although it is thought HMRC generally regard them as transparent. Such arrangements should therefore be avoided if clarity as to source or situs is required.

Should the arrangement be in the form of a limited partnership, it is definitely transparent for income tax purposes (ITTOIA 2003, s 848). For CGT purposes the same result ought also to follow, as TCGA 1992, s 59 renders partnerships transparent. However, a limited partnership may, depending on its precise terms, come within the general definition of unit trust, and as such fall to be treated as a company for CGT purposes (IR Press Release 21 October 1987). Indeed, regulations expressly disapply this treatment as respects UK limited partnerships registered under the Limited Partnership Act 1907 (The Capital Gains Tax (Definition of Unit Trust Scheme) Regulations 1988 (SI 1988/266)).

Anti-avoidance legislation

The offshore fund legislation

4.5 One anti-avoidance code, and one only, is targeted at offshore funds, namely the code referred to above, TA 1988, ss 757–64, described in Chapter 71. It was first enacted in 1984 when the top rate of income tax was 75% and capital gains were taxed at 30%. It applies to what are called non-qualifying offshore funds and deems the gain realised on the disposal of an interest in such a fund to be income. What it does not do is deem an apportioned part of the income of the fund to be that of the investor on an arising basis.

A non-qualifying offshore fund is any fund which is not certified by HMRC as having distributor status. As is described in para 71.9, a fund can have distributor status if it pays out at least 85% of its income as income or if its income is nil or less than 1% of the average value of its assets. If it has distributor status it is only subject to the anti-avoidance legislation described in Chapter 71 insofar as the proceeds of any sale include an equalisation element.

Sections 739 and 740

4.6 Superficially, TA 1988, s 739 might be thought to apply to any given investor's share of the income of a fund. However, a Commissioners case prior to the introduction of the offshore fund legislation is generally understood to have decided to the contrary principally on the grounds that the motive defence described in Chapter 58 applies. In the light of *IRC v Willoughby* [1997] STC 995, this must be right, for offshore funds are standard investment products bought for investment reasons (cf para 58.20). Any doubt that may now remain is dispelled by the offshore fund legislation itself, which provides a comprehensive code for taxing offshore funds in the same way as the life policy legislation did in *Willoughby*.

In their response to representations made by professional bodies as regards the new s 741A motive defence HMRC pointed they did not intend to apply s 739 to offshore funds. However, they reserved the right to do so should the regime be abused beyond the apparent intention of Parliament.

CGT

4.7 No CGT legislation is targeted specifically at offshore funds. But TCGA 1992, s 13 has to be considered (see Chapter 66). That section applies to any fund in corporate form if it would be a close company if UK resident. The issue of whether it can apply to a fund in unit trust form is one of some difficulty as, for s 13 to apply, the entity has not merely to be a company for CGT purposes but also close within the meaning of TA 1988, ss 415 and 416 (TCGA 1992, ss 13(1) and 288(1)). Although the contrary is arguable, it may be suggested the better view is that the deeming in TCGA 1992, s 99 is wide enough to make a unit trust treated as a company close if it would be close were it in fact a company.

In practice, s 13 is not of concern to portfolio investors both because the funds they invest in are most unlikely to be close and because they are likely to come within the de minimis exemption from s 13 (see para 66.13).

Planning

Distributor funds

4.8 Since it distributes its income, a distributor fund offers no income sheltering possibilities. However, assuming s 13 is not in point, it does enable any gains in the fund to be deferred. But this advantage is more apparent than real, for gains in the onshore equivalent are similarly exempt. Under TCGA 1992, s 100, gains realised by authorised unit trusts and investment trusts are exempt, as are those in open-ended investment companies (SI 2006/964, regs 98 and 100).

Non-qualifying funds

4.9 Investment in a non-qualifying offshore fund brings two income tax advantages:

(1) Assuming the fund is not transparent for income tax purposes (para 4.3), there is a deferral in that the income in the fund is rolled up tax-free and is not charged on the investor unless and until he disposes of his interest.
(2) The deferral is converted into avoidance if by the time of realisation the individual has become non-resident. As the gain is income, the CGT rule that the individual must be non-resident for at least five complete tax years does not apply (cf Chapter 27).

A non-qualifying fund operates as a CGT deferral, in the same way as a distributor fund, thereby postponing any charge until realisation. But the deferral carries a price inter alia for two reasons:

(a) The gain charged on realisation is an income gain, and as such is neither tapered nor indexed. Had the investor held the assets directly any gains would have enjoyed those reliefs.
(b) On death there is a deemed disposal, but the gain then accruing is charged (TA 1988, s 757(3)). There is no tax-free updated base cost.

The practical result of the above points is that if the growth in a non-qualifying fund is capital rather than income, the tax treatment may be unattractive, although it remains the case that CGT is deferred, the tax not being payable at all if the investor is non-resident when he disposes of his interest in the fund.

Offshore trusts

4.10 Non-qualifying offshore funds can be a useful investment for offshore trusts. This is for two reasons. The first is that, as described in Chapter 2, the anti-avoidance legislation applicable to the income of offshore trusts is normally less severe than that applicable to gains. The offshore fund legislation converts what would otherwise be capital gains into income even if the underlying growth in the fund is mainly capital. The second reason is that provided the fund is not transparent, UK investments may be held without the additional income tax on dividends or interest payable by offshore trustees with UK beneficiaries (cf para 34.14).

A point sometimes raised is whether, if an offshore trust invests in a mutual fund, the purchase is an associated operation for the purposes of TA 1988, s 740 (see Chapter 56) with the result that the trust's share of the fund's income is included in its s 740 relevant income. The motive defence would not confer protection if it did not apply on creation of the trust (cf Chapter 58). But unless the fund is transparent for income tax purposes the argument that the fund income is relevant income is without merit, for TA 1988, s 762 specifically provides that the offshore income gain is relevant income for the purposes of s 740. This is an express provision as to the application of s 740 to non qualifying mutual funds which, it may be suggested, precludes other treatment.

Private funds

4.11 The above discussion has focused on quoted funds. In practice small private funds are not uncommon. Provided the fund falls within the definition of offshore fund given above (para 4.1), tax treatment is generally as described in this chapter. However, TCGA 1992, s 13 does apply if it is close, and a unit trust which is privately held may more readily be characterised as transparent for IHT purposes (see para 31.13).

A variety of techniques are suggested to overcome the s 13 problem. One such is protected cell companies, which are allowed by the laws of certain jurisdictions. The theory is that each pool of investments belongs to a given group of shareholders and the liabilities of one pool or cell cannot be recovered from the other cells. It is suggested that such a company is not within s 13, provided there are sufficient cells to keep all investors below the 10% threshold. Such companies have not, however, been the subject of judicial analysis and it is far from clear that the tax or general legal treatment will be as intended.

Comparison with offshore trusts

4.12 Non-distributing offshore funds offer the following advantages over a private offshore trust:

(a) An offshore trust cannot achieve a tax-free roll-up of income and gains unless the settlor is wholly excluded. An individual can achieve a tax-free roll-up by investing in a fund and still be able to take the proceeds at the end.

(b) Even where an offshore trust does operate as a tax-free roll-up, tax on any eventual distribution can be increased by the CGT supplemental tax (para 63.29). There is no equivalent with an offshore fund.

(c) As standard commercial investments, offshore funds and life policies may be less provocative to HMRC and carry lower compliance costs.

The drawbacks include the following:

(i) A trust enables assets to be tied up for several generations. An interest in an offshore fund is simply an asset which has to be given away, bequeathed or otherwise dealt with.

(ii) With an offshore fund, normally the only income and gains able to be sheltered is that from portfolio investments. Private company shares, land, and other one-off assets cannot generally be so sheltered.

Chapter 5

Life policies

Introduction

5.1 This chapter deals with the sheltering possibilities offered by offshore life policies. The use of life policies in both onshore and offshore tax planning is widespread, and many schemes, particularly as regards IHT, revolve around them. This chapter deals with the use of offshore life policies as a specifically offshore tax shelter.

General

5.2 An offshore policy is a policy issued by an offshore life office which does not trade in the UK. Like any policy such policies can effectively be investment vehicles. This is because the sum payable on the maturity or surrender of the policy is with profits or unit linked. Where a policy is with profits, the policyholder shares in the profits of the life office, usually in the form of bonuses credited to the policy annually. Where the policy is unit linked, the sum payable on maturity or surrender is linked to the performance of an underlying fund. Units in the fund are allocated to the policy and the value of those units determines the amount payable.

In substance, unit linked policies resemble a managed portfolio of investments, but whatever the apparent substance, the legal reality of insurance products is that the policyholder owns not a portfolio of investments but merely a right in contract against the life office. Should the life office become insolvent, the policyholder is simply an unsecured creditor.

The arrangement must, of course, be a life policy. But a life policy need have little or no mortality risk. Thus in *Fuji Finance Inc v Aetna Life Insurance Co Ltd* [1997] Ch 173, the sum payable on surrender was essentially the same as that which would have been payable had the life assured died at the time of the surrender. This, the Court of Appeal held, did not prevent the policy from being life assurance.

In England a life policy is only valid if the person effecting the policy has an insurable interest (Life Assurance Act 1774, ss 1 and 3). In broad terms this normally means the life assured has to be that of the person effecting the policy or his spouse. In other jurisdictions, and in particular in some offshore jurisdictions, there is no such restriction and accordingly it is possible to effect life assurance on one or more third party lives. This gives offshore life assurance considerably more flexibility than in England, although in practice a life office would be unlikely to write a policy with significant mortality risk on the life of a stranger.

Tax treatment

General principles

5.3 Since the life office is offshore and does not trade in the UK, it is not subject to tax on the income and gains from the investments backing the policy, save insofar as tax is withheld in countries of source.

In the policyholder's hands, the policy is a capital asset. Thus in the absence of the chargeable event legislation described below, the proceeds on maturity or surrender would be free of income tax. The same is true of partial surrender. An HMRC attempt to characterise regular, annual, partial surrenders as income failed before a Special Commissioner (*Sugden v Kent* [2001] STC (SCD) 158).

Although capital, life policies are not chargeable assets for CGT purposes (TCGA 1992, s 210(2)). The only exception is where the policy has at any time been acquired for actual consideration (s 210(3)). Where for this reason the policy is chargeable, a disposal takes place both when the policy is assigned and on receipt of the sum assured (s 210(10)).

The chargeable event legislation

5.4 This code, ITTOIA 2005, Part 4, Chapter 9, was drafted principally with onshore policies in mind but, with modifications, it applies equally to offshore policies. It counters the tax sheltering potential of policies by treating the gain realised when the policy matures or is surrendered as income. It also covers partial surrenders. This legislation differentiates qualifying from non-qualifying policies, but offshore policies are by definition non-qualifying. The legislation is analysed in Chapter 72.

Other anti-avoidance legislation

5.5 It was held in *IRC v Willoughby* [1997] STC 995 that TA 1988, s 739 does not apply to the income from funds backing a life policy (see para 58.20). The CFC legislation cannot apply to an offshore life office provided the bulk of its business is with unconnected persons (cf para 67.8). The life office's gains could only be attributed to UK participators under TCGA 1992, s 13 if it were close (cf Chapter 66).

Personal portfolio bonds

5.6 It is possible for a policy to be linked solely to its own fund, and for that fund to be managed by the policyholder or his investment adviser. Such policies are known as personal portfolio bonds.

HMRC consider that personal portfolio bonds, being personalised rather than forming part of a collective scheme of investment, should not benefit from what they regard as the favourable tax regime applicable to life assurance. Initially they took the case of *IRC v Willoughby* (supra) to the House of Lords, seeking to tax the income of a personal bond fund under TA 1988, s 739. Then, having lost, they introduced punitive anti-avoidance legislation imposing an annual charge on the holder of such policies (ITTOIA 2005, ss 515–526; see para 72.11).

Connected persons

5.7 A policy-holder can be connected with a company held in a fund linked to his policy within the meaning of the income tax and CGT definitions (TCGA 1992, s 286; TA 1988, s 839). This is the position where on the facts the policy-holder and the life office act together to secure or exercise control of the company. So too the settlor of a trust owning the policy is connected with the company if he and the life office so act together (*Foulser v MacDougall* [2005] STC (SCD) 374, affirmed (on a different point [2006] STC 311)).

Tax planning

Deferral

5.8 At its most basic, an offshore policy which is with profits or unit-linked secures a deferral of tax. Subject to withholding tax, income and gains accrue and are reinvested gross in the fund backing the policy. Tax is not payable by the policyholder under the chargeable event legislation, until the policy matures or is surrendered.

Should the policy mature on the death of the policyholder, the gain charged is not the difference between the proceeds and the base cost, but the difference between the base cost and the surrender value immediately prior to death. Accordingly, if the surrender value is less than the maturity value as it may be where there is a significant element of life cover, the mortality gain (the difference between the surrender value and the maturity value) is tax-free. At one time the gain on the maturity or surrender of a life policy was tax-free if the policy was held in trust and the settlor was already dead. But now if the settlor is dead, the gain on a policy in trust is subject to tax at the rate for trusts if the trust is UK resident. If the trust is non-resident the gain on maturity is not taxable as it arises. It is treated as relevant income for the purposes of TA 1988, s 740 which means tax liability arises if capital is distributed to a UK beneficiary (see Chapter 56).

Life policies are not as attractive from a CGT standpoint, for the gain on the policy is an income gain with no taper or indexation relief. But it remains the case that the fund backing the policy is a gross fund, thereby securing deferral of gains.

Non-residence

5.9 The deferral of the tax on the income and the gains reinvested in the policy fund becomes a complete shelter if the policyholder is an individual who becomes non-resident before the policy matures or is surrendered (ITTOIA 2005, s 465(1); see para 72.5). Because the gain is taxed as income, the CGT requirement of being non-resident for at least five complete tax years does not apply (cf para 27.7).

Partial withdrawals

5.10 A unique feature of the tax regime for life policies is that a partial surrender of up to 5% of the premium may be taken tax-free each year (see para 72.2). The ability to take such surrenders is often referred to as the ability to take tax-free 'income'. In fact it is a misnomer to say that the 5% surrenders are tax-free because the amount of the surrender is included in computing the benefit value when the policy matures or is sold or is fully surrendered (ITTOIA 2005, s 492(1)(b); see para 72.4). Strictly therefore, it is only another form of deferral, and once the total of tax-free partial surrenders equals the premium, future partial surrenders are immediately chargeable to tax.

What is undoubtedly true, however, is that the 5% withdrawals enhance the deferral otherwise implicit in the policy. This enhanced deferral becomes a complete shelter if by the time of maturity or surrender the policyholder is non-resident. Such is also to a large extent achieved if by the time of maturity or surrender the policy is held in an offshore trust, and the person who transferred the policy to the trust is then dead. As noted above, the gain in that event is only chargeable insofar as distributions are made to UK beneficiaries.

Trusts

5.11 Life policies can be an attractive and tax-efficient mode of investment for existing trusts, particularly where the policy is written under a law which does not require the policyholder to have an insurable interest. One example is given in relation to settlor-interested trusts in para 7.13.

Personal portfolio bonds

5.12 As noted above, if a personal portfolio bond is caught by the anti-avoidance legislation directed at such policies, the tax consequences are severe. Policies with an element of self-selection should therefore be avoided unless they fall within the exceptions to the legislation.

In fact those exceptions do give some flexibility. It is true that the investments backing a bond will rarely, if ever, be able to be private assets such as chattels, land, or private company shares. But it may be possible to have an individual portfolio of quoted investments provided the selection is not by the policyholder but solely by an investment manager. The manager may be nominated by the policyholder provided his actual appointment is by the life office (cf para 72.14).

Self-selection by the policyholder himself is allowed if the investments which may be selected are confined to unit trusts, open-ended investment companies and other mutual funds (see para 72.13). Now that so many mutual funds exist, this gives wide scope for a policyholder who is keen to self-select, although care is needed both over the wording of the contract and the actual selection of the investments to ensure they really do steer clear of the anti-avoidance legislation.

Comparison with offshore trusts

5.13 Offshore policies offer the following advantages as compared with offshore trusts:

(1) The income and gains within the policy fund accrue gross even though the person providing original funds (the policyholder) can benefit. With a trust the person providing the funds (the settlor) has to be totally excluded.
(2) The 5% withdrawals are tax-free. With a trust any distribution to a UK-domiciled resident is potentially taxable.
(3) Even when the gain on the maturity or surrender of a life policy is taxed, there is no notional interest on the tax, as there is with CGT capital payments (cf para 63.29).

The drawbacks include the following:

(1) A trust can protect assets for several generations. A policy does not of itself do that.
(2) A trust can shelter all forms of assets, whereas assets which can back policies are restricted by the rules relating to personal portfolio bonds.
(3) The charges made by life offices are often opaque and may be high.
(4) Life policies can be subject to aggressive selling, which may make it difficult to identify the real advantages for any particular individual.

Section III

Existing Trusts

Chapter 6

Existing settlements

Introduction

6.1 Many offshore settlements created by UK domiciliaries exist. This chapter explains what tax planning potential they continue to offer and what (if any) steps should be taken to counteract recent legislative changes in the UK. This chapter should be read in conjunction both with subsequent chapters in this section, and also with the analysis of trust distributions in section IV of this Part.

It is assumed in this chapter that the settlor of the trust had an actual UK domicile when he created the settlement, or was deemed to be UK domiciled for the purposes of IHT (cf para 30.14). It is also assumed that the terms of the trust exclude the settlor and his spouse and that neither of them do in fact benefit from the trust. Existing settlor-interested trusts are considered in the next chapter.

Discretionary trusts

6.2 Offshore discretionary trusts created by UK domiciliaries are more common than might be supposed. Typically the assets could be protected from 10-yearly charges by business property relief or the trust may be long-standing, trustees and beneficiaries regarding 10-yearly IHT charges as an acceptable price to pay for flexibility. It is likely that the changes made by FA 2006 will increase the number of offshore discretionary trusts.

Inheritance Tax

6.3 Offshore discretionary trusts are unaffected by the 2006 changes, continuing to be subject to the regime of 10-yearly and exit charges described in Chapter 43. The IHT imposed on these trusts is normally unenforceable against the trustees in their home jurisdiction as it is imposed by a foreign revenue law (cf *Government of India, Ministry of Finance (Revenue Division) v Taylor* [1955] AC 491). But HMRC do not regard themselves as precluded from attempting to recover the tax, and few offshore trustees would now wish to be non-compliant.

In certain respects, the changes in FA 2006 have improved the position of offshore discretionary trusts. Most notably, the creation of interests in possession is now without IHT consequences. As is described in the next paragraph, such interests can be useful in income tax planning. Perhaps more important is the HMRC argument that trustees who allow a beneficiary to use property rent-free have given him an interest in possession (SP 10/79). The result of FA 2006 is that any such notional interest in possession is now without IHT consequences so long as first created by discretionary trustees after 22 March 2006.

Income tax

6.4 As described in Chapter 2, offshore discretionary trusts operate as an income shelter. The sheltering is restricted to foreign source income at trust level, but UK source income may be sheltered by holding the investments through an offshore holding company (see Chapter 9). Sheltering occurs so long as the income is accumulated and can continue indefinitely as offshore jurisdictions do not restrict accumulation.

Should capital be distributed to UK beneficiaries, or benefits in kind be conferred, a tax charge arises under TA 1988, s 740 on the value distributed or the benefit conferred by reference to the retained income (see Chapters 13 and 56). But the rate of tax is no greater than the rate which would have been payable when the income arose had the trust been UK resident and it is avoided if the recipient beneficiary is non-resident (cf para 14.2). Non-residence may be a price a beneficiary is prepared to pay if substantial income has been rolled-up offshore and he wishes to access it tax-free.

An alternative approach where large amounts of income have been rolled-up is not to distribute capital, but for the trustees to pay UK beneficiaries current income as it arises. If there is a large class of beneficiaries it can be spread around, and much may be absorbed by personal allowances and basic rate-bands.

This is particularly so where there are infant beneficiaries, provided the settlor is dead or they are not his children (cf para 59.8). Should the figures be greater a reduction in tax on dividend income may be achieved by appointing interests in possession in favour of the intended recipients over the shares concerned. This will secure the Schedule F dividend rates (para 12.2). These are effectively nil or 25% if the shares are in UK companies. Arguably the case of *Manninen* [2005] All ER (EC) 465 means the same rates apply on foreign dividends, at least insofar as from the European Union and the European Economic Area (cf para 49.15). But, subject to that, the rates on non-UK dividends are 10% and 32.5%.

In the past, appointment of interests in possession for these purposes was rendered unattractive by the IHT consequences. But as explained above, FA 2006 means this drawback has now gone. However, one advantage which FA 2006 has taken away is that such interests do not secure CGT rebasing should the holder of the life-interest die (TCGA 1992, s 72(1A)).

Accumulation and maintenance trusts

6.5 The term 'accumulation and maintenance trust' is used here to describe trusts which enjoy the protection of IHTA 1984, s 71 (see para 44.8) prior to the vesting of the absolute interests or interests in possession. Insofar as those interests have vested, the trust is more properly described as fixed interest or, in the case of absolute vesting, there is no longer any trust at all.

Accumulation and maintenance trusts offshore are either as originally settled or result from subsequent appointment by the trustees. As is explained in Chapter 42, the protection afforded by s 71 is now available only to those accumulation and maintenance trusts in existence on 22 March 2006, and it is therefore these which this part of the present chapter considers.

All such accumulation and maintenance trusts will slip into the discretionary trust regime on 6 April 2008 or, if earlier, should interests in possession arise at any time before then but after 22 March 2006. This result is only avoided if the capital vests absolutely in the beneficiaries on attaining 18. A higher age for absolute vesting can be specified but the price for this is a small tax charge when vesting does occur (see para 44.9). Further, the share of each beneficiary must be fixed, and only he can enjoy capital and income from his share.

Once an accumulation and maintenance trust has moved into the discretionary trust regime, its IHT and income tax treatment will be as described above in relation to discretionary trusts. A point to keep in mind is that 10-yearly anniversaries arise by reference to the original creation of the settlement rather than 6 April 2008. But as is explained in para 44.10, on the first 10-yearly anniversary after 6 April 2008 the effective rate will be reduced to reflect the period of s 71 protection. A point also to stress is that the discretionary trust regime applies even after interests in possession have arisen, provided such arising is after 22 March 2006 (see para 44.10).

Between now and 5 April 2008, the big decision for the trustees of offshore accumulation and maintenance trusts is whether to accept the movement into the discretionary trust regime on 6 April 2008, or whether to alter the trust by appointment so as to meet the conditions for continuing s 71 protection. For most offshore trusts the answer is clear as the price of continuing s 71 protection is absolute vesting. In most cases this will be contrary to the underlying rationale of the trust and, assuming the beneficiary is UK resident, it may well result in a benefit under TA 1988, s 740 and a taxable capital payment under TCGA 1992, s 87. As described in para 63.29, the latter can result in a 64% rate of tax.

But the reasons for not securing continuing s 71 protection are not just negative. The result of an accumulation and maintenance trust moving into the discretionary trust regime on 6 April 2008 is that the property will enter into that regime without the 20% entry charge that is normally the price of doing so. As is described in Chapter 43, that entry charge existed as much before FA 2006 as afterwards and its absence in the present context is a genuine relieving provision in FA 2006.

Assuming accumulation and maintenance trusts existing on 22 March 2006 are left as is, sooner or later the beneficiaries will come into their interests in possession. Although for IHT purposes such vesting is now a non-event, for income tax purposes it is still a real change. The income ceases to be capable of accumulation and so able to be sheltered and instead becomes that of the life-tenant. Assuming the life-tenant is UK resident it thus becomes taxable, albeit at the more favourable dividend rates referred to in para 6.4 above if the income is dividend. But one advantage of FA 2006 is that this taxability can, if desired, be terminated without IHT consequences for, assuming they have power to do so, the trustees can simply reappoint the funds on discretionary trusts, or even give income interests to other beneficiaries. As explained in para 43.14, the property in such cases remains within the relevant property regime and there is no exit charge.

Such flexibility is of course not possible if the accumulation and maintenance trust is one of those, rare offshore, where the capital vests absolutely in the beneficiaries when they attain 25 or some lesser age. As indicated above, absolute vesting can have unfortunate tax consequences. In most cases such can be avoided before capital vests if the trustees make an advance for the benefit of the beneficiary onto new trusts. The ultimate authority for such advances is *Pilkington v IRC* [1964] AC 612 and local advice should be taken as to whether such an exercise is in fact permissible under the trust's proper law. For CGT reasons, the new trusts should not involve the creation of a separate settlement (see para 65.6).

Fixed-interest trusts

6.6 Fixed-interest trusts are trusts where the trust fund is subject to one or more interests in possession. Such interests may have been conferred when the trust was created, or be the result of vesting under accumulation and maintenance trusts. Alternatively, interests in possession can arise by appointment by the trustees.

Inheritance Tax

6.7 As described in para 44.1, until 22 March 2006, all interests in possession were, for IHT purposes, equated with ownership of the underlying trust assets. This treatment is retained for interests in possession existing as at 22 March 2008 and for certain interests in possession, known as transitional serial interests, immediately following the determination of such existing interests. But otherwise, apart from exceptions immaterial to offshore tax planning (see paras 44.3 to 44.5), the equation with ownership of the underlying assets does not apply to interests in possession arising or created after 22 March 2006.

FA 2006 has presented trusts subject to interests in possession on 22 March 2006 with a potentially serious IHT problem. Assuming the property remains settled, there is an IHT charge when that interest in possession or any successive transitional serial interest ends, as at that point the trust property enters into relevant property regime. This is so even if the ending is during the lifetime of the holder of the interest and, in that respect, is in contrast to the law prior to FA 2006. Under that prior law, the inter vivos termination of an interest in possession qualified for PET treatment if the termination was followed by another interest in possession or by accumulation and maintenance trusts. In a nutshell, FA 2006 has deprived existing interest in possession trusts of the ability to avoid IHT by inter vivos terminations, and in that respect represents a new and additional tax burden. Whereas existing accumulation and maintenance trusts have been allowed to move into the relevant property regime without tax charge, that facility has not been afforded to existing interest in possession trusts.

The changes in FA 2006 also raise issues with the spouse exemption. Until 22 March 2006, the spouse exemption applied on the termination of an interest in possession if the property vested absolutely in the former life-tenant's spouse or if a new interest in possession arose in her favour. This was so whether the termination was inter vivos or on death. The position now is that the spouse exemption continues to apply if the property vests absolutely in the life-tenant's spouse. But should she take only an interest in possession, the spouse exemption is only available if the existing interest terminates on the life-tenant's death or if her interest otherwise qualifies as a transitional serial interest – ie if the existing interest terminates before 6 April 2008 (see Chapter 44).

Under the terms of FA 2006 there are four possible solutions to these problems. One is to vest the property absolutely in one or more of the beneficiaries. If that beneficiary is the former life-tenant or his spouse, the vesting is without IHT consequences, and otherwise PET treatment is secured (see para 44.7 below). But as with accumulation and maintenance trusts, both income tax and CGT, and non-tax considerations, are likely to render absolute vesting unattractive.

The second is to do nothing. This may be particularly attractive if the life-tenant is young. In such event during his life-time the trust fund will remain free of the 10-yearly charges under the relevant property regime. Further, if on his death his spouse takes a life-interest the spouse exemption still applies and entry into the relevant property regime is deferred until her interest terminates, as her interest counts as a transitional serial interest (see para 44.2). It is true that the trust fund is at risk of IHT at 40% when he dies or (as the case may be) his spouse dies. But given normal mortality, the tax regime is likely to be very different by the time this happens, and the cost of premature death can be safeguarded by life assurance.

The third solution is to take advantage of the rules relating to transitional serial interest. As explained in para 44.2, it is possible to secure PET treatment on the replacement of the existing interest in possession with another interest in possession. But such replacement must be effected before 6 April 2008 and (except where the trust fund comprises life policies) the exercise can be done once only. A further drawback is that the problem posed by FA 2006 is not cured, but merely postponed into another life interest. Nonetheless such a solution may be attractive if the present life-tenant is elderly and the proposed holder of the transitional serial interest young, for example a child or grandchild.

A fourth and in many ways attractive solution is to effect a managed movement into the relevant property regime. There is no reason why every seven years the existing life-tenant's nil-rate band should not be used to effect the tax-free appointment of an appropriate proportion of the fund onto discretionary trusts (assuming the life-tenant's nil-rate band is otherwise available). A more radical solution is possible if and to the extent that the trust fund is invested in assets eligible for business property relief (IHTA 1984, ss 103–114). In such event an appointment onto discretionary trusts is without IHT consequences, although it does have to be remembered that IHT is chargeable if the life-tenant dies within seven years at a time when the trust no longer retains the business assets (IHTA 1984, s 113A).

It should be noted that both the third and the fourth solution require the former life-tenant to be completely excluded from benefit under the settlement. If he is not, the trust property remains comprised in his estate under GWR rules (para 47.3).

Income tax

6.8 Unless and until action of the kind described above is taken, the income of an existing life-interest trust is taxed as that of the life-tenant and so, assuming he is UK resident, it is not sheltered (cf para 12.2). The income remains unsheltered should a transitional serial interest be appointed, assuming that that life-tenant is also UK resident.

Should the action taken be to appoint the funds into the relevant property regime, income tax treatment will depend on what trusts are appointed. Should those trusts be interest in possession the income will remain taxable, assuming again the new life-tenant is UK resident. But should the trusts be discretionary, income sheltering will be achieved as respects foreign income. The position will be as described above in relation to discretionary trusts.

Capital Gains Tax

6.9 Hitherto the discussion in this chapter has not considered CGT. In reality CGT is an important factor, itself requiring careful planning.

Attribution of gains to the settlor

6.10 Although the income of the settlement is not taxed as that of the settlor, capital gains may be. As is explained in Chapter 60, capital gains are taxed as the settler's under TCGA 1992, s 86 if his children or their spouses are beneficiaries or receive a benefit. The same result can follow if the settlor's children and their spouses are excluded, but his grandchildren and their spouses are not. In this event the gains are taxed as those of the settlor if the settlement was made after 17 March 1998 or if it has become tainted in the sense described in Chapter 61.

In all these cases where the trust gains are taxed as those of the settlor, so also are gains realised in any underlying company. As is described in para 66.24, company gains can be attributed to the trust, and thus to the settlor if the trust owns more than 10% of the company.

Reimbursement of the settlor

6.11 The assessment of capital gains on the settlor creates an important practical issue, namely that although he bears the tax, the benefit of the gain accrues to the trust, from which he and his spouse are excluded. There is a statutory right of reimbursement (TCGA 1992, Sch 5 para 6) but as this is merely a right conferred by an English statute, it is far from clear that it is enforceable against a trust governed by foreign law. The issue is discussed in para 60.13, and, if the statutory right is not enforceable, the trustees may simply be unable to reimburse the settlor. Some settlors may, as a result, face ruin.

In one Jersey case, the Royal Court sanctioned a variation to overcome this difficulty, but in that case the facts were extreme and the family unanimous (see para 60.13). It is far from clear that the same approach could be taken generally.

Exceptions to the settlor charge

6.12 The attribution of gains to the settlor does not apply to every settlement of which his children or grandchildren are beneficiaries. Self-evidently it ceases when he dies, it being expressly provided that the charge is not made in the year of death (see para 60.2). So too the charge ceases to be made if the settlor becomes non-resident and remains so for at least five complete tax years.

These considerations means that the attribution of gains to the settlor is not a permanent issue for the trust. If realisation of gains can be delayed until the settlor is dead or non-resident, attribution on an arising basis is avoided. In view of the number of deferrals in the CGT code, such delay is not as difficult to achieve as might be supposed.

A point which also needs to be borne in mind is that in any tax year it is only the net gains of the trust or of any underlying company which is attributed to the settlor, any losses accruing to the entity concerned being deducted. At trust level, brought forward losses are also allowed (see para 60.11). This means that, with careful management, trusts holding portfolio investments can often avoid the charge. A further point is that even if in a tax year net gains do arise, any personal losses of the settlor can offset them (see para 60.12).

Avoiding the settlor charge

6.13 Absent emigration of the settlor, the simplest method of avoiding the settlor charge is to exclude those beneficiaries who cause it to arise. In the case of pre 17 March 1998 settlements this may be a practical possibility – as, provided the settlement is untainted, grandchildren can be left in as beneficiaries (see para 60.5). But if children and their spouses are to be excluded, the exclusion needs to be effected with care. As is explained in paras 60.9 and 60.20, it needs to extend to companies and to actual or possible civil partners.

An alternate approach to avoiding the settlor charge is to avoid returns taxed as capital gain. This may not be practical in cases where the trust is already locked into investments pregnant with gain. But where this is not so, it is possible to design an investment strategy which largely or wholly avoids capital gains. This subject is dealt with in Chapter 8.

A final point arises if the settlement is subject to an interest in possession which subsisted on 22 March 2006, or to a transitional serial interest. If, in such case, the interest holder dies while still entitled to the interest, the assets in the trust are rebased without tax charge (TCGA 1992, s 72).

Settlements not subject to the settlor charge

6.14 As settlors die or emigrate, the number of trusts subject to the settlor charge will fall. Indeed many trusts already are not subject to it. But although such trusts are free of CGT on an arising basis, CGT is still an issue which has to be considered.

The reason for this is that gains realised in the trust or any underlying company go into the s 87 pool, from whence they can render taxable capital distributions or benefits conferred on UK resident beneficiaries. This subject is discussed in Chapters 55 and 65, and the key point to note is that the top rate of tax on such distributions can be 64% rather than the normal 40% (see para 63.29).

It is tempting to conclude from this that returns taxed as capital gain are as unattractive when gains are not assessed on the settlor on an arising basis as where they are. But in practice such conclusion is likely to be wrong.

One reason for this is that most existing settlements already have substantial s 87 pools, not to mention pools of s 740 relevant income and offshore income gains (cf Chapter 13 and para 63.13). This means capital distributions to UK beneficiaries are likely to be taxable in any event, regardless of what return the trustees now generate. Indeed in many cases where underlying companies are involved the aggregate existing pools may exceed the value of the trust fund.

The second reason is that if an offshore trust is of any size it is unlikely that capital distributions to UK beneficiaries will be seen as a likely scenario. As is explained in Chapter 14, the more likely strategies are distributing capital to non-residents or confining what is distributed to current income.

But there will undoubtedly be cases where these factors are not in point. In those cases, the investment strategies referred to above may be followed – in other words, investing for income returns as explained in Chapter 8. In addition it should be borne in mind that tax-free rebasing will occur should any interest in possession subsisting on 22 March 2006 be retained until death, as is also the position with transitional serial interests.

Capital distributions

6.15 As just foreshadowed, a key issue for many existing trusts is whether, and if so how, tax-efficient distributions may be made to UK beneficiaries. A variety of strategies do exist. The subject is covered in detail in Chapters 13 and 14 below.

Is the settlement worth retaining?

6.16 Some may argue that the issues discussed earlier in this chapter mean that existing offshore settlements should be wound up and the capital distributed to the beneficiaries. A further factor deployed in support of such argument is the cost of administering a trust offshore, although with efficient providers this factor should not be of great importance.

In appropriate cases, winding up should certainly be considered. One such case is where the principal beneficiary or beneficiaries have emigrated and will remain non-resident for at least five complete tax years. Here, distributions of capital will be free of UK tax and should the beneficiary(ies) in due course become non-domiciled, the capital can eventually be taken entirely out of the UK tax net. But even on this scenario there are potential drawbacks to watch. One is the possible impact of local tax in whatever country the beneficiaries have moved to. Another is that if the settlor is still alive and resident in the UK, any capital gains triggered on winding up the structure will be taxed as his.

A second scenario where winding up may be considered is where the trust's income and gains pools are non-existent or modest and little or no further gain will be triggered on distributing the current investments in specie. Here, winding up the trust may be attractive if the fund is modest in size relative to fees or if the housing or other capital needs of the beneficiaries outweigh the advantages of offshore sheltering.

But these circumstances apart, winding up an existing offshore trust is unlikely to be attractive. In part this is because such winding up is likely to trigger capital gains. But more important is the fact, explained in Chapter 2 above, that an offshore trust is still an actual or potential tax shelter. Assuming that the trust permits accumulation of income, income is sheltered and once the settlor is dead or non-resident, so too are gains.

Chapter 7

Existing settlor-interested settlements

Introduction

7.1 This chapter looks at the classic offshore trust created by UK domiciliaries in the 1980s, namely the trust where the settlor is a beneficiary, often the life-tenant. Trusts of this sort were created during the period before 1991 when all gains realised by offshore trustees were free of tax on an arising basis. Mostly they were created as a CGT shelter. Many have substantial realised or latent gains and this chapter discusses whether such settlements are worth retaining and, assuming they are, how UK tax may best be minimised. It assumes the trust was created before 17 March 1998 and that the settler is UK domiciled.

Tax treatment

Income tax and CGT

7.2 Settlements where the settlor or his spouse are actual or potential beneficiaries now confer no income tax or CGT advantage. This is because income and gains in both the settlement and in any underlying holding company are assessed as the settlor's as they arise. Liability on income is under TA 1988, s 739 and ITTOIA 2005, s 624 (see Chapters 55 and 59). Liability on offshore income gains is under s 739 as applied by TA 1988, s 762(5)(a) (see para 71.25). Liability on capital gains is under TCGA 1992, s 86 (see Chapter 60). It is triggered both where the trustees make actual disposals and also if they fall foul of the trustee borrowing rules (see Chapter 62).

Inheritance tax

7.3 Settlements where the settler is a beneficiary do not confer any IHT advantage either. Thus if the settlor is life tenant the trust assets are treated as his for IHT purposes (IHTA 1984, s 49). This is so even after the changes made by FA 2006, as the settlor's life interest was in existence on 22 March 2006 (cf para 44.1 below). In the event of the settlor's death, the trust incurs liability to IHT at his estate rate save insofar as the trust assets are relieved from IHT by reliefs such as business property relief. Liability to IHT is also avoided if, on the settlor's death, his spouse takes a life interest, for a spouse's life interest in such circumstances is a transitional serial interest and so equated with absolute ownership (see para 44.2). But IHT then has to be faced on the spouse's death. A further point is that the spouse exemption does not apply if the spouse is non-domiciled (IHTA 1984, s 18(2)).

In the relatively rare cases where the settlor is only a discretionary beneficiary the settlement is liable to the IHT relevant property regime of ten-yearly and exit charges (see Chapter 43). In addition the property is likely to be treated as comprised in the settlor's estate under the gift with reservation rules save insofar as it was settled before 18 March 1986 (see para 47.3).

Accumulated gains

7.4 Despite the fact that trust gains are currently assessable on the settlor on an arising basis, the trust may well have a s 87 pool of trust gains. Such is the position if the trust or any underlying company realised gains before 17 March 1998 and those gains have not previously been allocated to capital payments. Gains in this pool become chargeable under TCGA 1992, s 87 insofar as capital is distributed to the settlor or any other beneficiary who is resident and domiciled in the UK (see Chapter 63). The rate of tax is 64% (see para 63.29).

Terminating the settlement

7.5 Since settlor-interested trusts now confer no tax advantage, the primary tax planning issue for the trustees is whether the settlement should be wound up and the capital distributed to the settlor or another member of his family. On the face of it, this is an attractive course of action, for it enables the settlor or another member of his family to regain control of the assets and avoids the fees and costs chargeable by the trustees. But in reality there may be significant tax obstacles, specifically two:

(1) If there is a s 87 or a Sch 4C pool of trust gains, such will result in a CGT charge at 64% on the recipient of the distribution insofar as he is resident and domiciled in the UK.
(2) There may be latent gains in the current assets, which will be charged on the settlor on an arising basis when the assets are sold or distributed in specie.

As a result of these two points, terminating the settlement only makes sense in the following situations:

(a) The settlement has neither a s 87 nor a Sch 4C pool of trust gains and has not received capital from another settlement which does. If in such a case there are also no latent gains, there is no disadvantage in distributing the entire trust fund to the settlor or to other UK resident beneficiaries.

(b) There are no latent gains and the settlement is being terminated by distribution to one or more non-resident or non-domiciled beneficiaries. In such a case the distribution is not charged (paras 63.22 and 64.7). If the recipients are relying on non-residence, they must remain non-resident for a least five complete tax years (see paras 63.23 and 64.12).

It may also be possible to terminate the settlement without tax cost if there are no latent gains and the pool of trust gains is a s 87 pool, whose amount is less than the value of the trust fund. In that event an amount equal to the pool may be distributed to non-resident or non-domiciled beneficiaries in one tax year. This will wash out the gains, enabling a tax-free distribution of the balance of the capital in the next tax year. But such a strategy is not possible if there are latent gains, for terminating the trust will involve realising those gains, and the ensuing charge on the settlor. Nor is it possible if the pool is a Sch 4C pool or if distributions from the settlement are taxable by reference to another settlement's Sch 4C pool. In such case gains in the Sch 4C pool are not washed out by the distribution to the non-resident or non-domiciliary (see Chapter 64).

In connection with these various strategies it should be remembered that if trust assets are held through a holding company, the latent gains to be considered include both those on the shares in the company and those on the company's investments (see Chapter 9). There is now no relief for gains distributed by the company within two years of being realised, although if the settlor is charged under TCGA 1992, s 86 on the corporate gains, such tax may be able to be set against any tax payable by him in respect of a distribution by the company within the three- or four-year period referred to in s 13(5A) (see para 66.17).

Inheritance tax consequences

7.6 If the trust is wound up, any distribution to the settler or his spouse is without IHT consequences provided he is life tenant (IHTA 1984, s 49). This is because his life interest subsisted on 22 March 2006, with the result that the settled property is treated for IHT purposes as his (cf para 44.1).

In cases where the settlor is life tenant and the distribution is to another beneficiary, the distribution will be a PET (IHTA 1984, s 3A). FA 2006 has preserved PET treatment where a beneficiary becomes absolutely entitled to the trust property on the termination of an interest in possession which subsisted on 22 March 2006 (see para 44.7). The result is that IHT is avoided provided the settlor survives seven years. In general, a distribution to a beneficiary who is not the settlor is good IHT planning for it removes the property from the settlor's estate and avoids IHT provided he survives seven years.

Should the trust be discretionary, the distribution results in an IHT exit charge of up to 6%, the rate depending on the value of the fund and how recent the last ten-year anniversary was (see paras 43.6). If the recipient is not the settlor, the distribution is also a PET under the gift with reservation rules unless the settlement was made before 18 March 1986 (FA 1986, s 102(4); see further para 47.10).

Immigration to the UK

7.7 The likelihood is that existing trust gains or latent gains will make termination of the trust unattractive. In that event immigration of the trust to the UK may be considered.

The tax and other consequences of immigration are discussed in Chapter 11. But such a step brings little advantage, for the trust income and gains remain attributed to the settlor (ITTOIA 2005, s 624; TCGA 1992, s 77). Indeed there is one drawback, namely that gains are locked into charge, for the trust cannot subsequently leave the UK without a deemed disposal of all its then assets at market value (TCGA 1992, s 80; see para 28.8). If the trust remains offshore, CGT on an arising basis is avoided should the settlor die or emigrate.

Exclusion of the settlor

Inheritance tax

7.8 Exclusion of the settlor is a topic which, even if previously rejected, requires revisiting as a result of FA 2006 in all cases where the settlor has a life interest. Prior to 22 March 2006, the trustees could have avoided the IHT potentially chargeable on the settlor's death by terminating his interest inter vivos and ensuring he was completely excluded from future benefit. If the ensuing trusts were interest in possession or accumulation and maintenance trusts, the exercise was a PET.

FA 2006 has changed these rules, in that PET treatment is not available on the inter vivos termination of the settlor's interest in possession unless on such termination the settled property vests absolutely in a beneficiary (see para 44.7). Instead, if the property remains settled, it moves into the relevant property regime, regardless of the form which the trusts following the life interest take. As such it suffers an entry charge at 20% insofar as the settlor's nil rate band is exhausted (see para 43.2).

FA 2006 has, however, afforded a measure of transitional relief, in that, in common with other interests in possession subsisting on 22 March 2006, termination of the settlor's life interest is eligible for PET treatment if such termination is before 5 April 2008 and on termination another beneficiary takes an interest in possession. In all such cases, the successor life interest is a transitional serial interest and thus, for IHT purposes, equated with ownership of the trust assets (see paras 43.2 and 44.7). A transitional serial interest also arises if on the settlor's death his spouse takes a successive life interest and, since as a result the spouse's interest is equated with absolute ownership, the spouse exemption applies.

But, however the transitional serial interest arises, it carries an important drawback. This is that, assuming the property remains settled, IHT has to be faced when the interest terminates, whether on death or inter vivos, for at that stage the settled property will inescapably move into the relevant property regime. The tax charge will be at 40% if the termination is on the successor life tenant's death or within three years of death, and otherwise at inter vivos rates.

As with other life interest trusts (para 6.7), the decision the trustees have to make is whether to buy themselves time before entering the relevant property regime by terminating the settlor's life interest before 5 April 2008 and appointing a successor life interest. It is not an absolute solution in that, as just indicated, the relevant property regime and the initial entry charge will kick in once that successor life interest ends. But should the settlor and his spouse be elderly, and the successor life-tenant young, the time bought will, on normal life expectancy, be substantial and worthwhile.

In some cases, it may be appropriate to terminate the settlor's life interest and move straight into the relevant property regime, either by appointing discretionary trusts to follow the settlor's life interest or by deferring any appointment until after 6 April 2008. Such a strategy is appropriate where the entry charge can be avoided. This will be so where the property appointed is within the settlor's nil rate band or where it is eligible for business property relief (IHTA 1984, ss 103–114). But in the latter event the trustees will need to retain the property for seven years if a charge is to be avoided in the event of the settlor's death (see ibid s 113A).

Matters are altogether easier if the trust is already discretionary and the settlor is interested merely as a discretionary object. In such case his exclusion is, as before FA 2006, a PET. Further, both before and after his exclusion the trust is in the relevant property regime, and is so subject without now having to incur the cost of an entry charge.

Income tax and CGT

7.9 One clear advantage of terminating the settlor's life interest is that trust income, and that of any underlying company, ceases to be taxed as his provided that, when his life interest is terminated, he and his spouse are excluded from any other possibility of benefit under the settlement. However, if the settlor is life-tenant and the termination is by appointing a transitional serial interest before 5 April 2008, the advantage may be more apparent than real. This is because that interest will entitle the new life-tenant to the income as it arises, and so render it taxable as his if he is UK resident (cf para 12.2). Exclusion of the settlor therefore only avoids income tax if the new trusts are discretionary or, assuming a life interest is appointed, if the new life-tenant is non-resident or without other income.

Should the settlor be merely a discretionary beneficiary, the income tax advantage is more easily achieved, for the trust is already discretionary. Once the settlor is excluded, the income is sheltered if accumulated.

Exclusion of the settlor does not of itself prevent capital gains in the trust and any underlying company being assessed as his. To achieve this result his children and their respective spouses must be excluded as well. So too must his grandchildren and their spouses if the settlement has become tainted in the sense explained in Chapter 61. In some family contexts exclusion of the children as well as the settlor may be a logical step. But where this is not so, the continuing CGT disadvantage of the settlement has to be faced. In such cases the best means of overcoming it is, where possible, by investment for returns taxed as income, as discussed in Chapter 8.

Points to watch

7.10 If the settlor is to be excluded it is essential that he and his spouse are excluded under the terms of the trust from any possible benefit and do not, in fact, receive benefit. As just explained, such is necessary for income tax reasons, and it is also required on account of the IHT gift with reservation rules (see para 47.3).

Exclusion of the settlor should not be effected by the settlor releasing or assigning his life interest, for such is a disposal of the interest on which any gain is chargeable (TCGA 1992, s 85). Market value will normally be substituted and while in most cases overriding powers vested in the trustees will render this nominal, such will not always be so. The prudent course of action is for the exclusion to be effected by the trustees in exercise of powers conferred on them. If they have no such powers the chances are the settlor's interest does have value and the exercise should not be attempted at all.

Should reliance be placed on the IHT transitional rules by appointing a transitional serial interest before 5 April 2008, it must be remembered that the benefit of those rules can be taken once only. In other words, one transitional serial interest cannot be followed by another. The particular trap is that if the trust has been reorganised since 22 March 2006, and the settlor's interest in possession as at that date replaced by another, the latter is a transitional serial interest. It cannot be replaced by a further transitional serial interest.

Inaction

7.11 When all is said and done, the decision may be to leave the trust as it is. Several planning points arise if that course is taken. Many are applicable to all forms of settlement and so are listed in Chapter 10. A few others are more specific.

CGT rebasing on death

7.12 Assuming the settlor is life tenant all unrealised gains will be eliminated on his death for on the death of the life tenant the assets in the trust are rebased without charge to tax (TCGA 1992, s 72). Thereafter, should his spouse take a successive life interest and retain it until her death, a further tax-free rebasing of the trust assets for CGT purposes is secured (TCGA 1992, s 72(1B)(a)(ii)). This goes to reduce the capital gains otherwise passing into the trust's s 87 pool (cf Chapter 13) and arises because the spouse's interest is a transitional serial interest.

Investment

7.13 If the settlement is retained as is, there is no particular tax reason to invest for income as against gains or vice versa, for both income and gains are taxed as the settlor's on an arising basis. However, investment in roll-up funds is best avoided for such can result in doubling up of tax (see Chapter 71).

Offshore life assurance may offer a tax efficient investment medium if the trust has liquid assets. As is described in Chapter 5, offshore life policies can be written on any lives, and so if the trustees take out a policy written on a third party life or lives, tax liability on the settlor is avoided provided the individual(s) concerned survive the settlor. In such a case, the proceeds of the policy are simply s 740 income in the trust, not taxed unless distributions are made, and even then free of notional interest.

In the result, a life policy offers a convenient means of rolling up income and gains until after the settlor dies, without exposing him to tax liability. The one important point to watch is that the policy must not be a personal portfolio bond, for if it is the settlor will be subject to the punitive annual charge (see para 72.16).

The use of a life policy can go even further than just rolling up income and gains. As is explained in para 5.10, up to 5% of the premium can be taken tax-free each year, and, if it is so taken it is capital as a matter of trust accounting. Accordingly, it does not result in an income tax charge on the settlor qua life-tenant and indeed may be distributed to him if there is power to distribute capital. Such 5% withdrawals do of course increase the gain on the maturity of the policy, but this may be regarded as acceptable, given that that gain is merely a s 740 gain.

Capital distributions

7.14 As already noted, capital distributions remain taxable by reference to any s 87 or Sch 4C pool (see Chapter 13). Planning strategies for avoiding such charge are outlined in Chapter 14.

Holding companies

7.15 Many trusts hold their investments through an offshore holding company. The use of such company has advantages and drawbacks, summarised in Chapter 9. But if a trust in which the settlor is life-tenant has a holding company in place, such can offer a means of repatriating any gains pool in the company to the settlor at relatively low cost in tax. This is achieved if the company pays a dividend. Such dividend is taxed as the settlor's income but, as explained in para 12.2, the rate of tax is 32.5%. A 25% rate may be secured if the company is first made UK resident (see para 11.7) but as such a step brings all the company's income and gains into corporation tax, it is unlikely to be worthwhile if the company is going to have a continuing investment function (see further Chapter 11).

In practice, the company's reserves may well include retained income as well as gains. The latter will have been taxed as the settlor's under TA 1988 s 739, and so should not be taxed again if, on distribution, they are the settlor's income (cf para 55.23). Indeed, in such cases this factor makes a distribution of this sort attractive if termination of the settlor's life interest is in prospect.

Chapter 8

Capital gains and income

8.1 This chapter explains how the return achieved by an offshore trust or its underlying company may be taxed as income rather than capital gain. As is explained in Chapters 2 and 7 an income return is normally advantageous insofar as the beneficiaries and settlor are resident and domiciled in the UK and the settler and his spouse are excluded from the trust.

Bond portfolios

8.2 The traditional method of investing for income is to invest in fixed-interest securities. Here the return is, by definition, income. On the sale of the security between interest payment dates the accrued interest is a matter of general law received as part of the capital sale proceeds. But helpfully the accrued interest scheme deems the accrued interest element in the sale price to be income also (TA 1988, s 713).

Some fixed-interest securities are wholly free of CGT, notably UK government securities and corporate securities which fall within the definition of qualifying corporate bond (TCGA 1992, s 115). Unfortunately, save in relation to corporation tax, a security is only a qualifying corporate bond if it is denominated in sterling and is non-convertible (ibid s 117). This means that most fixed-interest securities in a global portfolio are subject to CGT.

It might be thought that in practice this would not matter as, by being fixed-interest, such securities would be unlikely to generate capital gains. Unfortunately this is not always so, as currency gains are subject to CGT. Any gain on an asset denominated in a foreign currency is computed by comparing the sterling equivalent of its acquisition cost, fixed by exchange rates at the date of acquisition, with the sterling equivalent of the proceeds of disposal, fixed as at the date of disposal (see *Capcount Trading v Evans* [1993] STC 11). It follows that if a bond is denominated in a currency other than sterling, appreciation of that currency against sterling results in a capital gain.

It might be thought that even this, overall, ought not to result in gains, as bonds denominated in currencies which depreciate against sterling result in losses. Such losses are allowable in computing gains in offshore trusts (see paras 60.11 and 63.5). But while in many cases this may avoid net gains, it is not always a complete solution. One reason is that losses are only relievable on a current-year or brought forward basis (TCGA 1992, s 2(2)); if, therefore the disposals at a gain proceed the disposals at a loss, the latter are unrelieved.

A second point is that, if the portfolio is in an underlying company, losses are relieved only on a current year basis and cannot be relieved against any gains at trust level (see para 66.8).

But the main reason for not adopting a strategy of investment in bonds is quite simply commercial. The price of avoiding capital gain is the avoidance of capital growth. In commercial and investment terms this is unacceptable and, even supposing some bond element is appropriate, prudent allocation policy normally dictates growth investments as well.

High yielding shares

8.3 In constructing portfolios, it is usually possible to identify shares with a high dividend yield. Generally the yield reflects greater risk and so, while some such shares may perform well and generate capital gains, others do not and result in offsetting losses.

Unfortunately constructing a portfolio round such shares is open to many of the same objections as apply to bond portfolios. Two further drawbacks have also to be kept in mind. One is that there is no CGT exemption analogous to that for UK government securities and qualifying corporate bonds. The other is that the higher risk normally inherent in high-yielding shares means that diversification requirements may make it difficult commercially for more than a small proportion of a portfolio to be invested in such shares.

Non-distributor offshore funds

8.4 As is explained in Chapter 5, offshore funds are mutual funds resident outside the UK. Unless the fund is certified by HMRC as a distributor fund, the gain on any disposal or redemption is deemed to be income for UK tax purposes (see Chapter 71). This is so regardless of whether growth in the value of the fund reflects income or gains on the underlying investments.

This deeming of a capital gain to be income in many ways represents the complete answer to those seeking a return which is treated as income for tax purposes rather than capital gain. The completeness of the answer is enhanced by the fact that the growth of the hedge-fund industry means that a large proportion of global investment offerings are now in mutual fund form. Most such funds roll up their income and capital gains and so could not be certified as having distributor status. Indeed few are so certified, as narrow UK tax concerns are relatively unimportant to the global investment community.

Most professional asset managers now have their own mutual funds, which investors can invest in as an alternate to bespoke management. Many investment professionals consider that the return on a house's own funds can be better than that on equivalent bespoke management. Indeed some houses recommend smaller clients to buy their managed funds instead of using bespoke managers.

It follows from this that trustees or an underlying company can achieve an income return with full diversification by investing in a suitable selection of non-distributor funds. There are certain practical points to watch, most notably to ensure that the fund is a collective investment scheme in the sense that that term is used in the Financial Services and Markets Act 2000 (cf para 4.1). A further point is that the fund should not be closely held as otherwise there is a risk capital gains in the fund will be apportioned to investors under TCGA 1992, s 13. But these points, which are discussed further in Chapter 4 do not detract from the general advantages of non-distributor funds.

Offshore life policies

8.5 Offshore life policies are a more sophisticated form of wrapper than offshore mutual funds. But in tax terms their effect is the same, for the return is deemed to be income under the chargeable event legislation. That legislation is explained in Chapter 72, and life policies generally are considered in Chapter 5.

Life policies have two potential drawbacks which must be watched. One is that the trustees' own investment manager should not normally manage the investments underlying the policy, since otherwise the policy may fall foul of the severe anti-avoidance legislation directed at personal portfolio bonds (see para 72.11). The other is that life policies can incur greater costs than other investment vehicles, costs which should be carefully probed before a life policy strategy is adopted.

Underlying companies

8.6 Where trustees hold the trust investments through one or more wholly-owned holding companies, the shares in such companies are assets which can result in chargeable gains on a sale or liquidation. But as is discussed more fully in Chapter 9, value can be extracted from holding companies by dividend and, as a result, holding companies in the present context result more in an opportunity than a threat. Surplus value can be extracted by dividend prior to any sale or liquidation and if so it is income in form.

Dividends of this kind have two particular advantages. One is that they potentially inflate the total of s 740 relevant income, assuming the trust is discretionary. This in turn means there is more relevant income to match against capital distributions and thus less likelihood of distributions being taxed at the rather higher CGT rates (cf Chapter 13). Second, should the trust be fixed-interest, the dividend does pass to the life-tenant rather than being retained in trust. But the higher rate of tax is the dividend rate of 32.5%.

Direct investment

8.7 Many trusts hold not professionally managed portfolios but specific assets, for example real estate or holdings in private companies. With investments of this sort, capital gains may be difficult to avoid if, as no doubt is the hope, capital growth is achieved.

Two points can, however, be kept in mind as possible mitigation. One is that investments held by the trust directly are eligible for taper relief (TCGA 1992, s 2A and Sch A1). Accordingly, if the asset is shares in a private trading company, reduction of the taxable element of the gain to 25% may be achieved. Offshore trustees with direct holdings in trading companies should, so far as possible, always ensure the investment qualifies for business taper. Second, investments held through a holding company do not attract taper, but still enjoy relief for indexation. Over the years, indexation is a most valuable reduction in the gain on assets whose performance is steady rather than spectacular.

A final point, relevant to shares representing a controlling interest, is to remember that the trustees may be in a position to procure dividends. Such dividends, if commercially feasible, are income and may reduce any capital gain on the shares. Should the paying company be UK resident the dividend is taxable in the hands of the trustees as UK source income (or in the hands of the life-tenant if there is an interest in possession). But these results may be avoided if the UK shares are held through an offshore holding company.

Illiquid trusts

8.8 For many existing trusts, the preceding discussion is theory rather than practice in that the trust is already invested in assets showing substantial accrued gains or requiring retention for commercial reasons. In such cases an investment strategy generating a return which in tax terms is income may not be practical. But the points made in this chapter should be kept in mind and implemented if, when, and to the extent possible. Planning with existing offshore trusts is often incremental, exploiting opportunities as and when presented by legislative change or family circumstances.

Chapter 9

Underlying companies

Introduction

9.1 Offshore trustees frequently hold the trust assets through one or more wholly-owned offshore companies. For the most part the reason for this is not tax but the practical advantages of owning the trust investments through a company. This chapter addresses the tax issues raised by the use of holding companies and considers how far such companies are appropriate.

Tax issues

Company residence

9.2 As is explained in Chapter 38, the company is resident where the board meet, provided all decisions are put before the board and the directors properly discharge their duties under the relevant company law. There is no objection if most or all decisions are on the recommendation or request of the settlor or the beneficiaries. But the board must give genuine consideration to all such matters and any request should be put in the first instance to the trustee shareholders. They should then, if thought fit, communicate it to the directors.

Board meetings should be properly minuted and requests and recommendations recorded in writing. If, in fact, the directors and trustees stand aside and let a UK resident settlor or beneficiaries run the company, HMRC may have grounds to contend that the company's residence is in the UK.

Attribution of income

9.3 If the settlor or his spouse are beneficiaries under the trust the question arises of whether the company's income can be attributed to him. It is generally accepted that attribution is not possible under the settlement code in ITTOIA 2005, Part 5, Chapter 5 (see para 59.24).

But even if Chapter 5 does not apply, s 739 does have to be addressed. As is described in Chapters 54 and 55, this section applies both where income becomes payable to a non-resident entity as a result of the transfer alone and where it becomes so payable as a result of the transfer and one or more associated operations (s 739(1)). As a result it applies to holding company income, for the vesting of assets in the trustees is the transfer and the incorporation and funding of the company are associated operations (cf *Corbett's Executrices v IRC* (1943) 25 TC 305).

Attribution of gains

9.4 If the trust gains are attributable to the settlor under TCGA 1992, s 86, the gains so attributable include any which would be apportioned to the trust under TCGA 1992, s 13 if the trust were resident (see para 66.24). As a result, such of the company's gains as are attributable under s 13 are included in the trust gains.

Benefits and capital payments

9.5 If the company's gains and income are not taxed as the settlor's on an arising basis, their taxability as and when UK resident beneficiaries receive benefits or capital payments from the trust has to be considered. The position with gains is the same as where gains arise directly to the trust, in that the company's gains are included in the trust's s 87 pool (or in a Sch 4C pool insofar as the s 87 pool has been carried into a Sch 4C pool) (cf para 66.24). So too income in the company is likely to be relevant income for the purposes of s 740, although this is not always so (see paras 13.2 and 57.3).

Benefits in kind

9.6 The risk of benefits in kind being taxed under ITEPA 2003 arises in the same way as with directly-owned companies, if either the settlor or a beneficiary can be said to be a shadow director (see Chapters 53 and 69). It used to be thought there was little risk in this area, for the most they can do is make requests to the trustees, it being up to the trustees to communicate with the directors if they think fit. Unfortunately, as is described in Chapter 53, a recent case has widened the definition of the term shadow director and on one view at least a settlor or beneficiary could be caught if the actual directors regularly take account of his views.

Double counting

9.7 The accretion of value represented by the company's income or gains is only at the disposal of the trustee shareholders if it is paid in dividend or if the company is sold or liquidated. Inevitably this means the same accretion of value is income or gains twice, often being income once and gains once. The result is that potential liability can arise twice on the settlor if gains and/or income is taxed as his. It also means that relevant income and trust gains can be doubled up under the benefits and capital payments codes.

The general rule is undoubtedly double taxation and it is for this reason that in tax terms holding companies are generally regarded as unattractive. But some reliefs from the double taxation exist in law and practice and as a result it is necessary to consider the different situations which can arise separately.

Company income taxed as the settlor's

9.8 As noted above, if the settlor or his spouse are beneficiaries under the trust, income in the company is likely to be taxable as his under TA 1988, s 739. Should the company be sold or liquidated, any gain then accruing is assessable on the settlor under TCGA 1992, s 86 (see Chapter 60). No credit exists, either in law or in practice, for any tax he previously bore under s 739 on the income in the company.

The position is otherwise should the company pay the income to the trust in dividend. Prima facie such dividend is assessable on the settlor both under s 739 and under ITTOIA 2005, s 624. But it is generally thought that in a straightforward case, HMRC would not seek to assess the dividend again under either s 739 or ITTOIA 2005, s 624. Passages in *Tax Bulletin* 40 stating that income is not in practice assessed under both s 739 and the former TA 1988, Part XV are consistent with this although it has to be said not explicit. In fact as is explained in para 55.19 such double assessment may be precluded in law for s 739 will have deemed the income in the company to be that of the transferor for all purposes of the Income Tax Acts.

Company gains assessed on the settlor

9.9 As described in para 66.25, tax assessable on the settlor on a distribution from the company may be offset by tax assessed on him under TCGA 1992, s 86 in respect of any gain realised by the company. But this relief is a limited relief, for it only applies if the distribution takes place within a three to four-year period after the gain is realised. Further, while it applies both to dividends and to liquidation distributions, it does not apply if the company is sold.

In all cases where this relief is not in point, double tax results. If the company is liquidated after the three or four-year period or sold at any time, any gain is chargeable on the settlor in full. As described in para 66.25, there is not even a deduction of tax from gain, for the settlor does not make the disposal occasioned by the sale or liquidation (cf s 13(7)).

Company income or gains not assessed on the settlor

9.10 If the company income and/or gains are not taxable as the settlor's, UK tax only comes into issue if the trustees make a distribution to a UK-resident beneficiary, whether as income or capital, in the latter event liability being under TA 1988, s 740 or TCGA 1992, s 87 or Sch 4C (see Chapter 13). In law, income and gains accruing to both the trust and the company are included in the s 740 relevant income and in the s 87 pool of trust gains. Strictly therefore the aggregate relevant income and trust gains are doubled.

In one situation, this doubling up should be avoided. This is where income in the company is paid up as dividend to the trust and then distributed by the trust as income. Here the income will genuinely have been paid away at both stages and so, on HMRC practice if not law, it is never relevant income (see para 57.9).

This situation apart, it is said that in practice HMRC do not double count for the purposes of s 740: in other words if income of the company is paid up in dividend to the trust and retained there, there is only one lot of relevant income (see para 57.15). But while this practice, if such it be, may accord with law, it is not published. Certainly it does not apply to gains, or where income in the company is realised at trust level by way of gains in a sale or liquidation.

Loans

9.11 It is often said that in practice the points made above are not serious, for the company can be capitalised by loan from the trust and accordingly money can be passed back to the trust by loan repayment, without doubling-up of the kind referred to above. This is true. But what it ignores is that if the company's investments do well, in time sufficient income and gains are generated to repay the loan in full. All that is then left is the shares showing substantial unrealised gain.

Another solution sometimes canvassed is for the company to fund the trust by upstream loan – ie by loan to the trust. Insofar as this was ever a satisfactory solution, it has been rendered dangerous by the rules as to trustee borrowing, for an upstream constitutes trustee borrowing. This means it results in a deemed disposal of the company shares and any other assets held directly by the trustees if the trustees make a loan or effect a capital distribution (see Chapter 62). It also causes any s 87 pool in the trust to be converted into a Sch 4C pool such as more readily results in gains being allocated to UK beneficiaries (see Chapter 64).

Other tax disadvantages of a holding company

Company residence and benefits in kind

9.12 When trustees use a holding company it is necessary to worry about company residence and benefits in kind. If the trustees hold the investments directly, issues as to the central management and control of the company and shadow directors simply do not arise.

Tax credit

9.13 UK or foreign tax borne by a holding company cannot be credited against UK tax charged on distributions from the trust. Where the investments are held directly by the trustees, credit for UK and foreign tax may be claimed by the life-tenant if the trust is then subject to an interest in possession (see para 12.2). Otherwise credit for UK tax may be allowed under ESC B18 (see para 12.7).

Unrelieved losses

9.14 Use of a company may well generate unrelieved losses for CGT purposes, whether in computing the settlor's liability under TCGA 1992, s 86 or trust gains under s 87. This is because TCGA 1992, s 13 does not, in general, allow losses to be apportioned (see para 66.8). All that is possible is that losses in the company may be set on a current-year basis against gains apportioned from the same company or from another company in which the trust concerned is also a participator. Losses cannot be carried forward in the company insofar as they exceed gains in the year concerned and, more importantly, losses in the company cannot be set against gains realised by the trustees.

The practical result of this is that in a trust and company structure there may be substantial unrelieved losses. This problem simply does not arise if the company or companies are dispensed with for then all losses and gains arise at trust level.

Loss of taper relief

9.15 For the purposes of s 13 the company's gains are computed with the benefit of indexation but without taper (s 13(11A)). Now that inflation is low, indexation can be less attractive than taper, particularly where the base cost of the asset is small or business taper applies. Gains accruing to the trustees, by contrast, are computed with the benefit of any applicable taper relief.

Unexpected capital payment

9.16 A somewhat technical problem to note is that a payment from the trustees to the company may count as a capital payment to UK resident individuals. The problem arises because a capital payment to a non-resident company counts as a capital payment to any UK resident individual who controls it (TCGA 1992, s 96). By concession, the problem does not arise if, as is normal, none of the shares in the company is owned by a UK individual (TCGA 1992, s 96(10); ESC D40). If, however, the settlor or a beneficiary owns some shares and the trust the rest, a non-arm's length payment from the trustees to the company does count as a capital payment to the settlor or beneficiary, for the trust holding is attributed to them in determining whether they control the company (TA 1988, s 417(3)(b), (c)) (see further para 65.13).

Updated base cost on death

9.17 If the trust is an interest in possession trust, its assets may receive a tax-free updated base cost for CGT purposes on the death of the life tenant (TCGA 1992, s 72). This is so if the interest subsisted on 22 March 2006 or is a transitional serial interest (see Chapter 44). Where investments are held through a holding company, the new base cost does not extend to the underlying investments. This can be particularly unfortunate should the company vest in UK beneficiaries absolutely on the death of the life tenant, for then they will potentially be subject to tax on the unrealised gains in the company under TCGA 1992, s 13 when it realises its assets.

Trustee borrowing

9.18 As noted above, an upstream loan from the company to the trust is trustee borrowing. If the trustees do not apply the loan for normal trust purposes, any subsequent distribution or loan by the trustees triggers a complete or partial disposal of all the trust assets (see further Chapter 62).

A related risk arises if the trustees borrow money from another source and transfer it to the company. Here too there is a deemed disposal unless the transfer is structured as a subscription for shares or securities in the company (see para 62.10).

Tax advantages of a holding company

9.19 Although holding companies are often regarded as unattractive in tax terms, they do have some tax advantages. On occasion these justify the formation of a company and they can certainly ameliorate the problems posed by existing corporate structures.

Role of dividends

9.20 Payment of dividends by the company may lessen tax on distributions to UK beneficiaries. This is particularly so if the trust income is not assessable as the settlor's and the recipient beneficiary has an interest in possession. This subject is discussed in para 14.9.

Section 739

9.21 One advantage of a holding company arises where the settlor is a beneficiary of the trust. Here the settlement code catches the trust income, but income in a company is only attributed to the settlor if s 739 applies. Section 739 can be avoided if the company is bought replete with investments (see para 55.12) and so here there is a structure in which the settlor can be a beneficiary without having income attributed to him on an arising basis.

UK assets

9.22 Where the trust has UK assets, use of a company means that tax on UK dividends and interest if the trust is not settlor-interested is restricted to the tax (if any) withheld on interest (FA 1995, s 128; see further para 34.14). Exemption from UK tax obtains in respect of bank and building society interest in that such interest may be paid gross to an offshore company (TA 1988, s 481; Income Tax (Building Societies) (Dividends and Interest) Regulations 1990 (SI 1990/2231), reg 4(1)(g)).

In appropriate cases, these are real advantages. This is not so with interest, as plenty of offshore investments exist which pay interest gross. But with dividends, the advantage is clear, and relevant where the trustees wish commercially to hold shares in UK companies. It is true that the same advantage can be achieved by investing in the UK through an offshore mutual fund in corporate form (cf Chapter 4) but there may be good commercial reasons why such is unattractive. This is the position where the trust investment is one or more large or controlling holdings or where it is designed to pick stock on a bespoke basis.

UK income of a non-resident company which is not dividends or interest is normally subject to basic rate income tax (22%) (see para 34.4). The main category of income affected by this is rental income and the practical result here is that interposition of a company reduces the rate of tax from 40% to 22%. But in practice deductions such as interest often render this point unimportant as the deductions may result in little taxable income.

Retention of income

9.23 Where the trust is a fixed-interest trust, use of a company enables de facto accumulation to be achieved. If income and gains are retained in the company, there is no trust income to which the life tenant is entitled.

This can be attractive in some family situations. However such a strategy can have trust law implications. The basic duty of trustees of fixed-interest trusts is to maintain a balance between life tenant and remaindermen providing the life tenant with a reasonable income. It is arguable that trustees can only permit income to be rolled-up in the company with the concurrence of the life tenant and certainly they would need to be given genuine consideration to his interests before doing so.

Trustee borrowing

9.24 As explained in para 62.20, borrowing by a holding company does not count as trustee borrowing for the purposes of TCGA 1992, Sch 4B. This means all the risks entailed in that schedule are avoided. As a result where borrowing is needed to pay for an investment, holding the investment through a company may be attractive.

Existing companies

9.25 The above discussion has assumed the trustees are considering whether or not to incorporate a company to hold the trust investments. Difficult issues arise where the trust's investments are already in a company and the factors discussed earlier in this chapter are felt to render a company unattractive.

Can the company be dispensed with?

9.26 The first step is to consider whether the company can be eliminated without tax cost. This is possible if there is no net latent gain on either company's shares or its investments. It is also possible if commercially the company can be sold as a going concern and its shares are free of gain. In all such cases consideration should be given as to whether the company should be retained.

Assuming the shares in the company do show a gain, it is normally worth keeping the company in being, for eventually 40% of the latent gain on its shares will drop out of charge under taper relief. But it is prudent to avoid future growth in the company, and in this regard it helps if new investments are effected outside the company in the direct name of the trustees. This, however, may be difficult if all value in the trust is held through the company. Consideration may be given to making loans from the company to the trust but, as noted in para 9.11 above, such will be trustee borrowing within TCGA 1992, Sch 4B. In such a case it is therefore necessary to avoid being caught by Sch 4B. This is best done if the proceeds are spent on ordinary trust assets and that the trustees themselves do not make distributions or loans (see further Chapter 62).

Distributions

9.27 Assuming the company is kept in being, issues will arise as to whether the trustees should receive the company's income and gains by way of dividend or leave them in the company, thereby increasing the potential gain on any disposal of the shares. It is difficult to generalise but some relevant considerations are as follows:

(1) In general distribution of the company's income as income is prudent, for at worst it is relevant income for the purposes of s 740. This avoids it being double-counted and if retained at trust level it is relevant income in the hands of the trustees rather than inflating the potential gain on the company shares.

(2) Distribution may be particularly attractive where the trust has a UK-resident and domiciled life tenant, for, as noted in para 9.20, dividends are assessable on him as they arise and attract tax at 32.5%. However this presupposes the trustees' wish to distribute value to him. If they do not, distributions by the company will need to be avoided.

(3) Dividends may be less attractive if some or all of the beneficiaries are UK-resident but not domiciled, for capital distributions from the trust to them can be taxable by reference to relevant income but not by reference to s 87 or Sch 4C gains (cf Chapters 19 and 20. Should a non-domiciliary be life-tenant, the dividends are taxable on the remittance basis and the 32.5% rate does not apply.

Chapter 10

Traps and pitfalls

10.1 As will be apparent from the preceding chapters of this book, many tax traps exist for offshore trustees and their beneficiaries. This chapter lists some of the more general points to look out for.

The long tail of relevant income and trust gains

10.2 It should be remembered that the income taken into account as relevant income, and the gains in a s 87 pool, can go back as far as 10 March and 6 April 1981 respectively. The practical effect of this is that much research may be needed to confirm that a distribution really will be tax-free and there is clearly a danger old income or gains may be overlooked.

There are two exceptions to the long tail. One is that if the settlor was non-resident or non-domiciled the cut-off date for capital gains is 17 March 1998 (see para 63.14). The second is that any gains or income assessed on the settlor on an arising basis are excluded. It should be noted that gains are unlikely to have been so assessed before 17 March 1998 on account of the transitional provisions for pre-1991 settlements (see Chapter 61) and that income within s 739 but not remitted can be relevant income for the purposes of s 740 if the settlor is non-domiciled (cf para 57.12).

Trustee borrowing

10.3 The rules relating to trustee borrowing and transfers of value present real difficulties for offshore trustees (see Chapter 62). The best practical advice is that trustees should not borrow. If they do borrow any proposed course of action thereafter needs to be reviewed to check it is not a transfer of value within the meaning of TCGA 1992, Sch 4B or, if it is, that the borrowing has been applied for normal trust purposes.

A particular danger is where the trustees borrow from an underlying company. If they use the money borrowed to lend down to another company, or to distribute or lend to a beneficiary, such is a transfer of value for the purposes of Sch 4B. A deemed disposal of the trust assets will thereby be triggered.

Should there be a Sch 4B transfer, not merely are the ensuing gains assessable on the settlor on an arising basis if the trust is within s 86, but gains in the settlement's s 87 pool are carried into a Sch 4C pool. This has two disadvantages, namely that they cannot be washed out by distributions to non-residents or non-domiciliaries and can be allocated in full to the beneficiaries of any other settlement to which the settlement transfers funds. Inter alia this last point means that a s 87 pool in excess of the value of the trust fund may still all be taxable. Sch 4C is discussed further in Chapter 64.

Tainting

10.4 The rules as to tainting are not nearly as significant as they once were (see Chapter 61). However, if breached they could bring a pre-1998 grandchildrens' settlement within TCGA 1992, s 86 and so result in gains being attributed to the settlor on an arising basis. If therefore the settlor is alive and is, or may become, resident and domiciled in the UK, tainting should be avoided unless in any event the grandchildren and their spouses are all wholly excluded.

Unexpected s 13 gains

10.5 As explained in para 66.23, gains in a close company can be apportioned under TCGA 1992, s 79B to trustee participators if the company is resident in a country with which the UK has concluded a double tax treaty and the gains are treaty protected. The same result follows if the trustees are participators in a UK company and that company is a participator in the company resident in the treaty jurisdiction. As with all gains so apportioned, the gains come within TCGA 1992, s 86 if that section applies to the settlement and otherwise they constitute trust gains within s 87.

Section 13 does not apply to gains realised on assets used by the company for the purposes of a trade. But otherwise its ambit is very wide, extending to any participator with more than 10% of the company concerned. Many trustees hold shares in UK private companies and, until the enactment of TCGA 1992, s 79B, were not concerned with what went on in foreign subsidiaries of such companies. Now, however, they should be, for s 79B means any gain on non-trading assets is apportionable to the trust. Because this applies only where the gain is treaty protected, the gains caught will tend to be those realised by bona fide foreign subsidiaries rather than by purely offshore subsidiaries. The latter are not treaty protected and so are outside s 79B.

Offshore funds

10.6 As explained in para 8.4, investment in offshore funds can represent good tax planning for some forms of trust, particularly children's trusts. However, for other trusts there are dangers, specifically two explained in Chapter 71:

(1) Offshore income gains are not washed out by distributions to non-residents.
(2) Where the trust is a settlor-interested trust, on a strict reading of the legislation, the offshore income gain could be taxed twice or even three times. Such trusts should therefore avoid offshore funds.

UK real estate

10.7 Offshore trustees holding UK land, whether directly or through a company, need to keep TA 1988, s 776 in mind. This section applies if the land is acquired or developed with the sole or main object of realising a gain on its disposal. It is expressed to apply for the purposes of preventing tax avoidance, but the Court of Appeal has held that a tax avoidance purpose is not a pre-requisite for its operation (*Page v Lowther* [1983] STC 799).

Section 776 applies as much to non-resident as resident holders of UK land. In practice, HMRC frequently invoke it where non-residents sell developed or developable land even where, on the face of it, the preconditions for the section are not met. They have power to direct the purchaser to withhold tax, but this power is only exercisable once the land is under contract (TA 1988, s 777(a); *Pardoe v Entergy Power Development Corpn* [2000] STC 286).

The real sting in s 776 lies in s 776(8). This applies where the opportunity of realising the gain was provided by some other person and requires the provider to be assessed instead of the person who actually realises the gain. It is clear this sub-section applies where a person such as the settlor diverts the opportunity to make a profit to an offshore trust or company (*Yuill v Wilson* [1980] STC 460). The true ambit of s 776(8) is unclear, particularly how far it applies merely to those who introduce a purchase to an offshore entity. But what is clear is that it is unwise for the settlor or beneficiaries to be involved in any way in the buying or selling of land by the trust or any underlying company.

Benefits to the settlor

10.8 It must be remembered that if the settlor is alive and resident in the UK, inadvertence can cause gains to be assessed as his even if such is not already the position under TCGA 1992, s 86. This is so if in any tax year he or his immediate family receives a benefit (cf TCGA 1992, Sch 5 para 2(1)(c)).

In relation to income the same result can follow if he or his spouse receive a benefit (TA 1988, ss 739 and 742(2)(c)). More seriously the receipt by the settlor of a capital sum or the making or repayment of a loan can cause the whole income in the structure to be assessed as his for ever or, in the case of a loan to the settlor, until the loan is repaid (TA 1988, s 739(3); ITTOIA 2005, s 633; see paras 55.10 and 59.9). Great care is therefore required in all dealings as between the settlor and the trust.

Benefits to the settlor could also trigger liability under the pre-owned asset rules if conferred after 6 April 2005 (see Chapter 70). Those rules are most likely to come into issue if the trust or any underlying company owns land or chattels of which the settlor has partial use or enjoyment. Such use or enjoyment would be in breach of trust if the settlor is not a beneficiary, but that does not necessarily mean it does not happen, particularly where the asset is abroad. The pre-owned asset rules would come into issue if the use did not amount to a reservation within the meaning of the GWR rules (see further Chapter 47).

Benefits in kind

10.9 A benefit conferred on a UK resident beneficiary may be taxable otherwise than as a capital payment or s 740 benefit. Such liability arises should the employment income rules taxing benefits in kind be in point. These rules are considered in Chapter 69 and need to be kept in mind where the trustees own an offshore company of which a beneficiary could be a shadow director (see Chapter 53). They may also come into issue if a UK beneficiary is an actual employee of a company in which the trust is interested. In such cases particular dangers attach to loans and distributions of shares or securities in specie.

Should a distribution or other benefit be taxable as a benefit in kind it is not taxable under TA 1988, s 740 or TCGA 1992, s 87 as those sections only catch payments and benefits which are not otherwise taxable.

Beneficial interests

10.10 No UK resident beneficiary should effect a disposal of a beneficial interest in an offshore trust. Should he do so, the transaction is subject to CGT, for the exemption for beneficial interests does not apply unless the trust is UK resident (TCGA 1992, s 85). A particular sting is that normally the beneficiary has a nil acquisition cost, for the creation of an interest under the terms of a settlement does not involve a corresponding disposal and so market value is not substituted (TCGA 1992, s 17(2)). An exception to this is where the trust has emigrated from the UK without previously having been non-resident, for then beneficial interests are rebased (TCGA 1992, s 85(3)).

A beneficiary disposes of his beneficial interest if he sells it, gives it away, or releases it. Save in the case of a sale, market value is substituted, for the transaction is not at arms length (TCGA 1992, s 17(1)). In many instances where an interest is released, market value is nil, for the interest is either discretionary or subject to overriding powers. But save where this is clearly so transactions in beneficial interests should be avoided.

Schemes to avoid the charge on beneficial interests have in the past involved repatriating the trust to the UK prior to the sale of the beneficial interest, or repatriating the trust and then emigrating it again. These schemes are now blocked, the former completely (TCGA 1992, s 76(1B)) and the latter wherever there are unallocated trust gains outstanding at the time of the emigration (ibid, s 85(10)).

Transfers between trusts

10.11 The transfer of all or part of the trust fund from one trust to another gives rise to CGT difficulties, particularly the issue of whether the two settlements are separate and the possibility that the transfer is a capital payment to a beneficiary if made in exercise of a power to benefit that beneficiary. This and related issues are discussed in paras 63.29 and 65.6.

A further issue is raised by the rules as to trustee borrowing. Should the transferor trust itself have a Sch 4C pool of gains, or have received funds from another trust which is a relevant settlement in relation to such a pool, the effect of the transfer will be to render the gains in the Sch 4C pool assessable on the beneficiaries of the transferee trust. The practical result is that the trustees of the transferee trust need to review the Sch 4C position of the transferor trust before accepting the transfer. The same considerations apply if the transfer is itself a Sch 4B transfer, ie if the transferor trust then has outstanding trustee borrowing for in such circumstances the effect of the transfer is to convert the transferor's trusts s 87 pool into a Sch 4C pool. All this is explained in Chapter 64.

Should the advance be into a pre-existing UK settlement further adverse consequences may follow. The exercise will render capital distributions from the UK settlement, hitherto tax free, taxable by reference to the gains pools in the offshore settlement (see paras 63.26 and 64.8). A similar analysis is likely to obtain as respects s 740 relevant income (see para 56.22). An additional consequence is that any disposals of beneficial interests under the UK settlement will become chargeable (TCGA 1992, s 76(1A)(b)).

Separate funds

10.12 A trust in separate funds can give rise to difficulties in that, unless a sub-fund election has been made, it has a single s 87 pool of gains.

Accordingly gains realised in one fund can be allocated to capital payments from another. This issue and possible solutions is discussed in para 63.28. A similar problem can arise with s 740 relevant income (para 56.15).

Involuntary vesting

10.13 Some offshore settlements, particularly older ones, provide for one or more beneficiaries to become absolutely entitled on attaining a specified age or on a specified event. Common examples are accumulation and maintenance settlements which confer absolute interests, or fixed-interest settlements where the remainderman takes absolutely.

Such settlements can be a disaster in tax terms. In the case of the death of the life-tenant, the settled fund may suffer IHT at 40% and then the net proceeds received by the beneficiary may be taxed at 40% under TA 1988, s 740 or 64% under TCGA 1992, s 87. In the case of absolute vesting under an accumulation and maintenance trust there will be the latter charges and, unless a hold-over election is possible, the total of trust gains will be inflated by any gains on the deemed disposal occasioned by the absolute entitlement (TCGA 1992, s 71). A further misfortune arises if the settlor was non-domiciled but the recipient beneficiary is not, for then the assets are propelled straight into the IHT net.

These difficulties may be avoided if the funds are able to be and are appointed on new trusts prior to absolute vesting. Where there is not an overriding power, recourse has to be had to express or statutory powers of advancement. Normally these can be used, for avoidance of the tax penalties can be viewed as sufficient benefit to the beneficiary. But if the exercise amounts to an advance to a new trust, HMRC are likely to contend it is a capital payment (see para 65.6) and generally it is essential to take specialist advice, both as to local trust law and as to UK tax.

Civil partnership

10.14 As explained in paras 55.28 and 59.3, a trap exists where the settlor of any settlement whose income is not currently assessed as his under TA 1988, s 739 or ITTOIA 2005, s 624 enters into civil partnership. In such case, the income does become assessable as his unless the terms of the settlement, as well as excluding the settlor and his spouse, also exclude any civil partner. Where, therefore, civil partnership of the settlor is in prospect, amendment to the trust deed should be made in advance of the ceremony.

As a matter of strict construction this point applies in relation to s 739 even where the settlor is not in civil partnership (see para 55.28) and it also arises as respects the attribution of gains (see para 60.9). For this reason any new settlement should expressly exclude civil partners in the same way as spouses. As explained in para 60.9, HMRC have said informally they will not take any point on the non-exclusion of civil partners in relation to settlements existing on 23 November 2005. But prudent trustees will undoubtedly wish to exercise powers of appointment or exclusion so as to put the matter beyond doubt as a matter of law.

Chapter 11

Trust immigration

Introduction

11.1 This chapter reviews the tax consequences and possible planning opportunities which arise when an offshore trust becomes UK resident. It assumes the settlor and beneficiaries are resident and domiciled in the UK.

How a trust becomes UK resident

11.2 A non-resident trust becomes UK resident if the non-resident trustees retire and UK trustees are appointed in their place. The tests of what renders a trust UK resident are explained in para 37.2.

If the trust is governed by English law, there is no trust law obstacle to appointing English trustees (cf para 28.2). Should the trust be governed by foreign law, that law determines whether the foreign trustees can validly resign in favour of UK trustees. But most trusts contain express powers to appoint trustees in any part of the world and in that event there is unlikely to be difficulty although the point should be checked with local lawyers.

A trust governed by foreign law retains the foreign law as its governing law notwithstanding the appointment of UK trustees. Most trusts contain power to change the governing law and it may be thought this power should be exercised on immigration to replace the foreign law with English law. As a general rule that temptation should be resisted as English trust law tends to be more restrictive than its offshore counterparts. A particular example is the English restrictions on accumulation which, despite discussion, have still not been repealed.

Income tax

Discretionary and accumulation and maintenance trusts

11.3 Once a discretionary or accumulation trust becomes UK resident, its worldwide income is assessable on the trustees. As a general rule the rate of tax is the 40% rate for trusts, although the first slice of trust income enjoys basic or lower rate tax (TA 1988, s 686D). Dividends not within the £500 first slice are taxed at the dividend rate. In the case of foreign dividends this means tax at the rate of 32.5% (TA 1988 s 686(1A)). In the case of UK dividends, the tax credit mechanism means that tax on the actual amount of UK dividends is 25% (TA 1988 s 686; ITTOIA 2005, s 397). The first slice is normally £1,000, but it is reduced if the settler has made other settlements (TA 1988, s 686E).

The position post-immigration contrasts with the position pre-immigration in that foreign income is brought into charge to tax. The tax exposure on UK income is unaffected as UK tax payable by non-resident trustees is not restricted to tax withheld where the trust has UK beneficiaries (FA 1995, s 128(5); see 34.15). Dividends received by foreign trustees do not enjoy a tax credit but are treated as received net of the dividend ordinary rate (ITTOIA 2005, s 399(4)). The net position is thus the same.

Once the trust becomes UK resident, income distributions by the trustees fall within the provisions of TA 1988 s 687. This requires tax at the 40% rate for trusts to be withheld from any distribution and paid over to HMRC. The trustees are entitled to offset this tax against any tax paid by them under TA 1988 s 686 on the trust income as it arises. But in the case of UK dividends the tax eligible for the offset is only the 25% tax actually paid by the trustees. If s 687 tax exceeds the post-immigration s 686 tax, the excess may be offset against s 686 tax on UK income charged while the trust was non-resident (s 687(3)). But there is no s 686 tax on prior foreign income and so if that income is distributed after the assumption of residence there is a s 687 cost to the trustees (albeit recouped by the beneficiary when he offsets the s 687 tax withheld against his personal tax).

Fixed-interest trusts

11.4 As described in para 12.2, the income of a fixed-interest trust is taxed as that of the life-tenant. Accordingly, tax treatment is determined by his residence status, rather than that of the trustees, and immigration of the trust has little impact. However, once the trust is UK resident, the trustees are accountable for basic or lower rate tax on behalf of the beneficiary.

In one respect immigration does alter tax treatment. Certain categories of foreign capital receipt are deemed to be income, for example offshore income gains (see Chapter 71). These are not assessable on the trustees while non-resident but become chargeable at the rate for trusts once the trust immigrates (TA 1988 s 686A).

Settlor-interested trusts

11.5 Should the trust be settlor-interested all the trust income is taxed as the settlor's if he is UK resident (see Chapter 59). These rules apply regardless of the residence status of the trustees, so are unaffected by the immigration of the trust. Immigration does cause TA 1988 s 739 to cease to apply (cf Chapters 54 and 55), but this is normally not significant as in relation to trusts s 739 is largely co-terminous with ITTOIA 2005, s 624.

Trust capital distributions

11.6 The general rule is that capital distributions by the trust once it is resident are free of income tax. This, however, is subject to the following exceptions:

(1) If the recipient is a minor child of the settlor, liability may arise under ITTOIA 2005 s 629 (see para 59.8). This applies equally whether the trust is resident or non-resident.
(2) Outstanding offshore income gains on immigration are allocated to distributions of capital when the trust is resident until exhausted. This is because the rules as to offshore income gains described in Chapter 71 apply (see TCGA 1992 s 89(1) and para 11.8 below).
(3) Distributions of capital when the trust is resident may be taxed under TA 1988 s 740 insofar as the trust accumulated foreign income whilst it was non-resident and such income has neither been taxed as the settlor's on an arising basis nor allocated to a prior s 740 benefit (cf para 56.20).
(4) Distributions of capital may also be taxed insofar as income has been retained in a company owned by a trust. Provided the company is foreign registered this is so whether it remains non-resident or immigrates, as for s 740 purposes a foreign registered company is deemed non resident (s 742(8)).

This last point is potentially a trap should an underlying company immigrate with the trust, for immigration will expose the company's profits to corporation tax. There is no provision crediting that tax against any s 740 tax.

Capital gains tax

Section 86 trusts

11.7 Should an immigrating trust be within TCGA 1992 s 86 while non-resident, its gains, while non-resident, are taxed as those of the settlor. Section 86 is explained in Chapter 60 and applies if the settlor, his children, or in some cases, his grandchildren, are beneficiaries. Effectively it results in a tax charge of 40%.

When such a trust immigrates, the gains continue to be taxed as the settlor's if the settlor and his spouse are beneficiaries (TCGA 1992 s 77). If the trust is a children's or grandchildren's trust from which the settlor and his spouse are wholly excluded, gains cease to be assessable as the settlor's and are taxed as those of the trustees. But the rate is still 40%.

Other trusts

11.8 Should the trust not be within s 86, the effect of immigration is to bring trust gains into charge to tax in the hands of the trustees at the rate of

40%. Such gains are not allocated to capital payments. Tax on the latter would be at the personal rate of the beneficiary and as a result the effect of immigration may be to increase tax insofar as the trustees make distributions of capital to UK resident and domiciled beneficiaries whose CGT annual exemption or lower-rate bands are available.

An exception to the rule that capital payments by the resident trustees are not taxable is made if, when the trust immigrates, it has outstanding trust gains in a s 87 pool (TCGA 1992 s 89). As described in para 63.19 these may be allocated to capital payments after immigration. The same applies if the trust has a Sch 4C pool or has received, or while resident receives, capital from another trust which has such a pool (para 64.8). Supplemental tax is applicable so the rate of tax may be as high as 64%.

Beneficial interests in trusts

11.9 The exemption for disposals of beneficial interests in trusts does not apply if the trust has previously been non-resident (TCGA 1992 76(1A)). Accordingly, the position in this regard remains the same as when the trust was non-resident (see further para 10.10).

Trustee borrowing

11.10 The rules as to trustee borrowing in TCGA 1992 Sch 4B and 4C apply to resident trusts which have previously been non-resident. On a strict reading this is so even if there are no outstanding gains from the non-resident period or if all such gains have been allocated to capital payments (see para 62.19).

The result of this should the trustees effect a Sch 4B transfer while resident, is a complete or partial disposal of all the trust assets. Should the trust be settlor-interested, the ensuing gain is assessed as the settlor's under TCGA 1992 s 77. Otherwise it is assessed on the trustees and taxed at 40%.

There is an argument, discussed in para 64.13, that the transfer also has the result of creating a Sch 4C pool, with the result that the gain is effectively taxed for a second time in the hands of beneficiaries in receipt of capital payments. Pending clarification of this risk, trustees who have immigrated should take particular care to avoid a Sch 4B transfer.

Rebasing on immigration

11.11 In contrast to some jurisdictions, the UK does not rebase the assets of immigrants. The result is that a gain realised on the disposal of an asset acquired prior to immigration includes the pre-immigration proportion of the gain.

Thought should therefore be given to re-basing prior to immigration. Such could be achieved by selling and buying back assets, although if this is done, the possible impact of the *Ramsay* principle on the purchase and buy back should be considered. In the case of shares and securities more than 30 days must elapse between the two transactions (TCGA 1992, s 106A(5)). An alternate method of re-basing is to create a new settlement and transfer the assets to it.

Re-basing will generate trust gains for the purposes of s 87 and so is of little point if capital is likely to be distributed to UK resident and domiciled beneficiaries, or if capital has been distributed to such beneficiaries and is as yet unmatched with trust gains. As noted below, re-basing must be undertaken in the tax year prior to immigration rather than in the year of immigration itself.

Assets showing a loss should not be re-based. This is because the loss is allowable once the trust is UK resident.

Emigration

11.12 Should the trust re-emigrate, then, in contrast to immigration, there is a deemed disposal of its assets at market value (TCGA 1992 s 80 and 185; see para 28.8). The practical result is that once the trust moves to the UK, its gains are locked into charge to UK tax. This is often cited as an argument against immigration.

Year of immigration

11.13 As with individuals, income tax is charged on trusts by tax years. The trust is taxable in the year of immigration on its full income of that year as the law does not allow tax years to be split. ESC A11, which provides for split years, is expressed as applying only to individuals.

Trustees are liable to CGT in a tax year if they are resident in the UK during any part of the year (TCGA 1992 s 2(2)). In contrast to individuals, this has never been abrogated by any split-year concession (cf ESC D2). As a result any gain realised in the tax year of immigration is chargeable even if realised prior to immigration. As just noted, this needs to be borne in mind if consideration is being given to pre-immigration rebasing.

Inheritance tax

11.14 Immigration does not affect the IHT status of a trust. The matter remains governed by the domicile of the settlor when the settlement was made and the situs of the assets (see Chapter 46).

Underlying companies

11.15 Should the trustees own one or more companies, their position should be considered if the trust immigrates. On certain scenarios immigration of a company may be considered even if the trust remains non-resident.

Becoming resident

11.16 As explained in Chapter 38, a company resides where the central management and control of its business is exercised. In the normal case such management and control is exercised by the board and the company resides where the board meets. Accordingly, moving the company to the UK is achieved if the foreign directors resign and a UK board which meets regularly in the UK is appointed in their place.

Now that UK registered companies are deemed to be UK resident (see para 38.27), an immigrating company is ipso facto registered under foreign law and governed by that law. English company law does not allow the re-registration or re-domiciliation of foreign companies, and so the immigrating company has to remain subject to foreign law. Once the company has immigrated advice on UK company law formalities for foreign registered companies should be taken.

Immigration should always be considered where the owning trust is itself immigrating. This is because ownership by a UK shareholder can in certain cases make it more difficult to establish that central management and control has remained with the Board offshore (cf para 38.23).

Income

11.17 Once a foreign company becomes UK resident, its worldwide income comes into charge to corporation tax at 30%, or at a lesser rate if the small companies rate applies (TA 1988 s 13). UK dividends do not, however, become taxable as UK dividends are not subject to corporation tax (TA 1988 s 208).

Any dividends the company pays to the now resident trust attract the one-ninth tax credit (ITTOIA 2005, s 397). Since the abolition of ACT this has been so regardless of what, if any, corporation tax has been born by the profits out of which the income is paid. The one-ninth tax credit results in an effective rate of tax on actual dividends of 25% for higher rate individual taxpayers and for discretionary and accumulation trusts. This treatment contrasts with the position while the company is non-resident. Here the rate of tax on the actual amount of dividends is the Schedule F higher rate (32.5%) for individuals and trusts. There is no one-ninth tax credit.

TA 1988 ss 739 and 740 continue as a matter of law to apply to the company's income after immigration as, for the purposes of ss 739 and 740, a foreign-registered company is deemed non-resident (cf para 54.10). It appears HMRC can subject the company income either to corporation tax or to income tax under s 739, but cannot tax the same income twice. In practice the corporation tax is given as a credit against the income tax (cf para 55.16).

As noted above (para 11.6) there is no provision crediting the corporation tax against any tax charged under s 740 on a distribution from the trust. This potential double tax is an argument against immigrating an underlying company unless when UK resident the company distributes its profits as income.

Company gains

11.18 Once the company becomes UK resident, attribution of gains under TCGA 1992 s 13 (see Chapter 66) ceases. Instead its gains are subject to corporation tax at 30% or, if applicable, the small companies rate. Frequently this will represent a tax reduction as s 13 gains apportioned to resident individuals or trusts may be taxed at 40%. The gains continue to be indexed rather than tapered.

It is often said that gains realised by resident companies are taxed twice, once by the company and again when the shareholder realises his shares. Insofar as this is still true, the same normally applies with non-resident companies by virtue of s 13. The point is considered in relation to s 13 in para 66.16.

Year of immigration

11.19 Corporation tax is charged by accounting periods. A new period starts when a company becomes UK resident (TA 1988 s 12(2)(a)) and so from then its income and gains are fully subject to corporation tax.

Planning

11.20 As the above discussion has made clear, the decision as to whether a trust should immigrate turns on several factors. There is one non-tax consideration which may favour immigration. This is that the settlor or the beneficiaries may desire a degree of input into the management of the trust or an underlying company which is only consistent with them being directors or trustees. In such a case it may be prudent to accept the commercial logic of this rather than have continuing conflict with the tax demands of an offshore structure. At worst this kind of tension can lead to involuntary immigration with risk of failure to comply with consequent reporting requirements.

In the case of companies there is one noteworthy tax argument which may favour immigration in appropriate cases. This is that, as noted above, dividends paid by a resident company attract less tax than those paid by a non-resident company in that the effective rate is 25% rather than 32.5%. This is material where the shareholder is UK resident or is a non-resident trust which is either settlor-interested with a UK settlor, or is fixed-interest with a UK life-tenant. If in such case a distribution is going to be made, tax is less if the company has immigrated. The subject is considered further in para 14.9.

Section IV

Trust Distributions

Chapter 12

Income distributions

Introduction

12.1 As offshore trusts mature, UK beneficiaries increasingly want to enjoy some benefit. Absent non-residence, enjoying benefit, whether in income or capital form, normally results in at least some UK tax. This chapter explains how income distributions to UK resident and domiciled beneficiaries are taxed and the next chapter deals with distributions of capital. Planning suggestions are offered in Chapter 14.

This chapter assumes the settlor is or was resident and domiciled in the UK but that the trust income is not assessable on him under TA 1988, s 739 or ITTOIA 2005,s 624 (see Chapters 55 and 59). It should also be remembered that distributions to a minor child of the settlor are taxed as the settlor's income under ITTOIA 2005, s 629 to the extent of the current or retained income (see para 59.8). This also is assumed not to be in point here.

Fixed-interest trusts

12.2 Many offshore trusts settled by UK domiciliaries are fixed-interest. This means one or more beneficiaries are entitled as of right to the income. The general rule is that the life-tenant is treated as directly entitled to the underlying income. Thus if the underlying assets are in the UK he has UK source income and if they are abroad he has foreign income. These principles were established in the 1920s in the leading cases of *Singer v Williams* [1921] 1 AC 41 and *Baker v Archer-Shee* [1927] AC 844.

An important practical result of these cases is that the life-tenant enjoys the same income tax treatment as if he had owned the assets personally. This is significant in relation to dividends as it means a UK resident and domiciled life-tenant enjoys the dividend rates of 10% and 32.5% (TA 1988, s 1A(1A) and 1B). Further, in the case of dividends paid by a UK company, the tax credit applies, so that the effective rates of tax on the actual dividend paid are nil basic rate and 25% higher rate.

The general rule only applies, however, insofar as the proper law of the trust follows that of England and treats the life-tenant as having a specific equitable interest in each and every trust investment. Some other systems of law do not view the matter this way and consider that what the life-tenant has is the right to have the trustee account to him for the balance of the income after expenses. If this is the position, the source of the life-tenant's income is his right against the trustee and is a new source (*Archer-Shee v Garland* [1931] AC 212). The various advantages noted above do not therefore apply.

It is settled that the law of New York is of the latter kind (*Archer-Shee v Garland* (supra)). So also is the law of Scotland (see FA 1993, s 118 and the Inland Revenue Press Release "*Finance Bill – Scottish Trusts*" 9 July 1993). But as is well known, the trust law of must offshore jurisdictions is or follows English law, and so for trusts governed by such laws the general rule as stated above applies. But the point may perhaps be live with jurisdictions such as Liechtenstein where the local trust law has a purely statutory basis and draws on American as well as English ideas.

Whichever form the trust takes, a deduction is made for the trustees' expenses and remuneration in computing the life-tenant's income (*IRC v Berrill* [1981] STC 784, 797). This is not really consistent with the idea that the life-tenant is entitled to the income from inception, but is based on old cases and well-established law (see for example *Macfarlane v lRC* (1929) 14 TC 532). The expenses which may be deducted are not merely those which are income expenses as a matter of general law but also capital expenses insofar as the trustees are empowered to and do charge them against income (*Carver v Duncan* [1984] STC 556, 656 per Oliver LJ).

Insofar as the trust income is foreign, the life-tenant should, assuming he is UK resident, enter it as his income on the Foreign Pages of the tax return. UK income is entered on the Trusts etc Pages.

Distributions from trust capital

12.3 A series of cases on English trusts has established that where trustees are required or empowered to top-up the life tenant's income out of capital, the payments thereby made are taxable as annual payments. The leading case is *Cunard's Trustees v IRC* (1945) 27 TC 122. Here if the income fell short, the trustees were empowered to apply such portion of the trust capital by way of addition to the income as they in their absolute and uncontrolled discretion saw fit. The Court of Appeal held that the purpose of the top-up payments out of capital was an income purpose and that as such they fell to be treated as the life-tenant's income despite having been made out of capital.

This principle can apply equally in relation to foreign trusts. In applying it, the nature of the life-tenant's interest has to be ascertained under the appropriate foreign law and then the question of whether a given receipt is income or capital is ascertained under English Law. Thus in *Inchyra v Jennings* [1965] 2 All ER 714, the trustees were required to distribute 1% of the value of the trust fund annually to the life tenant. This was capital under the Canadian proper law of the trust, but under English law it fell to be characterised as income.

There has been no decided case where this principle has been applied otherwise than to regular payments explicitly made to top up income. Nor, in relation to fixed-interest trusts, has it applied otherwise than to payments to the life-tenant, although in *Inchyra v Jennings* it is fair to say the recipient of the capital was life-tenant in just one quarter of the fund.

Discretionary trusts

New source

12.4 The principle in *Baker v Archer-Shee* plainly has no application to discretionary trusts. Indeed it could be argued that a distribution from a discretionary trust is not subject to income tax at all on the grounds that it is a voluntary payment by the trustees or that it lacks recurrence. These arguments, however, were rejected in relation to distributions from a foreign discretionary trust in *Drummond v Collins* (1915) 6 TC 525, on the grounds that such payments were income arising from possessions out of the UK within the former Schedule D Case V. In relation to UK trusts, *Cunard's Trustees v IRC* (supra) established that discretionary income distributions from a UK resident trust are assessable as annual payments (*IRC v Berrill* [1981] STC 784, 797 per Vinelott J).

What is clear from these authorities is that the discretionary trust is the source and thus that the distribution has a source separate from that of the underlying income in the trust. It is reasonably clear that distributions from a UK discretionary trust are now taxable under ITTOIA 2005, s 683 as annual payments not otherwise charged, and indeed ITTOIA 2005, ss 684(3) and 686(2) expressly assume this to be so. It may be on a strict reading of *Drummond v Collins* that income distributions from a foreign discretionary trust are income not otherwise charged within ITTOIA 2005, s 687, but even if so, there is little discernible difference between the two heads of charge.

An income distribution from a foreign discretionary trust should be entered in Box 5 of the Foreign Pages of the tax return.

Capital or income

12.5 *Drummond v Collins* did not address the issue of when distributions by discretionary trustees are income and when they are not. There is little direct authority on this in relation to non-resident trusts and somewhat confusing case law in relation to UK trusts.

In relation to UK trusts, the starting point is *Cunard's Trustees v IRC* (supra). Although this case concerned payments to a life-tenant, the payments were, as just noted, discretionary in the sense that the trustees had a discretion as to whether to make them. Accordingly, the principle that can be extrapolated from the case is that in deciding whether a distribution from a discretionary trust is income, it is necessary to look at the purposes of the distribution.

Essentially these were the points taken by HMRC in what is now the leading case on the subject, *Stevenson v Wishart* [1987] STC 266. Here discretionary trustees had power to make either capital distributions or income distributions. An elderly beneficiary became ill, and over a three-year period the trustees made regular payments totalling in excess of £100,000 to meet terminal nursing-home fees. These payments were made out of trust capital in exercise of a power over capital.

HMRC argued that the payments had the character of income and should therefore be taxed as the beneficiary's income. The Court of Appeal rejected this, stating that terminal care is normally funded out of capital and that no issues as to income could possibly have arisen if a single capital sum had been appointed at the outset. The Court also stressed the fact that the power exercised had been a power to appoint capital. The mere fact of recurrence was not itself sufficient to make the payments income, *Cunard's Trustees* being distinguishable because the power exercised was not an express power to top up income.

It may be suggested that in the light of *Stevenson v Wishart*, the law is as follows:

(i) A payment out of income in exercise of a power to distribute income is always income.
(ii) A payment out of capital in exercise of a power to distribute capital is normally capital.
(iii) But this may be displaced if the payments are recurrent and their purposes are an income purpose.
(iv) General living expenses may be an income purpose. But terminal care is not and nor, on the authority of *Stevenson v Wishart*, are advances of capital to which the beneficiary is contingently entitled.

Accumulations

12.6 As will be apparent from the above, the nature of the power being exercised and the question of whether the funds distributed are capital or income is important. In this context, the issue of accumulations has to be considered. The effect of accumulation is to turn income into capital, most accumulation clauses directing that the accumulations be treated as trust capital for all purposes. Once accumulation is made, a subsequent distribution of the accumulated fund is a distribution of capital (*Stanley v IRC* [1944] 1 AII ER 230). Accordingly, it is only income of the recipient if it can be made so under the principles described above.

Trusts differ in the detail of the provisions relating to income. In some cases there is a trust to accumulate with a power to distribute, and in others there is a long-stop trust to distribute with power to accumulate. Whichever the case it needs to be remembered that a power has to be exercised within a reasonable period – conventionally by the end of the year following that in which the income arises unless there are indications to the contrary (see for example *Re Allen-Meyrick's Will Trusts* [1966] 1 All ER 740).

If the trust is to accumulate and no distributions are in fact made, the income is plainly accumulated. But if the trust is to distribute there must be a positive decision to accumulate if accumulation is to be achieved. The decision can be inferred from slight evidence, for example the trust accounts. But if it is clear the income has not been accumulated, the position remains that the income must be distributed. If there is a fixed default beneficiary the income is his and taxable as his, but otherwise, if there is a discretion, the discretion remains exercisable on the basis that all the income must be paid out (see *Re Locker's Settlement Trusts, Meachem v Sachs* [1978] 1 All ER 216). In such an event, what is distributed is still income and so taxable as such even though the trustees may be paying it later than they should have done.

ESC B18

12.7 The effect of the trust being the source of the beneficiary's income in the case of distributions from a discretionary trust, means that there is, as a matter of law, no credit given to the beneficiary for tax borne by the trustees. With a fixed-interest trust this issue does not arise, as the income is that of the beneficiary at the outset, at least where the proper law follows English law and treats him as equitably entitled to the income.

Where the trustees are resident in the UK, the potential double taxation of discretionary trust distributions is addressed by TA 1988, s 687, which requires the trustees to operate deduction at source in relation to income distributions and offset the tax due on the distributions against tax on their income as it arose. Section 687 does not cover the position where UK trustees have suffered foreign tax, but ESC B18 allows credit for the foreign tax to the beneficiary insofar as the foreign income arose in the tax year of the payment or the five previous years.

Section 687 is not expressly limited to UK trusts, but it is generally assumed that it is so limited so as to accord with the territorial limitations applicable to income tax (see Chapter 30 above and ESC B18). It follows that distributions to UK beneficiaries by a non-resident discretionary trust are potentially double-taxed. This is particularly noteworthy in relation to trusts with UK income in that the trustees are taxable on that income at 40% or the trust dividend rate and the beneficiary then suffers further tax on the net sum distributed, again at 40% if he is a higher-rate taxpayer.

This anomaly is also addressed by ESC B18, for it allows the beneficiary to take the same credit for the trust's UK tax as would have applied under s 687 if the trust had been UK resident. To obtain this treatment, the trustees must be fully compliant in that their self assessment returns must be up-to-date and all tax due on UK income paid. The UK tax credited can be that for the tax year of the distribution or the previous five tax years. The operation of the concession is in the hands of the Centre for Non-Residents to whom a claim must be made. ESC B18 indicates that income is set against distributions on a last in first out basis, and that foreign and UK source income is treated as distributed rateably.

What ESC B18 does not allow, in relation to non-resident trusts, is credit for foreign tax on foreign income. This therefore is unrelieved if distributions are made to UK residents.

Insofar as the trust income includes UK dividends, the trust tax credited to the beneficiary is restricted to the actual tax paid by the trustees and does not extend to the one-ninth tax credit attaching to the dividend under the UK imputation system. The beneficiary, however, is taxed on the actual distribution he receives from the trustees, and therefore the ESC B18 calculation is a deduction of the actual tax paid by the trustee on the dividend from the tax due from the beneficiary on the distribution. Now that the dividend rate applicable to trusts is 32.5%, the tax paid by the trustee is 25% of the dividend received. It follows that where the beneficiary is a basic-rate taxpayer, the credit eliminates tax. Should he be a higher-rate taxpayer, the credit reduces the tax on the distribution from 40% to 15%.

Insofar as the trust's UK income is other than dividends, the fact that the general rate applicable to trusts is now 40% means that the ESC B18 credit eliminates tax at beneficiary level insofar as the trust income is UK source and the income distributed arose after 6 April 2004.

The reference in ESC B18 to trust tax for the previous five tax years being allowed is curious for normally, under the principles described above, retained income which is more than a year or two old will have been capitalised. This does not of itself mean a distribution of such capitalised income is per se capital in the hands of the beneficiary: as described above it could be income if distributed on a recurrent basis for an income purpose. But of their nature such cases are rare and the issue which therefore arises is whether ESC B18 implicitly allows a taxpayer to treat what would otherwise be a capital distribution as income and take the benefit of the concession. In practice it is often treated in this way.

Chapter 13

Capital distributions

Introduction

13.1 This chapter explains how income tax and capital gains tax are computed when the trustees of an offshore trust distribute capital to a beneficiary resident and domiciled in the UK. It is assumed the trust was created by a settlor resident and domiciled in the UK and that it is not protected by the s 741 motive defence (see Chapter 58).

The issue of whether a distribution is capital or income is addressed in the previous chapter. In this chapter, it is assumed that as a result of applying the principles there described, it has been established that the distribution is capital.

The rules described in this chapter also apply where a beneficiary resident and domiciled in the UK enjoys trust assets in specie. As is described in Chapters 56 and 65, it is now difficult to argue that for tax purposes such enjoyment does not equate to an annual capital distribution equal to the rent or interest foregone.

Capital distributions are rendered taxable by reference to relevant income and pools of gains. Potentially there are three types of gain pool, namely offshore income gains, s 87 capital gains, and Sch 4C pools. In broad terms these gain pools are all computed in the same manner, the detailed rules being explained in Chapters 63 and 64 and para 71.19.

The basic rule is that a capital payment is taxed first by reference to relevant income and only if there is none is it necessary to look at pools of gains, offshore income gains being taken before s 87 and Sch 4C gains. Should the distribution be taxed by reference to relevant income or offshore income gains, it is taxed as income. It is taxed as a capital gain insofar as matched with gains in a s 87 or a Sch 4C pool.

Should the distribution be to the settlor, it cannot be taxed by reference to relevant income (see para 56.10). It can be taxed by reference to s 87 gains if such gains accrued before 17 March 1998 and the settlement was made before 19 March 1991 (see para 13.11 below). As is explained in Chapter 71, it may also be taxable by reference to offshore income gains.

Relevant income

13.2 It follows from the above that the first stage in determining the taxability of a capital distribution to a beneficiary other than the settlor, is to ascertain whether there is relevant income. The concept of relevant income is explained in Chapter 57. It has to be ascertained in relation to any given benefit or distribution what non-resident entities are capable of generating relevant income in relation to the recipient beneficiary and which (if any) have in fact generated such relevant income.

Chapter 57 explains that in answering these questions many technical issues arise, some of which, if advanced, would favour the taxpayer. In appropriate cases where the amounts at stake justify significant professional costs, it is worth investigating some or all of these points. There is nothing wrong in doing so provided full disclosure is made of how s 740 liability has been arrived at or, if as a result of these points there is nil liability, how that conclusion has been reached.

But in the generality of trust cases, the pragmatic approach is undoubtedly to treat the trust as having a notional pool of s 740 relevant income or, where there is a holding company, treat the trust and company as together having a single combined pool. In normal cases, the pool will simply be the income of past years which has (a) not been used in expenses (b) not been distributed as income and (c) not been allocated to prior distributions in charging tax under s 740. As described in para 56.20 only distributions to UK residents are taken into account for these purposes.

If the trustees are well advised they will have maintained a computation of their s 740 relevant income. If they have not, such will need to be prepared and, quite apart from ascertaining the tax treatment of any particular distribution, it should be prepared so as to facilitate future planning. The computation needs to go back to the inception of the trust or, if later, 10 March 1981. In most cases, trust or company accounts should in practice give the necessary information, the relevant income being income which has been accumulated or retained.

Trust advances

13.3 Even in a simple case there may be one situation in which relevant income outside the trust/company structure has to be considered. This is if the trust has received an advance from another trust. Here income in that trust is relevant income in relation to the distribution, save insofar as it arose after the advance and the beneficiary receiving capital from the subject trust is wholly excluded from it (see para 57.13).

Income excluded

13.4 Although, as indicated above, the pragmatic approach should in the simple case be to treat the trust as having a single s 740 pool, there are certain instances where this approach should not be taken.

One such case is if the income arose in a fund from which the beneficiary was excluded and could never be a beneficiary. In contrast to gains, strictly there is no single pool of relevant income and so if the recipient beneficiary could never in fact have benefited from income it should not be treated as relevant income in relation to him. The better view is that the same is true if the income has been segregated in banking terms and he has been excluded from it subsequently or it has been distributed to another beneficiary (see para 57.13).

A second instance of income being excluded is where there is a holding company and the company has paid retained income up to the trust. Here double counting is unlikely to be required (see para 57.15).

Income included

13.5 There are also cases where additional amounts need to be included in the total of relevant income. One is where the trust or company holds fixed-interest securities sold between interest periods. Here the accrued interest scheme requires the accrued interest element received as part of the proceeds to count as relevant income (see para 57.6). So too if capital has been distributed to a non-resident, offshore income gains may move across to being s 740 relevant income. This complex point is explained in Chapter 71. A further example concerns gains on life policies, which in certain circumstances are also deemed to be s 740 income (see para 72.14).

Dry trusts

13.6 It is common to encounter what are sometimes called dry trusts. These are trusts which do not or are not thought to have any s 740 relevant income. Such can be for one of three reasons:

(1) No income has ever arisen as for example where the sole trust asset is a property which has never been let or shares in a UK company which has never paid dividends.
(2) The trust is an interest in possession trust, which means by definition income cannot be retained.
(3) All income which has ever arisen has been used in expenses or distributed to beneficiaries as income.

Dry trusts are frequently encountered and if a trust has hitherto been dry it is often felt prudent to keep it dry so as to avoid tiresome s 740 computations for the future. A trust will not of course be dry to the extent it owns shares in underlying, non-resident companies unless those companies too are dry. Nor will it be dry if it has received accrued interest or, in the case noted above, if offshore income gains have moved across to being relevant income.

The charge to tax

13.7 Assuming there is relevant income, the s 740 distribution is taxed as the income of the recipient beneficiary. It should be entered at Box 6.5 of the

Foreign Pages of the recipient's return. In practice the uncertainties over s 740 highlighted both here and in Chapters 56 and 57 render it desirable to explain in Box 39 or in a covering letter the basis on which liability has been calculated. HMRC in any event expected to be advised of the entity to which the relevant income accrued.

In some cases, the trust's retained income may be relevant income in relation to more than one distribution and sometimes it may also be taxable on an arising basis under TA 1988, s 739. Here the rule is that the income is apportioned on a just and reasonable basis (see para 57.12). Whatever basis is adopted should be explained in relevant tax returns. In general it may be suggested that allocation should be done on a year by year basis and as between s 740 distributions, should within each year be on a pro rata basis.

If when all the required calculations have been done, the capital distribution is less than the relevant income allocated to it, the distribution is fully taxable under s 740 and the notional s 740 pool is correspondingly reduced. But should the distribution exceed the relevant income for the tax year of the distribution and for previous years, it is necessary to go to the next stage, which is to look at the pools of gains. It is always necessary to go to the pools of gains where the distribution is to the settlor.

Offshore income gains

13.8 As indicated at the beginning of this chapter the first pool to look at is the pool of offshore income gains. It may well be the trust's pool has been computed and kept up to date, and certainly the relevant information is asked for in Form 50 (FS) (at Part E). But if the pool has not been computed, the computation needs to be effected. The start date is 1 January 1984 or, if later, the inception of the settlement.

Computing the pool

13.9 The pool comprises offshore income gains, ie gains realised on the disposal of non-distributor offshore funds. Such gains are included if they were realised by the trust or any underlying company at any time since the inception of the trust, or if later since 1 January 1984. The computational rules are mainly those applicable in computing s 87 pools of capital gains and are described in para 71.19 and Chapter 63. In practice the most difficult issue in computing the pool is identifying which investments really are offshore funds and confirming they do not have distributor status.

The pool will have been reduced by any distributions of capital made in prior years not taxed under s 740. As described in para 71.19 such distributions are taken into account even if made to non-residents or non-domiciliaries.

The pool may be larger than might be thought. This is because there is no equivalent to TCGA 1992, s 86 attributing offshore income gains to the settlor on an arising basis. As is explained in para 71.25, TA 1988, s 739 does apply to offshore income gains in excess of capital payments to UK residents if the trust is settlor-interested, but at least on a strict reading of the legislation does not prevent offshore income gains going into the pool as well and so potentially being taxed twice. However, it may be suggested that the potential double taxation would entitle taxpayers in practice to omit gains taxed under s 739 from the pool, provided this is fully disclosed.

The tax charge

13.10 The excess of the distribution over relevant income is taxed as an offshore income gain to the extent of the offshore income gains in the pool as at the end of the tax year in which the distribution is made. There is no specific box in the self-assessment return for distributions treated as offshore income gains and the amount should therefore be entered in Box 6.5 of the Foreign Pages with details given in Box 39 as Additional Information. Should the settlement have made more than one distribution of capital in excess of any s 740 relevant income in the year concerned, the pool is allocated between the distributions, the allocation being pro rata if the aggregate distributions are greater than the pool. As just noted, distributions to non-residents or non-domiciliaries count for these purposes, albeit not taxed.

Should the capital payment or payments exceed both the relevant income and the offshore income gains, it or they are carried across to the s 87 and Sch 4C pools. Conversely, if the capital payment(s) are fully absorbed by the offshore income gain pool, the offshore income charge concludes the taxation of the distribution(s). The balance of gains in the offshore income gain pool is then carried forward.

Capital gains

13.11 Section 87 and Sch 4C come into issue and subject the distribution to capital gains tax insofar as (a) it has not been taxed as income under the rules described above and (b) an applicable s 87 or Sch 4C pool exists at the end of the tax year in which the distribution is made.

The gains pool

13.12 As with offshore income gains, the trustees may well maintain an up-to-date computation of their s 87 pool. Such is contemplated by Part H of Form 50 (FS). But if they do not, a full computation is necessary. The relevant rules are explained in Chapter 63. Essentially what is required for each tax year is a computation of the net gains (after allowing for indexation, taper, and losses) on which the trustees would have been chargeable if UK resident.

Gains in underlying companies apportionable under TCGA 1992, s 13 are included (see para 66.24) and express rules deal with transfers between settlements.

It might be thought that as a result of TCGA 1992, s 86, there would normally be no gains to go into a s 87 pool, for s 86 attributes gains to the settlor on an arising basis unless he, his children and his grandchildren are excluded (see Chapter 60). But in fact most existing offshore settlements do have a s 87 pool, for s 86 was not enacted until 1991, and did not generally apply to pre-1991 settlements until 17 March 1998 (see Chapter 61). Accordingly, most long-standing offshore settlements have a s 87 pool. Further gains inevitably go into the s 87 pool if the settlor is dead, non-domiciled or non-resident (see para 63.13).

The normal rule is that the distributing settlement will have a s 87 pool and not a Sch 4C pool. But as is described in Chapter 64, it will have a Sch 4C pool if, after 21 March 2000, the trustees have fallen foul of the artificial rules in TCGA 1992, Sch 4B relating to trustee borrowing. In such case they have a Sch 4C pool comprising the gains realised under Sch 4B plus their s 87 pool, as at the end of the tax year they fell into Sch 4B (or, if later, as at 8 April 2003). Gains arising thereafter go into a new s 87 pool.

The s 87 and Sch 4C pools will have been reduced insofar as gains have been allocated to prior-year capital payments. For the purposes of s 87, but not those of Sch 4C, capital payments to non-residents or non-domiciliaries are taken into account (cf paras 63.22 and 64.7).

Matching the pools

13.13 Should the settlement have both a s 87 and a Sch 4C pool, gains in the two pools are matched to the distribution on a first-in, first-out basis (see para 64.10). Where the trust has made other distributions not taxed as income in the same tax year, the gains in the pools are allocated to the distributions pro rata. As just noted, distributions to non-residents and non-domiciliaries are taken into account in relation to s 87 pools but not in relation to Sch 4C pools.

Should the distribution or distributions not taxed as income be less than the pool(s) or part thereof allocated to them, the part not taxed as income is taxed in full as capital gain in the tax year of the distribution and the taxation of the distribution is concluded. But should the distribution or distributions exceed the pool(s), the excess is carried forward and dealt with under the rules described in the next section.

Sch 4C and relevant settlements

13.14 In most cases that should be the end of the matter as respects the tax liability of the beneficiary in the year of distribution. But there is one exception. This is where the distributing settlement is what is called a relevant settlement in relation to the trustee borrowing rules – ie it has directly or indirectly received capital from another settlement which is itself already a relevant settlement under those rules (see para 64.7). In such cases there is a floating Sch 4C pool, computed as described in Chapter 64, which can be attributed to capital payments from any relevant settlement until exhausted. Accordingly, in the unlikely event that the distributing settlement is a relevant settlement in relation to the Sch 4C pool of another settlement, the gains able to be allocated to the distribution include those in that Sch 4C pool.

The tax charge

13.15 As already indicated, if a distribution is taxed under s 87 or Sch 4C, the tax charged is CGT. The distribution should be entered in row 11 of Capital Gains pages of the tax return and details of the trust and the computation given as additional information under Box 8.22. In contrast to the income tax charges described earlier in this chapter, tax may be inflated by notional interest. The rules are described in para 63.29, and any notional interest is entered at Box 8.9 of the Capital Gains pages.

Surplus distribution

13.16 Even after all the above calculations, a part of the capital distribution may be left. This will be so if it exceeds the relevant income and all the gains pools capable of being allocated to it. In such case the surplus is tax-free if the distribution has terminated the settlement. But if the settlement continues, the excess distribution is carried forward and taxed by reference to the relevant income and the gains pools of the following tax year.

To the extent that there is relevant income in that tax year, it and any further distributions made in that year are taxed as income. Should the brought-forward and current year distributions exceed the relevant income, they are taxed as offshore income gains insofar as the settlement has realised any in the year, pro rata if in excess of such offshore income gains. The surplus is taxed as capital gains to the extent of any s 87 or Sch 4C gains realised in the year, again pro rata if the brought-forward and current year distributions exceed the current year s 87 and Sch 4C pool. Insofar as there is such excess, the excess is carried forward to the next tax year and the process repeated. This goes on until either the settlement ends or all distributions have been matched with relevant income or with pools of gains.

IHT

13.17 In many cases a distribution also occasions an IHT exit charge. This subject is covered in Chapter 43.

Chapter 14

Planning points

Introduction

14.1 This chapter outlines some techniques for minimising the income tax and capital gains tax charged on capital distributions. As in the rest of this section, it is assumed the settlor is UK resident and domiciled or at least was when he made the settlement.

Distributions to non-residents

Complete distribution

14.2 The only completely satisfactory means of conferring tax-free benefit on the beneficiaries is to make distributions to non-residents. This avoids the charges under s 740, s 87 and Sch 4C, because those charges only arise insofar as the recipient beneficiary is resident in the UK. If the distribution is of the entire trust fund, the tax problems of the settlement are at an end.

Given that the settlor is or was UK resident and domiciled, the intended object or objects of the trustees' discretion may not be non-resident. However, if the fund is large enough and the desire to distribute is strong enough, emigration may be an acceptable price for the beneficiaries to pay for freedom from tax. As described in Chapter 27, sheltering trust distributions is a potential reason for tax-driven emigration.

But if this strategy is to be adopted, the following points, noted in Chapter 32, must be remembered.

(1) To avoid CGT, emigration needs to be for at least five complete tax years.
(2) No distribution should be made in the tax year of emigration or in that of return.
(3) Emigration should not be to a country which does or might tax the distribution.

A further point arises if the settlement is one where gains are assessable on the settlor on an arising basis (see Chapter 60). In such a case any latent gains in the settlement when the trust fund is distributed will be charged on the settlor, for there is a deemed disposal when a beneficiary becomes absolutely entitled to the trust property (TCGA 1992, s 71). Complete distribution is normally, therefore, only attractive if there are no latent gains or the settlement is not one where the gains are assessable on the settlor on an arising basis.

Some resident beneficiaries

14.3 In practice, even if one or more of the beneficiaries is or is prepared to become non-resident, others will not be. In this event complete distribution to the non-residents will result in family inequality.

There are two possible solutions. One arises where there is a s 87 pool of stockpiled gains but no relevant income. Here an amount equal to the s 87 pool may be distributed to the non-resident beneficiaries in one tax year (those beneficiaries being non-resident for at least five complete tax years). This will wash out the s 87 pool (see para 63.17). In the next year the balance of the trust fund is distributed tax-free to the UK beneficiaries. The distribution has to be in the following tax year as otherwise gains are allocated to the distributions pro rata (see para 63.16). Assuming there is no attribution to the settlor, any latent gains should be realised before the distribution to the non-residents, so that they too may be washed out by the distribution to the non-residents.

The reason why it is postulated that there is no relevant income is that although a distribution to a non-resident is not chargeable, it does not wash out relevant income (see para 56.18). It may however be that if accumulated income has at all times been kept in a separate fund, and that fund is distributed to a non-resident, such will render the income unavailable thereafter and so wash it out. This is discussed further in para 57.13.

The technique of washing out gains does not work either if the settlement has a Sch 4C pool rather than a s 87 pool, or if another settlement's Sch 4C pool can be allocated to it. The reason is the same as with s 740, namely that while Sch 4C distributions to non-residents are not chargeable, gains are not allocated to them (see Chapter 64).

A point also to remember is that a distribution to non-residents does not wash out offshore income gains. They cease to be taxable under s 87 but instead become relevant income for the purposes of s 740 (see para 71.27). This means they will be taxable on the ensuing distribution to resident beneficiaries.

The second solution to the problem of some resident beneficiaries is to distribute the entire trust fund to the non-residents. It can then be left to them to compensate other members of the family. This is a risky strategy, for if there is any understanding or obligation on the non-residents to benefit the other members of the family, the exercise may fall to be characterised as a distribution to them for the purposes of ss 740 and 87 (see paras 56.21 and 65.4). If there is no such understanding or obligation, the UK residents may lose out.

Partial distributions

14.4 In practice the only distribution made may be a distribution of part of the trust fund to non-residents, the balance of the trust fund being retained.

If this course is taken one point should kept in mind. This is that if the distribution exceeds any s 87 pool as at that time, gains realised in subsequent years will be allocated to it. If by then a non-resident recipient has resumed UK residence and domicile, a tax charge will result (see para 63.22). A tax charge does not result, however, by reference to income accumulated in the retained fund, for s 740 only applies if the recipient is resident at the time of receipt. Nor does this problem arise with Sch 4C pools as Sch 4B gains are not allocated to non-residents.

It may be that in the following tax year, a further partial distribution is made to the UK beneficiaries. As noted above, this will be free of tax provided the prior year's distribution washed out any s 87 pool to date and there is no relevant income, Sch 4C pool or pool of offshore income gains. However, it may not remain free of tax for should income be accumulated or gains realised in the future, such will result in a tax charge.

This result may be avoided in relation to s 87 pools of capital gains or offshore income gains if in the prior tax-year, the part of the trust fund which is not going to be distributed is resettled on the trusts of a separate settlement. This works because a transfer to another trust carries with it gains which are undistributed at the end of the tax year concerned, but not excess capital payments (see para 63.27). However, a number of points need to be noted:

(1) The distribution to the non-resident beneficiaries has to be sufficient to wash out the gains realised by the resettlement as well as the stockpiled gains.
(2) It must be clear the transferee settlement is a separate settlement (see para 63.28).
(3) The resettlement must not itself amount to a capital payment (see para 65.6).

It is arguable that that such a resettlement would not prevent accumulated income in the resettlement from being relevant income in relation to the distribution from the original settlement (see para 56.17). If so, such accumulation would still result in a tax charge on the UK beneficiaries.

Short-term non-residence

14.5 The five-year rule does not apply to income tax. Accordingly, a trust with only relevant income can make a tax-free distribution to a beneficiary who is non-resident for only one complete tax year (as to which see para 27.4). However, this strategy is not without risk, for even if there is no pool of gains at the time of the distribution, gains realised by the trust in the future will cause the distribution to be taxed at that stage, assuming the beneficiary is then UK resident.

Non-domiciled beneficiaries

14.6 It is comparatively unusual for any of the beneficiaries under a settlement created by a UK domiciliary to be non-domiciled yet resident in the UK. But should such be the case, distributions to the non-domiciliary are free of capital gains tax and enable gains in any s 87 pool to be washed out. The position is the same as on distributions to non-residents (see para 63.22). The same applies to offshore income gains, for, if the recipient is UK resident, s 740 is not applied (see para 71.27).

If there is relevant income the position is more complicated, since s 740 requires such income to be allocated to any distribution before gains (see para 13.2). A distribution to a non-domiciliary is only free of liability under s 740 to the extent that the trust's relevant income does not include UK source income and the benefit is not received in the UK. This issue is discussed further in para 56.23, and, in general, it may be difficult to ensure that a distribution to a non-domiciliary is tax-free if there is retained income.

Small distributions

14.7 A distribution to a non-taxpaying beneficiary is free of income tax to the extent of his personal allowance (£5,035 in 2006–07). Should there be no relevant income or offshore income gains in the trust, a distribution equal to the basic annual exemption (£8,800 in 2006–07) is free of CGT, assuming the beneficiary's annual exemption is otherwise available. If, however, the trust has no s 87 or Sch 4C pool, the distribution is carried forward and taxed as and when the trustees do realise gains or accumulate income. Since in that year the beneficiary's personal allowance or annual exemption may have been used, it is better not to make small distributions unless, in the tax year concerned, there is relevant income or a s 87 or Sch 4C pool to cover it.

In theory it is possible to use both a beneficiary's personal allowance and his annual exemption. But this is only possible if the relevant income is wholly absorbed by the personal allowance, for otherwise the distribution is taxed as income until the relevant income is exhausted. The better method for securing both the allowance and exemption is to ensure there is no relevant income by distributing income as income, and then (assuming there are pools of gains) making modest capital distributions equal to the annual exemption.

Losses

14.8 Tax may be avoided on a distribution if the existence of relevant income means it is taxable under s 740 and the recipient beneficiary has trading or other income tax losses. In such a case the losses may be set against the recipient's s 740 notional income in the same way as against other income. The same applies if the capital distribution is taxed as an offshore income gain. With capital gains, however, the position is otherwise. Section 87 and Sch 4C gains cannot be set against the recipient's capital losses (TCGA 1992, s 2(4)).

Role of dividends

14.9 Planning opportunities arise insofar as the relevant income or the value represented by gains is in an underlying company. These opportunities involve the company paying the income or accrued gains to the trust as dividend.

Increase s 740 relevant income

14.10 The simplest illustration of the role of dividends is where the trust has a substantial s 87 or Sch 4C pool of old gains, resulting in a tax charge at rates of up to 64% on any distribution to a UK resident and domiciled beneficiary. Here a dividend paid by an underlying company owned by the trust is relevant income. As such it is allocated first to any capital distribution to a UK beneficiary (see para 56.28) and so it ensures that the rate of tax on such distribution cannot exceed 40% until the total of the dividend and other relevant income is exceeded.

Increase income payments

14.11 Taxation of a benefit under s 740 still results in a tax charge of 40%. But there is one method by which this position may be improved. This is if the recipient beneficiary is appointed a life-interest in the shares concerned before the dividend is paid. In such case, the dividend then becomes the recipient beneficiary's income and is taxed at the dividend upper rate of 32.5%, which applies as much to foreign dividends as UK dividends. Despite the fact that this tax rate is lower than on a capital distribution it still has to be applied as ss 740 and 87 apply only to benefits and distributions not otherwise taxed as income.

Immigrate the company to the UK

14.12 The position can be improved still further where there is a UK life-tenant if the company immigrates to the UK before the dividend is paid. In such case the effect of the company being UK resident is that it becomes subject to corporation tax (see para 11.15). A concomitant of this is that any dividend attracts the one-ninth tax credit, thereby reducing the effective rate of tax for higher rate taxpayers to 25% (para 11.17). If repatriation of offshore profits is desired, 25% may be regarded as a not unacceptable price to pay.

A company should not of course be immigrated to the UK unless all other implications have been considered (see paras 11.15 to 11.18). Immigration is less attractive without appointment of a life-interest for, although the effective tax paid by the trust is then only 25%, any subsequent distribution of income is taxable as a new source (see para 11.6).

How much can be paid in dividend?

14.13 The techniques described above only work insofar as the dividend paid by the company is income. Should the company have immigrated, the matter is governed by the corporation tax rules as to what constitutes a distribution (TA 1988, s 209). Otherwise the issue is as discussed in para 33.3. Any distribution of realised profits, whether capital or income, should be income unless the company is in liquidation. Greater difficulty may be encountered if it is desired to go beyond this, and in such cases careful consideration is required both of the company's proper law and the case law referred to in para 33.3.

Non-domiciled beneficiaries

14.14 Dividends may be unattractive if some or all of the beneficiaries likely to benefit from the trust are non-domiciled. This is because to them capital payments are free of CGT, whereas income distributions may be taxed if remitted, and s 740 can be difficult for non-domiciliaries to wholly avoid (see para 56.23).

Free use of property

14.15 The Court of Appeal has held that interest-free loans represent annual capital payments for s 87 purposes equal to the rent or interest foregone (para 65.7). It must be assumed the same reasoning applies to the free use of property and to s 740 (para 56.11).

Despite this, trustees may still be tempted to benefit beneficiaries by interest-free loans or the free use of property. Such has the merit of at least initially resulting in only a modest tax charge. But in the long-run it is normally a strategy that cannot be recommended, for effectively it results in charges under ss 740 and 87 both when the free use is allowed and then when the capital is distributed. The total tax bill is greater than if the capital is distributed at the outset.

A different view may of course be taken if the trustees envisage the capital may eventually be distributed to non-residents.

Sometimes the charge under s 740 or s 87 is avoided by requiring the beneficiary to pay interest or rent. If this is done, the interest or rent is both taxable as UK source income of the trustees and also goes to increase relevant income with double taxation potentially resulting. In addition the beneficiary has to withhold tax, lower-rate tax in the case of interest, and in the case of rent, basic-rate tax under TA 1988, s 42A unless the landlord is within the non-resident landlord scheme (cf para 34.6 and 34.13).

CGT minimisation techniques

14.16 One or two specific techniques exist for minimising the charge under s 87 or Sch 4C.

Distributions to charity

14.17 HMRC accept that capital distributions to charities are relieved by the CGT exemption for charities and yet a distribution to charity washes out an amount of gains in any s 87 pool equal to the distribution (see para 65.5). If the distribution to charity is made in one tax year and the balance of the trust fund is distributed in the following year, CGT on the latter distribution is reduced or eliminated to the extent of the distribution to the charity. But this technique does not carry out relevant income, so the subsequent distribution would be taxed under s 740 if there is such income. If the subsequent distribution is not of the whole trust fund, it will become taxable if income is retained or gains realised in the future (cf para 14.4 above).

HMRC's practice in relation to charities and s 87 was announced before the enactment of Sch 4C. However, it may be argued that it should not also apply to Sch 4C.

Generate relevant income

14.18 Since a capital distribution is taxed first by reference to relevant income, the rate of tax on a distribution may be reduced from 64% to 40% if relevant income can be generated. This is in point if the trust has a s 87 or a Sch 4C pool but no or insufficient relevant income or offshore income gains.

An obvious context to use the technique is where the trust owns an underlying company. The point has already been explained in para 14.9 above.

Split the trust fund

14.19 This technique takes advantage of the fact that if part of the trust fund is transferred to a new settlement, the gains in the s 87 pool as at the end of the tax year of the transfer are split pro rata between the two trusts (see para 63.26). If the gains pool equals half the value of the original trust fund a distribution by the trustees of that trust of half the trust fund will be fully taxable. But, if in a prior tax year half the trust fund has been transferred to another trust, a complete distribution from one or other trust is taxable as capital gain as to only 50%.

This technique cannot be used if the trust has outstanding borrowing within the meaning of TCGA 1992, Sch 4B, for then the transfer will trigger a Sch 4B deemed disposal and carry the s 87 gains into a Sch 4C pool (see

Chapter 62). Nor can it be used if the settlement has an existing Sch 4C pool for such pools are not split pro rata (see para 64.7).

This technique does not apply to relevant income, and any such income is therefore likely to be allocated to the distribution in toto (cf para 56.16). As with similar exercises described in para 14.4 above, it must be ensured the two trusts are truly separate and that the transfer between the two trusts cannot be characterised as a capital distribution.

A sub-fund election within TCGA 1992, Sch 4ZA achieves the same result as splitting the trust fund in the manner described above. The ability to make such an election is not confined to UK trusts. But the restrictions in Sch 4ZA render it unlikely that sub-fund elections will be widely used in practice.

Section V

Non-domiciliaries

Chapter 15

Foreign assets

Introduction

15.1 Those whose domicile is outside the UK but who are resident in the UK enjoy favourable tax treatment. This section outlines the planning opportunities open to them. Technical issues, including the law as to domicile, are explained in Part B in Chapters 30, 39, 42 and 45 and 46.

As is explained in para 39.13, the government is currently reviewing the use of domicile as a connecting factor and the tax treatment of non-domiciliaries. However, although the review has now been in progress since 2002, consultation proposals have not yet been issued. This section is therefore based on the law as it currently stands.

This chapter covers the foreign investments of a non-domiciliary and the income they generate. UK investments are dealt with in Chapter 17, UK houses in Chapter 21 and employment earnings in Chapter 23.

The basic rules

Inheritance tax

15.2 The foreign situs assets of an individual who neither is nor is deemed to be domiciled in the UK, are excluded property and so outside the scope of IHT (see para 30.10). This means the investments of such a non-domiciliary are free of IHT provided they are kept outside the UK.

Capital gains tax

15.3 Capital gains realised on the disposal by a foreign domiciliary of his foreign situs assets are not taxable unless the proceeds of the disposal are remitted to the UK (see para 41.1). Although remittance is caught whether effected in the year of disposal or subsequently, capital gains tax is not in issue if the proceeds of disposal are kept abroad permanently.

Income

15.4 Provided the non-domiciliary makes the requisite claim, foreign source investment income is not taxed unless remitted to the UK (see

Chapter 40). As with capital gains, a remittance is taxable whether effected in the year of receipt or subsequently, and so tax is avoided provided the income is kept abroad permanently.

Deemed income

15.5 Non-domiciliaries are not subject to the accrued interest scheme as respects foreign securities (see para 40.20). They are subject to the regime taxing offshore income gains as income (see Chapter 71) but, as with ordinary capital gains, a charge only arises if the proceeds of the disposal are remitted to the UK. They are also subject to the regime taxing deep discount as income (ITTOIA 2005, ss 427–460), but here too the remittance basis applies (ITTOIA 2005, s 428(3)).

Practical issues

UK spending

15.6 The effect of the basic rules just described is that the foreign investments of non-domiciliaries are free of UK tax provided they and the proceeds and income they generate are kept abroad. For some non-domiciliaries this is entirely sufficient as a tax-planning strategy. Typically such a non-domiciliary would be working in the UK and generating his UK spending needs from his UK earnings. In such cases the simple technique of keeping his investment portfolio abroad is cheap and does not require elaborate, tax-driven, financial planning.

But for the majority of non-domicilaries UK spending money needs in part at least to be funded from abroad and in addition there may be good commercial reasons to invest in the UK. This means it may not be possible to keep the assets and income entirely free of exposure to UK tax. However, a variety of techniques do exist whereby funds can be brought to or invested in the UK without tax consequences. The relevant techniques are discussed in Chapters 16 and 17.

Situs

15.7 It is easy to state that all investments should be foreign situs. It is not, however, always easy to achieve this in practice.

There are two reasons for this. The first is that the common law, which determines situs for the purposes of IHT, is derived from old cases whose facts bear little relation to modern investment products. The second is that express, and in some respects counter-intuitive, rules apply to CGT. The common law rules are explained in Chapter 31, and the statutory CGT rules in Chapter 32.

A solution to the problem posed by the CGT situs rules is to hold the assets in an offshore trust (see Chapter 19). Difficulty with the IHT situs rules are avoided if the trust holds the investments through an underlying company (see para 45.3).

Source

15.8 Source is a different concept from situs, and, as with IHT and situs, the matter is largely governed by old case law. Details are given in Chapter 34D.

A particular trap is represented by income arising in the Republic of Ireland (ITTOIA 2005, s 831(5)). The remittance basis does not apply, which means such income is taxable in full even if not remitted. The point applies to mutual funds resident in Ireland as here any dividends have an Irish source if the fund is in corporate form. Capital gains are not subject to this rule.

Change of domicile

15.9 It goes without saying that the advantages described above cease if the individual becomes domiciled in the UK. The circumstances in which this may happen are explained in Chapter 39.

With IHT, the potential problem is much worse on account of the concept of deemed domicile. If any individual is resident in the UK during all or part of 17 out of 20 tax years (including the current year) he is deemed to be domiciled in the UK. This rule is explained in para 30.14 and it means that once the seventeenth year commences, all the non-domiciliary's assets become fully subject to IHT.

Under current law and practice, it is possible for a non-domiciliary to avoid the IHT consequences of acquiring an actual or a deemed UK domicile by making an offshore settlement before he does so. This is as explained in Chapter 19. An offshore settlement does not, in general, avoid the income tax and CGT consequences of acquiring an actual UK domicile for, assuming the settlement is settlor-interested, income and gains are assessed on a UK settlor on an arising basis.

The long arm of remittance

15.10 Although in this chapter it is pre-supposed that investments and the income they generate are not brought to the UK, remittance to the UK can happen inadvertently. It is important to avoid such traps and ensure that if funds are required in the UK, the techniques described in Chapter 16 are used.

Reinvestment

15.11 Once an item of income or gains has arisen, it is taxable insofar as any subsequent remittance can be traced back to it. The detailed rules are explained in para 40.5, but at its simplest, it means that remitting the proceeds of a foreign investment bought out of foreign income or gains is taxable. This does not apply if the income or gains arose prior to the assumption of residence (para 40.6) or if the remittance is effected after residence ceases. Other methods of overcoming this problem in relation to income are discussed in Chapter 16.

Currency gains

15.12 It should be remembered that foreign currency bank accounts are assets for CGT purposes, a disposal occurring whenever money is withdrawn. Should the currency have appreciated against sterling, a gain accrues. This point is explained in para 41.3 and means that the remittance of what to the uninitiated may appear as capital untainted by income or gain, in fact carries an element of capital gain.

The foreign currency accounts of non-domiciliaries at banks outside the UK are an exception to the CGT rule that the situs of the debt is determined by the residence of the debtor (see para 32.12). They are, as one would expect, foreign situs and eligible for the remittance basis as respects currency gains.

Settlement of liabilities

15.13 Remittance occurs not simply if money is bought to the UK, but if it is used to settle a UK liability. These rules are explained in para 40.5. The example often given is of a non-domiciliary who uses foreign income or gains to settle his UK butcher's bill in the UK: this is a taxable remittance even though the money never passes through the non-domiciliary's UK bank account.

A related point arises with credit cards. Settlement of a UK credit card is a remittance regardless of where the credit card has been used. So too even if the credit card is foreign and paid off abroad, remittance occurs insofar as the credit card is used in the UK or to settle UK liabilities (including purchases at UK airports).

Investment

15.14 Remittance occurs where funds are brought to the UK for investment as much as where they are used for spending. It is sometimes argued that the capital nature of investment may preclude this, but it is difficult to find support in the authorities (cf para 40.5).

It follows that portfolio managers who use a non-domiciliary's foreign income or gains to effect settlement in the UK, are effecting a taxable remittance. This is so even if the investment being bought is foreign, and remittance also occurs if the fund manager holds funds on client account in the UK. The better view is that the purchase of a UK situs investment where settlement is made abroad does not occasion remittance of the purchase price. But the subsequent sale of such an investment would be a taxable remittance if settlement was in the UK or if the proceeds otherwise reached the UK (see para 40.5).

EU Savings Directive

15.15 Three Member States of the European Union, namely Luxembourg, Belgium and Austria have opted for withholding tax rather than exchange of information. The same applies inter alia to Jersey, Guernsey, the Isle of Man, the British Virgin Islands and Switzerland. Under the terms of the Directive, withholding tax falls to be applied on interest payments to non-domiciliaries even if not remitted, provided the non-domiciliary is resident in the UK. However, most affected offshore jurisdictions are taking the position that the unremitted interest of non-domiciliaries is not caught. The subject is discussed in Chapter 50, as are the mechanics for recovering tax withheld.

Apart from Luxembourg, Belgium and Austria, the Member States of the EU are applying exchange of information, as are the Cayman Islands. Details of interest payments made to non-domiciliaries in such countries are therefore disclosed to HMRC.

There are many jurisdictions not within the Savings Directive, for example Bermuda, the Bahamas and all Far Eastern jurisdictions.

Chapter 16

Bringing money to the UK

Introduction

16.1 This chapter outlines the techniques which non-domiciliaries can use to bring money to the UK without incurring an income tax or CGT charge. The underpinning technical analysis is given in Chapters 40 and 41.

This chapter deals with investments and investment income. Planning for employment income is explained in Chapter 23.

Segregate capital and income

Separate bank accounts

16.2 As is described in para 40.6, it is well settled that if capital is held in one foreign account and all the income it generates is credited to a second, remittance to the UK from the capital account is not taxable as a remittance of income. In other words, to determine whether a remittance is of income, the exercise required is not economic equivalence but tracing. For these purposes funds count as capital if held prior to the assumption of UK residence or acquired subsequently by inheritance or gift (cf para 40.6). It is sometimes suggested that the two accounts should be at separate banks, but the leading case indicates this is not necessary (*Kneen v Martin* (1934) 19 TC 33).

Capital gains and offshore income gains

16.3 The main problem with operating separate bank accounts is that of capital gains and offshore income gains. If the capital account is a portfolio, it is of its nature likely to generate such gains. If a remittance is made from the capital account, a proportion of these gains will be included in the remittance (cf paras 41.1 and 71.15). Indeed, as described in para 41.3, the same problem may arise if the capital account is simply fixed-interest securities or bank deposits, for foreign currency is a chargeable asset for CGT purposes. The problem is further enhanced by the rule, described in para 41.1, that capital losses occurring on foreign situs assets are not allowable to non-domiciliaries.

One consequence of this is that non-distributor offshore funds are unattractive to non-domiciliaries, as it is those funds which generate offshore income gains (see Chapter 71). It is much better for a non-domiciliary to hold funds with distributor status, for then the return is or is mainly income which can be received into a separate bank account. But even if this is done the problem of ordinary capital gains remains.

One solution is to invest solely in sterling deposits or in sterling fixed-interest securities which are exempt from CGT either as government securities or as qualifying corporate bonds (TCGA 1992, s 115). This may be appropriate for non-domiciliaries in the UK on a short-term basis or with modest funds, but as a rule is too restrictive in investment terms.

A second solution is to operate three accounts, one income, one the proceeds of assets disposed of at a gain, and the third other capital. Remittance to the UK takes place from the third account, which by definition has to be in sterling. This solution certainly works, but it is cumbersome in practice and carries the risk that ultimately there will be insufficient funds in the third remittance account.

A third solution is to transfer the assets concerned to a settlo r-interested offshore settlement. This is discussed in Chapter 19.

Practical issues

16.4 A point to stress about using separate bank accounts is that income should be credited directly to the income account. If it is not, issues then arise as to whether its subsequent removal from the capital account to the income account is sufficient to prevent remittances from the latter being taxable (cf para 40.5).

In practice many foreign banks find operating segregated bank accounts difficult. Mistakes are made, even in jurisdictions such as Jersey and Guernsey which are very familiar with the technique. An audit often reveals some tax as due to HMRC. Where this is so it may be possible to correct the error and treat it as having never been made (see para 40.6). But otherwise repairs to the non-domiciliary's relevant tax return or other corrective action should be initiated.

Cessation of source

16.5 It is well established and accepted by HMRC that source-ceasing works in relation to the income of non-domiciliaries. The technical underpinning of the technique is described in para 40.7. The essence is that foreign income is not taxable if it is remitted in a tax year after that in which the investment or bank account generating the income is sold or closed. It follows that the income of a portfolio can over a period of years be paid into an income account and then all investments in the portfolio are sold. Remittance from the income account in a subsequent tax year is not then taxable as income.

An attraction of the technique is that it offers a means of avoiding the CGT problem described above. The capital or portfolio account need not be remitted and so the fact that it contains capital gains is immaterial. If the income account is denominated in sterling, its remittance in the tax year after all the investments and bank accounts in the capital account are sold or closed is entirely tax free.

Source-ceasing is a further reason for non-domiciliaries to invest in offshore funds which have distributor status as distinct from those which do not. This is because source ceasing can protect the income from the former but it has no application to offshore income gains.

Practical issues

16.6 If source ceasing is to be used, it is essential to identify what the source of the income is so that its cessation can be ensured. One of the assets whose source has to be ceased is any bank account used for the capital account or its portfolio. Such account should be closed shortly before the end of the tax year in which the source ceasing is effected, any interest on it having been credited directly to the income amount. The income account should also be closed, the sums in it being moved to a new account which becomes the capital account and is operated with a new income account. Many advisers believe these accounts should be at a different bank, or at least at a different branch of the bank. But case law indicates that strictly this is not necessary. The procedure is explained in more detail at para 40.10.

Settlement of debts

16.7 Anti-avoidance legislation deems a remittance to occur if foreign income or gains are used to settle a UK bank borrowing, or if they are used to settle a foreign bank borrowing which has been or is used to fund remittances to the UK (see para 40.12). But the legislation does not block all arrangements involving debts.

Foreign bank loan

16.8 Money borrowed from a foreign bank and brought to the UK does not result in a taxable remittance unless and until principal of the loan is paid off out of foreign income or gains. The fact that income or gains are used to service the interest is immaterial (providing payment of the interest is made abroad). So too there are no tax consequences if foreign income or gains are used to pay off the loan after the individual has ceased to reside in the UK.

This technique is often used to fund house purchases and is discussed in para 21.4 in that context. The principal difficulty is that the interest may turn out to be UK source income of the lender, an issue discussed in paras 33.6 to

33.10. If it does have a UK source, the borrower, ie the non-domiciliary, is required to withhold 20% tax and account for such tax to HMRC (see para 34.6).

This difficulty may be avoided if the lending bank is based in a jurisdiction giving the country of residence sole taxing rights over the interest, and a direction to pay interest gross is obtained under SI 1970/488. Such direction does, however, have to be renewed every five years (CNR DT Guidance Note 8).

Other debts

16.9 It is widely believed that a non-domiciliary who owes money to a UK creditor who is not a bank does not effect a taxable remittance if he effects settlement to a foreign account of the creditor. This is so even if the goods or services being paid for were delivered or rendered in the UK. The technical analysis behind this belief is explained in para 40.16. In practice it is sometimes used to settle school or even professional fees. HMRC take the view that remittance does occur if a cheque is handed to the supplier in the UK, albeit then presented abroad.

Gifts abroad

16.10 There are two respects in which the making of gifts abroad can enable funds to reach the UK without tax.

Gift of income or capital gain

16.11 It is now well settled that a gift abroad of foreign income or gains converts the income or gains into capital in the hands of the donee. As such it can be remitted free of tax. The relevant case law is described in Chapter 42. As there explained, the gift must be perfected abroad and the donee must not give the money or financial equivalence back to the donor. A great advantage of the gift abroad technique is that it embraces capital gains and deemed income as well as actual income.

Of itself a gift abroad does not enhance the spending power in the UK of the donor. But as the case of *Grimm v Newman* [2002] All ER (D) 93 (Nov), [2002] EWCA Civ 1621 established, the donee can be the non-domiciliary's spouse and can use the gifted money to buy her half share in a UK house owned 50:50 by the couple. Further applications of the principle are discussed in para 42.6 and would certainly include funding of the donee's spouse's own spending in the UK.

It is sometimes suggested the same principle can be invoked if a gift is made to a settlor-interested offshore trust and the trust then brings the money to the UK to invest. Although technically there may be some doubt about this (see para 42.8), it is the experience of at least some practitioners that HMRC accept this is effective to convert the income or gains into capital in the hands of the trust. It is of course essential that the gifted money does not find its way back to the donor while in the UK and it is prudent to avoid financial benefit to him.

Gift prior to sale

16.12 A gift abroad may also be considered when an asset pregnant with gain is likely to be sold. Here a gift of the asset to a settlor-interested trust eliminates the gain without raising remittance issues. This is because the trust acquires the asset at an updated base cost while the donor, although realising a gain, does not realise any amount capable of being remitted (see further para 41.8).

A caveat

16.13 Making gifts abroad has IHT consequences if at the time of the gift the non-domiciliary is deemed domiciled for IHT purposes (see paras 30.9 to 30.14). Unless reliefs apply, a gift into settlement is an immediately chargeable transfer, whatever the form of the settlement (see para 43.2). An outright gift to another individual is taxable should the donor fail to survive seven years (IHTA 1984, s 3A). But an outright gift to the donor's spouse is normally without IHT consequences. Such a gift is an exempt transfer unless the recipient spouse has neither an actual nor a deemed UK domicile (IHTA 1984, s 18).

Even if the donor does not have a deemed UK domicile at the time of the gift, the future impact of the gift with reservation rules should be kept in mind. These rules are discussed in Chapter 47, and they mean any UK assets in a settlor-interested trust at the time of the settlor's death are subject to IHT. So too the inter vivos exclusion of the settlor, or capital distributions to other beneficiaries, may be potentially exempt transfers.

Regardless of deemed domicile, gifts also require consideration of the pre-owned asset rules discussed in Chapter 70. Where the gift is into a settlor-interest discretionary trust, these rules are unlikely to come into issue, because the property in the trust is subject to a reservation (see para 70.17). A gift to a spouse is outside the rules (see para 70.14). But a gift to another individual which is used to fund the purchase of land or chattels used or enjoyed by the donor in the UK is likely to be caught by the pre-owned asset rules, unless the gift is of cash made more than seven years before use or occupation begins (see para 70.16).

Chapter 17

UK investments

Introduction

17.1 This chapter outlines how non-domiciliaries may hold UK investments without incurring adverse tax consequences. It is assumed that the funds required to buy the UK investments have been brought to the UK without triggering a taxable remittance (see Chapter 16) and that the non-domiciliary has not yet acquired an IHT deemed domicile (see para 30.14).

Basic tax treatment

17.2 A non-domiciliary holding UK assets in his personal name enjoys none of the tax advantages outlined in Chapter 15. Instead his tax exposure in respect of such assets is the same as that of the ordinary taxpayer both resident and domiciled in the UK. Thus income and capital gains are fully taxable on an arising basis and the assets are exposed to IHT. The latter comes into issue should the non-domiciliary die and results in a charge at the rate of 40% insofar as the UK assets exceed the nil-rate band (£285,000 in 2006/07). IHT also comes into issue on gifts to trusts and on other gifts should the non-domiciliary fail to survive seven years.

IHT mitigation

17.3 A number of strategies exist for managing or avoiding the IHT exposure on UK assets.

Timely realisation

17.4 IHT only comes into issue if UK assets are held at the moment of charge – ie on death or when a gift is made. If, therefore, all UK assets have by then been sold and the proceeds converted to cash or other assets abroad, the charge is avoided.

With gifts this is a relatively easy procedure to implement as the timing of the gift can be anticipated. But realisation prior to death carries the difficulty that the date of death is not normally known in advance. The practical solution normally adopted is to retain the UK assets while the individual is of reasonable age and in good health and cover the risk of untimely death by term assurance. The assets can then be sold when age or illness render life expectancy modest.

An alternate solution to life assurance applies where the individual is married or in civil partnership. Here spouses may bequeath the UK assets to each other, leaving action to remove the assets from the UK to be taken by the survivor after the first death. This works provided sufficient time elapses between the two deaths. The IHT spouse exemption should be fully available, for that exemption is only restricted to £55,000 if the transferor spouse is UK domiciled or deemed domiciled and the recipient is not (IHTA 1984, s 18(2)).

Value reduction

17.5 Instead of selling the UK assets, their taxable value can be reduced. A liability secured on an asset goes to reduce the value of that asset for IHT purposes rather than the value of the estate generally (IHTA 1984, s 162(4)). The liability must have been incurred for full consideration (IHTA 1984, s 5(5)), but self-evidently, borrowing secured against an asset is plainly within the rule. Accordingly, at its simplest, the acquisition of UK assets with borrowed money secured on them reduces the potential IHT exposure. This technique, and the potential pitfalls, is explained in relation to UK houses in Chapter 21.

IHT reliefs

17.6 The potential use of general IHT reliefs should not be forgotten. One, the spouse exemption, has already been mentioned and merits consideration wherever UK assets are directly held by a married non-domiciliary.

A second relief is that for potentially exempt transfers, ie outright gifts within seven years of death. Term assurance can cover the risk of untimely death. There is, however, one caveat: the donor should not use or otherwise benefit from the gifted assets or any asset bought by the donee in replacement of it. If he does, he is likely to fall foul of the GWR rules or, if not them, the pre-owned assets rules (see Chapters 47 and 70).

A third and most important relief is business property relief. This now covers all unquoted shares providing the company is a trading company not dealing in land or securities (IHTA 1984, s 105). It is applicable to all individuals and confers protection from GWR charges as well as ordinary IHT charges. In practice it should be applicable in most cases where the UK investment is shares in a private trading company. There are points to watch, most notably that the shares must be owned for at least two years (IHTA 1984, s 106) and that the relief may be partially lost if the company also holds investment assets (IHTA 1984, s 112).

Authorised Funds

17.7 One important category of UK investment is free from IHT in the hands of non-domiciliaries, namely units in an Authorised Unit Trust and shares in an open-ended investment company. Although mainly considered in relation to non-resident non-domiciliaries, these reliefs apply equally to resident non-domiciliaries. They are explained further in para 30.11.

Remove the asset from the UK

17.8 There are certain classes of asset which can be removed from exposure to IHT by simple export from the UK. The most obvious example is chattels such as pictures or fine furniture. A chattel owned by a non-domiciliary is in charge to IHT if in the UK but not if it is elsewhere.

The ability to confer IHT protection by removal from the UK for certain assets may extend to intangibles. As is described in paras 31.9 and 31.6, shares in UK companies can, under the Companies Act 1985 s 188, be converted to bearer form by issuing warrants to bearer and a simple debt can be enshrined in a deed executed under seal. It is widely thought that the warrants to bearer are situate where found and that a deed under seal converts a simple debt into a specialty, with the result it too is situate where found. However, those undertaking such strategies should be aware that a judge has recently questioned the effectiveness of warrants to bearer to change situs (see para 31.9).

Both for these reasons and because of their inherent technical complexity such conversion exercises should only be undertaken with specialist advice. Whatever the form of the asset, removal from the UK is subject to the same issues as to timing as arise when the UK assets are sold and the proceeds removed from the UK.

Income tax and CGT

17.9 None of the above strategies confer protection from income tax on the income the UK assets generate whilst held in the UK. A further point is that the issue of warrants to bearer does not prevent any dividend paid by the UK company concerned from having a UK source and thus being taxed on an arising basis; as is explained in para 33.3, source is determined by the residence of the company.

The CGT exposure on any UK gains remains also, despite the above mitigation strategies. But the removal of a chattel from the UK converts any gain on the chattel to foreign situs, as there is no exit charge. This does not, of course, avail with UK shares, and, since 16 March 2005, use of warrants to bearer has, even if it works for IHT, not been effective to change situs for CGT purposes (see para 32.6). Nonetheless it should be remembered that shares or other assets qualifying for IHT business property relief may also attract the business rates of taper for CGT purposes (TCGA 1992, s 2A and Sch A1). This effectively reduces the rate of tax to 10% once the assets have been held for more than two years.

CGT may be a particular issue if a non-domiciled individual desires to avoid IHT by selling UK assets and removing the proceeds from the UK. Such sale will have a CGT cost if the asset is showing a gain. But the difficulty may be avoided if the sale and removal only takes place following inheritance by a surviving spouse, for then the asset is rebased on the first death (TCGA 1992, s 62).

Avoidance of CGT

17.10 As explained in Chapter 19, the UK assets held by an offshore trust are free of CGT so long as the settlor remains non-domiciled. Holding the UK assets in an offshore trust is therefore the best form of CGT mitigation. This is one of the several reasons for a non-domiciliary to form an asset-holding offshore trust.

Holding companies

17.11 Another method by which non-domiciliaries own UK assets is through a holding company registered in an offshore jurisdiction.

Inheritance tax

17.12 An offshore company avoids IHT because the relevant asset for IHT purposes is the shares in the company which are foreign situs (save in the most unlikely event that the shares are bearer shares physically kept in the UK).

CGT shelter

17.13 Provided UK residence on the part of the company is avoided, it also operates as a CGT shelter, for being non-resident it is outside the charge to CGT, save insofar as it is trading in the UK through a permanent establishment (TCGA 1992, s 10B). So too the non-domiciliary is not taxed on the company gains under TCGA 1992, s 13 as that section does not apply to non-domiciliaries (see para 66.4). Any gains in the company can ultimately be distributed free of charge to the non-domiciliary if such distribution is by dividend paid abroad prior to liquidation. On that scenario the cessation of source principle allows tax-free remittance to the UK in the tax year following that in which the company is finally dissolved (see para 40.7). Alternatively the shares in the company could simply be sold after the dividend and the dividend remitted in the tax year after the sale.

Income tax

17.14 The position as respects income if the company is non-resident is in contrast. Here TA 1988 s 739 deems the income of the company to be that of the individual, and insofar as the income has a UK source, tax is on an arising basis (see Chapter 55). Section 739 can on certain scenarios be avoided, notably if the company is bought by the non-domiciliary as a going concern (see para 55.12) or if the motive defence in ss 741 and 741A applies. But of their nature these scenarios are unlikely.

Company residence

17.15 Should a non-domiciliary own an offshore registered company directly, there is always a risk it may fall to be treated as UK resident under the central management and control test. But this result is avoided if the company is genuinely managed by the board in the offshore jurisdiction concerned (see Chapter 38). Should the non-domiciliary be on the facts a shadow director, the possible impact of the benefits in kind code should be kept in mind (see Chapters 53 and 69).

Mutual funds

17.16 As will be apparent from this chapter there is no completely satisfactory method for a non-domiciliary or a settlement created by him to hold UK investments. But in the case of portfolio investments a solution does exist. This is to acquire UK investments not directly, but through a mutual fund.

Offshore funds

17.17 The tax planning potential of offshore funds is explained in Chapter 4. For these purposes the fund should be a company, ie an open-ended company rather than a unit trust, for there is a slight risk some unit trusts may be fiscally transparent (see para 31.13). But provided the fund is in corporate form, its shares are the assets for IHT and CGT purposes and foreign situs. So too they are the source of any dividends and foreign income. The UK investments held by the fund are by definition free of IHT and the fund, being a foreign company, is not subject to UK income tax or CGT on its UK assets.

In short, an offshore fund in corporate form offers a wrapper which removes the tax drawbacks of portfolio investment in the UK without the problems attaching to holding companies.

For a non-domiciliary, an offshore fund with distributor status is preferable. This is because all or a significant part of the return is then foreign source income. Cessation of source means the latter can be remitted tax free in any tax year after that in which the shares in the fund are sold. The same is not true of non-distributor funds as there the return is offshore income gain wherein the relevant remittance rules are the CGT rules (cf para 71.15).

Irish funds should be avoided as the remittance basis does not apply to income arising in the Republic of Ireland (see para 40.1).

UK Authorised Funds

17.18 As explained in para 17.7, units in authorised unit trusts and shares in UK open-ended investment companies are not subject to IHT if held by a non-domiciliary or in a trust created by him. They are, however, subject to CGT on an arising basis if held directly by the non-domiciliary, as they are treated for CGT purposes in the same way as other UK assets. This normally renders them unattractive as direct investments for the non-domiciliary.

Another drawback of UK funds is that they generate UK source income. But some UK unit trusts or open-ended investment companies generate little or no income and if so these may be considered as an alternate to offshore funds. Their advantage is that the gain is taxed as capital gain regardless of what distributions the fund makes.

Chapter 18

Anticipating UK domicile

Introduction

18.1 This chapter identifies steps a non-domiciliary should take in anticipation of acquiring a UK domicile. As is explained in Chapter 39, he may never acquire an actual UK domicile, but once he has resided in the UK for all or part of 17 tax years he is deemed to be UK domiciled for IHT purposes.

Deemed and actual domicile

18.2 Discussion of steps in anticipation of UK domicile tends to be couched in terms of IHT and deemed domicile, for once the 17-year residence threshold is crossed, acquisition of the deemed domicile is inevitable. But it should not be forgotten that a non-domiciliary whose main home is in the UK acquires an actual UK domicile once it is clear as a matter of objective evidence that he intends that the UK will remain his main home permanently or indefinitely (cf para 39.3). Once that intention is formed he should notify HMRC he has a UK domicile and include his world income and gains on future returns.

HMRC do from time to time check an individual's domicile in an enquiry and while in practice they are slow to claim a change of domicile retrospectively, interest and penalties are due should they be successful in doing so. At least some more experienced advisers are of the view that HMRC are too slow to challenge long-stay residents who continue to assert foreign domicile. If nothing else it would not be surprising if at some stage greater scepticism is expressed on the part of HMRC.

Inheritance tax

18.3 The prime result of acquiring an actual or a deemed UK domicile is that the taxpayer's global assets become exposed to inheritance tax. It is of course possible for UK domiciliaries to mitigate that tax, for example by gifts more than seven years before death. But such strategies are not always possible and can entail complications arising out of the gift with reservation and pre-owned asset rules (see Chapters 47 and 70).

Fortunately for the non-domiciliary there is one strategy which enables these difficulties to be avoided. This is to create an offshore settlement before there is any risk of him having acquired an actual or a UK domicile. As is described in Chapter 45, the effect of the excluded property rules is that foreign situs property is excluded property provided the settlor had neither an actual nor a deemed UK domicile when he put funds into settlement. Subsequent changes in his domicile are, as the law now stands, immaterial.

The IHT advantages of a settlement, although not any income tax or CGT advantage, may be achieved even if the settlement is UK resident. This is because the residence of a trust is immaterial in determining excluded property status. However, as with all excluded property settlements it is essential that all the trust assets are foreign situs.

Income tax and CGT normally render a UK resident trust unattractive if the fund is of any size. But for modest funds, cost considerations may favour UK trusteeship particularly if some or all of the trustees are non-professional.

CGT

18.4 At one time the making of a settlement whilst non-domiciled also achieved lasting freedom from CGT even after the settlor's acquisition of an actual UK domicile. This is no longer so. Once the settlor becomes resident and domiciled in the UK, gains in an offshore trust are assessable on him on an arising basis under TCGA 1992, s 86 (see para 60.2). Further, and regardless of the settlor's domicile, capital payments to beneficiaries both resident and domiciled in the UK are taxable insofar as matched to trust capital gains or offshore income gains (see Chapter 63 and para 71.18).

There are two areas where CGT planning in anticipation of a change of actual domicile is still worthwhile. One concerns rebasing and the other trust distributions.

Rebasing

18.5 Under CGT rules, these is no rebasing when a non-resident becomes resident or when a non-domiciliary becomes UK domiciled. Accordingly, gains which come into charge on assets held at the time of the change of status include historic gains as well as gains accruing subsequently. The same applies to offshore trusts should gains become assessable on the settlor under TCGA 1992, s 86 on his becoming both resident and domiciled in the UK.

On the face of it these considerations indicate foreign assets should be rebased prior to the acquisition of a UK domicile. But in reality matters are not altogether simple. One reason is that rebasing triggers a gain, taxable if remitted. As is explained in para 41.12, the remittance of a gain is taxable even if effected after acquisition of a UK domicile.

The next point is that rebasing is not always easy to achieve. A sale and buy back is likely to entail stamp duty or other transfer taxes and there are also transaction costs. Shares cannot be bought back for at least 30 days (TCGA 1992, s 106A(5)) and, in the case of assets not dealt with on a recognised exchange, there is always the risk that a sale and rapid buy back will be vitiated under the *Ramsay* principle. A transfer to a spouse is not effective as such disposals are on a no gain, no loss basis (TCGA 1992, s 58).

Perhaps the best means of overcoming the difficulties is by gifting the assts into an offshore settlement, a strategy which also eliminates any previously unremitted gain in the value gifted (see para 16.12). Such a strategy also fits well with the IHT strategy of holding assets in an excluded property settlement. But UK assets should not be settled as such is an immediately chargeable transfer and, assuming the individual is UK resident, any gain crystallised on the transfer into settlement is chargeable on an arising basis.

A third issue with rebasing is that it is essential to be certain at the time the rebasing is effected that the individual concerned indeed still has an actual foreign domicile. If later it turns out he did not, the effect of rebasing is an immediate charge to CGT on the gain thereby realised. It may be difficult to achieve a sufficient degree of certainty as to domicile to justify crystallising gains, particularly where the context is one where the acquisition of a UK domicile is anticipated in the not too distant future.

In practice the solution to this difficulty is to regard rebasing as a matter to be kept under constant review. Subject to tax considerations in any other relevant jurisdiction, it is a prudent step for a non-domiciliary to consider before becoming resident at all. Thereafter it is a step which should be considered in any event in relation to assets which come to show a large latent gain, provided at the time it is done the individual's foreign domicile is still beyond doubt.

Losses

18.6 Rebasing should not be effected as respects assets showing a loss. This is because losses accruing to non-domiciliaries on foreign assets are not allowable (see para 41.1). Allowability is achieved once the individual is UK domiciled.

Trust distributions

18.7 Should the non-domiciliary be a beneficiary of an existing offshore trust, trust distributions prior to the acquisition of UK domicile should be considered. The issue arises because capital distributions to non-domiciliaries are not taxable under the various capital payments regimes, whereas capital payments to resident domiciliaries are (see paras 63.22, 64.9 and 71.18 to 71.26). Accordingly, it makes good sense to effect capital distributions before there is any risk of the recipient having acquired a UK domicile. This is so even if the recipient is a settlor, for while capital payments made to him after the acquisition of a UK domicile cannot be taxed by reference to current gains (as those are taxed on him on an arising basis), they can be taxed by reference to past gains (see para 63.20).

As with rebasing, this strategy is not one which should be implemented if there is any doubt about the recipient's actual domicile. The capital payment should never exceed the relevant pools of gains. If it does the excess is carried forward and set against future gains. If by then the recipient is both resident and domiciled in the UK, tax results (see para 63.22).

Should the recipient not be settlor, possible income tax exposure on the distribution under TA 1988, s 740 should be considered (cf Chapter 57). Where applicable, s 740 has priority to capital treatment.

Income tax

18.8 There is some scope for anticipatory planing with income tax but such planning is of a rather different nature as income arises and is potentially taxable on an annual basis. Two points are, however, worth making.

Tax-free remittance

18.9 In contrast to capital gains, remittances of foreign investment income are tax-free if effected in a tax year subsequent to that in which UK domicile is acquired (see para 40.19). Accordingly, should the acquisition of a foreign domicile be anticipated, foreign income can simply be kept abroad until the tax year after the acquisition is effected, and then remitted tax-free. Prudence dictates that the remittance should in fact be delayed until UK domiciled status has been agreed with HMRC.

Accelerating income

18.10 There may be some classes of foreign income whose receipt can be accelerated. This also should be considered when a change of domicile is anticipated. Perhaps the most obvious instance is foreign private companies controlled by the taxpayer or a settlor-interested trust, for here the timing of dividends is largely within the shareholder's control. If such acceleration is able to be combined with remittance after the acquisition of foreign domicile, a significant tax advantage may be secured.

Another class of income where acceleration may be achieved is offshore income gains (cf Chapter 71). However, here it should be remembered that the remittance rules are those applicable to CGT, so any remittance of the offshore income gain after the acquisition of UK domicile is taxable. Should the interests in offshore funds be held in trust, complex issues may arise, which are discussed in paras 71.18 to 71.26.

Exclusion of the settlor

18.11 Should the non-domiciliary be settler of an existing settlor-interested settlement, the issue of whether he should be excluded prior to him acquiring an actual UK domicile should be considered. On the face of it such exclusion is attractive for, assuming his wife is excluded as well, this prevents the income of the settlement being taxed as his under ITTOIA 2005, s 624 and so on the face of it preserves the trust's foreign source income from tax.

Unfortunately, in reality, matters are not as simple as this. One reason is that s 739 may still apply if the settlor has previously received capital sums while UK resident (see para 55.10). A second point is that exclusion does not confer CGT protection unless the settlor's children and in some cases grandchildren, are excluded as well (see Chapter 60). Finally, there is the argument that exclusion amounts to a PET for IHT purposes if it is effected when the settlor already has a deemed UK domicile (see para 47.10). This carries the risk of IHT exposure in the event of death within seven years, such as does not occur if the settlor remains interested until death.

Wider considerations

18.12 A non-domiciliary who is or may be acquiring a UK domicile should remember that domicile has wider implications than tax. It governs matters such as succession and marriage and, at least so far as English law is concerned, the effect of acquiring an English domicile is that these matters become governed by English law. The implications of this should be reviewed with care.

A related area concerns those systems of law where family assets are held for the family, perhaps by a senior figure, without differentiating individual ownership. A non-domiciliary interested in such structures should consider whether they are appropriate to growing connection to the tax and legal system of the UK. Certainly if he is likely to acquire a deemed or even an actual domicile, tax factors if no other are a strong argument in favour of securing certainty, in an English law sense, as to what assets he does own and what assets he does not.

Change of law

18.13 The current review of residence and domicile could result in long-stay non-domiciliaries becoming deemed domiciled in the UK for all tax purposes rather than just for IHT (cf para 39.13). Further, deemed domicile could be imposed after a period of residence shorter than 17 years.

Given these possibilities, the question arises of how far the planning techniques discussed in this chapter may be used to anticipate such change in the law. The short answer is that it is impossible to tell at this stage. The present government is committed to proceeding by consultation (see para 39.13) and present indications are that any change will be signalled in advance. Assuming this is indeed so, such will be the time for anticipatory planning. At this stage all that can be said is that rebasing for CGT purposes is likely on any view to make sense if such can be done by gift into settlement or otherwise without generating remittable gains.

What is certainly not clear is whether remittance of prior foreign income will be tax-free following any imposition of deemed domicile for income tax purposes, or whether the excluded property status of settlements created by a settlor who was non-domiciled when he created the settlement but now is not, will be preserved. However, as respects the latter point there must be at least some prospect of arrangements existing at a given date being grandfathered, and so to that extent excluded property settlements created now could turn out to have continuing future advantage.

Chapter 19

Creating offshore settlements

Introduction

19.1 Non-domiciliaries resident in the UK frequently create offshore settlements. For the most part those settlements are discretionary and the non-domiciliary and his spouse are included in the class of beneficiaries. During their lifetimes they are regarded as the principal beneficiaries. Such settlements are normally known as excluded property settlements as the property in them is, or at least is intended to be, excluded property for IHT purposes (cf Chapter 45).

This chapter summarises the tax advantages achieved by excluded property settlements and discusses their other implications. The next chapter focuses on the tax issues which arise once the settlement is up and running. Chapter 22 addresses the rather different issues which arise when a non-domiciliary wishes to make provision for his family.

Advantages

Inheritance tax

19.2 An excluded property settlement does not of itself confer any IHT advantage so long as the settlor has neither an actual nor a deemed UK domicile. But, as explained in para 18.3, should his actual or deemed domicile change, the assets in the settlement remain free of IHT. This is so regardless of the form of the settlement. The 2006 changes to IHT mean that this long-term protection is of increasing value.

CGT

19.3 Since the trustees of an excluded property settlement are non-resident, they are not subject to CGT. This freedom from tax extends to UK assets as well as to foreign assets save in the unlikely event the trustees are trading in the UK (see para 30.5). So long as the non-domiciliary retains his foreign domicile, the gains in the settlement cannot be assessed as his as they arise under TCGA 1992, s 86 (see Chapter 60), and nor are capital distributions to him able to be taxed under TCGA 1992, s 87 or Sch 4C (see Chapters 63 and 65).

As a result, an excluded property settlement offers a complete shelter for capital gains, so operating even where amounts representing the gain are distributed to the non-domiciliary and brought by him to the UK. As compared with assets owned personally the CGT advantages are therefore threefold:

(1) Gains realised on UK investments are sheltered.
(2) Gains on foreign situs assets are also sheltered. The difficulties posed by CGT remittance basis, discussed in para 16.3, are eliminated not by avoiding remittance, but by rendering the gain not taxable in the first place.
(3) The difficulties over the CGT situs rules noted in para 15.7 are not material since the gain is sheltered regardless of situs.

Remittance planning

19.4 Settling funds which represent unremitted foreign income or gains can, depending on the facts, permit tax-free remittance by the trustees thereafter (paras 16.11 and 42.8). Should a foreign situs asset be settled prior to disposal, remittance issues are wholly avoided, for a gain generated by a gift is incapable of remittance (see para 16.12).

Potential drawbacks

19.5 Although in almost all cases clearly advantageous, an excluded property settlement does have certain implications which should be kept in mind.

CGT exposure

19.6 Should the settlor become domiciled as well as resident in the UK, any gains in the settlement will be taxable as his as they arise (see Chapter 60). So too capital distributions to him will be taxable by reference to gains in the settlement arising before he became UK domiciled (see para 63.22). For this reason, the trust gains should be computed in each year and, if there is a risk that the settlor will at some stage become UK domiciled, a strategy for minimising tax on future distributions should be formulated (cf Chapter 14 and para 20.8).

Income tax

19.7 Making a settlement does not result in any income tax saving for the non-domiciliaries and can make remittance planning more complicated.

However, provided correct planning is put in place, the position is no worse than with directly owned assets. This subject is explained in Chapter 20. A particular point to note is that as the non-domiciliary is transferor, TA 1988, s 740 cannot render distributions of capital to him subject to income tax.

Although prima facie gains realised by non-resident trusts on the disposal of non-distributor offshore funds are taxed in accordance with the CGT capital payment rules, this is only so if under those rules the gain is matched on a current-year basis with distributions to the settlor or other UK-resident beneficiaries. Should this not be so, the gains are s 739 income, taxable on the settlor insofar as remitted (see para 71.25).

Other family members

19.8 In due course a non-domiciliary may wish to provide for his children or other family members. Such provision can be expensive if funded by an excluded property settlement. Should the recipients be resident in the UK, taxation of benefits under TA 1988, s 740 has to be considered, and should they be domiciled as well, CGT is in issue too. The position is as described in Chapter 22.

Loss of control

19.9 Creating a trust has important non-fiscal implications. A trust results in the trustee controlling the assets and being in the driving seat. If the non-domiciliary is unlikely to be able to accept this, there is a risk of the trust being a sham and the arrangement is best not entered into at all (see Chapter 51). However, in practice many of the concerns non-domiciliaries have may be allayed by reputable trustees and by including in the trust provision for a protector with power to remove and appoint trustees.

Personal law

19.10 At least in the eyes of English law, non-domiciled status means the non-domiciliary's personal law is not English. His personal law may impose forced heirship rules extending to lifetime gifts and it may also be characterised by community of property. Such rules may affect the capacity of the non-domiciliary to make the settlement.

Most offshore jurisdictions have express legislation validating settlements despite the settlor's personal law. But such legislation is only effective as respects assets in the jurisdiction concerned. Making a settlement can open the door to wide-ranging and expensive international litigation. In appropriate cases, careful advice should be taken at the outset.

Creating the settlement

Timing

19.11 Self-evidently, an excluded property settlement should be made before there is any risk of the non-domiciliary having acquired an actual or a deemed UK domicile. Deemed domicile should be watched in particular as the rules for computing means it can start sooner than expected (see para 30.14).

In view of the CGT advantages, the settlement should be made as soon as possible. Indeed some domiciliaries are advised to create a settlement before taking up UK residence.

Until 22 March 2006, the CGT advantages of an offshore settlement could be achieved without an IHT entry charge even if the non-domiciliary had acquired a deemed UK domicile. This was possible if the non-domiciliary or his spouse took an initial interest in possession, for then the settlement was without IHT consequences (see para 45.16). Now such a settlement propels the property straight into the relevant property regime and an IHT entry charge results (see para 43.14).

As is described in para 2.13, this entry charge can be avoided should IHT reliefs such as business property relief or normal expenditure out of income be in point, and so in such cases a deemed domiciliary who has previously failed to act can still consider an offshore settlement. Even though it will not have excluded property status, CGT protection is enjoyed unless and until the non-domiciliary acquires an actual UK domicile.

Assets settled

19.12 The assets transferred to the excluded property settlement should be foreign situs as otherwise an IHT entry charge may result (see para 46.2). The common law situs rules apply (Chapter 31) and, given the increasing areas of uncertainty, the status of each asset to be settled should be reviewed with care.

For the reasons given in para 18.6, it may not be appropriate to settle assets showing a loss. This is material should there be a likelihood of the settlor acquiring an actual UK domicile.

One kind of UK asset may be thought to represent an exception to the rule that UK situs assets should not be settled, namely holdings in authorised funds. As explained in para 30.11, these are excluded property if in the ownership of an individual with neither an actual nor a deemed UK domicile, with the result that their transfer into settlement does not result in an entry charge. Nonetheless there will not be many cases where the settling of holdings in authorised funds should be considered by a non-domiciliary, for any gain triggered by the disposal is taxable on an arising basis as the situs of authorised funds is in the UK for CGT purposes.

Form of trust

19.13 As noted at the beginning of this chapter, the trust should be discretionary so as to confer flexibility. As the objective is to continue funding the settlor he and his family should be in the discretionary class.

The IHT changes made in 2006 mean that the IHT treatment is the same even if the trust gives an initial life interest to the settlor. On certain scenarios such could have income tax advantages, in that it avoids distributions from the trust being a new source and so potentially complicating remittance planning (cf para 20.5). It also avoids a build up of income able to be taxed under TA 1988, s 740 on distributions to other beneficiaries (cf para 20.6).

Should the settlor take an initial life interest, flexibility may be preserved by giving the trustees overriding powers over capital. These are arguments that a settlement under which the settlor is life-tenant results in a charge under the pre-owned assets legislation (see para 70.24). This risk is avoided provided none of the trust investments are UK situs, or, if they are, they are held through an offshore holding company. It is also prudent to ensure that none of the investments is land or chattels used or enjoyed by the settler in specie.

Chapter 20

Existing excluded property settlements

Introduction

20.1 In the previous chapter, non-domiciliaries were recommended to create offshore settlements soon after becoming resident in the UK and certainly before there is any risk of a deemed or actual UK domicile being acquired. This chapter addresses planning techniques the trustees should adopt once the settlement is created and in particular how income and gains should be managed so as to ensure funds can be distributed to the settlor or other beneficiaries without tax charge.

In this chapter it is assumed the settlor is alive and resident in the UK, but has not attained an actual UK domicile. The settlement is assumed to be discretionary with the settlor among the beneficiaries. It is assumed the class of beneficiaries also includes persons who are resident and may perhaps be or become domiciled in the UK and that in due course, and particularly in the event of the settlor's death, some of those persons may benefit. In this latter regard it should be read with Chapter 22 which deals in general terms with how non-domiciliaries should confer benefit on UK resident family members.

Income tax

UK source income

20.2 The settlor of an excluded property settlement is chargeable to tax on an arising basis insofar as the trust or any underlying company receives UK source income and he is still alive and resident in the UK. Income is so taxed under TA 1988, s 739 and ITTOIA 205, s 624 (see paras 55.22 and 59.27). For this reason, UK source income and thus UK investments, should be avoided.

Avoiding UK investments also improves the position should TA 1988, s 740 be in point as respects benefits conferred on beneficiaries other than the settlor. Should any such beneficiary be resident but not domiciled in the UK, avoidance of UK source income means a benefit escapes tax under s 740 provided it is not received in the UK and the income in the trust or company is not brought to the UK (see para 56.23).

Benefiting the settlor

20.3 In many cases, the primary planning requirement for the trustees is to ensure that if they do decide to confer benefit on the settlor such can be in tax-free form even if the benefit is received in or brought to the UK. Assuming all the trust income is foreign source, this is primarily achieved by operating the techniques described in Chapters 16 and 40 to ensure that income is segregated and that, where necessary, source-ceasing and other procedures are used.

This exercise is, however, complicated due to the fact that a trust is involved, for the trust means income tax has to be considered at two levels. The first is the income arising to the trustees which is deemed to be that of the settlor under TA 1988, s 739 and ITTOIA 2005, s 624, albeit subject to the remittance basis (see paras 55.22 and 59.27). The second is distributions by the trustees. If the trustees make an income distribution it counts as income from a new source (see para 12.4). The better view is that this applies even if the recipient is the settlor if by reason of foreign domicile he has not been taxed on the income at trust level (see para 59.30). As the source is the trust the remittance basis applies, but as the trust is continuing, source-ceasing is not possible.

The practical result of this is that remittance planning and income segregation have to be effected at two levels. The trustees need to operate a capital and an income account, all income being credited directly to the income account and all capital receipts to the capital account. Should the settlor require funds to bring to the UK, capital should be appointed to him, the appointment being funded by a transfer from the trust capital account to the settlor's personal capital account. It goes without saying that both these accounts should be abroad so as to avoid IHT complications. So long as the appointment is in exercise of a power over capital it should not be income in the hands of the settlor (cf para 12.5) and he can safely remit.

In due course source-ceasing may be used at trust level in that if all the trust investments generating the income are sold, effectively the income account becomes a capital account from the start of the following tax year (cf para 40.7). If such account is used to fund a capital distribution to the settlor, again this may be remitted by him tax free.

In one respect operating these banking procedures is easier with a trust than where foreign assets are personally owned by a non-domiciliary. As explained in para 19.3, assets in trust are not subject to CGT whether on a remittance basis or otherwise, so long as the settlor remains non-domiciled. As a result no issues arise as to whether distributions of capital to the settlor are taxable as remittances of capital gain.

Holding companies

20.4 Where the trust investments are held through a holding company a further level of complexity is involved in operating remittance procedures. Dividends paid by the company to the trust are themselves income from a continuing source, namely the shares in the company. Even if such dividends are capitalised in the trust and distributed as capital to the settlor, tax still results if he brings the capital to the UK as the source of the dividends is continuing. This is so even if the underlying investments in the company have all been sold.

In practice underlying holding companies tend to be capitalised by loan. In such case, value can reach the trust in capital form by loan repayment. Accordingly advantage can be taken of segregation and source-ceasing if the company operates capital and income accounts and effects loan repayments by debiting its capital account. If the trust receives the repayment in its capital account, and makes a capital distribution to the settlor from that account, the settlor can remit to the UK without tax consequences.

Unfortunately this solution is not a complete answer, for if the investments perform well, the trust loan to the company will at some stage be cleared. In such case it is unwise for the company then to make a loan to the trust, for such is trustee borrowing triggering a deemed disposal should the trustees distribute capital or make a loan while the loan to them is still outstanding (see Chapter 62). Although such a disposal will not result in a charge to CGT on the settlor under TCGA 1992, s 86 because he is non-domiciled, a Sch 4C pool of gains will be created. As is explained in Chapter 64, such gains cannot be washed out by distributions to non-resident or non-domiciled beneficiaries. This could prove disadvantageous should capital at some stage need to be distributed to beneficiaries both resident and domiciled in the UK. For this reason the only way forward, where any shareholder loan is fully repaid, may be sale or liquidation of the company.

Life-interest

20.5 An alternate method of providing for the settlor is for him to retain or be appointed a life interest. Such is now without IHT consequences provided the settlement is created after 22 March 2006 or was discretionary in form on that date (see para 43.14). A life interest in the settlor may on one view result in a charge under the pre-owned assets legislation (see para 70.24), but this risk is avoided provided all the assets in the trust are foreign situs (see paras 19.13 and 70.26).

Should the settlor hold a life interest, the income from the trust investments is treated as his provided the proper law of the trust is based on English trust law (see para 12.2). He can keep the income segregated and abroad and, should the trust investments all be realised, he can remit his rolled-up income tax-free in a subsequent tax year as cessation of source applies (see para 40.7). Further, capital appointments from the trust to him will also be free of income and so able to be remitted.

Should the investments of such a life-interest trust be in a holding company, the company needs to keep capital and income in separate accounts. The income account should be paid up to the trust in dividend at which point it will be the income of the settlor as life-tenant. So long as the company is retained, cessation of source permitting tax-free remittance of the income will not be possible. But the structure will still be free of income.

A drawback of the life-interest solution is that it can result in much of the investment return in the trust enuring to the settlor. Should he have or have acquired a deemed UK domicile, this may result in IHT exposure. But if all that is being funded is his current expenditure, that issue is not material.

Section 740 issues

20.6 It needs to be remembered that, unless motive defence (described in Chapter 58) applies, benefits conferred on UK resident beneficiaries other than the settlor are potentially taxable under TA 1988, s 740. If the trustees maintain a separate income account containing the rolled-up income, such is relevant income by reference to which distributions to resident beneficiaries can be taxed. The fact that the income was deemed to be that of the settlor is immaterial if by reason of non-remittance it has not in fact been taxed as his (see para 57.12).

Wherever a settlement is or is likely to have UK beneficiaries, s 740 relevant income should be computed in the manner described in Chapter 13. The best solution to the potential s 740 difficulties is to distribute all the income abroad as income, for then it never has the chance to become relevant income. Such distribution does not result in tax if the recipient is non-resident. If the recipient is non-domiciled, tax is avoided provided that the income is not remitted. As just noted, the recipient of such distribution can be the settlor himself. Necessarily this solution of full distribution is achieved if the trust is subject to an interest in possession. From a s 740 standpoint, an interest in possession in the settlor is therefore helpful.

Even where the trust has already built up a pool of relevant income, the potential problems posed by s 740 are not without solution. One approach is to distribute an amount equal to the relevant income by way of capital distribution to a non-domiciled but resident beneficiary abroad. If this is done, it is strongly arguable that the distribution carries out the relevant income (see para 56.25), but as the recipient is non-domiciled the distribution does not result in a s 740 charge. The better view is that this remains the position even if subsequently and independently the beneficiary remits to the UK (see para 56.24). This technique has to be operated with a resident but non-domiciled beneficiary, rather than a non-resident beneficiary, as distributions to non-residents are ignored for the purposes of s 740 (see para 56.18). The recipient beneficiary cannot be the settlor as s 740 does not apply to the settlor (see para 56.10). Although, as indicated in paras 56.24 and 56.25 the efficacy of this technique could be debated, it certainly represents the better view and is a position which with full disclosure can and should be taken on tax returns.

It should be stressed that this technique does not work and results in a tax charge insofar as any of the relevant income was UK source or has been remitted by the trustees. This is because even the limited s 740 remittance basis does not apply to UK income or remitted foreign income.

An alternate technique, which also overcomes the problem of UK income, arises if the relevant income has been segregated in banking terms in a separate account. This effectively is what happens if the trust operates capital and income accounts for the benefit of the settlor. If this has been done it is strongly arguable that a distribution of such rolled up income, effected by debiting the income account directly in favour of the recipient, causes the income to cease to be relevant income even if no s 740 benefit is conferred. The income in the income account can be distributed to a non-resident beneficiary or to the settlor. In the latter event the settlor would need to keep the distributed money abroad unless the trust has previously operated complete source-ceasing.

This technique can also be used when making distributions abroad to resident non-domiciliaries other than the settlor to give an added argument that the relevant income has been carried out.

Accrued interest

20.7 One difficulty with operating the procedures just described concerns accrued interest on foreign securities – ie the accrued but unpaid interest brought into charge when the security is sold. On such a sale the interest element cannot be segregated and carried into an income account. This does not matter in planning for the settlor, for the foreign securities of non-domiciliaries are excluded from the accrued income scheme and this exclusion carries over into s 739 and ITTOIA 2005, s 624 (see paras 55.22 and 59.27). But the position is otherwise with s 740. Here the accrued interest is relevant income and there is no exclusion in respect of non-domiciled beneficiaries. As accrued income cannot be segregated, it cannot be stripped out either (a) by paying it away as income, or (b) by carrying it to a segregated income account and distributing that account to the settlor or a non-resident beneficiary.

For those reasons accrued interest represent a real practical problem when s 740 is being considered. There are two solutions. One is to deal with it in the manner described above in relation to s 740 relevant income which has not been segregated in banking terms – ie distribute an amount equal to it to a resident but non-domiciled beneficiary other than the settlor by way of capital distribution abroad. The other is to avoid accrued interest altogether. In investment terms this means avoiding all foreign fixed-interest securities. This may be impractical, but there is a method of achieving such a result in tax terms which is to hold all fixed-interest securities through offshore funds. To be on the safe side the fund should be in corporate form (see para 4.2) but provided this is done, the fund is a separate entity whose shares are unaffected by the accrued income scheme. The issue of whether such fund should be distributor or non-distributor is discussed below. It should not be Irish based, as Irish income does not attract the remittance basis (see para 20.9).

Capital gains

20.8 As noted in para 19.3 capital gains tax is not an immediate issue with excluded property settlements as gains are not taxed on an arising basis. But in one respect CGT is important. This is that capital gains realised since 17 March 1998 form a s 87 pool and are allocated to capital payments since that date. Allocation is made regardless of the residence and domicile status of the recipient and is made whether the recipient is the settlor or some other beneficiary. Should the recipient be resident and domiciled in the UK he is taxed by reference to the s 87 pool. The s 87 pool stops growing if the settlor becomes domiciled as well as resident in the UK, for then the gains are assessed on him on an arising basis under TCGA 1992, s 86. But the pool is still relevant to him, for once he is resident and domiciled, any capital payments to him are taxable to the extent of the past pool (see para 63.20).

There is no doubt that a settlement which has or may have UK resident and domiciled beneficiaries should maintain a computation of its s 87 pool in the manner described in Chapter 13. This is because, without such information, planning to eliminate the potential s 87 charge on distributions to UK resident and domiciled beneficiaries is impossible. As is described in Chapter 14, a variety of planning techniques do exist, most notably ensuring that any s 87 pool is eliminated by distributions to non-residents or non-domiciliaries, including the settlor himself.

In general it is inadvisable to distribute capital in excess of the s 87 pool to a non-resident or non-domiciled beneficiary if there is any risk of that beneficiary becoming both resident and domiciled in the future. This is because the excess becomes taxable if, by the time there are s 87 gains, the recipient is resident and domiciled (see para 63.22). It is unclear whether, if deemed domicile is introduced for all tax purposes, such would apply on acquisition of such deemed domicile. But there must be at least a risk of this so the point should be borne in mind on distributions to long-stay, non-domiciled residents.

As noted above (para 20.4), it is also important to ensure that the settlement does not fall foul of the rules as to trustee borrowing (see Chapter 62). Should it do so, gains in its s 87 pool are carried into a Sch 4C pool, where they cannot be allocated to distributions to non-residents or non-domicilaries and so remain taxable should a distribution be made to a beneficiary resident and domiciled in the UK (see Chapter 64).

Offshore funds

20.9 As is described in Chapter 4, capital gains realised on the disposal of distributor offshore funds are taxed as ordinary capital gains and go into the s 87 pool. The position is otherwise with capital gains realised on the disposal of non-distributor offshore funds, for these are taxed as offshore income gains. They form a separate OIG pool, capital payments being allocated to the OIG pool in priority to the s 87 pool (see para 71.19).

Advantages to excluded property settlements

20.10 Potentially, investing through non-distributor funds is optimal for an excluded property settlement, for such converts ordinary income into offshore income gain. As such it is no longer deemed to be the settlor's income under ITTOIA 2005, s 624 or TA 1988, s 739 and so even if distributed and remitted it is tax-free. So too a distribution to another UK resident beneficiary is tax-free provided that beneficiary is non-domiciled, for application of the CGT rules means the distribution is not taxed (para 71.19).

Offshore funds potentially confer two further advantages. One is that, as the fund is the entity, access to UK investments may be secured without entailing the tax consequences of UK source income or UK situs assets. As described in para 4.3, some ultra-cautious advisers would say these advantages only obtain if the fund is in corporate form. The second advantage is that pertaining to accrued income, discussed in para 20.7 above.

The s 739/s 740 trap

20.11 Unfortunately non-distributor funds entail two traps, as described in paras 71.24 to 71.27. The first is that unless an offshore income gain is distributed in the tax year in which it is realised, it becomes s 739 income (assuming the trust is settlor-interested). As such it becomes taxable if it is remitted, as it would be if it is included in a capital distribution to the settlor which he brings to the UK. The second, and less serious, is that if offshore income gains are matched with a distribution of capital to a non-resident they move across and become s 740 relevant income. This means that even if all the actual income has been stripped out as per para 20.6 above, there is still relevant income in the structure. In essence the problem is the same as with accrued interest.

Solutions

20.12 There are two solutions to the s 739/s 740 trap. The best is to ensure that offshore income gains are always matched with distributions to UK residents on a current-year basis. As tax on such distributions is not avoided unless the recipient is non-domiciled, the requirement is for the recipient to be the settlor or some other resident but non-domiciled beneficiary.

The second solution is to ensure that all offshore funds invested in have distributor status. This is not really a solution as it means forgoing what are otherwise the advantages of a return taxed as offshore income gain. But it may be appropriate in cases where investment in offshore funds is attractive to achieve exposure to UK markets or to deal with the accrued interest problem noted in para 20.7 above. In such cases, the income will by definition be distributed, and will therefore fall to be dealt with in the ways discussed above in relation to other trust income.

IHT

20.13 As noted elsewhere, exposure of the trust assets to IHT is avoided provided the assets are all foreign situs. Although in some respects source and situs differ, this in general points to the same conclusion as that noted above in relation to income tax, namely that UK investments should be avoided. However, as noted above, access to UK investments may be achieved indirectly via offshore funds.

If IHT alone is being considered, certain kinds of UK investments can be held. Thus IHT exposure is avoided if the investments are held through an underlying offshore holding company. So too, holdings in authorised funds are free of IHT if in an excluded property settlement (see para 45.11). But in all cases the result of such investments is to generate UK source income, with the tax consequences outlined above. Further, even if the settlor is no longer a beneficiary, UK income tax at trust level attaches to distributions from UK authorised funds held by the trustees (see para 34.15).

Assuming UK assets are avoided, the excluded property settlement is prima facie free of IHT. But there are traps to avoid.

Gift with reservation

20.14 As noted in para 47.10, it is reasonably clear a GWR charge is avoided on the settlor's death even if he then has an actual or a deemed UK domicile. But a point which should be kept in mind is that even if all the trust assets are foreign situs, the settlor could make a PET if he is excluded as a beneficiary or if during his life funds are distributed to other beneficiaries. The law in this area is notably unclear and there can be reasonable confidence that the point does not arise unless at the time of such exclusion or distribution the settlor has an actual or a deemed UK domicile. But if the settlor does have such an actual or deemed domicile, distributions to other beneficiaries of the kind referred to above are best avoided.

Sale of beneficial interest

20.15 As noted in para 45.9, excluded property status is lost if a UK domiciliary is entitled to an interest in possession and his entitlement was the result of a disposition made for money or money's worth. This rule only applies if the disposition occurred after 5 December 2005, but it needs to be kept in mind on trust reorganisations.

Initial life interest of the settlor and/or his spouse

20.16 Should a settlement made before 22 March 2006 be subject to an initial life-interest conferred on the settlor or his spouse, excluded property status is lost as from when neither of them first has an interest in possession if when the initial or the successive interest ends, the holder had a deemed or actual UK domicile. The point is explained in para 45.16.

Additions

20.17 As explained in para 45.8, HMRC consider additions to the settlement after the settlor has obtained an actual or a deemed UK domicile can jeopardise excluded property status. They may be wrong but additions in such circumstances should be avoided as the argument is not worth having.

Chapter 21

Houses

Introduction

21.1 This chapter analyses the tax problems which arise when non-domiciliaries own UK homes. It principally addresses the problems faced by non-domiciliaries who are resident in the UK, but in para 21.24 consideration is given to non-domiciliaries who are non-resident. It primarily addresses the problems faced by a non-domicilary making a new acquisition rather than the issues which arise with existing houses.

Direct ownership

21.2 The natural way for a non-domiciliary who is resident in the UK to acquire a UK or indeed any other home is in his direct ownership. From a tax standpoint this has the advantage that it can be protected from CGT by the private residence exemption (TCGA 1992, s 222). However, it must be remembered that where the UK residence is not on the facts the non-domiciliary's main residence, an election is required if the exemption is to apply (TCGA 1992, s 222(5)). This election must be made within two years of the time when the individual first has two or more residences (*Griffin v Craig-Harvey* [1994] STC 54). An individual is treated as having two or more residences even if one of them is leased, or one of them is abroad.

Disadvantages

21.3 Although protection can be obtained from CGT, direct ownership entails two drawbacks, one major and one minor. The minor problem is that the residence constitutes a UK asset of the non-domiciliary which means UK probate is required on his death. This is tiresome, particularly if he has no other assets.

The major problem is inheritance tax. As the home is UK situate it is subject to IHT regardless of the fact that the non-domiciliary has a foreign domicile. If the non-domiciliary dies while still owning it, tax is due at the rate of 40% insofar as it and any other UK assets he has exceed the nil-rate band, which currently (2006–07) stands at £285,000. Since non-domiciliaries tend to own quite valuable homes, this prospective tax burden is considerable.

Inheritance tax solutions

21.4 One solution to the IHT problem is the same as that for UK assets generally (para 17.4), namely to plan on the basis that the non-domiciliary will sell the house before he dies and remit the proceeds abroad, thereby converting the value back into excluded property. Life assurance can be used as protection against untimely death and these days the annual premium is normally less than the annual running costs of offshore trusts or companies. But this route does have one disadvantage in that selling and remitting the proceeds abroad does not secure excluded property status if the non-domiciliary has by then acquired an actual or deemed UK domicile.

A variant of this approach is for the non-domiciliary to leave the house to his spouse with her selling or remitting the proceeds abroad. But if this approach is taken it should be remembered that if at the time of his death he has an actual or deemed UK domicile and she does not, only £55,000 of the spouse exemption is available (IHTA 1984, s 18(2)).

At one time another way of overcoming the IHT difficulty would have been for the non-domiciliary to give the purchase price to members of his family abroad, with them then buying the house. This was never entirely satisfactory as it leaves the donees with IHT exposure should they die. Now it certainly cannot be recommended for, while the gift of cash may mean the gift is effective to circumvent the IHT gift with reservation rules, a pre-owned asset charge arises (see para 47.4 and Chapter 70).

A variant on this is for the non-domiciliary and other members of his family to acquire the house as tenants in common in equal shares. Provided they all occupy the house, gift with reservation and pre-owned asset difficulties should be avoided (see paras 47.5 and 70.20). Further, a multiplicity of nil-rate bands should confer IHT protection if any of the co-owners dies, at least so long as he has no other UK assets. But it may be questioned how workable a solution of this sort is in all save the simplest cases.

Mortgages

21.5 A relatively complex solution to the IHT problem is to rely on the IHT rule whereby liabilities charged on a particular asset are taken to reduce the value of that asset (IHTA 1984, s 162(4)). This rule means that if the house is subject to a mortgage which reduces the value of the net equity to below the nil-rate band, IHT is avoided provided the donor has no other UK assets.

A substantial mortgage against the property is probably the best method of overcoming the IHT problems posed by direct ownership, coupled with joint ownership by husband and wife so as to increase the tax-free net equity to a level which provides adequate security. The loss of income resulting from the payment of the interest can be compensated by investment abroad of the funds which would otherwise have gone into the house.

There can, however, be a problem with a substantial mortgage, and this arises from the mechanics of making interest payments. The simple method is to take the borrowing from a UK bank or building society, and meet the interest out of UK income. If this is done the interest may be paid gross without deduction of tax at source (TA 1988, s 349(3)). Many non-domiciliaries, however, have insufficient UK income for this purpose, and the issue which then arises is that the bringing of foreign income to the UK to meet the interest is a remittance of such income, thereby bringing it into charge.

There are three possible ways round this difficulty. One is to use the various procedures described in Chapter 16 to ensure that what is brought to the UK is not a remittance of income. This is to be recommended as it is straightforward. The next possibility is to make a back-to-back deposit with a foreign branch of the bank and offset the interest on that deposit against the interest chargeable on the loan. The difficulty here is that the existence of the deposit could perhaps give HMRC grounds for arguing that the loan is not in truth an incumbrance on the property and at the very least it would be more than arguable that the debt should be set rateably against the property and the deposit. A further point is that the deposit should not be made out of foreign income, for otherwise the whole exercise could amount to a constructive remittance (ITTOIA 2005, s 834; see para 40.14).

The third possible solution is for the borrowing to be from a foreign bank with the interest payments made directly to that bank abroad. The difficulty here is that the non-domiciliary may then be required to deduct lower rate tax at source under TA 1988, s 349(2), for the lender's usual place of abode is outside the UK. The question of whether deduction is required turns on whether the interest has a UK source. This issue is discussed in paras 33.6 to 33.10 and the conclusion must be that the interest is likely to have a UK source if the loan is secured as then the security is in the UK and the borrower is UK resident. The assumption should therefore be that deduction at source is required.

A way round this problem is for the borrowing to be from a bank in a country with which the UK has made a double tax treaty giving the country of residence sole taxing rights over interest. In such a case, application may be made every five years to HMRC for a direction to pay the interest gross (see the Double Taxation Relief (Taxes on Income) (General) Regulations 1970 (SI 1970/488) and CNR DT Guidance Note 8).

Private mortgage

21.6 It is sometimes suggested that the mortgage can be from a trust, company or individual connected to the borrower, with the result that the interest can be low or even nil. This raises four issues.

The first is that as the borrower is UK resident, the debt is likely to have a UK situs (cf para 31.4). This means it is potentially exposed to IHT if the lender is a trust or individual. That difficulty may perhaps be overcome by making the debt a specialty and keeping the deed abroad (see para 31.6). The difficulty is also overcome if the lender is a company but here benefit in kind issues would arise if the borrower could on the facts be said to be a shadow director and the interest rate is not commercial (para 69.10).

The second difficulty is that if no interest or non-commercial interest is charged, transfer pricing could perhaps be in point (see Chapter 68).

The third difficulty is that if the borrower has in the past in any way funded the lender the debt may be disallowed on death, and its repayment inter vivos treated as a PET. This is the result of FA 1986, s 103. This is old and complex Estate Duty legislation discussed in para 47.13 and, as there indicated, it should be avoided provided all funding of the lender was effected abroad by the non-domiciliary when he had neither an actual nor a deemed UK domicile. But care should be taken to avoid any possible risk under s 103 as on certain scenarios it could effectively result in a double charge to tax.

The final difficulty is that the loan may be a regulated activity for the purposes of the Financial Services and Markets Act 2000 (see Financial Services and Markets Act (Regulated Activities) Order (SI 2001/544) Article 61). This will be the position if it is secured on the property by first legal mortgage. Should this be the position, a criminal offence is committed unless the lender is authorised under FSMA 2000.

Direct trust ownership

21.7 Ownership by a trust settled by the non-domiciliary is a solution often adopted. By definition the non-domiciliary is a beneficiary of the trust and in practice he is normally the principal beneficiary. Sometimes the trust may be a pre-existing settlement, but in other cases it is a newly-formed trust whose sole asset is the property.

Probate

21.8 One advantage which trust ownership has over individual ownership is that a trust does not die. Probate issues will not therefore arise when the non-domiciliary dies.

Offshore trustees are sometimes reluctant to take legal title to a UK property in their name. If so, consideration may be given to using a UK or offshore nominee company. Provided it is clear such company really is a nominee no tax consequences will result.

Capital gains tax

21.9 Assuming he pays no rent, the non-domicilary's occupation of the property is an annual benefit equal to the rent forgone for the purposes of TCGA 1992, s 87 and Sch 4C, and also the offshore income gain legislation (paras 65.7 and 71.18 to 50). This does not matter so long as he is non-domiciled for in such event the payment is either ignored (Sch 4C) or is not taxable (s 87) (see paras 63.22 and 64.7).

The one risk which arises is if there is no pool of gains at the time of the occupation and by the time there are s 87 gains or offshore income gains the erstwhile non-domicilary is both resident and domiciled in the UK. In such case, the capital payment will then be taxable by reference to those gains (para 63.22). In practice this is unlikely to be a problem with ordinary capital gains as once the non-domiciliary is UK resident and domiciled these will be assessable on him on an arising basis under TCGA 1992, s 86 unless he and all other defined persons are excluded (see Chapter 60).

Any gain on the disposal of the property is not assessable on the trustees as they are non-resident. The gain will however go into the trust's s 87 pool. However this result is avoided if on the facts the house is the non-domiciliary's only or main residence and the trustees so claim. A claim may also be made if the house is not the non-domiciliary's main residence but is one of his residences. In such case the non-domiciliary and the trustees must also jointly elect that the house should be treated for CGT purposes as the main residence (TCGA 1992, s 225; *Sansom v Peay* [1976] STC 494). As with directly-owned properties such election should be made within two years of acquisition.

Should the house be the trust's sole asset, the effect of the election is that there will never be trust gains unless the proceeds of any sale of the house are invested.

Income tax

21.10 The non-domiciliary's occupation of the house will be a benefit for the purposes of TA 1988, s 740. But this does not matter, for as settlor he is transferor and so not within s 740 (see para 56.10).

Inheritance tax

21.11 The purchase of the house means that the trust holds a UK situs asset. The result is that the trust is exposed to IHT at rates of up to 6% as and when 10-yearly anniversaries occur (see further paras 43.3 and 46.3). The charge on 10-yearly anniversaries arises regardless of the form of the trust unless the settlement was created before 22 March 2006 and is subject to an interest in possession equated with absolute ownership (see Chapter 44).

Given that the settlor is a beneficiary, the gift reservation rules described in Chapter 47 mean that the house is in his estate for IHT purposes should he die. If, therefore, he dies before the house is sold, IHT at the death rates will be chargeable. The same result follows if he has an interest in possession equated with absolute ownership. As with direct individual ownership, it may be possible to cover the IHT payable on death by term assurance.

Prior to 22 March 2006 the issue arose of whether, by allowing the individual to occupy the house, the trustees were conferring on him an interest in possession, thereby triggering an exit charge under the IHT relevant property regime (see para 46.8). As a result of the changes in FA 2006 this issue is no longer relevant as the creation of an interest in possession does not displace the relevant property regime (see para 43.14).

Pre-owned assets

21.12 Provided the house is GWR property it is not caught by the pre-owned asset rules (see Chapter 70). The house will be GWR property if the trust is discretionary (see paras 47.3 and 47.7). Should the trust not be discretionary, the pre-owned asset tax could on one view come into issue if the settlor is life-tenant (see paras 70.22 and 70.24). Until this area is clarified such a scenario should therefore be avoided.

Borrowing

21.13 As with individuals, potential IHT exposure may be reduced if the trustees borrow. The encumbrance rule applies, so that if the borrowing is charged against the house it necessarily reduces the value of the house for IHT purposes, whether the charge in issue is a charge on death or a 10-yearly charge. In some cases it is not even necessary for the borrowing to be charged on the house. This is the position if the trust has no other assets for then the house is the sole asset and the borrowing ipso facto reduces the net value. Such analysis obtains even if the settler holds a life interest equated with absolute ownership, for, although as life-tenant he is deemed to be beneficially entitled, the trust is still a separate estate (*St Barbe Green v IRC* [2005] EWHC 14 (Ch), [2005] STC 288). It may be suggested the same reasoning ought to apply where the house is subject to GWR rules.

An advantage trustees have over individual owners is that being non-resident, they can pay the interest on any borrowing without deduction of tax even if the borrowing is from a foreign lender. It is generally accepted that this is so regardless of whether the loan is secured on the house (cf para 33.9). Remittance difficulties are avoided provided the interest is paid abroad and indeed if the trust has income and it has been properly segregated, this is a good way of using some of it. There is no constructive remittance provided no part of the income is used to repay principal (para 40.13).

Unless the settler holds a life interest equated with absolute ownership, borrowing is not rendered unattractive by the pre-owned asset rules. Although such borrowing is an excluded liability, it being such a liability is immaterial as excluded liabilities are not relevant to GWR property (see para 70.17).

Borrowing does, however, raise a problem and this is the CGT rules as to trustee borrowing (see Chapter 62). These are not a problem if the settlor and all beneficiaries likely to benefit are non-resident or non-domiciled as then any ensuing gain cannot be assessed on the settlor under s 86 and any capital payment is not chargeable (see Chapters 60, 63 and 64). But otherwise the rules must be kept in mind. They ought not to be in point provided the borrowing is applied directly in house purchase, for the house will be an ordinary trust asset (see para 62.7). But care is required if borrowing is to be used to fund building works or other expenses or if the house is sold.

A final point is that borrowing may not be as complete a solution to IHT exposure as with an individual. This is because the rate of tax on a 10-yearly charge in an excluded property settlement is computed on the basis of both the UK assets at the time of the charge and the foreign assets at the time the trust was created (see para 46.4).

Other beneficiaries

21.14 Rather different considerations apply where a trust buys a house for occupation by a beneficiary other than the settlor. The main points are explained in para 22.12.

Ownership through a company

21.15 Looked at purely from an IHT standpoint, the simplest way of overcoming the IHT difficulties with direct or trust ownership is for the house to be owned by a foreign-registered holding company in which the non-domiciliary owns all the shares. If this is done, the shares are the relevant asset for IHT purposes, and, being foreign situs, are excluded property. Unfortunately, despite these various advantages, corporate ownership cannot in general be recommended.

Company residence

21.16 The first difficulty is that as with all directly-owned companies care will be needed to prevent the company from being UK resident. As is described in Chapter 38, it is necessary to show that central management and control is exercised by the board of directors abroad. There may be difficulties in practice in demonstrating this where the sole asset is a UK house lived in by the controlling shareholder. If the company is found to be UK resident, the main practical consequence is that it is subject to corporation tax on any gain realised on the sale of the house. The corporate ownership means the private residence exemption is not available.

The earnings risk

21.17 A more compelling danger in using a company is that the non-domiciliary's occupation of the house may be taxable as a benefit in kind under ITEPA 2003, ss 97–113. Where it applies it normally results in notional earnings each year equal to 5% of the cost of the house over £75,000 (see

Chapter 69). This represents a very substantial tax charge, the assessable benefit being £46,250 annually on a house costing £1m.

There is no doubt that occupation of a UK residence can be charged under ss 97–113 if the non-domiciliary is an actual director or is an employee of the foreign holding company. This follows because any accommodation provided by the employer for an employee or his family is treated as provided by reason of his employment (s 97). But non-domiciliaries are not normally directors or employees of foreign holding companies, if only because a UK resident director or employee would jeopardise the non-resident status of the company. However, even where the non-domiciliary is not a director or employee, the occupation of the house may still be taxable under ss 97–113. This is because ITEPA 2003, s 67 defines the term 'director' as including any shadow director (*R v Allen* [2001] STC 1537). The meaning of the term 'shadow director' is considered in Chapter 53, and as there concluded it may be difficult for a non-domiciliary in occupation of the house to avoid being characterised as a shadow director.

Avoiding the earnings risk

21.18 One way to avoid the earnings risk is for the non-domiciliary to buy the house and then give it to the company. This does not occasion IHT, for he owns the shares. There is still a small employment income liability based on gross rateable value but a charge based on 5% of cost is avoided, for the cost is nil. However, there are difficulties in taking this route.

One difficulty is Stamp Duty Land Tax, which is chargeable on gifts to connected companies at a rate of 4% insofar as the value of the property exceeds £500,000 (FA 2003, s 53). Second, there is a concern over the IHT gift with reservation rules (as to which see Chapter 47). It is sometimes said that a gift to a company in which the donor owns shares is a gift with reservation and if so, the gifted property remains in his estate for IHT purposes. If this point is good at all, it lacks merit where the donor owns all the shares in the company for then there is no element of gift.

Another means of avoiding the earnings risk is suggested by the fact that the cost to which the 5% interest factor is applied is net of reimbursement by the actual or notional employee. As is discussed in para 69.6, the reality of house purchase for non-domiciliaries is that the non-domiciliary is providing the price. It ought to therefore be possible to structure the exercise to come within the reimbursement rule although it has to be said that as yet there is little evidence this is a tried or tested route.

Pre-owned assets

21.19 On the face of it, the pre-owned asset legislation should not be in issue where the non-domiciliary owns the house through a company as he owns all the shares. Assuming the house is the company's sole asset, the shares count as derived property, which means the beneficial ownership exemption applies (see para 70.22). Unfortunately there is one scenario where this may not be so, and this is if the company has significant commercial borrowings. In this situation, the value of the shares will be substantially less than the value of the house, and a proportionate income tax charge may arise. However, as explained in para 70.34, HMRC has, in another context, adopted an analysis which may effectively answer this point.

There is also a more fundamental point. In most cases where a company is used it is largely capitalised by shareholder loan, and in such cases the issue arises of whether the loan is derived property. If it is not, the only derived property is the shares, with a value which is vastly less than the house. Common sense indicates that in fact both the shares and the loan are derived property and thus that there is nothing in this point. HMRC do not agree, although they are prepared to achieve the same result by accepting that no notional rent should be attributable to the shareholder loan (see para 70.34).

Transfer pricing

21.20 The present transfer pricing rules are described in Chapter 68 and have applied for income tax purposes since 6 April 1999. There is an argument that a market rent can be imputed to a non-resident company if it owns a house occupied by a shareholder or by a beneficiary under a shareholding trust. As the company is non-resident, any such imputed rent would be chargeable to basic rate income tax. If this argument succeeded its effect would be almost as draconian as a benefit in kind charge. HMRC, however, do not take the point (see para 68.20).

Trust structures

21.21 In practice, companies owning houses are frequently owned not directly but by a settlor-interested offshore trust. The trust is normally discretionary.

Such structures do reduce the company residence and earnings risks, for it can be said that if anyone tells the directors what to do it is the trustees. But while this is a valid argument in relation to company residence (cf para 38.26) it is less compelling with shadow directorship. As explained in Chapter 53, an individual is a shadow if he gives non-professional advice which is regularly followed (*Secretary of State for Trade and Industry v Deverell* [2001] Ch 340).

Ownership of the company by a trust does raise the same pre-owned asset points as are described in para 21.19. The analysis is as given in that paragraph.

Using a trust also brings additional issues namely that the occupation of the house is a capital payment for the purposes of TCGA 1992, s 87 and a benefit for the purposes of TA 1988, s 740. But as explained above (paras 21.9 to 21.10), these ought not to pose problems provided the occupier is the settlor and remains non-domiciled.

Payment of rent

21.22 Many of the tax problems described above are avoided if the occupier pays a commercial rent to the company. The rent is of course taxable but such liability is offset by any expenses the company meets and, more importantly, by any interest charge if it borrows to buy the house. For transfer-pricing reasons (para 68.19) the borrowing should not exceed what can be secured on the house, but even with that limit, the interest and normal expenditure on repairs should offset the rent. Because the rent is commercial, the pre-owned asset charge which could otherwise result from the borrowing is avoided (cf para 70.9). The interest is deductible even if the borrowing is from a foreign lender.

Payment of rent may not be a complete solution to the earnings risk for, as noted in para 69.8, a charge can still arise if interest at the official rate on the purchase price of the house exceeds the rent. But even if on the figures this is the position, the charging of a commercial rent makes it much easier to show the occupier is not a shadow, particularly if the company is held in trust. Claiming tax where a market rent is being paid would hardly be an attractive position for HMRC to take.

A significant practical difficulty is funding the rent. The chances are the occupier will have insufficient UK income and if so, he will need to remit foreign income. Techniques described in Chapter 16 will need to be used. An intriguing possibility is whether remittance would occur at all if the rental payments were made offshore ie from a foreign bank account of the non-domiciliary to a foreign bank account of the owning company. The analysis of the cases on constructive remittance in para 40.16 provides an argument they would not.

Conclusion

21.23 The only clear conclusion is that there is no one method which is always right for structuring the ownership of UK houses. Each case has to be considered on its own facts. However, direct ownership gives rise to the fewest problems, the IHT risk being funded by life assurance. There is much to be said for the view that his UK home is the one asset a non-domiciliary resident in the UK should own directly.

Non-residents

21.24 Many individuals who own residential property in the UK are both non-resident and non-domiciled. At one time any accommodation available in the UK ipso facto made such an individual resident here, but this is no longer so (see para 36.10).

Direct ownership of the property results in IHT exposure in the same way and to the same extent as if the individual is UK resident. The techniques for avoiding the exposure while still retaining direct ownership are as described in para 21.2. One technique which has rather more potential is the mortgage solution, for since the individual is non-resident, deduction at source should not be required on any interest on a foreign loan. Further foreign income can be used to meet interest on a UK loan and indeed other expenses, for, since the individual is non-resident, remittances are not taxable. Further, non-residents are not caught by the pre-owned asset rules (para 70.25).

In practice, non-resident individuals normally hold UK residential property through offshore companies, owned either directly or in trust. This has the advantage, under current law, of potentially enabling Stamp Duty Land Tax to be avoided on a future sale.

For the reasons given above, there may be an individual who on the facts is a shadow director of the company. But as is explained in para 69.18 providing on the facts no duties of the hypothetical employment can be said to be performed in the UK, there are no notional earnings. Avoidance of duties may be easy if the shadow director is not the occupier, for example, where the occupier is a member of his family. But if the shadow director is the person who uses the house, HMRC could perhaps argue that such matters as organising repairs and insurance are duties, by definition performed in the UK. This danger, if such it be, may be avoided if the company appoints a managing agent to discharge those duties, so that the only obligations imposed on the occupier are negative ones such as avoiding damage to the property or annoyance to neighbours.

Since the individual is non-resident, company residence in a corporate ownership structure is unlikely to be an issue. Such risk as there is should be avoided if the director of the company and the trustees conduct themselves properly (cf Chapter 38).

Chapter 22

Gifts from abroad

Introduction

22.1 Non-domiciliaries frequently wish to make provision for members of their family or other individuals who are resident in the UK. Some such non-domiciliaries are themselves resident in the UK but often this is not so, the donor's sole connection with the UK being the one or more recipients of his bounty who live there. This chapter reviews appropriate planning strategies.

Outright gifts

Taxation of the gift

22.2 An outright gift or testamentary bequest by a non-domiciliary does not normally attract UK tax. The exceptions to this are as follows:

(1) Gifts or bequests by non-domiciliaries of UK situs property are subject to IHT. However, as is explained in paras 30.11 and 30.12, this does not apply to holdings in authorised funds and nor, should the non-domiciliary be non-resident, does it apply to FOTRA government securities. Further, any inter vivos gift is potentially exempt, which means IHT is avoided provided the non-domiciliary survives seven years.

(2) Should the non-domiciliary have a deemed UK domicile, his global assets are subject to IHT in the event of his death (see para 30.14). But inter vivos gifts are exempt if made more than seven years before death.

(3) CGT is in no circumstances be in issue if the property passes to the UK resident on the non-domiciliary's death (TCGA 1992, s 62).

(4) Otherwise any gain on the gifted property is chargeable should the non-domiciliary be resident in the UK and the property UK situs (see para 30.7). Holdover relief is not available save as respects business assets (TCGA 1992, s 165).

(5) CGT is not in issue on a gift of property outside the UK or if the non-domiciliary is non-resident (subject to the five-year rule noted in para 27.7).

(6) Neither ad valorem stamp duty nor Stamp Duty Land Tax is in issue on

a gift or bequest as those taxes are not chargeable on voluntary dispositions (save as respects gifts to connected companies) (see FA 2003, s 53 and Sch 3 para 1).

Benefit to the donor

22.3 The gifted asset remains in the donor's estate for IHT purposes if he reserves a benefit or enjoys a benefit from the asset, and the benefit subsists until his death. This means it is subject to IHT on his death if he has then acquired an actual or a deemed UK domicile (para 47.8). So long as he does not have such a domicile, IHT on his death is avoided if the property is excluded property in relation to him – ie provided it is foreign situs or a holding in authorised funds.

Should the reserved benefit end inter vivos, the ending is a potentially exempt transfer. Although the point is not certain, it seems reasonably certain this cannot apply to foreign situs property or holdings in authorised funds unless the donor is then domiciled or deemed domiciled in the UK (see para 47.9).

An obvious example where the gift with reservation rules are in point is if the gifted property is a house which the donor continues to use. This is so whether the house is in the UK or abroad, although in the latter case, gift with reservation issues should only arise if the donor acquires an actual or a deemed UK domicile.

There are exceptions to the IHT gift with reservation rules, described in paras 47.4 and 47.5. But if one of those are in point, the issue has to be considered of whether the benefit to the donor results in exposure under the pre-owned asset rules (see Chapter 70). Such exposure is avoided if and so long as the donor is non-resident or, so long as he has neither an actual nor a deemed UK domicile, if the asset enjoyed is excluded property (see paras 70.25 to 70.26). But where these conditions are not met, the pre-owned asset rules have to be considered. The main danger is where the asset enjoyed is not the same as the asset gifted, for then there is unlikely to be a reservation under the GWR rules (cf para 47.4). The pre-owned asset rules are precluded if the gift was of cash, but only if it was made before 6 April 1998 or more than seven years before the donor first used or enjoyed the asset that the donee bought with the cash (see para 70.16).

Taxation of the donee

22.4 Should the resident donee have an actual or a deemed UK domicile, the gifted assets will thereafter be in the IHT net, regardless of situs. Assuming he does not currently have an actual or deemed UK domicile, the same result will follow as and when he does acquire such a domicile. Any potential IHT exposure can of course be minimised by the normal IHT strategies open to UK domiciliaries such as gifts more than seven years before death or investment in property qualifying for reliefs such as business property relief.

So long as the recipient has neither an actual or a deemed UK domicile, the gifted assets are not exposed to IHT provided they are foreign situs or holdings in authorised funds at the moment of charge (ie on the death of the recipient or when he makes a gift). Assets situate outside the UK are free of IHT and there is no IHT charge on the removal of property from the UK. However, it has to be recognised that a long-stay non-domiciliary will inevitably acquire a deemed domicile in due course.

Should the resident recipient have an actual UK domicile, income and gains generated by the gifted assets are taxable as his as they arise. Assuming he is a higher-rate taxpayer, the rate of tax is normally 40%, but foreign and UK dividends qualify for the dividend rates and the effective rate on gains is reduced by taper.

Should the recipient be non-domiciled, tax on an arising basis applies as respects UK income and gains. Foreign income and gains are taxable only insofar as remitted to the UK. As is described in Chapter 16, avoidance of income tax on remittances is a practical possibility but such is more difficult as regards gains. Accordingly, some tax and also considerable compliance costs may have to be accepted as respects foreign gains.

There is currently no concept of deemed domicile for income tax and CGT purposes and so a recipient who is foreign domiciled at the time of the gift may be able to preserve it for a considerable period. The current consultation by the government may result in this being changed, however (see para 39.13).

Offshore settlement

22.5 As an alternative to the outright gift, the non-domiciliary may provide for the UK resident(s) by creating an inter vivos or testamentary offshore settlement.

Taxation of the gift

22.6 The taxation of any gift or gifts to the trustees is the same as with outright gifts, with one qualification. This is that an immediate charge to IHT at 20% is made if the non-domiciliary has a deemed UK domicile, save insofar as his nil-rate band is available or some other IHT relief is in point (see para 43.2). Should he not be deemed UK domiciled this charge is avoided insofar as the assets transferred to the trust are foreign situs or holdings in authorised funds (see para 46.2).

Ongoing taxation of the donor

22.7 Should the settlement be inter vivos, ongoing taxation issues may arise for the settlor. Inheritance tax falls to be considered should the settlor be an actual or potential beneficiary, for then the settlement is a gift with reservation (cf para 47.3). But this is of no consequence provided the settlor did not have an actual or a deemed domicile when he made the settlement, his interest subsists until his death, and all the settled property is then foreign situs or holdings in authorised funds. In such a case, the assets are protected from IHT by being excluded property (para 47.10). But should the settlement own other kinds of UK property when the settlor dies such will form part of his taxable estate as it is not excluded property. So too if, in such a case, the settlor ceases inter vivos to be a beneficiary, such may be a PET if he then has an actual or a deemed UK domicile (cf para 47.10).

Regardless of his residence status, there is no circumstance in which the trust income can be assessed as the settlor's if he and his spouse are wholly excluded from benefit by the terms of the settlement and never benefit or receive loans or repayment of loans from the trustees (see Chapters 55 and 59). But should he become resident and domiciled in the UK, the entire trust income will be taxed as his on an arising basis. Should he be resident but remain non-domiciled, UK source income is taxed on an arising basis and foreign source income is taxable insofar as remitted (see para 55.22).

Should the settlor be non-resident, the UK income of the settlement is assessable as his under ITTOIA 2005, s 624 (see Chapter 59). This may reduce rather than increase tax insofar as the settlor's lower rate bands and personal allowance are available. The better view is that attribution of the UK income to the settlor also captures the restriction of UK tax liability on dividends and interest to tax withheld, save perhaps where interest is paid gross (see FA 1995, s 128 and para 59.26).

The settlor is not exposed to CGT as respects the trust's gains unless and until he becomes both resident and domiciled in the UK. Should that occur, the trust gains will be assessable as his unless he, his children, his grandchildren, their respective spouses, and associated companies are all excluded (see Chapter 60).

Taxation of the trust

22.8 The trust is not subject to IHT provided the settlor had neither an actual nor a deemed domicile when he made the settlement and trust assets are all foreign situs or holdings in authorised funds. This exclusion of charge applies whether the trust is fixed-interest or discretionary (para 45.2). There are certain exceptions, described in Chapter 45, but none is likely to be material.

The trust is free of income tax on foreign-source income (see para 30.2). Assuming the trust is a discretionary or accumulation trust, any UK source income is, however, taxable at the rate for trusts. As there are UK beneficiaries this latter charge applies fully to dividends and interest (see FA 1995, s 128(5) and para 34.15). However, the UK tax is restricted to tax withheld insofar as the assets are held through an offshore holding company (see para 9.22), and, as described above, may be partially displaced if the settlor is a beneficiary.

The trust is not exposed to CGT save in the unlikely event that the trust assets include a UK business.

Taxation of the beneficiaries

22.9 Should a UK resident beneficiary be life tenant, the trust income is taxed as his (see Chapter 12). Provided the proper law of the trust follows English law, dividends received directly by trust attract the dividend rates if he is UK domiciled (para 12.2). If he is non-domiciled the remittance basis applies, remitted dividends attracting basic rate tax insofar as within the beneficiary's basic-rate band and otherwise the dividend higher rate of 32.5% (see para 40.2).

Should UK resident beneficiaries of an accumulation or a discretionary trust receive income distributions, such is taxable as a new source (see para 12.4). The remittance basis applies to a non-domiciled recipient, but tax-free remittance may be difficult to achieve as the trust is a continuing source (cf para 40.7).

A non-resident beneficiary is not subject to income tax at all, save as respects any UK source income to which he is entitled as life tenant (cf para 12.2).

Should capital be distributed to a UK resident beneficiary, the recipient may be subject to income tax under TA 1988, s 740 unless the motive defence applies (see Chapter 56). The motive defence is unlikely to be in point if one of the reasons for creating the settlement was to minimise UK tax for the beneficiaries. But if it was created for other reasons, such as to provide for the beneficiaries without allowing them access to the capital, the defence may be able to be invoked (see Chapter 58). In practice it is difficult to be sure of the outcome until the issue is tested with HMRC. Techniques for avoiding s 740 liability are as discussed in para 20.6.

Should s 740 not be in point, whether because the motive defence applies or for some other reason, a capital distribution may attract income tax under the offshore fund rules or under TCGA 1992, s 87 or Sch 4C (see Chapters 63, 64 and paras 71.18 to 71.27). However, such a charge only arises if the recipient is both resident and domiciled in the UK. But should this condition be met and time have elapsed between the matched gain and the distribution, the rate of tax can be as high as 64% (paras 63.29 and 64.11).

With careful planning it is possible to avoid the charges on capital distributions. Relevant techniques are discussed in Chapter 14 and also para 20.8.

There are two final points to note. One is that the free use of trust property by beneficiaries is taxable as a benefit or capital payment if the other conditions for the operation of TA 1988, s 740 or TCGA 1992, s 87 or Sch 4C are met (see paras 56.11 and 65.7). If there are no trust gains or income when the use occurs, liability is postponed until income is retained or gains are realised in the future. This last point can catch even a non-resident or non-domiciled user, for he is taxable under s 87 when gains are realised should he then be resident and domiciled in the UK (para 63.22).

The second point is that a capital distribution could have IHT consequences. This is so if the trust is discretionary and one of the following conditions is met:

(1) The distributed property is neither foreign situs nor holdings in authorised funds, or
(2) The settlor had an actual or a deemed UK domicile when he made the settlement, or
(3) The settlor is an actual or potential beneficiary. Here the charge would be a PET under the gift with reservation rules. The charge should only arise if at the time of the distribution the settlor has an actual or a deemed UK domicile (see para 47.10).

Absolute and settled gifts compared

22.10 It can be a difficult decision as to whether the provision the non-domiciliary makes for the UK residents should be absolute or settled. Often family considerations will be decisive, but where this is not so, the tax considerations outlined above should be reviewed.

Funds needed in the UK

22.11 If the funds being provided are needed for UK spending, outright gifts are preferable. This is because the tax rules pertaining to settlements are complicated and thus expensive in compliance. Such expense is not justified if the gifted money is going to be spent in the near term.

UK housing

22.12 Should the funds be required by the recipients to buy a UK home, IHT exposure may be inevitable for, absent somewhat artificial arrangements, use of an offshore company to ensure the value is in the form of foreign situs assets may carry unacceptable shadow director risks (see para 21.17). Inevitable IHT exposure removes one of the main advantages of a settled gift. A further drawback of a settled gift is that charges in respect of the occupation of the house under TA 1988, s 740 and TCGA 1992, s 87 or Sch 4C may be difficult to avoid.

For all these reasons, funds to enable the UK recipients to purchase UK homes may be felt to be best provided by outright gifts. Use of the house by the non-domiciled donor should be avoided on account of gift with reservation risks and the pre-owned asset rules, although occasional visits as a guest are acceptable (cf FA 1986, s 102A).

A trust may, however, be considered in the following scenario:

(1) The trust fund comprises only the house, for IHT reasons the trust being constituted by a gift of cash abroad which is then used by the trustee to buy the house.
(2) The trust has no other assets so there is no income and so no possibility of a s 740 charge.
(3) The house is the beneficiary's only residence, or a PPR election is made, for then provided the trustees so claim, the gain in the hands of the trustee is exempt (TCGA 1992, s 225; see para 21.9). This avoids any trust gains accruing for the purposes of s 87.

This solution results in exposure to IHT at a rate of up to 6% on every tenth anniversary of the trust (see para 43.3). No charge arises on the beneficiary's death as, even if he has an interest in possession, such is without IHT consequence as respects trusts created after 22 March 2006 (see para 43.14). The donor should be totally excluded from benefit so as to avoid any IHT charges under the GWR rules in the event of his death.

Providing income

22.13 Should the non-domiciliary's objective be to provide the UK resident(s) with income, a trust may be recommended. The advantages this confers are that long-term protection from IHT is secured and exposure to capital gains tax is avoided. Even if the beneficiary is non-domiciled and the gains are foreign situs, the trust may be preferred to an outright gift, for the trust offers complete CGT avoidance whereas outright ownership entails the complexities of the remittance basis (cf para 16.3).

It may be preferable for the UK resident to have a life interest. This has two advantages:

(1) Dividends are taxed at the dividend rates (save insofar as within his basic-rate band if he is non-domiciled).
(2) If he is non-domiciled each investment is a separate source (paras 12.2 and 40.7).

One disadvantage of a trust in these circumstances is that should capital eventually need to be distributed to a UK domiciled and resident beneficiary, the tax on stockpiled gains at 64% may have to be faced. This is material to the extent that capital is likely to be so distributed and the techniques for avoiding the charge on stockpiled gains are unlikely to be in point.

Long-term family fund

22.14 A wealthy non-domiciliary may simply intend to set up a long-term family fund. This could hold a pool of investments but it could also be the ultimate holding vehicle of a trading concern.

Here again, for IHT reasons if no other, a trust is to be recommended over direct ownership. It is likely that a discretionary trust will be appropriate, on the grounds that the trustees may wish to accumulate the income or retain flexibility as to who receives distributions. Such a trust should not, for IHT reasons, hold any UK investments directly.

Given the nature of the trust it will probably be recognised that capital distributions to resident and domiciled beneficiaries are too expensive, but this may not be material given the objective is a long-term family fund. If capital does have to be distributed to a resident and domiciled beneficiary, the size of the fund may make emigration worthwhile, at least five years being required to avoid CGT. In the meantime, income can always be paid to UK residents as current income.

A composite solution

22.15 In reality, the non-domiciliary seeking to provide for UK residents may do so by a combination of outright and settled gifts. A practical solution is to fund UK spending and house purchase by outright gifts, and income needs and long term family funds in settlement.

Should the settlor be a beneficiary of any inter vivos trust?

22.16 As what is envisaged is provision for others it may be regarded as illogical if the settlor is among the beneficiaries should he create a trust. However, should the settlor be non-resident, including him as a beneficiary does enable gains and income in the settlement to be washed out by distributions to him and there may be advantages as respects any UK income (para 22.7). Including the settlor also permits washing out if he is resident but non-domiciled, provided he retains his foreign domicile and, in the case of income, does not remit it.

Nonetheless there can be significant disadvantages in the settlor being a beneficiary:

(1) The gift with reservation points noted in paras 22.7 and 22.9 above. These mean IHT will result on his death should the trust directly hold UK assets (other than authorised funds). So too, should he acquire an actual or a deemed domicile, or possibly if he is UK resident, any release or termination of his interest is a PET, as is any capital distribution to another beneficiary.

(2) The fact that if he is or becomes UK resident, the income is assessable as his, on an arising basis if he loses his foreign domicile. This result would be avoided if he is wholly excluded from benefit but then the gift reservation issues just noted could arise.

(3) Should the settlor receive a capital distribution whilst still a beneficiary and resident in the UK, s 739(3) will (unless the motive defence applies)

deem the trust income to be his thereafter, regardless of whether he is subsequently excluded from benefit (paras 55.8 and 55.10). This result only occurs if the capital distribution is a payment, but it is also triggered if the payment is a loan or the repayment of a loan.

In the light of these factors, the settlor should not be a beneficiary if there is any risk of him becoming both resident and domiciled (or deemed domiciled) in the UK, and it is best avoided if there is a likelihood of him merely becoming resident in the UK. There is little risk if he is and will remain non-resident and non-domiciled.

Existing settlements

22.17 The funds the non-domiciliary wishes to see applied for the benefit of the UK residents may already be in a trust of which he is settlor and beneficiary. If he is UK resident, the trust may have been set up for the reasons described in Chapter 19 and operated in the manner indicated in Chapter 20.

Outright gifts

22.18 Any outright gifts the non-domiciliary wishes to make may be funded by distributions to him from the settlement. Such is only unattractive should he have a deemed UK domicile. Care must of course be taken to ensure that the assets concerned are foreign situs or holdings in authorised funds. It is also important that the non-domiciliary cannot, on the facts, be characterised as a conduit (cf paras 56.21 and 65.4).

Gifts effected by direct distributions by the trust to the UK resident recipient are rendered unattractive by CGT if the recipient is UK domiciled and otherwise by income tax under TA 1988, s 740, unless the motive defence applies.

Settled gifts

22.19 Any settled provision the non-domiciliary wishes to see made could be effected by the trustees of the existing settlement creating the requisite new settlement and transferring funds to it. This has one advantage, namely that that settlement may qualify for the motive defence whereas any new settlement made by the non-domiciliary himself may not. The original settlement could well have been set up for reasons wholly unconnected with UK tax and it would be a pity to lose that status.

There are, however, four possible disadvantages to using the existing settlement in this way:

(1) If the motive defence is not in point, capital distributions to the UK residents may be taxed by reference to income since the inception of the existing settlement or (if later) 1981. Such income may be considerable if the settlor is resident in the UK on account of the procedures described in Chapter 20.
(2) Should the recipient of any capital distribution be both resident and domiciled in the UK, CGT and the supplemental tax will be charged by reference to trust gains since 17 March 1998 or (if later) the inception of the existing settlement (see Chapter 63).
(3) Should the existing settlement, or any settlement from which it has received funds, have fallen foul of the rules as to trustee borrowing, it will have a Sch 4C pool which cannot be washed out by distributions to non-residents (cf Chapter 64).
(4) The points just made in para 22.16 above, are applicable where the settlor is resident in the UK and particularly where he may become domiciled there.

The general conclusion is that a distribution of the funds needed to the settlor and the making of a new settlement by him is more attractive if the motive defence is unlikely to apply to the original settlement. If it does apply, use of the existing settlement may be worth considering unless there is a risk of the settlor becoming resident and domiciled in the UK.

Foreign law and tax

22.20 All the above strategies are subject to the non-domiciliary's own law of succession and, if he is not UK resident, applicable tax wherever he is resident.

Particular problems may be posed if the succession law of his domicile imposes forced heirship, either on death alone or affecting inter vivos gifts as well. An unresolved issue is the UK tax status of a settlement which breaches applicable forced heirship rules and as a result could be upset by a UK resident heir of the settlor under the law of the settlor's domicile. Express anti-forced heirship legislation enacted by most offshore jurisdictions renders it unlikely that the jurisdiction of the settlement will entertain the forced heirship claim and if so, the problem may not be felt to be material. But not all offshore jurisdictions disapply forced heirship and in any event such disapplication may not protect assets in other jurisdictions which do recognise forced heirship. It may be the only complete solution for such a family is to settle what is freely disposable under the non-domicilary's proper law and satisfy the forced heirship claims by outright bequests.

Chapter 23

Earnings

Introduction

23.1 This chapter explains the planning opportunities available to non-domicilaries in respect of earnings from employment.

Overseas earnings

23.2 The basic rule is that non-domiciliaries, like other UK residents, are chargeable in full on their general earnings (ITEPA 2003, s 21). However, what are called chargeable overseas earnings are taxable only if remitted to the UK (s 22). Although this remittance basis is not as generous as that applicable to investment income, it gives some scope for planning.

Definition

23.3 Chargeable overseas earnings are what used to be called foreign emoluments. They require the following conditions to be met (ITEPA 2003, s 23(2)):

(a) the employer must be resident outside the UK and not resident in either the UK or Ireland (ss 23(2) and 721(1));
(b) the duties of the employment must be performed wholly outside the UK.

In determining whether any duties are performed in the UK, incidental duties may be disregarded (ITEPA 2003, s 39). In law the concept of incidental duties has been strictly defined: thus an airline pilot working for a foreign airline whose schedule includes occasional UK stopovers performs more than incidental duties in the UK (*Robson v Dixon* (1972) 48 TC 527). In practice HMRC regard visits to the UK by an overseas representative to report or training visits to the UK as incidental (IR 20 paras 5.7 and 5.8). Attendance by a director at UK Board meetings is not regarded as incidental and nor is responding to an email or telephone call from a worried client! (*Tax Bulletin* 76 (April 2005) pp 1202–03).

Planning

23.4 In some cases the non-domiciliary works exclusively abroad. Where this is the position the remittance basis may be secured by ensuring the employer is resident in a specific foreign territory and not in the UK. As a matter of law the employer may be a company controlled by the non-domiciliary, although here care should be taken to ensure the company really is resident in the foreign territory concerned (cf Chapter 38).

The more normal situation is where the non-domiciliary is working in the UK. If he is working full-time in the UK, there is little that can be done, as all his duties are necessarily UK-based. But if some of his duties are performed abroad, it may be possible to create two contracts, split contracts as they are sometimes called.

One of these contracts is with the UK employer and covers the UK duties. The other is with an associated foreign company and covers the foreign duties. The earnings under this contract are chargeable overseas earnings providing all the duties under it are in fact performed abroad. The split of earnings between the two contracts must be reasonable, as if it is not, an appropriate adjustment has to be made for tax purposes (ITEPA 2003, s 24). In determining what is reasonable particular regard must be had to the nature of and time spent on the UK duties and the foreign duties.

HMRC have recently reviewed their practice on split or dual contracts (*Tax Bulletin* 76 (April 2005) p 1201). Their position may be summarised as follows:

(1) They accept split contracts can be used in appropriate cases, and, where they are appropriate, the tax issues raised are whether non-incidental duties have been performed in the UK, and whether the spilt of earnings is commercial.
(2) HMRC do not consider split contracts are appropriate unless there are two distinguishable jobs. Unless there are two distinguishable jobs, HMRC are likely to argue there is in reality a single employment partially carried on in the UK and so wholly taxable on an arising basis. In particular HMRC take this line where the sole division of functions between the two employments is according as to where the functions are performed.
(3) Particular scrutiny is to be expected where originally there was a single employment or self-employment or where the job was originally advertised as one.
(4) If the two contracts are in reality one, the UK employer is responsible for PAYE and NIC on the whole.

Tax Bulletin 76 repays detailed study by those minded to take up split contracts. Both for tax and for commercial reasons it is important to remember that the contract or contracts adopted have employment as well as tax implications. Specialist employment law advice is essential, both in the UK and in the jurisdiction of the foreign contract.

Meaning of remittance

23.5 As noted above, chargeable overseas earnings are taxable if remitted to the UK. For the purposes of ITEPA 2003, the concept of being remitted to the UK is given an extended definition (ITEPA 2003, s 33). Earnings are treated as remitted to the UK if either of the following conditions is met:

(a) they are paid, used, or enjoyed in the UK; or
(b) they are in any manner or form transmitted or brought to the UK.

As a matter of language, this definition is wider than the comparable words of ITTOIA 2005, s 832 (see para 40.2). There the charge is simply on sums 'received' in the UK. It is true that 'received' has been judicially expanded in *Thomson v Moyse* (1960) 39 TC 291 in that Lord Radcliffe referred to the sums received in the UK being sums of money derived from the application of the foreign income to achieve the necessary transfer to the UK. But it is by no means clear that even in the light of *Thomson v Moyse* receipt under s 832 is as wide as under s 33. In particular, s 33 contemplates emoluments being enjoyed in the UK, whereas s 832 refers only to sums received in the UK.

Two cases are relevant, both decided on TA 1988, s 132(5), the predecessor to s 33, namely *Harmel v Wright* [1974] STC 88 and *Grimm v Newman* [2002] STC 1388. Both are analysed in Chapter 42. In *Harmel v Wright* (at p 97), HMRC submitted that s 132(5) 'can shed light on and possibly give some small extension to the word receipt', but Templeman J did not find it necessary to decide whether it in fact had this effect. In *Grimm v Newman*, the Court of Appeal did not distinguish receipt under what is now s 832 from receipt under what is now s 33 at all. They also relied on *Thomson v Moyse*. The conclusion therefore must be that such authority as there is gives little basis for construing s 33 as extending the basic word 'receipt'.

If the earnings are received in the UK after the taxpayer has died, the personal representatives are assessable (ITEPA 2003, s 13(4)(b). Similar rules as to constructive remittances as are found in ITTOIA 2005, ss 833 and 834 are set out in ITEPA 2003, ss 33 and 34. These rules are explained in para 40.12.

Not ordinarily resident

23.6 Different remittance rules apply if the taxpayer while being resident in the UK, is not ordinarily resident. The circumstances in which this in practice arises are described in para 36.13.

In such cases, the remittance basis applies to all general earnings in respect of duties outside the UK (ITEPA 2003, s 26). There is no requirement that the employer be non-resident and no requirement that the duties be performed exclusively abroad. Earnings are normally apportioned between duties abroad and duties in the UK on the basis of the number of working days spent abroad (SP 5/84 para 2).

It is essential that the remuneration for the foreign duties is paid abroad for otherwise the remittance basis is not in point at all (cf ITEPA 2003, s 33 and *Slattery v Moore Stephens* [2003] STC 1379). But the remuneration for both the UK and the foreign duties may be paid in a single sum and, provided paid abroad, the part time-apportioned to the foreign duties enjoys the remittance basis. Remittances are treated as being first of the UK earnings and so tax on the remittance basis does not result until remittances have exhausted the UK earnings (SP 5/84 para 3).

If a non-domiciliary is not ordinarily resident, the rules applicable to those not ordinarily resident are normally more attractive than those applicable to non-domiciliaries generally (cf *Slattery v Moore Stephens*, supra). In the short term it may therefore be prudent to structure arrangements to take advantage of them. But self-evidently this ceases to be so once the taxpayer is or is at risk of being treated as ordinarily resident.

Avoiding remittances

23.7 In Chapter 16, the many techniques available to non-domiciliaries to avoid taxable remittances are explained. Few of these avail for chargeable overseas earnings.

Do not bring the income into the UK

23.8 Self-evidently if chargeable overseas earnings are not brought to the UK at all, tax liability does not arise. To take advantage of this, it is necessary for the non-domiciliary to keep the earnings separate from other monies which are not taxable if remitted. If this is not done, authorities on the former Cases IV and V indicate that remittance from a mixed account will be treated first as a remittance of income until it exceeds the income paid into the account (cf para 40.5).

An exception to this is that remittance from a mixed fund of income taxed on an arising basis and income taxed on the remittance basis, is treated as being of the former until it is exhausted (cf para 40.5 and Inspector's Manual para 1568).

Cessation of source

23.9 At one time, cessation of source was effective to avoid liability under the former Schedule E, for such liability did not arise if the employment had ended in a prior tax year (*Bray v Best* [1989] STC 159). Now, however, post cessation earnings are treated as earnings of the last tax year in which the employment was held (ITEPA 2003, ss 22(3) and 30(3)).

Alienation abroad

23.10 *Grimm v Newman* [2002] STC 1388 has confirmed that a gift of earnings abroad, followed by remittance by the donee does not result in a tax charge. This issue, and the planning possibilities raised are discussed in Chapter 42.

Loans and overdrafts

23.11 As noted above, the rules as to constructive remittances, are specifically incorporated in ITEPA 2003. These rules are explained in para 40.12, and the various techniques there described for circumventing them are in point.

Remittance in specie

23.12 HMRC consider that non-monetary assets brought to the UK amount to a remittance if purchased out of the earnings (Employment Income Manual para 40302). This may be supported by the language of ITEPA 2003, ss 22 and 33 which refers to earnings as distinct from amounts being remitted to the UK. It contrasts with the equivalent CGT provision which does refer to 'amounts' (see TCGA 1992, s 12(2) and para 41.8).

Territorial limits

23.13 Earnings which arise before the individual is resident in the UK are not taxable even if remitted in a period of residence. This is because ITEPA 2003 only attaches to earnings for a year in which the employee is UK resident (ss 21 and 22 passim). However, earnings paid prior to the employment commencing would be caught if the employee is resident at the time of commencement, for ITEPA 2003, s 30(2) treats a prior payment as earnings of the first tax year of the employment.

Should remittance occur after a non-domiciled employee has acquired a UK domicile, a tax charge results. This is in contrast to the position under ITTOIA 2005, s 832 and follows because the rules in ITEPA 2003 do not in terms state that a tax charge only arises if the individual is non-domiciled at the time of remittance.

A more difficult issue is if remittance occurs after the employee is non-resident. If the employment ceased before he left the UK, the remittance is taxable for ITEPA 2003, s 30(3) relates it back to the last year of employment. The position ought to be otherwise if the employment continues at least until the tax year after emigration, for then even if relating back applies, it goes back only to a period of non-residence.

Deemed income

23.14 Certain anti-avoidance provisions treat cash or benefits to be earnings, notably sections charging accommodation and benefits in kind (see Chapter 69). In such cases, the result of such deeming is that the relevant territorial limits are those applicable to earnings generally (*R v Allen* [2001] STC 1537) (see further para 69.18).

Other types of legislation provide that a sum counts as earnings. In those circumstances territorial limits, and the availability or otherwise of the remittance basis, have to be gathered from the legislation in question (cf *Nichols v Gibson* [1996] STC 1008).

Section VI

Business

Chapter 24

Offshore subsidiaries

Sheltering income profits

24.1 UK companies and groups can shelter foreign income profits through offshore subsidiaries. There are many business activities which can be carried on in a low or nil tax jurisdiction, particularly in jurisdictions where employees can be accommodated in the jurisdiction itself or across the border in an adjoining high-tax country. Typical activities include international sales operations, investment services, insurance, banking and financial services, shipping, and holding company and treasury functions. If these activities are carried on by an offshore subsidiary, UK tax can in principle be avoided because the subsidiary is recognised as a separate entity by the UK tax code and UK tax does not attach to the foreign profits of non-residents (see Chapter 30).

Fiscal connection

Residence of subsidiaries

24.2 Since newly formed UK registered companies are ipso facto UK resident any offshore subsidiary necessarily has to be foreign registered (cf para 38.27). The residence of foreign registered companies is considered in Chapter 38. The matter is governed by the central management and control test and HMRC scrutiny may be expected where, as postulated here, tax avoidance is intended.

In practical terms the subsidiary should have a local board of directors who genuinely meet and give due consideration to all matters properly requiring decision by the board. The directors should be people who have the necessary skills to run the business. The UK parent's role should be confined to that of shareholder. Provided these steps are taken, any HMRC challenge to the residence of the subsidiary is unlikely to succeed.

Avoidance of taxable presence

24.3 It is self-evident that an offshore subsidiary is only an effective shelter if a taxable presence in high tax jurisdictions is avoided. The rules as to taxable presence vary from country to country. Local advice must be taken on the rules, and the offshore subsidiary's operations so structured that taxable presence in high tax jurisdictions is avoided.

In the UK, the issue of taxable presence turns on whether the non-resident is trading with the UK, in which case it is not taxable, or whether it trading in the UK, in which case it is. This issue is considered in para 33.12. If as is normally the case a company trading in the UK is so trading through a permanent establishment, the company is liable to UK corporation tax on profits attributable to the permanent establishment (TA 1988, s 11). The permanent establishment is assessable as the company's UK representative (FA 2003, s 150).

Profit diversion and transfer pricing

24.4 The essential tax function of offshore subsidiaries is to earn profits which would otherwise be realised by group members in high tax jurisdictions. There are two ways in which this is done. One is for an independent business activity to be carried on by the offshore subsidiary, most goods or services supplied to or from the subsidiary being supplied by or to independent third parties. The other is for the offshore subsidiary to provide services to other group members, or sell materials to them or buy finished goods from them for onward sale. In these latter scenarios the offshore subsidiary is potentially diverting profits which would otherwise be realised by other group members in high tax jurisdictions, and transfer pricing rules have to be considered.

Transfer pricing

24.5 Transfer pricing is an international issue, and most jurisdictions now have legislation requiring market value to be substituted for tax purposes on connected party sales. The UK is no exception, and the relevant legislation is discussed in Chapter 68. It is increasingly relied on by HMRC to counter avoidance. Its practical effect is to make it difficult to divert profits from the UK if goods or services are supplied to a UK entity at an overvalue or supplied by it at an undervalue.

Effective profit diversion

24.6 Profit diversion is not, however, completely precluded by UK and international transfer pricing legislation. Two kinds of operation are possible. The first is where the subsidiary provides genuine services for other group members, its profits being fair remuneration for those services. Thus the routing of materials purchased through an offshore subsidiary falls foul of transfer pricing if the offshore subsidiary is simply an invoicing company. But an offshore subsidiary may be an effective shelter if it is a purchasing company for the whole group, buying in bulk and selling on in small quantities as and when the materials are specifically required. Similar principles apply where the subsidiary is providing services such as marketing, group insurance, or finance, so long as the subsidiary's margin is comparable with those providing such services on an arm's length basis.

The other form of effective profit diversion is where goods or services are supplied to or from countries with less rigorous transfer pricing rules. Here it may be that goods and services can be supplied by a subsidiary in the jurisdiction concerned to other group members at below world prices, or supplied to it at above world prices. In this event neither the UK nor most other countries' transfer pricing rules say that the benefit of the over or undervalue must be taken in the group members in the high tax countries. Indeed, the essence of transfer pricing adjustments is that it should not be, for it is market value and no more which is substituted. Accordingly, provided the true market price can be proved, the under or over-value can be effectively sheltered by an offshore company, perhaps one formed specifically for the purpose.

Profits which may be sheltered

24.7 As a result of transfer pricing rules it may be said that offshore subsidiaries may principally be used to shelter three kinds of profit:

(1) Profits from business carried on with unconnected third parties.
(2) Profits resulting from genuine services provided on arm's length terms for other group members.
(3) Profits resulting from transactions with group members located in jurisdictions which do not have rigorous transfer pricing rules.

Avoiding the controlled foreign company legislation

24.8 Until 1984, company residence, taxable presence, and transfer pricing were normally all that had to be considered in deciding whether an offshore subsidiary was an effective tax shelter. Since then, a further factor has had to be allowed for, namely the controlled foreign company legislation (TA 1988, ss 747–756).

The controlled foreign company legislation is analysed in Chapter 67. It is targeted specifically at offshore subsidiaries which are not subject to a local rate of tax of at least three-quarters the equivalent UK tax. Its effect is to make the UK parent subject to corporation tax in respect of the subsidiary's profits.

Over the years the CFC legislation has been steadily strengthened with the result that many former loopholes have been eliminated. Thus it used to be possible to avoid the legislation by distributing 50% of profits but now the threshold is 90%.

There is however one exclusion which remains significant and this is where the subsidiary is engaged in exempt activities. To be engaged in exempt activities, the subsidiary must satisfy certain key conditions. Its business must not be an investment type business and if the business is dealing in goods, the subsidiary's trading partners must be unconnected and outside the UK. If the business is what the CFC legislation calls wholesale, distributive, financial, or service business, at least half its receipts must not be derived from connected persons or from UK residents. Perhaps more important, whatever the nature of its business, the subsidiary must have proper premises in the jurisdiction where it is based, together with adequate personnel there to effectively manage its affairs.

These conditions are described in more detail in para 67.8. If a subsidiary meets them liability under the CFC legislation does not arise. It might be thought that relatively few subsidiaries would meet these conditions but in fact this is not so. The conditions could, for example, be satisfied by an international sales subsidiary not dealing with the UK, or by an independent insurance subsidiary insuring unconnected non-UK clients or providing re-insurance on proper commercial terms.

The CFC legislation may also be precluded under European law if the CFC is established in the European Union or the European Economic Area and is not a wholly artificial arrangement. This is discussed in para 49.3.

Repatriation of profits

24.9 Even assuming transfer pricing and the CFC legislation do allow some sheltering, it is not enough to simply shelter income profits as they arise. Thought also needs to be given to whether and if so how they will be repatriated. Here recent legislative changes have made the position easier.

Dividends

24.10 If the profits of the subsidiary are paid up in dividend, such is an income receipt of the UK parent assessable to corporation tax under Schedule D Case V. Relief for underlying or withholding tax borne by the subsidiary may be claimed, insofar as such does not exceed the corporation tax otherwise chargeable (TA 1988, ss 790(6) and 797).

One way of avoiding the Case V tax is to accumulate profits in the subsidiary until the UK parent has trading losses or other losses relievable against general income. The profits can then be distributed in the accounting period when the losses arise and loss relief claimed. Unfortunately, the saving thereby achieved is more apparent than real, for the losses will not be available to set against other profits, for example profits of future accounting periods.

A somewhat artificial route for avoiding the Case V tax is for the subsidiary to become UK resident, and then pay the dividend (TA 1988, s 247). UK residence is achieved by appointing UK directors and holding the subsidiary's board meetings in the UK. The dividend is tax-free, for, as a distribution, it is excluded in computing the parent's taxable profits (TA 1988, s 208).

Sale or liquidation of the subsidiary

24.11 Should the subsidiary be sold or liquidated, the applicable tax is corporation tax on chargeable gains. The rate of tax is the same as on income profits and any gain may be offset against the UK company's capital or allowable income losses (TCGA 1992, s 8). The position ought therefore to be the same as with a dividend. In fact there are three reasons why this is not so:

(1) Indexation is allowed in computing gains accruing to UK companies (TCGA 1992, s 53(1A)). This saves tax to the extent that the UK company paid or subscribed significant amounts for the subsidiary.
(2) There is no relief for any underlying or withholding tax borne by the subsidiary.
(3) Dividends cannot be set against the capital losses of the recipient.

In appropriate cases the new and important relief for disposals of substantial holdings may be considered (TCGA 1992, Sch 7AC). This relief applies as much where the company invested in is non-resident as where it is resident (Sch 7AC para 26) and the term substantial connotes simply that the investing company must have owned 10% or more of the company invested in during two years prior to the disposal (Sch 7AC para 8). If the relief applies, any gain on the disposal is tax free. There is an anti-avoidance provision, but this only applies if arrangements have been put in place from which the sole or main benefit is exemption of the gain (Sch 7AC para 5). The arrangements can either be the acquisition of the company invested in or, more likely, the commencement or alteration of its trade.

The most important limitation on the new relief is that both the investing company and the company invested in must be trading companies or members of a trading group during the two years before and also immediately after the disposal (Sch 7AC paras 18 and 19). A trading company is one whose activities do not to a substantial extent include non-trading activities and a trading group is one where the activities of the group as a whole do not to a substantial extent include non-trading activities (Sch 7AC paras 20 and 21). Substantial is not defined in the legislation but the HMRC view is that it means more than 20% (*Tax Bulletin* 62 (December 2002, p 985)).

Sheltering capital gains

24.12 Offshore subsidiaries now offer more scope for sheltering capital gains than income profits. This is because neither the transfer pricing nor the controlled foreign company legislation applies to capital gains. It should, however, be remembered that market value must be substituted on any transaction between the offshore subsidiary and the UK group (TCGA 1992, s 17). If an offshore company is trading in the UK through a permanent establishment, assets used or held for the purposes of the trade or the permanent establishment are subject to corporation tax on chargeable gains (TCGA 1992, s 10B).

TCGA 1992, s 13

24.13 There is one legislative obstacle to sheltering capital gains and this is TCGA 1992, s 13. Where this section applies it apportions gains realised by the subsidiary to its UK parent, the apportionment being by the extent of the parent's interest if the subsidiary has multiple participators. Gains can be apportioned through a chain of offshore subsidiaries if there is an offshore group structure.

Section 13 is considered in Chapter 66. For present purposes the important point is that it only applies if the offshore subsidiary would be a close company if it were UK resident. The definition of close company is the standard definition in TA 1988 (ss 414–417). A company is close if five or fewer participators either control it or would be entitled to the greater part of its assets in a winding up. However, a company cannot be close if at least 35% of its shares are held by the public and dealt in on a stock exchange. More importantly a subsidiary is not a close company if its ultimate parent is not a close company.

The practical result of this definition is that the offshore subsidiaries of quoted groups are not close companies whereas the subsidiaries of privately owned groups generally are. Accordingly, offshore subsidiaries provide an effective CGT shelter for quoted UK companies or groups, but not for their unquoted counterparts.

But even for unquoted groups, the importance of s 13 should not be overstated for it does not apply to the trading assets of trading companies. A further point is that European law may prevent it from applying if the subsidiary is established in the European Union or European Economic Area and is not a wholly artificial arrangement (see para 49.3).

Section 13 is subject to double tax treaties in that if a subsidiary is resident in a treaty territory, a treaty provision giving the country of residence sole taxing rights precludes the section (see para 66.21). It is, however, fair to say that treaties are increasingly being renegotiated to remove this point (see para 66.22). Further, even when applicable, the point represents a trap insofar as the UK parent has trustee shareholders, for in such a case the appropriate proportion of any gain caught by s 13 must be apportioned through to the trustees under TCGA 1992, s 79B. This subject is described in para 66.23.

Offshore subsidiaries as holding companies

24.14 Multinational groups often group their foreign subsidiaries under an offshore holding company subsidiary. Such a strategy represents effective

CGT planning if the group is quoted, for it shelters any gains realised if the operating subsidiaries are sold or liquidated. Such an offshore holding company normally has one drawback, in that the controlled foreign company legislation has to be considered. A holding company can, however, accumulate dividends from the operating subsidiaries if it satisfies the CFC motive defence or the exempt activities test (see paras 67.8 and 67.17).

If these exceptions are not in point, profits can simply be accumulated in such operating subsidiaries as are not caught by the CFC legislation and realised in a sale or liquidation. The latter is tax-free since the gain is capital and accrues to the offshore holding subsidiary. Such an approach is, however, unattractive if the profits of the subsidiaries bear substantial local tax, for then the sale or liquidation means that tax cannot be offset against UK tax if the profits eventually reach the UK.

Criminal offences

24.15 Ever since 1951 the criminal law has had to be considered in relation to non-resident subsidiaries. Until 1988 it was a criminal offence for a resident company either to migrate or to transfer its business abroad without Treasury consent (TA 1970, s 482). The maximum penalty was imprisonment for two years or a fine of £10,000 and while prosecutions are not thought to have been brought, the criminal sanction was a powerful deterrent.

It is now no longer a criminal offence for a resident company to migrate or transfer its business abroad. But what is often forgotten is that the 1951 legislation created two other criminal offences, with the same penalties as described above, and these offences have not been repealed (TA 1988, s 765).

Continuing criminal offences

24.16 The present offences are directed not at companies migrating but at the subject matter of this chapter, namely resident companies with non-resident subsidiaries. The first offence is for a UK company to cause or permit a non-resident subsidiary to create or issue any shares or debentures (TA 1988, s 765(1)(c)). The second offence is for the UK company to transfer any shares or debentures in a non-resident subsidiary otherwise than to directors as directors qualifying shares (TA 1988, s 765(1)(d)). It is to be noted that whereas the issue offence extends to issues by sub-subsidiaries, the transfer offence does not catch transfers by the subsidiary of shares in sub-subsidiaries.

Treasury consent

24.17 As with the former migration offences, an offence is not committed if Treasury consent is first obtained. Treasury consent may be either a specific consent applied for in advance of the transaction concerned or one of the published General Consents.

The General Consents were reissued in 1988 (The Treasury General Consents 1988). Their wording is extremely complicated, so much so that some advisers ignore them and apply for specific consent in all cases. The main transactions permitted by the General Consents are as follows:

(1) Shares or debentures may be issued by any non-resident subsidiary to unconnected parties for full consideration.
(2) Shares or debentures may be issued by one overseas subsidiary to another if both are resident in the same country.
(3) Irredeemable shares may be issued for full consideration to the UK parent.
(4) Debentures may in certain circumstances be issued to the UK parent.
(5) Shares or debentures in the subsidiary may be transferred by the UK parent to unconnected parties for full consideration.
(6) Shares or debentures may be transferred on any terms to other members of the UK parent's group.

Minor amendments were made to the General Consents in 2000 to reflect the changes made by FA 2000 to the definition of the term group (Inland Revenue Press Release 26 July 2000 (see [2000] STI 1079; *Tax Bulletin* 46 (October 2000))).

Guidance notes for applicants for specific consent were published in 1988. The application should be made to the Treasury, and, in an emergency, to HMRC. The commercial reasons for the proposed transaction should be explained and in practice these are weighed against any loss of tax to the UK which the proposal would entail.

European relief

24.18 Neither the criminal offences nor the need to obtain Treasury consent apply if the transaction is movement of capital within EU Directive 88/361/EEC (TA 1988, s 765A). In such a case HMRC merely have to be notified of the transaction within six months of it happening.

As is explained in para 48.16, Directive 88/361/EEC has been superseded by Article 56 of the EU Treaty, but s 765A has not been updated. Article 56 applies to capital movements to third countries as well as to EU states (see para 48.21), and in Directive 88/361/EEC there is reference to the liberalising of capital movements involving third countries. It may be, therefore, that s 765A applies to all transactions otherwise within s 765 which are movements of capital.

In SP 2/92, the Revenue indicated they do not share this view. Paragraph 10 of that statement says in terms that s 765A applies only to movements of capital between EU Member States. If that is a correct construction of s 765A, it is likely to be compatible with European law as s 765 was enacted before 31 December 1993 (cf para 48.21).

In SP 2/92 HMRC state that Directive 88/361/EEC does not apply to movements of capital between Member States and the Channel Islands or the

Isle of Man. The Directive does not apply to movements between Gibraltar and UK residents because Gibraltar and the UK are regarded as the same state (SP 2/92 para 5).

Chapter 25

Parallel companies

Introduction

25.1 Parallel companies are an alternative to group structures. Instead of forming an offshore subsidiary, the shareholders in a UK company incorporate an offshore company in their direct ownership, its shareholding mirroring that of the UK company. Parallel companies are only a practical solution where the UK company is unquoted and normally they are only formed where the company has one or a small group of family shareholders.

A parallel offshore company has one great advantage over an offshore subsidiary. The controlled foreign company legislation does not apply to it, for that legislation can only attribute profits to corporate shareholders. A further advantage is that the criminal offences under TA 1988, s 765 should not arise, for these can only be committed by UK companies.

Parallel companies are, however, subject to the same rules as subsidiaries regarding such matters as taxable presence and transfer pricing (see paras 24.3 and 24.4). They also bring problems of their own, notably over company residence, shadow directors, section 739, capital gains, and the repatriation of profits.

Company residence

25.2 As with subsidiaries, parallel offshore companies have to be registered abroad, and their residence is governed by the central management and control test. This is discussed in Chapter 38, and while the position ought to be the same as with subsidiaries in practice it may not be.

The reason for this is that one or two controlling shareholders may be much more tempted to interfere in the affairs of a directly-owned offshore company than the board of a UK parent would be. Furthermore, HMRC may take more persuading that central management and control is not being exercised from the UK.

Practical steps to avoid the risk are outlined in paras 38.22 to 38.25. It is important that a parallel company of the kind being postulated here, which is genuinely trading, has a board of directors who are competent to and do demonstrably run the business. The board should meet regularly in the country where the company carries on business. The shareholders should maintain a proper distance, and requests they make to the offshore company should only be implemented after due consideration by the company's board at a properly minuted meeting. There is no objection to a shareholder being on the Board, but decisions relating to the business of the company must be taken at Board meetings in the offshore jurisdiction concerned.

Shadow directors

25.3 Even if the dangers of company residence are avoided a UK shareholder may still find he is at risk of being a shadow director. This issue is examined in Chapter 53, and as there explained *Secretary of State for Trade and Industry v Deverell* [2001] Ch 340 has made a finding of shadow directorship more likely. If a UK resident is a shadow director any benefits he receives from the company, whether in the UK or abroad, are taxable as earnings (see Chapter 69).

Section 739

25.4 TA 1988, s 739 is analysed in Chapters 54 and 55. There is no doubt that it applies when a foreign company is incorporated, and further that trading profits count as income for the purposes of the section (*Latilla v IRC* [1943] AC 377; *IRC v Brackett* [1986] STC 521). Accordingly, in the simplest of all cases, it applies where the proprietor of a wholly owned UK company incorporates an offshore trading company which diverts profits from the UK.

But s 739 does not apply in all cases. First there is the motive defence, discussed in Chapter 58. Here the UK shareholder has to show that the incorporation of the offshore subsidiary was a genuine commercial transaction with any tax avoidance being merely incidental. There are certainly cases where the defence can avail, for example, if there are good commercial reasons for having an operating company near where foreign profits arise, and yet exchange controls or some other factor make it preferable to base the company in a nearby offshore jurisdiction rather than in the actual country producing the profits. Another situation is where a local manager or joint venturer is to have a stake in a foreign operation and it is a genuine term of his participation that the company is based in a specific low tax jurisdiction.

A rather different context in which s 739 does not apply is where the UK individuals buy an existing company. Here s 739 is precluded because the transfer made by the individuals, namely the purchase of the shares, is not one by virtue of which profits accrue to the company (see para 55.12). This is a well recognised route for escaping s 739, but it must not be taken too far. The company must genuinely be a pre-existing company, and not one formed a few days before by offshore providers specifically for the purposes of being bought.

A third context where s 739 may be disapplied is under European Law if the fundamental freedoms are in point. This issue is discussed in para 49.3, and it may be particularly apposite if the company is resident in a Member State of the European Union or the European Economic Area.

Capital gains

25.5 Directly-owned offshore companies give rise to CGT problems, for their chargeable gains are apportioned to the UK resident participators. The apportionment is under TCGA 1992, s 13 and is on the basis of the extent of each participator's interest. While apportionment only applies to close companies, it catches virtually all parallel companies of the kind postulated in this chapter, since it is difficult to envisage such a company which is not close.

Section 13 is discussed further in Chapter 66. In certain business situations it is not of great importance, for gains accruing on assets used in a trade carried on by the company are not apportioned and nor are any gains assessable on the company by reason of its having a UK permanent establishment. So too currency gains are not apportioned if the currency is held for trade purposes. In certain cases s 13 may be precluded by European law (see para 49.3) and it is certainly excluded insofar as the company is resident in a jurisdiction with which the UK has concluded a double tax treaty, and the treaty gives the other country sole taxing rights over capital gains realised by its residents. But treaties are increasingly being renegotiated to preclude this point, and treaty protection does not in any event apply to trustee shareholders (TCGA 1992, s 79B; see para 66.23).

If none of the exceptions avails and charges do arise under s 13, the element of double taxation at least can be mitigated. Credit relief is available if the gain is distributed within a three- or four-year period of being realised (see para 66.17). The distribution may be by dividend or in a liquidation, and now that income and gains are taxed at the same rate, a timely dividend may be considered where a substantial gain otherwise within s 13 has accrued.

Repatriating profits

25.6 As with most offshore structures, profits sheltered in a parallel company are not without more at the disposal of the shareholders. Either the company must be sold or liquidated, or a dividend paid. In either event UK tax will be due.

Dividends

25.7 Should a dividend be paid, UK resident recipients are liable to income tax. Assuming the recipients are individuals or trusts, there is no credit for tax borne by the company. But the rates of tax are the dividend rates, i e 10% for basic-rate individual taxpayers and 32.5% for discretionary or accumulation trusts or higher-rate individual taxpayers (TA 1988, ss 1A(1A)(b), 1B, and 686(1A)).

Sale

25.8 Should the company be sold, TA 1988, s 740 is not in point (see para 56.13) so the tax which has to be considered is capital gains tax. This tax is ameliorated by taper relief – reducing the gain by 40% after ten years if the shares are non-business assets and by 75% after two years if they are business assets (TCGA 1992, s 2A).

Shares are business assets if the company is a trading company or the holding company of a trading group (TCGA 1992, Sch A1 paras 3 and 6). Provided the company is unlisted there has since 6 April 2000 been no restriction as to the size of the shareholding. A company or group is a trading company or group if the activities of the company or group do not, to a substantial extent, include non-trading activities (TCGA 1992, Sch A1 paras 22, 22A and 22B). Substantial is taken by HMRC as meaning 20% or more and a variety of factors may be looked at in applying the test, notably turnover, asset base and expenses, and time spent by directors and employees (*Tax Bulletin* 62 (December 2002) pp 982–986).

Business taper relief is available as much where the shares are in a non-resident company as a resident company. The major catch is that the trading condition has to be satisfied throughout the period of ownership or, if shorter, since 6 April 1998 (TCGA 1992, Sch A1 para 3). If this condition is not met a proportionate part of the gain attracts non-business taper. Problems can also arise with holdings of less than 25% in that these were not business assets prior to 6 April 2000 unless the owner worked full-time for the company and held at held at least 5% of the shares.

Provided however that all the various conditions are satisfied business taper does enable profits in a non-resident trading company not caught by s 739 to be realised at the effective rate of 10% after two years. This is an attractive and perhaps unanticipated result of the taper regime.

Liquidation

25.9 There is an argument that the proceeds of liquidation are taxable under TA 1988, s 740 but that section would only be in point if the shareholder was not the transferor (see paras 56.14 and 55.23). Should s 740 in fact be in point, the rate of tax is 40% and no credit is available for tax borne by the company. This is less attractive than either a dividend or a sale and the risk of s 740 being in point is a reason to avoid liquidation.

Should s 740 be inapplicable, the proceeds of liquidation are subject to capital gains tax. So long as the company qualified as a trading company or trading group, business taper should be available. But the liquidation may mean there is a period during which the shares are not business assets, particularly if trading ceases. In this event business taper is proportionately lost.

TA 1988, s 703

25.10 TA 1988, s 703 counters any income tax advantage resulting from transactions in shares, inter alia by requiring consideration received in capital form to be subject to income tax insofar as attributable to undistributed profits. It has been held applicable on the sale of a company (*IRC v Wiggins* [1979] STC 244). It does not apply unless HMRC serve a notice invoking it (s 703(3)).

Section 703 is subject to a motive or purpose defence in that it cannot be invoked in relation to transactions effected for bona fide commercial reasons or in the ordinary course of making or managing investments (s 703(1)).In general s 703 should not be in point on a straightforward sale or liquidation. However the generosity of business taper means it is of increasing interest to HMRC, particularly where the company concerned is offshore. There is a clearance procedure (TA 1988, s 707) and on any sale or liquidation consideration should be given as to whether to use it.

Other strategies

25.11 Perhaps the most effective means of bringing profits sheltered offshore to the shareholders is for the shareholders to emigrate permanently. As is described in para 27.13, there is no exit charge on emigration and CGT is avoided thereafter provided the emigrant remains non-resident for at least five complete tax years. An alternate solution may be to wait until the shareholders die, and then sell or liquidate the company with the advantage of the new CGT base value available on death (TCGA 1992, s 62). However, this strategy is only effective on liquidation if the circumstances are such that TA 1988, s 740 is avoided, for successors will not be protected from that section by being transferors. A futher point on either a sale or a liquidation is that TA 1988, s 703 still requires consideration.

Trust structures

Advantages

25.12 Ownership through an offshore trust offers a means of avoiding some of the difficulties otherwise attaching to parallel companies. As is explained in Chapter 2, an offshore discretionary trust from which the settlor and his spouse are wholly excluded should with appropriate care prevent liability arising under s 739. It follows from this that exclusion from s 739 may be achieved in relation to a parallel company if such a trust owns all the shares. Ownership through the trust also brings the further advantage that it is harder for HMRC to contend that the company is UK resident (cf para 38.26. The risks of somebody in the UK being found to be a shadow director are also reduced, but probably by not very much, so benefits to any such person should be avoided.

In the result, it may safely be said that in income tax terms, the ideal structure for sheltering foreign business profits is a non-resident company owned by a non-resident trust from which the settlor and his spouse are wholly excluded. Such sheltering of business profits may be part of a wider structure, in which the trust is also used to shelter investments, as is described in Chapter 2. Indeed, the business activities of the company may generate the funds from which the portfolio investments are purchased.

One matter which is not necessarily resolved by a trust ownership is how the profits are eventually to be repatriated. The problems in this area, and possible solutions, are discussed in Chapters 12 to 14. A particular point to note is that gains realised by a non-resident trust can be reduced by business taper in the same way as gains realised by residents.

In relation to capital gains TCGA 1992, s 13 operates to apportion the company's gains from non-trading assets to the trust. Sheltering it not achieved if the trust gains can be further attributed to the settlor under TCGA 1992, s 86 for then the gains attract tax on an arising basis (see Chapter 60). Indeed, in one respect, in such cases the trust makes s 13 exposure worse, for treaty-protected gains in the company can be apportioned to the trust and thence to the settlor (TCGA 1992, s 79B; see para 66.27). But where s 86 is not in point, CGT does not arise unless and until a resident beneficiary receives a capital payment.

Although on the face of it, the combined effect of ss 13 and 86 is unattractive, the difficulties in the context of trading companies should not be exaggerated. As noted above gains on most assets used in the company's trade are not apportionable (cf para 66.10).

Exclusion of the settlor

25.13 There is a price which has to be paid for a trust structure of this kind and this is that shareholders in the UK company are normally settlors and so have to be excluded. In some cases this is not a problem, as where the shareholders are already wealthy. Alternatively, the problem may be avoided if the initial capital settled in the trust comes not from the shareholders but from parents or even, if gains are to be sheltered, from more remote relatives. Such arrangements are discussed in para 2.16 and should be effective to prevent the shareholders from being treated as settlors providing any dealings between them and the offshore company are on commercial terms (see para 59.22). Assuming the settlor in such cases is not a parent or grandparent, CGT difficulties with ss 13 and 86 are also avoided.

Section 739 may pose greater problems for such arrangements in that liability extends to procurers of the offshore arrangements (see para 55.24). To minimise risk, the UK shareholders should as far as possible be distanced from the setting up of the offshore arrangements, and certainly they should not indirectly provide funds for the trust. The extended meaning of 'power to enjoy' should also be kept in mind as should the importance of ensuring that the UK individuals neither lend to nor borrow from the company or trust (cf paras 55.2 and 55.8).

The settlor as beneficiary

25.14 Despite these possibilities, there are undoubtedly cases where the UK shareholders must inevitably be the settlors and do not wish to be excluded from benefit. In these circumstances, the question arises of whether trust ownership still brings benefits.

The answer to this depends on whether s 739 will catch the company's profits. Prima facie it will, for the creation of an offshore trust, followed by the formation of an offshore company, does bring s 739 into play. Indeed, in cases such as this the chances of s 739 applying may be greater, for the creation of the trust is motivated by tax considerations, and thus in practice jeopardises any motive defence which may exist in relation to the company.

Fortunately, there is one situation in which a s 739 liability can be avoided. This is where the company is a pre-existing company, purchased by the trustees with the settled funds. As is described above (para 25.4), s 739 does not apply to the profits of such a company so long as funds are not injected into it. It would, of course, catch any dividends paid to the trust, but there is no obstacle to the indefinite retention of profits by the company. Eventually the profits can be brought to the trust as capital in a sale or liquidation, and if this is done no income accrues to the trust and so there is nothing to be taxed under s 739. There will, however, be a capital gain, and questions of taper relief, attribution under s 86, and TA 1988, s 703 would have to be considered at that stage.

Chapter 26

Employee benefit trusts

Introduction

26.1 The term 'Employee Benefit Trust', or 'EBT', encompasses a wide variety of trusts. The common factor is an intention to benefit employees, either by cash distributions or by buying, holding and in due course distributing shares in the employer company. A definition may be found in ESC A68. In the words of that concession 'Employee trusts are discretionary trusts created by funds provided by employers for the benefit of their employees, past, present or future or for the benefit of any dependant or relations of such employees'. According to UITF abstract 32 (see para 26.12 below) in the typical EBT the employer makes payments to the trust and the trust then uses assets accumulated from those payments to pay the employees for some or all of the services they have rendered to the employer.

In recent years, offshore EBTs have become common. They raise difficult tax issues, most of which have tended to be settled by negotiation rather than litigation. One case has resulted in litigation to the House of Lords, *Macdonald v Dextra Accessories Ltd* [2005] STC 1111.

Income tax and CGT

26.2 The test of trust residence is the same for an EBT as for any trust. For income tax purposes an EBT is non-resident if all the trustees are non-resident (FA 1989, s 110). For CGT purposes at least a majority of the trustees must be non-resident and the general administration of the trusts must be carried on abroad (TCGA 1992, s 69(2)). These tests are discussed further in Chapter 37 and, as there described, the income tax test will apply for CGT purposes as from 6 April 2007. Were an EBT to emigrate it would be deemed to dispose of its assets at market value for CGT purposes, just like any other trust (TCGA 1992, s 80).

Assuming an EBT is non-resident, then, as with any non-resident trust, trust gains are free of CGT in the hands of the trustees and liability to income tax is restricted to UK source income. UK source income accruing to the trustees is fully subject to tax, for inherently the trust will have UK beneficiaries. As such the conditions for relief under FA 1995, s 128 are not met (see para 34.15). The rate is the rate applicable to trusts (40%) or, in the case of dividends, the 32.5% dividend trust rate (TA 1988, s 686).

Section 739

26.3 A key issue with offshore EBTs is the extent to which anti-avoidance legislation applies. Logically the first section to consider is TA 1988, s 739 (for which see Chapter 55). This section, however, only applies if there is an individual transferor, and cannot therefore attribute EBT income to a corporate employer. Normally this will be the end of the matter save in the unlikely event that the employer is an individual or a partnership. But as described in para 55.24, a person can count as a transferor for the purposes of s 739 if he has procured or been associated with the transfer and there is authority that a controlling shareholder or shareholders may be caught in this way (*Congreve v IRC* [1946] 2 All ER 170). Accordingly, s 739 issues could arise where the employer company is controlled by one or perhaps a small group of shareholders.

But in such a case, reliance may be placed on two other features of s 739. The first is that liability does not arise unless the transferor receives a capital sum or has power to enjoy. If therefore the controlling shareholders are totally excluded and do not benefit, any possible attack under the section is excluded. Second, s 739 is subject to the motive test described in Chapter 58. If the EBT is set up for the commercial reason of motivating employees it ought to be within the motive defence. However, there is one general counter-argument. This is that the EBT is offshore rather than onshore and, in many cases, quite overtly designed to reward employees in a tax-efficient manner. A specific risk would also arise if a pre-existing EBT had emigrated for tax reasons, for emigration is an associated operation (para 54.4).

Settlement code

26.4 The settlement code in ITTOIA 2005, Part 5, Chapter 5 deems the income of a settlement to be that of the settlor if he is an actual or a potential beneficiary (s 624) or if he receives a capital sum, including the making or repayment of a loan (see Chapter 59). The settlor includes any person by whom the settlement is made, whether directly or indirectly (s 620). Since the definition of 'settlor' refers to a 'person' it is clear that a company can be within the definition but there is no provision deeming participators in a corporate settlor to be settlors. It is sometimes said that a company cannot be a settlor, for companies are not meant to confer benefit on third parties. But it may be doubted whether this is really so, particularly where the company's memorandum confers appropriate express powers.

The settlement code is subject to a bounty test: for an arrangement to be a settlement and for a person to be settlor there must be some element of bounty. This qualification is not statutory but derives from case law and its precise ambit is unclear (see para 59.17). At first sight it is difficult to see its relevance to an EBT, for in legal form an EBT is in essence no more than a discretionary trust under which, from time to time, gratuitous benefit will be conferred on a class of persons defined by reference to employment. Nonetheless HMRC said in *Tax Bulletin* 16 (April 1995 p 204) in relation to the application of the definitions now in ITTOIA 2005, s 620 to TCGA 1992, s 87 that a genuine commercial arrangement by a company to attract, retain and motivate good quality staff is protected by the bounty test.

It is unclear how far this practice can be relied on where an EBT is used in aggressive tax planning. There may be a risk if the employer's contributions would not satisfy the wholly and exclusively test for deductibility. HMRC may in particular seek to apply the settlement code if the settlor company is close and the participators can benefit.

If the bounty defence is or may not be in point, liability under the settlement code can be excluded in the same way as liability under s 739, namely by excluding the employer and any other person who could possibly be described as a settlor. It is also necessary to ensure that such persons do not receive or make loans to the EBT so as to avoid liability under ITTOIA 2005, s 633 (see para 59.9).

CGT – section 86

26.5 One anti-avoidance section requires consideration in relation to CGT, namely s 86. This attributes the gains of an offshore settlement to the settlor if he, his children, his grandchildren, or their respective spouses or any company controlled by any of them does or could possibly benefit. It is analysed in Chapter 60.

The term 'settlor' is defined in the same terms as in ITTOIA 2005, s 620 (see TCGA 1992, Sch 5, para 8) and for this reason that HMRC statement in *Tax Bulletin* 16 is equally applicable. Insofar as the bounty defence is not in point, liability under s 86 may be avoided by completely excluding the settlor and the other persons listed above.

In that connection, an interesting point is who the settlor is. Section 86 defines the settlor as any 'person' and thus on the face of it comprehends an employer company in an EBT context. However, TCGA 1992, Sch 5 then contains rules deeming participators in corporate settlors to be settlors where the company is close (paras 7 and 8). Clearly gains cannot be assessed on both the company and the participators, so the inference is that in the case of a close company, the company is not settlor. But does one then infer that no company is to be treated as settlor for the purposes of s 86, or can a non-close company still be settlor?

Inheritance tax

26.6 Since an EBT is a discretionary trust it is prima facie subject to the IHT regime of 10-yearly and exit charges (see Chapter 43). In fact this result is normally avoided, for provided certain conditions are met, a specific exemption prevents the settled property from being relevant property and so takes it outside the discretionary trust regime (IHTA 1984, ss 58(1)(b) and 86). This exemption applies whether the trust is onshore or offshore.

The conditions are laid down by IHTA 1984, s 86 and are as follows:

(1) The beneficiaries are restricted to employees or office holders and their spouses, relatives and dependants. Charitable beneficiaries are also allowed.
(2) The beneficiaries comprise all or most of the employees and office holders of the employer concerned.

Although these provisions take EBTs out of the 10-yearly and exit charges, there is one catch. This is that a special charge is made under IHTA 1984, s 72 if any of the following occurs:

(a) the settlement ceases to qualify under s 86;
(b) the trustees make a distribution to a person who has provided any of the settled property;
(c) the trustees make a distribution to any participator holding 5% or more of the shares or any class of shares. This applies where the provider of the settled property is a close company;
(d) the trustees make a disposition (other than a distribution) as a result of which the value of the settled property is diminished.

The special charge is 0.25% per quarter for the first 10 years since the trust was created, 0.20% per quarter for the next 10 years, 0.15% per quarter for the next 10 years and so on (IHTA 1984, ss 72(5) and 70(6)). In practical terms, the main significance of s 72 is that it prevents participators in the employer company from benefiting if that company is close and IHT protection is desired.

Conferring benefit

Distributions

26.7 The general rule is that a distribution from an EBT to an employee is earnings (*Brumby v Milner* [1976] STC 534). At one time a distribution after the employment had ceased escaped tax under the cessation of source rule (*Bray v Best* [1989] STC 159). But now this is no longer so, for ITEPA 2003, s 30(3) deems post cessation earnings to be earnings of the last year of the employment. In either event PAYE has to be operated by the employer unless the trustees themselves deduct and account for tax under PAYE regulations (ITEPA 2003, s 687). The payment will attract liability for National Insurance Contributions as well if it can be said to be derived from the employee's employment. (SSCBA 1992, s 3; Trusts and Settlements Manual para 5060). As offshore trustees cannot be required to operate PAYE, responsibility for accounting for tax under the PAYE system is likely to fall on the employer.

Should a distribution from an offshore EBT not be taxable as earnings, it is taxable as income if it is an income distribution (cf Chapter 12). If it is capital

HMRC may seek to invoke TA 1988, s 740. However as noted above, the motive defence may preclude this and, even if s 740 is in point, liability cannot exceed relevant income, ie the income in the EBT which has been accumulated and not distributed as income (see Chapter 56).

Another head of charge to consider is liability to CGT under TCGA 1992, s 87 (see Chapter 63). However, that section only applies if the EBT is a settlement in the sense that that term is used in ITTOIA 2005, s 620 and so the section is not in point if the bounty defence referred to in para 26.4 above is available. If defence is not available, supplemental tax could mean a tax rate of higher than 40% (see para 63.29).

Distributions to non-residents

26.8 A key issue is whether the tax on distributions may be avoided if the recipient is non-resident. It is fairly clear that if the employee himself emigrates *after* his employment ceases, any distribution to him is still treated as taxable earnings. This is because it relates back to the last year of his employment, when by definition he was within the territorial limits set out by ITEPA 2003. But what if he emigrates before his employment ends? In this situation he will be outside ITEPA 2003 if his employment continues at least into the tax year after emigration and all the duties of the employment are performed abroad. Logically therefore a distribution from the EBT should then be tax-free, as it should be following a cessation of such employment, for ITEPA 2003, s 30(3) merely relates a post cessation receipt back to the last year of actual employment. So too neither the income tax charge on trust income distributions nor TA 1988, s 740 will be in point as they apply only to UK residents.

In reality such exercises should not be undertaken without specialist advice. It has to be remembered that if a distribution is taxable as earnings it is the resident employer who is likely to have to pay the tax under the PAYE system. One argument HMRC may raise is that the distribution is partially referrable to and thus is earnings for years prior to the final year. Another point is that even if HMRC fail in showing that the distribution is taxable earnings, an issue would arise of whether it was taxable under some other head, for example as a termination payment under ITEPA 2003, s 403 (cf Trusts and Settlements Manual, para TSEM 5060). This section applies to any payment made in connection with the termination or variation of a person's employment, whether the payment is made to the employee or a relative and whether or not the payer is the employer. As payments caught count as earnings they are not within the general territorial limits of ITEPA 2003 in ss 14–43 (see ITEPA 2003, ss 7 and 403, ITEPA 2003 Explanatory Notes para 47 and *Nichols v Gibson* [1996] STC 1008).

Another avenue to explore in connection with distributions to non-residents is that a distribution to someone other than the employee is not normally taxable as earnings (*Barclays Bank Ltd v Naylor* (1960) 39 TC 256). It may be taxable as a benefit in kind under ITEPA 2003, s 203 if paid to his close family, but that charge is displaced if in the tax year concerned the employment no longer subsists (*Tax Bulletin* 65 (June 2003), 1037). This limitation is displaced in the case, for example, of the special rules applicable to loans and shares (ITEPA 2003, ss 188(2) and 446U(2); see Chapter 69). But otherwise a distribution may escape tax if it is made to a relative or dependant of a former employee. Here too, however, specialist advice is essential.

Sub-funds and loans

26.9 In practice EBTs frequently allocate or appoint sub-funds for particular employees and their families. This was done in *Macdonald v Dextra Accessories Ltd (see* [2003] STC 749) where key directors who were also shareholders took a very substantial proportion of their total remuneration packages by way of contribution to an offshore EBT. HMRC argued that the allocations in their favour either amounted to earnings in the general sense of the term or were taxable benefits within ITEPA 2003, s 203 (para 69.15). The Special Commissioners rejected both contentions principally because the EBT was a trust under which the trustees had discretions and could not, in a commercial sense, be compelled to comply with the wishes of the employees. HMRC did not appeal on this point to the High Court.

EBTs also in practice make loans to the employees and this too was done in *Macdonald v Dextra Accessories Ltd*. HMRC argued that the loans were taxable as earnings and this too was rejected by the Special Commissioners. For the most part the loans were at the official rate of interest, which would have precluded attack under ITEPA 2003, ss 173–191 (see para 69.10). But some loans were not. It may be suggested that such loans would not have been caught by ss 173–191 as an EBT does not fall within the categories of lender caught by those sections. Perhaps for that reason those sections do not appear to have been invoked in *Macdonald v Dextra Accessories Ltd* even in relation to at least one loan in the case which was interest-free. But it may be doubted whether HMRC would accept this (cf Trusts and Settlements Manual, para TSEM 5060).

Paying interest does of course result in taxable UK source income to the EBT. If the interest is retained in the EBT, and if s 740 is in point, such income is also s 740 relevant income.

Payments into the EBT

26.10 The rules and issues which apply in creating and funding an EBT are the same whether it is offshore or onshore.

Liability of employees

26.11 Employees do not receive taxable earnings when payments are made into the EBT for, so long as the trust is truly discretionary, no employee has any vested right (*Edwards v Roberts* (1935) 19 TC 618). The correctness of this decision is implicit in *Macdonald v Dextra Accessories Ltd.*

Deductibility

26.12 To be deductible, a contribution to an EBT has to satisfy both the general rules as to deductibility and also the specific rules in FA 2003, Sch 24.

A series of cases has established that under general rules a contribution to an EBT is deductible in the tax computation of the employer provided it is not once and for all and provided that it is made wholly and exclusively for the purposes of the employer's trade (see for example *Heather v P-E Consulting Group Ltd* [1973] 1 All ER 8; *Jeffs v Ringtons Ltd [1985] STC 809*; *Mawsley Machinery Ltd v Robinson* [1998] STC (SCD) 236). A deduction is not allowed for the initial payment setting up the trust, and thereafter the employer must not be under an obligation to make payments to the EBT, for then the payments would be taxable as income in the hands of the EBT.

Schedule 24 operates where a deduction would otherwise be allowed under the general rules just described. It prevents the employer from taking the deduction unless within nine months of the end of the accounting period the money is used by the trustees to meet qualifying expenses or provide qualifying benefits. Qualifying benefits are benefits which give rise to both an employment income tax charge and a NIC charge, or would do so if the duties of the employment were performed in the UK. Loans are excluded. Qualifying expenses are trustee expenses which would be deductible if incurred by the employer. Insofar as a deduction cannot be taken for the accounting period in which the money is paid to the EBT, it may be taken in a subsequent period insofar as qualifying benefits are then provided out of it. To the extent that such benefits are never provided a deduction is never available. Schedule 24 is thus both a timing provision and a provision which in some cases wholly denies relief.

Schedule 24 was enacted in response to schemes such as that in *MacDonald v Dextra Accessories Ltd*. The decision of the House of Lords that the former legislation (FA 1989, s 43) had broadly similar effect is not therefore of ongoing relevance.

IHT

26.13 If a payment into an EBT is deductible in computing profits it is not a transfer of value for IHT purposes (IHTA 1984, s 12). It is unclear whether for these purposes a payment counts as deductible only when it becomes deductible under the timing rules in FA 2003, Sch 24, or whether the issue of deductibility is considered regardless of timing.

In practice this issue may be avoided in many cases, as a disposition by a close company is not in any event a transfer of value provided the conditions of IHTA 1984, s 86 are met (para 26.6) and 5% participators in the settlor company cannot benefit otherwise than by payment in cash which is taxable as income (IHTA 1984, s 13).

Conclusion

26.14 An offshore EBT is clearly more attractive than an onshore EBT. This is because, at least in the normal case, income and gains can accrue gross. It is true that the eventual distributions are likely to be taxable. But the tax is no higher than the normal PAYE and NIC rates. There is no supplemental tax such as applies to distributions from family trusts taxed as capital gain. As in other situations EBTs are an example of tax being able to be deferred and thus able to generate a larger fund from which benefits are ultimately paid.

It remains to be seen how far the 2003 restrictions on deductibility will affect the popularity of EBTs. However what can be said is that the other tax advantages of offshore EBTs remain, particularly the apparent ability to accumulate tax-free income and gains. Furthermore, even if the EBT has to be funded out of taxed profits, Corporation Tax at 30% is less onerous than the combined rate of income tax and secondary national insurance contributions chargeable on an immediate payment of earnings.

Section VII

Emigration

Chapter 27

Individuals

Introduction

27.1 Migration is seen by many as a means of avoiding tax. Sometimes individuals go abroad in order to avoid a specific liability, for example CGT on a substantial gain or tax on a large capital payment from a trust. More often an individual decides to work or retire abroad in any event, and then seeks advice on how his plans may be used to minimise UK tax.

A point to stress is that most industrialised countries now have tax rates comparable to those obtaining in the UK. Furthermore, the hitherto lax enforcement procedures in many parts of the world are being tightened up. Accordingly, a migrant may not save overall tax if he goes to such traditional retirement countries as Spain or Portugal. To achieve a permanent reduction in tax it is necessary to move to a nil or low-tax jurisdiction. Some offshore jurisdictions restrict immigrants, but others still welcome newcomers.

Some individuals overcome the problem of where to go by not becoming resident in any country for tax purposes. Most countries define residency by days spent there, and it is therefore possible to avoid fiscal connection with any country by spending limited time in several. Local advice should be taken on the residency requirements of each country involved and it should be noted that severing fiscal connection with the UK can require a longer absence if the migrant does not move to one particular place (see para 27.4 below).

Becoming non-resident

27.2 An individual who leaves the UK is fully non-resident for tax purposes if three conditions are satisfied, namely:

(1) he is not resident in the UK;
(2) he is not ordinarily resident in the UK;
(3) his absence from the UK is not for the purpose of only occasional residence abroad (TA 1988, s 334).

The circumstances which make an individual resident in the UK are discussed in Chapter 36, as is the meaning of ordinary residence and occasional residence.

Year of departure

27.3 In law residence is determined for complete years of assessment, and accordingly all three conditions must be satisfied throughout a tax year before a taxpayer is non-resident for that year. But under ESC A11, HMRC allow non-residence to be backdated to the date of departure if one of two conditions is satisfied (ESC A11):

(1) the individual leaves the UK for permanent residence abroad, and becomes not ordinarily resident in the UK;
(2) the individual leaves the UK to work full time abroad under a contract of employment. Both the period of absence, and the contract, must subsist over a period which includes at least one tax year.

HMRC regard the question of whether work abroad is full time as one of fact, although they do note that the typical UK working week is 35–40 hours (*Tax Bulletin* 6 (February 1993)). Work in the UK in some unconnected occupation may cast doubt on whether the foreign job is full-time.

In practice non-residence is also backdated to the date of departure in the following situations:

(1) The individual leaves the UK to work abroad full-time on a self-employed basis (IR20 para 2.4).
(2) The individual is the spouse of somebody who has left the UK to work abroad full-time, either on a self-employed basis or as an employee (IR20 para 2.6).

Short absences

27.4 The conventional view is that an individual should not be resident in the UK for at least three complete tax years if he is to be certain of being non-resident for all tax purposes. The basis of this view appears to be that shorter absences are capable of being for the purposes of only occasional residence abroad, in which case income tax liability attaches as if the taxpayer were still resident (TA 1988, s 334). Alternatively, it is said the taxpayer may still be ordinarily resident in the UK, although as noted in para 36.5, it is difficult to reconcile this view with the case law.

There are two situations in which a taxpayer who is absent for a period including only one complete tax year should count as definitely non-resident. The first rests on practice rather than law. It is the same as one of the circumstances where non-residence is backdated to the date of departure, namely where the individual or her spouse goes abroad to work full-time. The absence must extend over at least one complete tax year and the individual is allowed to spend on average 90 days per year in the UK (IR20 paras 2.2–2.6).

The second situation is based on the decision in *Reed v Clark* [1985] STC 323. Here the taxpayer left the UK on 3 April 1978 and did not set foot here again until 1 May 1979. He retained accommodation in the UK, but throughout his period abroad, he had a permanent home and place of business in Los Angeles. Nicholls J held that on these facts the taxpayer was not resident in the UK and that his absence was not for the purposes of only occasional residence abroad. He also indicated that occasional residence is the opposite of ordinary residence, and accordingly it is implicit in the decision that the taxpayer was not ordinarily resident here either. Thus it may be said that a taxpayer is fully non-resident in a year of assessment if he does not set foot in the UK at all in the year and has a permanent home and place of business in one specific place abroad.

IR 20 indicates HMRC accept *Reed v Clark*, for under para 2.9 an individual absent from the UK for just a single tax year is treated as non-resident if he has gone abroad for a settled purpose. Indeed, in contrast to *Reed v Clark*, such an individual can visit the UK for up to 90 days per tax year. HMRC indicate that 'settled purpose' includes 'a fixed object or intention in which you are going to be engaged for an extended period of time'. Para 2.9 indicates that in such cases non-residence is treated as commencing on the date of departure.

Practice and procedure

27.5 Prior to self-assessment HMRC would, if supplied with the facts, give a formal ruling that an emigrant was indeed non-resident. This is no longer done, and now the general rule is that the individual must claim non-resident status by completing the non-residence etc pages of the self-assessment return for the year of departure (*Tax Bulletin* 29 (June 1997) p 425). HMRC may at that stage review the individual's residence status by way of enquiry into the return, but if they do not do so within the period allowed, the individual's non-resident status for the year in question cannot be challenged. This is not so, however, if incorrect information is given on the non-residence etc pages so care over their completion is important.

It is still possible to file Form P85 on or shortly after departure. If this is done, HMRC may simply make an in-year repayment on the basis of the information in Form P85. But such repayment does not bind HMRC as to the individual's residence status, which may therefore be enquired into when he files his return for the year of departure. Where however HMRC do enquire into the P85 before accepting non-resident status they do not in practice enquire into the matter again when the return for the year in question is filed (*Tax Bulletin* 29 (July 1997) 426).

CGT

27.6 The general rule is that CGT is not chargeable if the taxpayer is neither resident nor ordinarily resident in the UK throughout the year of assessment in which a gain accrues (TCGA 1992, s 2). Accordingly, a taxpayer can completely shelter capital gains by emigrating permanently in one tax year and realising the gains in subsequent years. This is so whether the gains arise on foreign situs or UK assets, and it is fair to say that migration is the simplest and most effective avoidance technique for the individual holding assets with substantial latent gains.

Short-term migration

27.7 Since 1998 there has been a very important restriction on the use of emigration to shelter capital gains. This is that the emigrant must not come back to the UK, or, if he does so there must be a specified number of tax years between the tax year of his departure and the tax year in which he returns. This rule is enacted by TCGA 1992, s 10A. It is normally described as requiring the emigrant to be non-resident for at least five complete tax years, and it was so announced at the time of the 1998 Budget (IR Press Release, 17 March 1998, 'Capital gains tax – temporary non residence'). But in fact the legislation (s 10A(1)(c)) says that fewer than five years must separate the year of departure and the year of return. On the face of it, this suggests four complete tax years is sufficient, although most advisers, for prudence, recommend five.

The legislation refers to the tax years between the year of departure and the year of return as intervening years. Gains and losses realised during intervening years are not taxed in those years but if the individual in fact returns within the prescribed period, they are all treated as accruing in the year of return. Gains so treated include gains that would have been attributed to the taxpayer under TCGA 1992, ss 86 and 13 (see Chapters 60 and 66) if he had in fact been UK resident in the intervening years, but not the gains of settlor-interested resident settlements (s 10A(2)(b)).

There are two important points to note about the s 10A procedure:

(1) Provided the settlor is in fact non-resident for longer than the specified period of four or five years, gains in the first and subsequent complete tax years following departure are free of tax. Section 10A bites only if the individual returns within the time specified.
(2) Should he so return the gains and losses of the intervening years all fall into the year of return, which means the normal CGT rule that losses cannot be carried back is effectively displaced. But this does not apply to losses attributed under s 13 (s 10A(6)).

Section 10A is subject to the following exceptions:

(i) It does not apply unless the emigrant has been resident in the UK for some part of at least four of the seven tax years preceding the year of departure.
(ii) The gains or losses treated as accruing in the year of return do not include gains or losses realised on assets acquired during the period of absence. This, however, does not inter alia apply to:
    (a) assets acquired from the individual's spouse;

(b) beneficial interests under settlements;
(c) new assets under roll-over and similar claims.

As with all extensions of territoriality, the issue arises of whether s 10A is compatible with European law. The cases referred to in para 49.16 indicate that it is.

When first enacted s 10A was expressed as subject to double tax treaties, and it was accepted by HMRC that a taxpayer had treaty protection if, during the intervening years, he was resident in a country whose treaty with the UK followed the OECD model and gave the country of residence sole taxing rights over most gains. This protection, of course, extended only to types of gain in fact allocated by the treaty concerned to the country of residence, and in the years following 1998 it became HMRC practice in Treaty negotiation to reserve the UK's right to tax gains realised within six years of departure. This provision is, for example, now found in the treaties with the United States, Canada, South Africa and France.

Since 16 March 2005 the issue has been academic, for now it is expressly provided that treaties cannot override the s 10A charge (s 10A(9C)). Further, s 10A also applies if during the intervening years the individual is non-resident under the tie-breaker clause in a treaty, as well as where he is non-resident under domestic law.

UK branch or agency

27.8 A second exception to the rule that non-residents are not liable to CGT arises where the non-resident is carrying on business in the UK through a branch or agency (TCGA 1992, s 10). In these circumstances gains are chargeable to the extent that they accrue on UK situs assets used for the purposes of either the branch or the trade. At one time the charge was restricted to trades carried on through a branch or agency, but since 1989 it has been extended to professions (s 10(5)).

A migrant may find he is trading in the UK through a branch or agency if he retains a UK business and runs it through a manager. Perhaps the most common example is farming but the problem can arise with any kind of business. A branch or agency trade also exists if the migrant is a partner in a UK partnership, for in law any one partner is the agent of all the others (Partnership Act 1890, s 5). Accordingly, the migrant is chargeable on his proportion of any gains realised by such a mixed residence UK partnership (cf TCGA 1992, s 59).

At one time, the charge on branch or agency gains could be avoided by removing the assets from the UK or by not disposing of them until after the branch or agency trade had ceased. These avoidance possibilities were blocked in 1989, and now a deemed disposal occurs if assets are removed from the UK or the branch or agency trade ceases (TCGA 1992, s 25(1)). Roll-over relief is not available on the disposal of branch or agency assets unless the new assets are also branch or agency assets (TCGA 1992, s 159).

Disposals in the year of departure

27.9 Gains accruing on disposals in the year of departure are chargeable even if the disposals occur after the taxpayer has left the UK. This is because CGT is chargeable even if the taxpayer is UK resident for part only of the tax year (TCGA 1992, s 2(1)).

In most cases ESC D2 used to exempt post-departure gains. This concession applied if in practice non-residence was backdated to the date of departure under ESC A11 (para 27.3 above). However, ESC D2 now only applies where the migrant was non-resident throughout at least four of the seven tax years prior to the year of departure. This effective withdrawal of ESC D2 took effect as respects departures on or after 17 March 1998.

CGT planning

Postponing disposals

27.10 CGT is avoided if a permanent emigrant delays any disposal until the tax year following that of his departure. The date of disposal for CGT purposes is normally the date of contract (TCGA 1992, s 28). Accordingly, if a disposal needs to be postponed until a subsequent tax year, no contract should be entered into until after the following 6 April.

It should be remembered that a contract can be oral, save where the asset disposed of is land in England and Wales. Save as respects such land, HMRC may contend in provocative cases that there is an oral contract prior to emigration. Care should be taken to avoid giving a factual basis to support such a contention.

Delaying a binding contract can be unacceptable commercially, but in such situations advantage may sometimes be taken of two exceptions to the rule that the date of the contract is the date of disposal. These exceptions are, first, that a disposal under a conditional contract only occurs when the condition is satisfied, and second, that where an option is granted, the disposal only takes place when the option is exercised (TCGA 1992, s 28(2)).

In theory conditional contracts are the better means of postponing a disposal, for both sides are bound. Unfortunately it is often unclear whether a contract is in fact conditional. A contract is only conditional if (a) the condition is precedent to performance and (b) it is contingent in the sense that neither party covenants to bring it about (*Eastham v Leigh* [1971] Ch 871). The best example of a conditional contract is one whose performance is subject to an unconnected third party consent, for example, the grant of planning permission.

The difficulties with conditional contracts mean that options are frequently used to postpone the date of disposal. Options can either be call options, whereby the purchaser is entitled to call on the vendor to sell the asset, or put options, under which the vendor can require the purchaser to buy the asset. The disadvantage in both cases is that only one side is bound. Sometimes this disadvantage is overcome by using cross options, i e having both a call and put option. If these options are exercisable at the same price and at the same time, it may be that HMRC could argue they constituted a concluded contract, entered into when the options are granted. But such an argument is inconsistent with *J Sainsbury plc v O'Connor* [1991] STC 318, CA. It is on any view much less convincing if the periods of exercise for the options are successive and the price varies slightly.

In appropriate cases, cross options merit serious consideration. However, HMRC scrutiny should be expected, particularly as to whether, notwithstanding the documentation, there was a binding oral agreement prior to emigration.

Company sales

27.11 Where the taxpayer sells a company he owns, CGT may be deferred under TCGA 1992, s 135 if the consideration is shares or loan stock rather than cash. In such case, the date of disposal for CGT purposes is deferred until the replacement shares or loan stock are disposed of. Over the years many individuals have emigrated before disposing of the replacement shares or loan stock and thereby sheltered gains.

It does however have to be remembered that the relief in s 135 is subject to a motive defence. Under TCGA 1992, s 137, the relief is precluded unless the exchange is effected for bona fide commercial reasons and does not form part of arrangements one of whose main purposes is the avoidance of CGT or corporation tax. In *Snell v Revenue and Customs Comrs* [2006] STC (SCD) 296, Special Commissioners held that the conversion of deferral into avoidance by emigration could be a tax avoidance purpose. If, therefore, the taxpayer has at the time of the exchange the purpose of becoming non-resident, s 137 relief is not available.

The moral of *Snell* is that an individual selling a company who thinks emigration might be attractive should not develop or investigate such plans until the sale is concluded. However, if on the facts the purchaser has only ever been prepared to pay in shares or loan stock, an intention to emigrate should not be material.

Section 137 is subject to a clearance procedure in TCGA 1992, s 138. It should be remembered that any clearance does not hold good unless all relevant facts and considerations are disclosed. If therefore an applicant for clearance has considered becoming non-resident such should be referred to in the application if certainty is to be achieved.

Business assets

27.12 It is difficult for an individual to use migration to shelter gains accruing on the disposal of an unincorporated UK business. This is because once he migrates, the business will be a branch or agency trade, and gains on the business assets will accordingly remain in charge.

There are two ways round this difficulty. One is to sell the business before migration and invest the proceeds in the assets of a new business situate abroad. In these circumstances roll-over relief is available (TCGA 1992, s 152). That relief is not clawed back when the individual migrates, and indeed it is even possible for the new assets to be purchased after migration. Since the new assets are foreign situs, no branch or agency charge can arise on their disposal, and accordingly, so long as the migrant remains non-resident, the gain is completely sheltered.

The second avoidance technique is to transfer the business to a company as a going concern prior to migration. If the transfer includes all the assets of the business and shares in the company are the sole consideration received by the individual, the gains on the business assets are rolled into the company shares (TCGA 1992, s 162). Since the shares are not a business, they can be sold after migration without fear of a branch or agency charge. To avoid attack under the *Ramsay* principle, the transfer to the company should take place before the sale is negotiated. It should also take place before migration, since otherwise the cessation occasioned by the transfer could result in a branch or agency charge (TCGA 1992, s 25(3)), although HMRC said in 1990 they would not take this point (*Taxation Practitioner* (May 1990) p 232).

Charges on migration

27.13 In contrast to companies and trusts, an individual does not suffer a deemed disposal of his assets when he migrates.

Certain other charges may, however, come into issue. One such arises if (1) the migrant has been the recipient of a gift and (2) a gain accruing on the making of the gift was held over under either of the two regimes for hold-over relief, namely that for business assets in TCGA 1992, s 165, and that involving trusts in TCGA 1992, s 260. If these conditions are satisfied, migration causes the held-over gain to be assessed on the migrant and charged at his marginal rate of tax (TCGA 1992, s 168).

Fortunately there are two important reliefs from this charge:

(1) the charge does not arise if migration occurs more than six years after the end of the year of assessment in which the hold-over disposal occurred (s 168(4));
(2) the charge is also avoided if the taxpayer goes abroad for full-time employment and returns within three years without having disposed of the asset (s 168(5)).

Another charge to consider is where the migrant has deferred a gain under the Enterprise Investment Scheme or the VCT scheme. In such a case emigration triggers a charge on the postponed gain, but only if it occurs within three years (TCGA 1992, Sch 5B para 3(1)(c) and Sch 5C para 3(1)(e)). The charge is not made if the emigration is for less than three years and for full-time employment.

It is unclear whether an argument could be run that these charges break European law. The cases discussed in para 49.16 indicate that European law could be breached if the emigrant moves to the European Union or the European Economic Area. On these scenarios, the implication of those cases may be that the held-over gain should not be charged until the asset is disposed of.

Income tax

27.14 Migration avoids UK tax on foreign-source income. In the year of departure only a proportion of foreign source income is in practice charged to UK tax. The liability is on the smaller of (a) the income in fact arising prior to departure and (b) an apportioned part of the income for that year (IR 20, para 6.15).

UK investment income

27.15 The tax treatment of UK investment income once the individual is non-resident is detailed in Chapter 34. UK investment income is fully charged in the year of departure, the exemption in FA 1995, s 128 for excluded income not applying in that year (ESC A11).

Business income

27.16 A migrant who has been engaged in a trade or profession in the UK is treated as permanently discontinuing the trade when he migrates (ITTOIA 2005, s 17). If in fact the business continues it is treated as newly started up. The individual remains in charge to UK tax if the business operations continue in the UK, for then he is trading in rather than with the UK (cf para 33.13 and *IRC v Brackett* [1986] STC 521). If as is normal the UK business operations amount to a branch or agency, the branch or agent is assessable as UK representative (FA 1995, s 127). Losses of the period of UK residence are able to be brought forward (ITTOIA 2005, s 17(3)).

Should the migrant be in partnership there is no discontinuance of the migrant's notional trade under the partnership if the partnership business is carried on wholly in the UK. But if this is not the case, the migrant suffers a discontinuance and recommencement of his notional trade (ITTOIA 2005, s 852).

Employment income

27.17 A non-resident is only liable to UK tax on employment income insofar as duties are performed in the UK (ITEPA 2003, s 27). Where some duties are performed in the UK and some not, the general rule is time apportionment by working days (cf SP 5/84). These rules apply whether the employer is foreign or UK-based and are subject to any applicable double tax treaty. Tax is recovered by the PAYE system and it is possible to obtain a direction as to the proportion of the earnings which are to be treated as taxable for the purposes of operating PAYE (ITEPA 2003, s 690).

In the year of departure, split year treatment may be claimed for earnings from an employment carried on wholly abroad, with the result that post-departure earnings from such employment are not taxable (IR 20, para 5.4). This inter alia protects individuals who emigrate and immediately take up a new foreign employment. As noted above, filing Form P85 may enable overdeducted PAYE tax to be repaid if the individual had a UK employment which ceased on departure.

Inheritance tax

27.18 A person leaving the UK remains liable to inheritance tax until three complete tax years have elapsed after he has acquired a domicile of choice in a new country. As is described in Chapter 39, he only acquires such a domicile of choice if he fixes his chief residence in the new country with the intention of remaining there permanently, unless and until something happens to make him change his mind. In order to demonstrate that a domicile of choice has been acquired, ties with the UK should be severed and any UK property sold.

A migrant remains liable to IHT until three tax years have elapsed because for IHT purposes he has a deemed UK domicile during that period (see para 30.14). Once the three-year period is up, the foreign situs assets of the migrant are removed out of the ambit of inheritance tax. UK situs assets are still chargeable, but this difficulty can be overcome by owning those assets through a foreign registered holding company (see para 17.12).

Once a migrant considers he has acquired a foreign domicile for IHT purposes, it is prudent to establish the position with the UK HMRC in case the migrant subsequently has to return to the UK. Means of achieving this are described in para 39.12.

As is described in para 30.13, there are certain assets where liability to IHT is not determined by domicile. The most notable is British government securities, most of which are outside the ambit of IHT provided the owner is not ordinarily resident. It follows that an emigrant can secure IHT protection by switching his assets to appropriate government securities once he has lost ordinary residence, regardless of domicile. Such switching should not, of course, be effected until the tax year after that of departure if it would result in capital gains being realised and nor should it effected if there is any likelihood of falling foul of TCGA 1992, s 10A (para 27.7 above).

Chapter 28

Migration of trusts

Introduction

28.1 The migration of a trust does not entail the UK trustees moving abroad, although if this happened, the trust would become non-resident. Instead, the UK trustees retire, non-residents are appointed in their place and the general administration of the trusts is moved abroad. As is described in Chapter 37, this makes the trust non-resident. For CGT purposes it is only necessary under current law to have a majority of trustees non-resident (TCGA 1992, s 69(1)). In practice, however, all the new trustees should be non-resident. This is currently the requirement for income tax and will be the requirement for both income tax and CGT from 6 April 2007 (see para 37.7).

Can the trust migrate?

28.2 The essence of trusteeship is a personal obligation binding the conscience of the trustee. The courts of equity enforce the trust at the instance of the beneficiaries, but in order to do so, the trustees need to be in jurisdiction. These fundamental principles mean difficult issues may be raised by the appointment of foreign trustees of an English trust.

Express power

28.3 There is little doubt that the courts will in appropriate cases sanction the appointment of non-resident trustees. There are several cases where this has happened, and in view of those cases it necessarily follows that the appointment of non-resident trustees can be expressly authorised by a settlement. Most modern settlements do contain such authorisation, coupled with a provision preventing the removal of a trustee on the grounds of absence for more than twelve months. It is generally accepted that such provisions make the appointment of a foreign trustee subject to the same considerations as apply where a resident trustee is appointed.

No express power

28.4 At one time the law where there is no express power is thought to have been summarised by Sir John Pennycuick V-C in *Re Whitehead* [1971] 2 All ER 1334 at 1337:

> 'the law I think has been quite well established for upwards of a century, that there is no absolute bar to the appointment of persons resident abroad as trustees of an English trust. I say "no absolute bar", in the sense that such an appointment would be prohibited by law and would consequently be invalid. On the other hand, apart from exceptional circumstances, it is not proper to make such an appointment. That is to say, the court would not, apart from exceptional circumstances, make such an appointment, nor would it be right for the donee of the power, apart from exceptional circumstances, to make such an appointment out of court. If they did, presumably the court would be likely to interfere at the instance of the beneficiaries. There do, however, exist exceptional circumstances in which such an appointment can properly be made.'

Two points follow from this dictum. First, it is plain that an appointment of foreign trustees can never be invalid in the sense that it is void. Accordingly, it is effective unless and until upset by the beneficiaries and thus, as they accept, binds HMRC. Second, according to Pennycuick V-C, the appointment is improper unless special circumstances exist.

The following cases are material in deciding what special circumstances suffice:

(1) In *Meinertzhagen v Davis* (1844) 1 Coll 335 the court approved the appointment of US trustees where the beneficiaries were US domiciliaries moving to the US.

(2) In *Re Long's Settlement* (1868) 19 LT 672 the court refused the appointment of New Zealand trustees where the beneficiaries were about to go, but had not yet gone, to New Zealand.

(3) In *Re Smith's Trusts* (1872) 26 LT 820 the court appointed Canadian trustees where the beneficiaries had lived in Canada since 1858.

(4) In *Re Liddiard* (1880) 14 Ch D 310 the court appointed Australian trustees where all the beneficiaries lived in Australia.

(5) In *Re Seale's Marriage Settlement* [1961] 3 All ER 136 Buckley J sanctioned an arrangement under the Variation of Trusts Act 1958 involving the appointment of Canadian trustees and an advance into an identical Canadian settlement where the beneficiaries had lived in Canada for many years.

(6) In *Re Weston's Settlements* [1969] 1 Ch 223 the Court of Appeal refused to sanction a similar arrangement in relation to Jersey. The beneficiaries were young, had only lived in Jersey for three months and could easily move.

(7) In *Re Windeatt's Will Trusts* [1969] 2 All ER 324, Pennycuick V-C distinguished *Re Weston* on the grounds that the beneficiaries had lived in Jersey for nearly 20 years.

(8) In *Re Whitehead's Will Trusts* [1971] 2 All ER 1334 itself Pennycuick V-C approved the appointment of Jersey trustees where the beneficiaries had lived in Jersey since 1959.

Modern decisions

28.5 The effect of these cases is that in the absence of an express power the only circumstances in which it is established as proper to appoint non-resident trustees is if the beneficiaries live in the jurisdiction in which the proposed trustees reside. Certain unreported decisions, however, suggest that this approach is too restrictive (see *Capital Taxes* [1992] 81). The decisions are as follows:

(1) In *Re Chamberlain*, an arrangement was approved under the Variation of Trusts Act 1958 for the export of a trust to Guernsey. The beneficiaries were domiciled in Guernsey and Indonesia.
(2) In *Richard v Hon A B Mackay* Millet J sanctioned an advance to a new Bermuda trust. The beneficiaries were all UK domiciled although some had Far Eastern connections.
(3) In *Re Beatty*, Vinelott J sanctioned the appointment of Jersey trustees of a Will trust, where one of the three principal beneficiaries lived in Australia and another was about to move to Spain.

In the latter two cases, both Millet J and Vinelott J drew a distinction between cases where the court is appointing new trustees and cases where the appointment is being made out of court. They suggested that in the latter situation Pennycuick V-C's language is too restrictive. All that is required is that the appointor can properly form the view that the appointment of non-resident trustees is for the benefit of the beneficiaries.

Millet J referred with approval to a decision of Mann J in Australia (*Re Kay, MacKinnon v Stringer* [1927] VLR 66). Mann J identified the two relevant considerations as being:

> 'First, that the proposed transaction should not put the trust fund at risk or deprive the beneficiaries of appropriate protection from a court armed with the necessary powers; and, secondly, that the transfer of funds or the appointment of foreign trustees is appropriate.'

Millet J then concluded:

> 'Certainly in the conditions of today, when one can have an international family with international interests, and where they are as likely to make their home in one country as in another, and as likely to choose one jurisdiction as another for the investment of their capital, I doubt that the language of Sir John Pennycuick is really in tune with the times. In my judgment, where the trustees retain their discretion, as they do in the present case, the court should need to be satisfied only that the proposed transaction is not so inappropriate that no reasonable trustee could entertain it.'

Where are we now?

28.6 It is tempting to conclude in the light of these three cases that Sir John Pennycuick's dictum in *Re Whitehead* can be disregarded. However, it is to be observed that none of the three cases concerned the typical and straightforward case where it is proposed to appoint non-resident trustees of an English trust, with exclusively UK beneficiaries. The three cases make it likely that such an appointment would, if challenged, be upheld as proper. But in none of the three cases was the point so decided on the facts, and the strong language of the Court of Appeal in *Re Weston's Settlements* must not be forgotten. For the present, caution, where there is no express power, should still be the watchword, coupled with a hope that the issue will soon be concluded by a properly reported decision directly in point.

Form of migration

28.7 Section 37(1)(c) of the Trustee Act 1925 must be watched when a trust migrates. It provides as follows:

> 'it shall not be obligatory, save as hereinafter provided, to appoint more than one new trustee where only one trustee was originally appointed, or to fill up the original number of trustees where more than two trustees were originally appointed, but, except where only one trustee was originally appointed, and a sole trustee when appointed will be able to give a valid receipt for all capital money, a trustee shall not be discharged from his trust unless there will be either a trust corporation or at least two persons to act as trustees to perform the trust;'

A trust corporation is a corporation entitled to act as a custodian trustee by rules made under the Public Trustee Act 1906 (Trustee Act 1925, s 68). Under these rules it must be incorporated under the law of the UK or some EU country and have a place of business in the UK. Such a corporation, therefore, will not be found in offshore jurisdictions.

As a result, the practical effect of s 37(1)(c) on trust migration is that the resident trustees do not get a good discharge unless there are at least two non-resident trustees. Until 1 January 1997, the non-resident trustees had to include at least two individuals, but the law was changed by the Trusts of Land and Appointment of Trustees Act 1996, Sch 3 para 3(12). If there is no good discharge, the resident trustees remain trustees and the trust is likely to remain resident (cf *Adam & Co International Trustees Ltd v Theodore Goddard* [2000] 2 ITELR 634).

Section 37(1)(c) can be excluded by express provision in the settlement (Trustee Act 1925 s 69(2); see also *London Regional Transport Pension Fund Trust Co v Hatt* [1993] PLR 227 and *Lewin on Trusts* (17th ed, 2000), 14–25).

HMRC used to take a point on s 37(1)(c) prior to 1 January 1997 where two individuals were not appointed. It may be assumed they would now take the point if two persons are not appointed.

Tax on migration

28.8 When a trust migrates the trustees are deemed under TCGA 1992, s 80 to have disposed of and immediately reacquired all the settled property at its market value immediately before the relevant time. The relevant time is the time at which the trustees become neither resident nor ordinarily resident in the UK. Since the deemed disposal takes place immediately before the relevant time, any gains on the deemed disposal accrue to the UK trustees rather than to their non-resident successors. Should the trust be settlor-interested and so within TCGA 1992, s 77, the gains are assessed as the settlor's.

The deemed disposal does not extend to UK situate assets which immediately after the relevant time are branch or agency assets of a trade carried on in the UK by the trustees: such assets remain in the charge by virtue of TCGA 1992, s 10. Nor does the deemed disposal extend to assets if, before the relevant time, gains accruing on them would have been protected by a double tax treaty (s 80(5)).

A further restriction prevents the trustees from claiming roll-over relief under TCGA 1992, s 152 if the new assets are acquired after the relevant time (s 80(6)). An exception is made where the trustees are trading in the UK and the new assets are branch or agency assets.

Reliefs

28.9 Relief from the s 80 charge is available where the trustees of a resident settlement become non-resident as a result of the death of a trustee. Under the law until 5 April 2007, this would happen if (1) the general administration of the trusts was already carried on abroad; (2) before the death there was an equal number of resident and non-resident trustees; and (3) the deceased trustee was resident. Where this relief applies the deemed disposal under s 80 is restricted to certain assets provided the trustees again become UK resident within six months, i e provided a non-resident trustee retires or a new resident trustee is appointed. The assets to which the charge is restricted are assets disposed of between the death and the resumption of UK residence and such assets (if any) as on the resumption of residence are protected from UK CGT by a double tax treaty.

Relief from the s 80 charge is also conferred where (1) the death of a trustee causes non-resident trustees to become UK resident and (2) the trustees again become non-resident within six months. In these circumstances the deemed disposal under s 80 is restricted to assets which the trustees acquired while resident and in respect of which a hold-over relief claim has been made.

Recovery of tax from past trustees

28.10 TCGA 1992, s 82 empowers HMRC to recover CGT assessed under s 80 from certain past trustees. They are able to invoke this section if the CGT is not paid by the migrating trustees within six months from the time when it becomes payable. That time is 31 January in the following year of assessment.

The tax may only be recovered from a past trustee if two conditions are satisfied. First, he must have retired within twelve months of the migration. Second, at the time of his retirement there must have been a proposal that the trustees might become non-resident. A retired trustee who has to pay the tax has a right of recovery against the migrating trustees.

Section 82 must be remembered whenever the trustee of a resident trust retires. If the export of the trust is even remotely in contemplation, he will need to see that he is satisfactorily indemnified against liability under this section. The section is open to criticism, for tax is recoverable from a past trustee whether or not he personally retired with a view to facilitating migration. Its effect is particularly harsh where a trustee is involuntarily removed, as can happen under many modern settlements.

European law

28.11 As a result of decisions of the European Court of Justice there is a live issue as to whether the s 80 charge is compatible with European law. This issue is discussed in para 49.16.

The bed and breakfast rule

28.12 Should the UK trustees sell shares prior to resigning in favour of non-resident trustees, the shares sold are not identified with shares of the same class acquired within the next 30 days if such acquisition takes place after the non-resident trustees are appointed (TCGA 1992, s 106A(5A)). This rule disapplies the normal anti bed and breakfasting rule in TCGA 1992, s 106A(5) and counteracts the scheme for avoiding the exit charge upheld in *Davies v Hicks* [2005] EWHC 847 (Ch), [2005] STC 850.

Other CGT consequences of migration

Disposals in year of migration

28.13 Gains accruing on disposals after migration but in the same tax year are fully chargeable. This is because gains are chargeable if the taxpayer is resident in the UK during any part of the year (TCGA 1992, s 2(2)). ESC D2 has never applied to trusts.

The chargeability of gains realised in the year of departure applies even if the new trustees are resident in a treaty territory whose treaty with the UK gives the territory sole taxing rights over capital gains. This has been the law since 16 March 2005 (TCGA 1992, s 83A as inserted by F(No 2)A 2005, s 33). Once a new tax year starts the overseas trustees are fully within the regimes for offshore trusts in TCGA 1992, ss 86 and 87 (see Chapters 60 and 63).

Capital payments

28.14 As is described in Chapter 63, the gains in a s 87 pool of a non-resident trust are attributed to beneficiaries who receive capital payments in the same year as the gains accrue, or who have received hitherto unallocated payments in earlier years. When a trust migrates it should be remembered that a capital payment is brought into account for these purposes if it was received when the trust was resident and was made in anticipation of a disposal by the trustees when non-resident (para 63.17). So too a capital payment received from a resident trust can be taxed by reference to a Sch 4C pool if made after or in anticipation of the Sch 4B transfer (TCGA 1992, Sch 4C para 9; see Chapter 64).

As explained in Chapter 65, capital payments include advances in specie and the free use of property. Furthermore, unless a sub-fund election has been made, a beneficiary is taxed even if the settlement is a single settlement divided into funds, and the gain accrues in a fund from which he is excluded. Thus a beneficiary who is paid out in full in anticipation of migration can be taxed in full on subsequent trust gains even though he cannot benefit from them.

Beneficial interests

28.15 As is explained in para 10.10, the exemption for disposals of beneficial interests under settlements does not apply if the trustees of the settlement are non- resident when the disposal takes place. TCGA 1992, s 85 gives a measure of relief where the settlement was formerly UK resident and has migrated. This relief applies to any beneficiary whose interest was created or acquired before the relevant time, that is, the date of migration. Where it applies, any gain accruing on a subsequent disposal of the beneficial interest is computed on the basis that the beneficiary acquired the interest at its market value at the relevant time. This does not apply if prior to being resident in the UK the trust was previously non-resident and at the relevant time it has unallocated trust gains within a s 87 or a Sch 4C pool (TCGA 1992, s 85(10)).

Trustee borrowing

28.16 So long as the settlement is UK resident and has not previously been non-resident, outstanding trustee borrowing within the meaning of TCGA 1992, Sch 4B in immaterial unless the settlement is settlor-interested within TCGA 1992, s 77 (see para 62.19). But this ceases to be so once the settlement becomes non-resident. Ideally any borrowing should be repaid before emigration or, if not, great care is needed to ensure the non-resident trustees do not make a transfer of value. This subject is discussed in Chapter 62.

Income tax implications

28.17 The emigration of a trust does not trigger recognition of income. However, the one exception is offshore income gains, as a disposal for the purposes of the offshore fund legislation takes place whenever it occurs for CGT purposes (see para 71.10).

Emigration does not affect the income tax exposure of actual income (as distinct from deemed income) if the trust is a fixed-interest trust, as such income is taxed by reference to the life-tenant (see para 12.2). That apart, emigration does operate to save UK tax on foreign income save insofar as the settlor is living and UK resident and he or his wife are beneficiaries (see Chapter 59). UK income remains in charge, unless the trust has no UK-resident beneficiaries (see para 34.15).

The split-year concession, ESC All, applies only to individuals.

When should a trust migrate?

28.18 In the 1980s many trusts migrated in order to shelter prospective gains from CGT. Migration has only occasioned a deemed disposal of trust assets since 1991: before then the only CGT consequence of migration was that any gain held over on the transfer of an asset into the trust became chargeable. Once the trust was non-resident, gains were free of tax on an arising basis, for it was also only in 1991 that the rules attributing gains to the settlor were introduced.

Since 1991 the migration of trusts has been much less common. The deemed disposal on migration means migration should generally only be considered where the trust is free of latent gains or where the tax charge on those gains is acceptable. Such is the position if the assets concerned are going to be sold in any event, particularly if further growth before sale is anticipated and after emigration the gains will not be attributed to settlor under TCGA 1992, s 86.

Where s 86 is in point after emigration, emigration may on any view be seen as pointless as exposure to CGT remains. It should however be remembered that s 86 only catches gains. If, therefore, the trust's return when non-resident will be mainly actual or deemed income, emigration may be attractive, provided the settlor and his spouse are wholly excluded. Methods of achieving returns taxed as income are discussed in Chapter 8.

Where s 86 is not point, for example because the settlor is dead, non-resident, or non-domiciled, emigration may still be regarded as unattractive on account of the taxes on distributions, described in Chapters 56 and 63 to 65. In the case of CGT this can be as high as 64%. But these drawbacks may be more apparent than real, as distributions are free of tax if the recipient is non-resident for at least five tax years (see para 14.2). The exposure of distributions to CGT is also avoided if the recipient is non-domiciled or if the trust return since emigration has been income.

Looking at the position overall, the arguments in Chapter 2 deployed in favour of newly created trusts being offshore apply equally to existing trusts. If therefore emigration is possible without significant tax charge, it should be given serious consideration.

Changes to trust residency rules

28.19 As described in Chapter 37, the changes to the trust residency rules taking effect on 6 April 2007 will mean some UK resident trusts will, for CGT purposes, become non-resident. Such trusts will be those settled by UK domiciliaries with a minority of trustees non-resident. Unless non-residence is attractive, the non-resident trustees should retire before 5 April 2007 to ensure that such trusts will be UK resident under the new rules (whilst still remaining UK resident under the old rules). Absent action, a CGT exit charge will be triggered as at 6 April 2007.

A similar point arises as respects trusts which are currently non-resident for CGT purposes but will be UK resident under the new rules. As described in para 37.12, the main categories of such trust are trusts relying on the professional trustee exemption and trusts with a minority of resident trustees. Unless action is taken before 5 April 2007 such trusts will be UK resident on 6 April 2007 and will not be able to become non-resident again without incurring the exit charge. The best method of countering this problem is to ensure that by 5 April 2007 all the trustees are in fact non-resident. In addition, where the professional trustee exemption is currently in point, care must be taken to ensure that general administration is carried on abroad once the UK professional(s) has or have retired.

Chapter 29

Company migration

Introduction

29.1 A UK resident company migrates when one of two conditions is fulfilled:

(1) it becomes non-resident under the central management and control test; or
(2) it becomes dual resident.

Central management and control

29.2 A company can now only become non-resident under the central management and control test if it is foreign registered (FA 1988, s 66; see Chapter 38). For such a company migration can be effected easily and without uncertainty, for all that is required is for the directors to cease meeting in the UK and commence meeting in a foreign territory. Provided the board meets in the new territory and properly discharges its functions the company will be resident there (see Chapter 38).

Dual residence

29.3 A company becomes dual resident if it is resident in the UK and some other country under their respective domestic laws, and under a double tax treaty between the UK and the other country it becomes treated as resident in the other country for the purposes of the treaty (FA 1994, s 249). A company becomes so treated if the place of effective management moves to the other country. Under this test both foreign and UK registered companies can become non-resident (para 38.28).

Criminal offences

29.4 Until 1988 company migration without Treasury consent was an offence. Now consent is no longer required, but migration does occasion certain tax and compliance consequences.

Tax consequences of migration

The deemed disposal

29.5 A company is deemed to dispose of its assets for CGT purposes immediately before it ceases to be resident (TCGA 1992, s 185). The fact that the disposal is before rather than on migration is significant, for it means any gains belong to the accounting period which ends with the migration. The cessation of residence in the UK is one of those events which causes an accounting period to end (TA 1988, s 12(3)(d)).

The deemed disposal and ensuing reacquisition take place at market value, and they extend to all the company's assets. There is, however, one exception and this is where the company continues to carry on a trade in the UK through a permanent establishment (s 185). In these circumstances assets situate in the UK and used in the trade or for the purposes of the permanent establishment are excepted from the deemed disposal. But this exception is not as generous as it appears, for the assets concerned remain within the charge to CGT even after the migration (TCGA 1992, s 10B).

Postponement of the charge

29.6 In certain circumstances gains accruing on the deemed disposal can be postponed. This is possible if, and only if, the migrating company is the 75% subsidiary of a UK parent (TCGA 1992, s 187). For the postponement to apply both the parent and the migrating subsidiary must give notice of election to HMRC within two years of the migration.

If an election is made, all the gains and losses arising in respect of the assets deemed to be disposed of are aggregated. The resultant figure is then treated as a single gain and this is treated as (a) not accruing to the migrating company but (b) accruing to the parent if and at such time as one of three events take place:

(1) the parent itself migrates, or
(2) the migrating company ceases to be a 75% subsidiary of the parent by reason of the parent disposing of some or all of its shares in the subsidiary, or
(3) the parent disposes of shares in the subsidiary after the latter has ceased to be a 75% subsidiary otherwise than on a disposal of its shares.

The postponed gain can also accrue to the parent if the subsidiary disposes of any of the assets which were subject to the deemed disposal (s 187). But such disposals only trigger a charge if they occur within six years of the migration, and, where some only of the assets are disposed of, only a proportion of the postponed gain is charged.

In certain circumstances the postponed gain can be reduced (s 187(5)). This happens where the subsidiary has allowable losses which have not otherwise been relieved and requires an election by both the parent and the subsidiary. This relief is of restricted effect because (1) allowable losses cannot accrue to non-residents save in respect of UK permanent establishment assets (TCGA 1992, s 16(3)) and (2) any losses accruing prior to migration will have already been relieved by a reduction in the postponed gain. As a result the relief appears to operate only if the non-resident trades in the UK through a permanent establishment and the losses accrue there.

Loss of roll-over relief

29.7 One of the quirks of roll-over relief is that new assets count as new assets even if the trader becomes non-resident before they are acquired (TCGA 1992, s 152 passim).

Unfortunately companies cannot take advantage of this, for when a company migrates no asset acquired subsequently can count as a new asset (TCGA 1992, s 185(2)). The only exception is the same as that made for the deemed disposal on migration: an asset can count as a new asset if (a) the company trades in the UK through a permanent establishment, (b) the asset is UK situate and (c) it is used in the permanent establishment.

European law

29.8 The issue of whether the deemed disposal on migration could be in breach of European law is discussed in para 49.16. *R v HM Treasury and IRC, ex p Daily Mail and General Trust [1988] STC 787* suggests it is not.

Compliance obligations

29.9 Although the criminal sanction preventing company migration has gone, some obligations still have to be complied with (FA 1988, s 130). These obligations are normal compliance obligations and failure to honour them results not in prosecution but in penalties.

Notifying HMRC

29.10 The following conditions must be satisfied by the company before it migrates:

(1) It must notify HMRC of (a) the time at which it intends to migrate and (b) the tax outstanding or payable in respect of accounting periods beginning before that time.

(2) It must make arrangements for securing the payment of all the tax and those arrangements must be approved by HMRC. If a dispute arises as

to the amount of the tax it is settled by the Special Commissioners. The tax outstanding or payable includes interest on tax and any corporation tax occasioned by the deemed disposal on migration. It also includes PAYE, and other tax deductible at source (s 130(7)).

The penalty for failing to comply with these obligations is a sum equal to the tax outstanding at the time of migration (FA 1988, s 131). This penalty may be recovered from:

(1) The migrating company itself.
(2) Any director of the migrating company or of any company which controls it.
(3) Any person who has instructed or directed the directors to cause the relevant obligations to be breached.

For a director or other person to be caught, he has to be a party to an act which to his knowledge will result in breach of the compliance obligations. But directors are rebuttably presumed to be parties to any act of the migrating company and they are also rebuttably presumed to know the effect of any act which in fact breaches the company's obligations. The term 'director' bears the same meaning as in the benefits-in-kind code and therefore includes shadow directors (s 131(6)(a); see further Chapter 53).

Revenue guidance notes

29.11 In 1990 HMRC (formerly the Revenue) published guidance notes for migrating companies, which explain how the compliance rules operate in practice (SP 2/90). The advance notification of migration should be sent to International Division (Company Migrations), Room 312, Melbourne House, Aldwych, London WC2B 4LL. Two or more months should be allowed. A resident solicitor or accountant should be appointed to act for the company after the migration and the unpaid tax should be secured by a guarantee from a bank or a suitable resident company. If the guarantee is to be unlimited, the tax liabilities do not need to be computed in detail, and as a result the approval will be speeded up.

Securing unpaid tax

29.12 The main method by which the outstanding tax is secured is by the compliance obligations just described (FA 1988, s 132). However, in case those provisions do not prove watertight, HMRC have further powers to recover tax due from the migrating company. The following persons may be required to pay any unpaid tax:

(1) Any company in the same group as the migrating company.
(2) Any individual who is or was a controlling director of either the

> migrating company or a company which controls it. A controlling director is a director who controls the company concerned. For these purposes, a shadow director counts as a director and control bears its close company definition in TA 1988, s 416 (s 131(6)).

HMRC may require these persons to pay the tax if the tax is outstanding more than six months after it is payable. Written notice must be served, specifying the amount of the tax and requiring payment within 30 days. No notice can be served more than three years after the amount of the tax has been finally determined.

Part B

Legal Framework

Section I

Territorial Limits

Chapter 30

Territorial limits of UK tax

Introduction

30.1 There is a presumption that all UK legislation is subject to territorial limits. Lord Scarman put the matter thus in *Clark v Oceanic Contractors Inc* [1983] STC, 35, 41:

> '… Unless the contrary is expressly enacted or so plainly implied that the courts must give effect to it, United Kingdom legislation is applicable only to British subjects or to foreigners who by coming to the United Kingdom, whether for a short or long time, have made themselves subject to British jurisdiction.'

Lord Scarman also cited *Re Sawers, ex p Blain* (1879) 12 Ch D 522. Here at p 526 James LJ referred to the:

> '… broad, general, universal principle that English legislation, unless the contrary is expressly enacted or so plainly implied as to make it the duty of an English Court to give effect to an English statute, is applicable only to English subjects or to foreigners who by coming into this country, whether for a long or short time, have made themselves during that time subject to English jurisdiction …'

In recent years, however, what has been emphasised is that the territorial principle is ultimately a rule of construction. Thus in *Agassi v Robinson* [2006] 1056, 1063 Lord Scott cited words of Lord Wilberforce in *Clark v Oceanic Contractors*, to the effect that British tax liability has never been exclusively limited to British subjects and foreigners resident in the jurisdiction. In all cases the question to be asked is 'who is within the legislative grasp, or intendment, of the statute under consideration'.

Income tax

30.2 It has long been accepted that income tax legislation recognises the territoriality principle. The position was encapsulated in one sentence by Lord Herschell in *Colquhoun v Brooks* (1889) 14 App Cas 493 at 503, a sentence subsequently approved by the House of Lords inter alia in *National Bank of Greece SA v Westminster Bank Executor and Trustee Co (Channel Islands) Ltd* [1971] AC 945 at 954. Lord Herschell's words were as follows:

> 'The Income Tax Acts, however, themselves impose a territorial limit, either that from which the taxable income is derived must be situate in the United Kingdom or the person whose income is to be taxed must be resident there.'

Source and residency

30.3 As will be apparent from Lord Herschell's dictum, the key issues are the residence of the taxpayer and where the income is derived from, or source as it is usually known. These concepts are considered in Chapters 36 to 38 and 33 respectively.

Exceptions and qualifications

30.4 There are four important qualifications to the general rule:

(1) The foreign source income of non-domiciled individuals resident in the UK is not taxed save insofar as remitted. This, the remittance basis, is explained in Chapter 40.
(2) UK source investment income arising to non-residents is for the most part exempt from UK tax save insofar as tax is withheld. This, the excluded income rule, is explained in para 34.14.
(3) In many instances, double tax treaties curtail the UK's taxing rights where the taxpayer is non-resident or the income is foreign source.
(4) In many cases, anti-avoidance legislation deems the income of a non-resident to be that of a resident. Prime examples are the CFC legislation and TA 1988, s 739 (see Chapters 55 and 67).

It is also to be stressed that, as the general rule is one of construction, specific legislative provisions can be construed as prevailing over it. *Agassi v Robinson* itself was an example of such construction process.

A further qualification concerns trusts. As is explained in Chapter 37, a mixture of case law and statute has attributed a residence to trusts for income tax purposes and as from 6 April 2007 the matter will be entirely governed by statute. But where a beneficiary is entitled as of right to the trust income, the residency of the trust is immaterial and instead income tax liability turns on the residence and domicile of the beneficiary. This principle is explained in paras 12.2 and 33.18. It does not apply to capital receipts which are deemed to be income. These are taxed as the trust's income whatever form the trust takes.

Capital gains tax

30.5 In contrast to income tax, the territorial limits of capital gains tax are, with limited exceptions, defined solely by residence. The basic rule is that a person is chargeable to capital gains tax in any tax year if he is resident or ordinarily resident in the UK during all or any part of the year (TCGA 1992, s 2(1)). In the case of companies, the charge is to corporation tax, for gains are included in total profits. All forms of trust (other than nomineeship) are treated as a separate taxable entity and so, in contrast to income tax, it is not necessary with fixed-interest trusts to look through to the beneficiaries.

Non-residents

30.6 There are two exceptions to the exemption of non-residents from CGT. The first is that an individual who emigrates but returns to the UK after less than five complete tax years remains subject to capital gains for his period of non-residence (TCGA 1992, s 10A). This rule is discussed in para 27.7.

The second is that a non-resident trading in the UK through a branch or agency is chargeable to CGT to a limited extent (TCGA 1992, s 10). The charge is on assets which are situate in the UK and used in the trade or held for the purposes of the branch or agency. The charge also applies to professions carried on in the UK (s 10(5)). In the case of companies, it operates where the trade is carried on through a permanent establishment (TA 1988, s 11; TCGA 1992, s 10B).

UK residents

30.7 There are two situations in which the liability of UK residents to CGT is qualified. The first is where a double tax treaty is in point and either exempts the gain from CGT or requires the UK to give credit for foreign tax.

The second concerns non-domiciled individuals. A non-domiciliary disposing of an asset situated abroad is liable to CGT only if and insofar as the gain is remitted. This, the CGT remittance basis, is conferred by TCGA 1992, s 12 and is explained in Chapter 41.

The CGT exposure of non-domiciliaries is also qualified in one other respect. Under TCGA 1992, s 16(4), a loss accruing to a non-domiciliary is not allowable if the asset disposed of is situated outside the UK. A point to stress is that the disallowance is absolute; it is not simply a question of allowing the loss to be set only against foreign situs gains.

Residence and situs

30.8 It is expressly provided that residence and ordinary residence have the same meanings for CGT as for income tax (TCGA 1992, s 9). The rules and practices described in Chapters 36 to 38 therefore apply. There are no special rules as to domicile and the general law described in Chapter 39 is in point.

The CGT legislation includes special rules as to the situs of assets. These are explained in Chapter 32.

Inheritance tax

30.9 The territorial limits of Inheritance Tax are expressed in terms of excluded property. There are several classes of asset which, if specified conditions are satisfied, are excluded property.

The IHT legislation gives effect to the excluded property concept by two principal rules:

(1) The estate of a person immediately before his death does not include excluded property (IHTA 1984, s 5(1)).
(2) No account is taken of excluded property which leaves a person's estate in determining whether an inter vivos disposition is a transfer of value (IHTA 1984, s 3(2)).

Foreign situs assets

30.10 Property which is situated outside the UK is excluded property if the beneficial owner is not domiciled in the UK. His residence, it may be noted, is immaterial. The common law rules described in Chapter 31 apply in determining the situs of property.

Authorised funds

30.11 FA 2003 created an important class of UK situs excluded property. A holding in an authorised unit trust or a share in an open-ended investment company is excluded if the owner is not domiciled in the UK (IHTA 1984, s 6(1A). This rule has applied since 16 October 2002 (FA 2003, s 186(8)). It will be noted that, as with foreign situs assets, eligibility for it is determined solely by domicile.

For these purposes the term open-ended investment company has the meaning given in s 236 of the Financial Services and Markets Act 2000. It must be incorporated in the UK. An authorised unit trust is a unit trust scheme approved under s 243 of the Financial Services and Markets Act 2000 (IHTA 1984, s 272). Open-ended investment companies and authorised unit trusts may be given the generic name authorised funds (see for example the Authorised Investment Funds (Tax) Regulations 2006 (SI 2006/964), reg 3).

UK bank accounts

30.12 A UK bank account is excluded property if it is denominated in foreign currency and the account holder is an individual who is neither resident nor domiciled in the UK (IHTA 1984, s 157).

This exemption is restrictive in that it applies only on death. It does not extend to sterling accounts and nor does it protect any account of a non-domiciliary who is resident in the UK. Such accounts represent a trap into which non-domiciliaries frequently fall.

UK government securities

30.13 Each issue of UK government securities is or is deemed to be subject to a condition that the stock is exempt from taxation if in the beneficial ownership of a person of a description specified in the condition (F(No 2)A 1915, s 47; F(No 2)A 1931, s 22; FA 1996, s 154; FA 1998, s 161). For IHT purposes, a government security is excluded property if it is in the beneficial ownership of an individual of a description specified in the condition applicable to its issue (IHTA 1984, s 6(2)).

What condition has to be met to secure this treatment is difficult to discern from the legislation. The original legislation allowed the government to issue gilts, which would be free of tax if the owner was neither domiciled nor ordinarily resident in the UK (F(No 2)A 1931, s 22; F(No 2)A 1915, s 47). FA 1940, s 60 allowed the Treasury, when issuing securities, to vary the conditions in F(No 2)A 1931, s 22 and subsequently FA 1996, s 154 allowed domicile to be disregarded. FA 1998, s 161 then deemed all gilt-edged securities previously issued without FOTRA conditions to have been issued with the FOTRA conditions with which 7.25% Treasury Stock 2007 was first issued. FOTRA conditions were defined as conditions as to exemption authorised by virtue of F(No 2)A 1931, s 22 (FA 1998, s 161(4)). The term gilt-edged securities was given the same meaning as in TCGA 1992, where it means all securities listed in TCGA 1992, Sch 9 (TCGA 1992, s 288(8)).

The published HMRC leaflet IHT18 states that since 6 April 1998 all British government securities except 3.5% War Loan 1952 have been exempt from IHT if the owner is not ordinarily resident in the UK. The IHT Manual is somewhat confusing on the subject. However at para IHTM 04306 it gives what it says is a definitive list of FOTRA securities. It also indicates that 3.5% War Loan is excluded property if, in addition to being not ordinarily resident, the owner is non-domiciled (para IHTM 04306).

In practice in most cases it may be felt reliance can be placed on the statement in IHT 18. But if it is important to be certain that government securities really are excluded property, prudence dictates confirming that the securities concerned figure both in the list in the IHT Manual and in the list in TCGA 1992, Sch 9 and what the precise conditions of their issue are.

It will be noted that government securities are not excluded property if the owner is not domiciled in the UK but resident there. This is because the determinant of exemption is ordinary residence not domicile.

Deemed domicile

30.14 For IHT purposes, an individual is domiciled in the UK in all cases where under the general law described in Chapter 39 he is in fact domiciled there. In addition a non-domiciliary is deemed to be domiciled in the UK if either:

(1) he was in fact domiciled in the UK at any time in the preceding three years; or
(2) he has been resident in the UK in 17 out of the 20 years of assessment ending with and including the current year.

In practice the 17-year rule gives rise to the greater difficulties. The principal reason for this is that a year counts towards the 17 years even if the individual is resident in the UK for only part of the year. This means long-stay residents cross the threshold sooner than they think and a year count should always be carried out to check the position. Another trap with the 17-year rule is that it applies on departures in addition to the three-year rule and means long-stay residents only lose deemed domicile after being non-resident for at least three complete tax years.

For years prior to 1993–94 available accommodation is disregarded in determining whether the individual was UK resident (IHTA 1984, s 267(4); FA 1993, s 208(5)). The issue of available accommodation is discussed in para 36.10, and it is still relevant in some cases. Thus a non-domiciliary who first became UK resident in 1989–90 acquires a deemed domicile in 2005–06 if UK resident in all years between. But in years prior to 1993–94 many non-domiciliaries were only treated as resident because of the available accommodation rule, particularly in the initial year of residence. In such cases, the residency position should be tested in the absence of available accommodation, initially under current HMRC practice, but also in law. As described in para 36.3, law on when an arrival first becomes resident may in some cases be more favourable than practice.

One or two old Double Tax Treaties displace the deemed domicile rules in certain cases. The treaties concerned are those with France, Italy, India and Pakistan (IHTM IHT13024). Where an individual is domiciled in one of these four countries the Treaty should be checked. HMRC take the position that the Treaties with Italy, India, and Pakistan do not displace the deemed domicile rules on inter vivos transfers (ibid).

Settlements

30.15 Special rules apply in determining whether, if the classes of asset listed above are settled property, they are excluded property and so outside the scope of IHT. These rules are described in Chapter 45.

Chapter 31

Situs of assets

Introduction

31.1 The situs of property is principally relevant to Inheritance Tax in that foreign situs property is not subject to that tax if it is owned by a person who is neither domiciled nor deemed domiciled in the UK, or by a settlement created by such a person (see paras 30.10 and 45.2). The IHT code does not provide rules for determining situs save only for one provision operating by implication, namely the rule that an individual's estate comprises all property to which he is beneficially entitled (IHTA 1984, s 5(1)). That apart, the matter is governed by the common law. The classic textbook treatment of the subject is in *Dicey and Morris, Collins on the Conflict of Laws* (14th ed, 2006) pp 1116–1132.

Situs is also material to capital gains tax, in that gains accruing on the disposal of the foreign situs assets of non-domiciliaries are subject to the remittance basis (see Chapter 41). So too the charge on non-residents carrying on business in the UK is restricted to UK situs assets (para 30.6). But in contrast to IHT, the CGT legislation enacts express situs rules and, as a result, the common law applies only to assets not covered by those rules.

This chapter deals with the common law, and thus addresses the situs rules applicable to IHT. The CGT rules are considered in Chapter 32.

Tangible property

31.2 Tangible property does not, in general, occasion difficulty under the situs rules. Not surprisingly it is situate where found. This applies both to real estate and to chattels (see for example (*IRC v Stype Investments* [1982] STC 625, 633 and *Young v Phillips* [1984] STC 520, 534, passim).

Intangible property

31.3 The general rule, as stated as Rule 120 in *Dicey*, is as follows:

> 'Choses in action generally are situate in the country where they are properly recoverable or can be enforced.'

This rule was cited with approval by the Privy Council in *Kwok Chi Leung Karl v Comr of Estate Duty* [1988] STC 728, 732. It is however only a general rule and it is modified and in some cases disapplied with respect to many types of intangible.

Debts

31.4 A debt is perhaps the most obvious kind of a chose in action. In accordance with the principle cited above the basic rule is that a debt is situated where it can be enforced (*Kwok Chi Leung Karl v Comr of Estate Duty* [1988] STC 728, PC). In the case of an individual this means the debt is situate where the debtor resides (*A-G v Bouwens* (1838) 4 M & W 171). This is so even if the debt is secured (*Payne v R* [1902] AC 552).

With companies the position is more complicated because, for the purposes of suit, a company resides wherever it carries on business in its own name. In this event the situs of any debt owed by the company is the place where, under the contract governing the debt, the obligation to pay falls to be performed. Thus the situs of a bank account is the branch at which the account is kept, for that is where the customer can withdraw his money (*R v Lovitt* [1912] AC 212). So too, debts under an insurance policy are situate where the policy monies are payable rather than at the company's head office (*New York Life Insurance Co v Public Trustee* [1924] 2 Ch 101, CA).

Negotiable instruments

31.5 A negotiable instrument is an instrument transferable by delivery or by delivery coupled with endorsement to the back of the instrument. A debt enshrined in a negotiable instrument is thus assignable by delivery of the instrument and upon such delivery the assignee obtains title good against the world. He does not have to give notice to or otherwise involve the debtor. Negotiable instruments are regarded as a form of chattel – ie the debt is the piece of paper. Accordingly their situs is governed by the rules pertaining to chattels and thus they are situate where found.

This principle was established as long ago as 1838 in the leading case of *A-G v Bouwens* (1838) 4 M & W 171. It has been affirmed in recent years in cases such as *Kwok* (at p 732) and *Young v Phillips* [1984] STC 520 p 534). However, those recent cases do indicate that for the principle to apply there must, where the document is situate, be a market in which its value can be realised.

An instrument is rendered negotiable and thus within this rule either by statute or by commercial custom. An example instanced in *A-G v Bouwens* is foreign bills of exchange traded on the Royal Exchange. But far and away the most significant category of negotiable instrument is the bearer bond – ie debt issued by a public authority or by a company in the form of bonds payable to bearer and expressed as transferable by delivery. This was exemplified in

Winans v R [1908] 1 KB 1022 (affirmed) [1910] AC 287, where foreign bonds payable to bearer and traded on the London Stock Exchange had been deposited in the Bank of England. These, the Court of Appeal held, were UK situs.

Specialties

31.6 A second exception to the basic rule regarding debts is that a specialty debt is situate where the deed enshrining the debt is found (*Stamp Comr v Hope* [1891] AC 476). The classic definition of a specialty debt is 'an obligation under seal securing a debt, or a debt due from the Crown or under statute' (*R v Williams* [1942] AC 541, 555). It follows that if a debt is enshrined in a deed, it is a specialty.

Because of the ease with which a debt can be enshrined in a deed, the specialty rule is artificial. Nonetheless it is firmly entrenched in long-standing case law (see for example *A-G v Bouwens*, supra). Further, it was affirmed by the Privy Council in *Kwok* (supra, at p 732) in the simplest terms: 'a specialty debt is situate where the deed is physically situate'. For this reason, it may be suggested, the rule is invulnerable to change otherwise than by statute. Periodically rumours circulate that HMRC are taking a case challenging the rule, but significantly no such case has ever in fact been brought in the High Court or before the Special Commissioners.

It is clear that a debt does not have to be secured to be a specialty: this is apparent from *Gurney v Rawlins* (1836) 2 M & W 87, where an unsecured obligation under seal to pay insurance monies was held to be a specialty and so situate where the policy was found. Equally it is also clear that a mortgage debt can be a specialty if the mortgage is by deed: see *Stamps Comr v Hope* [1891] AC 476. This latter case also shows that the execution of a deed containing an express covenant to repay the debt converts a simple debt into a specialty.

It is plain that in the case of a mortgage, the situs of the mortgagor's debt is determined by the nature of the debt rather than the situs of the land. Thus, in *Stamps Comr v Hope*, the debt was held situate in Victoria, where the deed was, rather than in New South Wales, where the land was. But where there are duplicate deeds securing the debt, the situs of the land, together with factors such as the residence of the debtor, may be taken into account in choosing which of the deeds determines situs: *Toronto General Trusts Corpn v R* [1919] AC 679.

It is widely thought that the physical location of the deed only determines the location of a specialty debt if that location is a jurisdiction which recognises the special nature of deeds. It follows that if a specialty is being relied on to determine the location of debt, it should be confirmed in the jurisdiction where it is kept that the concept of the deed is recognised there. Effectively this means the specialty must be kept in a common law jurisdiction and not, for example, in Jersey or Guernsey.

Shares

31.7 A share is part of the capital of a company, to be distinguished from a security or loan stock, which is an obligation of the company (*Singer v Williams* [1921] 1 AC 41). The basic rule is that a share is situated where it can be effectively dealt with as between the owner and the company (*Brassard v Smith* [1925] AC 371). For these purposes a share only counts as effectively dealt with if and at such time as the transferee becomes legally entitled to all rights of a member (*R v Williams* [1942] AC 541). The question of where a share can be effectively dealt with has to be determined by the constitution of the company. However, where only registration on the register of members constitutes a person a member as against the company, the situs of the register is the situs of the shares (*Brassard v Smith* [1925] AC 371).

Multiple registers

31.8 It may be that the company's constitution allows the maintenance of more than one registered office or the keeping of branch registers in two or more separate countries. In this event the choice between those countries is made on rational grounds, which in practice means selecting the country where the owner is more likely to deal in the shares (*Ontario Treasurer v Blonde* [1947] AC 24; *Standard Chartered Bank Ltd v IRC* [1978] STC 272). It is, however, important to distinguish multiple registry offices or branch registers from mere copy registers. This distinction was drawn in *Standard Chartered Bank Ltd v IRC*, where the company register was at its head office in South Africa, with a duplicate register listing UK members in the UK. The evidence was that a transferee only became a member as against the company when entered in the head office register and this meant the shares were situate in South Africa.

Bearer shares

31.9 There is no English authority directly in point on bearer shares. These are shares where simple delivery of the share certificate or other documents of title gives the transferee all rights of membership as against the company. Title to the shares is not subject to registration. Application of the rules relating to negotiable instrument described above (para 31.5) indicates that such shares are situated where the certificates or other documents are found, for the shares can only be dealt in there. Such has been held to be the law in Canada (*Secretary of State of Canada v Alien Property Custodian for United States* [1931] 1 DLR 890). This conclusion does not however extend to renounceable letters of allotment (*Young v Phillips* [1984] STC 520).

A UK company may issue share warrants to bearer. The effect of such warrants is that the bearer of the warrants is entitled to the shares, the shares being transferable by delivery of the warrant (Companies Act 1985, ss 188 and 355). On the basis of the above analysis it is argued such shares are situate where the warrants are found. However, in *Chandrasekaran v Deloitte & Touche Wealth Management Ltd* [2004] EWHC 1378 (Ch), [2004] All ER (D) 128 (Jun), Patten J suggested this may not be so where no obvious market exists for the shares in the foreign jurisdiction concerned (at para 16). However, he expressly forbore from deciding the point.

Transfers endorsed in blank

31.10 Bearer shares must be distinguished from registered shares whose certificates are endorsed with transfers executed by the shareholder in blank. In *R v Williams* [1942] AC 541, the testator had so endorsed his share certificates, and it was accepted that a delivery of the endorsed certificates was a good assignment of the shares, since it passed legal title to the assignee. The endorsed certificates were fully marketable in New York where they were kept by the testator. However, it is clear from the judgment of the Privy Council both in that case and in *Ontario Treasurer v Blonde* [1947] AC 24 that the situation of the certificates could not prevail over the location of the register, for delivery of the certificates merely conferred the right to registration. However, since in *R v Williams* there were two registers the situs of the endorsed certificates was material in deciding between registers on rational grounds, and resulted in the situs of the shares being in New York.

It is noteworthy that in *R v Williams* the registered owner of the shares was the person who held the certificates and signed the blank transfer. In *Stern v R* [1896] 1 QB 211, shares in US companies were freely marketable in England on delivery of a certificate with the transfer endorsed on the back completed. In contrast to *R v Williams*, the owner of the shares was not the person in whose name the shares were registered in the US. The Court held that, as the endorsed certificates were freely marketable in the UK, they fell to be treated in the same way as other negotiable instruments in accordance with *A-G v Bouwens* (1838) 4 M & W 171. The shares were thus rendered UK situate.

Unless the distinction noted above is a valid one, *Stern v R* is not consistent with *R v Williams*. The distinction, however, is not drawn in *R v Williams* or any of the other decided cases, and in the Canadian case of *Royal Trust Co v R* [1949] 2 DLR 153, *Stern* was not followed. *Stern* may be inconsistent with *IRC v Stype Investments (Jersey) Ltd* [1982] STC 625 in that the latter case indicates that the beneficial owner's right to nominee property has the same situs as the property itself (see para 31.1). But *Stern* was referred to without disapproval in *Winans v A-G* [1910] AC 27 and in *Young v Phillips* [1984] STC 520, 534.

HMRC consider that *Stern* is good law where the beneficial owner is not the registered holder of the shares (IHTM 27150). This does not apply if the registered holder is a good Marking Name or a Street Name – ie a financial institution such as a broker, bank or discount house.

Beneficial interests

31.11 A distinction has to be drawn between beneficial interests in the underlying property and personal rights against the trustee or legal holder of the property. In the case of the former, the relevant asset is the underlying property and its situs is the situs of the beneficial interest (*Re Clore* [1982] STC 625). But where the asset is a personal right, it is simply a chose in action and its situs is determined by the rules pertaining to choses in action.

The distinction is illustrated by Australian cases relating to unadministered residue. It was held that the residuary legatee is not entitled to any particular asset in the estate so long as administration is continuing, but instead merely has the right to compel due administration (*Sudeley (Lord) v AG* [1897] AC 11; *Stamp Duties Comr (Queensland) v Livingston* [1964] 3 All ER 692). Accordingly the situs of the residuary legatee's asset is not that of the assets in the estate, but the jurisdiction where the deceased was domiciled and the executors reside.

The principle was applied in a trust context in *Re Smyth, Leach v Leach* [1898] 1 Ch 89. Here the deceased owned a reversionary interest under an English trust holding Jamaican real estate. Romer J held that, as reversioner, the deceased owned merely the right to have the trust duly performed when the reversion fell in. As such, he held a chose in action situate in England rather than an asset in Jamaica.

It can be difficult to determine whether what a person owns is an interest in the underlying assets or a chose in action. However, an analogy may be drawn with the CGT concept of absolute entitlement. Should a person be absolutely entitled as against the trustee or nominee, or should two or more persons be jointly so entitled, the property is treated as theirs for CGT purposes (TCGA 1992, s 60). Case law has established that the interests have to be concurrent rather than successive, i e ownership as joint tenants or tenants in common, rather than life-tenant and remaindermen (see for example *Kidson v Macdonald* [1974] STC 54). But absolute entitlement is preserved even if several beneficial owners accept contractual fetters such as voting restrictions or pre-emption rights, provided it is clear that each co-owner remains entitled to recover at the end of the arrangement the same property as he put in (*Booth v Ellard* [1980] STC 555).

Assuming the CGT principles are a good analogy, the result is that a beneficiary becoming absolutely entitled to settled property ceases to own a chose in action but instead acquires an aliquot share in each trust asset, situate where those trust assets are situate (*Stephenson v Barclays Bank Trust Co Ltd* [1975] STC 151). But by analogy with the CGT cases, this would be displaced if the trust asset is land or private company shares until all the trust interests have vested absolutely (*Crowe v Appleby* [1975] STC 502; *Pexton v Bell* [1976] STC 301).

Partnership interests

31.12 It is well settled that a partner's interest is a chose in action situated where the partnership business is carried on. Case law establishes that the place where the business is carried on is not necessarily the same as the place where all or a majority of the partners reside (*Beaver v Master Equity* [1895]

AC 251; *Stamp Duties Comr v Salting* [1907] AC 449). The implication is that, provided the place where the business is carried on is correctly identified, the situs of the actual assets owned by the partnership is not relevant in determining the situs of the shares that the individual partners own.

Unit trusts

31.13 Unit trusts are a form of nomineeship. The trustee holds a portfolio of investments and cash. The units issued to the investors are equitable interests under the trust and each unit confers an undivided share in whatever the fund of the unit trust consists of from time to time (see *M&G Securities v IRC* [1999] STC 315, 319, per Park J).

For many tax purposes unit trusts are deemed to be separate fiscal entities. Thus for CGT purposes all unit trusts, wherever situate, are deemed to be companies, and the units shares (TCGA 1992, s 99). So too, special income tax rules apply to UK-resident unit trusts, both authorised and unauthorised (TA 1988, ss 468 and 469).

For Inheritance Tax purposes, however, there is no provision deeming the status of unit trusts. However, there is one very important indication, namely the rule that units in authorised unit trusts are excluded property if owned by a non-domiciliary or owned by a trust settled by a non-domiciliary (IHTA 1984, ss 6(1A) and 48(3A)). This is an indication that unit-holders are seen for IHT purposes as owning a chose in action constituted by their units rather than aliquot shares in each underlying investment.

Without this indication there would be difficulty in being certain that the unit-holder's asset is not an aliquot share of each underlying asset. The dictum from *M&G Securities* cited above may be referred to in this context. But at least in the normal case, the unit-holder is not entitled to call on the trustee to transfer investments of the unit trust to him in specie. He is merely entitled to call on the manager to redeem his units for cash. This, it may be suggested, places him on the chose in action side of the line on the basis of the cases cited in para 31.11 above.

The position may be otherwise if the unit-holder is entitled on redemption to call for an aliquot share of the unit trust's investments in specie (as was the position in the *M&G Securities* case itself). Here it may be suggested the situs of what he owns is much more likely to be that of the underlying investments. Despite IHTA 1984, ss 6(1A) and 48(3A), there must be real risk that situs would be that of the underlying investments.

Immobilised securities

31.14 The term 'immobilised securities' is a technical name for securities held in international settlement systems, principally Euroclear and

Clearstream. Euroclear is based in Brussels and Clearstream in Luxembourg. Originally Euroclear and Clearstream settled Eurobonds, but now they are used for a wide range of securities.

Major financial institutions hold cash and securities accounts at Clearstream and Euroclear. Securities in an institution's account are held either for its clients or itself, or for other institutions which themselves hold their securities for themselves or their clients.

Securities held on Euroclear and Clearstream are issued by crediting each participating institution's securities account with the amount of the stock it or its principals have subscribed for. Transfers are effected by debiting the securities account of the transferor and crediting that of the transferee. Corresponding debits and credits are made in the respective cash accounts of the institutions concerned. Interest and the proceeds of redemption are also paid through the cash accounts.

So far there is no paper in the system. However the company or governmental body issuing the security does issue a single instrument to a depositary, who then holds the instrument to the order of the clearing systems, ie Euroclear and Clearstream. This instrument is known as a global bond, and while in form it is a bearer bond, in substance it is never envisaged that it will leave the custody of the depositary. Further it is a single bond representing the whole issue: the depositary does not hold separate bearer bonds representing the separate holdings of each holder of the issue. In certain circumstances those holders are entitled to be issued with what are called definitive bonds, ie a physical bearer bond corresponding to their respective holdings. But normally such right arises only on default of the issuer or the clearing system.

The situs of immobilised securities is a much debated topic, of relevance to far wider issues than just tax. In a tax context, the debate has historically been expressed by reference to Eurobonds. The question is rendered complex by two factors in particular, namely the fact that Euroclear and Clearstream are governed by Belgian and Luxembourg law respectively and by the fact that there is no standard documentation package for immobilised securities.

No case law bears on the question. However the preponderance of textbook opinion is that the situs of immobilised securities is that of the clearing system in which they are held – ie Belgium or Luxembourg. This is the view taken in *Dicey* (at p 1125). It is also the conclusion reached, after extensive discussion with fellow lawyers, by *Joanna Benjamin* in her book *Interests in Securities* (Oxford, 2000) pp 158–9. In support of this view is the fact that Euroclear and Clearstream are registration systems on which the securities are effectively dealt. As such they are analogous to share registers, albeit that what is being dealt in is mainly debt rather than shares.

A contrary view fastens on the nature of the immobilised security and, where the securities are in fact debt, focuses on the position of the debtor. The debtor company or institution is under an enforceable obligation to pay interest and principal, and is also subject to default obligations such as that to issue definitive bonds. The whole bundle of obligations could be seen as a chose in action, situate where the issuing company resides.

A third view is that the relevant asset is the global bond, in which all holders of the security have an interest by virtue of the depositary holding it to the order of the clearing systems. As the global bond is in the form of a bearer bond, its situs on this analysis determine the situs of the security. This analysis, however, is rejected by both *Dicey* and *Benjamin*. In a technical sense, the fallacy in it is that the owners of the security are never entitled, even collectively, to have the global bond transferred to them. Instead, the most that they can require is the separate issue of definitive bonds (and the cancellation of all or a corresponding part of the global bond).

A further argument against the global bond determining the situs is that even though in form bearer, in practice it is never dealt in. As noted above (para 31.5), marketability is required for a negotiable instrument to determine situs. A final, practical, point, is that no investor is likely to know where the global bond is, many of them in fact being in London. It is difficult to see HMRC, or the Courts, being attracted by a solution which could damage the UK as a financial centre.

In the result, the choice as to situs is between the place of residence of the issuing institution and that of the relevant clearing system. Given that the clearing systems are outside the UK, the only practical area of difficulty is securities issued by UK companies or institutions. If it is desired to avoid UK situs assets, immobilised securities so issued should be avoided.

HMRC have given little guidance on this issue. In 1994 they did imply that investors holding Eurobonds would be treated as holding rights to and interests in a bearer security (see *Private Client Business* [1994], 139–40). This might be thought to imply that the situs of immobilised securities is that of the global bond. If so, it is at variance with the conclusions reached above, and, for the reasons there given, wrong. But HMRC's comments were prefaced by the caveat that the position depends on the terms of the issue. In any event their more recent comments indicate their position has altered, for in para IHTM 27077 of the Inheritance Tax Manual they say situs is determined by the terms of issue of the particular security in question.

ADRs and GDRs

31.15 Depositary receipts are issued by financial institutions. The institution concerned is holder of shares in a company, the shares being registered in either its name or that of a nominee. The institution issues depositary receipts to investors, each receipt representing a given number of the underlying shares. The depositary receipt concept was evolved in the United States, and the depositary is accepted as holding the underlying shares on trust for the owners of the receipts. Normally the depositary maintains a register on which the receipts are transferable but in the case of Global Depositary Receipts, a single receipt may be deposited with a depositary to the order of Euroclear and Clearstream. This then enables dealings in the GDRs to be cleared on those systems.

Given the trust relationship the logical conclusion, in the light of the previous discussion, would be that the investor's asset is the underlying shares rather than the depositary receipts. However, *Joanna Benjamin*, in her book *Interests in Securities* suggests that where depositary receipts are transferable on the register maintained by the financial institution, that register determines situs (see paras 11–14). In the case of GDRs traded on Euroclear or Clearstream, the same issues would arise as with other immobilised securities (see para 31.14).

Other financial products

31.16 Many financial products exist apart from those discussed above. Some raise equally difficult issues as to situs. But, in most cases, the difficulty is not identifying the relevant legal principles, but determining what legal relationships are entailed in the product. Careful analysis is needed, often on a case by case basis.

Chapter 32

CGT situs rules

Introduction

32.1 The situs of assets is relevant to CGT in two respects:

(1) Gains accruing to non-domiciled individuals on the disposal of foreign situs assets are taxable only insofar as remitted to the UK (TCGA 1992, s 12; see Chapter 41).
(2) Non-residents carrying on a trade or profession in the UK are taxed on gains accruing on certain assets situated in the UK (TCGA 1992, ss 10 and 10B; see para 30.6).

In contrast to Inheritance Tax, TCGA 1992 contains express statutory rules determining situs for the purposes of CGT. These rules, contained in TCGA 1992, ss 275–275C, form the subject matter of this chapter. The common law, as described in Chapter 31, applies only to assets whose situs is not covered by the statutory rules.

In view of the growing number of non-domiciliaries with personal investment portfolios, the rules are of considerable practical importance. In some cases the result they point to is unexpected, and for this reason they need to be watched with care.

Land

32.2 The situs of land is governed by the common law and thus is where the land is (cf para 31.2). However s 275(1)(a) does provide that the situation of rights or interests in or over immovable property is the same is that of the property itself. An exception is made for rights by way of security, which are therefore covered by the rules as to debts discussed below.

Tangible moveable property

32.3 As with land, the situation of tangible moveable property is left to the common law: it is where the property is (see para 31.2). This is a point which has to be watched by non-domiciliaries, for it means that the bringing of a chattel to the UK for sale results in any gain being taxed on an arising basis.

As with land, s 275(1)(b) provides that rights or interests over tangible moveable property have the same situation as the property itself.

Shares

32.4 For the purposes of the CGT situs rules, the term 'share' includes the interests in a company owned by the members if the company is of a kind which has no share capital (s 275(2)(a)). The term 'company' is defined for CGT purposes as including any body corporate or unincorporated association, but not a partnership (TCGA 1992, s 228(1)). As unit trusts are deemed for CGT purposes to be companies, save insofar as excluded by regulations, units in unit trusts also count as shares for these purposes (ibid s 99).

Municipal or governmental authority

32.5 A share or an asset treated as a share which is issued by a municipal or governmental authority has the situs of that authority (s 275(1)(d)). The same applies if the share is issued by a company created by such an authority.

UK incorporated company

32.6 Shares of a company incorporated in the UK are, in all circumstances, treated as situate in the UK (s 275(1)(da)). This follows the common law, save perhaps as to warrants to bearer. As is explained in para 31.9, it is widely believed the latter convert UK shares to foreign situs under the common law. Such is not the position for CGT purposes.

Registered shares

32.7 Registered shares are situate for CGT purposes where the register is situate or, if there is more than one register, where the principal register is situate (s 275(1)(e)). This follows the common law (see para 31.7) and is subject to the two rules just noted.

The term 'registered' is not defined. But by analogy with the common law, it presumably means shares where registration is required to constitute the holder a member as against the company.

Bearer shares

32.8 The CGT code makes no express provision as respects bearer shares, other than insofar as issued by a UK company or by a governmental or municipal authority. It follows that the common law applies (as to which see para 31.9).

ADRs and GDRs

32.9 The CGT code does not make express provision as to ADRs and GDRs (as to which see generally para 31.15). However, it may be suggested that if the underlying shares are registered in the name of the depositary or its nominee, they count as registered for the purposes of the above situs rules. This conclusion follows because it is difficult to see the owner of the ADRs or GDRs as otherwise than absolutely entitled to the underlying shares. Under TCGA 1992, s 60, property to which a person is absolutely entitled is treated as belonging to the beneficial owner.

Somewhat surprisingly HMRC consider that ADRs and GDRs involve two assets, namely the beneficial interest in the underlying shares and the depositary receipt itself (see Capital Gains Manual CG 50240–43). However, almost all the value is in the former asset and that, HMRC consider, has the same situs as the underlying shares.

Debts

32.10 The CGT situs rules differ most markedly from the common law in their application to debt. This is because, for CGT purposes, the basic rule is that a debt is situate in the UK if and only if the *creditor* is resident in the UK (TCGA 1992, s 275(1)(c)). This is so whether the debt is secured or unsecured, and is in contrast to the common law, where the basic determinant is the residence of the *debtor* (see para 31.4). But although the basic CGT rule looks to the creditor, there are important exceptions and these, cumulatively, make the basic rule the exception rather than the rule.

Judgment debts

32.11 A judgment debt is treated as situate where the judgement is recorded (s 275(1)(k)).

Non-domiciliary bank accounts

32.12 A bank account owned by a non-domiciliary who is resident in the UK is not situated in the UK unless it is in sterling or, if not in sterling, if the branch at which it maintained is in the UK (s 275(1)(l)). If follows that all non-UK foreign currency accounts of non-domiciliaries are situate outside the UK and so eligible for the remittance basis.

Debentures

32.13 The term debenture is not defined for CGT purposes. It therefore bears its common law meaning. That meaning is itself not wholly clear but the definition in *Halsbury* is that a debenture is a document which either creates or acknowledges a debt (*Halsbury's Laws*, vol 7(2) para 1533). It can be registered or bearer and in the latter event is negotiable (ibid para 1537). Section 275(2)(b) extends the definition in one respect, in that in relation to a person other than a company, the term debenture includes securities.

The situs rules as to debentures are similar to those pertaining to shares. They are as follows:

(1) debentures issued by a municipal or governmental authority (or by a body created by such authority) are situated in the country of that authority;
(2) debentures of a UK company are situate in the UK;
(3) registered debentures of any other kind are situated where the register is situated or, if there is more than one, where the principal register is situated.

Bearer bonds

32.14 As with bearer shares, the CGT rules make no express provision for bearer bonds (cf para 31.5). The rules listed above are, however, in point in two respects. First, government bonds are plainly securities if not debentures and so fall in the category of governmental debentures situate in the country of such government. Second, bonds issued by UK companies are situated in the UK assuming, as will almost invariably be the case, they can correctly be characterised as debentures.

But there remains an important category of bearer bond not covered by the above rules. This is bonds issued by non-UK companies and these, therefore, are covered by the basic creditor rule and so are situate in the UK if the creditor, ie the owner of the bond, is UK resident.

Immobilised securities

32.15 The difficulties over establishing the common law situs of immobilised securities are explained in para 31.14. The application of the CGT situs rules is equally difficult.

The first point is whether, when immobilised, government or municipal bonds still count as issued by the governmental or municipal authority. It is difficult to avoid the conclusion that they do. The second point is similar and is whether debt issued by a UK company counts as debentures of that company when immobilised. Here too it is difficult to see the answer as being other than affirmative and, if so, there is nothing in the CGT situs rules preventing bonds issued by UK companies from having a UK situs.

The third and most difficult point concerns bonds issued by foreign companies. Here what the company itself issues or commits itself to issue is normally bearer in form, albeit that transfers of the stock are effected through Euroclear and Clearstream. In those circumstances can it be said that registered debentures exist? There is much to be said for the answer being negative and, if so, the practical result is that most foreign corporate bonds owned by non-domiciliaries resident in the UK have a UK situs under the basic creditor rule noted above.

This last is a surprising conclusion, and hardly one would expect was intended. The reference in TCGA 1992, s 275 to registered debentures dates back only to 2005. Before then the term used was 'registered securities', which term may not have raised the same difficulties where securities are immobilised. This is because the primary meaning of 'security' is a debt or claim, the payment of which is in some way secured (see *Singer v Williams* [1921] 7 TC 419, 431 per Viscount Cave). It may thus be easier to describe bonds held through Euroclear and Clearstream as registered securities then as registered debentures.

A possible solution to the problem (if such it be) may be suggested by s 275(2)(b). As noted above this provides that, in relation to a person other than a company, references to debentures include securities. The context indicates this is intended to cover debt where the issuer is not a company. But the words 'in relation to a person other than a company' could be wide enough to refer also to the holder of the debt, and if so the position as respects non-domiciliaries resident in the UK in relation to foreign immobilised securities is the same as it was before the 2005 changes.

Intellectual property

32.16 Patents, trademarks, and registered designs are situated where they are registered or, in the case of multiple registration, where any register is situate (s 275(1)(h)). Licences or other rights are situate in the UK if exercisable there (ibid). Copyright, design right, and franchises therefrom are situate in the UK if exercisable in the UK or if any right derived therefrom is exercisable in the UK (s 275(1)(j)).

Goodwill

32.17 The goodwill of a business is situate where the business is carried on (s 275(1)(g)).

Other intangibles

32.18 The CGT situs of many forms of intangible property is given by the rules described above. But where this is not so, s 275A provides that the intangible is for CGT purposes situate in the UK if at the time it is created it is subject to UK law (s 275A(3)). An intangible is treated as being subject to UK law if it or any right or interest forming part of it is governed by or enforceable under UK law (s 275B(2)).

Options and futures

32.19 An option or future which is not subject to UK law is deemed to be so subject, and thus situate in the UK, if the underlying subject mater is treated as UK situate under any of the CGT situs rules other than s 275A itself (s 275A(8)). Although the wording of s 275A is obscure, it appears that the same result follows with options and futures where the underlying subject matter is an intangible whose situs is deemed to be in the UK under s 275A itself.

For the purpose of these rules, the terms 'future' and 'option' bear the meanings given to them in the corporation tax rules pertaining to derivative contracts (s 275B(3); FA 2002 Sch 20). Thus a future is a contract for the sale of property at an agreed date and price (Sch 20 para 12(6)). The term 'option' includes warrants, warrants being defined as instruments entitling the holder to subscribe for shares or corporate debt (Sch 20 para 12(8), (9)). A contract is neither a future nor an option if it provides for cash payment rather than the delivery of any property (Sch 20 para 12(10)).

Intangibles not subject to UK law

32.20 Should an intangible be neither in fact subject to UK law, nor deemed to be so under s 275A, its situs is not affected by s 275A. Unless therefore the intangible falls within one of the categories described earlier in this chapter, its situs for CGT purposes is governed by the common law. In broad terms such intangibles are choses in action, the situs of which under common law is where they are enforceable. As explained in para 31.3, this is normally the place of residence of the person against whom the right is enforceable.

Relevance to non-domiciliaries

32.21 Many investment products are intangibles which are neither shares nor debt. As such their CGT situs is likely to be governed by the rules just described. In some cases, the result will be that investment products thought to be non-UK situate are, for CGT purposes, in fact situate in the UK. Careful analysis of the product in question is required.

Co-owners

32.22 TCGA 1992, s 275C expressly provides that a co-ownership interest has the same situs as that of the underlying asset.

Chapter 33

Source

Introduction

33.1 The word 'source' is the colloquial term used to discuss whether income arises in or is derived from the UK. Thus income has a UK source if it arises in the UK and a non-UK source if it does not. As will be apparent from paras 30.2 to 30.4, the source of income is significant. The foreign-source income of non-residents is not (bar anti-avoidance legislation) taxable and that of resident non-domiciliaries is taxable only if remitted.

There is much case law on what constitutes the source of income. An important preliminary observation is that the source of investment income is not necessarily the situs of the asset generating the income: thus dividends are sourced not where the shares are situate but where the paying company is resident.

Rental income

33.2 Rental income has a UK source if the land is in the UK, and a foreign source if it is not. Foreign rental income is computed in the same way as UK rental income, but treated as a separate letting business (ITTOIA 2005, s 265).

Dividends

33.3 Dividends and other distributions from a company have a UK source if the company paying the dividend is UK resident (ITTOIA 2005, s 382). This is so even if the company paying the dividend is registered abroad or the shares are otherwise foreign situs (*Bradbury v English Sewing Cotton Co Ltd* [1923] AC 744). Conversely, if a now rare non-resident UK registered company (see para 38.27) pays a dividend, that has a foreign source.

Should a foreign entity not fall to be treated as a company for UK tax purposes, the source of any income is the underlying assets or business of the entity, the income arising to the owners of the entity when it arises in the entity. The circumstances in which a foreign entity falls to be treated as transparent are considered in Chapter 35.

A distribution paid by a foreign company is not taxed as income if it is a dividend of a capital nature (ITTOIA 2005, s 402(4)). In determining whether a dividend is income or capital, it is necessary to determine the nature of the receipt under the proper law of the company concerned and then English law is applied to determine whether a receipt of that nature is income or capital (cf *Inchyra (Baron) v Jennings* (1965) 42 TC 388, 400 per Pennycuick J).

This is illustrated by two decisions of the House of Lords. First, in *IRC v Reid's Trustees* [1949] 30 TC 431, a dividend paid out of capital profits by a South African company was held to be income for the corpus of the asset, namely the shares, remained intact. Second, in *Rae v Lazard Investments Co Ltd* [1963] 41 TC 1 a distribution by a Maryland company in what was essentially a form of reconstruction was held to be capital, for it was a return of capital under the proper law of the company concerned.

When it comes to the second stage of applying English law, form has traditionally prevailed, with the result that a payment is income if it cannot be characterised a reduction of capital, a repayment of share premium, or as paid in liquidation. But recent cases have shown some tendency to look behind the form and consider the substance. *Rae v Lazard Investment Co Ltd* was one example, and another is *Courtaulds Investments Ltd v Fleming* (1969) 46 TC 111 where Buckley J treated the repayment of a share premium reserve in an Italian company to the shareholders as capital. What does however remain clear is that any straightforward distribution of realised profits otherwise than in liquidation is income. This is so whether the profits were income profits or realised on the sale of capital assets. *IRC v Reid's Trustees* is authority for this and no later case has called the proposition into question.

The specific UK rules determining what, for income tax purposes, counts as a distribution are not in point as they apply only where the company is UK resident (ITTOIA 2005, s 382). However, the cases on UK company distributions decided before the introduction of that system are good law in determining how receipts from foreign companies should be taxed. Indeed such cases were cited in *Rae v Lazard Investment Co Ltd.*

Partnerships

33.4 ITTOIA 2005, s 848 provides that, where a trade or profession is carried on in partnership, the partnership is not to be treated as a separate entity for income tax purposes. Section 848 applies to all partnerships, including non-trading partnerships. It follows that the source of a partner's share in the income is not the partnership contract but the underlying assets or business (*Memec plc v IRC* [1998] SC 754, 763, CA).

Contractual rights

33.5 Where on the facts a contract is not mere machinery but has an independent vitality it is the source of payments made under it (*Memec plc v*

IRC, supra). Where the rights are to income, the source of such income is where the contract is enforceable (*Alloway v Phillips* [1980] STC 490).

Interest

33.6 Determining the source of interest can be difficult. The matter is governed by case-law rather than statute.

The cases

33.7 The leading case is colloquially known as the Greek case, *National Bank of Greece SA v Westminster Bank Executor and Trustee Co (Channel Islands) Ltd* (1970) 46 TC 472. Here a Greek bank had issued bonds guaranteed by another Greek bank. The bonds were secured on Greek assets and on the facts the funds to pay the interest would have had to come from Greece. Principal and interest were payable in London or in Greece by cheque drawn on London. However, retrospective Greek legislation meant the only place where the debt could be enforced had come to be the guarantor's branch in London.

The House of Lords held that the interest did not have an English source, pointing out that the mere substitution of an English guarantor was not sufficient to move the source of the interest. The reasoning in the House of Lords concluded with the following cryptic sentence:

> 'the bond itself is a foreign document, and the obligations to pay principal and interest to which the bond gives rise were obligations whose source is to be found in this document.'

In an earlier case, *IRC v Viscount Broome's Executors* (1935) 19 TC 667 an individual resident in both Kenya and England had incurred a debt to a Kenyan resident. The security was in both Kenya and England and under the terms of the contract the interest was payable in Kenya. But when the debtor died his executors were English and they paid interest in England out of English assets. Finlay J stated that the interest has a UK source if paid by a UK resident out of a source in the UK and decided that on the facts those conditions were both met.

A third case is *Hafton Properties Ltd v McHugh* [1987] STC 16. Here a UK company purchased a US property subject to two mortgages. One of the mortgages it took over and serviced in the US out of the US rental income. The other it paid off, funding the payment with a short-term unsecured facility from a Swiss bank, which it serviced from the UK out of its UK resources. The Special Commissioner decided that the interest on the first loan did not have a UK source, whereas the interest on the Swiss facility did. His decision on these points was not appealed.

Factors to take into account

33.8 It is clear from these cases that the place where the payment of the interest is enforceable is not decisive of where the source of the interest is. Had the place where payment was enforceable been decisive, the source of the interest in the Greek case would have been in the UK as that was the only place where payment could be enforced.

It is also clear, secondly, that the place of the debtor's residence is not decisive either. All three cases listed above make it clear that other factors have to be looked at as well. Had place of residence been decisive, the Greek case could have been decided on the simple ground that Greece was where the original debtor and the guarantor resided.

A third point is that the source of funds and the place at which payment is made are important. This is particularly apparent from *IRC v Broome's Executors* where, in formulating the test he applied, Finlay J referred back to Lord Herschell's classic definition of territoriality in *Colquhoun v Brooks* (1889) 2 TC 490, 499 (see para 30.2 above). Here Lord Herschell makes it clear that if the taxpayer is not resident in the UK, 'that from which the taxable income is derived' must be situate in the UK if income is to be taxed.

A factor which appears not to be relevant is the situs of the debt: in the Greek case, Lord Denning's judgment in the Court of Appeal makes it clear the bond in question was a bearer bond (see 46 TC 472, 486). Yet that fact had no bearing on the eventual decision in the House of Lords and, indeed, the case does not disclose where the bonds were physically situate.

Another factor which is not relevant is the proper law of the debt. This too is apparent from the Greek case, where earlier litigation makes it clear that the proper law had been held to be English (*Adams v National Bank of Greece* [1960] 2 All ER 421). Yet despite this Lord Hailsham LC was still able to conclude, in the passage cited above, that the bond was a 'foreign' document. The unimportance of proper law is also indicated by *IRC v Broome's Executors*, where proper law is not mentioned at all.

An issue which is less clear is whether the source of interest is determined once and for all when the debt is first created, or whether it can move. In *Hafton Properties Ltd v McHugh*, the Special Commissioner cited the Greek case as signifying a disinclination to view source as peripatetic. In fact on a close reading it does not do this, but merely focuses on the fact that the location of the obligation could not change merely because changes in Greek law meant that the only way the debt could be enforced was against the guarantor in London. *IRC v Broome's Executors* indicates source can be peripatetic, in that in that case it is clear Finlay J was looking purely at the position of the executors and how they funded the interest rather than at the position before the original debtor died.

Conclusion

33.9 As a result of the above analysis the conclusion must be that in determining the source of interest it is necessary, as in the Greek case, to look at all the facts. *IRC v Broome's Executors* was not cited in the Greek case. But its conclusion is entirely consistent with the Greek case, namely that one must look at both the residence of the debtor and at the place where the interest is paid and how it is funded.

Practice

33.10 In *Tax Bulletin 9* (1993) 100 HMRC state that their view on the location of source is based on the Greek case. They extrapolate from the case four factors which they regard as important, namely the residence of the debtor, the source from which the interest is paid, where it is paid, and the nature and location of any security. HMRC state that if all four factors point to the UK, the interest has UK source. What is not indicated in *Tax Bulletin* is the position if some only of the factors are in the UK but a reasonable inference is that HMRC would not necessarily assert a UK source.

At one time HMRC took the view that interest payable by a UK company would not have a UK source if it was paid abroad to a non-resident in foreign currency under a foreign specialty, with no security in the UK (IR letter 22 January 1980). Subsequently HMRC revised their view and stated that a loan to a UK company normally does give rise to taxable interest (IR letter 17 February 1982), regardless of whether there is a specialty.

More recently, the Inspector's Manual (at para 3940) refers with approval to *Tax Bulletin 9* and lists the four factors enumerated above. It then refers to the proposition that 'interest paid by a UK resident should generally be paid under deduction of tax'.

The Manual says this proposition should be modified in two respects. One is that interest paid by a foreign branch of a UK company is regarded as having a foreign source if the loan was raised for the purposes of the foreign branch's business, and conversely that interest paid by the UK branch of a foreign company is regarded as having a UK source if the loan was raised for the purposes of the UK branch's business. The second modification is that interest paid by a UK resident individual is not regarded as having a UK source if it is payable abroad on an overseas loan which (a) was taken out to buy an overseas asset or for some other overseas purposes, and (b) is not secured on UK property. Interestingly, and in contrast to companies, the Manual does not suggest the contrary is true – ie that interest on a loan taken out by a foreigner in the UK to buy UK property has a UK source.

It is plain from this that HMRC practice is and has for many years been in a muddle. Nonetheless it is fair to say that practitioners advising the corporate sector do generally adopt the so called proposition in the Manual and advise treating payments of interest by UK resident companies to foreign lenders as having a UK source. But such does not really advance the argument as (absent a foreign branch) most interest is likely to be paid in the UK and/or out of UK funds.

The correct stance for practitioners to take, it may be suggested, is to avail themselves of the Manual in those cases where it plainly says interest is not regarded as having a UK source. Otherwise it is to be stressed that the Greek case represents the law, and that the *Tax Bulletin* article stands as a considered

HMRC statement of the effect of the case. Thus it may be concluded that interest paid in the UK by a UK resident to a non-resident has a UK source. But conversely interest paid by a UK resident to a non-resident abroad out of funds abroad does not, even if the circumstances are outside those suggested in the Manual.

Reform

33.11 In December 2003, the government initiated a consultation on replacing the present rules as to the source of interest with a statutory rule. This did not result in legislation.

Trading income

Non-residents

33.12 The profits of a trade carried on by a non-resident have a UK source and so are taxable if he is trading in the UK (ITTOIA 2005, s 6(2)). If, however, he is merely trading with the UK, there is no UK source and the trade is not taxable in the UK.

The basic test

33.13 The test of whether or not a person is trading in the UK is a common law one. At one time the place where the contracts of sale were made was thought to be decisive (*Grainger & Son v Gough* [1896] AC 325, 3 TC 462). If the contracts of sale were made in the UK the trade was carried on in the UK and if they were not it was not. Now, however, it is clear that this is only the position where the trade is pure merchanting. The general test is where the operations take place from which the profits in substance arise (*Firestone Tyre and Rubber Co Ltd v Llewellin* [1957] 37 TC 111). Thus a manufacturing trade is carried on in the UK if the manufacturing takes place here and a trade involving the provision of services is carried on in the UK if the services are performed here (cf *IRC v Brackett* [1986] STC 521).

In *IRC v Hang Seng Bank Ltd* [1990] STC 733 at 739 the Privy Council gave useful guidance. Lord Bridge expressed himself as follows:

> 'The broad guiding principle … is that one looks to see what the taxpayer has done to earn the profit in question. If he has rendered a service or engaged in an activity such as the manufacture of goods, the profit will have arisen or derived from the place where the service was rendered or the profit making activity carried on. But if the profit was earned by the exploitation of property assets as by letting property, lending money or dealing in commodities or securities by

buying and reselling at a profit, the profit will have arisen in or derived from the place where the property was let, the money was lent or the contracts of purchase and sale were effected.'

The case concerned the question of whether, for Hong Kong tax purposes, profits generated by dealing in certificates of deposit were arising in or derived from Hong Kong. But Lord Bridge's observations apply equally to the distinction between trading in and with the UK (cf *Yates v GCA International Ltd* [1991] STC 157 at 172 and *IRC v HK-TVB International Ltd* [1992] STC 723 at 729). In the latter case Lord Jauncey affirmed that the proper approach is to ascertain what were the operations which produced the relevant profits and where those operations took place.

Non-trading activities

33.14 Case law has established that two forms of activity do not amount to trading in the UK:

(1) Purchasing goods or services in the UK for use in the business abroad (*Sulley v A-G* (1860) 2 TC 149).
(2) Representative offices, sales promotions, or after-sale services, provided the contracts of sale and other trading activities are made or carried on abroad (*Greenwood v FL Smidth & Co* (1922) 8 TC 193 HL).

Extent of charge

33.15 If a non-resident is trading in the UK, the profits are fully in charge to UK tax if the trade is carried on wholly in the UK. But if the trade is partly carried on abroad, only the profits arising from the part carried on in the UK are taxable (ITTOIA 2005, s 6). This gives statutory effect to previous practice as published in *Tax Bulletin 18* (August 1995 p 238).

In such cases, there is obviously scope for disagreement in determining what proportion of the overall profit is attributable to the UK. In practice HMRC apply the same criteria as are laid down in the Permanent Establishment Article of Double Tax Treaties. Accordingly, it is necessary to ascertain what the profits of the UK operation would be if it was a separate enterprise dealing on arm's length terms with the rest of the business (*Tax Bulletin 18* (August 1995) p 238). Accordingly, the transfer-pricing criteria discussed in Chapter 68 apply.

Branch, agent, or permanent establishment

33.16 Assuming the trading in the UK is being carried on by an individual through a branch or agency, the branch or agent is assessable on behalf of the non-resident as his UK representative (FA 1995, s 126). In the case of companies the charge is to corporation tax and arises if the trade is being carried on through a permanent establishment (TA 1988, s 11(1)). Certain types of investment trade carried on by a non-resident through a broker or investment manager are excepted from these charges. This is discussed further in Chapter 34.

Resident trading abroad

33.17 The converse question as to whether a non-resident is carrying on a trade in the UK is whether a UK resident trading abroad can ever be said not to be carrying on the trade, at least in part in the UK. An old Scottish case is generally taken as authority that he cannot and that the profits of the trade are fully in charge to UK tax (*Ogilvie v Kitton* (1908) 5 TC 338). But where a partnership is trading wholly or partly abroad and is controlled and managed abroad, a partner who is resident in the UK but not domiciled there can treat his share of the trading profits arising outside the UK as relevant foreign income (ITTOIA 2005, s 857). As such they attract the remittance basis described in Chapter 40.

Income from trusts

33.18 The discussion of trust distributions at para 12.2 indicates that the source of a life-tenant's income is the underlying investments if the trust is governed by English law or a law which in this matter follows English law. Should the governing law be New York law or a law which is similar to New York law, the life-tenant's asset is a right as against the trustees to have the trust duly administered and the net income paid over to him or applied for his benefit. So too a discretionary beneficiary has merely a right against the trustee to have the trust duly administered and the right to such income as the trustee decides to give him.

The result is that where the trust's proper law follows English law the source of the life-tenant's income is that of the underlying income, determined as per the rules outlined earlier in this chapter. In other trust cases, the location of the source of the beneficiary's income is wherever the beneficiary's rights as against the trustee can be said to be located.

There is little direct authority on where such source is located. However in *Drummond v Collins* (1915) 6 TC 525, 534, the Court of Appeal described the US trust fund at issue in that case as a 'possession' in America. Also relevant is *Memec plc v IRC*. Here, at first instance, Robert Walker J said that the exercise of the trustee's discretion is regarded as creating a new source of income (see [1996] STC 1336, 1351). So too in *Inchyra (Baron) v Jennings* (1965) 42 TC 388 Pennycuick J described the source of the beneficiary's income as the trust estate, together with the right to have that estate applied for her benefit.

The inference to be drawn is that the source of the payments a beneficiary receives under a discretionary trust is located where the trustees reside and exercise their discretion.

Distributions from mutual funds

33.19 As described in Chapter 4, non-UK mutual funds represent an increasingly large part of most investment portfolios. For the most part mutual funds are in form either open-ended investment companies or unit trusts.

OEICs

33.20 As an open-ended investment company is a company, any income paid out to the investor is dividend. The location of its source is therefore determined by the rules given in para 33.3 above.

Unit Trusts

33.21 In contrast to CGT, the income tax code does not deem non-resident unit trusts to be companies. As a matter of general law, the legal form is that each unit-holder owns an undivided share in the investments and cash which from time to time comprise the funds in the unit trust (*M & G Securities v IRC* [1999] STC 315, 322, per Park J). Accordingly the issue is whether the source of the unit-holder's income is the underlying investments or his right against the trustee or manager of the unit trust.

A unit trust differs from a private, family trust in that the relationship is a mix of trust and contract. But as the case of *Memec plc v IRC* [1998] STC 754 shows, the family trust cases may be applicable in commercial contexts. The identity of the unit-holder's income should therefore be determined in accordance with the principles applicable to life-interest trusts, described in para 33.18 above. In other words if, as a matter of construction, the unit-holders are entitled to have the income after expenses paid out to them, the source is the underlying investments. But if the terms of the unit trust require the income to be retained and invested, any distributions are a new source, located where the trustee resides and the payment is made.

At first sight, this latter conclusion may be inconsistent with HMRC practice, as published in the Inspector's Manual (IM 1517). This states that:

> 'Normally a United Kingdom resident shareholder in a foreign unit trust is assessable under Case V by reference to his share of the income of the fund whether this is paid out to him in cash or used to purchase additional units.'

However, the inconsistency may be more apparent than real, for the Manual does not refer to retention and reinvestment of the income but to its application in paying up further units. The distinction is admittedly one of form rather than substance, but in the case of additional units, the unit-holder does receive something, whereas with simple accumulation he does not. A further point is that foreign unit trusts are included in the offshore fund legislation (see para 71.3). If all foreign unit trusts are transparent, this would be otiose, as none would in any event operate as an income shelter.

That unit trusts which simply accumulate are in practice to be regarded as opaque may be reinforced by HMRC's general observations on entity characterisation in *Tax Bulletin 83* (as to which see further para 35.8). The two points to which particular attention is paid in determining whether an entity is opaque or transparent are who carries on the business and whether the amount of profits to which members are entitled depends on a decision of the entity or its members. Both these factors point to a unit trust being opaque if it is able to accumulate its profits and is not required to distribute them or pay up further units.

The conclusion that certain types of unit trust are opaque is, of course, without prejudice as to how capital receipts on the sale or redemption of units are taxed. As described elsewhere (Chapters 4 and 71), unless the fund is a distributor fund these are subjected to income tax under the offshore fund legislation.

Immobilised securities

33.22 Immobilised securities are discussed in relation to situs in para 31.14. No special rules apply to determine where the source of the interest they generate is located. The matter should thus be determined by the principles outlined in para 33.8. The choice is between the residence of the issuing company and the situs of the relevant clearing system (ie Belgium or Luxembourg) (cf para 31.14). As the latter is abroad, this means issues as to source really only arise with securities issued by UK companies.

In practice, as is noted in para 33.8, it is generally accepted that if the borrowing company is a UK company, the interest has a UK source. It never seems to have been suggested that the holding of securities through Euroclear and Clearstream moves the source of the interest abroad. As explained in para 34.6,TA 1988, s 349(3)(c) removes the requirement to deduct tax at source on quoted Eurobonds, but it does not mean the interest ceases to have a UK source.

ADRs and GDRs

33.23 It is generally accepted that the source of dividends received by the holders of American Depositary Receipts and Global Depositary Receipts is the underlying shares. As a matter of law, this may be regarded as correct, for the owner of the ADR or GDR has a specific entitlement to dividends in the same sense a life-tenant does under an English trust.

Chapter 34

UK income of non-residents

Introduction

34.1 This chapter details what tax is suffered by non-residents on UK source investment income and how such tax is secured. The issue of whether income has a UK source is addressed in the previous chapter.

Basic charging rules

Individuals

34.2 In the absence of specific relieving provisions, the basic rule is that non-resident individuals suffer both basic and higher rate tax on their UK-source income. In general personal allowances are not available, but the benefit of the allowances may be claimed by Commonwealth citizens, nationals of the European Economic Area and residents of the Channel Islands and the Isle of Man (TA 1988, s 278(2); FA 1996, s 145).

Trusts

34.3 Non-resident discretionary or accumulation trusts are charged at the rate for trusts on their UK source income (see TA 1988, s 686 and *IRC v Regent Trust Co Ltd* [1980] STC 140). This liability extends, as respects all forms of trust, to capital receipts treated as income for the purposes of the rate applicable to trusts insofar as such receipts have a UK source (TA 1988, s 686A).The position of trusts is considered further in para 34.15.

Companies

34.4 A non-resident company is not subject to corporation tax save insofar as it is trading in the UK through a permanent establishment (TA 1988, s 11). If it is so trading, the corporation tax charge is on profits attributable to the permanent establishment and on gains realised on property used or held for the purposes of the permanent establishment (TA 1988, s 11AA; TCGA 1992, s 10B).

UK income of other non-resident companies, however, is not outside the charge to tax. The residual liability to income tax remains. There is no provision imposing higher rate tax (cf TA 1988, ss 1(2) and 6(2)), so the liability is to lower rate tax in the case of UK savings income and to basic rate tax in the case of other UK income such as rental income (cf TA 1988, s 1A).

Withholding taxes

34.5 In many instances the UK secures basic or lower rate tax by requiring deduction at source (cf TA 1988, s 4(1) (1A)).

Interest

34.6 The principal section requiring deduction at source is TA 1988, s 349. Section 349(2)(c) applies to yearly interest paid to a person whose usual place of abode is outside the UK. It requires the person by or through whom the interest is paid to deduct lower rate tax and account for it to HMRC. If he fails to deduct, he is still accountable to the HMRC and cannot recoup out of future payments to the non-resident.

There are a number of exceptions to section 349(2)(c), of which the following are the most important in the present context:

(a) In its terms it does not apply to short interest, ie interest on a loan which cannot last more than a year.
(b) It does not apply to relevant foreign income (s 349(3)(za)). This means it only applies if the interest has a UK source (ITTOIA 2005, s 830).
(c) Interest paid by banks in the ordinary course of their business is expressly excluded (s 349(3)(b)).
(d) Interest on all quoted Eurobonds is exempted (s 349(3)(c)). For this purpose the term 'quoted Eurobond' means any security issued by a company which is listed on a recognised stock exchange and carries interest (s 349(4)).
(e) Interest on all gilt-edged securities is payable gross (TA 1988, s 50(A1)). Interest on other public revenue dividends (other than local authority stock) is, however, subject to withholding (s 349(3C)).
(f) The element of discount on the redemption of deep discount securities is not subject to withholding tax (ITTOIA 2005, ss 427–460).
(g) Section 349 does not apply to building society interest (TA 1988, s 477A(7)).
(h) Section 349 does not apply to interest paid by a dealer in financial instruments who is authorised under the Financial Services and Markets Act 2000 (s 349(3)(i)).
(i) Even where tax on interest may otherwise be withheld, this is subject to the applicable double tax treaty if the recipient of the interest is resident in a treaty country. In such cases the recipient may apply for the rate of

withholding tax to be reduced to the level prescribed by the treaty (see Double Taxation Relief (Taxes on Income) (General) Regulations 1970 (SI 1970/488) and Centre for Non-Residents (CNR) Guidance Note 8).

Although bank interest is excluded from section 349(2)(c), deduction at source is required under other rules if the recipient is either an individual or a discretionary or accumulation trust (TA 1988, s 481(4)). This rule, however, is displaced in the case of an individual if he declares to the bank that he is not ordinarily resident in the UK and includes his name and address in the declaration (TA 1988, s 481(5)(k)).

The rule is displaced in the case of a non-resident trust if the trustees declare that they are not ordinarily resident in the UK and do not have any reasonable grounds for believing that any of the beneficiaries are (TA 1988, s 481(5)(k)). For the purposes of this provision, the term beneficiary means an actual or potential beneficiary who is, will, or may become entitled to the income of the trust, or a person who is the object of any discretion over income (TA 1988, s 482(5A)). It is unclear whether the reference to potential beneficiaries extends the definition to persons who could be added as beneficiaries in exercise of a power to that effect, but HMRC's view is that it does not (see the Financial Intermediaries and Claims Office Newsletter No 3, January 1999).

Deduction at source in respect of building society interest is governed by The Income Tax (Building Societies) (Dividends and Interest) Regulations 1990 (SI 1990/2231). Interest may be paid gross if the recipient is a non-resident individual and makes a declaration to the building society to that effect giving his name and address (regs 4(1)(a) and 11). Interest paid to companies is paid gross, as is interest paid to the trustees if all persons beneficially interested are non-resident (reg 4(1)(b), (g)).

The EU Savings Directive of 3 June 2003 does not impose any obligation on UK payers to withhold tax. As is explained in Chapter 50, this is because the UK has opted for exchange of information (Reporting of Savings Income Information Regulations 2003 (SI 2003/3297)).

Dividends

34.7 Strictly-speaking, dividends are not subject to deduction of tax at source. Instead the general rule in the UK is that a tax credit mechanism operates (TA 1988, s 231).

This rule does not, however, apply to non-residents unless the non-resident in receipt of the dividends is an individual within one of those categories of non-resident individual eligible for the personal allowance (ITTOIA 2005, s 397). Instead non-residents are treated as having paid tax at the dividend ordinary rate of 10% (ITTOIA 2005, s 399). In the case of non-resident companies, this discharges liability to UK tax. Non-resident discretionary or accumulation trusts are treated as receiving the dividends grossed up by tax at the dividend ordinary rate (s 399(4)). The trustees are then liable to UK tax on the gross dividend at the dividend trust rate of 32.5% with credit for the 10% tax treated as paid. The effective rate of tax on the net dividend is therefore

25%. Grossing-up also applies to dividends received by non-resident individuals, but the reliefs described below (para 34.14) mean that this is of academic significance only.

Save where a treaty provides to the contrary the tax treated as withheld cannot be recovered, but equally no tax is withheld from the dividend itself. This absence of withholding tax on dividends is one of the factors which makes the UK attractive for inward investment, meaning as it does that the only tax on profits distributed to non-resident investors is corporation tax on the UK company's profits.

Authorised investment funds

34.8 A distribution from an authorised fund is either shown as interest or as dividend. In the latter event the rules applicable to dividends described above are in point. But should the distribution be shown as interest, the general rule is that lower rate tax must be deducted at source under TA 1988, s 349 (2) (The Authorised Investment Funds (Tax Regulations 2006 (SI 2006/964) (reg 26)). But this is disapplied if a reputable intermediary receives the interest on behalf of a non-resident or if the recipient is an individual and has made a declaration in the prescribed form that he is non-resident (regs 26(4), 27 and 30). Fixed-interest trusts can satisfy this latter condition if the life-tenant is non-resident. Such a declaration may be made by the trustees of a discretionary trust if the trustees are also non-resident and all actual or potential beneficiaries known to the trustees are non-resident (regulations 30(6) and 32).

Other income

34.9 TA 1988, s 349(1) requires deduction at source from other categories of income, notably annual payments and patent royalties. Other legislative provisions apply section 349 to further kinds of income paid to persons whose usual place of abode is outside the UK, for example copyright royalties (TA 1988, s 536). The instance most frequently encountered used to be rent, where the tenant had to deduct tax at source if he made payment direct to a non-resident landlord. Now, however, rental payments are governed by the rules as to UK representatives described at para 34.13.

UK representatives

34.10 Many non-residents investing or trading in the UK use a UK representative of some kind. Such a representative may be a fund manager managing a portfolio, or a property professional looking after investment property. In either event the issue arises of whether the representative is assessable to tax on behalf of the non-resident.

Two sets of provisions have to be considered as regards this. One, FA 1995, ss 126, 127 and FA 2003, s 150, applies where the non-resident is carrying on any trade, profession or vocation in the UK. The other, TA 1988, s 42A, applies to rental income. It is to be stressed that, apart from these two sets of provisions the investment income of a non-resident cannot be assessed in the name of a UK resident

Traders in the UK

34.11 FA 1995, s 126 applies to the branch or agency through which a non-resident individual or trust carries on the trade, profession or vocation in the UK. The branch or agency is what is called the non-resident's 'UK representative' and is assessable by virtue of FA 1995, s 126(2) on behalf of the non-resident in respect of:

(a) trading profits arising directly or indirectly through the branch or agency, and
(b) income and capital gains from property or rights used by, or held by or for the branch or agency.

As UK representative, the branch or agency is under the same compliance obligations as the non-resident principal (FA 1995, Sch 23). The UK representative has an express right to a full indemnity from the principal.

FA 2003, s 150 makes comparable provision in relation to companies trading in the UK through a permanent establishment. The permanent establishment is the UK company's representative for the purposes of corporation tax as respects the establishment's chargeable profits.

Investment income

34.12 It is to be stressed that these rules do not catch investment income or gains unless the income or gain accrues on assets of the branch or agency or permanent establishment. In theory they can apply where the investment activities themselves amount to trading in the UK. But in practice in such cases the UK representative is normally protected from assessment as a representative.

In the case of individuals and trusts, this is because FA 1995, s 127 exempts certain types of agent in respect of certain types of transaction. These exemptions are as follows:

(a) A person not carrying on the regular agency of the non-resident is not a UK representative of the non-resident.
(b) A broker is not a UK representative in relation to transactions carried out through him if he is acting in the ordinary course of business on normal commercial terms, and he is not otherwise the non-resident's representative.

(c) An investment manager is not a UK representative in relation to investment transactions carried out through him if the transactions are carried out in the ordinary course of business on normal commercial terms.

For the purposes of the last of these exemptions, 'investment transaction' is defined in FA 1995, s 127(12) as follows:

(i) transactions in shares, stock, futures contracts, options contracts or securities of any description (excluding futures or options relating to land). A contract is not prevented from being a futures or option contract merely because obligations are settled by a payment of a sum of money (section 127(13));
(ii) buying or selling foreign currency or the placing of money at interest.

The Treasury has power to add other kinds of transaction, but no power to delete any category of transaction. The power has been used to add certain swap contracts (SI 2003/2172).

The exemption for investment managers is excluded if the manager is the non-resident's agent for other purposes (section 127(3)(f)). It is also necessary for the manager to act in what is called an independent capacity (section 127(3)(c)). This means the relationship between them must be at arm's length (section 127(18)). In practice HMRC regard that test as satisfied inter alia where less than 70% of the manager's business comes from the non-resident or persons connected with him (SP 1/01, paras 18, 19).

A further requirement is that the investment manager and persons connected with him must not together have an interest amounting to 20% or more in the non-resident's relevant excluded income (section 127(4)). For these purposes the relevant excluded income is income derived from investment transactions carried out though the manager which are otherwise exempt under FA 1995, s 128 (see para 34.14 below). This complex exception is explained more fully in SP 1/01 at paras 24–31. Even where it applies it only exposes the manager to tax on the proportion of the income in which he is interested, and self-evidently it is of no relevance where the non-resident and the portfolio manager are quite unconnected.

Similar provisions are made for companies in that a non-resident company is not regarded as having a permanent establishment where it carries on UK business through an agent of independent status acting in the ordinary course of such business (FA 2003, s 148(3)). Brokers and investment managers count as agents of independent status if the various conditions set out above for brokers and investment managers acting for individuals and trusts are met (FA 2003, Sch 26).

Rental income

34.13 TA 1988, s 42A applies where the usual place of abode of the person receiving the rents is outside the UK. The test based on usual place of abode differs from the tests of residence and ordinary residence which are used elsewhere in the UK tax code. In some cases, a person with his usual place of abode outside the UK may be resident here, as where he has no home in the UK but makes regular visits in excess of 90 days per tax year.

Section 42A is largely an enabling section, permitting the necessary regulations to be made. The regulations in question are The Taxation of Income from Land (Non-residents) Regulations (SI 1995/2902). Somewhat confusingly, these regulations are expressed in terms of non-residents, but the term 'non-resident' is defined as a person who has his usual place of abode outside the UK.

Regulation 3 defines the UK representative of the property owner as:

(a) such person as the Board of Inland Revenue prescribe by notice, or (if none is prescribed)
(b) such agent of the non-resident as receives or has control of the rent, or (if there be none)
(c) the tenant.

The UK representative is required to make quarterly and annual returns. The quarterly return is a calculation of basic rate tax due on rent paid for the quarter and is accompanied by payment of the tax. Where the agent makes the return, deductible expenses are allowed in calculating the tax (reg 9). Where the tenant makes the return, the tax is calculated on the gross amount of the rent (reg 8). The UK representative is entitled to an indemnity from the non-resident in respect of any tax he pays (TA 1988, s 42A(3)). If the tenant is the UK representative, he does not have to deduct tax if the rent is less than £100 per week.

The non-resident can receive rent gross under the non-resident landlord scheme. To do this, he must make application to the Board and inter alia satisfy them either that he has complied with all his UK tax obligations to date, or that he has so far had none (reg 17). The non-resident must undertake to operate self-assessment in respect of his rental income and otherwise comply with his tax obligations. Any authorisation the Board give for payment gross is revoked if these undertakings are breached. The non-resident landlord scheme is administered by HMRC Centre for Non-Residents.

Non-residents investing in UK rental property are treated as carrying on a UK property business (ITTOIA 2005, s 269(1)). The profits are computed in the same way as trading profits, and this means inter alia interest payable on loans to purchase or improve the property is allowable (ITTOIA 2005, ss 272 and 29). Such interest is allowable even if it is paid abroad by the non-resident owner in such a way that the obligation to withhold does not arise. But if the loan is from a connected party, it may fall foul of the transfer pricing legislation unless it is on commercial terms (TA 1988, Sch 28AA; see also *Tax Bulletin* October 1998 p 579).

It used to be said that for interest to be allowable the loan had to have been incurred to fund the acquisition or improvement of the property. Borrowing for non-business purposes on the security of let property did not give rise to interest relief. But now it appears HMRC sees such borrowing as withdrawal of working capital and so may accept the ensuing interest as a deduction providing total borrowing does not exceed the cost of the property (see *Taxation* vol 154 (3 March 2005) p 539).

Excluded income

34.14 As described above, the basic rule is that, in law, non-residents are fully liable to UK tax in respect of their UK income. However, this is displaced in the case of what is called 'excluded income'. Excluded income is defined in FA 1995, s 128(2) and FA 2003, s 151(2) and consists principally of dividends and interest. It does not include rental income.

The significance of excluded income is that the non-resident's tax liability cannot exceed what it would be if the only tax chargeable on excluded income is such tax (if any) as is withheld. However, in making this computation, personal allowances cannot be claimed. In HMRC's view this relief does not exempt the income, which still has to be included on the non-resident's tax return (Financial Intermediaries and Claims Office Newsletter No 7, March 2000).

It is to be noted that any income protected from assessment by the broker and investment manager exceptions described above is also excluded income. This means that, even if a non-resident's investment activity amounts to a trade, the profits are not subject to UK tax provided that the trade is conducted through an unconnected investment manager or broker (Statement of Practice SP 1/01, para 14).

Not surprisingly, income cannot count as excluded income if it is income in relation to which the non-resident has a UK representative who is not protected by the exception for brokers and investment managers (FA 1995, s 128(2)(b)). Accordingly the position is reached that income is not excluded if it arises from deposits or shares held or used for the purposes of a trade, profession or vocation carried on through a branch or agency in the UK, unless the representative charge is precluded by the exceptions for occasional agents, brokers, or investment managers.

Trusts

34.15 A more important exception to the relief for excluded income is that it does not apply to the income of a discretionary or accumulation trust unless the trust satisfies the conditions described above for interest to be paid gross (FA 1995, s 128(5)). As there noted, these conditions exclude trusts with UK-resident beneficiaries, but this exclusion does not, in the HMRC's view, extend to trusts where the present class of beneficiaries does not include UK residents but UK residents could be added in future.

In considering whether to pay the tax due on UK source income, trustees with UK beneficiaries should keep in mind the rule in international law that the courts of one country will not enforce the revenue claims of another

(*Government of India v Taylor* [1955] AC 491). The English Court of Appeal has recently affirmed this is a fundamental principle of English law (*QRS 1 Aps and others v Fransden* [1999] STC 616). If, therefore, offshore trustees pay the UK tax they may be meeting an unenforceable liability and could thereby be acting in breach of trust. In practice, however, most modern trusts contain express power to pay taxes even if not enforceable, and normally such power may be relied on, both because some or all of the beneficiaries are physically in the UK and because it removes what may be a potential embarrassment to the trustees which could inhibit their ability properly to discharge their duties. But in cases of doubt, and more particularly where there is no express power, local legal advice should be taken.

There is no doubt HMRC can and do expect to recover tax due under UK law from non-resident trustees, not merely on what would otherwise be excluded income, but also on any other UK source income the trustees might receive. The rate of tax is the same as that for resident discretionary or accumulation trusts, namely the rate applicable to trusts, now 40%, or the dividend trust rate (TA 1988, s 686(1AA)). The latter is 32.5% (ibid s 686(1A)), but UK dividends received by non-resident trustees are treated as grossed-up by tax at the dividend ordinary rate (10%) and this tax is treated as having been paid (ITTOIA 2005, s 399). The effective rate of tax on dividends is thus 25%.

The above rules do not of course apply if the trust is a fixed-interest trust, in which event, excluded income is free of tax if the life-tenant is non-resident (see para 12.2). Nor do they apply if the trust is settlor-interested and the settlor is non-resident, at least insofar as the income is dividends (see para 59.26).

The first £1,000 of the income of discretionary or accumulation trusts is taxable only at the basic, lower, or ordinary dividend rate (TA 1988, s 686D). This applies to non-resident as well as resident trusts, but is subject to anti-fragmentation rules (TA 1988, s 686E). In the case of non-resident trusts, the starting rate is applied in disregard of the trust's foreign income (see s 686D(2) and *Tax Bulletin* 78 (August 2005) p 1215). In other words, the first £1,000 of the trust's UK income attracts the starting rate, regardless of how much foreign income the trust has.

Non-resident discretionary or accumulation trustees who hold their UK investments through a non-resident company avoid the difficulties described above. Such a company enjoys the same reliefs for excluded income as a non-resident individual (FA 2003, s 151). This is one reason why trustees may consider forming such a company, but other factors also require consideration (see Chapter 9).

Chapter 35

Characterisation

Introduction

35.1 As will be apparent from the discussion of situs and source, a key issue in offshore tax planning can be deciding how, for UK tax purposes, a foreign entity should be characterised. This chapter outlines the salient principles to be derived from the decided cases.

Companies

35.2 Two well established principles apply in determining whether a foreign entity is treated as a company for UK tax purposes.

The first is that, by comity of nations, English law recognises the juristic status of bodies established under foreign law. Lord Hanworth MR put the matter thus in *Dreyfus v IRC* (1929) 14 TC 560 at 576;

> 'If there has been a body established by foreign law, the courts will recognise the juristic status of that body and thus the Court says that the principle of the liability of members of a foreign corporation to third parties is to be referred to the law under which that corporation was established, and if the law does show it was established as a separate entity effect should be given to it.'

The second is that, in determining what a foreign entity is, it is necessary to look at its characteristics as determined by the foreign law and then determine what, under English law, an entity with those characteristics would be. This principle was summarised by Dyson J in *R v IRC, ex p Bishopp* [1999] STC 531 at 545 in the context of determining the status of a Jersey LLP as follows:

> 'It is common ground that, in determining whether a Jersey LLP is a partnership for purposes of United Kingdom taxation, the nature of the rights, obligations and other features of the organisation must be determined according to Jersey law; but the characterisation of its status, i e whether a body of that kind should be treated as a partnership or not the United Kingdom (see *Rae* (*Inspector of Taxes*) *v Lazard Investment Co Ltd* [1963] 1 WLR 555, 41 TC 1).'

Partnerships

35.3 The issue of whether a foreign entity or arrangement is a partnership is determined in the same way as it is determined whether it is a company. It is necessary to identify the characteristics of an English or Scottish partnership and then investigate the extent to which those characteristics are shared by the foreign entity or arrangement in question (*Memec plc v IRC* [1998] STC 754, 764, per Peter Gibson LJ).

It follows that, just because an arrangement is called a partnership in the relevant foreign country, application of English law to the various rights and obligations may lead to the conclusion that for tax purposes it is not. In *Memec plc v IRC* a German silent partnership gave the silent 'partner' a contractual right to share in the active 'partner's' profits and the obligation to bear a proportion of losses up to the amount of its capital contribution. The Court of Appeal held that this was not a partnership. So too in *R v IRC, ex p Bishopp* [1999] STC 531 HMRC had indicated in an informal pre-transaction ruling that a Jersey LLP should be regarded as a company. The court refused to review HMRC's ruling.

Trusts

35.4 Common law jurisdictions recognise trusts and their trust law is based on English law. What is characterised as a trust in a common law offshore jurisdiction therefore falls to be so characterised in England. However, many offshore jurisdictions have by legislation allowed forms of trust to be created which are not recognised as valid at common law. The most notable example is the non-charitable purpose trust. No decided case exists on how such a trust would be characterised in England but, if the issue did arise, the principles referred to above would be applied (see for example *Memec plc v IRC* [1998] STC 754, 764).

Many offshore jurisdictions expressly allow the settlor to reserve extensive powers, for example to direct investment, to direct distributions, and to hire and fire trustees. The issue powers of this sort raise is whether, in a common law jurisdiction such as England without the relevant legislation, the relationship would be characterised not as a true trust but as one of nomineeship. It is, however, unlikely this would be the correct analysis provided the trustees are left with genuine responsibilities over the trust assets. Authority for this is cases such as *Perry v Astor* [1935] 19 TC 255 where, even though a trust was revocable, it was still treated as a trust for tax purposes. In such cases it is of course essential that the trustees do genuinely and independently discharge the functions reposed in them. If they do not, such inertia may, when coupled with the extensive powers reserved to the settlor, render a sham finding likely (see Chapter 51).

Foundations

35.5 Foundations are characteristic of civil law jurisdictions and are now being introduced to various common law jurisdictions by statute. In offshore tax planning, the foundation normally encountered is the Liechtenstein Stiftung.

The key characteristics of the Liechtenstein Stiftung are laid down in Liechtenstein legislation (Personen und Gesellschaftsrecht Articles 552–570). The Stiftung does have legal personality and is liable for debts only to the extent of its assets. It is administered by the Foundation Council. But it holds its assets for purposes specified by the Founder or as laid down in by-statutes. The true analysis of the Stiftung is, it may be suggested, that it does not own its assets beneficially, but is bound to apply them for the specified purposes. As such it is analogous to a fiduciary relationship, the issue being whether on the facts it is nomineeship or to be equated with a true trust. This, it may be suggested, turns on the construction of the by-statutes.

There is no English case law on how a foundation should be characterised, and nor is there published HMRC practice. However the experience of at least some practitioners is that HMRC take the kind of approach indicated above.

It is sometimes said that the definition of settlement in IHTA 1984, s 48(2) deems a foundation to be a trust for IHT purposes in that it refers to dispositions whereby property is held on various kinds of trust and then extends the definition to dispositions under which the property 'would be so held if … the disposition were regulated by the law of any part of the United Kingdom …'. It may however be suggested that, of itself, s 48(2) does not have this effect. Either a foundation is analogous to a trust, in which case it is so treated for English tax purposes generally. Or it is not, in which case s 48(2) does not apply either.

Opaque or transparent

35.6 An issue related to, but different from, the characterisation of entities, is whether an entity or arrangement is opaque or transparent. This issue normally arises in connection with income tax.

Case law

35.7 The leading case on transparency is *Memec plc v IRC* [1998] STC 754, which, as noted above, revolved around a German silent partnership. The issue was whether the source of the silent partner's income was the dividends received by the silent partnerships or his contractual rights against the silent partner.

Both at first instance and in the Court of Appeal, the test applied was whether the silent partnership was mere incidental machinery or had independent vitality. At first instance [1996] STC 1336 Robert Walker J said:

> 'Transparency is normally associated with a situation where the ultimate recipient of the income has a beneficial interest in it from the start, and moreover the income is not transmuted at some intermediate stage by the need for the trustees to exercise a discretion or by its being packaged so as to reach the ultimate receipt in the form of a fixed annuity.'

HMRC practice

35.8 HMRC have published the practice they adopt in deciding, for income tax purposes, whether an entity is opaque or transparent. This practice is now set out in *Tax Bulletin 83* (June 2006), having previously been in *Tax Bulletins 39* and *50*.

HMRC stress that the issue of whether an entity is opaque or transparent is not necessarily the same as determining whether it is a company or a partnership. However, HMRC express themselves as having regard to *Memec plc v IRC* and itemise several factors they consider relevant. The most important are whether any business is carried on by the entity or by the persons having an interest in the entity and whether those persons are entitled to share profits as they arise or whether the distribution of profits requires a decision by the entity or its members.

In *Tax Bulletin 83*, HMRC list entities on which they have given a view. The list does not include foundations, whether in Liechtenstein or elsewhere.

Section II

Residence and Domicile

Chapter 36

Residence of individuals

Introduction

36.1 The issue of whether in law a taxpayer is resident in the UK is subject to certain limited statutory provisions, but otherwise the question is governed by case law. In the event of dispute, the issue is determined by the appellate Commissioners. The taxpayer can appeal to the High Court and beyond, but the courts will only interfere if (i) the Commissioners' decision is not based on the evidence before them or (ii) they misdirect themselves in law (*Reed v Clark* [1985] STC 323, 336; *Shepherd v Revenue and Customs Comrs* [2006] STC 1821). The result is that the law is characterised by great uncertainty, for it consists not of clear rules, but of judgments determining whether the Commissioners were entitled to find as they did.

For years, much of the uncertainty has been removed in practice, for in IR 20 HMRC publish a clear statement of when, and when they do not, regard a taxpayer as resident. HMRC follow these rules as if they had statutory force, and for that reason it is sufficient for most taxpayers simply to follow them. However, the law is still important, both because HMRC practice may not be applied in tax avoidance cases, and because, with due notice, HMRC practice can and does change.

In 1993 an attempt was made to simplify the law. In the Budget of March 1993, the then Chancellor announced he was abolishing one of the most distinctive features of that law, namely the available accommodation rule. As is explained below, the actual legislation (FA 1993, s 208) did not in terms achieve this but the gap is filled by HMRC practice.

In the 2002 Budget the Chancellor announced a review of the rules of residence and domicile. This is still ongoing.

The complexities of the subject make a clear exposition of the law of residence as it currently stands difficult to achieve. In this chapter the approach taken is first to consider the common law meaning of the terms resident and ordinarily resident. The limited specific statutory rules are there addressed and lastly HMRC's practice is summarised.

Residence: case law

Levene and Lysaght

36.2 The basic common law rule is that the term 'resident' bears its normal dictionary meaning. The matter was put thus by Viscount Cave in *Levene v IRC* [1928] AC 217, 222:

> '… the word "reside" is a familiar English word and is defined in the Oxford English Dictionary as meaning "to dwell permanently or for a considerable time, to have one's settled or usual abode, to live in or at a particular place". No doubt this definition must for present purposes be taken subject to any modification which may result from the terms of the Income Tax Act and Schedules, but, subject to that observation, it may be accepted as an accurate indication of the meaning of the word "reside".'

The two leading cases were decided in the 1920s, namely *Levene v IRC* (1928) 13 TC 486 and *Lysaght v IRC* (1927) 13 TC 511. In both, the taxpayers were British subjects who had sold their homes in the UK. Mr Levene left the UK in December 1919, and then spent the following times in the UK:

1920–21	19 weeks
1921–22	21 weeks
1922–23	20 weeks
1923–24	20 weeks
1924–25	22 weeks

During this time Mr Levene owned no permanent home abroad, although in January 1925 he did take a lease of a flat in Monaco. Until then he stayed in hotels. His visits to the UK took place in the summer months when he also stayed in hotels. During his time in the UK he attended to family matters and took medical advice.

In *Lysaght*, the taxpayer was a director of a substantial family company in England. In 1920 he gave up his home in England and moved permanently to a house he had acquired in Ireland. However, he came to England for a week every month to attend board meetings and during these visits stayed at the same hotel in Bath. Days spent in the UK were as follows:

1922–23	101 days
1923–24	94 days
1924–25	84 days

In both cases the Special Commissioners decided the taxpayer was resident in the UK for the years in issue. In Mr Levene's case they reached this conclusion having regard to his past and present habits of life, the regularity and length of his visits to the UK, his ties with the UK, and his freedom of attachments abroad. In Mr Lysaght's case no reasons were given. The Special Commissioners' decisions were upheld in the House of Lords as being ones they could properly reach, although in *Lysaght* it is clear the House would equally have upheld the opposite conclusion and Viscount Cave actually dissented.

Those coming to the UK

36.3 *Levene* and *Lysaght* make it clear an individual can be resident in the UK even if he is only in the UK for a relatively small part of the year and his permanent home is abroad. But it is noteworthy that both cases concerned British nationals who had emigrated from the UK. The result would very likely have been different had Mr Levene and Mr Lysaght been individuals coming to the UK. Such was expressly recognised by Viscount Cave in *Levene* and has also recently been acknowledged by a Special Commissioner (*Shepherd v Revenue and Customs Comrs* [2005] STC 644 at para 58). That it is right is also indicated by several old first instance decisions:

(1) In *IRC v Zorab* (1926) 11 TC 289 the taxpayer was an Indian national who had moved to Europe, staying in hotels. When in England he stayed in the same hotel and was in fact in England from 1 November 1920 to 3 October 1921, from 22 July 1922 to 20 January 1923, from 21 June 1923 to 11 December 1923, from 21 May 1924 to 18 October 1924, and from 12 May 1925 to 24 November 1926. The Special Commissioners found he was non-resident and Rowlatt J refused to interfere, regarding the taxpayer as a 'mere traveller'.
(2) In *IRC v Kinloch* (1929) 14 TC 736, the taxpayer was a British national who had moved to India on marriage in 1909. Her husband died in 1916. She spent 66 days in the UK in 1921–22, 40 days in 1922–23, 177 days (including illness) in 1923–24, 5 months 12 days in 1924–25, 145 days in 1925–26, 141 days in 1926–27 and 156 days in 1927–28. She always stayed in the same hotel, and her visits were occasioned by the fact that her son was at school in the UK from 1921. HMRC challenged her residence for 1924–25, and the Special Commissioners held she was non-resident. HMRC did not appeal, but raised the issue again for 1927–28. The Special Commissioners found that the continuance and length of her visits meant she was then resident and once again Rowlatt refused to interfere.
(3) In *Withers v Wynyard* (1938) 21 TC 724 the taxpayer was a British actress who at all times owned the lease on a London flat. She was in the United States acting from November 1931 until April 1933 at which point she returned to act in a play in London. She left London again on 7 July 1933, and apart from a further visit on 1–24 September, did not return until July 1934 when she returned permanently. HMRC eventually accepted she was non-resident in 1932–33, and the General Commissioners found she was also non-resident in 1933–34. Laurence J refused to interfere.

These cases indicate that those coming to the UK can spend well over 90 days per year here without becoming resident. *Kinloch* indicates that, at a certain point, residence may be assumed but not until a number of years have elapsed.

Those leaving the UK

36.4 For those leaving the UK, it is clear *Lysaght* is close to the line beyond which in law they cannot be resident. But how close is not clear from any of the speeches in the House of Lords. Some guidance may however be obtained from two contrasting cases, namely *IRC v Brown* (1926) 11 TC 292 and *IRC v Combe* (1932) 17 TC 405. In *Brown* the taxpayer was a British national who had moved abroad in 1919 and thereafter lived in hotels in England and on the continent. In 1924–25 he spent just two and a half months in England and the

Special Commissioners found he was not resident. Rowlatt J refused to interfere, on the grounds that the facts would have allowed a finding either way. *Brown* therefore indicates that a residence finding is possible if a British émigré spends as little as two and a half months in the UK.

In *Combe*, the taxpayer left the UK to work in New York on 3 May 1926, and returned from New York on 10 October 1928, but was abroad for much of the remainder of 1928–29. His days in the UK were 52 in 1926–27, 175 in 1927–28, and 181 in 1928–29. The General Commissioners in Scotland found he was not resident in the three years, and while this finding was not directly at issue on appeal in the Court of Session, it was not called into question. The case shows that even if a finding of residence is possible with stays of as little as two and a half months, a finding of non-residence may equally be possible with visits of close to six months.

Consistent with these cases is *Shepherd v Revenue and Customs Comrs* [2006] STC 1821. Here the taxpayer was an airline pilot who spent half the year outside the UK flying. He decided to move to Cyprus and rented a flat there from October 1998. He argued that in 1999–2000 he was non-resident, on the grounds that he was in the UK for less than 90 days. His day count (excluding days of arrival and departure) was in fact found to be 80 days, but he continued to maintain and use his UK residence. His job, from which he retired in April 2000, required him to be in the UK before and after each flight. He spent just 77 days in Cyprus and was not granted an immigration permit until February 2000. The Special Commissioner concluded there was no distinct break in the pattern of the taxpayer's life in October 1998, and that the most that could be said was that he was resident in Cyprus as well as in the UK. On this basis she found he had remained UK resident in 1999–2000. The High Court refused to interfere.

Ordinary residence: case law

36.5 The leading authority on the meaning of ordinary residence is *Shah v Barnet London Borough Council* [1983] 1 All ER 226, which related to student grants rather than tax. The House of Lords decided that foreign students who were allowed into the UK on education visas for a limited period were ordinarily resident here. Lord Scarman stated the law as follows ([1983] 2 AC 309 at 343):

> 'Unless, therefore, it can be shown that the statutory framework or the legal context in which the words are used requires a different meaning. I unhesitatingly subscribe to the view that "ordinarily resident" refers to a man's abode in a particular place or country which he has adopted voluntarily and for settled purposes as part of the regular order of his life for the time being, whether of short or of long duration.'

Logically the term 'ordinarily resident' presupposes the individual is 'resident' and then, as Lord Scarman implies, requires an added quality to make it 'ordinary'. However, certain tax legislation, most notably TCGA 1992, s 2, proceeds on the assumption that an individual can be ordinarily resident without being resident.

It may be suggested, however, that residence is indeed a precondition of ordinary residence. The authority for this proposition is *Levene v IRC*, which concerned ordinary residence as well as residence. Since the taxpayer was held to be resident, the issue of whether an individual could be ordinarily resident without being resident did not directly fall for decision. But Viscount Cave's speech includes the following passage ([1928] AC 217 at 225):

> 'The expression "ordinary residence" is found in the Income Tax Act of 1806 and occurs again and again in the later Income Tax Acts, where it is contrasted with usual or occasional or temporary residence; and I think that it connotes residence in a place with some degree of continuity and apart from accidental or temporary absences. So understood, the expression differs little in meaning from the word "residence" as used in the Acts; and I find it difficult to imagine a case in which a man while not resident here is yet ordinarily resident here.'

Viscount Cave's speech was expressly concurred in by Lord Atkinson; and Lord Buckmaster concurred in the dismissal of the appeal. If, as may be suggested, this represents the law, an individual can never be ordinarily resident without being resident. It has to be accepted, however, that if this view is right, Parliament enacted such legislation as TCGA 1992, s 2 under a mistaken view of the law. But it must be pointed out that this view was shared by Special Commissioners in *Reed v Clark* [1985] STC 323 and in *Shepherd v Revenue and Customs Comrs* [2006] STC 1821, 1833. In the former case the Special Commissioners reviewed all the relevant authorities, including *Levene*, and concluded as follows:

> 'From the speeches in *Levene* and *Lysaght* we would draw the conclusion, first that to be resident in this country for a tax year a person must live here for part of that year, though not necessarily in his own place of abode, and second, that the concept of ordinary residence involves actual residence, in the sense referred to with the added quality of continuity.'

On appeal to the High Court, Nicholls J did not deal with the term ordinary residence, but his remarks on occasional residence, and specifically the passage cited in para 36.7, give no grounds for supposing he would have disagreed with the Commissioners.

Ordinary residence and habitual residence are interchangeable terms. The question of whether the individual is lawfully present in the UK is irrelevant in determining ordinary residence (*Mark v Mark* [2005] UKHL 42, [2005] 3 All ER 912 para 31).

Express statutory rules

36.6 Four specific statutory rules as to residence are laid down in TA 1988, ss 334, 335, and 336.

Occasional residence abroad

36.7 Section 334 applies to an individual if:

(1) his ordinary residence has been in the UK, and
(2) he has left the UK for the purpose of only occasional residence abroad.

Where s 334 applies, the individual is charged to income tax as if he were still residing in the UK. The section is of very limited impact, and there is no reported case where it alone has resulted in liability to tax. This is because an individual is normally found to be still resident in the UK if he has left the UK for only occasional residence abroad. Thus in *Levene v IRC*, the taxpayer was found to have left the UK for only occasional residence abroad, but equally he was resident in the UK all along. Conversely, in *IRC v Combe* (1932) 17 TC 405, the taxpayer's three-year absence in New York was not found to be for the purposes of occasional residence abroad.

The leading case on occasional residence is *Reed v Clark* [1985] STC 323. Here the taxpayer was absent for only a little over a year, but there was a distinct break in the pattern of his life and throughout his absence he had made his permanent home and place of business in California. On these facts Nicholls J decided his residence in California was not occasional. He considered that ordinary residence is the converse of occasional residence, observing that 'a person's occasional residence is contrasted with his usual (or ordinary) residence'. He then made the following comments (at 345):

> 'In my view a year is a long enough period for a person's purpose of living where he does to be capable of having a sufficient degree of continuity for it to be properly described as settled. Hence, depending on all the circumstances, the foreign country could be the place where for that period he would be ordinarily and not just occasionally resident. I appreciate that this construction may give little scope in practice for the operation of [s 334] as an independent charging provision. But having regard to the origin of the section in the earliest days of income tax at the end of the eighteenth century I do not find this consideration sufficiently compelling to require the language in [s 334] to be given some different meaning.'

Section 334 does not apply to CGT. This presumably is because ordinary residence alone (if such is possible) renders a person subject to CGT (TCGA 1992, s 2).

Full-time work abroad

36.8 Section 335 allows available accommodation in the UK to be disregarded in determining residence if the taxpayer works full-time abroad. For this section to apply, the taxpayer must either be self-employed and no part of his business can be carried on in the UK, or he may be an employee, in which case no more than incidental duties may be performed in the UK. Incidental has been strictly construed, and thus a KLM pilot whose flights occasionally included a UK stop-over was held to perform more than incidental duties in the UK (*Robson v Dixon* [1972] 3 All ER 671).

'Full-time' is not defined and there is in law no fixed number of hours which is required as a minimum. If the taxpayer is an employee there is no reason why the employer cannot be a company controlled by him. But evidentially it may be harder to prove that the employment really is full-time.

HMRC regard a working week of 35–40 hours as full-time, and may accept a lesser time commitment depending on local conditions. In certain circumstances several part-time jobs can together be regarded as amounting to full-time work (IR 20, para 2.5; *Tax Bulletin* 6 (February 1993)). A UK directorship may not preclude full-time employment abroad but it would be scrutinised.

Temporary residents

36.9 Section 336 of TA 1988 is headed 'Temporary Residents in the United Kingdom' and it applies to any person who 'is in the United Kingdom for some temporary purpose only' and not with the intention of establishing his residence here. Such a person is not treated as resident for the purposes of determining taxable earnings from employment, and he is not charged to tax as a person residing in the UK in respect of relevant foreign income under ITTOIA 2005 (s 336(1)). An exception to these rules is, however, made if the person has in fact resided in the UK for six months or more in a tax year. Similar provisions are made in relation to CGT by TCGA 1992, s 9(3).

Although s 336 has been in the income tax legislation since the Napoleonic Wars, it has been the subject of little case law and its meaning is far from clear. Two points in particular have arisen. The first is the meaning of 'temporary purposes' and the second is whether s 336 is a relieving section (ie relieving persons who would otherwise be taxable as residents of certain tax consequences arising therefrom) or whether by implication it enacts a substantive rule as to residence.

On this latter point, the meaning of the section itself appears clear: it does not enact a rule as to residence but merely confers relief for certain purposes. Such was affirmed by the majority of the Court of Session in *Lloyd v Sulley* (1884) 2 TC 37 and by Lord Warrington in *Levene* and it is also implicit from the facts of *Lysaght* and *Levene*. Those two cases concerned liability to tax on income of a kind not specifically mentioned in s 336, and it is noteworthy that in neither case was temporary residence a central issue. A further point is that when CGT was enacted in 1965, the draftsman did not think s 336 governed the rules as to residency. Thus, what is now the TCGA 1992, s 9(1) provided that 'resident' has the same meaning as for income tax, and then what is now s 9(3) enacted a provision exempting temporary residents from charge in the same terms as s 336.

As regards the first point, the meaning of 'temporary purposes', one authority is directly in point, namely *Cooper v Cadwalader* (1904) 5 TC 101. Here an American had taken a lease of a shooting-lodge in Scotland, and he spent a continuous period of two months there each year during the grouse-shooting season. His principal residence was in New York. The Court of

Session affirmed the finding of the General Commissioners that he was resident in the UK, and upheld assessments made on him under Schedule D. The question then arose of whether he was exempted by what is now s 336(1). All three judges who gave reasoned opinions held that it did not apply as the shooting-lodge was a residence and so meant he was in the UK with the view or intent of establishing his residence here. Lords Adam and McLaren then gave an additional reason for s 336(1) not applying, namely that coming to Scotland year after year for the shooting season was not a temporary purpose. In a significant passage Lord McLaren observed that 'temporary purposes means casual purposes as distinguished from the case of a person who is here in pursuance of his regular habits of life'.

Lord McLaren's words were applied in *Shepherd v Revenue and Customs Comrs* [2006] STC 1821 at para 16. That case indicates that an individual who is in the UK to carry out duties of his employment is not in the UK for temporary purposes.

That the approach taken in *Cooper v Cadwalader* represents the correct construction of 'temporary purposes' is also indicated by some of the cases concerned with individuals without available accommodation. Thus in *IRC v Brown* (1926) 11 TC 292 the Commissioners' decision, upheld by Rowlatt J, included findings that the taxpayer's stays in UK hotels were for temporary purposes only. Similarly in *Levene*, Viscount Cave observed that Mr Levene's purposes when spending several months a year in hotels abroad were only temporary. The conclusion which may be drawn is that frequent or even lengthy visits to the UK to stay in hotels are visits for temporary purposes.

The question it would be most helpful to have an answer to is whether in *Lysaght*, the taxpayer's regular monthly visits for board meetings were for temporary purposes. This question was not answered in the House of Lords speeches, but the reference in *Shepherd* to employment duties suggests the monthly visits were not for temporary purposes as attendance at board meetings was part of the taxpayer's duties as director.

Available accommodation

36.10 Until 5 April 1993, the key concept in the legal meaning of residence was that of the permanent or settled abode. Thus, as repeated cases affirmed, if the taxpayer occupied a house or flat in the UK he was, in the absence of specific statutory provision, resident here. It did not matter if the house or flat was one of several homes round the world (*Lloyd v Sulley* (1884) 2 TC 37) and, indeed it was clear that a taxpayer counted as resident if he only spent a month or two in each year at his UK residence (*Cooper v Cadwalader* (1904) 5 TC 101). Provided the house or flat was available to the taxpayer he did not need to own it, and so a taxpayer could become resident here if accommodation was made available to him by a company he controlled (*Lowenstein v De Salis* (1926) 10 TC 424). The one exception was that noted in para 36.8 above, namely that available accommodation was disregarded if the taxpayer worked full time abroad.

FA 1993, s 208 introduced amendments to s 336 and TCGA 1992, s 9 with effect from 1993–94 onwards. These amendments provide that the existence or otherwise of available accommodation must be disregarded in determining whether an individual is in the UK for some temporary purpose and not with a view or intent of establishing his residence here.

As a matter of strict construction these amendments have little effect on the law of residence. Their effect is merely to reverse the principal ratio of *Cooper v Cadwalader*, namely that s 336 did not apply because the existence of the hunting-lodge meant the taxpayer did have the intention of establishing his residence in the UK. The amendments do not reverse the subsidiary reasoning of Lords Adam and McLaren, namely that visits to the UK are not made for temporary purposes if made in pursuance of the taxpayer's regular habits of life. Strictly, therefore, the scope of the amendments may in law be limited, for in reality many foreigners with houses or flats in the UK come here regularly year in year out for business or recreational purposes. Their visits are part of the regular habits of their life, and thus, on the *Cooper v Calwalader* test, fall outside s 336.

A further issue is whether even in this limited respect the amendments changed the law as to residence. In a sense this is an absurd question, for the amendments are to ss 9(3) and 336, which, as noted above, do not as such govern the meaning of residence. But s 208(4) makes an amendment to the IHT deemed domicile rules in IHTA 1984, s 267 (see para 30.14). Until 1993–94, s 267(4) provided that available accommodation was disregarded in determining whether the taxpayer had been resident in the UK in 17 out of the last 20 years. Section 208(4) repealed this disregard and is comprehensible only on the basis that the rest of s 208 is concerned with the substantive law of residence. There is thus inconsistency, if not ambiguity, in s 208 and the issue therefore arises of whether statements in Hansard can be taken into account in construing it (*Pepper v Hart* [1992] STC 898).

In *Shepherd v Revenue and Customs Comrs* [2006] STC 1821, the Special Commissioner held not, on the grounds that the words inserted into s 336 are not in fact ambiguous and do not lead to absurdity (para 71). However, it appears that her comments were directed at the point of whether s 336 applied only to temporary visitors rather that on whether FA 1993, s 208 amended the law as to residence at all.

That the then Government intended s 208 to change the law of residence is indicated by the Budget Press Release on 16 March 1993, which first announced the change. This opens with the following words:

> 'The Chancellor proposes in his Budget to abolish the available accommodation rule.'

It later stated, in para 4, that:

> 'the Chancellor's proposal will mean that no account will be taken of the availability of accommodation in the UK in determining whether an individual here for a temporary purpose only is resident for tax purposes.'

That this was the intention was confirmed when the Finance Bill was in Committee stage (HC Official Report, 24 June 1993, cols 590–91). Mr Michael Stern referred to the difficulties over the scope of s 336 and asked the Financial Secretary to the Treasury, Mr Stephen Dorrell, to confirm that:

> 'the purpose of [s 208] as set out in the Budget Press Release is achieved by [s 208] as drafted.'

Mr Dorrell replied that the Revenue had always regarded s 336 as having illustrative value. Hence, he said:

> 'it is not necessary in [the Revenue's] view to go any further in [s 208] which already fully achieves its objectives.'

Mr Dorrell then referred to the available accommodation test as 'a spurious test of residence' and concluded that 'this is why it should be abolished'.

Mr Dorrell's statements were clear and unequivocal and it may thus be argued that they satisfy the conditions laid down in *Pepper v Hart* for Parliamentary material to be taken into account. Accordingly, by this somewhat roundabout route the conclusion may be reached that s 208 did alter the law as to residence.

But even if that is so what is plain is that, as the Special Commissioner pointed out in *Shepherd*, s 336 still on its terms only applies to temporary visitors, and nothing in the material cited above displaces this. It follows therefore that available accommodation should as a matter of law still be taken into account in relation to persons who visit the UK as part of the regular order of their life. For that reason, s 208 is in law be of only limited effect although as noted below in practice its application is much wider.

HMRC practice

36.11 Current HMRC practice is set out in Part I of IR20. In one or two places this specifically refers to extra-statutory concessions and so is subject to the rubric applicable to all concessions, namely that the benefit of the concession is not given where an attempt is made to use it for tax avoidance. Otherwise IR20 is a clear statement of practice made to all the world which can therefore be relied on by taxpayers (cf *R v IRC, ex p MFK Underwriting Agents Ltd* [1989] STC 873 at 892 per Bingham LJ).

The current edition of IR20 was issued in December 1999. It provides clear practical rules in many areas where the law is uncertain. Its overall effect is to make the number of days spent in the UK virtually the sole test of residence.

Residence

36.12 The main points of IR20 as regards residence are as follows:

(1) A taxpayer is always regarded as resident in the UK in a tax year if he is here for 183 days or more in the year (para 1.2).

(2) A taxpayer is also regarded as resident in the UK if he is here for an average of 91 or more days per tax year (paras 2.7 and 3.3). The average may be taken over a period of up to four years and is determined by a

fraction of which the denominator is the total number of days in the period under review and the numerator is the number of days in the period spent in the UK. This fraction is then multiplied by 365 to give the average number of days per year in the UK over the period.

(3) For the purposes of both the 183 and the 91 day rule, days of arrival and departure are not normally counted as days spent in the UK (para 1.2).

(4) Persons coming to the UK are divided into three categories, namely:

   (i) Those intending to live in the UK permanently or remain at least three years, who are regarded as resident from arrival (para 3.1).

   (ii) Long-term visitors, ie persons intending to remain indefinitely. They are regarded as resident from arrival if they own or lease accommodation here or have come here for a purpose which will involve remaining for at least two years (para 3.7).

   (iii) Short-term visitors, who are simply subject to the 183 and 91 day rules (para 3.3). The 91 day rule treats a visitor as resident in the UK if over a four-year period his average number of days in the UK per tax year exceed 90. In such a case, residence commences from the fifth year or, if earlier, from when the visitor decides to spend more than 90 days per year in the UK.

(5) A person is regarded as intending to remain here if he is here on a continuing basis and any departures are for holidays or short business trips (para 3.1).

(6) An individual leaving the UK is regarded as non-resident if he satisfies the 183 and 91 day rules and falls into one of the following categories:

   (i) He emigrates permanently (para 2.8).

   (ii) He or his spouse leave the UK to work full time abroad under a contract of employment or on a self-employed basis for a period which includes at least one complete tax year (paras 2.2, 2.4 and 2.6).

   (iii) He goes abroad for some other settled purpose which lasts for at least one complete tax year (para 2.9).

(7) An individual going abroad without satisfying any of the above three conditions is treated as remaining resident. However, if in fact he satisfies the 183 and 91 day rules for three complete tax years, his status can be reviewed (para 2.9).

Ordinary residence

36.13 IR20 asserts that an individual may be ordinarily resident without being resident. However, the only example given is that of the individual who takes a long holiday and does not set foot in the UK during a full tax year (para 1.3). Otherwise in all cases where a departing individual is regarded as non-resident, he is also regarded as losing ordinary residence.

An arrival is regarded as ordinarily resident from the date of arrival if:

(a) he is coming to the UK permanently (para 3.1);

(b) he is a long-term visitor who intends to remain in the UK for at least three years;

(c) he is a long-term visitor who owns or leases accommodation for at least three years on arrival or in the same tax year as arrival (para 3.11); or
(d) he is a short-term visitor who intends at the outset to be in the UK 91 or more days per year over at least the next four tax years.

As will be apparent, to a large extent the question of whether an immigrant is treated as ordinarily resident on arrival turns on what he says he intends. Perhaps for this reason a surprisingly large number of arrivals in the UK are initially treated as not ordinarily resident. Such a person subsequently becomes ordinarily resident as follows:

(a) Long-term visitors are treated as ordinarily resident from the tax year following the third anniversary of their arrival, assuming they remain that long. Ordinary residence starts earlier if they buy or lease accommodation for three years or more or otherwise decide their stay will be for more than three years (paras 3.9 and 3.10).
(b) Short-term visitors are treated as ordinarily resident from the start of the fifth tax year if average annual visits exceed 91 days or more per year for more than four tax years.

HMRC practice and the law

36.14 HMRC practice is helpful and in almost all cases should be followed when questions of residence are at issue. However, in three respects it may be harsh:

(1) It will not always be the case that a taxpayer whose average visits are between 91 and 180 days per year will be resident. If the taxpayer has a permanent home abroad, is foreign, and has no business interests in the UK, a contrary finding would, it is suggested, be quite open to the appellate Commissioners. *IRC v Lysaght* and the cases discussed in para 36.3 above are in point.
(2) The authorities provide no basis for the proposition that a person who makes visits of between 90 and 180 days per year becomes resident at the outset if he then intends such visits. *Kinloch v IRC* [1929] 14 TC 736 is to the contrary.
(3) As noted above, it is doubtful in law whether it is possible to be ordinarily resident without being resident.

A more pertinent observation is that available accommodation is hardly mentioned. In practice this is extremely important and means that available accommodation may normally be ignored. There would appear to be only two exceptions to this:

(1) In determining whether a taxpayer has gone abroad for permanent residence. Here all that is required is that the retention of UK accommodation is consistent with living abroad permanently or for at least three years (para 2.8).

(2) In determining whether a longer-term visitor becomes resident or ordinarily resident in the first three years.

The practical result of HMRC practice is that days spent in the UK are the determinant of residence. Under this practice an individual may spend a considerable amount of time in the UK, particularly when it is remembered that days of arrival and departure do not normally count as days in the UK. In theory it is possible for an individual living abroad to fly into London to work on Tuesday morning and leave on Friday night every week for 45 weeks in the year and still be non-resident. HMRC have given no view on such individuals, although it is apposite to remember that in IR20, the practice on days of arrival and departure is prefaced by the word normally.

In *Tax Bulletin* 52 (April 2001) HMRC reviewed the position of one category of mobile workers, namely those whose home and settled domestic life is in the UK, but whose work such as lorry driving or selling causes their time in the UK to be under the 90-day limit. The HMRC view is that such individuals do remain UK-resident. The position of such individuals is in a sense the reverse of the person living abroad who visits the UK regularly and it may be the *Tax Bulletin* article impliedly confirms that HMRC accept the non-resident status of the latter category of person.

Compliance

36.15 Under self-assessment, individuals self-certify their residence status. HMRC no longer give residence rulings save where such is necessary to obtain relief from foreign tax under the terms of a double tax treaty. The notes to the non-residence pages include a questionnaire to enable individuals to determine their residence status. Both these notes, and the non-residence pages themselves, echo IR20 and emphasise that days spent in the UK are virtually the sole test.

It is open to HMRC to check an individual's residence status as part of an enquiry into a return under TMA 1970, s 9A. The matter is immune from investigation once the 12-month period for enquiries into the return has expired unless the individual has made inadequate or fraudulent disclosure. In practice HMRC also regard themselves as bound if they investigate an individual's residence status for PAYE coding or repayment purposes (*Tax Bulletin* 29 (June 1997) 425).

Residence is ultimately an issue of fact and HMRC in an enquiry are entitled to any information bearing on this. Such information can include passports, personal and business diaries, accounts with financial institutions, and itemised telephone bills (see *Morris v Roberts* [2005] EWHC 1040 (Ch); [2006] STC 135, 145). Individuals sometimes claim that in practice HMRC will never catch up with them if they exceed the relevant day-counts. The breadth of information potentially available makes this an unwise approach to take.

Departure and arrival

36.16 In law an individual counts as resident in the UK throughout a tax year if he is resident for part of the year. But by concession a new arrival is treated as resident only from the date of arrival if prior to arrival he was not ordinarily resident (ESC A11). This concession does not apply to CGT unless the new arrival has previously been non-resident for at least five complete tax years (ESC D2).

Those departing from the UK are by concession treated as becoming non-resident on departure if they go abroad permanently (ESC A11). This concession does not apply to CGT unless the individual was non-resident throughout at least four of the seven tax years preceding that of his departure (ESC D2). Those who go abroad to work full-time for a period which extends over at least one complete tax year are regarded as non-resident for income tax purposes from the date of their departure until the date of their return. The law and practice relating to short-term and permanent emigration are discussed in detail in Chapter 27.

Double tax treaties

36.17 A double tax treaty is material in determining residence if an individual is resident in the UK for UK domestic tax purposes and in a treaty state for the domestic tax purposes of that state. Where this happens, the treaty lays down rules for determining which state the taxpayer resides in for the purposes of the treaty.

The rules in most treaties follow those in Article 4 of the OECD Model Convention. These rules are as follows:

(1) If the individual has a permanent home available to him in only one state he is resident in that state.
(2) If he has a permanent home in both states, he is resident in the state with which his personal and economic relations are closer ('centre of vital interests').
(3) If he does not have a permanent home in either state, or his centre of vital interests cannot be determined, he is resident in the state where he has a habitual abode.
(4) If he has a habitual abode in both states or neither state, he is a resident of the state of which he is a national.
(5) If he is a national of both states or neither state, his residence is settled by mutual agreement between the two HMRC authorities.

In international tax planning treaties are often far more important than UK domestic law in determining residence, for once an individual is resident in a foreign state under a treaty, the treaty generally only allows the UK taxing rights over certain UK source income and gains. But in offshore planning, treaties are less significant, for few genuine low-tax jurisdictions have any sort of treaty with the UK. Two which do, Jersey and Guernsey, have only restricted treaties, which do not include an OECD-type residence article.

Chapter 37

Residence of trusts

Introduction

37.1 The residence of trusts is material to income tax and CGT but not, in general, to IHT. As is described in Chapter 45, the liability of trusts to IHT turns on the nature of the assets and the domicile of the settlor rather than the residence of the trustees.

Until 5 April 2007, the income tax rules are different from those pertaining to CGT. As from 6 April 2007, there is a common test of residency, albeit enacted by different legislation in relation to the two taxes.

Capital gains tax: until 5 April 2007

37.2 The basic rule is that a trust is UK resident unless two conditions are satisfied (TCGA 1992, s 69(1)):

(1) All or a majority of the trustees are either not resident or not ordinarily resident in the UK.
(2) The general administration of the trusts is ordinarily carried on outside the UK.

The trustees

37.3 The first of these conditions requires an investigation of the residence status of each of the trustees. With individual trustees this is not normally a problem, since individual offshore trustees tend to live and work in a particular offshore jurisdiction. It should be noted that a trustee is counted as not resident both if he is non-resident or if, being resident, he is not ordinarily resident. With corporate trustees, the central management and control test described in Chapter 38 has to be watched, particularly where the corporate trustee is a subsidiary of a UK group. The residence status of offshore corporate trustees has, however, rarely if ever been attacked in practice.

This first condition renders it essential to be clear who all the trustees are. Such an issue arises where the settlement has been appointed in separate funds, each with their own trustees. Unless a sub-fund election has been made such funds remain a single settlement for CGT purposes save insofar as any given fund is transferred to a new settlement on exhaustive trusts. The residence of such a multi-fund settlement is determined by looking at the trustees of all the funds, and, if half or more of this aggregate body are UK resident, so too is the settlement as a whole. As a result a fund with wholly foreign trustees can be sucked into UK residence, as happened in *Roome v Edwards* [1981] STC 96. The same would have happened in *Green v Cobham* [2002] STC 820 had not the appointment of one of the funds been set aside under the Hastings-Bass principle (see para 52.5).

General administration

37.4 As regards the second requirement, nobody really knows what constitutes the general administration of the trusts. Inheritance tax cases have drawn a distinction between the dispositive and the administrative powers of trustees (see especially *Pearson v IRC* [1981] AC 753, [1980] STC 318, HL). It may be suggested in the light of this that the general administration of the trusts relates to matters carried out in exercise of the trustees' administrative powers. It would thus include the making and management of trust investments, trust accounting, and the operating of the trust bank account.

A different analysis is that general administration equates with effective management, the term used in the tie-breaker clauses of double tax treaties to determine the residence of companies. The meaning of this term is discussed in para 38.28. In a trust context it could mean the place where the shots are called – ie the place where the trustees make their decisions. Or it could mean the place where the trust is in fact administered ie where the books are kept, where the postal address of the trustees is, and where decisions are implemented.

Whatever the correct test, it is clear is that both decision making and implementation should, to be safe, be outside the UK. If this is done it is difficult to see any HMRC attack on the general administration point succeeding and indeed, the experience of practitioners is that the issue is one the HMRC have fought shy of raising.

Professional trustees

37.5 An exception to the general rule relating to the residence of trusts is made for trustees who carry on the business of managing trusts (TCGA 1992, s 69(2)). Such a person may be treated as non-resident in relation to a particular trust if all the settled property is derived from a person who was neither resident nor domiciled in the UK when he transferred the property to the settlement. If as a result of the operation of this rule all or a majority of the trustees are or are treated as non-resident, the general administration of the trusts is deemed to be carried on abroad.

The effect of this exception is to ensure that when it applies, the trust is non-resident. It enabled trust companies and professional trustees to attract foreign trust business to the UK and should be read in conjunction with the income tax rules relating to mixed-residence trusts described below.

To qualify for this exception, the trustee must itself carry on a business which includes the management of trusts. This means the exception is *not* available if the trustee is simply an employee of a person carrying on such a business. So too if the trustee is a partner in a business which includes the management of trusts he ceases to qualify for the exception when he retires (*Green v Cobham* [2002] STC 820). The exception could also be jeopardised if, in a group structure, one company performs the sole function of acting as trustee, with all management and administration being carried on by another group member.

Income tax: until 5 April 2007

37.6 There is no general rule determining the residence of trusts for income tax purposes. However, the various charging provisions are expressed in terms of the person receiving the income or, in the case of certain categories of deemed income, the trustee or trustees in receipt of it. Under the Interpretation Act 1978, s 6, the singular includes the plural. It follows that a trust is resident in the UK if there is one trustee and he is resident in the UK or if there are several trustees and all are resident in the UK (cf *Dawson v IRC* [1989] STC 473, HL).

Mixed-residence trusts occasioned difficulty. In *Dawson v IRC* (supra) the trust had one resident trustee and two non-resident trustees. The trustees were in receipt of foreign investment income, and HMRC assessed the resident trustee under Schedule D Case V. Schedule D applied to foreign income if the person receiving it was resident in the UK (TA 1988, s 18). The House of Lords held that trustees receive income jointly and that they could only be described as persons resident in the UK if all reside there.

As a result of *Dawson v IRC*, the law was changed and now FA 1989, s 110 governs the position where one or more trustees is resident in the UK and one or more is not. Such a trust is treated as UK resident if the settlor was resident or domiciled in the UK when he made the settlement or at any time when he provided funds for the settlement whether directly or indirectly. If the settlement has more than one settlor, this test is applied to each of them and the trust is UK resident if any of them was resident or domiciled in the UK when he made the settlement or provided funds. Only if none of those conditions is met is the trust non-resident, ie only if all those who have provided funds were at all material times neither resident nor domiciled in the UK.

The income tax rules as to the residence of trusts are easier to deal with than their CGT counterparts as they focus solely on the residence status of the trustees and do not require an investigation of where the general administration of the trusts is carried on. For UK domiciled settlors they are more onerous as they require all the trustees to be non-resident rather than merely a majority.

Trust residency from 6 April 2007

37.7 The rules as to trust residency which apply from 6 April 2007 are enacted by TA 1988, s 685E and TCGA 1992, s 69. Section 685E has been inserted by FA 2006, Sch 13, and s 69 has been amended into the form it will take from 6 April 2007 by FA 2006, Sch 12.

Although the residency rules are separately enacted for CGT and income tax, their language and effect are the same. In essence the new legislation adopts the rules hitherto applicable to income tax.

The new rules

37.8 As from 6 April 2007 a trust will be resident in the United Kingdom if:

1. All the trustees are resident in the UK (TCGA 1992, s 69(2A); TA 1988, s 685E(3)).
2. One or more of the trustees is resident in the UK and the settlor satisfies specified conditions as to his residency or domicile (ss 69(2B) and 685(4)).

The specified conditions are that the settlor was UK resident or domiciled at any time at which he provided value to the settlement, or otherwise effected a transaction which rendered him settlor. It will be noted that it is that time which is looked at: the settlor's subsequent acquisition of UK residence or domicile is immaterial. But in the case of multiple settlors each is looked at and even if only one fails the residence and domicile test, a mixed residency trust is UK resident.

Who is settlor

37.9 For both income tax and CGT purposes, the term settlor is defined. As with the residency rules, the legislation is separate for the two taxes, but its effect is the same. The definition applies for other purposes as well, and as such is referred to elsewhere in this book. But it has not supplanted the definition used in anti-avoidance codes such as ITTOIA 2005, Part 5 Chapter 5 or TCGA 1992, s 86 (as to which see Chapters 59 and 60).

The core rule in the new definition is in TA 1988, s 685B(1) and TCGA 1992, s 68A(1). It is that a person is a settlor if he has 'made' or is treated as having made the settlement.

Sections 68A and 685B do not explain what is meant by making a settlement. However they do give instances of where a person is treated as making a settlement. Thus a person is treated as making a settlement if he makes it indirectly if he provides property for the purposes of the settlement. If a person makes the settlement pursuant to reciprocal arrangements with someone else, the other person is treated as making the settlement.

In general these cases where a person is treated as making a settlement mirror those where a person is deemed to be settlor in ITTOIA 2005, s 620 and TCGA 1992, Sch 5 para 8 (see paras 59.8 and 60.2). One is therefore left wondering whether there are any circumstances in which a person falls outside the provisions deeming him to have made the settlement and yet has 'made' it within the normal unexpanded meaning of the term. One possible instance is where the settlement is not bounteous. Under the pre-existing anti-avoidance definitions, the use of the word 'provide' indicates some element of bounty must be involved (see para 59.20).

Sections 68C and 685D deal with variations of a will or intestacy which are treated for CGT purposes as having been effected by the deceased (TCGA 1992, s 62(6)). If the result of the variation is that the property becomes or remains settled, the rules identifying the settlor are as follows:

1. If the property is not settled under the will or intestacy, the person or persons making the variation are treated as settlor or settlors of the trust thereby constituted (sub-s (2)).
2. If the property is settled under the will or intestacy the deceased is treated as settlor of any settlement resulting from the variation (sub-s (5) and (6)).

Transfers between settlements

37.10 It is expressly provided under the new rules that when property is advanced or appointed from one settlement to another, the settlor or each settlor of the transferor settlement is treated as having made the transferee settlement or a proportionate part of it (TCGA 1992, s 68B; TA 1988, s 685C). In such a case the settlor's residency and domicile is tested at the time when he provided property to or otherwise constituted himself settlor in relation to the transferor settlement (s 68(2C); s 685E(5)). This, it may be suggested, is a logical provision, in that it focuses on the moment when the settlor conferred bounty, regardless of the vehicle through which he initially did so.

An issue of difficulty with this rule is whether it also requires the residence and domicile of the settlor of the transferor settlement to be tested as at the time of the transfer between the settlements. This turns on whether the settlor can, within the language of the new sections 68B and 685C, be said to have 'made' the transferee settlement and, if so, whether he did so at the time of the transfer. Superficially that language indicates he can: thus sections 68B(3)(a) and 685C(3)(a) state that the settlor of the transferor settlement is 'from the time of the [transfer]' treated as having made the transferee settlement. However, close inspection of the language suggests it is doing no more than deem the settlor to be settlor of the transferee settlement at all times following the transfer. It does not bring forward the time at which he is deemed to have made the transferee settlement to any time other than when he made the transferor settlement.

Branch, agency, or permanent establishment

37.11 A new and menacing provision is contained in TCGA 1992, s 69(2D) and TA 1988, s 685E(6). It applies to any non-resident person who acts as trustee in the course of a business which he carries on in the UK through a branch, agency, or permanent establishment. In such a case that trustee is deemed to be UK resident.

The terms 'branch', 'agency', and 'permanent establishment' are not defined, and nor are any criteria laid down by which it will be judged whether a non-resident trustee is carrying on business in the UK. However, it is to be assumed that the general law determining whether non-residents are trading in the UK through a branch or agency will be in point. The key question is normally whether a trade is being carried on in the UK, a branch or agency being inferred if it is. As is explained in para 33.13, over the years two key tests have been propounded as to whether trading is taking place in the UK, namely where the contracts of sale are made and, more recently, where the profit-making activities are in substance carried on.

It will be apparent that these tests *could* catch non-resident trustees who either agree to take on new business in meetings in the UK or discharge significant trusteeship functions while in the UK. The latter might include meeting beneficiaries and/or the managers of investments. There is also danger in group structures if employees of UK group members concern themselves too much with overseas trusts of which non-resident group members are trustee, and in particular if the UK employees are able de facto to commit the non-resident trustee.

Where a non-resident trustee infringes this condition in relation to one trust, it is not clear whether he is deemed UK resident in relation to just that trust or in relation to all trusts of which he is trustee. It may be suggested the former is the better reading.

Commencement and transitional

37.12 As indicated above, the new rules come into force on 6 April 2007. This allows trustees time to consider whether their residence status will change for either CGT or income tax purposes and if so what action to take. Since the new legislation most replicates the existing income tax law, it is the CGT residency of any given trust which has to be looked at.

The two critical points of difference between the new rules and the existing CGT rules are as follows:

1. If the settlor fails the residence/domicile test, just one resident trustee will make the trust UK resident. Under present law, a UK resident trustee does not make the trust UK resident for CGT purposes provided a majority of the trustees are non-resident and the general administration of the trusts is carried on abroad.
2. If the settlor does pass the residence/domicile test, the trust will be non-resident under the new law if just one trustee is non-resident. Under

present law, a majority of trustees need to be non-resident and the general administration of the trusts carried on abroad.

An equally important point of change is that the present s 69(2) is not replicated in the new legislation. Section 69(2) is the provision described in para 37.5 above which deems a trust with a UK trustee to be non-resident if the settlor was neither resident nor domiciled in the UK when he made the settlement and the trustee is acting as trustee in the course of a business which includes the management of trusts. This, the professional trustee exemption, is therefore being scrapped. When what is now Sch 12 was produced in draft for consultation in early 2006, it included proposals for an enhanced professional trustee exemption. This proposal was dropped, allegedly on the grounds it infringed EU competition law.

The result of the various points noted above is that a significant number of trusts which are currently non-resident for CGT purposes will become UK resident on 6 April 2007. This result is avoided if, between now and then, the trusteeship is restructured so as to ensure the trust is non-resident under both the present and the new law. This is achieved if all the trustees are non-resident and (until 6 April 2007) the general administration of the trusts is carried on abroad.

Action before 5 April 2007 is essential, for if a trust is allowed to slip into residency when the new law takes effect, subsequent emigration will trigger an exit charge under TCGA 1992, s 80 (see para 28.8). Save when a trustee dies, there is no relief for this charge even in the case of short periods of UK residence.

Protectors

37.13 Protectors are persons who are not trustees but have certain powers in relation to the trust. They generally have the power to appoint new trustees and often they are given the power to dismiss trustees. Their consent may be required to the exercise of major dispositive powers over capital and they may also have power to add or exclude beneficiaries.

A question which may be raised is whether, if the protector of an offshore trust is UK resident, his residence can make the trust as a whole UK resident. At present this question is academic, in that it has not been raised in any reported case, but the fear of it leads most advisers to recommend against a UK protectorship.

In fact these fears are ill-founded. Two distinct points have to be distinguished. The first is whether the protector can be classed as a trustee for tax purposes generally. It is highly unlikely that he can be so classed, for the trust property is not vested in him, and he does not have power to initiate action, but merely power to veto proposals put up by the trustees proper. Such risk as there is is reduced if the matters which require the protector's consent are restricted to major fiduciary appointments or advances of capital. The trustees should be unfettered in their discretions over income and investment.

The second point is whether the existence of a UK protector could mean, for CGT purposes, that under the law relevant until 5 April 2007, the general administration of the trusts was not carried on abroad. In theory there could be situations where this would come about, as where a UK protector made all investment decisions and managed funds on behalf of the trustees. But this should not occur in practice, and it is difficult to see any protector, whether UK resident or not, as being involved in the general administration if, as just suggested, his consent is required only to major fiduciary dispositions.

Chapter 38

Residence of companies

Introduction

38.1 The companies which feature in offshore tax planning are almost always incorporated under the law of an offshore jurisdiction. But even if incorporated in an offshore jurisdiction, a company is not effective in offshore tax planning if it is found, as a matter of UK law, to be resident in the UK.

In the UK there is no statutory test for determining where a foreign registered company resides. Instead the matter is governed by case law. The early authorities concern multi-national companies or groups operating for the most part in colonial contexts. More recent cases, decided in the last 20 years, have applied the principles there developed to the modern offshore world.

Central management and control

38.2 The test to be applied in determining company residence was formulated in *De Beers Consolidated Mines Ltd v Howe* [1906] AC 455. Here Lord Loreburn stated that 'a Company resides where its real business is carried on'. He then said that 'the real business is carried on where the central management and control actually abides'. In the later case of *Unit Construction Co Ltd v Bullock* [1960] AC 351, Lord Radcliffe said that this test must be treated as being 'as precise and unequivocal as a positive statutory injunction.'

The facts in *De Beers* concerned a company incorporated under South African law, whose general meetings took place in Kimberley. Its business involved the mining of diamonds in South Africa, and the sale of those diamonds in London. Its directors were divided between London and South Africa but a majority, including two of the three life directors, resided in England. Both under the company's regulations, and in practice, meetings of the London directors had primacy. In particular, the case stated shows instances where the South African directors referred matters to and took instructions from London.

The appellate Commissioners found that the company was resident in the UK, on the grounds that the head and seat and directing power of the company were situate there. In the House of Lords, the taxpayer argued that the company's registration meant that it resided in South Africa. Lord Loreburn, who gave the only reasoned speech, rejected this. In applying the central management and control test, the decisive factor was how the company in fact conducted its affairs rather than what was prescribed under its internal regulations or bye-laws. On this basis it was inescapable that the company was resident in the UK for, to paraphrase Lord Loreburn, real control of practically all the important business of the company was exercised by the directors in London.

Location of business

38.3 Central management and control is not necessarily exercised where the company's business is located. In one of the earliest cases, all the company's business was in India, where it was managed by a local director on behalf of the Board. Most of the shareholders were resident in India. The company did not own premises in London but the Board met there and on the facts the local director could only act in India by authority of the Board and could at any time be recalled. On these facts the Court of Exchequer decided that the company was resident in England (*Calcutta Jute Mills Co Ltd v Nicholson* (1876) 1 TC 83).

This point was discussed by the Court of Appeal in a recent criminal case, *R v Dimsey* [2001] UKHL 46, [1999] STC 846. The facts of this case are considered below (para 38.17), but the Court emphasised that the central management and control test is a composite test 'designed to identify where the decisions of fundamental policy are made as opposed to the place where the day-to-day profit earning activities are undertaken'.

Shareholder control

38.4 Central management and control must also be distinguished from shareholder control. As the Court of Appeal pointed out in *R v Dimsey* (at p 860), shareholders collectively have the power to ensure that the affairs of the company are conducted in accordance with their wishes, that power being exercised through general meetings. But they do not exercise central management and control of the company's business.

Role of directors

38.5 Assuming a company is being run constitutionally, central management and control of its business is exercised by its directors sitting as a board. Such was described as the paradigm of central management and control in *R v Dimsey* (at p 860). So too in *Wood v Holden*, Park J observed that in all normal cases, central management and control is identified with the control which the board has over the company's business and affairs (see [2005] EWHC 547 (Ch), [2005] STC 789, at para 21). As a result, he said, the principle almost always followed is that a company is resident in the jurisdiction where its board meets. Park J's analysis of the law was approved in the Court of Appeal (see [2006] EWCA Civ 26, [2006] STC 443, 460, at para 27).

Unconstitutional control

38.6 In the first half of the twentieth century, several cases on company residence reached the courts. In all the cases, legal control of the company's business was vested in the directors and it was either found or assumed that what happened in practice accorded with what was required constitutionally. In *Unit Construction Co Ltd v Bullock* [1960] AC 351, the question arose of what the position is if practice diverges from the company's constitution.

The facts were that the taxpayer had incorporated three East African subsidiaries, and, under their articles, the boards of these companies had to meet locally and manage the companies. In fact losses ensued and the board of the taxpayer became so exasperated that they appointed their own man as chairman of the subsidiaries, and ran the East African operation themselves through him. Minutes of board meetings of the local board were written up, but it is clear from the Special Commissioners' findings that the directors never sat round a table or took decisions as a board (see 38 TC 712, 717). At most they merely rubber-stamped decisions already taken in London, the local board minutes being written up after the event.

The case arose because the taxpayer wished to set the East African losses against its own profits. This in turn meant establishing that the subsidiaries were UK resident and so the remarkable position was reached of the taxpayer arguing for UK residence and HMRC resisting this. The Commissioners found in favour of the taxpayer on the grounds that real control and management was at all times exercised by the parent board in London.

Both the High Court and the Court of Appeal held that only authorised and constitutional management and control were material in determining where central management and control lay, and they accordingly quashed the Commissioners' decision. Their decisions were, however, themselves reversed by the House of Lords. As Lord Loreburn pointed out in *De Beers* itself, it is actual conduct that counts in determining a company's residence rather than what should happen under the company's constitution.

In the half century following *Unit Construction Co Ltd v Bullock*, there was uncertainty over how far the decision went. This has now been resolved by *Wood v Holden*. In his analysis of the law approved by the Court of Appeal, Park J referred to four earlier cases where central management and control had been found to lie with the directors. He then contrasted those cases with *Unit Construction Co Ltd v Bullock* in the following terms (see [2005] EWHC 547 (Ch), [2005] STC 789 at para 27 and [2006] STC at para 26):

> 'whereas in *Unit Construction Co Ltd v Bullock*, the parent company itself exercised central control and management of the African subsidiaries, effectively by passing the local boards altogether, in the four cases the parent companies or their equivalents, while telling the local boards what they wished them to do, left it to the local boards to do it.'

Dual residence

38.7 In the early twentieth century, one of the most difficult issues with the central management and control test was whether, and if so, in what circumstances a company can be resident in two territories. The problem first arose in *Swedish Central Rly Co Ltd v Thompson* [1925] AC 495. There the company was UK registered and simply received rent from a railway line it had long since built in Sweden. In 1920, taking advantage of *De Beers*, it removed decision-making powers to Board meetings in Sweden and as a result HMRC conceded that central management and control abided there. But the secretary, the company seal, and the company's bank account remained in London, and three directors and the secretary periodically met there. The Commissioners found that the company was resident in England as well as in Sweden and the House of Lords held that such dual residence was possible in law.

The principle thus established was considered in *Egyptian Delta Land and Investment Co v Todd* [1929] AC 1. In this case, a UK registered company had removed all its functions to Egypt, save those which, as a UK registered company, it was required to have in England. Had the courts decided it was resident in England, they would have effectively decided that under the pre-1988 law, no UK company could ever be non-resident. In fact the decision of the Commissioners, affirmed by the House of Lords, was that the company was non-resident. Many people have found this case difficult to distinguish from the *Swedish Railway* case, but in fact it is not. As Lord Radcliffe pointed out in *Unit Construction Co Ltd v Bullock* [1960] AC 351, in the Swedish case the company did little, and of that little, the functions performed in London were a large part. In the Egyptian case, by contrast, the facts disclosed a large business run wholly in Egypt.

This issue of dual residence was directly in point in *Unit Construction Co Ltd v Bullock* [1960] AC 351, for it had been conceded by HMRC that the three subsidiaries were on any view resident in Kenya. The House of Lords regretted that this concession had been made and, although not essential to the decision, discussed how the dual residence cases should be reconciled with the central management and control test. Lord Radcliffe said they were either an exception to the central management and control test, arising where the facts do not enable central management and control to be identified at all, or result simply from central management and control genuinely being exercised from two territories. It may be suggested that the latter explanation is to be preferred, given that the facts in some dual residence cases are virtually identical with those in *De Beers* itself (see, for example, *Union Corpn Ltd v IRC* (1952) 34 TC 207, 259).

Wood v Holden

38.8 *Wood v Holden* is now the leading case on company residence in an offshore context. At first instance, [2005] EWHC 547 (Ch), [2005] STC 789, Park J delivered an exhaustive analysis of the law and his judgment and reasoning were upheld in the Court of Appeal ([2006] STC 443). HMRC sought leave to appeal to the House of Lords, but their application was refused.

Facts

38.9 *Wood v Holden* concerned schemes to avoid CGT on the sale of a private UK trading company, Greetings. These schemes were devised and orchestrated by Price Waterhouse, the taxpayer's UK accountants, who were providing both tax and corporate finance advice.

The taxpayers were at all times resident and domiciled in the UK. Originally they owned 96% of Greetings, the remaining shares being owned by independent outside shareholders.

In 1995, the taxpayers gave all their shares in Greetings to a newly-formed UK holding company, Holdings. That company was owned as to 51% by the taxpayers or UK trusts, and as to 49% by CIL. CIL was a BVI company administered in Geneva. It was itself owned by offshore trusts created by the taxpayers. As the law stood in 1995, the gift of the shares in Greetings to Holdings attracted hold-over relief under TCGA 1992 s 165. The onward sale by CIL of its shares in Holdings would not have resulted in CGT exposure as the capital structure of CIL meant it was outside TCGA 1992, s 13 as that section then stood (cf Chapter 66).

FA 1996 made changes to s 13 before Holdings had been sold and as a result of those changes any gain realised by CIL on the sale of its shares in Holdings would have been attributed to the taxpayers under the combined effect of TCGA 1992, ss 13 and 86 (see para 66.24). Price Waterhouse therefore devised the following steps to avoid this result:

(1) On 18 July CIL acquired a Dutch company, Eulalia Holding BV. The seller of this company was the ABN Amro group, and at all material times AA Trust, a subsidiary of ABN Amro, was managing director and, it would appear, sole director of Eulalia.
(2) On 23 July 1996, CIL and Eulalia signed an agreement whereby CIL sold all its shares in Holdings to Eulalia for £23m plus overage. The purchase price was left outstanding on the terms of a loan agreement signed on 23 or 24 July.

Thereafter the following took place:

(1) On 5 and 6 August 1996, Eulalia engaged Price Waterhouse to provide tax advice and advise in connection with the sale of its shares in Holdings.
(2) On 30 September 1996, Price Waterhouse introduced to Eulalia a purchaser for its shares in the sum of £30m.
(3) On 21 October 1996 Eulalia and the other shareholders sold their shares to the purchaser.

It was intended that the steps devised by Price Waterhouse in 1996 would avoid CGT for the following reasons:

(a) Eulalia was effectively managed at the ABN/Amro office in Holland.
(b) As such it was a resident of the Netherlands under the UK/Netherlands double tax treaty.

(c) This meant, as HMRC conceded, that TCGA 1992, s 13 could not apply to gains realised by Eulalia (cf para 66.21).
(d) Eulalia was not resident in the UK under the central management and control test.
(e) As such the disposal of the shares in Holdings from CIL to Euaia was a no gain/no loss disposal by virtue of the combined effect of TCGA 1992, ss 14 and 171 (see para 66.14). This meant that for s 13 purposes the gain was carried forward to the ultimate sale by Eulalia, where it was treaty protected.

The Special Commissioners

38.10 HMRC attacked the scheme devised by Price Waterhouse at one point only. They argued that Eulalia was resident in the UK on 23 July 1996. They further conceded or contended that CIL was on that date non-resident with the result that TCGA 1992, s 14 did not operate to render the sale of Holdings shares by CIL to Eulalia a no gain/no loss disposal. This left the way open for TCGA 1992, ss 13 and 86 to attribute it to the taxpayers.

The Commissioners found the facts pertaining to the residence of Eulalia were as follows:

(1) The key date was 23 July 1996. However, it was accepted the subsequent events leading up to the sale of 21 October 1996 were of evidential value.
(2) On 23 July 1996 two individuals representing AA trust, the corporate director of Eulalia, did resolve to buy the shares in Holdings from CIL. However, there was no evidence that they had any materials before them explaining the transaction or how the price had been arrived at.
(3) Between 30 September and 16 October 1996 there were exchanges between Eulalia on the one hand and Price Warehouse and the solicitors acting for the vendors on the other, culminating in AA Trust approving the draft sale documentation on 16 October 1996.
(4) No officer of AA Trust was asked to give oral evidence as to what had in fact happened in 1996. However, one of its officers gave uncontroverted evidence that AA Trust's general practice was to have documents it was asked to enter into as corporate director reviewed by legal counsel. It would consider whether they were in the interests of the company concerned and not detrimental to the position of AA Trust.

The Special Commissioners decided that on 23 July 1996, Eulalia was resident in the UK. Their reasoning is encapsulated in the following two passages at paras 132 and 133 of their decision:

> 'There is no evidence that any consideration was given by Dutch Trust Company of the basis on which the price of £23.7 million was fixed. There is no record of any explanation having been provided by the firm of chartered accountants who had produced the draft agreement containing that figure or of

any advice being requested or given. Neither is there any evidence of any consideration being given as to the price by [the BVI company, by its director, or by the Swiss manager].

We conclude that the Appellants have failed to satisfy us that the central control and management of [the Dutch company] was not in London from 18 July 1996 when [the BVI company] became its shareholder. The only acts of management and control of [the Dutch company] were the making of the board resolutions and the signing or execution of documents in accordance with those resolutions. We do not consider that the mere physical acts of signing resolutions or documents suffice for actual management. Nor does the mental process which precedes the physical act. What is needed is an effective decision as to whether or not the resolution should be passed and the documents signed or executed and such decisions require some minimum level of information. The decisions must at least to some extent be informed decisions. Merely going through the motions of passing or making resolutions and signing documents does not suffice. Where the geographical location of the physical acts of signing and executing documents is different from the place where the actual effective decision that the documents be signed and executed is taken, we consider that the latter place is where "the central management and control actually abides." '

The High Court judgment

38.11 The taxpayers appealed to the High Court. Park J allowed the appeal on the basis that:

> 'On the proper understanding of the law the only correct conclusion capable of being reached on the basis of the materials which the Commissioners had before them was that Eulalia was resident in the Netherlands.'

Park J was satisfied, on the basis of the facts found by the Commissioners, that AA Trust did, as managing director of Eulalia, genuinely resolve on 23 July 1996 to buy the shares in Holdings from CIL, and did in October 1996 genuinely decide to sell those shares to the outside purchaser. The fact that the decisions may have been taken on the advice of Price Waterhouse in the UK, and as part of an overall scheme, did not alter the fact that the decisions had been taken.

The essence of Park J's judgment is that the genuine nature of the decisions was enough. In an interesting aside, it is clear that he regarded as irrelevant the issue of whether, in taking the decisions, AA Trust had sufficient information to properly discharge what its duties as director would have been under English law.

Court of Appeal

38.12 In the Court of Appeal, HMRC contended that the Special Commissioners had determined Eulalia's residence as a question of fact, and that accordingly Park J had had no power to interfere with their decision. Under

Edwards v Bairstow [1956] AC 14, Park J had to be satisfied either that the Special Commissioners had applied the wrong test or that they came to a conclusion which could not properly be reached on the basis of the right test. The Court of Appeal, however, agreed with Park J that the only conclusion open to the Commissioners was that Eulalia was resident in the Netherlands.

In the Court of Appeal's judgment two decisive facts led to this result (para 40):

(1) The directors of Eulalia were not bypassed in July and October 1996 as they did in fact execute the relevant documents.
(2) The Commissioners found that the directors 'accepted' the July purchase agreement and as a result must in fact have decided to execute it.

Like Park J, the Court of Appeal recognised that the Eulalia transactions were part of a pre-planned tax saving scheme and that Price Waterhouse expected AA Trust as managing director to implement its advice. But this, the Court considered, was not relevant. So too the Court of Appeal regarded it as irrelevant that AA Trust may have reached the decisions without proper information or consideration. As Chadwick LJ put it (at para 43) 'ill-informed or ill-advised decisions taken in the management of a company remain management decisions.'.

Earlier offshore cases

38.13 Prior to *Wood v Holden*, several cases since 1990 had also interpreted the central management and control concept in the context of facts familiar to offshore practitioners. Two of these cases were among the four cited with approval in Park J's summary of the law in *Wood v Holden*, namely *Re Little Olympian Each Ways Ltd* and *Untelrab Ltd v McGregor* [1996] STC (SCD) 1.

Re Little Olympian Each Ways Ltd

38.14 In *Re Little Olympian Each Ways Ltd* [1994] 4 All ER 561, Lindsay J had to decide whether a Jersey company had become ordinarily resident in the UK for the purposes of the law relating to service out of the jurisdiction. The company had been struck off the register in Jersey but had since been restored to conduct English litigation. The directors were four partners in a Jersey firm of lawyers, and evidence was given that half the shares were owned by the estate of a Greek intestate and the other half by a Foundation. In practice a UK resident purported to give instructions to the board, and was one of the signatories to the company's bank account. But the company's board did meet and it was the source of instructions to the English solicitors regarding the litigation.

Lindsay J found that the company was not ordinarily resident in the UK. The basis for his decision was his acceptance of evidence from one of the directors to the effect that he would act in accordance with the UK resident's instructions provided they were consistent with Jersey company law and the interests of the actual shareholders. Lindsay J also observed that the UK resident had no constitutional power to impose his wishes on the Board since he was not in fact a shareholder.

Untelrab

38.15 In *Untelrab Ltd v McGregor* [1996] STC (SCD) 1 the Unigate group had incorporated an offshore finance subsidiary which over the years made loans to other group members. The loans resulted from telexed requests from the group head office and the evidence was that none of the requests were improper or unreasonable, but, if any had been, or not been in the interests of the company, they would have been refused. If the group had insisted, the directors would have resigned.

The Special Commissioners found that Untelrab's board did meet, in Bermuda, and transacted the company's business there. The proposals from head office were discussed and the board would have refused to carry out any proposal which was improper or unreasonable. The Commissioners also found that Unigate group policy was to devolve decision-making to the subsidiaries. On these facts the Commissioners found Untelrab was not resident in the UK, and HMRC did not appeal.

R v Crown Court at Kingston

38.16 *R (on the application of IRC) v Crown Court at Kingston* [2001] STC 1615 is a criminal case which is also of interest, despite not being referred to in *Wood v Holden*. Here HMRC prosecuted an accountant who had advised in connection with complex offshore corporate schemes, inter alia involving the transfer of the residence of companies owned by a Swiss resident from the UK to Guernsey. The Crown Court threw the prosecution out and its decision was affirmed by the Divisional Court.

The key issue was the state of the accused's knowledge at the relevant time. However as a preliminary to considering that issue, the Divisional Court made some general observations on when central management and control may be found to abide with a controlling shareholder. It said:

> 'Notwithstanding the ultimate "foreign" ownership of the shares of the company, it will be resident for tax purposes in the offshore jurisdiction in question if the appointed directors genuinely determine its affairs in that jurisdiction. If, however, they simply obey the instructions of the ultimate owner of the company's shares who remains in another jurisdiction, the central management and control, and therefore the residence of the company for the purposes of its tax liabilities, will be the location of the ultimate owner of its shares. The difficulty here is to distinguish between the situation in which the directors act as mere ciphers, simply doing as they are told by the ultimate owner of the company, and the situation in which the directors have explained to them by the

ultimate owner of the company's shares that certain transactions are in the interests of the company, and decide on the basis of the information given to them that the company should enter into them.'

Later it said:

> 'Minutes of both board and general company meetings are often drafted in advance of the meeting to which they relate. There is nothing improper in the use of such drafts, provided the meeting does deal with the business before it in the manner indicated in the draft, and that, in the case of a board meeting, the directors present do have the discussions and make the decisions indicated by the draft. It is one thing for directors to take into account the wishes of the ultimate shareholder of their company or the advice of its advisers, as indicated by a draft resolution; it is another for them to act without regard to the company's interests or their own judgement, but solely because they are instructed to do so by their ultimate shareholder.'

R v Dimsey

38.17 *R v Dimsey* was also a criminal case. Like *Wood v Holden*, it was a decision of the Court of Appeal [1999] STC 846, and as in *Wood v Holden*, permission to appeal on the company residence point was refused by the House of Lords (see [2001] UKHL 46, [2001] STC 1520 at para 26).

Facts

38.18 Dimsey was a Jersey resident whose Jersey company inter alia provided company formation and administration services. One of his clients was Chipping, a UK resident for whom he formed three companies, two of which were used in trading activities and one of which held investments. In the early 1990s Chipping was investigated by HMRC and made what later turned out to be only partial disclosure, claiming to be a consultant in relation to the two trading companies and not referring to the investment company.

In due course Chipping pleaded guilty to the common law offence of cheating the public revenue and both he and Dimsey were convicted of conspiracy. It appears from the Court of Appeal judgment that the cheating charges inter alia related to the profits of the three companies, the prosecution case being that on the facts the companies were UK resident. Accordingly the issue of the residence of the companies went to the jury and, as they convicted Dimsey, they must have concluded the companies were UK resident.

Court of Appeal decision

38.19 In the Court of Appeal, Dimsey argued that the trial judge had misdirected the jury as to company residence. The manner in which the trial judge put the matter was as follows:

> 'You may think that possibly the simplest way of formulating a test in the circumstances of this case is are you sure that Chipping was in reality managing and controlling these companies or may it have been Dimsey or some other person or persons.'

The particular objection which Dimsey took to this approach was that it implied it would have been sufficient for the companies to be UK resident for Chipping to be concerned with day to day management. The Court of Appeal rejected this objection, stating that the key factual issue was whether or not it was Dimsey who managed and controlled the companies, with Chipping acting merely as a consultant. This, the Court of Appeal said, was plainly before the jury.

At first sight, the Court of Appeal judgment is disturbing. In part this is because it does not refer to the directors of the offshore companies at all, still less considering where they met and if so what decisions they reached. Further it is clear that Dimsey signed contracts on behalf of the companies and dealt with invoices and banking matters.

However, on closer examination this concern is more apparent than real. The passages from the trial judge's summing up cited by the Court of Appeal show that the prosecution case was that the business of the companies was really conducted by Chipping in the UK. The defence case was that 'their real business was conducted by Mr Dimsey in Jersey and that Chipping was only a consultant'. In other words, the issue of whether and if so where the boards met does not seem to have been raised by the defence at all, presumably, it is to be inferred, because the boards did not meet or were bypassed. If so, *Dimsey* is a *Unit Construction Co Ltd* type case, where the board is not the determinant of company residence. The issue therefore was who in reality exercised management and control and where did they do it. So analysed, *R v Dimsey* is consistent with the cases cited above.

HMRC practice

38.20 HMRC first published their practice in 1983 (SP 6/83). The current statement of practice was issued in 1990 (SP 1/90). Three points require comment.

First, it is stressed that company residence is ultimately a question of fact, turning on where central management and control is in fact exercised. It means HMRC will, in a disputed case, investigate the facts of how the company has operated, studying Board minutes and other documents and, if available, interviewing witnesses.

Second, HMRC indicate the approach they adopt in investigating the factual position. First, they try to ascertain whether the directors of the company in fact exercise central management and control. Next, if the directors do exercise central management and control, HMRC seek to determine where they in fact do this. Lastly, in cases where the directors apparently do not exercise central management and control, HMRC look to establish where and by whom it is exercised.

The final point to emphasise about HMRC practice is that they sound a warning about company residence in a tax-avoidance context. HMRC examine the facts particularly closely where 'it appears that a major objective underlying the existence of certain factors is the obtaining of tax benefits from residence or non-residence'.

At the time of writing, SP 1/90 has not been updated to reflect *Wood v Holden*. Given that HMRC fought *Wood v Holden*, it is a reasonable inference that, on the criteria set out in SP 1/90, HMRC thought Eulalia was UK resident. To that extent, therefore, what is said in SP 1/90 needs to be qualified. However, in its emphasis on the factual position, and in particular where offshore avoidance is involved, it is still a salutary warning.

Practical conclusions

The position now

38.21 Despite SP 1/90, it is now clear from *Wood v Holden*, and the other recent cases cited above, that an offshore company is resident where its board meet if the board do meet and give genuine consideration to the transactions put before them. It is not necessary for them to meet more often than there are transactions for them to consider and from a company residence standpoint, it is not necessary for them to consider and understand the transactions in detail. All that is required is that they be satisfied the transactions proposed are in the interests of the company, in accordance with its governing law, and proper. Provided the directors give genuine consideration to these issues, it is immaterial that the transactions are proposed by the shareholder or some third party and that the board never in fact refuses 'requests' made by such persons.

Practical steps

38.22 In practice prudent advisers ensure the boards of offshore companies go further than this. Two steps in particular are prudent:

(1) The board should meet, at a minimum, yearly or half-yearly and conduct a genuine review of the company's business and investments.
(2) In reaching any decision the board should have sufficient material before it to properly discharge its duties as a matter of the applicable company law and should have genuine understanding of that material. Even if not necessary to establish company residence, failure to conform with such practice exposes the directors to personal risk under the applicable company law.

In addition, the following common sense steps are essential:

(a) Board meetings should be properly minuted, the minutes reflecting reasoning as well as simply decisions.
(b) All directors minuted as present must in fact have been present.
(c) Any requests from the shareholder or third parties are expressed as requests for consideration rather than instructions.
(d) In the case of complex transactions, the main terms and draft documents are considered and approved by the board well in advance of actual signing.
(e) Any instructions as to implementation are given by or on behalf of the board.

Company residence elsewhere

38.23 As a result of *Wood v Holden*, it is probably fair to say that meetings of the directors will, even if the above guidelines are not followed, only fail to determine company residence in two circumstances. One is if the directors do not meet, as in *Unit Construction Co Ltd v Bullock* and, it is suggested above, *Dimsey*. The other is if, as suggested in *Wood v Holden*, the directors simply sign the documents mindlessly, without even thinking what the documents are (see [2006] STC 443 at para 36). In cases such as this, *R v Dimsey* is a salutary warning of the risks directors run if the result is that the company is thereby rendered UK resident.

Telephonic meetings and written resolutions

38.24 In terms of how meetings are conducted, there is plainly no difficulty under UK company residence rules if the meetings are telephonic, provided none of the participating directors is in the UK. Written resolutions signed by all the directors are in practice frequently used, partly because the participation of all the directors is then proved. It is reasonably clear from *Wood v Holden* that the mere signing by the directors of written agreements was sufficient and if so, the signing of an antecedent written resolution plainly is as well. But in cases of controversy, most practitioners regard it as helpful to have the evidence of properly minuted meetings and certainly, if written resolutions are to be used, it must be clear on the facts that each director understands what he is agreeing to and why it is in the interests of the company. A further point is that no director should sign or consider a written resolution whilst in the UK.

UK resident directors

38.25 In the light of the decision in *Wood v Holden*, the issue may be raised of whether the board of an offshore company can include UK resident individuals. In theory there should be no objection to this, provided the board does meet outside the UK, and is the genuine decision-making forum. But extra care is needed, particularly where the UK resident owns or is interested in shares in the company. In such cases, HMRC scrutiny must be anticipated and to counter this it must be clear on the facts the board is the decision-making body and that it gives any necessary instructions.

Trustee shareholders

38.26 Where the shares in offshore companies are held in an offshore trust *Re Little Olympian Each Ways Ltd* (para 38.14 above) suggests there is an added line of defence against the company being found to be UK resident. This is that if anybody is constitutionally authorised to give 'instructions' to the directors it is the trustee shareholders. Nonetheless, as central management and control is ultimately a question of fact, the residence of a company could be found to be in the UK if both directors and trustees stand aside in favour of a UK resident settlor or UK resident beneficiaries. For this reason, and because it accords with trust and company law, any requests or suggestions from the settlor or the beneficiaries should be directed to the trustees. The trustees can then, if thought fit, communicate with the directors (even if in reality the same individuals are involved).

UK registered companies

38.27 As a result of legislation enacted in 1988, incorporation is the test of residence for UK registered companies (FA 1988, s 66). The case law on central management and control is therefore of relevance only to foreign registered companies.

There is one exception to the incorporation rule. This exception operates if the UK registered company was carrying on business before 15 March 1988 and had become non-resident before then pursuant to a general or a specific Treasury consent obtained under now repealed provisions of TA 1988, s 765. If the consent was a specific consent, the company can remain non-resident regardless of where it is based, and it only becomes UK resident if it in fact becomes resident under the central management and control test.

If the consent was a general consent, a further condition has to be satisfied. This condition is that the company was taxable in a foreign territory. By 'taxable' is meant being liable to tax on income by reason of domicile, residence, or place of management, but not simply being liable to a flat-rate sum or fee (see FA 1988, Sch 7, para 5 and SP 1/90, para 6). Provided a company which migrated before 15 March 1988 pursuant to a general consent was taxable in a foreign state it may remain non-resident, but only so long as it is so taxable. There was in fact only ever one general consent, which applied where the company was formed after 1951 to carry on new business and over half its share capital was owned by non-residents.

The exception for companies which became non-resident pursuant to a specific consent applies also to companies which migrated after 15 March

1988 pursuant to a specific consent applied for before then. Such a company does however have to have commenced business before then.

Dual resident companies

38.28 A company is generally referred to as dual resident if the following conditions are satisfied:

(1) It is resident in the UK under UK domestic law whether as a UK registered company or under the central management and control test.
(2) It is liable to tax in some other state by reason of residence, domicile, or place of management.
(3) There is a double tax treaty between the UK and the other state.
(4) Under the tie-breaker clause in the treaty it is treated as resident in the other state for the purposes of the treaty.

In the OECD Model Treaty, the test under the tie-breaker article is where the company's place of effective management is situated. In *Wensleydale's Settlement Trustees v IRC* [1996] STC (SCD) 241, a Special Commissioner considered that the place of effective management is where the shots are called, implying realistic positive management. HMRC consider that the place of effective management may, in some cases, differ from the place of control (SP 1/90, para 22).

In *Wood v Holden* [2005] EWHC 547 (Ch), [2005] STC 789, the taxpayer argued that even if Eulalia was resident in the UK under the central management and control test, its place of effective management was in the Netherlands. The Special Commissioners rejected this argument, holding that on the facts of the case there was no difference between effective management and central management and control. The Court of Appeal found it very difficult to see how, in the circumstances of the case, the effective management test and the central management and control test could lead to different results (see [2006] STC 443 para 44).

The normal case of a dual resident company is a UK registered company whose effective management is in the treaty state. But a foreign registered company can also be dual resident, as was argued in *Wood v Holden*. According to HMRC, an example of a dual resident foreign registered company would be where the company's business is run by executives abroad with the final directing power resting with a non-executive board in the UK.

A company which would otherwise be dual resident is deemed for all UK tax purposes to be non-resident (FA 1994, s 249). This rule applies whether or not the company has hitherto claimed relief under the treaty concerned. It is not of great relevance to offshore tax planning, for few offshore jurisdictions have double tax treaties in the UK with tie-breaker clauses as to residence. But *Wood v Holden* is a case where it could have been in point.

Chapter 39

Domicile

What is domicile?

39.1 Domicile is a legal status whose primary role is as a connecting factor. It determines whether English or some foreign law regulates personal relationships, e g marriage, legitimacy and succession. Domicile has been adopted by the UK tax system as a factor limiting the UK tax jurisdiction but it should be remembered that it is a general legal concept, and not one created merely for tax purposes.

An individual can have only one domicile at any time: a domicile of origin; a domicile of choice; or a domicile of dependency. The place in which an individual is domiciled is not necessarily a nation in a political sense, but any geographical area governed by a single system of law (*Re Fuld's Estate (No 3)* [1968] P 675 at 682–684). Thus an individual is domiciled in 'England' or 'Scotland', rather than in 'the United Kingdom' and in one of the several states which make up such federal countries as Australia or the United States.

The concept of domicile evolved in relation to individuals and for tax purposes is material only in relation to individuals. It has been held that a company has a domicile where it is registered, but no aspect of corporate tax liability turns on domicile (cf *Gasque v IRC* (1940) 23 TC 210).

Domicile of origin

39.2 An individual acquires a domicile of origin when he is born (*Henderson v Henderson* [1967] P 77, [1965] 1 All ER 179). Normally, this is his father's domicile at the date of his birth, but if his parents are unmarried, it is the mother's domicile. A domicile of origin continues unless and until the individual acquires either a domicile of dependency or a domicile of choice: upon his acquiring one or other, that will remain his domicile until abandoned. If it is abandoned without another domicile of choice or dependency being acquired, the domicile of origin revives (*Udny v Udny* (1869) LR 1 Sc & Div 441).

A person's domicile of origin is often described as having an adhesive quality. The reasons why the domicile of origin is said to be adhesive are twofold. First, the burden is on whoever alleges a person has acquired a domicile of choice to prove it. Second, although the standard of proof is the civil standard it is variously said either that the burden is heavy (*Winans v A-G* [1904] AC 287, 291) or that the acquisition of a domicile of choice is regarded as a serious matter, not to be lightly inferred from slight indications or casual words (*Re Fuld's Estate (No 3)* [1968] P 675 at 684; *Buswell v IRC* [1974] 2 All ER 520, [1974] STC 266). This second point may, however, be called into question by *Bheekhun v Williams* [1999] 2 FLR 229. Here the Court of Appeal affirmed that the burden of proof is on the person who alleges a change of domicile but it weighed the evidence in the case on the ordinary civil balance of probabilities.

Domicile of choice

39.3 The modern law on domicile of choice is founded on Scarman J's judgment in *Re Fuld's Estate (No 3) Hartley v Fuld* [1968] P 675. In a much-quoted passage, he said that an individual acquires a domicile of choice if he fixes his chief residence in the new country and intends to reside there 'indefinitely' or for an 'unlimited time'. This formulation was followed by the Law Commission in their 1987 report on the law of domicile (Cmnd 200). That report states the individual must both reside in the new country and have an intention 'to make his home in [the new] country permanently or indefinitely'. This passage of the Law Commission's report was cited with approval in Lady Hale's speech in *Mark v Mark* [2005] UKHL 42, [2005] 3 AII ER 912 (at para 39), and as a result now has the authority of the House of Lords.

An individual can acquire a domicile of choice once he has attained the age of 16.

Residence

39.4 It is to be stressed that the acquisition of a domicile of choice involves the fact of residence as well as an intention. For these purposes it is clear that a residence only counts if it is the person's sole or chief residence. Thus in *Plummer v IRC* [1988] 1 All ER 97, [1987] STC 698, a young lady who intended to reside permanently in Guernsey did not acquire a domicile of choice there because her chief residence was in England, her home in Guernsey being on the facts merely secondary. So too in *IRC v Duchess of Portland* [1982] STC 149, a lady failed to abandon an English domicile of choice because, although she did not intend to remain permanently in England, her chief residence was there. But retention of accommodation in the country of origin does not negative the acquisition of a domicile of choice elsewhere if on the facts the new country is the main home (*Shaffer v Cilento* [2004] EWHC 188 (Ch), [2004] All ER (D) 122 (Feb)).

Intention

39.5 Two Court of Appeal decisions have clarified what is meant by permanently or indefinitely.

The more recent, *Cyganik v Agulian* [2006] All ER (D) 372 (Feb) concerned a Greek Cypriot who died in 2003 having lived in the UK for 43 years. The Court of Appeal cited passages in Scarman J's judgment in *Re Fuld*, to the effect that the necessary intention is lacking if the individual intends to return to the land of his birth 'upon a clearly foreseen and reasonably anticipated contingency', such as the end of his job. But the position is otherwise if what he has in mind is only a vague possibility, such as making a fortune or some sentiment about dying in the land of his fathers. Applying this test, the Court of Appeal decided that the individual in *Cyganik v Agulian* was still domiciled in Cyprus.

The other, much earlier, decision of the Court Appeal is *IRC v Bullock* [1976] STC 409. Here the taxpayer, who was Canadian, had come to England in 1932 to serve in the RAF, and he had married an English woman in 1947. He had lived in England since 1932, and HMRC asserted for 1971–2 and 1972–3 that he had acquired an English domicile of choice. His wife, who was four years younger, would not contemplate moving to Canada, but the evidence was the taxpayer would go back there if she predeceased him. The Court of Appeal decided in these circumstances that he still had a Canadian domicile.

In the course of reaching this decision the Court of Appeal reviewed nineteenth century cases as well as *Re Fuld*. The Court concluded that a domicile of choice is only acquired if the individual 'intends to make his home in the new country until the end of his days unless and until something happens to make him change his mind' (at p 415). The existence of a contingency on which he would return to his country of origin negatives the necessary intention provided the contingency is not doubtful or indefinite and there is a sufficiently substantial possibility of it happening.

Return to the country of origin

39.6 Despite what is said in some of the passages cited above, the intention which has to be proved is the intention to remain permanently or indefinitely in the new country. It does not have to be proved that the contingency on which the individual would leave entails his return to his country of origin (*Cyganik v Agulian* [2006] All ER (D) 372 (Feb) para 49)). But it is important that the individual has the necessary intention to remain in one particular country as his main home: it is not sufficient to acquire a domicile of choice if the individual is unclear which of several countries he will finally settle in even though he has no intention of ever returning to his country of origin (cf *Surveyor v IRC* [2002] STC (SCD) 501).

Evidence of intention

39.7 A person only acquires a domicile of choice in the new country if his intention to remain there is firm and settled (*Re Clore, Official Solicitor v Clore* (No 2) [1984] STC 609). Another way of putting the same point is that the intention must be clear and unequivocal (*Cyganik v Agulian* at para 51). What an individual intended has to be ascertained as a fact by a process of inference from all the available evidence (*Cyganik v Agulian* at para 13). All that the individual has said and done must be looked at. Account can be taken of what the individual said and did after the alleged change of domicile as well as what he said and did before (*Bheekhun v Williams* [1999] 2 FLR 229). The task which has to be undertaken was described in graphic terms by Megarry J in *Re Flynn; Flynn v Flynn* [1968] 1 All ER 49, 51:

> 'In one sense there is no end to the evidence that may be adduced; for the whole of a man's life and all that he has said and done, however trivial, may be prayed in aid in determining what his intention was at any given moment in time. The state of a man's mind is as much a fact as the state of his digestion, but, as Harman LJ is reputed to have observed, "the doctors know precious little about the one and the judges know nothing about the other". The difficulty is as old as the Year Books and the celebrated dictum of Brian CJ in 1477, uttered in theological terms which have waned in fashion: "*Le Diable n'ad conusance de l'entent de home*". All that the courts can do is to draw inferences from what has been said and done; and in doing this, too much detail may stultify.'

Statements the person has made are not necessarily conclusive in determining whether he has acquired a domicile of choice. Thus in *Wahl v A-G* [1932] 147 LT 382, HL, a German applied for British naturalisation and stated to the Home Secretary that he intended to reside permanently in the UK and had no intention of leaving it. This, however, was held to be insufficient to displace other evidence that a domicile of choice had not been acquired. Statements to HMRC that the individual intends to remain indefinitely in the UK are not conclusive as to domicile either. Nor even are statements in an HMRC affidavit that the deceased was UK domiciled if there is no evidence that the issue had been properly considered by the person swearing the affidavit (*Buswell v IRC* [1974] STC 266; *Re Furse; Furse v IRC* [1980] STC 596).

The acquisition of nationality and a passport in the new country can point to the acquisition of a domicile of choice there but it is not conclusive evidence. Thus in *Bheekhun v Williams* [1999] 2 FLR 229 the deceased was a Mauritian who had come to the UK in 1960, and chose to retain a British passport when Mauritius became independent in 1968. The trial judge and the Court of Appeal accepted evidence that the deceased was then considering remaining in the UK and concluded he had acquired a UK domicile of choice. But in *F v IRC* [2000] STC (SCD) 1, an Iranian exile with long-standing UK connections, including a UK home, obtained indefinite leave to remain in the UK in 1980 and British citizenship and a passport in 1982. On the evidence he intended always to return to Iran when it was safe to do so, and had acquired a British passport merely for travel convenience. On these facts, a Special Commissioner found he retained his Iranian domicile.

The fact that the individual is in the new country illegally does not, per se, prevent him from acquiring a domicile of choice there although it is clearly relevant in determining his intention (*Mark v Mark* [2005] 3 All ER 912).

Abandonment

39.8 A domicile of choice may be abandoned. For this to happen, the country of choice must cease to be the individual's main residence and he must cease to intend to resume main residence there (*Re Flynn; Flynn v Flynn* [1968] 1 All ER 49; *IRC v Duchess of Portland* [1982] STC 149). The change of intention need not be a positive decision not to return but may simply be a withering of intention so that at some point it can be said the intention has gone (*Shaffer v Cilento* [2004] EWHC 188 (Ch), [2004] All ER (D) 122 (Feb)). Nonetheless, the absence of intention must be unequivocal and, as with the acquisition of a domicile of choice, is not to be lightly inferred.

A practical question of some importance is whether a UK national who has acquired a foreign domicile of choice loses that domicile if he has to return to the UK for medical reasons and eventually dies there. The Special Commissioner's decision in *Allen v Revenue and Customs Comrs* [2005] STC (SCD) 614 indicates the domicile of choice is not lost if the foreign home is kept and maintained ready for occupation and it is clear on the facts the individual would return there, if, for example, the family members caring for him would accompany him.

Domicile of dependency

39.9 A domicile of dependency can be attributed only to a child under 16. A child's domicile of origin is displaced by a domicile of dependency if the domicile of the parent upon whom the child's domicile depends changes. If this happens the domicile of choice, which the parent thereby acquires, becomes the child's domicile of dependency. On attaining 16 a domicile of dependency is retained by the child as a domicile of choice. But if the child does not live in the territory and never intends to live there, this acquired domicile of choice is forthwith abandoned. Normally in these circumstances the child's domicile of origin revives but if he is living in a third territory with the intention of remaining there, that territory becomes his domicile of choice (*Re Scullard, Smith v Brock* [1957] Ch 107).

The domicile on which a child under 16 normally depends is that of his father, but his mother's domicile is the relevant domicile if the child is illegitimate, the father is dead, or the parents are separated and the child has no home with the father (see Law Commission report on the Law of Domicile, Cmnd 200 (1987) pp 4–5).

Until 1974, a married woman did not enjoy an independent domicile but took her husband's domicile as a domicile of dependency. This rule was abolished in 1973 (Domicile and Matrimonial Proceedings Act 1973, s 1). A married woman's domicile is now determined independently in the same way as that of her husband. But a woman who on 1 January 1974 had her husband's domicile, as a domicile of dependency, retained that domicile as a domicile of choice and must abandon it before she can acquire, or reacquire, her own domicile (*IRC v Duchess of Portland* [1982] Ch 314, [1982] STC 149).

Establishing an individual's domicile

39.10 In practical terms it is frequently important for a taxpayer to establish with HMRC what his domicile is. In many cases it is necessary to do this before entering into a particular transaction, for the domicile of the taxpayer will affect the form the transaction takes.

Retaining a foreign domicile of origin

39.11 If the issue is whether a UK resident with a foreign domicile of origin has acquired a UK domicile of choice, the matter may be tested by ensuring that the taxpayer has some unremitted foreign income. As is described in Chapter 40 such income is not taxable unless the taxpayer is UK domiciled. Claims for non-domiciliary treatment should be made on form DOM 1, form P86 or on the individual's tax return. If a claim is made prior to the submission of the return HMRC will respond with a ruling (*Tax Bulletin* 29 (June 1997) 425). If a claim is made on an individual's tax return, it will be conclusive as respects the year of the return provided sufficient information is given and HMRC do not raise an enquiry within the year following the 31 January deadline for submission of the return. The taxpayer's domicile is at large in future years if HMRC enquire into the returns for those years.

In practical terms, the best way of substantiating a claim that the taxpayer does not intend to remain in the UK indefinitely is if he keeps a home or other property in his country of origin. Property in the country of origin is not however conclusive if other evidence clearly points to the acquisition of a domicile of choice in the UK (*Bheekhun v Williams* [1999] 2 FLR 229). Another important practical step is that the taxpayer makes a will under the law of the country of origin, for if that country is indeed his domicile, its law governs the devolution of his estate. It also helps if it is his wish to be buried there (*Anderson v IRC* [1998] STC (SCD) 43).

If there is a change in the relevant facts in any tax year, the individual in his return for that year should tick box 29 of the non-residence etc pages. Should it be concluded that as a result of the change the individual has acquired a UK domicile, HMRC may, depending on the circumstances, treat the change as deferred until the beginning of the following tax year (*Tax Bulletin* 29 (July 1997) p 426). If an individual fails to tick box 29 when he should have done, it would be open to HMRC to raise an enquiry after the one-year enquiry window has closed.

Acquiring a foreign domicile of choice

39.12 The contrary situation is where a UK domiciliary migrates and wishes to establish a foreign domicile of choice. In this situation HMRC will not give a hypothetical ruling, and so the best solution is for the taxpayer to wait until three complete tax years have elapsed and then make a gift of foreign situs assets in excess of the IHT nil-rate band to a trust.

It is necessary to wait for three complete tax years because, for IHT purposes, a UK domicile is deemed to persist for three years after it is in fact lost and is retained if the taxpayer has been resident in the UK in 17 of the last 20 years of assessment (see para 30.14). Provided the gift consists of foreign situs assets, IHT will be chargeable unless the taxpayer has lost both his actual and his deemed UK domicile. Accordingly, if in fact HMRC do not seek to charge IHT, it will be clear that they accept he has acquired a foreign domicile.

In practical terms, HMRC are prepared to accept that migrants from the UK have acquired a foreign domicile if the facts warrant this. One point, however, is important. Once the three-year period has elapsed, the foreign domicile of the taxpayer should be established immediately. This safeguards the position if, later, the taxpayer has to return to the UK for medical or other reasons, for, once he has returned, it may be difficult to prove he intended to remain abroad indefinitely.

Proposals for change

39.13 The 1987 Law Commission paper referred to above proposed changes to the law of domicile (Cmnd 200), but so far no action has been taken to implement these proposals. The proposals were enshrined in a draft bill, the main points of which were as follows:

(1) The domicile of origin should be abolished.
(2) A child's domicile should be that of the country with which he is most closely connected. In the absence of evidence to the contrary, this country would be presumed to be the country where his parents are domiciled.
(3) On attaining adulthood, a person should retain his childhood domicile unless and until he acquires another domicile.
(4) An adult should acquire a new domicile if he is present in a new country and intends to remain there for an indefinite period. He should keep that domicile unless and until he acquires another one.

In 1988 HMRC published a consultative paper containing proposals which would, if implemented, have removed domicile as a connecting factor for income tax and CGT (Inland Revenue 'Residence in the United Kingdom' July 1988). These proposals were withdrawn in 1989.

In the 2002 Budget, the Chancellor announced a review of the rules of residence and domicile. A background paper, containing no proposals but a review of current law and international comparisons, was published in April 2003. The next stage was said to be a consultation paper setting out possible approaches to reform (2004 Economic and Fiscal Strategy Report (March 2004) para 5.103). No announcement has been made as to when this will be issued.

Section III

The Remittance Basis

Chapter 40

Investment income

Relevant foreign income

40.1 The remittance basis applies to what ITTOIA 2005 calls relevant foreign income (ITTOIA 2005, s 831). Relevant foreign income is defined in ITTOIA 2005, s 830 as income arising from a source outside the UK which is chargeable under one of a number of specified provisions.

The principal categories of income which, if the source is foreign, are relevant foreign income are as follows:

(1) Trade profits
(2) Foreign rental income
(3) Interest
(4) Dividends paid by non-resident companies
(5) Deep discount
(6) Royalties
(7) Annual payments and other income not otherwise charged

In determining whether income arises from a source outside the UK, and thus is relevant foreign income, the normal rules as to source apply. These rules are explained in Chapter 33.

The remittance basis does not apply to relevant foreign income arising in the Republic of Ireland (ITTOIA 2005, s 831(5)).

In addition to the remittance basis applicable to relevant foreign income, the remittance basis also applies to certain categories of employment income and to CGT. The remittance basis for employment income and CGT is enacted in legislation which in some respects differs from that applicable to relevant foreign income. It is considered in Chapters 23 and 41.

The charge to tax

40.2 The remittance basis applies for any tax year if the recipient of the income makes a claim to that effect for the year concerned under ITTOIA 2005, s 832(1) (ITTOIA 2005, s 878(2)). Once a claim is made it covers all the taxpayer's relevant foreign income for the year. An individual may make a claim if he is either not domiciled in the UK or if he is not ordinarily resident in the UK. Both these terms bear their normal common law definitions, discussed in Chapters 36 and 39. In particular there is no concept of deemed domicile such as applies to inheritance tax.

Assuming a claim is made, the charge on relevant foreign income is made on:

> 'the full amount of the sums received in the United Kingdom in the tax year in respect of the income.'

This is enacted by ITTOIA 2005, s 832(1), the central charging provision of the remittance basis. It is further provided, by s 832(2) that:

> 'it does not matter whether the income arises in the year in which the claim is made or arose in an earlier year in which the person was UK resident.'

Remittances form part of the taxpayer's total income and so are subject to higher or basic rate tax as appropriate. The lower rate and dividend ordinary rate are not available as those rates do not apply to dividends and interest taxed on the remittance basis (TA 1988, s 1A(4)(a)). Remittances of foreign dividends do however attract the dividend upper rate (TA 1988 s 1B). Until 5 April 2005, that rate was not applicable to income computed on the remittance basis, but the position was changed inadvertently as part of the rewrite resulting in ITTOIA 2005 (see *Tax Bulletin 84* (August 2006) p 1303). Foreign dividends are treated with UK dividends as comprising the highest part of a taxpayer's income (TA 1988 s 1A(5)).

As remittances are included in total income, personal reliefs, the starting rate, and other deductions from total income are available. Accordingly, a non-domiciliary with no UK income can make modest tax-free remittances of income by utilising his personal allowance.

If the remitted income has suffered foreign tax, double tax relief is allowed, but on the basis that the income is grossed up by the foreign tax (TA 1988, s 795(1)). In some cases, the credit for foreign tax can mean remittance of the income occasions little or no UK tax, particularly if the taxpayer is not thereby brought into the higher rate band.

The remittance basis is wholly on a current year basis. In other words, the charge under s 832(1) is on the amounts remitted to the UK in the year concerned.

History

40.3 Prior to 6 April 2005, the remittance basis applied to income chargeable under Cases IV and V of Schedule D. Case V included an extended definition of remittance, but in the leading case of *Thomson v Moyse* [1961] AC 967, the House of Lords held that the charge under both Case IV and Case V was on the full amount of the actual sums received in the UK. Apart from the redundant word 'actual' this is the same language as that now used by ITTOIA 2005, s 832(1).

The remittance basis applicable to Cases IV and V originally applied to the foreign income of all taxpayers and dated back to the first enactment of income tax. Since 1974 it has applied only to non-domiciliaries and to

Commonwealth and Irish citizens not ordinarily resident in the UK. It had been progressively withdrawn from other categories of taxpayer between the years 1914 and 1974.

It will be observed that ITTOIA 2005 has in one respect widened the categories of taxpayer eligible for the remittance basis. It now applies to all those who are not ordinarily resident in the UK and not just to such persons who are Commonwealth or Irish citizens.

As the language of s 832(1) replicates the effect of the language formally applicable to Cases IV and V, it may be inferred that the very substantial body of case law on the meaning of 'received' under Cases IV and V remains good law. Indeed, given that ITTOIA is simply a rewrite, any other conclusion would be most surprising.

Meaning of 'received'

40.4 At one time a very technical view was taken of whether income had been received in the UK for the purposes of Cases IV and V. In *Hall v Marians* (1935) 19 TC 582 and *IRC v Gordon* (1952) 33 TC 226 the taxpayer had had accounts with the National Bank of India both at its London branch and at its Colombo branch. The taxpayer overdrew at the London branch, and from time to time the overdraft was transferred to the Colombo branch where it was cleared out of the taxpayer's foreign income. The House of Lords held that there had been no remittance of that income.

Hall v Marians and *IRC v Gordon* were reversed by what is now re-enacted as ITTOIA 2005,ss 833, 834 (see para 40.14 below). But in *Thomson v Moyse* (1958) 39 TC 291 an even more technical analysis found favour in the Court of Appeal. In *Thomson v Moyse*, the taxpayer had drawn cheques on his New York bank in favour of his UK bank, and the UK bank had bought the cheques and immediately credited the taxpayer's account with the sterling proceeds. Its agents in New York then presented the cheques through their New York bank, and the UK bank was credited in New York with the proceeds in dollars, which it sold in New York to the Bank of England for sterling. The Court of Appeal held that the taxpayer's US dollar income had not been remitted to the UK, on the grounds that the dollars had been sold by him to the London bank in New York.

This decision was reversed in the House of Lords. Lord Radcliffe stated that Cases IV and V were concerned simply with the turning of income which has arisen in a foreign country into the expendable resources of the taxpayer in the UK. He encapsulated the principles which should apply as follows:

> 'the computation … depends simply on the question, what is the amount of sums which have been or will be received in the United Kingdom in the year of assessment. No doubt proper construction of those words requires that the sums computable must be "of" the income, by which I would understand "sums of money derived from the application of the income to achieving the necessary transfer". But that is all. If sterling sums are received, and are so attributable, that is enough for liability.'

Thomson v Moyse represents a practical approach to the remittance rules and undoubtedly ended certain highly technical avoidance schemes. However, apart from *Hall v Marians* and *IRC v Gordon*, earlier decisions in favour of the taxpayer were left standing and these form the basis of current planning techniques for non-domiciliaries. As noted above, the language of ITTOIA 2005, s 832(1) effectively replicates the result of *Thompson v Moyse*, and so it is to these techniques that attention must now be turned.

Do not bring the income to the UK

40.5 It goes without saying that if income is not remitted the charge under s 832(1) does not arise. Accordingly, no liability arises if income is spent abroad or simply reinvested abroad. The foreign domiciliary who does not need to spend his foreign investment income in the UK is thus able to accumulate that income abroad wholly free of UK tax.

Apart from ITTOIA 2005, ss 833 and 834 (para 40.16 below), there is no concept of constructive remittance. Early in the twentieth century HMRC argued that life assurance companies who made up accounts showing unremitted foreign income as an asset must be treated as having remitted it. This argument, however, was rejected by the House of Lords (*Gresham Life Assurance Society Ltd v Bishop* [1902] AC 287).

Where HMRC were more successful was in establishing that if a remittance is made from a mixed fund, it is presumed to be income to the extent that income has been paid into the fund. This was established in *Scottish Provident Institution v Allan* (1903) 4 TC 591, where the taxpayer had sent money out to Australia for investment on mortgage. Substantial amounts of interest had accrued and both this and the repayments of principal had been intermixed. In remitting money back to England the company's Australian agents designated the remittances as repayment of principal but this was held to be ineffective in the House of Lords. In a memorable phrase, Lord Halsbury LC observed that 'the mere nicknaming the sum received' could not alter the taxability of what was in substance profit earned abroad.

In practice a non-domiciliary often uses a mixed account to fund both foreign and UK spending. An issue often raised is whether, if foreign spending precedes UK spending, it should be regarded as having drawn off income rather than capital in the account. Logical application of *Scottish Provident Institution v Allan* suggests this is the right analysis. But there is neither authority nor published HMRC practice on the point.

An account may also consist of some income taxed on the arising basis and some on the remittance basis. In practice HMRC treat the income taxed on the arising basis as remitted first (Inspector's Manual, para 1568). Dicta in *Roxburghe's Executors v IRC* (1936) 20 TC 711 suggest this accords with the legal position.

A point which must be remembered is that income counts as remitted if it is received in the UK; it does not have to be received by the taxpayer personally. Thus, receipt by some third party on the taxpayer's instructions counts as remittance (*Timpson's Executors v Yerbury* (1936) 20 TC 155, CA). This means that a remittance occurs if the taxpayer draws a cheque on his foreign bank account in favour of a UK supplier of goods or services. So too settling a UK credit card is a remittance, as is the use of a foreign credit card in the UK.

Mere reinvestment of foreign income abroad does not amount to remittance, although if the investment is sold outside the UK, the income is remitted if and when the proceeds are received in the UK (*Patuck v Lloyd* (1944) 26 TC 284; *Walsh v Randall* (1940) 23 TC 55). If the investment is in bearer form or is a chattel and physically brought to the UK no remittance then occurs (*Scottish Widows' Fund Life Assurance Society v Farmer* (1909) 5 TC 502, CS). But the income does count as remitted when any asset brought to the UK is sold in the UK (*Scottish Provident Institution v Farmer* (1912) 6 TC 34).

It is sometimes suggested that if a large one-off remittance is made from a mixed fund to meet capital expenditure such is a remittance of the capital in the fund and so tax-free. Such a proposition lacks authority and is of doubtful validity for income is taxable even if capitalised prior to remittance. This is apparent from the cases noted above where the income has been invested and the proceeds of sale brought into the UK.

Remittance does not occur just because a non-domiciliary receives a cheque in the UK which he later credits to a foreign bank account. But remittance does occur if the cheque is presented in the UK or, in HMRC's view, if it is given away in the UK or passed in the UK to a third party in settlement of a debt (Inspector's Manual para 1564).

Capital and income accounts

40.6 The procedure of operating capital and income accounts circumvents the decision in *Scottish Provident Institution v Allan*, for it enables the taxpayer to demonstrate that what is remitted is not income. The procedure requires the taxpayer to have two bank accounts, one of which is credited with income receipts and the other only with capital. Remittances to the UK are made only from this second account.

HMRC challenged the capital and income account procedure in *Kneen v Martin* (1934) 19 TC 33. Here the taxpayer was a UK citizen who commenced residence in the UK in 1925. She had two bank accounts at the New York office of the Bankers Trust Company of New York. One was credited with the income from her US investments, and the other, from which remittances to the UK were made, with the proceeds of capital realisations. The Special Commissioners found she had not remitted income and this finding was affirmed in the Court of Appeal. The key findings of the Special Commissioners were as follows:

> 'the proper inferences for us to draw were that the actual sums remitted to the [UK] were all derived from the proceeds of realisation of investments owned by [the taxpayer] before 1925 and not from income, or the proceeds of realisation

> of investments acquired out of income, arising since that date, and that she was not resident in the United Kingdom before 1925. We also thought it a reasonable inference that the investments sold had been largely replaced by other investments acquired out of income arising in America.'

House of Lords approval to capital and income account procedures may be inferred from Lord Radcliffe's remark in *Thomson v Moyse* that the sum remitted must be income. ITTOIA 2005, s 832(1) adopts this approval, for it requires that the sums received in the UK must be 'in respect of the income'.

The findings in *Kneen v Martin* show that the capital and income accounts may be at the same branch of the foreign bank, and that it matters not that the accumulated foreign income is reinvested abroad. It is, however, important to remember that the capital account cannot contain the proceeds of all investments sold; it can only be credited with proceeds of investments not directly or indirectly acquired out of foreign income. This is an application of the principle in *Patuck v Lloyd*, noted above.

The obvious example of investments not acquired out of income is inherited investments or investments acquired out of inherited capital; as is noted in Chapter 42, a gift is capital in the hands of the donee even if made out of the donor's income. The passage from the Commissioners' decision in *Kneen v Martin* cited above suggested that money also counts as capital if it represents or is derived from income which arose prior to UK residence. This is now confirmed by ITTOIA 2005, s 832(2), which is limited to income arising in years in which the taxpayer was UK resident.

It is not unknown for foreign banks to misunderstand a non-domiciliary's instructions and debit a remittance to the UK to the wrong account. Where this occurs the non-domiciliary can require the bank to correct the position by appropriate book entries and, as against HMRC, the remittance is treated as if it had come from the account originally specified by the non-domiciliary (*Roxburghe v IRC* (1936) 20 TC 711).

Cessation of source

40.7 It is a well-established principle that income cannot be taxed in a year of assessment unless the source from which it is derived exists during that year. This principle was established in the 1920s in *National Provident Institution v Brown* (1921) 8 TC 57, HL and *Whelan v Henning* (1926) 10 TC 263. In many instances, for example post cessation trading receipts, it has been abrogated by statute, but otherwise, as *Bray v Best* [1989] STC 159, HL affirmed, the principle remains good law.

Practice

40.8 On the basis of the cessation of source principle a well-established practice of avoiding tax on remittances has grown up, whereby an investment is sold or a bank account closed in one year of assessment, and the income it produced remitted in the following year. It is clear from the notes on the non-residence etc pages of the tax return (p NRN5) that HMRC do not regard such a remittance as taxable. Indeed in para 4.17 of the 1988 Consultative Document 'Residence: the scope of UK Taxation for Individuals' it was stated that the following procedure prevents income being regarded as a 'remittance':

> 'closing an account or selling an income producing asset in one year, and remitting accumulated income in the next when there is no longer a source of income that can be charged to tax.'

This practice has been widely exploited as a tax-avoidance strategy. But two questions do have to be considered in relation to it. The first is whether the practice is soundly based in law, and thus whether HMRC could, with due notice, change it. The second is when a new bank account is a separate source.

Legal basis

40.9 On the face of it, the practice is not soundly based in law, for ITTOIA 2005, s 832(2) expressly provides that a remittance is taxable even if the income arose in an earlier tax year. However this initial impression is false, for nothing in ITTOIA 2005 suggests it has abolished the source doctrine. Indeed, ITTOIA 2005, s 830 uses the word 'source' in defining the various categories of relevant foreign income.

The point may be confirmed by comparing the provisions in ITTOIA 2005 with the equivalent provisions of ITEPA 2003 dealing with employment income. ITEPA 2003, s 22(3)(b) makes it clear that a remittance of earnings is taxable whether or not the employment is held at the time of the remittance. There is no equivalent provision in ITTOIA 2005, s 832(2).

Under the former Cases IV and V there was at one time doubt about the cessation of source procedure on account of *Diggines v Forestal Land, Timber and Railways Co* (1930) 15 TC 630. At the time to which that case related, taxpayers other than non-domiciled individuals were taxed on the arising basis on the average of the preceding three years under Rule 1 of Case V on income from stocks, shares, and rents, and on a remittance basis under Rule 2 on income from other foreign possessions. The taxpayer company held shares in several foreign companies, and the Court of Appeal decided each holding was a separate source, with the result, following *Whelan v Henning*, that if a given holding yielded no dividends in a year of assessment no tax was exigible for that year in respect of the holding. The House of Lords reversed this decision, deciding that no further sub-division of Case V beyond Rules 1 and 2 was appropriate. Rule 1 referred to 'the full amount' of the income from stocks, shares and rents, and this the House of Lords decided meant tax under Rule 1 could be charged provided any stocks, shares, or rents produced income in the year concerned.

The division of Case V into Rules 1 and 2 was abolished in 1940, but under TA 1988, s 65(5)(b) the charge under the unified Case V was still on 'the full amount' of sums received in the UK. On the face of it, it could be argued that the ratio of *Diggines* applied to the effect that all sources within Case V had to cease before remittance in a subsequent year could be tax free.

In fact such a conclusion is almost certainly wrong. In 1926, FA 1926, ss 29–31 replaced the three-year average with the preceding-year basis. Section 30 enacted what became TA 1988, s 67 to the effect that where in a year of assessment the taxpayer ceased to possess all or any part of a particular source of income, that source or part was treated separately. These rules were considered obiter by the House of Lords in *Goodlass Wall and Lead Industries Ltd v Atkinson* (1950) 31 TC 447, HL, and in three out of the four reasoned speeches they were construed as precluding income arising from assets the taxpayer had ceased to possess in one year being included in the measure of Case V liability the following year. In other words, they impliedly overruled *Diggines*. They were expressed in terms of income arising, but s 67(6) applied them to the remittance basis as if references to income arising were references to income received. So applied and construed they were generally regarded as providing a sound legal basis for cessation of source.

At one time it was suggested that this conclusion was not the end of the matter, for one result of the introduction of self-assessment on 6 April 1996 was to abolish the preceding-year basis and the closing rules in s 67 that went with it. Section 67 was repealed for new sources from 6 April 1994 and for continuing sources from 6 April 1998 (FA 1994, ss 207(4), 218 and Sch 20, para 7). If, therefore, the closing rules no longer applied, the implied overruling of *Diggines* had gone, and accordingly it could be argued that the *Diggines* ratio was revived in full force.

It is, however, improbable that this is the correct construction of the 1994 legislation, for it was clear from the transitional rules in s 218 and Sch 20 that that legislation affirmed the proposition, implicit in s 67, that each investment or bank account is treated as a separate source. Accordingly, as with ITTOIA 2005, there is clear legislative intent that 'source' should continue to be construed in the same way as under s 67.

Bank accounts

40.10 The question is sometimes raised of whether there is a new source if a bank account is closed and the money is transferred to a new account at the same branch of the bank. In law, a bank account is a contract between banker and customer under which the bank borrows the money from the customer on terms to repay it (see eg *Hart v Sangster* (1957) 37 TC 231). The argument is therefore that nothing changes if one account is closed and another opened at the same branch.

This argument is almost certainly wrong if one account is a deposit account at interest and the other a current account producing no interest. In such a case there is authority that the deposit account is a separate source (*Cull v Cowcher* (1934) 18 TC 449). The true principle appears to be that the source in the case of bank accounts is the deposit of the money on the agreed contractual terms (*Hart v Sangster*, supra). There is therefore a new source if there is any difference between the terms of the old account and the new.

The cautious course if cessation of source is being relied on is undoubtedly to have the old and new accounts at separate banks or at separate subsidiaries of the same bank. If this is not done, the money should pass into a non-interest bearing current account between the closing of the original account at interest and the opening of a new one. It is better too if the terms of the two interest-bearing accounts differ.

In practice difficulties of this sort tend only to arise in the Channel Islands or the Isle of Man, where banks are within the UK system. Elsewhere money at interest tends to be deposited for fixed periods at the end of which it is repaid. In such cases, repayment is plainly the end of the source, for even if the money is redeposited, the rate of interest is refixed.

Alienation abroad

40.11 The general rule is that a tax liability does not arise if the non-domiciled recipient of income gives it away abroad and the donee then remits the money to the UK. The frontiers of this principle were clarified by a recent professional negligence case, *Grimm v Newman* [2002] STC 1388. The relevant case-law and some practical issues are discussed in Chapter 42.

Constructive remittances

40.12 As noted above (para 40.4), the cases of *Hall v Marians* (1935) 19 TC 582 and *IRC v Gordon* (1952) 33 TC 226 established that remittance did not occur if a non-domiciliary settled a UK debt by payment to a foreign bank account of the creditor. These decisions were reversed in relation loan transactions by what is now ITTOIA 2005, s 833 and in addition provisions were introduced to counter back-to-back arrangements.

Loan transactions

40.13 Section 833 provides that income is to be treated as received in the UK if the taxpayer uses it outside the UK to satisfy a UK-linked debt. A UK-linked debt is any of the following:

(a) the principal or interest of any loan made to him in the UK;
(b) the principal of any loan made to him outside the UK, the proceeds of which are brought to or received in the UK;
(c) the principal of any loan made to satisfy any debt within (a) or (b) above; this covers the actual scheme in *Hall v Marians* and *IRC v Gordon*.

Section 833(5) applies s 833 in cases where a loan made outside the UK is satisfied before the money lent is brought to the UK. In such a case the remittance takes place not when the debt is satisfied but when the money is received in the UK.

Interest on a foreign loan

40.14 There is one noteworthy gap in the list of constructive remittances, namely, that the use of foreign income to pay *interest* on a loan made abroad does not count as a remittance even if the proceeds of the loan are brought to the UK. Accordingly, a widely used avoidance technique has grown up, whereby non-domiciliaries borrow money abroad, spend it in the UK, pay interest out of foreign income, and eventually clear the loan either out of capital, or when they have ceased to be UK resident. Such loans can be safely secured on foreign situs assets, provided the latter have not been purchased out of foreign income.

A point of difficulty can, however, arise with this technique, namely whether, when paying the interest the non-domiciliary is required to deduct tax at source under TA 1988, s 349(2)(c). That subsection requires deduction at source where yearly interest with a UK source is paid to a person whose usual place of abode is outside the UK (see para 34.6). Where a non-domiciliary has a foreign loan, the lender's place of abode will ipso facto be abroad and the interest will almost always be yearly interest. Accordingly, s 349(2) applies if the interest has a UK source (as to which see para 33.6).

Back-to-back arrangements

40.15 ITTOIA 2005, s 834 counteracts back-to-back arrangements. It applies if the following conditions are met:

(a) A person, referred to as the borrower, is indebted for money lent to him.
(b) Income is used by the borrower in such a way that money or property representing it is held by the lender on behalf of or to the account of the borrower.
(c) The circumstances under which it is so held are such that it is available to the lender for the purpose of satisfying or reducing the debt by set-off or otherwise.
(d) The amount of the borrower's debt to the lender or the time at which the debt
is to be repaid depend in any respect on the amount or value so held by the lender.

Where all these conditions are met, the income which has been applied as per condition (b) above is treated as having been applied in satisfaction of the debt for the purposes of the rules described above as to loans. In other words, assuming the debt is a foreign debt, remittance occurs insofar as the money lent has been or is in the future remitted to the UK.

Although s 834 or its predecessor, TA 1988, s 65(8) is often invoked by HMRC, a number of points need to be kept in mind. The first is that it applies only if the amount of the debt or the timing of repayment is in some way dependent on the deposited income. In other words a deposit which serves merely to offset the interest on the debt is not caught, provided the sole consequence of withdrawing the deposit is restoration of the interest to a commercial rate.

A second point is that s 834 contemplates that the same person, namely the borrower, both incurs the debt and applies the income in the back-to-back deposit. It follows that if a third party, for example a company or trust, provides the back-to-back deposit, s 834 does not apply. On a strict reading this is so even if the borrower is interested in the company or trust so that the income is deemed to be his under TA 1988, s 739 or ITTOIA 2005, s 624. But it may be an argument could be mounted that the deeming in ss 739 or 624 is wide enough to attribute the acts of the company or trust in depositing the money to the borrower.

A third point is that s 834 contemplates the back-to-back deposit being held by the lender. There is at least an argument that if the lender is one bank, and the recipient another bank, the subsection does not bite even if the two banks are in the same group. A contrary argument would arise if the bank receiving the deposit had given an express or implied counter-indemnity to the lending bank for such counter-indemnity could then be said to be property representing the back-to-back deposit.

No case on s 834 or 65(8) has yet been litigated and for that reason taxpayers should scrutinise its language with some care before accepting any HMRC argument it applies. Equally care should be taken to avoid its possible ramifications in structuring financing arrangements.

Exports of other debts

40.16 As will be apparent from the above the rules as to constructive remittances in ss 833 and 834 are expressed as applying to debts for money lent. They are not expressed as applying to debts generally and as a result, the question arises of whether the reasoning of *IRC v Gordon* remains good law where a debt incurred in the UK for goods or services is settled by payment to a bank account of the creditor abroad. Prima facie it does. The only reason for doubt is that in *Thomson v Moyse* (1958) 39 TC 291 *IRC v Gordon* was criticised. However it was not in terms overruled.

Assuming it still stands it offers a means of incurring expenditure on UK goods and services without effecting a taxable remittance. It is widely believed that HMRC accept this analysis, and thus that settlement of a debt for UK goods and services to a bank account outside the UK does not result in a taxable remittance. But as noted above, HMRC do consider that remittance occurs if the debt is settled by cheque and the supplier receives the cheque in the UK before presenting it abroad (Inspector's Manual para 1564).

Not ordinarily resident

40.17 The rules as to constructive remittance apply only to persons who are ordinarily resident in the UK (s 833(1)). In other words they do not catch anybody who is relying on non-ordinary residence to secure the remittance basis. More importantly they do not catch a non-domiciliary if he turns out not to be ordinarily resident.

The importance of a claim

40.18 As noted above, relevant income foreign income only enjoys the remittance basis if the taxpayer makes a claim for the tax year concerned. Once made the claim covers all relevant foreign income for the year, but a separate claim is required for each subsequent year.

Under the former Cases IV and V the claim that was required was simply that the taxpayer was non-domiciled or not ordinarily resident. In practice such claim was made by ticking Box 9.3 or 9.5 of the Non-residence etc pages of the Tax Return. This simply claims non-ordinary resident or non-domiciled status. Boxes 9.3 and 9.5 have not altered following the enactment of ITTOIA 2005, and so it seems a reasonable inference that ticking them is sufficient to constitute a claim. This is supported by TMA 1970, s 42, which requires claims to be included in the return, and by the notes to the Non-residence etc pages. On page NRN 4–5, these refer to claiming foreign domicile, and then direct that box 9.5 be ticked.

The normal time limits for a claim are 31 January five years and ten months after the end of the tax year (TMA 1970, s 43(1)). It might be thought this prejudices the many non-domicilaries who through ignorance or naivety do not make a tax return at all, for, as the time limit passes, all their undisclosed foreign income would be assessed by default on an arising basis. In fact this result ought to be avoided, for TMA 1970, ss 36(3) and 43C allow effect to be given on any default assessment or amendment to any claim which the taxpayer would have been entitled to make had he filed his return on time.

In one respect, the emphasis on a claim may have an unforeseen result. On a strict reading of ITTOIA 2005, ss 831 and 832, the rules in s 832 only apply in a tax year if a claim is made for that tax year. Among the rules is s 832(2) which provides that the taxable remittance for the year includes the income of past years. On a literal reading it follows that if for a tax year no claim is made, any remittances of past income in that year are tax free, albeit at the cost of any relevant foreign income in that year being taxable on an arising basis. This conclusion follows from the particular language of s 832(2) and would be difficult to spell out, if it could be spelled out at all, from the former language applicable to Cases IV and V.

This conclusion suggests there may be circumstances in which ticking box 9.5 may not be appropriate, although if this course is taken, it should be noted that box 9.5 refers also to capital gains. Although strictly the CGT remittance basis is not subject to a claim, it would be unwise not to tick box 9.5 if reliance is being placed on the remittance basis to shelter gains. If in such case it is not desired to claim the remittance basis for income, the better course may be to tick box 9.5 and strike the reference to income (with perhaps some comment under additional information to make the position clear beyond peradventure).

There is at least one scenario in which there may be good and totally unprovocative reasons not to claim the remittance basis. This is where the taxpayer is a basic-rate taxpayer whose only foreign income is dividends. Here the effect of claiming the remittance basis is to increase the rate of tax from 10% to 22.5% (see para 40.2 above).

There is a useful discussion of what, on any view, is a procedural mess in *Taxation* (Vol 157 No 4071, pp 543–5, 17 August 2006).

Change of status

40.19 Should the taxpayer become non-resident, a claim under ITTOIA 2005, s 831 would not be competent as, by virtue of his non-residence, none of his foreign income would be chargeable. As such he would have no relevant foreign income. In the absence of a claim remittance in any tax year subsequent to that of departure is tax-free.

In logic the same result follows should the taxpayer remain UK resident and acquire a UK domicile. In any tax year subsequent to the change of status, a claim under s 831 would not be competent as the taxpayer would not then be non-domiciled. Accordingly income remitted in any tax year after that in which UK domicile is acquired is free of tax.

This analysis accords with HMRC's view of what the position was under Cases IV and V (see *Taxation Practitioner* (December 1992) p 541). It may be presumed that the rewrite in ITTOIA 2005 has not altered this view.

If the taxpayer's domicile changes during the year of assessment, HMRC practice is to split the year in two (*Taxation Practitioner* (December 1992) p 541). As a result the remittance basis applies before the change but unremitted income can be remitted tax free after the change. However, this practice of splitting the year may not be in accordance with law, for income tax is an annual tax charged by years of assessment. The charge under s 832 if the taxpayer makes a claim is on the full amount 'of the sums received' in the UK in the year. ITTOIA 2005, s 831 makes no provision for splitting a year, and so in the year of change either the remittance or the arising basis must apply throughout. It is suggested the remittance basis should apply, for an individual who is not domiciled in the UK during part of a year satisfies the precondition of not being domiciled in the UK in that year, albeit for only some of the time.

Deemed income

40.20 The UK tax code contains many provisions deeming what would otherwise be capital to be income. In many cases this deeming extends to sums arising abroad. In such cases the application of the remittance basis can be a matter of difficulty.

The principal points to note are as follows:

(1) The remittance basis does not, in the absence of special provision, apply to deemed income at all. This is because the remittance basis is expressed as applying only to relevant foreign income as defined in ITTOIA 2005, s 830. The biggest trap here is non-resident life policies, the gains on which do not attract the remittance basis (see Chapter 72). Such policies should therefore be avoided by non-domiciliaries.

(2) The remittance rules do apply when a non-domiciliary disposes of a material interest in a non-qualifying offshore fund. But the relevant rules are the CGT rather than the income tax rules (TA 1988, s 761(5); para 71.15). This means that techniques such as segregation of income and cessation of source cannot be used.

(3) The discount on a foreign deep discount security is relevant foreign income, for ITTOIA 2005, s 830 expressly so provides. On the face of it this allows the remittance basis, but as discount and principal are also inseparable here it is difficult to see how segregation of income and cessation of source can apply.

(4) The accrued interest scheme (TA 1988, ss 710–728) does not apply to non-domiciliaries insofar as interest on the securities concerned would be taxable on the remittance basis (s 715(1)(j)). This is an exemption and means the accrued interest is free of income tax even if the proceeds of disposing of the security are remitted to the UK. CGT, however, may be an issue (see Chapter 41).

Chapter 41

Capital gains

Introduction

41.1 The remittance basis for CGT is enacted by TCGA 1992, s 12. Section 12(1) is expressed as applying 'in the case of individuals resident or ordinarily resident but not domiciled in the United Kingdom'. It provides that CGT is not charged on the disposal of assets situated outside the UK, 'except that the tax shall be charged on the amounts (if any) received in the United Kingdom in respect of those chargeable gains, any such amount being treated as gains accruing when they are received in the United Kingdom'.

Section 12(2) extends the meaning of 'received'. It treats as received in the UK 'all amounts paid, used, or enjoyed in or in any manner or form transmitted or brought to the United Kingdom'. It also incorporates the provisions as to loans and back-to-back deposits in ITTOIA 2005, ss 833 and 834 (as to which see para 40.12).

Section 12 contrasts with the remittance basis for relevant foreign income in ITTOIA 2005, s 832, for whereas the latter effectively neither defines nor extends the concept of receipt, s 12(2) does. Section 12(2), however, in all material respects replicates ITEPA 2003, s 33(2), which applies to remittances of overseas earnings. As is explained in Chapter 23, it is unclear whether ss 12(2) and 33(2) add anything to the basic meaning of receipt. HMRC, however, do consider it is open to them to argue that a given set of circumstances amounts to the remittance of a gain under s 12(2), even though it would not amount to a remittance for the purposes of s 832.

Section 12 requires each gain to be looked at separately to see if it has been remitted. Losses accruing to non-domiciliaries are not allowed if incurred on the disposal of a foreign situs asset, so there is no possibility of using losses to abate what is able to be remitted.

Section 12 is not subject to claim. CGT is referred to against box 9.5 of the Non-resident etc pages, but in logic it applies even if that box is not ticked. Failure to tick the box would not found an argument that a foreign situs loss should be allowed, as the disallowances of such losses depends on the fact of foreign domicile rather than being tied to the remittance basis.

Situs of assets

41.2 The question of whether the asset disposed of is situated outside the UK is determined by the CGT rules as to situs. These are explained in Chapter 32.

Computation of the gain

41.3 As with all gains on foreign assets, the gain accruing to a non-domiciliary is computed by comparing the proceeds of disposal converted into sterling at exchange rates prevailing at the date of disposal with the acquisition costs, these each being converted to sterling at the rate prevailing when incurred (*Bentley v Pike* [1981] STC 360; *Capcount Trading v Evans* [1993] STC 11). It is not possible to express the gain in foreign currency and simply convert that amount to sterling.

The disposals generating remittable gains include withdrawals from foreign currency accounts at non-UK banks insofar as the currency concerned has appreciated against sterling. This follows because for CGT purposes foreign currency is an asset (TCGA 1992, s 21(1)(b)). The normal rule that simple debts are exempt in the hands of the original creditor does not apply to foreign currency bank accounts (TCGA 1992, s 252(1)). The result is that any withdrawal from a foreign currency account is a disposal, for there is a disposal of a debt by the creditor whenever a debt is wholly or partially satisfied (TCGA 1992, s 251(2)). The only exception to these rules arises where the account represents currency acquired for personal expenditure abroad, including expenditure on a residence abroad (TCGA 1992, s 252(2)).

As explained in para 32.12, the foreign bank accounts of non-domiciliaries are treated as foreign situs for CGT purposes. But non-domiciliaries cannot treat all bank accounts containing a given foreign currency as a single asset, as SP 10/84 does not apply to them.

Indexation

41.4 Until 5 April 1998, indexation was computed by reference to the month in which the disposal occurred and the gain taxed on remittance was the gain after allowing the indexation allowance. Where a gain which accrued before 5 April 1998 is remitted after that date, the full indexation allowance remains allowed. As with all non-corporate taxpayers, indexation on disposals after April 1998 is frozen as at April 1998 (TCGA 1992, ss 53(1A) and 54(1A)).

Taper

41.5 Taper relief is available to non-domiciliaries. It is computed by reference to the time for which the asset has been held as at the date of the disposal (TCGA 1992, Sch A1 para 16(4)). It is not, however, allowed until the year in which the gain is remitted, for it is only at that point that the gain comes into the non-domiciliary's total of chargeable gains within TCGA 1992, s 2. It follows that if in that year the taxpayer's gains do not exceed his losses, any taper relief is lost. It is unclear what the position is if part only of the gain is remitted. On a strict reading of TCGA 1992, s 2A the whole taper relief on the disposal is allowed at that stage. TCGA 1992, Sch A1 para 21 does provide for apportionments, although if read literally only where the legislation otherwise directs an appointment to be made.

Mixed funds

41.6 It is easy enough to see that a gain has been remitted if the proceeds of disposal are paid into a separate account and eventually find their way to the UK. But what is the position if the taxpayer has one or more mixed accounts? Such accounts may receive income as well as asset realisations and may be used to fund reinvestment or foreign spending.

As is explained in para 40.5, remittances are presumed to be income insofar as income has been credited to the account. Thereafter the HMRC view is that remittances are gain in the proportion that the gains bear to the total amount in the account (Notes on Non-Residence etc pages, p NRN6).

Avoiding remittance

Segregating gains

41.7 As with the remittance basis for relevant foreign income it is clear that the non-domiciliary who simply spends or reinvests the proceeds of any disposal abroad escapes tax on those gains. The use of the words 'amounts received' in s 12(1) leaves no room for any concept of constructive remittance. However, an issue which does arise is whether only the gain need not be remitted or whether the entire proceeds of disposal of the asset must be kept abroad. As is indicated above, the latter is the approach taken by HMRC. It accords with common sense, for whereas income is distinguishable from the income-producing asset, gain and base cost are a single indivisible sum, separated only by the artificial CGT computation rules. This approach is widely understood to have been upheld in an unreported case by a Special Commissioner.

It is clear from this that there is no justification for using separate bank accounts to segregate gain and base cost, and purporting to avoid CGT by remitting only from the latter. However, where separate bank accounts can be used is to separate the proceeds of disposals realising a chargeable gain from the proceeds of exempt assets or assets realised at a loss. Remittances from the latter are, self-evidently, not remittances of any gain and so are free of CGT.

Gifts and remittance in specie

41.8 The use of the word 'amounts' in s 12(1) indicates that money must be brought to the UK. The equivalent word in ITTOIA 2005, s 832(1) is sums, and since for the purposes of s 832(1) a sum is treated as received in the UK when an asset brought to the UK is sold, so too in such circumstances an amount should be treated as received in the UK.

The use of the word 'amounts' has a further significance: if on a disposal or deemed disposal there is no consideration, any gain accruing cannot be remitted for there is no amount in respect of the chargeable gain capable of being received in the UK. This applies particularly on gifts.

This point offers scope for avoidance where a foreign situs asset is likely to be sold. If prior to any binding contract for sale the asset is transferred to an offshore trust the gain is effectively rendered tax-free even if remitted. Because the disposal to the trust is one of gift, no CGT liability can arise at that stage and thereafter the asset is in the trust where CGT is also avoided provided the settlor is non-domiciled (see para 60.2). These results follow even if the trust is settlor-interested and there is no reason why, after the sale, part of the proceeds cannot be appointed back to the settlor. CGT will only arise on capital distributions if the recipient is resident and domiciled in the UK (see para 63.22). To avoid attack under the *Ramsay* principle, the sale should not have been agreed on when the gift into trust is made. A reasonable time should elapse after the sale before any appointment to the settlor is made.

Cessation of source

41.9 The cessation of source technique is plainly not available to CGT, because the concept of source has no application to CGT.

Alienation abroad

41.10 As with income tax, remittance does not occur if the non-domiciliary gives away the proceeds of an asset abroad, and the donee remits the proceeds. This is established by the Court of Appeal decision in *Grimm v Newman* [2002] STC 1388 which turned on the comparable wording applicable to earnings. However, the money must not be channelled back to the donor and nor must he otherwise receive financial equivalence.

The clarification of the law resulting from *Grimm v Newman* has rendered alienation abroad perhaps the most effective means of bringing the value represented by gains to the UK without tax charge. Some of the practical issues which arises are discussed in para 42.4.

Change of residence

41.11 It is clear that the charge under s 12 cannot arise if the non-domiciliary remits gains which have accrued prior to the tax year in which he becomes UK resident; this follows because s 12(1) applies only to amounts received in respect of gains accruing while the taxpayer is resident. It is also clear that a charge does not arise if the non-domiciliary has ceased to be resident at the time of remittance. This follows because the remittance is treated as a gain accruing at the time of remittance, and as such the basic rule in TCGA 1992, s 2 means the amount cannot be chargeable.

As is described in para 27.7, TCGA 1992, s 10A treats gains realised during a period of non-residence as accruing in the tax year of return if fewer than five tax years separate the year of departure from the year of return. Since s 10A applies to all gains which would otherwise have accrued during the period of absence, it catches gains remitted then. However as the basic requirement for the operation of the CGT remittance is residence in the year of the actual disposal, s 10A does not, it may be suggested, catch remittance of gains realised during the tax years of absence.

Change of domicile

41.12 An interesting question is what happens if remittance occurs while the taxpayer is resident but after he has acquired a UK domicile. Here the HMRC view is that, in contrast to income tax, the gain is in charge (CGT Manual, para 25311). This view is understood to be supported by a decision of General Commissioners, and it turns on whether the opening words of s 12(1) 'in the case of individuals resident or ordinarily resident but not domiciled in the UK' qualify the latter part of the subsection. As a matter of construction, it is suggested the section could be read either way.

Chapter 42

Alienation abroad

Introduction

42.1 It has long been recognised that a gift abroad by a non-domiciliary of income or gains converts the gifted property into capital in the hands of the donee. Accordingly, no tax charge arises if the donee then brings the money to the UK.

The precise boundaries of this principle were uncertain and it was also unclear how far it applied to CGT and employment income given the wider express definitions of remittance (see paras 41.1 and 23.6). The case of *Grimm v Newman* [2002] STC 1388 highlighted and ultimately clarified many of the issues.

The early authorities

42.2 The alienation abroad principle was established by two cases in the 1930s, *Timpson's Executors v Yerbury* (1935) 20 TC 155 and *Carter v Sharon* (1936) 20 TC 229. In the former case, the taxpayer was life tenant under a New York trust and directed the trustee to pay part of the income to her children who were also resident in the UK. The trustee bought in New York sterling drafts drawn on a bank in London and posted them to the children in England who then cashed them. The Court of Appeal decided on these facts that the taxpayer was still entitled to the income when it reached the UK, and accordingly that she had effected a taxable remittance.

The key point was the finding of entitlement. The Court decided that entitlement when the income reached the UK resulted in a tax charge on account of what became TA 1988, s 59(1). This was a general rule for Sch D and provided that tax under Sch D must be charged on and paid by 'the persons receiving or entitled to the income'. It is separately re-enacted in the different charging provisions of ITTOIA 2005 (see for example ss 8, 371 and 404).

The Court of Appeal left open what the position would have been had the taxpayer alienated the income before it left New York. This point arose for decision in *Carter v Sharon*. Here the taxpayer's agent in California sent a bank draft drawn on a London bank to her daughter in the UK, but in this case the evidence was that the gift was complete once the draft was posted in California. On these facts, Lawrence J decided the taxpayer was *not* taxable on the sums in question. His reasoning is encapsulated in the last sentence of his judgment where he said:

> 'I so construe [TA 1988, ss 65(5) and 59(1)] when read together that they only apply to income from foreign possessions which is either received by the taxpayer in this country or to which he is entitled at the time it comes to this country.'

As noted in para 40.4 the House of Lords in *Thomson v Moyse* (1958) 39 TC 291 gave a practical construction to the remittance rules. However, it is clear that *Carter v Sharon* was not disapproved. Commenting on it and *Timpson's Executors v Yerbury* Lord Radcliffe said:

> 'What was in issue was whether what was received in this country had been received by the taxpayer at any stage. The decisions turned on the rules of English law as to the effectuating of voluntary dispositions of property.'

Harmel v Wright

42.3 In *Harmel v Wright* [1974] STC 88, Templeman J placed an important but entirely logical gloss on the alienation abroad principle. In that case the taxpayer had used his foreign employment income to subscribe for shares in one foreign company, which lent the money to a second foreign company, which in turn lent the money to the taxpayer who brought it to the UK. The Special Commissioners found that the taxpayer had received the income in the UK and this finding was upheld by Templeman J. He characterised the circumstances of the case as peculiar, but observed that emoluments had come in at one end of a conduit pipe and passed through certain traceable pipes until they came out the other end to the taxpayer.

Templeman J's reasoning is encapsulated in the following passage:

> 'In my judgement on the peculiar circumstances of this case – and I say nothing about other cases where it may be possible that money does, en route, disappear and it is not possible to follow with the same certainty as in the present case – the sums which the taxpayer eventually receives represent and are the emoluments which start off from his South African employers in the first place.'

As is apparent from the facts, *Harmel v Wright* concerned earnings rather than relevant foreign income. However, Templeman J rested his decision on the general meaning of 'remittance' rather than on the extended definition applicable to earnings (as to which see para 23.6).

Grimm v Newman

42.4 In *Grimm v Newman*, the taxpayer made gifts abroad to his wife of $786,000 in October 1991 and January 1992. The gifts were funded out of the taxpayer's foreign earnings. In February 1992 the taxpayer and his wife contracted to buy a house and they completed the transaction in March 1992.

They bought as joint tenants in equity. Mrs Grimm funded £386,983 of the price by remittance from the money given to her abroad and Mr Grimm funded the balance partly in cash and partly by a loan of £300,000 secured on the whole property. As between the spouses, this loan would have fallen to be discharged exclusively out of Mr Grimm's share of any sale proceeds.

Mr and Mrs Grimm lived in the house as their home. Somewhat later Mr Grimm was the subject of a back duty enquiry by HMRC and as part of an overall settlement, he conceded that the sum of £386,983 brought in by Mrs Grimm was as a taxable remittance of his foreign earnings. He then brought a negligence action against the UK tax adviser.

As part of his decision on that issue Etherton J decided at first instance that HMRC had a strong argument that Mrs Grimm's remittance was taxable under both the rules relating to earnings and under Sch D Case V. His reasoning was not clear, but he appears to have approached the case on the basis that if Mr Grimm benefited from the remittance by his wife he would be taxable on it. He said that there was such a benefit because Mr Grimm was joint tenant of the house and accordingly he had the right to occupy a much larger house than he could otherwise have afforded and would acquire his wife's share by survivorship if she pre-deceased him without severing the joint tenancy.

Etherton J's decision was appealed to the Court of Appeal. On appeal, Mr Grimm did not adopt Etherton J's reasoning for saying there had been a taxable remittance. Instead he argued Mrs Grimm's remittance was clearly traced from and identified with Mr Grimm's gift and that her remittance was part of a prearranged scheme in which he confidently expected she would effect the remittance. Effectively therefore his argument was based on the *Ramsay* principle and *Harmel v Wright*.

The Court of Appeal, by a 2:1 majority, considered they had to decide whether Mrs Grimm's remittance was a taxable remittance of Mr Grimm's earnings and then decided it was not. They rejected Mr Grimm's arguments to the contrary, giving five reasons for doing so:

(1) Mr Grimm's gift to Mrs Grimm was perfected abroad, Mr Grimm retaining neither beneficial interest in nor contractual control over the gifted money.

(2) For Mr Grimm to be taxable on the remittance he would have himself needed to receive in the UK the monetary or financial equivalent of what he gave, which he did not.

(3) *Harmel v Wright* was distinguishable because Mr Grimm did not himself receive any traceable financial equivalence in the UK.

(4) Nothing in the legislation entitles a remittance by one spouse to be treated as a remittance by the other.

(5) The fact that the money was used by Mr and Mrs Grimm to satisfy their joint and several obligation to the vendor of the property was immaterial.

The present position

42.5 *Grimm v Newman* has made the following points clear as respects alienation abroad:

(1) As required by the original Case V cases, the gift must be completed abroad.
(2) The fact that the donee is the recipient's spouse is immaterial.
(3) There appears to be no difference between relevant foreign income on the one hand and employment income and capital gains on the other as to the requirements which must be satisfied.

Certain other conclusions may also be drawn:

(1) It appears from the reference in *Grimm v Newman* to monetary or financial equivalence that a remittance by the donee would be taxable if money identifiable with the gift was received back by the donor in the UK or if he received financial equivalence in the broader sense. The tenor of *Grimm v Newman* and *Harmel v Wright* suggests such receipt must be pursuant to a prearranged scheme devised at the time of the initial gift.
(2) The reference in *Grimm v Newman* to whether the donor retained a beneficial interest in the gifted money or a contractual right of the control indicates that if these features are present when the gifted money reaches the UK, the remittance would be taxable. However the judgment is far from clear on the extent of this point.
(3) The abandonment of the broader benefit point which appealed to Etherton J indicates that non-financial benefit such as use of a house by the donor in specie may be ignored.

Practical situations

42.6 *Grimm v Newman* has clarified the law in certain situations which arise in practice, but doubt still exists over others.

House purchase

42.7 The facts of *Grimm v Newman* itself make it clear that if a husband gives his wife half the price of a UK house to be acquired jointly the remittance is not taxable provided the gift is completed abroad and the husband has no interest in or control over the gifted money. The same it may be suggested is true if the wife buys the UK house in her sole name, and the husband provides the entire price by gift abroad. It is true he may benefit by subsequently living in the property, but this is benefit in the non-financial sense.

Trusts

42.8 It is clear there is an effective alienation if the settlor makes a gift abroad to a trust from which he is wholly excluded. A subsequent remittance to the UK by the trustees, or by a beneficiary following a distribution, would plainly not be taxable as remittance of the settlor's income. But the position may be more complex if the settlor is a beneficiary.

Here it is to be noted that in *Grimm v Newman*, the Court of Appeal did attach weight to the fact that Mr Grimm had no beneficial interest in the money after the gift. This is not the position where the gift is to a settlor-interested trust, for the settlor, even if only a discretionary beneficiary, plainly does have some sort of interest. Accordingly trustees in such a case who bring the money into the UK to invest may be exposing the settlor to the risk of a taxable remittance. In practice, although not as a matter of strict legal analysis, the risk may be greater if the money is used to purchase an asset from which the settlor benefits, for example a house he lives in.

Should the trustees of such a settlor-interested trust make a distribution abroad to another beneficiary, a subsequent remittance by that beneficiary would be most unlikely to be taxable as the settlor's income, for the settlor would no longer have any interest in the gifted money. But what if the distribution is to the settlor? Here there is plainly risk if the settlor subsequently remits, both because self-evidently he is and has at all times been interested in the money and also because an extended *Harmel v Wright* argument would be available to HMRC.

It is unclear how far in practice HMRC would take points of this sort. But the clarification in *Grimm v Newman* has increased their chances of success should they choose to do so.

Companies

42.9 Similar issues arise where a non-domiciliary, or a settlor-interested trust he has funded, use income or gains to fund an offshore company, either by subscribing for shares in it or making a loan to it. What is the position if the company then brings the money to the UK for investment?

On the face of it such remittance should not be taxable, for the remitted money is the property of the company, and neither the non-domiciliary or the trust have any interest in it as such. Further Templeman J in *Harmel v Wright* suggested that it was only the conduit-pipe feature of that case which rendered the remittance taxable. The implication is that had one of the companies simply brought the money to the UK and invested it, the remittance would not have been taxable.

However *Grimm v Newman* has raised some doubts in this area, for the Court of Appeal did raise the issue of whether Mr Grimm still had legal control of the gifted money. In the case of a directly owned company, the non-domiciliary does retain control, in his capacity as shareholder. On this ground, therefore HMRC may have an argument a subsequent remittance by the company is taxable. The point would not however arise if the company is owned by a trust, for here the trustees have legal control, even if the trust is settlor-interested.

Section IV

Inheritance Tax and Settlements

Chapter 43

The relevant property regime

Introduction

43.1 As explained in Chapter 45, an offshore settlement is fully within the ambit of IHT unless the settler had neither an actual nor a deemed UK settlement at the time the settlement was created. So too offshore settlements created by non-domiciliaries are caught by the tax if (with some exceptions) the settlement holds UK assets.

The general rule is that all such settlements are covered by what may be referred to as the relevant property regime. The regime may be so designated because the property to which the principal provisions apply is termed relevant property (IHTA 1984, ss 64–69). Prior to 22 March 2006 many kinds of settlement were outside the relevant property regime. FA 2006 greatly reduced the categories of settlement so excepted, most exceptions now being transitional.

As all offshore settlements created by UK domiciliaries are caught by IHT, an understanding of the relevant property regime is important to offshore tax planning. The present chapter therefore outlines the IHT treatment of such settlements. The next chapter covers the exceptions to the relevant property regime. Chapter 45 deals with the territorial limits to the IHT charges on settled property, and Chapter 46 with how the relevant property regime applies to excluded property settlements.

The entry charge

43.2 When property is settled it becomes relevant property. An immediately chargeable transfer occurs save insofar as specific reliefs such as business property relief or normal expenditure out of income are in point (IHTA 1984, ss 21 and 104). In general the rate of tax is 20% (IHTA 1984, s 7(2)). But in certain circumstances the rate may be either less or greater.

The rate is less insofar as the settlor's nil-rate band is available. In 2006–07 that band is £285,000 and in 2007–08 it will be £300,000 (FA 2005 s 98). It is available provided the settlor has not made any other chargeable transfers in the sven years prior to the transfer of assets to the settlement (IHTA 1984, s 7(1)).

The rate is greater should the settlor die within five years of transferring the assets to the settlement (IHTA 1984, s 7(4)). It is the full death rate of 40% should he die in the first three years. Otherwise it is 32% in Year 4, and 24% in Year 5.

Settlements frequently arise on death by virtue of provisions in the deceased's will. There is no reason why testamentary settlements cannot be or become non-resident. Save insofar as exemptions apply, property passing into settlement on death is charged at the death rates of IHT – ie 40% once the nil-rate band is exhausted. Assuming the death occurs after 22 March 2006, the general rule is that such property enters the relevant property regime. But as is explained in para 44.4, an exception is made if and so long as the property is subject to an immediate post-death interest ie an initial interest in possession following the death.

The 10-yearly charge

43.3 The 10-yearly charge has always been the key feature of the relevant property regime. It is made on the tenth anniversary of the date on which the settlement commenced and on each 10-yearly anniversary thereafter (IHTA 1984, ss 61 and 64). This date is used even if on the date the settlement commenced the settled property was not relevant property but only became so subsequently. The charge is made on the value of the relevant property, ie on all the property in the settlement save insofar as a specific relief, such as business property relief, or one of the exceptions noted in Chapter 44 is in point (IHTA 1984, s 64). The rate is three-tenths of the lifetime rate of IHT (IHTA 1984, s 66). As the latter is currently 20%, the 10-yearly rate is 6%.

In many cases the rate is less. This is because the mechanics of determining the rate involve postulating a hypothetical transfer, and then determining what three-tenths of effective lifetime rate on that transfer would be. As the hypothetical transfer presupposes a nil-rate band, the result is that normally three-tenths of the effective rate is somewhat less than 6%. Indeed, if the value of the settlement as a whole is below the nil-rate band, the effective rate, and thus the tax, on the 10-yearly anniversary may be nil.

But unfortunately the benefit of the nil-rate band is not always available, or wholly available. This is for the following reasons:

(1) The hypothetical transfer presupposes previous transfers equal to chargeable transfers made by the settlor in the seven years prior to the creation of the settlement (IHTA 1984, s 66(5)(a)).
(2) It also presupposes that previous transfers equal to any amounts on which an exit charge was made in the previous ten years under the rules described below (ibid s 66(5)(b)).
(3) The amount comprised in the hypothetical transfer includes not merely the relevant property in the settlement on the 10-yearly anniversary, but also property comprised in any other settlement made by the same settlor on the same day, this property being valued as at the date the settlements were made (ibid s 66(4)(c)).
(4) The amount comprised in the hypothetical transfer includes as well the value of any property in the settlement which was not within the relevant property regime when settled and has remained outside that

regime at all times since (ibid s 66(4)(c)). This also is taken at its value when first settled. The main example of such property is excluded property (see para 46.4).

Many settlements, both onshore and offshore, still exist which were created before 27 March 1974, this being the date of the introduction of IHT (or Capital Transfer Tax as it was then known). In any such case, no account is taken of the transfers made by the settlor in the seven years prior to the creation of the settlement, and nor is account taken of other settlements created by the same settlor on the same day, or of settled property which has never been relevant property (IHTA 1984, s 66(6)).

Additions

43.4 Should the settlor have added property to the settlement, such addition may impact on the rate of tax on subsequent 10-yearly anniversaries. This is the position if the settlor's total chargeable transfers in the seven years prior to the creation of the settlement is less than his total in the seven years prior to the addition. In such case the greater cumulative total is used in computing the effective rate at subsequent 10-yearly anniversaries (IHTA 1984, s 67). However, in computing the settlor's cumulative total as at the date of the addition, his previous transfer or transfers to the settlement are ignored (ibid s 67(5)).

On the 10-yearly anniversary next following an addition, the rate of tax on added property is reduced. This is so whether the property was added by the settlor or someone else. The rate is reduced by as many fortieths as there are complete quarters in the 10-year period during which the property was not comprised in the settlement or not relevant property (IHTA 1984, s 66(2)).

Accumulations

43.5 Many settlements subject to the relevant property regime generate income and often such income is accumulated. This is particularly so with offshore trusts, for almost all offshore trust laws are free of fetters on accumulation such as are found in the English Law of Property Act 1925, s 164.

HMRC practice is to treat accumulated income as becoming added to the trust on the date on which accumulation is made (SP 8/86). It is so treated for the purposes of the fortieths rule described above. It cannot however be characterised as added by the settlor, as additions by the settlor are only taken into account if by way of chargeable transfer. As respects income which is in hand pending decision by the trustees, HMRC practice is not to treat it as a taxable trust asset at all.

The effect of the above practices is that on a 10-yearly anniversary IHT can be reduced by determining what part of the value is attributable to accumulations over the past ten years and when such accumulations were made. The tax can also be reduced by delaying decisions as to what to do with income in the period leading up to the 10-yearly anniversary. However this process should not be taken too far as otherwise de facto accumulation or distribution may occur (see para 12.6).

The exit charge

43.6 As well as the 10-yearly charge, the relevant property regime imposes exit charges (IHTA 1984, s 65). An exit charge is made when property in the settlement is distributed to beneficiaries or when the trustees enter into a depreciatory transaction.

In any such case, the amount charged is the amount by which the value of the property in the settlement is reduced. The rate of tax is based on the effective rate charged at the last anniversary – i e the rate of 6% or less (IHTA 1984, s 69). But the actual rate used is a fraction of that effective rate, the fraction being as many fortieths as there are complete quarters since the last 10-yearly anniversary (s 69(4)). It follows that in the first quarter following an anniversary there is a nil charge, and indeed it is provided that an event during that quarter is not returnable as an occasion of charge at all (s 65(4)).

Should property have been added to the settlement since the last 10-yearly anniversary, the rate of tax on the anniversary is adjusted for these purposes to what it would have been had the settlement then included the added property (IHTA 1984, s 69(2)). In the event that the added property is included in the distribution occasioning the exit charge, the rate of tax on the property is reduced to reflect the number of complete quarters since the anniversary and before the property was added to the settlement. These rules would seem to apply both where the added property is a genuine addition and where it is the result of accumulation.

Before the first 10-yearly anniversary

43.7 Should the exit charge occur before the first 10-yearly anniversary, the exit charge is based on the value of the property when settled, account also being taken of chargeable transfers made by the settlor in the previous seven years, settlements made by him on the same day, and property comprised in the settlement which has never been relevant property (IHTA 1984, s 68). The ensuing rate, of 6% or less, is then reduced to a fraction, this being as may fortieths as there are complete quarters since the settlement commenced.

Property ceasing to be relevant property

43.8 The rules as to the exit charge state that the charge is made whenever property ceases to be relevant property. Prior to FA 2006, property ceased to be relevant property not merely when it was distributed to beneficiaries absolutely, but also when it was appointed on fixed interest or accumulation and maintenance trusts as such trusts were then outside the relevant property regime. Now however they are in the relevant property regime, insofar as appointed after 22 March 2006. As a result, exit charges where the property remains settled are rare. The principal example is property appointed on charitable trusts.

Income distributions

43.9 An exit charge is not made should a distribution be payment which is the income of any person for the purposes of income tax (IHTA 1984, s 65(5)(b)). The same result follows if the payment will be the income of any person or, should the recipient be non-resident, if it would be his income were he UK resident.

This rule self-evidently protects income distributions from the exit charge, although as it is expressed in terms of payments, it is unclear whether it relieves distributions in specie. A more interesting question is whether it relieves capital payments taxed under TA 1988, s 740. The answer would appear to be that it does, as such payments are treated for all purposes of the Income Tax Acts as income (TA 1988, s 740(2)(a)). However, an exception would be made if, through insufficiency of relevant income, the payment is taxed as a capital gain under TCGA 1992, s 87 or Sch 4C as then the payment is not treated as income (cf para 56.28 and Chapters 63 to 65). But this exception would itself not be in point if the payment were taxed as an offshore income gain, for then again it is treated as income (see para 71.19).

An interesting point would arise if, at the time of distribution, there is neither relevant income nor any gains pool with which to match it. In such case, an exit charge would still not be in point if it could be said it 'will' be the income of the recipient – ie that it will be if and when there is relevant income.

Identifying the settlement

Definition of settlement

43.10 As will be apparent, the relevant property regime requires identification of the settlement, the property comprised in it, and the date on which it commenced.

In contrast to income tax and CGT, the term 'settlement' is defined for IHT purposes (IHTA 1984, s 43(2)). It means any disposition or dispositions of property whereby the property is held either:

(a) for persons in succession, or
(b) for any person subject to a contingency, or

(c) on trust to accumulate the income and/or distribute it at the discretion of the trustees.

On the face of it this definition indicates that for IHT purposes separate settlements exist inter alia if:

(1) part of a trust fund is held on discretionary trusts and part on fixed-interest trusts, or
(2) property is added to a trust on separate occasions, whether by one settlor or by several.

It is however now clear that the legislation should not be read in this way. In *Rysaffe Trustee Co (CI) Ltd v IRC* [2002] EWHC 1114 (Ch), [2002] STC 872, Park J held (at para 20) that the issue of whether there is one settlement or several is to be answered in accordance with the general understanding of trust practitioners. The reference in s 43 to dispositions comprehends cases where property is contributed to the settlement on more than one occasion. Park J's analysis was approved by the Court of Appeal (see [2003] EWCA Civ 356, [2003] STC 536, 541, para 25).

That this is right is confirmed by provisions in the relevant property regime. Thus the rules noted above as to additions contemplate a single settlement. So too the rules as to property comprised in the settlement not being relevant property imply that property subject to different trusts can be in the same settlement as relevant property.

Commencement of the settlement

43.11 As indicated above, the commencement of the settlement is the date from which 10-yearly anniversaries are computed. The general rule is that the date on which a settlement commences is the date on which property is first comprised within it (IHTA 1984, s 60).

Property moving between settlements

43.12 Where property is appointed or advanced from one settlement to another, it is treated for the purposes of the relevant property regime as remaining comprised in the transferor settlement. This means that 10-yearly anniversaries in respect of the transferred property are computed by reference to the commencement date of the original settlement (IHTA 1984, s 81).

The settlor

43.13 The term 'settlor' is defined for IHT purposes in substantially the same terms as ITTOIA 2005, s 620. Reference should therefore be made to the discussion in para 59.18. Where under the rules described above the commencement of the settlement is treated as deferred until the termination of the settlor's spouse's interest in possession, she is treated as settlor (IHTA 1984, s 80).

Life interests

43.14 Unless an interest in possession is one of those covered by the rules described in the next chapter, settled property subject to such an interest is relevant property and so subject to the rules described above. As a result the creation of a fixed interest inter vivos settlement occasions an entry charge and thereafter it is subject to 10-yearly charges. This is so even if the settlor or his spouse is the life-tenant (save in the unlikely event that the trust is a disabled trust (para 44.5)). So too, an exit charge is levied on any distribution of the settled property even if the recipient of the distribution was previously life-tenant. This result too is only avoided if his life-interest fell within one of the mainly transitional categories described in the next chapter.

One advantage that the present regime has, in contrast to that before FA 2006, is that the creation of a life-interest within an existing settlement is a non-event for IHT purposes. This is as explained in para 43.8 and follows because the property is relevant property both before and after. So too the termination of a life-interest is a non-event unless the life-interest is one of those detailed in the next chapter in which event the termination is immediately chargeable or potentially exempt.

In the long run these changes will make the IHT treatment of trusts simpler. But in the short-term, the transitional provisions described in the next chapter render the complexity formidable.

Chapter 44

Exceptions to the relevant property regime

Interests in possession existing as at 21 March 2006

44.1 Until 22 March 2006, settled property in which an individual enjoyed an interest in possession was not relevant property and thus was outside the regime of 10-yearly and exit charge described in the previous chapter (IHTA 1984, ss 58 and 59). Instead, the individual was for IHT purposes treated as owning the property in which the interest subsisted (ibid s 49). Thus it was taxed at the death rate if the interest subsisted until his death, and any inter vivos termination of the interest was taxed as a lifetime transfer of value.

An interest in possession which subsisted immediately prior to the announcement of the 2006 changes on 22 March 2006 remains subject to the old law so long as it subsists (IHTA 1984, s 49(1A)). In other words, the holder of the interest continues for IHT purposes to be treated as owning the trust property and it is not relevant property. But subject to the transitional provisions noted below, grandfathering under this head ceases once the interest ceases, and this is so even if on such cessation the beneficiary becomes entitled to another interest in possession in the same property.

Transitional serial interests

44.2 The 2006 legislation provides a period of two years, ending on 5 April 2008, during which interests in possession existing on 22 March 2006 can be replaced with another interest in possession. Such new interests in possession are referred to as transitional serial interests and remain governed by the old law – in other words the interest holder is treated for IHT purposes as owning the settled property and it is not relevant property. The new interest in possession may be held either by the owner of the original interest (as on a trust reorganisation) or by some other beneficiary.

For this treatment to be secured three conditions must be met (IHTA 1984, s 49C):

(1) The new interest, ie the transitional serial interest, must arise at the same moment as the interest existing on 22 March 2006 ends.
(2) That moment must be on or before 5 April 2008.
(3) Both the transitional serial interest and the interest existing on 22 March 2006 must be in the property comprised in the settlement.

Careful reading of those conditions indicates that an interest in possession is only a transitional serial interest if it takes effect on the termination of the interest subsisting on 22 March 2006. In other words, an interest is not a transitional serial interest if it replaces an earlier transitional serial interest, even if such replacement is before 6 April 2008.

It is unclear on the wording of the legislation whether the interest subsisting on 22 March 2006 must be terminated in its entirety or whether it can be terminated as respects some of the settled property but not the rest. So too it is unclear whether transitional serial interest has to subsist in all the settled property in which the original interest subsisted. It is however thought that HMRC accept that, in such cases, any ensuing interest is a transitional serial interest although as at the time of writing this has not been publicly confirmed.

There are two circumstances in which an interest in possession is a transitional serial interest even if it arises after 5 April 2008. One is if the interest arises on the death of the holder of the interest subsisting on 22 March 2006 and is held by the deceased's spouse (IHTA 1984, s 49D). The other applies to policies of life assurance held in interest in possession trusts on 22 March 2006. In such a case, subsequent interests in possession in the policies are transitional serial interests indefinitely, unless and until non-interest in possession trusts supervene (IHTA 1984, s 49E). Each interest must be held until death for this treatment to apply to the successive interests.

Post 22 March settlements

44.3 There are two circumstances in which interests in possession in settlements created after 22 March 2006 are subject to the old law. Neither is common in offshore contexts.

Immediate post-death interests

44.4 An immediate post-death interest is an interest in possession arising on a death after 22 March 2006 and created by the will or intestacy of the deceased (IHTA 1984, s 49A). Such interests are subject to the old law regardless of how long after 22 March 2006 the death occurs and regardless of who the life-tenant is and what trusts take effect on his or her death. The result is that the settled property is treated as owned by the life-tenant and is not relevant property.

It should be noted that this treatment ceases once the immediate post-death interest ends. This is so even if the interest-holder becomes entitled to another interest in the same settlement or the successive life interest is held by his or her spouse.

Disabled person's interest

44.5 The second category of interest in possession which is subject to the old law is the disabled person's interest (IHTA 1984, s 49(1A)(b)). That term means an interest in possession to which a disabled person is entitled, the term disabled person requiring the disability to exist when the property is transferred into settlement (IHTA 1984, ss 89(4) and 89B(c)). For these purposes, an individual counts as disabled if incapable under the Mental Health Act 1983 or if in receipt of an attendance allowance or disability allowance (ibid s 89(4)).

The term disabled person's interest also includes the settlor's life interest under a settlement created by him in reasonable anticipation of his incapacity (IHTA 1984, s 89A). The term extends as well to the deemed interest in possession which subsists in discretionary trusts where during the life of a disabled person over half of any applications of the settled property must be for his benefit (IHTA 1984, s 89).

The provisions relating to disabled person's interest are not confined to UK resident trusts. It will be interesting to see whether any offshore trusts take advantage of them.

Meaning of interest in possession

44.6 All the above exceptions to the relevant property regime apply only if the beneficiary in fact holds an interest in possession. That term is not defined in the legislation. Case law indicates that the holder of the interest must have a present right of present enjoyment (*Pearson v IRC* [1980] STC 318 HL). In other words any income of the settled property must be his as it arises. Should the trustees have power to accumulate the income, or pay it to other beneficiaries, it is not his as it arises, for the trustees must have reasonable time within which to consider and, if thought fit, exercise those powers (cf para 12.6).

The normal form of interest in possession is a life interest. But an entitlement to income for a term of years or during somebody else's life is also an interest in possession. It is clear too that an interest is not prevented from being an interest in possession just because the trustees have overriding powers over the capital. What matters is that the holder is entitled to all income that arises before the power is exercised.

An area of controversy has been whether an interest in possession is created if trustees simply allow a beneficiary to use property, as where the trustees provide the beneficiary with a home. HMRC's view is that such bounty can result in an interest in possession unless the beneficiary pays at least some consideration (SP 10/79). Case law indicates that if the settlement obliges the trustees to allow the beneficiary to occupy the property he does indeed have an interest in possession (*IRC v Lloyds Private Banking Ltd* [1998] STC 559). But he has no such interest if his occupation is in the discretion of the trustees. A Special Commissioner so decided in *Judge v Revenue and Customs Comrs* [2005] STC (SCD) 863, a decision not appealed by HMRC.

Effect of the interest in possession exceptions

44.7 The effect of an interest in possession being equated with absolute ownership under the above rules is that on its termination a transfer of value occurs. Such is chargeable (once the life-tenant's nil-rate band is exhausted) at 40% if the termination is on death and otherwise at life-time rates.

The IHT charge is avoided if the termination is inter vivos and the property vests in the life-tenant absolutely for then nothing changes for IHT purposes. So too, tax is avoided if the life-tenant's spouse takes absolutely or if his life-interest is followed by a transitional serial interest in her favour. This result is an application of the spouse exemption and, as generally with that exemption, is precluded if the life-tenant has an actual or a deemed UK domicile and his spouse does not (IHTA 1984, s 18). The main application of the spouse exemption will be where the holder of a life-interest subsisting on 22 March 2006 dies and his spouse takes a successive life-interest (para 44.2 above).

There is one further scenario under which, the termination of life-interest equated with, absolute ownership does not result in tax. The transfer is potentially exempt if the termination is inter vivos, and another beneficiary who is not the life-tenant's spouse takes absolutely. The same result follows should such a beneficiary take a successive life-interest which is a transitional serial interest – ie if the termination is before 5 April 2008. But as with all potentially exempt transfers, tax is chargeable if the former life-tenant dies within seven years of the termination.

Accumulation and maintenance trusts

44.8 Accumulation and maintenance trusts represent a further exception to the relevant property regime, albeit also transitional. Such trusts were a feature of the original CTT legislation. For a trust to qualify one or more beneficiaries had, on or before attaining 25, to become entitled to the settled property or to an interest in possession in it (IHTA 1984, s 71(1)(a)). Until then the income had to be accumulated save insofar as used for the maintenance, education, or benefit of beneficiaries under 25 (ibid s 71(1)(b)).

An accumulation and maintenance trust created on or after 22 March 2006 is within the relevant property regime and thus does not qualify for any special treatment. This is so whether the accumulation and maintenance trust is by way of original settlement or by appointment under existing trusts.

Accumulation and maintenance trusts created before 22 March 2006 remain outside the relevant property regime until 5 April 2008. During that period they thus remain immune from any 10-yearly charge otherwise applicable and likewise there is no exit charge should any absolute interests or interests in possession arise. But on 6 April 2008, all such accumulation and maintenance trusts become relevant property and so thereafter are caught by 10-yearly and exit charges (FA 2006, Sch 20 para 3). But uniquely, and generously, no entry charge is made on this deemed entry into the relevant property regime (FA 2006, Sch 20 para 3(3)).

Exceptions

44.9 There are two limited circumstances in which an accumulation and maintenance trust remains outside the relevant property regime after 6 April 2008. One is if the terms of the trust, either original or as varied before 6 April 2008, require the beneficiaries to take absolute interests on or before attaining 18 (FA 2006, Sch 20 para 3(1)). The other is if they take absolute interests on or before attaining 25 (IHTA 1984, s 71D).

The second scenario is provided for by IHTA 1984, s 71D(3)–(5). The language of these subsections is somewhat obscure, but what they appear to require is that each beneficiary's share in the settled property must be fixed before 6 April 2008, and that thereafter only he can benefit from the income and capital of his share (see s 71D(6)). This second scenario is not wholly free of tax, for on absolute vesting a tax charge is made. This tax charge is essentially a relevant property exit charge, the effective rate of 6% or less being reduced to as many fortieths as there are complete quarters between 6 April 2008 or (if later) the beneficiary attaining 18 on the one hand and absolute vesting on the other (IHTA 1984, ss 71E and 71F).

Implications of becoming relevant property

44.10 It is unlikely that either of these circumstances in which an accumulation and maintenance trust can continue beyond 6 April 2008 will be widely used by offshore trustees, in view of the fact they require absolute vesting. The assumption must therefore be that offshore accumulation and maintenance trusts will slip into the relevant property regime on 6 April 2008. Should they do this the following computational points should be noted:

(1) As per normal relevant property rules, 10-yearly charges will arise on 10-yearly anniversaries of the creation of the settlement, and not on 10-yearly anniversaries of when accumulation and maintenance status ceased. If the settlement conferred an initial life interest on the settlor or his spouse, the 10-yearly anniversaries are, as noted in para 43.11, anniversaries of the occasion of when such interest or successive interest terminated.

(2) On the first 10-yearly anniversary to occur after 6 April 2008, the charge will be reduced by one fortieth for each complete quarter of the 10-year

period prior to 6 April 2008 (IHTA 1984, s 66(2)), as during those quarters the property will not have been relevant property.

(3) Should some beneficiaries have attained interests in possession before 22 March 2006, the initial settled value represented by such interests will be included in the hypothetical transfer used to determine the rate of tax (cf para 43.3). This is because such value will never have been relevant property.

(4) On an outright distribution after 5 April 2008 but prior to the first 10-yearly charge thereafter, the rate of tax will be based on what the rate would have been on the previous 10-yearly anniversary had the trust not then been an accumulation and maintenance trust (IHTA 1984, s 69(2)(b) and para 43.6). But that rate will be reduced by so many fortieths as elapsed between that notional 10-year anniversary and 5 April 2008.

(5) Should the trust have been created less than 10 years before 5 April 2008, the rate of tax on any distribution after that date, but before the first 10-yearly anniversary, will be based on the value initially settled, but reduced by so many fortieths as there are complete quarters between the creation of the settlement and 6 April 2008.

One important point emerging from all this concerns interests in possession which vest after 22 March 2006. All will be within the relevant property regime. Even those vesting between 22 March 2006 and 6 April 2008 are so treated, for no transitional provision takes them out of such status. No vesting, however triggers an exit charge. This follows from the express provisions of Sch 20 para 3(3), referred to above.

Bereaved minor trusts

44.11 One very limited form of accumulation and maintenance trust can be created after 22 March 2008 and be outside the relevant property regime. This is the bereaved minor trust (IHTA 1984, s 71A). This is unlikely to be of relevance to offshore tax planning as such a trust can only arise under the will or intestacy of a parent of a bereaved minor or under the Criminal Injuries Compensation Scheme. The property must vest absolutely in the minor on attaining 18 (s 71A(3)(a)). But vesting can be delayed until 25, at the price of an exit charge when vesting does occur similar to that described above in relation to accumulation and maintenance trusts after 5 April 2008 (IHTA 1984, s 71D).

Chapter 45

Excluded property and settlements

Introduction

45.1 This chapter explains when property comprised in a settlement is excluded property and thus free of Inheritance Tax. In general the rules apply both where the property would, if not excluded, be relevant property, and where one of the exceptions to the relevant property regime described in Chapter 44 is in point.

Foreign situs property

45.2 Foreign situs property is excluded provided the settlor was not domiciled in the UK when the settlement was made (IHTA 1984, s 48(3)(a)). This rule applies regardless of the form of the settlement and even if the settlor is among the beneficiaries. It also applies regardless of subsequent changes to his domicile.

Situs

45.3 The common law rules as to situs apply in determining where the settled property is situated (see Chapter 31). A point to stress is that the asset looked at is the asset held by the trustees. Thus in the common case of a trust holding its investments through an offshore holding company, the relevant asset is the shares in the company as distinct from the investments the company holds.

Domicile

45.4 The rules as to deemed domicile described in para 30.14 apply in determining what the settlor's domicile is at the time the settlement was made. However this is not so if the settlement was made before 9 December 1974 save insofar as property has been transferred to the settlement after that date (IHTA 1984, s 267(3)).

Who is the settlor

45.5 The term 'settlor' bears its normal IHT meaning (IHTA 1984, s 44(1)). As explained in para 43.13 this is itself in substantially the same terms as the income tax anti-avoidance definition in ITTOIA 2005, s 620 (as which see para 59.18). It is expressly provided that where more than one person is settlor, the settled property is treated as comprised in separate settlements (ibid s 44 (2)) but this is only insofar as circumstances so require.

In *Hatton v IRC* [1992] STC 140, 159, Chadwick J pointed out that circumstances would so require if it has to be determined whether any of the settled property is excluded. He further commented that where each settlor provided an identifiable or proportionate part of the settled property, each is settlor of a notional settlement comprising what he has provided. But where what is provided cannot be sensibly apportioned or partitioned, each settlor can be treated as settlor of the whole lot. Thus, on the facts of the case, where a reversionary interest had been settled as part of a pre-planned arrangement, both the original settlor and the settlor of the reversion fell to be treated as a settlor of the entire funds comprised in the notional composite settlement.

Initial interest of the settlor or his spouse

45.6 A testamentary settlement is not treated as made on the settlor's death if his spouse takes an initial interest in possession. Instead, it is treated as made by her when her interest in possession ends (IHTA 1984, s 80). In such case foreign situs assets are only excluded property if the deceased was non-domiciled when he died and the spouse is non-domiciled when her interest ends (IHTA 1984, s 82). This rule, however, applies only for the purposes of the relevant property regime described in Chapter 43. Accordingly, provided the settlor was non-domiciled when he died, foreign situs property is excluded on the termination of the spouse's interest even if she is then UK domiciled or deemed domiciled. Only following her death, when the property falls into the relevant property regime, is excluded property status lost.

A similar rule applies where on the making of the settlement the settlor takes a disabled person's interest. His domicile has to be tested both when the settlement is made and when his interest ends.

In relation to settlements made before 22 March 2006 the rule described above operated in all cases where the settlor or his spouse took an initial interest in possession. The continuing impact of this rule in such cases is extremely complex and is explained in para 45.16 below.

Property moving between settlements

45.7 As described in para 43.12, property which is advanced or resettled from one settlement into another is treated for the purposes of the relevant property regime as remaining comprised in the first settlement (IHTA 1984, s 81). Here the rule determining the excluded property status is that the settlor of the first settlement must have been non-domiciled when that settlement was made, and the settlor of the second settlement must have been non-domiciled when the second settlement was made (IHTA 1984, s 82).

The natural reading of this rule is that one looks just at the domicile of the actual settlor of the transferee settlement when that was made, and the domicile of the actual settlor of the transferor settlement when that was made. However it is sometimes suggested that, in addition, the domicile of the settlor of the transferor settlement has to be tested as at the time of the transfer, on the grounds that the transfer of itself renders him settlor of the transferee settlement. The result would be that excluded property status is lost if by then he has acquired an actual or a deemed UK domicile.

It may be that this analysis is right if the transferor settlement was created with a view to making the transferee settlement, for the applicable definition of settlor, in IHTA 1984, s 44 includes any person who has provided funds indirectly for the purposes of or in connection with the settlement. But, as was affirmed in *Fitzwilliam v IRC* [1993] STC 502, those words connote there must be at least a conscious association of the provider of the funds with the settlement in question (per Lord Keith at p 516). It follows that if the transfer of funds between the settlements is by the trustees of the transferor settlement as an independent exercise of discretion, the settlor of the transferor settlement does not become settlor of the transferee settlement.

As noted above, s 82 applies only in relation to the relevant property regime. If therefore a trust is outside that regime the issue of who the settlor of the transferred property is, and when his domicile must be tested, is governed by general principles. It is, however, unclear what answer those principles give. One view is based on the proposition that the trusts in the new settlement are read into the original settlement (*Pilkington v IRC* [1964] AC 612). This carries the implication that the settlor of the original settlement remains settlor of the transferred property. The other view is that as per the analysis in *Rysaffe* (para 43.10 above) the transferee settlement is the settlement and its settlor is the settlor. As a matter of common sense the former analysis is clearly more attractive, but if so, the question may be asked as to why s 81 was felt to be necessary at all.

Additions after change of domicile

45.8 As noted above, under the terms of s 48(3), the settlor's domicile is tested only at the time when the settlement is made. However HMRC take the position that if, after he has acquired an actual or a deemed UK domicile, the settlor adds to the settlement, its excluded property status is jeopardised (see *Tax Bulletin 27* (February 1997) p 398). The extent of the jeopardy is gauged by applying the provisions as to separate settlors in s 48(3) and the reasoning of Chadwick J in *Hatton* (para 45.5 above). If therefore the added property can be separated out it, in HMRC's view, represents a non excluded property settlement. If the property cannot be separated out, the implication is that HMRC would regard the whole settlement as having lost its excluded property status.

Although HMRC's view has the attraction of logic, it is very difficult to support as a matter of construction. This is because HMRC's position is based on the proposition that, for IHT purposes, a settlement is made in relation to any particular asset at the time when that asset is transferred to the trustees. But the case of *Rysaffe v IRC* [2003] EWCA Civ 356, [2003] STC 536 indicates that such reasoning is in error. As noted in para 43.10, at first instance Park J expressly held that, where property is added to an existing settlement, both the original fund and the added property form a single settlement for IHT purposes (see [2002] EWHC 1114 (Ch), [2002] STC 872, 892). The Court of Appeal upheld Park J's judgment and nothing in their judgment indicates disagreement with this point.

There are also two further arguments against HMRC's view. One is that s 44(2), and *Hatton*, deal on their terms with the position where there are two settlors, not where there is one settlor who just changes his status. Second, the relevant property regime expressly provides that the commencement of a settlement is when property first becomes comprised in it (IHTA 1984, s 60). It thus implies that other property can subsequently become comprised in the same settlement.

Purchased interest

45.9 There is one circumstance in which the conduct of the beneficiaries causes excluded property status to be lost. This arises when a disposition is made for a consideration in money or money's worth and, as a result, an entitlement to an interest in possession arises, either directly or indirectly. If the holder of that interest in possession is UK domiciled, the trust property is not excluded property (IHTA 1984, s 48(3B)).

This provision does not apply if the disposition took place before 5 December 2005. But where it does apply, it operates for all time, even if the UK domiciled holder of the interest in possession ceases to be entitled to that interest or becomes non UK domiciled. When read strictly, this rule is expressed in terms of the UK domiciliary being entitled to an interest in possession in 'the' property which would otherwise be excluded property. It is therefore arguable that if his interest terminates, and then the property comprised in the settlement is sold, the provision no longer bites.

This provision needs to be watched wherever excluded property settlements with UK beneficiaries are reorganised, for the consideration given can be in money's worth. In other words, the consideration can be other interests under the same trust. Further the consideration does not have to have been given by the UK domiciliary who has acquired the interest in possession.

In practice, inadvertent falling foul of this provision is likely to occur under international trusts based in onshore jurisdictions rather than with offshore trusts. This is because the latter, at least where non-domiciliaries are involved, tend to be discretionary.

The term 'interest in possession' bears its normal meaning and is not restricted to interests existing on 22 March 2006 or transitional serial interests.

UK situs of excluded property

45.10 The categories of UK asset listed in para 30.11 to 30.13 which are capable of being excluded property if owned by an individual can also be excluded property if settled.

Authorised Funds

45.11 The rules in relation to authorised funds are the same as those which apply to foreign situs assets. Accordingly, shares in a UK open-ended investment company or units in an authorised unit trust are excluded if the settlor had neither an actual nor a deemed UK domicile when he made the settlement (IHTA 1984, s 48(3A)). The terms open-ended investment company and authorised unit trust have the meanings discussed in para 30.11.

Two of the provisions described above do not operate in relation to AUTS and OEICs. One is the rule, described in para 45.7, which requires the domicile of the settlor of both the transferee and the transferor settlement to be tested when property has been transferred between settlements (IHTA 1984, s 82). However, the settled property is still treated as comprised in the first settlement (IHTA 1984, s 81) and so the relevant domicile in testing excluded property status is that of the settlor of that settlement when it was made.

The other rule is the rule described in para 45.6 above, which tests the domicile of both the actual and notional settlor when an initial interest in possession of the settlor or his spouse has caused the making of the settlement to be postponed until the ending of the initial interest or the spouse's successive interest (IHTA 1984, s 82). In this case, however, the settled property is still treated as having been settled by the holder of the successive or initial interest when that interest ends (IHTA 1984, s 80). It is to be inferred that the excluded property status of holdings in authorised funds under the relevant property regime has to be judged by the domicile of the notional settlor at that time rather than that of the actual settlor when the original settlement was made.

The rules described in para 45.9 above relating to interests in possession acquired for consideration by UK domiciliaries apply also to holdings in authorised funds (IHTA1984, s 48(3B)).

FOTRA securities

45.12 Should FOTRA securities be settled the ordinary residence of the beneficiaries is the criteria for determining excluded property status (cf para 30.13). The basic rule is that the securities are excluded property if all the known persons for whose benefit the capital or income of the settled property has been or might be applied are not ordinarily resident (IHTA 1984, s 48(4)(b)). This condition requires the whole settlement to be looked at, and not just the trusts on which the FOTRA securities are held. Should the settled property have been transferred from another settlement the other settlement must be taken into account too, unless the transfer was before 19 April 1978 (IHTA 1984, s 48 (5)).

These conditions are stringent and inter alia bar FOTRA securities from being excluded property where the only UK resident beneficiaries are long-stop beneficiaries who are realistically most unlikely in fact to benefit (*Montagu Trust Co (Jersey) Ltd v IRC* [1989] STC 477). But it appears that wide powers of adding beneficiaries do not breach the conditions as it is not known who might be added. Such is implicit in the Court of Appeal's decision in *Von Ernst and CIE SA v IRC* [1980] STC 111 where possible objects of a charitable trust were potentially at issue.

The domicile of the settlor is immaterial to the excluded property status of FOTRA securities. However, it can come into issue in determining whether investment into such securities triggers an exit charge under the relevant property regime (see para 46.11).

There is one situation in which the ordinary residence of all the known beneficiaries does not have to be looked at. This is if the securities are subject to an interest in possession and that interest is one of the those still equated with absolute ownership of the underlying assets. In such case, only the life-tenant need be non ordinarily resident (IHTA 1984, s 48 (4)(a)). As is explained in Chapter 44, an interest in possession is equated with absolute ownership where it existed on 22 March 2006 or where it is a transitional serial interest, an immediate post-death interest, or a disabled person's interest.

Foreign currency bank accounts

45.13 The relief afforded to non-domiciliaries who are also non-resident in respect of foreign currency bank accounts (see para 30.12) is in limited circumstances extended to settlements (IHTA 1984, s 157). It applies where the settlement is subject to an interest in possession, if the interest holder is non UK resident and non UK domiciled. However, the relief only applies if, in addition, the settlor was non-domiciled when he made the settlement and the trustees are non-resident and non-domiciled.

Where it applies, the relief is of limited application as it only removes the account from charge on the life-tenant's death. It does not relieve liabilities under the relevant property regime and so is not in point as respects life interest settlements created after 22 March 2006 unless the life interest is an immediate post-death interest or a disabled person's interest.

Loss of excluded property status

45.14 In general the changes to IHT made by FA 2006 will not cause existing settlements to lose excluded property status. This is because the test as to whether settled property is excluded has always been the same for all forms of settlement. There are however two exceptions.

Government securities

45.15 As described in para 45.12 above, UK government securities which qualify for FOTRA treatment attract excluded property status if the settlement is subject to an interest in possession which is still, for IHT purposes, equated with ownership by the life-tenant of the underlying assets and the life-tenant is not ordinarily resident.

In practical terms the result is that FOTRA securities held by interest in possession trusts on 22 March 2006 qualify for excluded property status so long as the interest in possession existing on 22 March 2006 subsists or it is replaced by a transitional serial interest. But once those conditions cease to obtain the much more rigorous rules hitherto applying only to non-interest in possession settlements are in point. As a result some settlements may lose excluded property status.

Initial life interest of the settlor and/or his spouse

45.16 A much more important area in which the 2006 changes impact on the excluded property status of existing settlements is where the settlor or his spouse has an initial interest in possession or where one of them has an initial interest in possession and the other takes an immediately successive interest in possession. Until 22 March 2006 IHTA 1984, s 80 provided in such cases that the settlement was not treated as made for the purposes of the relevant property regime until the life interest or the successive life interest ended. Whichever spouse held that final life interest was treated as settlor. Section 80 applies to settlements created after 22 March 2006 only insofar as the initial interest is an immediate post-death interest or a disabled person's interest. Section 80 does, however, continue to apply in full to initial interests and successive interests under settlements created before 22 March 2006.

The significance of this latter point to excluded property status is that IHTA 1984, s 82 applies to cases within s 80. It prevents foreign situs settled property from being excluded property unless the settlor was non-UK domiciled when he made the actual settlement and he, or as the case may be his spouse, was non-UK domiciled when the notional settlement is made on termination of the interest or successive life interest.

The fact that s 80 has since 22 March 2006 applied only to immediate post-death interests and disabled persons interests means that for inter vivos settlements created thereafter, s 82 is not in point. In other words, an initial life interest vested in the settlor or his spouse is irrelevant to excluded property status (save in the unlikely event that the trust is a disabled person's trust).

However, as section 80 continues to apply to settlements created before 22 March 2006, s 82 continues to apply in such cases to determine excluded property status. This is so even if the successive life interest arises after 22 March 2006. However, both s 80 and s 82 apply only for the purposes of the relevant property regime. It follows that, for so long as the settled property is not relevant property, the excluded property status of foreign situs property continues, as before, to be determined solely by the general rule in IHTA 1984, s 48(3) – ie the domicile or deemed domicile of the settlor when the settlement was made.

The result of this last point is that, again as before 22 March 2006, foreign situs property is not subject to IHT on the termination of the initial or the successive life interest provided the settlor had neither an actual nor a deemed UK domicile when the settlement was created. This follows because, under the terms of s 80, the property is not for the purposes of the relevant property regime treated as settled at all until the initial and successive life interest end. As such the property cannot until then be relevant property.

Thus far the changes made by FA 2006 do not alter the excluded property status of existing settlements. But the position is otherwise once the initial life interest of the settlor has terminated or (where his spouse takes a successive life interest) that interest has terminated. If at that point the settlor or his spouse has an actual or a deemed UK domicile and the property remains settled, excluded property status is lost. Should the initial or successive life-interest be followed by a transitional serial interest, the loss of excluded property status is deferred until after that further interest has ended, for until then the property is not relevant property. But in all other cases the loss of excluded property status is immediate. This is a change from the pre-2006 law for, under that law, excluded property status was preserved where the subsequent trusts were fixed interest and so not relevant property.

In some cases within ss 80 and 82, the initial interests of the settlor and (where relevant) his spouse ended before 22 March 2006 at a time when the holder of the interest had an actual or a deemed UK domicile. Should such a trust have been subject to an interest in possession on 22 March 2006, foreign situs property will be excluded when that interest ends and when any transitional serial interest ends. This is because, while such interests subsist, the property is still not relevant property (see Chapter 44). But after that interest or those interests end, the property becomes relevant property provided it remains settled, even if the trusts at that stage are still fixed interest. At that point excluded status is lost.

Where, on 22 March 2006, the trust in such a case was subject to accumulation and maintenance trusts the trust becomes relevant property once any life interest vests or, if later on 6 April 2008. This is because the assets then become relevant property (see para 44.7). At such point foreign assets lose excluded property status.

Authorised Funds

45.17 One bizarre feature of s 82 is that it is expressed as applying only in determining the excluded property status of foreign situs property. As explained in para 45.11, it does not apply in determining the status of holdings in authorised funds. However this point does not, it may be suggested, have great practical significance, for what s 82 does is to require the domicile or deemed domicile of the actual settlor at the time of the actual settlement to be taken into account. It thus presupposes that the effect of s 80 on its own is to require excluded property status to be tested, for the purposes of the relevant property regime, by reference to the notional settlement rather than the actual settlement. On its own s 80 does not obviously have this effect, but s 82 indicates that this is how it should be construed. Assuming that is right, the domicile or deemed domicile of the holder of the initial or successive interest when that interest ends is still the relevant domicile for the purposes of the relevant property regime, albeit on its own rather than in conjunction with the relevant domicile on creation of the settlement. Accordingly, existing settlements will lose excluded property status as respects authorised funds in the same circumstances as those just described in relation to foreign property.

Chapter 46

Excluded property and the relevant property regime

Introduction

46.1 The interaction of the relevant property regime with excluded property is of some complexity. This chapter explains the main points. It should be read with the general explanation of the relevant property regime in Chapter 43.

Entry charge

46.2 The rules which apply in determining whether property transferred to a trust is excluded and thus free of the entry charge are those relating to individuals described in para 30.9 to 30.13 above. Accordingly, if the individual is non-domiciled, the property is excluded if it is foreign situs or holdings in authorised funds. FOTRA securities may be transferred without charge provided the individual is non-resident (regardless of domicile).

Interestingly, and in contrast to reliefs such as business property relief, there is no 'claw-back' should the individual making the transfer die within seven years having in the meantime acquired an actual or a deemed UK domicile or (in the case of FOTRA securities) become UK resident. Nor is there a 'claw-back' if at the moment of such death the property is not excluded. Excluded property status in all these circumstances is tested solely at the time of the transfer into the settlement.

10-yearly charge

46.3 If on a 10-yearly anniversary all the property in a settlement is excluded property there is no charge. The result follows because the charge is made only on relevant property and that term excludes excluded property (IHTA 1984, s 58(1)(f)).

If, on a 10-yearly anniversary, some only of the property is excluded only the part which is not excluded is charged. But in this situation the computational rules are of some complexity. As explained in para 43.3, the rate of tax is determined by a hypothetical transfer taking account of assumed previous transfers. The way in which the excluded property rules work in relation to this hypothetical transfer are not entirely logical.

The hypothetical transfer

46.4 The hypothetical transfer self-evidently excludes all excluded property in the settlement at the time of the anniversary. But the other two elements in the hypothetical transfer do not disregard excluded property, namely the initial value of the initial property settled in any settlement made by the same settlor on the same day and the value, immediately after it became comprised in the settlement, of any property which was not then relevant property and has not since become relevant property.

The reason why these two elements include excluded property is that they postulate simply the value of the property rather than any amount on which tax is in fact charged. The second of the two elements is significant as it encompasses all property which was excluded when it became comprised in the settlement unless it or property which represents it has at some stage ceased to be excluded property. The only way such cessation can occur is if the property is so invested by the trustees as to cease to be excluded property. Unless this happens the result is that the chargeable UK assets on a 10-yearly charge attract tax even if their value is small and on its own within the nil-rate band.

Accumulations

46.5 This point arises even if the value of the property transferred to the settlement was small, or even if all that value comprised chargeable UK assets. The reason is that the rule is expressed in terms of assets becoming comprised in the settlement. As is explained in para 43.5, HMRC's view is that income becomes comprised in the settlement if and when accumulated. If, therefore, such income arises outside the UK and is never brought to the UK, it is property comprised in the settlement which has never been relevant property. As such it is included in the hypothetical transfer in the manner described above.

Assumed previous transfers

46.6 As the first component in the assumed previous transfers is chargeable transfers made by the settlor, gifts by him of excluded property are ignored (cf para 43.3).

The second component, namely amounts on which exit charges were imposed in the previous ten years, also excludes excluded property for, as is explained below, the amount on which an exit charge is charged is the diminution in the value of the relevant property. As explained above, the term 'relevant property' excludes excluded property (IHTA 1984, s 58(1)(f)).

Reduction by fortieths

46.7 As described above, once the rate of tax on the 10-yearly anniversary has been arrived at, it is applied to such of the property as is not excluded. But where property which has previously been excluded is involved that may not be the end of the matter. This is because the rate is reduced as respects any particular item of property if that property was not relevant property throughout the previous ten years (IHTA 1984, s 66(2)). The reduction is by one fortieth for each complete quarter between the last 10-yearly anniversary and the date on which the property became, or last became, relevant property. The practical application of this, in relation to excluded property settlements, is that the rate of tax on non-excluded assets will not be the full rate unless those assets or the assets they represent have been non-excluded throughout the previous ten years. If for part of that time the value they represent was excluded property, fortieth reductions fall to be made.

The exit charge

46.8 As the exit charge is levied on the amount by which the value of the relevant property is reduced, a distribution of excluded property is not subject to the charge (IHTA 1984, s 65(2)). But if what is distributed is not excluded, the same computational complexity arises as with the 10-yearly charge.

Exit charge before the first 10-yearly anniversary

46.9 As is explained in para 43.7, the rate of exit charge on non-excluded property before the first 10-yearly anniversary assumes the same hypothetical transfer as on a 10-yearly anniversary save that previous exit charges are ignored and the hypothetical transfer is taken as the value of the settled property when it became comprised in the settlement (IHTA 1984, s 68(5)). This latter reference takes no account of whether such property is chargeable and so embraces excluded property. It follows that the value of excluded as well as non-excluded property when settled is taken into account in computing the rate of the exit charge on any non-excluded assets. For the reasons given above (para 46.5) accumulations are so taken into account as well, even if of foreign income at all times kept abroad.

Also as explained in para 43.7, the rate of the exit charge before the first 10-yearly anniversary is as many fortieths of what would otherwise be the rate as there are complete quarters which have elapsed since the making of the settlement. A further reduction is made if the property comprised in the exit charge has not been relevant property throughout that period (IHTA 1984, s 68(3)). The number of fortieths is reduced by each complete quarter during which the property was excluded. In other words, if the non-excluded property comprised in the exit charge represents property which was previously excluded, the rate of exit charge is correspondingly reduced.

Between 10-yearly anniversaries

46.10 As is explained in para 43.6, the rate of tax on an exit charge in the ten years following any 10-yearly anniversary is as many fortieths of the rate on the anniversary as complete quarters have elapsed since the anniversary. However, for this purpose, the rate on the anniversary is recomputed if since the anniversary any property has become relevant property, such property being treated in the recomputation as having been relevant property at the time of the anniversary (IHTA 1984, s 69(2)). This means that if any property which was excluded on the anniversary has ceased to be so, such is taken into account. Further it is so taken into account even if subsequently it has returned to excluded property status.

This last rule is a rule which potentially increases the rate. As with exit charges before a 10-yearly anniversary, the rate is reduced if the non-excluded property comprised in the exit charge represents property which was not relevant property throughout the period since the most recent 10-yearly anniversary. In such case, reduction is the same – complete quarters during which the property was excluded property are ignored in computing fortieths (IHTA 1984, s 69(2)).

Unexpected exit charges

46.11 As the basic rule is that an exit charge is made whenever property ceases to be relevant property, the switching of non-excluded property into excluded property prima facie occasions a charge. Such switching occurs if cash banked in the UK is moved abroad, if chattels or bearer instruments are moved out of the UK, or if UK assets are used to buy excluded property investments.

In the case of property which is or becomes excluded by being foreign situs, an exit charge in these circumstances is expressly precluded (IHTA 1984, s 65(7)). However, this express relief does not extend to authorised funds and as a result it follows that an exit charge is triggered if an excluded property settlement uses UK funds to buy holdings in authorised funds. Nor does the express relief apply where excluded property status results from investment in FOTRA securities unless the settlor was non UK domiciled when he made the settlement (IHTA 1984, s 65(8)).

Chapter 47

Gifts with reservation

Introduction

47.1 The gift with reservation legislation (FA 1986, ss 102–104) is primarily of significance in domestic UK IHT planning. It prevents individuals from giving away assets from which they subsequently derive benefit. However, it is of significance to non-domiciliaries in that at the very least it can result in expensive and often avoidable tax charges on UK assets. It also has a further import, namely that if property is subject to a reservation it should be outside the pre-owned asset rules. These rules are described in Chapter 70, and they too are of potential and expensive impact. For all those reasons some treatment of the gift with reservation rules here is necessary.

The great difficulty with the rules is that their language is obscure and, although contained in a modern statue, it in fact replicates nineteenth century legislation (*Ingram v IRC* [1999] STC 37, 41 per Lord Hoffmann). Until 5 April 2005, this obscurity caused less trouble than one might have expected. But now the pre-owned asset rules mean it is often as important for taxpayers to be certain facts come within the GWR rules as that they do not, and for that reason the many obscurities of construction assume greater importance.

This chapter briefly outlines the rules and the many exemptions. It then reviews in rather more detail their application to non-domiciliaries.

The charge to tax

47.2 The GWR rules are in issue if at any time in the relevant period, property is subject to a reservation. The relevant period ends on the individual's death and starts seven years before then (FA 1986, s 102(1)). It thus falls to be ascertained retrospectively.

A charge to tax arises if on the individual's death the property is subject to a reservation. In this event he is treated as beneficially entitled to the property immediately before his death (s 102(3)). It is thus included in his estate for IHT purposes (IHTA 1984, ss 4 and 5).

A charge to tax also arises if during the relevant period – i e within seven years of death – the property ceases to be subject to a reservation. In this event the individual is treated as having made a disposition of it by potentially exempt transfer (s 102(4)). That notional transfer is then brought into account on the death in accordance with the general rules relating to such transfers (IHTA 1984, s 3A).

When is property subject to a reservation?

47.3 The first prerequisite for property to be treated as subject to a reservation is that the individual must have disposed of it by way of gift (s 102(1)). The term gift is not defined and sits uneasily with the transfer of value concept by reference to which IHT is otherwise structured. HMRC consider the term includes sales at an undervalue and interest free loans, the gift in the former case being the undervalue and in the latter case the interest forgone (IHT Manual IHTM14316 and 14317). Most transfers which are exempt transfers for IHT purposes are expressly excluded, most notably transfers to spouses and transfers to charities and similar worthy causes (s 102(5)). Gifts before 18 March 1986 are also excluded (s 102(1)).

The second pre-requisite is that one of two further conditions must be met:

(a) the donee must not have assumed possession and enjoyment of the property, or

(b) the property must not have been enjoyed to the entire exclusion, or virtually the entire exclusion, of the donor, and of any benefit to him, by contract or otherwise.

It has never been entirely clear, in the second condition, what situations are covered by the words 'by contract or otherwise' and what situations are not. A benefit obtained by the donor by virtue of operations associated with the gift is deemed to be obtained by contract or otherwise (FA 1986, Sch 20 para 6(1)(c)).

The typical cases where the rules apply are where the donor gives a house away and goes on living there, or where he gives a chattel away and continues to use it. It has been held that property in trust is subject to a reservation if the settlor is a discretionary object (*IRC v Eversden* [2005] EWHC 136D (Ch), [2002] STC 1109; affd [2003] EWCA Civ 668, [2003] STC 822). It is generally thought that the ability to add the settlor as a beneficiary is at least at risk of having the same result. A joint account is a gift with reservation if one of the account-holders funded it and it is unrestricted as to withdrawals (*Sillars v Revenue and Customs Comrs* [2004] STC (SCD) 180).

Until 22 March 2006, the termination of an interest in possession did not constitute a gift of the trust property by the life-tenant, at least insofar as the termination was by act of the trustees rather than disposition by the life-tenant. But now the termination is treated for the purposes of the GWR rules as a gift of the underlying settled property, with the result that the exercise is a gift with reservation if the terms of the settlement allow benefit to be conferred on the former life-tenant (FA 1986, s 102ZA). This only applies insofar as the termination is on or after 22 March 2006, and, as a result of the changes made to trust taxation by FA 2006 Sch 20, applies only where the life interest existed on 22 March 2006 or is otherwise equated with ownership of the underlying assets (see Chapter 44).

Tracing

47.4 One of the quirks of the legislation, perhaps reflecting its antiquity, is that it presupposes that the item of property given away is the self-same item of property as is subject to the reservation. Thus in the paradigm case, a house is given away, and the donor goes on living there. If the donee has sold the property given to him and bought some other property, the latter is not prima facie capable of being subject to a reservation.

In reality there are tracing rules (Sch 20 para 2). On the face of it these cover sales etc for they provide that any property acquired by the donee as consideration for a sale, is itself to be treated as the gifted property. But in fact it is generally accepted they do not have this result. This is for two reasons. The first is that the tracing rules are expressly disapplied where the gifted property is a sum of money in sterling or any other currency (para 1(2)(b)). The second is that the rules as to substitution expressly state that the whole GWR legislation applies on a sale as if the proceeds were the property comprised in the original gift (Sch 20 para 2(1)). As such they come within the rule that tracing is disapplied on cash gifts.

The correctness of this as a general proposition is accepted by HMRC (IHT Manual IHTM14372; Capital Taxes and Estate Planning Quarterly [1992] No. 2, 26). HMRC consider that if the cash is subsequently used to acquire other property which the donor then uses, such may be caught if the acquisition is associated with the gift. But the example of this that the IHT Manual gives suggests a restricted application, namely where the gift of cash is followed by the donee using the cash to purchase the donor's house, which the donor then continues to live in (IHTM14372).

The tracing rules just described do not apply where the gift is into settlement. Here the property to which the rules are applied are the assets comprised in the settlement from time to time (Sch 20 para 5). But if property is distributed from the settlement it is then treated as comprised in the gift (para 6(2)). The implication of this is that it is treated in the form it is when distributed, as then gifted by the donor to the donee. Accordingly, it is thereafter subject to the individual substitution rules.

Similar tracing rules apply where the gift with reservation is occasioned by the termination of a life interest (Sch 20 para 4A).

Exceptions

Full consideration

47.5 Land or chattels are not property subject to a reservation if the donor is paying full consideration for his occupation or use (Sch 20 para 6(1)). In the case of rent, the rent should be reviewed to market rent at regular intervals. This exemption also applies where the gifted property is an undivided share in the land and thereafter both donor and donee occupy it (FA 1986, 102B(4)).

Change of circumstances

47.6 In the case of land, there is a limited exception where the donor is a relative of the donee and his occupation results from a change in circumstances.

Carve-out

47.7 It is now settled that in applying the GWR legislation it is necessary to look precisely at what is gifted. It is possible to divide property by interest as well as physically, and if on the facts only one interest is given, the GWR rules are not brought into play simply because the donor retains another interest (*Ingram v IRC* [1999] STC 37).

This rule means that the retention of a reversionary interest does not of itself mean a gift into settlement is a gift with reservation (*Stamp Duties Comr NSW v Perpetual Trustee Co Ltd* [1943] AC 425; IR letter dated 18 May 1987). However it may be suggested that there would be a reservation in the gifted property if the settlor was a discretionary object under the antecedent trusts.

The carve-out doctrine should in logic also be in point where the settlor is the initial life-tenant of the settlement, so that what he gives away on the creation of the settlement is the reversion. The gift of the reversion would itself be subject to a reservation if there were powers to appoint capital to the settlor or otherwise enable him to benefit from it.

The carve out rule has been disapplied as respects gifts of interests in land after 9 March 1999 (FA 1988, s 102A). If in such a case the donor retains a significant right or interest, the property disposed of is deemed to be subject to a reservation.

Territorial limits

Death

47.8 If property is subject to a reservation on death, the donor is treated as beneficially entitled to it regardless of his domicile. Territorial limit is therefore arrived at by application of general IHT rules.

Common sense indicates that the property concerned can only be excluded property in relation to the donor if, and only if, at the time of his death the donor neither is nor is deemed to be domiciled in the UK. However, it does have to be observed that IHTA 1984, s 6(1) provides that property is excluded if the person beneficially entitled to it is non-domiciled; in the case of an absolute GWR the person in fact beneficially entitled is the donee. There is therefore an argument that property comprised in a GWR can only be excluded property if the donee has neither an actual or deemed UK domicile. This argument is almost certainly wrong, for the effect of the GWR legislation is that there are competing beneficial entitlements – the deemed one of the donor and the actual one of the donee. In such a case IHTA 1984, ss 5(1) and 6(1) do, when read together, indicate that the status of property as excluded is determined by the domicile of the person whom it is sought to charge, ie that of the donee in the case of the donee's death, and that of donor in the case of the donor's death.

Inter vivos gifts

47.9 Where the reservation ends inter vivos, the rule that the notional disposition is a PET in theory leaves no room for the excluded property concept. Before a disposition can be a PET it must be a transfer of value, and once it is a transfer of value it is by definition not a disposition of excluded property (IHTA 1984, s 3(2)). Accordingly, on a strict reading of the legislation, the inter vivos ending of a reservation is a PET, and so subject to IHT if the donor fails to survive seven years, regardless of where the donor is domiciled and indeed regardless of whether he has any connection whatever with the UK.

It is inconceivable that this reading of the legislation would find favour in the courts if the matter was litigated. As is described in Chapter 30, UK tax legislation is subject to territorial limits. However, it can be a matter of some difficulty to identify what those limits are if they are not precisely defined by legislation. In the present context the obvious solution would be to say that the ending of a reservation would only be a PET if at that time the donor has an actual or deemed UK domicile or the property would not be excluded in the hands of a non-domiciliary. But it is not impossible that a looser connection with the UK would be held to be sufficient, for example, simply residence in the UK.

A point which also arises is the same as that arising on the donor's death, namely whether, assuming the excluded property concept is relevant at all, the relevant domicile is that of the donor or the donee. So far no guidance on these problems arising from the inter vivos termination of a reservation has been given in decided cases. Pending such guidance the safest course is ensure that any reservation subsists until the donor's death, particularly where the donor is resident in the UK.

Settled property

47.10 Should the reservation subsist until the settlor's death, the natural reading of the IHT legislation is that the settled property rules apply to determine whether it is excluded property in relation to him. This result follows because once property is settled, those rules prevail over the free estate rules (IHTA 1984, s 48(3), (6)). Accordingly, provided the donor was non-domiciled when he made the settlement, the question of whether the property to which he is treated as beneficially entitled under the GWR rules is excluded is determined regardless of whether he has subsequently acquired an actual or a deemed UK domicile.

Shortly after the GWR legislation was first enacted HMRC stated in published correspondence that they shared the above analysis (*Law Society Gazette*, 10 December 1986). During 2001, however, they made it known in unpublished correspondence that they were reviewing their practice on the point. An announcement was widely expected in the 2002 Budget but none was forthcoming. Subsequently para 2.8 of the residence and domicile paper published in April 2003 (see para 39.8) affirmed the 1986 position, which is now also reflected in the IHT Manual (para IHTM 14396). The analysis published in the *Law Society Gazette* in 1986 therefore remains good and it is generally accepted taxpayers are entitled to rely on it. In any event it may be argued strongly that it represents the correct construction of the legislation.

Should the settlor's reservation end inter vivos, the same issue arises as with free estate as to whether the excluded property concept has any place at all. Assuming it does, the issue would then arise of whether the test should be whether the property is excluded property under the settled property rules, or whether, in applying the excluded property concept, it should be treated as in the donor's free estate.

Parity of reasoning with the position on death suggests the former is correct. HMRC, in the IHT Manual, say a charge should be considered in circumstances where the donor has acquired a UK domicile prior to the PET (IHTM 14396). There is no suggestion that such a charge should be considered where he has not acquired an actual or a deemed UK domicile.

There is little doubt the inter vivos termination of the settlor's interest as a beneficiary under a discretionary trust is to be avoided where he has acquired an actual or deemed UK domicile. Such termination would occur where the settlor is wholly excluded or releases his interest as a beneficiary or, in respect of capital distributions, if such are to another beneficiary (cf FA 1986, Sch 20 para 5(2)).

Where the reservation is triggered by the termination of an interest in possession equated with absolute ownership (para 47.3 above), excluded property status on the death of the former life-tenant is determined in accordance with whether or not, under the settled property rules, the trust property is excluded. This is because FA 1986, s 102ZA applies only for the purposes of the GWR rules. An ending of the reservation inter vivos raises the same issues as the ending of any other reservation inter vivos.

Application to offshore tax planning

UK domiciliaries

47.11 For UK domiciliaries the gift with reservation rules apply in foreign contexts in the same way as they do domestically. Particular points to notice are that they treat the settlor as beneficially entitled to settled property on his death if he is a discretionary beneficiary and that use by the settlor of foreign property previously given away, for example a house, may trigger the rules.

Should a foreign house used by the settlor be in trust, it will be property subject to a reservation even if he is not a beneficiary, unless he pays a commercial rent for it.

Non-domiciliaries

47.12 There are two principal danger areas for non-domiciliaries. The first is where the non-domiciliary has made a gift in specie and the gifted asset is in or is brought to the UK. If following this the donor uses or enjoys the property, the rules are in point. This issue would arise with a chattel if the donor gives the chattel away in the UK or abroad and the chattel is then placed by the donee in the donor's UK house. The issue can also arise with UK houses insofar as the non-domiciliary gives the house, or a share in it, away and continues using it. But what is unlikely to be caught is a cash gift abroad which the donee then applies in buying a UK house later used by the donor (see para 47.4).

The second risk area is settlements. Should a settlement of which the settlor is a discretionary object hold UK investments directly, those investments are exposed under the GWR rules. Subject to the nil-rate band, those investments are subject to IHT in the event of the settlor's death. This is so even if the settlor is not resident in the UK. Authorised Funds would not, however, be caught for they are excluded property in the hands of a non-domiciliary or a settlement created by a non-domiciliary (see para 30.11).

An offshore holding company to hold UK assets may avoid the non-domiciliary being exposed under GWR rules. This is so if the gift by the non-domiciliary is to a trust and the trust forms the company, for then the asset comprised in the settlement is the company shares. The position is otherwise if the non-domiciliary's gift is direct to the company for then the rules are applied to the gifted property rather than the company shares. Use of a company may of course have other drawbacks, as discussed in para 17.15 and in Chapter 9.

Debts and encumbrances

47.13 The general IHT rule is that liabilities are taken into account in valuing an individual's estate insofar as incurred for consideration in money or money's worth (IHTA 1984, s 5). A liability which is an encumbrance on a particular property, for example a mortgage, goes to reduce the value of that property (IHTA 1984, s 162(5)). This has particular relevance to non-domiciliaries, and means that a debt charged on UK situs property reduces the value of that property.

Disallowance of debts

47.14 In one situation, debts are disallowed. The relevant legislation is FA 1986, s 103 which applies insofar as the money or other asset lent was derived from or funded by the person to whom it refers to as the deceased. It is a badly worded provision copied from old Estate Duty legislation. It is a provision which taxpayers can fall foul of through inadvertence and therefore requires close analysis. In the interests of clarity, this discussion is expressed in terms of borrower and lender rather than deceased and lender.

Property derived from the borrower

47.15 The key concept is property derived from the borrower. This is defined in s 103(3) as any property which was the subject matter of a disposition made by the borrower. It also includes any property which 'represents' the property which was the subject matter of such a disposition. Such representation can be direct or indirect and may be by virtue of one or more intermediate dispositions.

Certain dispositions by the borrower are excluded. Under s 103(4) such exclusion applies if the disposition was not a transfer of value. This principally excludes dispositions which do not diminish the value of the borrower's estate (IHTA 1984, s 3) but it also excludes any arm's length transaction not intended to confer gratuitous benefit as dispositions of that sort are deemed not to be transfers of value (IHTA 1984, s 10).

The exclusion is, however, itself precluded if the disposition was part of associated operations which included either:

(a) another disposition by the borrower which is not for full value, or
(b) a disposition by another party which reduces the value of the borrower's estate.

A difficult issue with the definition of property derived from the borrower is what happens if the original property is sold or exchanged for other property. Such could happen commercially or where the transferee under the original disposition transfers it to a company in return for a loan or shares. It is clear in such cases that the proceeds of sale or, as the case may be, the shares or loan are derived property as they are representative property. However, it may be argued that the original property ceases to be derived property, on the following grounds:

(1) It is inherent in the structure of s 103 that property acquired for full value is not derivative property.
(2) Section 103 was enacted with the GWR rules in FA 1986, s 102, which make it clear that when the gifted property is sold or exchanged it ceases to be the GWR property (FA 1986, Sch 20).

The disallowance on death

47.16 Should the money or other asset lent to the borrower be derived from him within the above definition, it is not a deduction for IHT purposes on his death. This is the principal charging provision of s 103, contained in s 103(1).

In principal, the disallowance is only to the extent that the money or other property lent was derived from the deceased. However there is a qualification to this (FA 1986, s 103(2)). This is that the disallowance is to the extent of any property owned by the lender and derived from the borrower unless the borrower can show that his disposition of that property to the lender was not made with reference to or in order to facilitate the loan.

Repayment

47.17 The borrower is treated as making a potentially exempt transfer if he repays a loan which would under the above rules be disallowed on his death (FA 1986, s 103(5)). It is to be noted that this deemed transfer is potentially exempt even if the lender is a trust or other entity to which actual transfer by the borrower would not be potentially exempt.

Territorial limits

47.18 An individual with neither an actual nor a deemed UK domicile is not normally concerned with s 103 on his death, for his assets are not in any event exposed to IHT. However this is not true of most categories of UK asset (see Chapter 29) and so a debt which would otherwise diminish the value of his UK estate is not allowed if it falls foul of s 103.

Section 103 is material to an individual who on his death does have an actual or a deemed UK domicile, in that where it applies it precludes a deduction against his worldwide estate. However, there is one potentially valuable limitation if at the time the individual made the gift to the lender he had neither an actual nor a UK domicile. Such gift is ignored for the purposes of s 103 if the gifted property was foreign situs, for such a gift will not have been a transfer of value and so is excluded from the dispositions which generate derived property. This result is precluded if the gift falls foul of the associated operations rule described above, but that rule should certainly not be in point if all the borrower's dispositions to the lender predate his acquisition of any actual or a deemed UK domicile.

Where the territorial limits of s 103 are less clear is where the loan is repaid inter vivos. As such repayment is deemed to be a PET, the same issues as to territoriality arise as with the GWR rules (para 47.9 above). It seems reasonably clear that a PET is triggered if the borrower then has an actual or a deemed UK domicile.

Practical implications

47.19 Section 103 needs to be watched where a settlor is considering borrowing from a settlement he has created. It applies even if the loan is fully commercial, and it is in point whether the loan is of cash or some other asset. It does not, it may be suggested, apply to a lease of land, as a lease is neither a debt nor an incumbrance, such as alone triggers the section.

As noted above, section 103 may in many cases be inapplicable to non-domiciliaries, although this is an area where great care is needed. Section 103 does not apply if the borrower is a company controlled by the individual who made the original disposition, or his spouse or other relative. But onward transmission by such persons to the original disponor would be unlikely to be effective.

Section V

European Law

Chapter 48

The fundamental freedoms

Introduction

48.1 Member States of the European Union have consistently reserved for themselves competence over direct taxation. For this reason neither the rates of tax nor the rules for determining the tax base are harmonised in the Union. Nonetheless, in a plethora of decisions, the European Court of Justice ('the ECJ') has applied Community law to direct tax, founding its jurisdiction on the fundamental freedoms conferred by Articles 39–60 of the Treaty.

Limited areas of direct tax are covered by directives, most notably the mergers directive of 23 July 1990, the parent and subsidiary directive of 23 July 1990, the directive of 3 June 2003 dealing with interest and royalty payments between associated companies, and the savings income directive also of 3 June 2003. All save the last concern relationships between EU companies. The savings directive is considered in Chapter 50. It impacts on the offshore world because the UK's Overseas Territories and Crown Dependencies are being required to operate its provisions in relation to interest payments.

Nonetheless the principal area where EU law has potential impact on the subject-matter of this book remains the ECJ's interpretation of the freedoms. Two of those freedoms, freedom of movement for workers, and freedom to provide services, are of little direct relevance here. But the position is otherwise with the freedom of establishment and the freedom of movement of capital.

A point which should be made at the outset is that this is a developing area where there are many questions to which it is difficult to predict an answer. Moreover, in some instances, decisions of the ECJ have gone further than one might have expected on the basis of purely English canons of construction. For this reason much of this chapter and the next one are speculative. Nonetheless, the inevitable conclusion is that the ECJ decisions to date are certainly of relevance to some areas covered in this book, and that future decisions could affect the subject matter of this book profoundly.

Primacy of European law

48.2 A point which should be emphasised is that, in the UK, European law has primacy. The matter was put thus by Lord Nicholls in *Re Claimants under Loss Relief GLO* [2005] UKHL 54, [2005] STC 1357 at para 16:

> 'The second basic principle concerns the interpretation and application of a provision of United Kingdom legislation which is inconsistent with a directly applicable provision of Community law. Where such an inconsistency exists the statutory provision is to be read and take effect as though the statute had enacted that the offending provision was to be without prejudice to the directly enforceable Community rights of persons having the benefit of such rights. That is the effect of section 2 of the European Communities Act 1972, as explained by your Lordships' House in *R v Secretary of State for Transport, Ex p Factortame Ltd* [1990] 2 AC 85, 140, and *ICI plc v Colmer* (*Inspector of Taxes*) [1999] 1 WLR 2035, 2041.'

The practical effect of this was then stated by Lord Nicholls in the following terms: (ibid para 17):

> 'When deciding an appeal ... the appeal commissioners are obliged to give effect to all directly enforceable Community rights notwithstanding the terms of [the relevant UK legislation]. Accordingly, if an inconsistency with directly enforceable Community law exists, formal statutory requirements must where necessary be disapplied or moulded to the extent needed to enable those requirements to be applied in a manner consistent with Community law.'

Freedom of establishment

48.3 Article 43 (formerly Article 52) of the EC Treaty prohibits restrictions on the freedom of establishment of nationals of a Member State in the territory of another Member State. The prohibition is expressly extended to the setting up of branches, agencies, or subsidiaries. The freedom also includes the right to pursue activities as a self-employed person and the right to set up companies or firms. The term 'firm' includes any legal person governed by private law save for those which are non-profit-making. It is expressly provided that companies or firms having their registered office, central administration, or principal place of business in the Community must be treated in the same way as natural persons.

Several decisions of the ECJ make it clear that a person is exercising the right of establishment if he owns shares in a company established in another Member State which gives him definite influence over the company's decisions and allows him to determine its activities (see for example *Baars v Inspecteur* [2000] 2 ITELR 660, 681). Thus 100% owned companies are undoubtedly comprehended.

It is unclear whether the right to take up and pursue activities as a self-employed person can only be infringed if the person is in fact carrying on activity as a self-employed person or merely because he might do so. It has, however, been said by the ECJ that a restriction on the right of establishment is prohibited even if it is 'of limited scope or minor importance' (*de Lasteyrie du Saillant v Ministère* [2004] 6 ITELR 666, para 43).

A tax charge on emigration to another EU country infringes the freedom insofar as the emigrant intends to carry on business in the new country as a self-employed person (ibid). Such a restriction also infringes the freedom if the emigrant holds controlling interests in companies registered in his country of origin, even if such companies are managed elsewhere (*N v Inspecteur*, 7 September 2006, Case C-470/04).

Host country restrictions

48.4 The obvious kind of restriction Article 43 counters is the host country discriminating against nationals of other Member States doing business there. Thus in *Metallgesellschaft v IRC* [2001] STC 452, the ability to pay dividends under a group income election under the former ACT regime was at issue. The election could be made if the parent was resident in the UK and not if it was not. As a result, groups with a UK parent enjoyed a cash-flow advantage in that payment of corporate tax by the subsidiary was delayed. The ECJ held that this restricted the freedom of EU parent companies to establish in the UK and thus breached Article 43. As a result UK subsidiaries of EU groups who paid ACT on group dividends have a right to restitution against HMRC equal to the time cost represented by the accelerated payment (*Sempra Metals Ltd v IRC* [2005] EWCA Civ 389, [2005] STC 687).

Restrictions in the country of origin

48.5 It is now well established that restrictions in the country of origin must also comply with Article 43. In a UK context, this is illustrated by *ICI v Colmer* [1998] STC 874. Here ICI was a 49% consortium partner, the consortium asset being a holding company with 23 subsidiaries, 4 resident in the UK, 6 in other Member States and 13, a majority, in non-EU countries. Under the then UK domestic law (now TA 1988, s 402(3)), ICI could have claimed loss relief in respect of its share of the losses of the UK subsidiaries, but only if a majority of the subsidiaries were UK resident. The ECJ held that this restricted the freedom of the consortium members to establish, through the holding company, in other Member States and so potentially infringed Article 43.

Baars v Inspecteur [2000] 2 ITELR 660 is another illustration of country of origin restrictions. There the Dutch wealth tax gave an exemption for substantial holdings in trading undertakings established in The Netherlands. The taxpayer owned a substantial holding in an Irish undertaking. This did not qualify for the wealth tax relief as the undertaking was not Dutch. The ECJ held that this difference in treatment breached Article 43. It confirmed that the substantial shareholding gave the taxpayer definite influence or management rights and so constituted establishment.

Two recent UK cases

48.6 Two widely-publicised UK cases have concerned country of origin restrictions. In *Marks & Spencer plc v Halsey* [2006] STC 237 the rule at issue was the ability of a UK company to offset against its profits losses incurred by UK subsidiaries but not those incurred by subsidiaries established in other Member States. This was held to breach Marks and Spencer's freedom to establish in other EU countries despite the fact that profits in the foreign subsidiaries were not taxable in the UK. So too in *Cadbury Schweppes plc v Revenue and Customs Comrs* (2006), 20 September, [2006] All ER (D) 48 (Sep), ECJ (Case C-196/04) the UK's CFC legislation (see Chapter 67) was held to infringe the freedom. The ECJ regarded it as irrelevant that the effect of apportionment is no more than to expose the profits of the foreign subsidiaries to the same tax as is payable by UK subsidiaries (ibid). What matters is that under the CFC legislation the UK parent is 'taxed on profits of another legal person'.

Is discrimination required?

48.7 An issue which has been canvassed is whether Article 43 requires restrictions to be discriminatory or not. Discriminatory restrictions in the host country are those which treat persons from other Member States less favourably. In the country of origin discriminatory restrictions are those which treat nationals established in the home country less favourably when they exercise their right to establish in other Member States. It has been suggested that even a non-discriminatory restriction can breach Article 43 (see *R (on the application of Professional Contractors Group Ltd) v IRC* [2001] EWCA Civ 1945, [2002] STC 165).

It now appears that while the issue with host country restrictions is whether they discriminate, the issue with country of origin restrictions is whether they hinder (*Cadbury Schweppes v IRC* supra, at para 42). Further, the issue is not merely whether they hinder establishment in other Member States by comparison with the country of origin, but whether they hinder establishment in some foreign Member States as distinct from establishment in others.

Countervailing tax advantage

48.8 The fact that the party whose freedom of establishment is allegedly infringed may enjoy some countervailing tax advantage is disregarded. Thus, in a case originating in Germany, certain reliefs enjoyed by German registered companies were denied to the permanent establishments of foreign companies (*Compagnie de Saint-Gobain v Finanzamt* [2000] STC 854). Conversely, permanent establishments could remit profits to their foreign head office without suffering withholding tax, whereas withholding tax was chargeable on dividends paid by German subsidiaries to foreign parents. The ECJ held that this latter advantage did not prevent the non-application of the reliefs to permanent establishments from infringing Article 43.

Defences

48.9 The fact that a restriction discourages freedom of establishment does not make it inevitable that it is struck down. The ECJ will uphold it as permissible if it pursues a legitimate objective compatible with the Treaty and is justified by what are called 'overriding or imperative reasons of public interest' (*Cadbury Schweppes plc v CIR* (Case C-196/04); *Marks & Spencer plc v Halsey* [2006] STC 237, para 35). But in all such cases the application of the restriction must be appropriate to the attainment of its objective and not go beyond what is necessary.

Abusive practices

48.10 The ECJ regards it as well settled that Community law cannot be relied on for abusive ends (*Halifax plc v Revenue and Customs Comrs* (Case C-255/02) [2006] STC 919, 962, para 62). Accordingly a measure restricting freedom of establishment is capable of being upheld where it specifically relates to wholly artificial arrangements aimed at circumventing a Member State's legislation (*Cadbury Schweppes plc v CIR* (Case C-196/04) para 51). A case by case analysis is required and it is clear that exercise of the freedom is not of itself abuse (*X v Riksskatteverket* [2004] STC 1271, 1289 paras 42–45).

Tax avoidance

48.11 It is well settled that protection of a Member State's tax revenue is not sufficient to justify a restriction (*Cadbury Schweppes v CIR*, para 49). So too it is irrelevant that the target of a restriction is transactions designed solely to exploit a favourable tax regime offered by another Member State. But a restriction is permissible if it is confined to transactions which are wholly artificial and it may also be justified if it prevents evasion or secures effective fiscal supervision (*X v Riksskatteverket* (supra) para 51). But here, as everywhere, the restriction must not go beyond what is necessary.

Coherence of the tax system

48.12 The concept of coherence of the tax system is illustrated by *Bachmann v Belgium* [1994] STC 855. Here Belgian tax law allowed a deduction for pension and life assurance contributions provided the life insurer was Belgian. Foreigners working in Belgium with life and pension arrangements elsewhere challenged the restriction to Belgian providers. The Belgian defence was that the exemption was part of a single regime under which benefits were taxed when paid, the regime thus operating as a deferral. The ECJ accepted the tax on benefits could not readily be enforced if the insurer was foreign and held that that factor, coherence of the tax system, meant Article 43 was not breached.

Subsequent cases, however, have established that coherence of the tax system is a narrow concept. There must be a tax advantage on the one hand and the offsetting of that advantage by a tax charge on the other. Both the taxpayer and the taxes concerned must be the same (*Bosal Holding BV v Staatssecretaris van Financiën* [2003] STC 1483, 1503, paras 29 and 30). A further point is that even if coherence of the tax system is a valid ground for a restriction, the restriction must be proportionate (*X v Riksskatteverket* [2004] STC 1271, 1281 para 72).

Territoriality

48.13 It is accepted by the ECJ that a Member State may tax residents and non-residents differently. However, any tax advantage available solely to resident taxpayers must be based on objective factors apt to justify the difference in treatment (*Marks & Spencer plc v Hasley* [2006] STC 237, para 38).

It is also accepted that the principle of territoriality enshrined in international tax law has to be respected (ibid at para 39). Thus a Member State can reserve for itself the right to tax unrealised appreciation on capital assets held by an emigrant at the time of emigration, for it is in accordance with the principle of fiscal territoriality that capital appreciation is taxable where the taxpayer resided while it accrued. But any such tax on unrealised appreciation must be deferred until the emigrant sells the assets and be reduced to the extent of any depreciation in value between emigration and sale. Further guarantees or security for the tax cannot be demanded at the time of emigration (*N v Inspecteur*, 7 September 2006, Case C-470/04).

In *Marks & Spencer plc v Halsey* [2006] STC 237, the territoriality principle was accepted as potentially allowing the restriction of loss relief to losses incurred by UK subsidiaries. Three arguments led to this conclusion, namely the fact that profits of non UK subsidiaries were not attributed to Marks and Spencer, the fact that without the restriction the losses might be relieved in the states of both the parent and the subsidiary, and the fact that without restriction losses might end up being offset in the Member State with the highest rate of corporate tax.

Proportionality

48.14 As indicated above (para 48.9), even if a restriction is justified, it must not go beyond what is necessary. If it does go beyond what is necessary the issue arises of whether the whole restriction is struck down, or whether it is disapplied on a case-by-case basis. In the first of the follow up cases to the ECJ decision in *Marks and Spencer v Halsey*, Park J decided the latter was correct (*Marks & Spencer plc v Halsey* [2006] STC 1235).

Freedom of movement of capital

48.15 Article 56 (formerly Article 73b) prohibits all restrictions on the movement of capital and on payments between Member States.

Meaning of movement of capital

48.16 The predecessor EU legislation to Article 56 was the former Article 67 of the Treaty, which required Member States to progressively abolish all restrictions on the movement of capital. In 1988, Directive EC/361/EEC gave effect to that requirement. Article 1 of the Directive required capital movements to be classified in accordance with Nomenclature in Annex 1. Although the Directive has been superseded, the ECJ has repeatedly stated that the Nomenclature has indicative value in defining what is meant by movement of capital (*Trummer (Reference for a preliminary ruling)* (C-222/97); *D v Inspecteur* [2005]: C-376/03 STC 1211 para 24).

Annex 1 has 13 main headings, each with several sub-headings. For present purposes the most important heads are the following:

I Direct Investment
II Investments in Real Estate
XI Personal Capital Movements, the sub-heads of which include gifts and endowments and inheritances and legacies
XII Other capital movements

Illustrations

48.17 Several tax cases illustrate the breadth of what is meant by movement of capital. Among them are the following:

(1) In *Heirs of Barbier v Inspecteur* C-364/01, [2003] ECR 1–5013, the taxpayers were the heirs of a Dutch national who had been a long term resident of Belgium. He owned legal title to land in the Netherlands as nominee for companies to whom he had previously contracted to sell the economic interest. Dutch legislation imposing taxes on death charged real estate in Holland regardless of the residence of the deceased. But while residents were taxed on the basis of economic ownership, a non-resident was taxed on the full value of land registered in his name even if he had no economic interest in it. The ECJ stated (at para 58) that investments in land, the transfer of land by the owner to a company in which he owns all the shares, and the inheritance of land are all movements of capital. The Dutch restrictions breached Article 56 as they discouraged the purchase of land by residents of other Member States and the transfer of its financial ownership to others.

(2) In *Ministre des Finances v Weidert* C-242/03, [2005] STC 1241, Luxembourg law allowed a deduction for Luxembourg residents who

invested in Luxembourg companies, but not a deduction where they invested in foreign companies. The ECJ held this breached Article 56 as it discouraged both investment by Luxembourg residents in companies established in other Member States and the revising of capital by such companies in Luxembourg.

(3) In *EC Commission v Belgium* C-478/98, [2000] STC 830 the Belgian government had issued loan stock on the Eurobond market through German banks on terms that Belgian nationals could not subscribe. Interest was payable gross and the reason for banning Belgian nationals was concern that Belgians would not declare the interest. The ECJ held this restriction fell foul of Article 56, as its effect was to dissuade residents of Belgium from subscribing to a loan issued abroad (ie in Germany). The ECJ stated that measures taken by a Member State which dissuade its nationals from obtaining loans or making investments in other Member States are restrictions on the free movement of capital.

(4) In *Re Manninen* [2004] STC 1444, the Finnish system of taxing dividends allowed Finnish shareholders full credit for corporate tax, the company being liable to pay extra tax if the tax credit on the dividends exceeded the tax otherwise payable by the company. But the credit did not apply on dividends received by Finnish investors from foreign companies. As in *Weidert*, the ECJ held this breached Article 56 both because it deterred Finnish investors from investing in companies in other EU countries and because it discouraged such companies from raising capital in Finland.

(5) In *Van Hilten v Inspecteur* (Case C-513/03), the ECJ stated that an inheritance consists of the transfer to one or more persons of the estate left by the deceased. It is therefore a movement of capital except where its constituent elements are confined to a Member State (paras 41 and 42). A mere transfer of residence is not, by contrast, a movement of capital (ibid para 49).

Exceptions

48.18 Article 56 is subject to Article 58 (formerly Article 73d). Article 58(1)(a) reserves the right of Member States to differentiate between taxpayers who are not in the same situation as respects residence or where their capital is invested, and Article 58(1)(b) allows Member States to take all requisite measures to prevent infringement of national law, in particular in the field of taxation. Article 58(2) states that the provisions as to movement of capital are also without prejudice to restrictions on the right of establishment which are compatible with the Treaty. But both Article 58(1) and Article 58(2) are curtailed by Article 58(3), which provides that measures and procedures adopted under Article 58(1) and 58(2) must not constitute arbitrary discrimination or disguised restrictions on the free movement of capital.

In *Manninen*, the ECJ provided a reconciliation of Articles 58(1)(a) and 58(3). Article 58(1)(a) allows unequal treatment, but Article 58(3) prohibits arbitrary discrimination. It follows that if there is difference in treatment, it must concern situations which are not objectively comparable or be justified by overriding public interest grounds. But in any case, the difference in treatment must be proportionate (*Manninen*, para 29). In effect, therefore, Article 58(1)(a) does no more than import defences in any event available as a matter of general principle, as described in paras 48.9 to 48.13 above. This point was implicit in earlier cases such as *X and Y v Riksskatteverket* [2004] STC 1271, 1293, para 72 and *Staatssecretaris van Financien v Verkooijen* C-35/98, [2002] STC 654, 694, para 53.

As with freedom of establishment, it is clear there are certain situations where Member States can distinguish between residents and non-residents. Such discrimination is possible if it takes the form of an exempt first slice which is allowed to residents in taxing wealth but is not allowed to non-residents. The rationale of this is that the state of residence taxes the global wealth of residents, but only the locally situate assets of non-residents. An exception could however be made if all of the non-resident's assets are in the State concerned (*D v Inspecteur* C-376/03, [2005] STC 1211).

In relation to Article 58(1)(b) it is settled that the requisite measures it allows to Member States do include measures to ensure fiscal supervision or combat illegal activities such as tax evasion (*EC Commission v Belgium* [2000] STC 830, 852, para 38). However, here as everywhere else, any measure relied on must be proportionate, must be appropriate for its purpose, and must not go further than is necessary to achieve that purpose (ibid para 41).

Overlap with Article 43

48.19 When a resident of one Member State forms a company in another Member State, the exercise is both establishment and movement of capital. In such cases, the ECJ has applied Article 43, exploring Article 56 only where the owner has insufficient control to amount to establishment (see for example *X v Riksskattverket* [2004] STC 1271).

It might be thought that in such cases Article 43 outs Article 56. But Article 58(2) expressly states that Article 56 is 'without prejudice' to restrictions on establishment which are compatible with Treaty. A contrary conclusion is on one view indicated by the Advocate General in *Cadbury Schweppes* in that he states that, as the UK's CFC legislation engages the freedom of establishment, the Treaty provisions relating to freedom of movement of capital are not in point. But this is not reflected in the judgment of the ECJ itself for this states simply that, as any restriction on the movement of capital is the inevitable consequence of the restriction on establishment, the former does not require independent examination (see para 33 of the judgment).

Extension to non-EU countries

48.20 The issue of how far the fundamental freedoms extend to transactions involving non-EU countries is of growing importance. A number of cases pending in the ECJ will undoubtedly clarify the issue, but even now some important points can be made.

The Treaty itself

48.21 It is well settled that the freedom of establishment in Article 43 is breached only if the restrictions at issue restrict establishment in other Member States. Thus in *ICI v Colmer* [1998] STC 874, ICI could not rely on Article 43 to claim the losses as, even with the EU subsidiaries counted as UK subsidiaries, a majority were still outside the EU (see *ICI v Colmer* [1999] STC 1089).

The position is otherwise with freedom of movement of capital. Here Article 56 states that all restrictions on movement of capital are prohibited not merely as between Member States but as between Member States and third countries as well.

At least one ECJ decision has applied Article 56 to third country movements, albeit not in the context of tax. In *Sanz de Lera, criminal proceedings against*: C-163/94, C-165/94 and C-250/94 [1995] ECR 1–4821 Spanish law made it a criminal offence to take currency abroad without prior authorisation. Mr Sanz de Lera was found with currency in his car whilst driving to Geneva, and was prosecuted. The ECJ held that the requirement of prior authorisation breached Article 56.

The extension of Article 56 to third countries is subject to one important restriction. Under Article 57(1) it is without prejudice to national restrictions existing on 31 December 1993 involving direct investment, real estate, establishment, the provision of financial services, or the admission of securities to capital markets. The matters so particularised echo certain items in the list in the Nomenclature in the Annex to Directive 88/361/EEC (para 2.11 supra) and it is plain that if a transaction amounts to a movement of capital and is not one of those particularised, it is not caught. Thus in *Sanz de Lera*, the Spanish exchange control restrictions had existed on 31 December 1993, but as physical export of bank notes is not one of the matters listed in Article 57(1), the Article did not avail. Further, the ECJ said Article 57(1) is precisely worded, with the result:

> 'no latitude is given to Member States regarding … the categories of capital movement which may be subject to restrictions.'

A further potential limitation on the application of Article 56 to third countries is that the EU Council may adopt measures relating to the matters referred to in Article 57(1) (Article 57(2)). However, unanimity is required if freedom of movement to or from third countries is to be detracted from.

It is likely that Article 57(1) applies both where the legislation currently containing the restriction was enacted before 31 December 1993 and where the legislation now in force is, in substance, identical to earlier legislation in force on that date or relaxes such legislation. The ECJ so held in relation to comparable transitional provisions in Article 70 of the Austrian accession treaty (*Konle v Austria*: C-302/97, [1999] ECR 1–3099). This principle would not however apply if the current legislation differs in approach or establishes new procedures (ibid).

To date, there has been no suggestion in judgments of the European Court that a different approach to Article 56 should be taken as between capital movements within the EU and capital movements to countries outside the EU. However, in one pending case, the Advocate General has noted that, within the EU, freedom of capital is a constituent element of economic and monetary union. He could not, therefore, 'exclude that a Member State may be able to prove that a restriction of capital movements with third countries is justified on a given ground, in circumstances where this ground would not amount to a valid justification of a restriction in purely intra-Community capital movements' (*Test Claimants in the FII Group Litigation v IRC* (Case C-446/04) para 121).

In the UK the extension of Article 56 to third countries is at issue in *NEC Semi-Conductors Ltd v Revenue and Customs Comrs* [2006] EWCA Civ 25, [2006] STC 606. The point in this case is whether the requirement in the ACT group income election regime that the parent be a UK company was in breach of Article 56 and, if it was, whether it was saved by Article 57. The Court of Appeal was of the view that the case should be referred to the ECJ on this point. But it deferred the referral until it was clear there would be no appeal to the House of Lords on other issues in the case or, if there were such an appeal, that the Court of Appeal's decision on those issues were upheld.

Associated territories

48.22 Annex II to the Treaty lists a number of non-European territories which are dependent on or associated with EU members. They include the Netherlands Antilles and some, but not all, of the British Overseas Territories. Those listed include the Cayman Islands, the Turks and Caicos Islands, the British Virgin Islands, and Bermuda.

The significance of the associated territories is that Article 182 of the Treaty provides for association between them and the EU. Among the objects of such association are freedom of establishment (Article 183(5)). The EU Council is required to lay down detailed rules and procedures (Article 187).

Council Decision 2001/822/EC, the Overseas Association Decision, gives effect to this requirement. Articles 44–46 of that Decision are inter alia headed rules of establishment, but do not add to what the Treaty says. In contrast to the Treaty, the Decision does specifically refer to capital movements but in terms much more restricted than Article 56 of the Treaty. All that is covered is payments in freely convertible money. The Decision also contains a tax carve-out clause (Article 55). This inter alia entitles competent authorities to distinguish between taxpayers who are not in the same situation as regards residence or where their capital is invested.

It appears the Decision gives the governments of Annex II territories standing in the ECJ. This is apparent from *Government of the Cayman Islands v Commission of the European Communities* ([2002] CILR 91; *Spitz and Clarke: Offshore Service*, Cases vol 4 p 167). Here the Cayman Islands sought unsuccessfully to delay promulgation of the EU Savings Directive.

As just noted, neither Article 182 of the Treaty nor the Overseas Association Decision apply to European territories. Instead, the basic rule is that the provisions of the Treaty apply in full to European states for whose external relations a Member State is responsible (Article 299(4)).

The UK is responsible for the external relations of Gibraltar, which is a colony, and for those of the Crown Dependencies, ie the Channel Islands and the Isle of Man. But the Crown Dependencies are carved out of the Treaty, for under Article 299(6)(c) the Treaty applies to them only to the extent listed in the third protocol to the 1972 Act of Accession. The third protocol principally deals with agricultural products and inter alia does not import the fundamental freedoms into the Crown Dependencies (*Roque v Lieutenant Governor of Jersey* (1998) Case C-171/96). Gibraltar by contrast is fully subject to the EU law, save for certain aspects relating to turnover tax and agricultural products (see 1972 Act of Accession Article 28; and *Commission of the European Communities v United Kingdom* (Case C-349/03, 21 July 2005).

If and, insofar as the European and non-European associated territories can be said to be third countries, Article 56 should extend to capital movements between them and Member States. In 1992 the UK expressed the view that the predecessor to Article 56 (Directive EC/361/EEC) did not apply to movements of capital between the UK and Gibraltar, but this was on the basis that Article 299(4) required Gibraltar to be treated as part of the territory of the UK (SP 2/92 para 5). It is difficult to see this reasoning as applicable to other dependent or associated territories.

European Economic Area

48.23 The European Economic Area ('EEA') is constituted by the Agreement on the European Area which first came into force on 1 January 1993. The parties are the Member States of the EU and three member countries of the European Free Trade Area, namely Iceland, Liechtenstein and Norway.

The significance of the EEA is that the Agreement confers the four fundamental freedoms in broadly similar terms to the EU Treaty. Thus Article 31 of the Agreement provides that there shall be no restrictions on the freedom of establishment of nationals of any EEA state in any other EEA state. So too Article 40 provides that there shall be no restrictions on the movement of capital belonging to persons resident in EEA states and no discrimination based on nationality or on the place of residence of the parties or on the place where the capital is invested.

Article 40 has been applied by the ECJ in *Ospelt v Schlossle Weissenberg Familien Stiftung*: C-452/01, [2003] ECR 1–9743 where the transaction at issue was a transfer of land to a Liechtenstein foundation. *Ospelt* is considered in more detail at para 48.27. The judgment makes it clear that Liechtenstein's adherence to the EEA agreement renders inapplicable the rules in Article 57(1) of the Treaty about legislation in force on 31 December 1993.

Three decided cases

48.24 Most cases on the fundamental freedoms have involved business. However, several demonstrate the potential application to private clients, and three in particular may be noted.

X and Y v Riksskatteverket

48.25 *X and Y v Riksskatteverket* [2004] STC 1271 originated in Sweden. Swedish law allowed a form of roll-over relief where shares in one company were transferred to another company in the same direct or indirect ownership. However, under Swedish law, this relief could not be claimed if the transferee company was foreign or if it was a Swedish company owned by a foreign company. In the *X and Y* case, X and Y asked for a pre-transaction ruling that, despite Swedish domestic law, the roll-over relief would apply on a proposed transfer of shares in a Swedish company they owned to a Swedish company owned by a Belgium company. The Belgian company was itself owned by X and Y. The Swedish tax authorities contended strongly that a tax advantage would accrue to X and Y and that there were strong tax avoidance reasons for the transaction.

The ECJ considered the position both where the transferee company was foreign and where, as on the facts of the case, it was a Swedish company owned by a foreign company. The Court held that on both scenarios the Swedish law breached Article 43 provided the foreign company was an EU company and the Swedish taxpayer had definite influence over the foreign company's decisions and could determine its activities.

It then went on to consider Article 56 where the transferee was a foreign company and the Swedish taxpayer did not have such influence and held that in such case the Article was infringed. The rationale was that the inability to secure roll-over relief on a transfer to another EU company was 'liable to dissuade those liable to Swedish tax on gains from transferring shares at undervalue to transferee companies established in other Member States in which they directly or indirectly have a holding'. Such dissuasion was, in the view of ECJ, a breach of Article 56.

Tax authorities argued in relation to both Article 56 and Article 43 that the deferral implicit in the roll-over relief meant that coherence of the Swedish tax system could only be maintained if the recipient company was Swedish and Swedish controlled so that the deferred gain could eventually be taxed. The ECJ rejected this, giving two separate reasons. One was that the Swedish/Belgian tax treaty in any event allocated taxing rights. The other was that a blanket restriction on roll-over relief was disproportionate, in that the concern of the Swedish legislation was that the gain would drop out of charge if the taxpayer emigrated. This risk, the ECJ said, could be countered by a more specific restriction.

De Lasteyrie du Saillant

48.26 *De Lasteyrie du Saillant v Ministèrie* [2004] 6 ITLR 666 was a French case, again concerning capital gains. Under French law, unrealised capital gains on shares were charged to tax on the emigration of the owner insofar as the shares represented (in broad terms) a holding of more than 25% in the company. The charge was postponed if the taxpayer deposited funds to secure the tax and if, in such case, five years elapsed without the asset being sold, the tax ceased to be chargeable. The taxpayer emigrated to Belgium, which has a generally favourable regime for taxing gains.

The ECJ held that the exit charge breached Article 43. It emphasised that a restriction on freedom of establishment is prohibited even if of limited scope or minor importance. It then concluded that the recognition of unrealised gains on emigration would, at the very least, have a dissuasive effect on French residents wishing to establish themselves in another Member State. The ECJ was pressed with the mechanism for deferring and ultimately avoiding the tax if the shares were retained but concluded that that procedure itself constituted a restriction.

A point which was raised but is not clear from the ECJ judgment is whether the taxpayer was simply emigrating to Belgium or whether he was proposing to exercise his right of establishment then as a self-employed person. The ECJ pointed out that factual issues were for the national courts, and that the French courts had seen fit to make a reference.

The more recent case of *N v Inspecteur* (Case C-470/04) suggests that the reasoning in *de Lasteyrie* may not be as wide as at first thought. As described in para 48.13 above, it appears from that case that the departing Member State can tax the unrealised gains of an emigrant, but only if such tax is in fact deferred until the assets are sold.

Ospelt

48.27 *Ospelt v Schlossle Weissenberg Familien Stiftung*: C-452/01, [2003] ECR 1–9743 was a case originating in Austria. Austrian legislation made the transfer of agricultural or forestry plots the subject of prior government authorisation. It further provided that the transfer of agricultural plots would not be authorised if it was contrary to the preservation and creation of an economically healthy medium or small size agricultural estate. In particular authorisation could not be given if the plot would be withdrawn from agriculture, combined into a large estate or hunting area or if the acquirer himself was unlikely to cultivate the plot or had insufficient specialist knowledge to do so.

The taxpayer, Ms Ospelt, was a Liechtenstein national who owned a castle and 43,000m² in Austria, in which she resided. Most of the land was agricultural plots leased to farmers. In April 1998 Ms Ospelt sought authorisation to transfer the whole property to a Liechtenstein foundation under which she was first beneficiary. The application was refused and, in litigation initiated by Ms Ospelt, reference was made to the ECJ.

The first question referred was whether Article 56 applied to rules whereby transactions in agricultural plots could be subject to restrictions in the public interest in relation to an EEA country, as noted above. To this the ECJ responded in the affirmative, holding that the EEA States are in exactly the same position as EU Member States. Further, the EEA agreement covered restrictions existing when it came into force as well as subsequent ones.

The second question was whether, assuming the Austrian restrictions were within Article 56 or its equivalent they could be justified as being in the public interest. Here, perhaps unsurprisingly, the ECJ's view was that prior approval of transfers of agricultural land is prima facie in the public interest, in that it helps preserve agricultural communities and maintain a distribution of land ownership which allows the development of viable farms. But equally, the ECJ held, the rules must not go beyond the objective pursued. The ECJ construed the Austrian rules as enabling authorisation to be refused where the transferee would not farm the land himself. This, the ECJ decided, was excessive as farming by tenant farmers would equally achieve the desired objective. On this ground, therefore, Ms Ospelt won.

The facts of this case are far removed from tax. The prime significance of the case is that the transferee was a Liechtenstein foundation. No point was taken in the ECJ that the transferee was such a foundation or that the transferor was first beneficiary.

Chapter 49

Impact of European law on anti-avoidance legislation

Introduction

49.1 The ECJ's decision in *Cadbury Schweppes* (12 September 2006, Case C-196/04) has confirmed that the fundamental freedoms described in the previous chapter will in certain circumstances strike down UK anti-avoidance legislation. Although much remains unclear pending further cases in the ECJ, this chapter summarises some points that can be made at this stage.

Non-resident companies

49.2 Non-resident companies are, as a matter of domestic law, outside the scope of UK tax save insofar as investing or trading in the UK. Nonetheless, where such companies are owned by UK residents, anti-avoidance legislation attributes their income and gains to UK residents. The main examples are the CFC legislation, TA 1988, s 739 and TCGA 1992, s 13, discussed in Chapters 67, 55 and 66 respectively. The issue raised by ECJ cases discussed in the previous chapter is how far such anti-avoidance legislation is now itself invalid.

Companies resident in the EU

49.3 As described in para 48.6, the decision in *Cadbury Schweppes* establishes that the CFC legislation restricts the freedom of establishment. However, in that case, the ECJ also held that the legislation thwarts wholly artificial arrangements with no purpose other than to remove profits from the scope of UK tax. As such the restriction it contains can be justified on the grounds of overriding public interest (cf para 48.9 above). But as with all such restrictions, it must not go beyond what is necessary to achieve this and so if, as a matter of construction, the legislation does extend beyond wholly artificial arrangements it falls to be disapplied. This is so even though the intention to obtain a reduction in the UK tax may have been 'central to the reasons for incorporating the CFC'.

The ECJ considered that the resolution of this issue turned on the construction of the CFC motive defence in TA 1988, s 748(3) and remitted that point to the UK courts. But, as the discussion of that subsection in para

67.17 indicates, it does not confine the CFC legislation to 'wholly artificial arrangements'. Thus para (a) of s 748(3) asks whether the reduction of UK tax was one of the main purposes of the transactions and para (b) asks whether a main reason for the company's existence is diversion of profits from the UK. There is nothing about whether or not the arrangements are wholly artificial.

It may therefore be concluded that the CFC legislation is likely to be held to breach Article 43. As to how great the breach is depends on what is meant by 'wholly artificial arrangements'. The *Cadbury Schweppes* judgment indicates that the criteria the ECJ had in mind is whether or not the CFC has 'an actual establishment intended to carry on genuine economic activities' in the host State. However, what is not clear is how it is judged whether a CFC meets this test. On the one hand the ECJ states that a CFC should be seen as a wholly artificial arrangement if is a 'fictitious establishment' or it is a 'letterbox or front subsidiary'. On the other the ECJ states that any findings must be based on objective factors with regard, in particular, to the extent to which the CFC physically exists in terms of premises, staff and equipment.

A practical conclusion would be that if the CFC is genuinely managed in the host country it is unlikely to be wholly artificial if it has such premises, staff and equipment as are appropriate to its business. An issue not addressed by the ECJ is what the position is if the CFC's business is not intensive as to labour or premises, for example if it is a finance or asset-holding company. This question will no doubt be tested in future litigation and, in particular, in other CFC cases pending before the ECJ. But it would perhaps be surprising if artificiality is tested otherwise than by what is appropriate to the business the CFC carries on.

Assuming the CFC legislation does indeed infringe Article 43 on the lines indicated above, a point to stress is that the legislation as a whole is not struck down. It is merely disapplied to the extent that it purports to catch arrangements which are not wholly artificial. This is clear from the final sentence of the ECJ's ruling and is supported by Park J's judgement in *Marks and Spencer v Halsey* [2006] STC 1235 (cf para 48.14 above).

Many advisers now consider that the reasoning in *Cadbury Schweppes* applies equally to s 739. The result is that s 739 falls to be disapplied in all cases where the transferee company is not a wholly artificial arrangement. Such disapplication is likely to have a greater impact on s 739 than on the CFC legislation. This is because s 739 does not have the exempt activities concept found in the CFC legislation and, more important, because of the terms of its motive defence.

As described in Chapter 58, that defence has been reformulated since 5 December 2005 (TA 1988, s 741A). But under both the original legislation and the reformulation, there is nothing which confines s 739 to wholly artificial arrangements. The first limb of the defence looks solely at whether the purpose of the transfer was tax avoidance, and while the second limb does refer to genuine or bona fide commercial transactions, it then focuses on whether the transactions were designed for tax avoidance. Further, such compatibility as the second limb may have had with *Cadbury Schweppes* under the original s 741 has gone under the new s 741A, as that section requires any tax avoidance purpose to be incidental, and excludes many types of transaction which are in fact commercial (see para 58.15).

There remains TCGA 1992, s 13. Unlike s 739 this is not subject to a motive defence at all, being precluded only where a gain is realised on an asset used for the purposes of the non-resident company's trade (s 13(5)(b)). In the light of the *Cadbury Schweppes* judgment it must be disapplied unless the non-resident company whose gains are being apportioned is a wholly artificial arrangement. Indeed, one form of apportionment could turn out to be wholly inoperative, namely that under TCGA 1992, s 79B whereby treaty-protected gains are apportioned directly to trustee shareholders (see para 66.23). It may be argued that there is no overriding pubic interest to justify that legislation at all and, if so, it may be wholly inoperative in relation to EU companies.

Prior to *Cadbury Schweppes*, there was one highly significant potential argument. This was that anti-avoidance legislation such as ss 739 and 13 does not, in general, result in more tax than would have been payable had the income or gain accrued to a UK resident. But now it is clear that this fact is not relevant. As noted above in para 48.6, in *Cadbury Schweppes*, the ECJ expressly disallowed the argument that the tax Cadbury Schweppes was required to pay under the CFC legislation was no greater than the tax the CFC would have suffered if UK resident.

European Economic Area

49.4 As noted in para 48.23, the fundamental freedoms extend also to the EEA. It follows that the analysis given above applies also to companies in the EEA. This may prove significant in the context of offshore tax planning as Liechtenstein is a member of the EEA.

Outside the EU and the EEA

49.5 As noted in para 48.21 above, Article 43 does not extend to companies which are not resident in either the EU or the EEA. The freedom of movement of capital in Article 56, however, does, and the issue is what in practice this will mean to the CFC legislation and ss 739 and 13. As is explained in para 48.21, ECJ guidance on this issue is still awaited.

Pending such guidance the following thoughts may be offered:

(1) It may be argued that Article 56 does not apply at all if the non-resident company represents establishment in the overseas territory by its owners. But, as is pointed out above, the references in Articles 57(1) and 58(2) to establishment render this unlikely to be right.
(2) It is likely that those Articles, and Article 58(2) in particular, render it unlikely that a justification upheld in relation to Article 43 would not also apply to Article 56. Thus wholly artificial arrangements designed solely to avoid tax are most unlikely to be protected by Article 56.
(3) As explained in para 48.21, it is an open issue as to whether the ECJ

will be more ready to uphold restrictions on third-country movements of capital than restrictions on movements within the EU.

(4) There is also an issue, discussed in para 48.22, as to whether the British Overseas Territories and the Crown Dependencies will, in relation to the UK, count as third countries. As many key offshore jurisdictions fall within these categories, this point is of some significance.

(5) Also, as explained in para 48.21, certain categories of restriction in force as at 31 December 1993 must be respected. As one of those categories is direct investment and another is establishment it is difficult to argue that non-resident companies controlled from the UK are not comprehended.

On the face of it, this last point leaves the CFC legislation, s 739, and s 13 unscathed in relation to third countries all such provisions predate 31 December 1993. But, at least in relation to ss 739 and 13, the position may not be so simple.

As respects s 13, this is because significant changes were introduced in 1996, inter alia preventing the section from being disapplied where the gain was distributed, and extending the ambit of s 13 to all participators rather than just to shareholders (FA 1996, s 174). It is difficult to see these changes as rendering s 13 identical to its form in 1993 or as relaxing it. If so, the ECJ's reasoning in *Konle* (para 48.21 above) suggests that the 1996 extensions of s 13 would not be protected or, possibly, the effect of the 1996 changes may have been to remove the protection from s 13 in its entirety. A further point to make is that s 79B, the section attributing treaty-protected gains to trustee shareholders, is entirely post-1993 and so not on any view protected.

Until this year, section 739 had not seen significant post-1993 amendment. But the changes to the motive defence represented by s 741A have altered this. As described in Chapter 58, the effect of those changes is to remove protection from certain commercial structures and deprive an innocent transaction protected by s 741/s 741A of such protection if a subsequent tax driven associated operation takes place. As with the 1996 changes to s 13, it may be concluded that this extension of s 739 is not protected as a pre-1993 measure or, possibly, that s 739 has lost its pre-1993 protection entirely.

For these reasons, the fact that ss 13 and 739 were enacted well before 1993 may not be a complete bar to Article 56 being invoked. But as indicated above, Article 56 will not be in point if the company concerned represents a wholly artificial arrangement. It is difficult to regard this as anything other than a very high hurdle to jump if the company concerned is in an offshore jurisdiction.

Trusts

49.6 Like non-resident companies, non-resident discretionary or accumulation trusts are outside the scope of UK tax save insofar as investing in the UK. But again, as with companies, anti-avoidance legislation can attribute the income or gains of the trust to UK residents as they arise. The legislation in question, TA 1988, s 739, ITTOIA 2005, s 624 and TCGA 1992, s 86 is discussed in Chapters 64, 68 and 69. In contrast to companies there is no guidance from the ECJ as respects trusts.

Characterisation of trusts

49.7 The definition of what constitutes establishment does, it may be suggested, render it unlikely that the formation of a trust amounts to establishment. But the transfer of assets by the settlor to the trust is a movement of capital. The conclusion that trusts are comprehended by Article 56 is reinforced by the inclusion of gifts and endowments in the Nomenclature in the Annex to the 1988 Directive. On almost any view, a trust represents a gift to the beneficiaries or an endowment in their favour. A further point is that in a sense trusts are comparable to foundations. In *Ospelt* (para 48.27 above) the transfer of assets to a foundation proved to be a movement of capital.

An objection that may nonetheless be raised is that, as trusts are not creatures of the civil law, the provisions of the European Treaty will not recognise them. It is difficult, however, to see this being a sustainable position as at least three EU countries include trusts in their domestic law (UK, Ireland, and Cyprus). Others recognise trusts in the sense of having ratified the Hague Convention on trusts.

Settlor-interested trusts

49.8 It may be regarded as unlikely that legislation attributing the income or gains of a trust to the settlor if he is a beneficiary infringes Article 56. This is because such legislation applies equally to trusts based in the UK. Thus TCGA 1992, s 86 is replicated by ibid s 77, and ITTOIA 2005, s 624 applies as much to resident as to non-resident trusts. Nothing in *Cadbury Schweppes plc v IRC* indicates a measure is restrictive if it attributes the income of both residents and non-residents alike to a UK taxpayer.

It is possible that this difficulty could be circumvented by arguing that the anti-avoidance legislation bears more severely where non-resident trusts are involved, in that as a matter of practice it is more difficult for the settlor to enforce his right of indemnity. Indeed, in the case of UK trusts some or all of any income tax assessable on the settlor is secured at source or assessed by HMRC on the trustees directly.

But even if points such as this gave grounds for differentiation, a further point has to be faced. This is the fact that the settlor of a settlor-interested trust is usually regarded as the principal beneficiary and in many cases is the person whose wishes are listened to, and who receives distributions should he ask for them. In these circumstances would the trust be regarded as a genuine gift or endowment? Or, looking at the matter another way, would there be much greater risk of it being seen as abusive?

Trusts in the EU and the EEA

49.9 Assuming the settlor and his spouse are excluded, no UK anti-avoidance legislation attributes the income of a trust to a UK resident on an arising basis. But the position is otherwise with gains, for TCGA 1992 s 86 applies where the beneficiaries of a non-resident trust include the settlor's children or grandchildren. There are clearly good grounds for supposing that if the creation of a trust is a movement of capital at all, Article 56 is breached by s 86, for, in its application to children's and grandchildren's settlements, s 86 has no equivalent as respects UK trusts.

It would certainly not be a defence to Article 56 that the tax payable by the settlor under s 86 is now normally the same as the trust would pay if UK resident. As noted in para 48.6 above, that point has been concluded by *Cadbury Schweppes*. But the issue of whether a trust could be seen as abusive, and/or as contrary to the purpose of Article 56 is still at large. Such arguments would plainly be easier for HMRC to run if all the beneficiaries were UK resident and the whole exercise was tax driven. But these points would be weaker if the beneficiaries were spread around the world and if, on the facts, the chosen jurisdiction had expertise in trust administration and suitable trust laws. Cyprus and Ireland within the EU could be cited here, along with Liechtenstein in the EEA.

Assuming s 86 were held to be a restriction, it would be difficult for the UK government to justify it as proportionate. In part this is because it lacks a motive defence, and in part because it visits the tax not on the persons who benefit from the gain (ie the beneficiaries) but on the settlor. The proportionate response, it may be said, is to tax gains when distributed – ie TCGA 1992, s 87 (see Chapter 63).

Trusts outside the EU and the EEA

49.10 As already noted, Article 56 applies on its terms to movements of capital between EU and third countries. In logic, therefore, if it disapplies s 86 in relation to the EU it should also do so elsewhere. It is no defence that s 86 was enacted before 1993, as gifts and endowments are not one of the kinds of capital movement to which the protection for pre-1993 restrictions applies (see para 48.21).

But it must still be a strong possibility that, as suggested in para 48.21, the ECJ would find it much easier to justify restrictions by overriding public interest where third countries are involved, particularly where those third countries are perceived as offshore. In addition there is the point, made in para 48.22, as to whether the Crown Dependencies and British Overseas Territories would, in relation to the UK, be seen as third countries at all.

Distributions

49.11 As suggested above, the taxation of distributions, while perhaps a restriction, could be seen as a proportionate response to non-resident trusts.

But even if so, two provisions in the relevant codes may be seen as vulnerable. One is the rule, applicable to TA 1988, s 740 (Chapter 56) that tax on benefits does not give credit for tax suffered by the income matched with the benefit (cf para 56.8). The other is the rule, applicable to TCGA 1992, s 87 (Chapter 63) that tax is inflated by notional interest (see para 63.29). If this is justified at all, it may be said that the interest should be at commercial rates rather than 10%.

Trustee borrowing

49.12 It can cogently be argued that the rules as to trustee borrowing described in Chapter 62 are without justification or, if they can be justified, that the legislation is wholly disproportionate. The legislation does apply to UK resident settler-interested trusts and so, for the reasons given above, it may have to be accepted that Article 56 cannot be invoked against it in respect of settler-interested offshore trusts. But even if that is so, it may be argued strongly that Article 56 is in point with other trusts, particularly those where any gain triggered under the trustee borrowing rules is assessed as the settlor's on an arising basis.

As the trustee borrowing rules were first enacted in 2000, they would not on any view be saved in relation to non-EU countries as pre-1993 restrictions.

Other applications

Thin capitalisation

49.13 The ECJ has held that thin capitalisation rules which discriminate between transactions between parties in the same Member State and parties in different Member States breach Article 43 (*Lankhorst-Hohorst GmbH v Finanzamt Steinfurt* [2003] 5 ITELR 467). The 2004 amendments to the UK's transfer pricing legislation reflect this decision (see Chapter 68).

Hold-over relief

49.14 The UK currently has two forms of hold-over relief, namely gifts of business assets and gifts involving discretionary trusts (TCGA 1992, ss 165 and 260). Both are precluded if the recipient is non-resident. The *X and Y* case indicates that this restriction is vulnerable in the ECJ as being in breach of the freedom of establishment and the freedom of movement of capital. As Article 56 is not restricted to Member States, the issue may come to be raised of whether the vulnerability extends to all transfers to non-residents, and not just to transfers to EU or EEA residents. In that context it does have to be recognised that ss 165 and 260 were both first enacted well before 1993. But the transaction involved where hold-over relief is claimed, namely a gift, is not one of those caught by the saving in Article 57(1) for pre-1993 restrictions.

Foreign dividends

49.15 The present UK rules for taxing foreign dividends in part at least reflect EU law, for the dividend rates of 10% and 32.5% apply to foreign dividends as well as to UK dividends. But *Re Manninen* [2004] STC 1444 indicates this does not go far enough, in that it appears from that case that the UK should be allowing on foreign dividends an equivalent to the tax credit enjoyed by UK dividends (see para 48.17). This would reduce the tax rate on the actual dividend to nil basic rate and 25% higher rate. It is unlikely, however, that *Manninen* will be of significance in offshore contexts, for the judgment in the ECJ predicates that the company has born corporate tax at least equal to the tax credit. That precondition does not normally obtain if the paying company is offshore.

The applicable freedom in *Manninen* was the freedom of movement of capital and this indicates that the reasoning extends to dividends paid by companies outside the EU. But if so, the point which has to be addressed is that the UK system for tax dividends has been in place since the early 1970s, the changes in 1997–8 reducing the differential treatment as compared with foreign dividends rather than the reverse. Accordingly, if the purchasing of third country shares can be said to be direct investment, the UK regime may be protected as a pre-1993 restriction (cf para 48.21). In *Test Claimants in the FII Group Litigation v IRC* (Case C-446/04) the Advocate General indicated that the ownership of shares amounts to direct investment if it gives the owner lasting and direct links with the company, allowing him to participate effectively in the management of the company or its control.

Emigration and exit charges

49.16 Currently the UK imposes an exit charge on companies and trusts which cease to be UK resident (see Chapters 28 and 29). Individuals are not subject to an exit charge save as respects held-over gains (see para 27.13). However, individuals returning before five complete tax years have elapsed are taxed on their return on gains realised in the interim (see para 27.7).

It may well be that the charges on individuals would be upheld as justified by the need to protect tax revenues and proportionate. As explained in para 48.26, in *de Lasteyrie* the ECJ indicated that taxing individuals on return after a brief stay abroad may be acceptable. So too, in *X and Y*, the ECJ indicated an exit charge on deferred gains could be an appropriate method of preventing exploitation of the deferral relief at issue in that case. *N v Inspecteur* (7 September 2006, Case C-470104) indicates that it would be lawful for the UK to tax any gain accrued at the time of emigration, provided the tax is delayed until the assets in question are sold.

A point which should be stressed is that *de Lasteyrie* and *N v Inspecteur* both turned on the freedom of establishment and thus are only in point on emigration to the EU. The recent case of *Van Hilten*, discussed in para 48.17, indicates that the emigration does not of itself engage the freedom of movement of capital. If so, exit charges on emigration to countries outside the EU (and EEA) would be permissible.

The position in relation to company emigration is complicated by *R v HM Treasury ex p Daily Mail and General Trust plc* [1988] STC 787. This was decided under the old law whereby UK registered companies could become non-resident but had to apply for Treasury Consent before doing so (cf para 29.1). The ECJ held this did not breach Article 43 as the transfer of central management and control was not within it. Nowadays, any emigrating company is foreign registered or dual resident (see Chapter 29). But it may be that the same reasoning would apply, and if so exit charges on companies and arguably trusts would be saved.

Trust emigration does not normally involve any legal person moving abroad, but instead the retirement of UK trustees in favour of foreign trustees and the transfer of the trust assets to them. As such, in a literal sense, a movement of capital is involved. If indeed the exercise is a movement of capital, the immediate and blanket charge on emigration is, on the face of it vulnerable. Further the transfer to foreign trustees does not, on the face of it, come within the categories of capital movement where pre-1993 restrictions are preserved (cf para 48.21).

Inheritance Tax

49.17 In general IHT is not characterised by the kind of rules that potentially fall foul of European law. However, several detailed rules may be open to objection. Two in particular may be noted.

One is the rule that if trustees are non-resident, the settlor may be called on to pay any tax for which the trustees are liable (IHTA 1984, s 201(1)(d)). As this does not apply where the trust is resident, it could be seen as a restriction.

The second is the rule disallowing the spouse exemption where the donor is UK domiciled and the donee is not (IHTA 1984, s 18(2)). A gift between spouses is fairly clearly a movement of capital as gifts are included in the Nomenclature in the Annex to the 1988 Directive. It follows that if the relevant elements of territoriality are present Article 56 may be breached. But given that the ECJ case law is expressed in terms of residency, it may be the breach would arise only if the donor spouse was resident in the UK and the recipient spouse was not. If both are UK resident, a gift between them does not involve any movement of capital between Member States.

Enforcing European law

49.18 In the commercial sector, a plethora of cases are resolving how ECJ decisions should be applied in practice. The ECJ has said that compliance with a tax provision which is contrary to EU law entitles the taxpayer to reimbursement or reparation for the financial loss thereby caused (*Metallgesellschaft Ltd v IRC* [2001] STC 452, 493, para 96). The precise form of the remedy is a matter for national courts.

The House of Lords has now held that the primary forum for giving effect to claims that UK legislation breaches EU law is the appellate commissioners (*Re Claimants under Loss Relief GLO* [2005] UKHL 54, [2005] STC 1357). Thus the freedoms should be invoked when filing, or by separate claim, and when contested by HMRC taken to appeal using the normal appeal process. If the case is one relating to closed years, the first stage should be to seek to bring an appeal or claim out of time. If this fails, and only if this fails, should the taxpayer litigate in the High Court.

In the event of a claim in the High Court, the issue arises of what, if any, limitation period applies. The Court of Appeal has held that the applicable period is the normal period of six years from the date on which the cause of action accrues (*Deutsche Morgan Grenfell Group plc v IRC* [2005] EWCA Civ 78, [2005] STC 329). FA 2004, s 320 in any event imposes a six-year time limit on tax claims arising out of mistake of law.

On a hearing by the Commissioners, the Commissioners are fully empowered to make a reference direct to the ECJ for a preliminary ruling. Under Article 234 of the treaty, such reference may be made if the Commissioners consider that a Decision of the ECJ on the point at issue is necessary to enable them to give judgment. A reference is however only appropriate if there is real doubt on the point or to achieve uniformity (*Trinity Mirror plc v Customs and Excise Comrs* [2001] EWCA Civ 65, [2001] STC 192, paras 50–54 per Chadwick LJ; *NEC Semi-Conductors Ltd v IRC* [2003] EWHC 2813 (Ch) [2004] STC 489 para 70 per Park J). It appears that an application of EU law can be forced during an enquiry by applying to the Commissioners under TMA 1970, s 28A(4) or FA 1998, Sch 18 para 33 for a direction that HMRC give a closure notice (*Vodafone 2 v Revenue and Customs Comrs* [2005] EWHC 3040 (Ch), [2005] STC 1530).

In practice

49.19 It is extremely difficult to gauge whether, and if so when, European law points should be taken in practice. Over the last decade or so, the development of ECJ jurisprudence has furnished the basis for arguments which would have at one time seemed unimaginable. There is a distinct risk of further developments opening up still more avenues, which in particular cases could be time-barred by the time any ECJ judgment is handed down. Equally many of the points which may look like possible arguments now could be closed off by future decisions. In such cases the result of taking a point on European law may simply be an expensive argument with HMRC plus (if tax has not been paid) interest and surcharges.

Any decision as to how far European law points should be taken in filing is therefore a matter of judgement. What is clear is that if an item of income or gains is omitted in reliance on European law, full disclosure must be made of the facts and reasons for the omission. On that basis, in the present stage of the jurisprudence, it would not be unreasonable to file on the basis that European law inter alia furnishes an actual or possible defence against the following:

(1) TA 1988, s 739 and TCGA 1992, s 13 in relation to companies within the EU and EEA which are not 'wholly artificial arrangements'.
(2) TA 1988, s 739 and TCGA 1992, s 13 in relation to companies in third countries, but only insofar as those sections apply by virtue of amendments introduced since 1993 and the company concerned does not represent 'wholly artificial arrangements'.
(3) TCGA 1992, s 79B (treaty protected gains apportioned to trustees).
(4) TCGA 1992, s 86 in relation to settlements from which the settlor and his spouse are wholly excluded.
(5) TCGA 1992, Sch 4B (trustee borrowing).
(6) The exit charge on trust emigration (TCGA 1992, s 80).
(7) The disallowance of holdover relief on disposals to non-residents.

Chapter 50

The EU Savings Directive

Introduction

50.1 The EU Savings Directive (2003/48/EC) was promulgated on 3 June 2003 and came into effect on 1 July 2005. The system created by the Directive is complex and in many respects characterised by uncertainty. The object of the present chapter is to explain the system in outline and highlight those aspects of relevance to the subject matter of this book.

The Directive

What income is caught

50.2 The Directive applies to interest paid or credited to an account (Article (6(1)(a)). The term 'interest' is not defined, but it is made clear that to be caught interest must relate to a debt claim, whether secured or unsecured. Interest on securities bonds and debentures is expressively included.

Not surprisingly, the Directive also applies to accrued interest – ie interest accrued or capitalised at the sale, refund, or redemption of a debt claim (Article 6(1)(b)).

Certain receipts from mutual funds are treated as interest (Article 6(1)(c) and (d)). The mutual funds affected are UCITS within the 1985 UCITS Directive (85/611/EEC) and undertakings for collective investment established outside the EU. The payments caught are distributions representing interest accruing to such entitles and payments on the redemption of shares or units. But payments of the latter kind are only caught if the fund is more than 40% invested in debt claims. The 40% threshold falls to 25% after 1 January 2011.

The initials 'UCITS' abbreviate the term 'undertaking for collective investment in transferable securities'. The 1985 directive specifies that an undertaking is only a UCITS if its sole object is the collective investment in transferable securities or other liquid financial assets of capital raised from the public. The undertaking must be open-ended, ie units must be redeemable at net asset value. The UCITS Directive expressly states that the undertaking can be constituted by contract (a common fund), by trust law (a unit trust), or as a company. Under the Directive a UCITS can only carry on business in the EU if authorised by its Member State.

A point to stress is that the Savings Directive does not apply to dividends (save those from mutual funds referred to above). Nor does it embrace other categories of income.

Which recipients are caught

50.3 The Directive applies only where the person to whom the interest is paid or for whom it is secured is an individual (Article 2(1)). However, an individual can displace the Savings Directive in relation to a given payment if he provides evidence that he is not the beneficial owner.

The Directive does not apply to all individuals. It applies only where the recipient is resident in a Member State, and that state is different from that of the payer of the interest (Article 8).

On whom does the Directive impose obligations

50.4 The Directive imposes obligations on those whom it terms paying agents. A paying agent is any economic operator who pays interest to or secures the payment of interest for the immediate benefit of the individual (Article 4(1)). The economic operator is paying agent whether he is the debtor, or is charged by the debtor with paying the interest on its behalf.

The directive also imposes obligations on what may termed residual entities. Such an entity is caught if it is established in a Member State and interest is paid to it or secured by it for the benefit of an individual or individuals resident in a Member State (Article 4.2). In such circumstances the Directive deems it to be the paying agent in relation to such interest.

An entity falls to be treated as a residual entity under these rules unless it can show it is a legal person, a UCITS recognised in accordance with Directive 85/611/EEC, or that its profits are taxed under the general arrangements for business taxation. What is meant by general arrangements for business taxation is not defined. An entity which would otherwise be treated as residual may elect to be treated as a UCITS for the purposes of the Directive.

What obligations does the Directive create

50.5 The first obligation imposed is that the paying agent must follow procedures laid down by its Member State to enable it to determine whether a payment of interest is to or is being secured for an individual resident in another Member State (Article 3(1)). The agent must then establish the identity and residence of the individual concerned (Article 3(2)(3)). For contractual relationships entered into after 1 January 2004, this requires the individual's passport or identity card and, if he has one, his tax identification number. Looser requirements are imposed on relationships existing as at 1 January 2004.

The second obligation is that the paying agent must give information to the competent authorities of its Member State (Article 8). This information must include the name and address of the individual receiving the interest or for whom it is secured. It must also include the account number or other identification of the source of the interest. The competent authorities of the paying agent's Member State are then obliged to communicate this information to the payee's Member State (Article 9). This provision for onward transmission is the teeth of the Directive. Communication is required at least once a year.

A third obligation imposed on paying agents arises where the payee is a residual entity established in another Member State. In such case, the paying agent must notify its competent authorities of that payee. Those competent authorities then notify the competent authorities of the residuary entity's state (Article 4(2)).

Transitional provisions

50.6 The Directive includes two important transitional rules.

Withholding tax

50.7 During the transitional period three EU Member States, Belgium, Luxembourg and Austria, are not obliged to provide information to other Member States (Article 10). Instead those three countries levy withholding tax on interest or payments treated as interest made to individuals resident in other Member States (Article 11). The rate of withholding is 15% until 2008, 20% from then until 2011, and 35% thereafter.

The withholding tax is shared as to 25% to the Member State of the paying agent and 75% to the Member State of residence. The transfer to the Member State of residence is envisaged as a block transfer and must take place within six months of the end of the tax year in the paying agent's Member State.

Should the payment from Belgium, Luxembourg or Austria be to a residuary entity in another Member State, the paying state has the option to impose withholding tax (Article 11(5)). This does not apply if the residuary entity agrees to disclosure of its details.

The Directive makes it clear that an individual can opt out of the withholding tax procedure by expressly authorising the paying agent in Belgium, Luxembourg or Austria, to operate the exchange of information procedure in relation to him (Article 13(1)(a)). He can also do so if he applies to the tax authorities of his Member State and they issue him with a certificate (Article 13(2)).

Where tax is withheld, the Member State of residence is obliged to give a tax credit, the credit taking the form of repayment if the tax withheld exceeds the tax due under national law in the country of residence (Article 14). Other

Member States are obliged to operate the normal information giving procedures in relation to payments to individuals in Belgium, Austria and Luxembourg.

The duration of the transitional period is defined elusively (Article 10(2)). It ends when the European Counsel agrees unanimously that the United States is committed to exchange of information and when agreements providing for exchange of information on request have been entered into between the EU and all of Switzerland, Liechtenstein, San Marino, Monaco, and Andorra. The former condition in particular effectively means a unanimous decision of the European Council is needed before the transitional period can end.

Negotiable debt securities

50.8 Domestic and international bonds and other negotiable debt securities are excluded from the Directive if issued or approved before 1 March 2001 (Article 15). This exclusion continues until 31 December 2010 or (in the unlikely event that it is earlier) the end of the transitional period applicable to withholding tax. The exclusion may continue after 2010, but only as respects paying agents in the three Member States operating withholding tax.

Extension to third countries

50.9 Article 17 of the Directive provided that the Directive came into force on 1 July 2005. However this was dependent on two conditions being satisfied. The first was that Switzerland, Liechtenstein, San Marino, Monaco, and Andorra reached agreement with the EU to apply equivalent measures to those contained in the Directive. The second was that agreement or arrangements were in place with dependent or associated territories providing for automatic exchange of information, or, during the transitional period, withholding tax. The term dependent or associated territories was defined as the Channel Islands, the Isle of Man and dependent or associated territories in the Caribbean. Bermuda and other British overseas territories outside the Caribbean were thus excluded.

On 27 October 2004, it was announced the EU had reached agreement with Switzerland, on the basis that Switzerland would operate the withholding tax procedure, but providing for exchange of information in request in cases of tax fraud and the like (IP/04/1315) [2004] STI 2306). Subsequently in 2005, the Council of Ministers confirmed that all the preconditions listed above had been met, agreements being in place with Switzerland, Liechtenstein, Andorra, Monaco and San Marino and also with Jersey, Guernsey, the Isle of Man and the Caribbean overseas territories of the UK and the Netherlands (HMRC press release 1 July 2005, [2005] SWTI 1200).

The agreements with the Crown Dependencies and overseas territories

50.10 Jersey, Guernsey and the Isle of Man reached agreement with the EU on a common form of tax information agreement to be entered into with each of the EU Member States to give effect to the Directive. These agreements provide that during the transitional period, Jersey, Guernsey and the Isle of Man are operating the withholding tax procedure, with the counterpart EU states providing exchange of information. At the end of the transitional period Jersey, Guernsey and the Isle of Man are committed to exchange of information. The Tax Information Agreements between these territories and the UK have been brought into force by statutory instrument (SI 2005/1261; SI 2005/1262; SI 2005/1263).

In the Caribbean, the Tax Information Agreement with the BVI is in similar form to those with the Channel Islands and the Isle of Man and this provides for the BVI to operate withholding tax. The Netherlands Antilles and the Turks and Caicos Islands have also opted for withholding tax during the transitional period. The Cayman Islands, Montserrat, Aruba and Anguilla have agreed to exchange of information from the start. In the case of the Cayman Islands, there is no obligation of the UK to provide information to Cayman

As noted above, Bermuda is not within the Savings Directive as it is not in the Caribbean. The Bahamas is outside the Directive as well, as it is an independent state. Gibraltar counts as part of the UK for EU purposes, which means the Directive strictly does not apply to payments between Gibraltar and the UK. However a Tax Information Agreement between the UK and Gibraltar came into force on 1 April 2006 (SI 2006/1453). It is equivalent to the agreements described above, providing for Gibraltar to operate withholding tax save insofar as the UK recipient of the interest opts for exchange of information.

A point to stress about all Tax Information Exchange Agreements is that, like the Directive, they impose obligations in the overseas or dependent territory only where the interest is paid or secured for an individual resident in a Member State of the EU. They do not impose obligations on payments to persons outside the EU, even if such persons reside in other overseas or dependent territories which have concluded Tax Information Agreements with EU countries.

As respects the Crown Dependencies and the various Caribbean jurisdictions operating the Savings Directive, collective investment schemes established in the relevant jurisdiction are only required to operate the Savings Directive if UCITS equivalent. Guidance issued by particular jurisdictions amplifies what schemes in the jurisdiction should be regarded as UCITS equivalent.

Implementation in the UK

50.11 As a Directive, the Savings Directive does not have direct effect. This meant the UK, like other Member States had to bring in legislation implementing it.

The regulations

50.12 The main implementing legislation in the UK is the Reporting of Savings Income Information Regulations 2003 (SI 2003/3297). These were amended in 2005 to reflect the fact that Tax Information Agreements extend the obligation to provide information to the Crown Dependencies and overseas territories described above (Reporting of Savings Income Information (Amendment) Regulations 2005 (SI 2005/1539).

The Regulations follow the Directive, as they are bound to do. The main points of clarification are as follows:

(1) A paying agent is any person established in the UK who makes savings income payments in the course of his business or profession to a relevant payee or a residual entity (reg 3).
(2) A relevant payee is an individual resident in a prescribed territory (reg 7).
(3) The term prescribed territory means another Member State or certain of the territories described above, namely Aruba, BVI, Gibraltar, Guernsey, the Isle of Man, Jersey, Montserrat and the Netherlands Antilles (reg 2).
(4) A residual entity has the meaning given in the Directive (reg 4). A paying agent must presume an entity is a residual entity unless the entity produces official evidence to show otherwise. Residual entities established in the UK are designated receiving agents (reg 6).
(5) Savings income has the meaning given to interest payments in the directive and thus, like the directive, excludes dividends (reg 8). Distributions from mutual funds are excluded if less than 15% of the fund is invested in debt claims.
(6) The information and reporting requirements imposed on paying agents and receiving agents are as laid down in the Directive.
(7) The transitional provision for negotiable securities applies.

Credit for withholding tax

50.13 FA 2004, ss 107–115 give effect to the obligation imposed on the U.K. to give credit for withholding tax. It applies to withholding tax levied in Belgium, Luxembourg and Austria, and also to withholding tax levied in the other territories with which Tax Information Exchange Agreements have been concluded. It is expressed in terms of savings income, but as in the regulations this term is defined as interest payments within the meaning of the Directive.

Should the savings income be income as a matter of UK tax law the withholding tax is treated as tax deducted at source. Should it exceed the income tax the individual is otherwise liable for in the tax year concerned, the excess is set against any CGT liability he may have and otherwise it must be repaid (FA 2004, s 108). In certain cases, savings income is capital as a matter of UK tax law, for example on the disposal of a distributor mutual fund. In such case, the tax withheld is treated as a payment of CGT. If it exceeds the

CGT for which the individual is otherwise liable it is set against his income tax liability for the year and, if it exceeds that too, it is repaid (FA 2004, s 109).

Application to trusts

50.14 The application of the Directive to trusts is far from clear. However on its language three points may be made:

(1) Should an interest in possession trust receive a payment of interest, the life tenant is the individual for whom it is secured.
(2) Should a discretionary or accumulation trust receive an interest payment, there is no individual for whom it is secured, as no individual is entitled to any payment unless the trustees decide to give it to him.
(3) Should a discretionary or accumulation trust make a distribution such is not an interest payment. It is neither interest in fact, nor within the extended definition in the Directive.

The effect of the above is that discretionary and accumulation trusts are outside the Directive, a proposition which currently seems generally accepted. Interest in possession trusts are within it, but two problems are raised.

The first is the position of interest payments which, while interest payments under the Directive, are not in fact the life-tenant's income. It may be suggested the Directive does not catch these, as there is no individual for whom they are secured. Examples are accrued interest and the proceeds of disposal of mutual funds.

The second is whether trustees are a residuary body. On the face of it two factors suggest they are. One is the general tendency of UK tax law to see a trust as an entity, and the other is the tendency of people in civil law jurisdictions to see trusts as entities. If so, the trustees would be a residuary entity and so liable to operate the Directive as deemed paying agent.

Two final points may be noted:

(1) A fixed interest trust is only caught by the Directive if the life-tenant is resident in the EU or in one of the territories to which the Directive has been extended.
(2) The Directive may create problems for trusts whose trustees are individuals resident in the EU. In such case, the individual would have to show he is not beneficial owner, but that would only displace the Directive insofar as the interest payment is income of a life-tenant or the trust is indeed a residuary entity (cf Article 2).

Non-domiciliaries

50.15 Non-domiciliaries resident in the UK are affected by the Savings Directive insofar as they hold bank accounts or other interest generating assets in the EU or in the various other countries and territories which have been brought within the Savings Directive. Where the source country is operating exchange of information, the information is simply passed to the UK. This will be the position wherever the foreign paying institution considers the non-domiciliary has a permanent home in the UK.

The position where the source country or territory is operating withholding tax is more complex. This is because, unless the non-domiciliary remits, the interest is not taxable in his state of residence, ie the UK.

The Directive makes no express provision for the position where the interest is not taxable in the home state. However, as noted above, there is the procedure in Article 13.2 allowing an individual to displace withholding where he obtains a certificate from the tax authorities in his home state. In addition there is the credit mechanism described above. The requires the home state to credit or repay the tax withheld – despite the fact it will only have received 75% of such tax from the source state or territory.

The inference from all this is that non-domiciliaries should either obtain a certificate from HMRC or accept withholding and claim a repayment or, as they are entitled to do, authorise the paying agent abroad to exchange information. As respects the first of these options FA 2004, s 113 carries into UK law the mechanism for issuing certificates, although it does not place HMRC under any obligation to issue a certificate in any particular case.

As noted above, credit for withholding is provided by FA 2004, s 108 and 109. Section 108 in its terms provides for credit even where an exemption or relief prevents the interest from being taxable and is thus reasonably clear in applying to unremitted interest. Section 109 is less clear but, it may be suggested, must be construed as giving effect to Article 14. Article 14 makes it clear the UK must repay the tax withheld if it exceeds the UK tax due. One is thus left with the bizarre position that the UK must pay the tax withheld on unremitted interest even though it receives only 75% of that tax. Having initially given incorrect information in the notes to the non-residence etc pages of the tax return, HMRC now accept the correctness of this analysis (*Tax Bulletin 84* (August 2006) p 1304).

An interesting question is whether such repayment would itself be remittance, being expendable resources in the UK (cf para 40.4) or whether it is the result of an effective alienation abroad (cf Chapter 42). The former is perhaps more likely.

What is happening in practice is that some at least of the withholding territories are taking the position that if the paying agent is satisfied non-remittance means income is not taxable in the UK, withholding need not to be operated. Thus the Guidance issued by Jersey, Guernsey, and the Isle of Man indicates at para 32 that retention tax should not inter alia apply to payments made to:

> 'An individual where it is known to the paying agent that the individual benefits in their Member State of residence from an exemption from income tax; or where because of non-remittance of interest to an individual's Member State of residence no liability to income tax arises in that country of residence.'

This is amplified in the following terms in para 34:

'The bullet point in paragraph 32 above leaves open the question how the paying agent is expected to know that an individual benefits from exemption from income tax etc. For some existing customers, the paying agent may have an understanding of and/or documentary evidence confirming the customer's tax status. Reliance on self-certification by a customer also may be appropriate, where the paying agent has no contrary evidence and where the assertion is consistent with the paying agent's understanding of the customer's circumstances. In other cases the customer may have in their possession documentation from a tax authority or other source which would assist in confirming their tax status or they might be asked to provide a letter confirming that status endorsed by a professional third party such as a lawyer or accountant. The ultimate responsibility will rest with the paying agent. It will be for the paying agent to decide whether they have sufficient information in order for them to know that no tax liability arises but, unless evidence exists to the contrary, those able to take advantage of the sixth bullet point in paragraph 32 may be considered to have arranged their affairs in a tax efficient manner.'

Section VI

General

Chapter 51

Sham trusts

51.1 If a trust is characterised as a sham, the legal analysis is that the trustee holds the assets not on the trusts laid down in the trust instrument, but as nominee of the settlor. A finding that a trust is a sham is often the result of family litigation and in that context can be serious for the trustee, for he may end up being found to have misapplied money that was not his, particularly where the settlor is dead. But the importance of the sham concept in a fiscal context is emphasised by the criminal case, *R v Allen* [2001] STC 1537.

What is a sham?

51.2 In English law the generally accepted definition of what constitutes a sham was given by Diplock LJ in *Snook v London and West Riding Investments Ltd* [1967] 2 QB 786, 802. His words are as follows:

> 'As regards the contention of the plaintiff that the transactions between himself, Auto Finance and the defendants were a "sham", it is, I think, necessary to consider what, if any, legal concept is involved in the use of this popular and pejorative word. I apprehend that, if it has any meaning in law, it means acts done or documents executed by the parties to the "sham" which are intended by them to give to third parties or to the court the appearance of creating between the parties legal rights and obligations different from the actual legal rights and obligations (if any) which the parties intend to create. One thing I think, however, is clear in legal principle, morality and the authorities (see *Yorkshire Railway Wagon Co v Maclure* (1882) 21 Ch D 309 and *Stoneleigh Finance Ltd v Phillips* [1965] 2 QB 537), that for acts or documents to be a "sham", with whatever legal consequences follow from this, all the parties thereto must have a common intention that the acts or documents are not to create the legal rights and obligations which they give the appearance of creating'.

Further elucidation of what is meant by sham was given by the Court of Appeal in *Hitch v Stone* [2001] STC 214, 230. Here Arden LJ stressed that an inquiry as to whether a document is a sham requires a careful analysis of the facts and then said the authorities establish the following points (at paras 65–69):

> 'First, in the case of a document, the court is not restricted to examining the four corners of the document. It may examine external evidence. This will include the parties' explanations and circumstantial evidence, such as evidence of the subsequent conduct of the parties.

Second, as the passage from *Snook* makes clear, the test of intention is subjective. The parties must have intended to create different rights and obligations from those appearing from (say) the relevant document, and in addition they must have intended to give a false impression of those rights and obligations to third parties.

Third, the fact that the act or document is uncommercial, or even artificial, does not mean that it is a sham. A distinction is to be drawn between the situation where parties make an agreement which is unfavourable to one of them, or artificial, and a situation where they intend some other arrangement to bind them. In the former situation, they intend the agreement to take effect according to its tenor. In the latter situation, the agreement is not to bind their relationship.

Fourth, the fact that parties subsequently depart from an agreement does not necessarily mean that they never intended the agreements to be effective and binding. The proper conclusion to draw may be that they agreed to vary their agreement and that they have become bound by the agreement as varied (see for example *Garnac Grain Co Inc v HMF Faure and Fairclough Ltd* [1966] 1 QB 650 at 683–684 per Diplock LJ …

Fifth, the intention must be a common intention (see *Snook*).'

The Jersey Court of Appeal has defined how the principles formulated in *Snook* and *Hitch v Stone* apply to trusts. In *MacKinnon v The Regent Trust Company* [2005] JCA 066 Southwell P said (at para 20):

"In order to succeed in showing that the three settlements are shams [the Plaintiff] must establish that:

(i) both [the settlor] and [the trustee] intended that the true position would not be as set out in the settlement deeds, but that either the settlements were invalid and of no effect or that the assets of the settlements were held for [the settlor] absolutely so that the assets were simply held to her order, and

(ii) both [the settlor] and [the trustee] intended to give a false impression to a third party or parties (including other beneficiaries and the Courts) that the assets had been donated into the settlements and were held on the terms of the deeds".

The plaintiff in *MacKinnon* sought leave to appeal to the Privy Council, but leave was refused. It is thus clear that a trust is only a sham if both the settlor and the trustee share the shamming intention and both intend to deceive third parties.

Some offshore cases

51.3 A number of cases illustrate how in practice the sham concept has been applied to offshore settlements. A point these cases emphasise is that in determining whether a trust is a sham, it is not simply a question of looking at what happened when the trust was created. It is also necessary to look at the subsequent conduct of the parties to see whether their conduct signifies a true trust or whether in reality they are behaving as nominee and absolute owner.

Rahman

51.4 The first case, *Abdel Rahman v Chase Bank (CI) Trust Co Ltd* [1991] JLR 103 (*Spitz and Clarke: Offshore Service Vol 1*, p 433) concerned a Middle Eastern settlor who wished to protect his assets from forced heirship claims. On English legal advice, a trust was formed, which inter alia gave the settlor right to revoke the trust as respects one-third of the assets in any one year. The income was payable to the settlor, he had power of appointment over what was to happen after his death, and the trustee had power to appoint all the capital back to him, exercisable solely in his interest.

The dispossessed heirs duly attacked the trust after the settlor's death, and their principal line of argument was that the trust fell foul of an old Jersey maxim '*donner et reteinr ne vaut*'. This maxim applies where a donor retains power to dispose of what he has given or where what is given remains in his possession. The Royal Court in Jersey held that the maxim applied to trusts, and that the Rahman trust did indeed fall foul of it. This aspect of the decision has been reversed in relation to offshore trusts by the Trust Law (Jersey) Article 8A.

What is of significance in the present context is that the Royal Court went on to consider how the settlor and the trustee in fact conducted themselves. After a lengthy review of the facts the Court concluded the trust was a sham in the following terms:

> 'Therefore, having taken into consideration the whole of the evidence and documentation, we were able to reach but a single and unanimous conclusion. KAR retained dominion and control over the trust fund throughout his lifetime. The settlement was a sham in the sense that it was made to appear to be what it was not. The *don* was a *don* to an agent or nominee. The trustee was never made the master of the assets. KAR intended to and in fact retained control of the capital and income of the trust fund throughout his lifetime and used the trust and the deed of appointment made under the trust to make testamentary dispositions. In our opinion, KAR's advisers and the trustee lent their services to the attainment of his wishes.'

The factual findings which led the Royal Court to this conclusion included the following:

(1) Chase Bank in Switzerland opened the trust account on terms requiring it to make or change investments on the direction of the settlor.
(2) The settlor negotiated and gave instructions for the replacement of Chase by Advicorp as investment manager in May 1978.
(3) $1m was diverted from money due to the trust in February 1978 on the orders of the settlor. Similar diversions were made subsequently.
(4) Chase Bank took investment instructions from the settlor.
(5) The settlor orally stated the trust fund was his own money to use as he wanted.
(6) Reversionary beneficiaries were not told about the trust.

(7) All distributions were made on the settlor's orders, without the trustee considering which power was being exercised or executing proper documentation.
(8) The settlor regularly took money from the trust bank without consulting the trustee.
(9) On the evidence there was no circumstance in which the trustee would have refused a request from the settlor.
(10) The trustees made loans to settlor's wife on the instructions of the settlor on terms that only the settlor could call in the loans.
(11) The trustees acted in relation to a Liechtenstein Establishment to the order of the settlor.
(12) Advicorp managed the investment on the instructions of the settlor and in practice regarded themselves as answerable to him.

Allen

51.5 The second case is *R v Allen* [2001] STC 1537. Here, as part of a tax investigation, the accused had been asked to list his assets and he had omitted any reference to assets held in two offshore trusts. Subsequently those trusts came to the attention of HMRC, and they prosecuted the taxpayer, inter alia claiming that the trust assets should have been included in the list of his assets. The basis of this claim was that the trusts were shams, so that the accused was beneficial owner of the assets held by the trustees.

The accused was convicted in a jury trial in London, and appealed to the Court of Appeal on the grounds that the jury had been misdirected by the trial judge. This appeal was rejected on the grounds that there was overwhelming evidence that the assets were the accused's 'to dispose of as he would' (see *R v Dimsey* [1999] STC 846). The accused treated the assets as his and there was 'no question of the trustees possessing any real power or discretion in the matter'. The evidence is not set out in the report of the case, but once again, the key point is what in practice happened after the alleged trusts were created.

Abacus

51.6 *Re Abacus (CI) Ltd* [2004] 6 ITELR 368 was one of many cases arising out of the litigation between Grupo Torras SA and Sheikh Fahad Mohammad Al Sabah. According to the case report, Grupo Torras was, between May 1988 and June 1990, defrauded of $430m of which $120m was Sheikh Fahad's share.

Sheikh Fahad had previously created a Jersey discretionary trust, known as the Esteem Trust, for the benefit of himself, his second wife and their son. US$1m was comprised in the initial settlement in August 1981, and in April 1982, Sheikh Fahad added further cash which was used to acquire the family's main home. Sheikh Fahad added much more substantial value to the trust between 1988–1992, starting with a gift of £5m in 1989–90. By the time *Re*

Abacus was heard, Grupo Torras and Sheikh Fahad's trustee in bankruptcy had recovered all assets added to the settlement after 1988, by virtue either of proprietary claims or under a Pauline action in Jersey. There remained the assets settled in 1981 and 1982 and this Grupo Torras sought to secure in *Re Abacus*.

Their primary attack was that the trust was a sham. However, it was clear on the facts that the trust was a bespoke trust drawn up by London solicitors with the advice of Counsel to achieve specific tax planning and asset protection objectives. There was evidence that the settlor had understood he was putting the trust assets beyond his legal control, for he rejected advice that other assets of which he did wish to retain control should be settled. The terms of the trust were expressly modified to ensure it did not fall foul of the 'donner et retenir ne vaut' maxim. The trustee was a reputable trustee company whose files and evidence disclosed no evidence it took on the trusteeship on any basis other than that set out in the trust deed.

Given this evidence it is scarcely surprising that the Royal Court concluded, as it did, that the trust was not a sham. The only serious point Grupo Torras was able to advance was that one attendance note of the solicitors referred to the settlor having 'control' of the trustees. However, the Royal Court construed this note as referring to the ability of the settlor to remove the trustees rather than any ability of his to control their actions.

In reaching its conclusion, the Royal Court affirmed that it is legitimate to take account of subsequent conduct in ascertaining what was intended when the trust was set up ([2004] 6 ITELR 368, 462). In this context the Court was pressed with the fact that the trustee had always implemented requests made by Sheikh Fahad and also with evidence that on occasion proposed transactions had been put to the trustee virtually as a fait accompli on a take it or leave it basis.

The Court accepted that this was correct on the facts but also found that the trustee had always given genuine consideration to the requests or transactions put to it. This, the Court held, confirmed the trustee had, at the time the settlement was executed, intended to act as a proper independent trustee.

In the course of reaching its decision, the Royal Court issued trenchant general observations on the relationship between trustee, settlor and beneficiaries. It initially cited *Letterstedt v Broers* (1884) 9 App Cas 371 as authority for the basic proposition that all trustee powers must be exercised only in the interests of the beneficiaries. It then explained the duty of the trustees in dealing with requests by the settlor or beneficiaries in the following terms:

> 'In our judgment there is nothing untoward in beneficiaries making requests of a trustee as to the investment of the trust fund, the acquisition of properties for them to live in or for the refurbishment of properties in which they already live. In our judgment many decisions of this nature are likely to arise because of a request by a beneficiary rather than because of an independent originating action on the part of a trustee. The approach that a trustee should adopt to a request will depend upon the nature of the request, the interests of other beneficiaries and all the surrounding circumstances. Certainly, if he is to be exercising his fiduciary powers in good faith, the trustee must be willing to reject a request if he thinks that this is the right course. But when a trustee concludes that the request is reasonable having regard to all the circumstances

> of the case and is in the interests of the beneficiary concerned, he should certainly not refuse the request simply in order to assert or prove his independence. His duty remains at all times to act in good faith in the interests of his beneficiaries, not to act against those interests for improper reasons.
>
> In our judgment, where the requests made of trustees are reasonable in the context of all the circumstances, it would be the exception rather than the rule for trustees to refuse such requests. Indeed, as Mr Journeaux accepted, one would expect to find that in the majority of trusts, there had not been a refusal by the trustees of a request by a settlor. This would no doubt be because, in the majority of cases, a settlor would be acting reasonably in the interests of himself and his family. This would particularly be so where there was a small close-knit family and where the settlor could be expected to be fully aware of what was in the interests of his family.'

The approach implicit in this passage was endorsed by the English Court of Appeal in *Charman v Cahrman* [2005] EWCA Civ 1606, [2006] 1 WLR 1053 (see especially para 70). The conclusion which may be drawn is that a trust cannot be attacked as a sham just because on the facts the trustee has always accommodated the wishes of the settlor or beneficiaries. For conduct to be evidence of sham, an additional element has to be present, namely failure when any given request is made to give it genuine consideration.

Minwalla

51.7 *Minwalla v Minwalla* [2004] EWHC 2823 (Fam), [2005] 7 ITELR 457 was a bitterly contested divorce case in England, in which the former wife of an Asian businessman was claiming capital in ancillary relief proceedings. The husband had for many years owned a Panamanian company administered in Jersey which received his earnings, discharged payments on his behalf, and held assets. In 1998 the husband had settled a Jersey discretionary trust to which the company was transferred and the trustees also acquired a second company which owned the London flat in which the couple lived. The trust was discretionary and the only named beneficiary was a charity. The trustee held two contradictory letters of wishes from the husband which appeared to bear the same date.

In the ancillary relief proceedings the husband argued the trust and the companies had nothing to do with him and should be left out of account. In the English High Court, Singer J rejected this, holding the trust was a sham.

The following two passages in his judgment indicate the facts which led him to that conclusion.

> 'What are the factors here that support the proposition that the trust is a front, and that H, at least, had no intention of treating it as such? First, the assets of the trust comprise only the shares in DM and the shares in MM. As to the former, it is clear that H has treated the bank accounts of DM as if they were his own. He has caused to be paid into them the funds to which he was entitled under his various consultancy agreements with Cathay Pacific. He has withdrawn money from those accounts as if it were his own. No formal trading accounts for DM have been drawn up, at least since the execution of the trust deed in 1998.

> Transfers have been made from DM to MM, without any accounting ever being undertaken between the two companies. Transfers have been made from DM to Jealott Investments Limited, as if the money were H's own funds to move around as he chose, which is precisely as he has always regarded them, a practice from which the trustees/directors have been unwilling or unable to restrain him.'
>
> 'In his testimony in Jersey Mr Morgan conceded in answer to questions from Mr Kingscote that DM was in truth H's alter ego; that H had total investment control over that company and, in Mr Morgan's own words, H treated DM as his own "personal fiefdom". Not only had Mr Morgan never seen any consultancy agreement between H and DM, he had not until this summer seen any of DM's bank accounts, and could not be sure at which banks accounts were operative. He was until shortly before he gave evidence in July wholly ignorant about a series of three agreements between Cathay and DM concluded as long ago as May 2001 under which DM would receive up to a total of $4,750,000 in one-off fees contingent upon securing certain deals, plus an annual fee income until April 2006 of $850,000.'

The judge was faced with the requirement that for a trust to be a sham both the settlor and the trustees must have so intended. However, he founded himself on an earlier English case, *Midland Bank v Wyatt* [1995] 3 FCR 11, in which the judge had held the test was satisfied if one of the parties to the sham 'merely went along with the shammer, not either knowing or caring about what he or she was signing'. Singer J held that the trustees satisfied the test, observing that they did not attempt at any stage to rein him in.

Singer J also gave a trenchant statement of what is and is not effective in an offshore context (at para 51):

> 'The nature and structure of sophisticated offshore arrangements such as have been deployed by [the husband] is well understood in this Division. No doubt the professional advisers and trustees of wealthy individuals wish honestly to strive to construct a network of interwoven trusts and companies able successfully to withstand the scrutiny of the internal revenue services of the parts of the world relevant to the interested parties. That shelter is dependent upon there being properly constituted corporate and trust structures in place; and there being a level of competence and of formality in the production of minutes of board meetings, powers of attorney and so on. There must also be supporting evidence (if and when questions arise which must be answered) for the proposition that proper consideration has been given by the trustees to the exercise of their discretionary powers. Two divergent letters of wishes do not fit anywhere into such a structure. I do not see how any professional trustee can properly have in his possession two such contemporaneous documents without there being the clearest instructions in writing as to which prevails.'

Minwalla is not a wholly satisfactory case, as the husband did not attend the ancillary relief hearing and the trustees were not represented. However a clearer contrast with *Re Abacus (CI) Ltd* could not be imagined, as almost all the features that in the latter case led the Royal Court to uphold the trust were absent. It is also to be observed that in *Re Abacus (CI) Ltd*, the Royal Court endorsed the proposition that a trustee has the necessary intention if he goes along with the sham neither knowing or caring what he is signing (see [2004] 6 ITELR 368, 400, at para 58).

As the trust in *Minwalla* was a Jersey trust, Singer J's order fell to be enforced in the Royal Court in Jersey. As an interesting postscript to the English case, the Royal Court asserted trenchantly that it is a matter for Jersey law as to whether a Jersey trust is a sham and reiterated the applicable principles as set out earlier in this chapter. Nonetheless, it ended up by enforcing the English judgement, on the grounds that the trustee had voluntarily submitted to the jurisdiction of the English Court (*CI Law Trustees Limited v Minwalla* [2005] JRC 099).

Consequences

51.8 Even though it may be difficult to prove a trust is a sham, the consequences if the allegation is upheld are severe. Thus in *Rahman, Abacus* and *Minwalla*, the result was or would have been that the assets were at the disposal of the creditors, or as the case may be, the heirs or the former wife. A question of particular difficulty for any trustee would be if after the death or bankruptcy of the settlor he had incurred fees or even made distributions in accordance with the fictitious trust. In all probability the trustee would have to make these good, for he would have been dealing with the property without the authority of the beneficial owner.

Allen was a tax case and it illustrates the obvious point that if a trust is a sham any hoped-for fiscal advantages are not achieved. Perhaps more seriously, it demonstrates that criminal liability can arise as well.

Minimising risk

51.9 Examination of the facts of the cases described above shows the risk areas to avoid. The classic danger is where the settlor is a non-domiciliary from a civil law country who thus has little familiarity with trusts. The trustee is a bank who manages his assets, and submits a standard form trust document. The bank says that although this document confers wide discretion on the trustee, in practice nothing will change and the settlor's wishes will continue to be followed. The only difference will be that on the settlor's death the assets will devolve in accordance with the trust and not in accordance with the heirship rules of the settlor's home country or his will. Once the trust is set up, the reality is that in fact nothing changes, and the trustee in practice regards itself as bound by settlor's instructions. Indeed, as in *Minwalla*, he may often be referred to as 'the client' and his wishes as 'instructions'.

There is no doubt that such a trust is vulnerable to a sham attack. The best way of avoiding such risk is to ensure:

(a) The settlor fully understands what a trust is and, in particular, that it is the trustee who is in the driving seat.

(b) A trust is in fact the kind of legal relationship the settlor wishes to enter into.

(c) Once set up, the trustee behaves as a trustee. That is not to say he cannot follow the settlor's wishes, but it must be clear that the settlor can do no more than make requests, to which, on each occasion, the trustee must give genuine consideration.

Chapter 52

The Hastings-Bass principle

Introduction

52.1 Over the last few years what is now referred to as the *Hastings-Bass* principle has occasioned much discussion. It is of particular relevance to offshore tax planning in that many of the cases have been generated by tax blunders in one offshore jurisdiction or another.

Hastings-Bass

52.2 *Re Hastings-Bass* [1974] 2 All ER 193 concerned an advance by the trustees of an English settlement under the Trustee Act 1925, s 32. The advancing trust was a fixed-interest trust created in 1947 under which (in the events which happened) the trust fund was held on trust for a father for life with an absolute reversion to his eldest son. A trust in this form, as the law then stood, would have attracted estate duty at 73% on the death of the father. Accordingly in 1958, during the lifetime of the father, the trustees transferred part of the trust fund to another trust created in 1957 under which the son took an immediate life interest with gifts over to his children.

Following the decision in *Pilkington v IRC* [1964] AC 612, it became clear that the then rules as to perpetuity rendered the gifts over void as respects the advanced fund. On the death of the father HMRC claimed estate duty on the grounds that what could actually be achieved by the advance, namely a life interest to the son, was different from what the trustees had intended, namely an out and out transfer to the 1957 settlement. The trustees had therefore not properly understood what they were doing with the result that the s 32 power had not been validly exercised.

The Court of Appeal rejected this contention on the grounds that the prime consideration in the trustees' minds had been the benefit to the son in saving the estate duty and accelerating his interest. What happened to the capital after his death was incidental.

In the course of reaching this conclusion the Court of Appeal summarised its conclusion on the legal issues raised in what has become a much quoted passage:

> 'To sum up the preceding observations, in our judgement, where by the terms of a trust (as under s 32) a trustee is given a discretion as to some matter under which he acts in good faith, the court should not interfere with his action notwithstanding that it does not have the full effect which he intended, unless

> (1) what he has achieved is unauthorised by the power conferred upon him, or (2) it is clear that he would not have acted as he did (a) had he not taken into account considerations which he should not have taken account, or (b) had he not failed to take into account considerations which he ought to have taken into account.'

In the Court of Appeal's view *Hastings-Bass* was a case where the trustees would have acted as they did even had they appreciated the impact of perpetuities law.

Other formulations of the principle

52.3 The *Hastings-Bass* principle has been considered in pension cases as well as cases involving private trusts. In *Mettoy Pensions Trustees Ltd v Evans* [1991] 2 All ER 513, 555, Warner J expressed the principle in positive form as follows:

> 'I have come to the conclusion that there is a principle which may be labelled "the rule in *Hastings-Bass*". I do not think that the application of the principle is confined, as Mr Nugee suggested, to cases where an exercise by trustees of a discretion vested in them is partially ineffective because of some rule of law or because of some limit on their discretion which they overlooked. If, as I believe, the reason for the application of the principle is the failure by the trustees to take into account considerations that they ought to have taken into account, it cannot matter whether that failure is due to their having overlooked (or to their legal advisers having overlooked) some relevant rule of law or limit on their discretion, or is due to some other cause.'

Later he said:

> 'In a case such as this, where it is claimed that the rule in *Hastings-Bass* applies, three questions arise: (1) what were the trustees under a duty to consider? (2) did they fail to consider it? (3) if so, what would they have done if they had considered it?'

In one of the most recent cases, *Sieff v Fox* [2005] EWHC 1312 (Ch), [2005] 3 All ER 693, Lloyd LJ formulated the principle as follows (at para 119):

> 'The best formulation of the principle seems to me to be this. Where trustees act under a discretion given to them by the terms of the trust, in circumstances in which they are free to decide whether or not to exercise that discretion, but the effect of the exercise is different from that which they intended, the court will interfere with their action if it is clear that they would not have acted as they did had they not failed to take into account considerations which they ought to have taken into account, or taken into account considerations which they ought not to have taken into account.'

Offshore trusts: UK tax errors

52.4 The *Hastings-Bass* principle has been invoked in five cases to cure tax blunders on the part of offshore trustees or their advisers, in four of them successfully.

Trustee residence

52.5 In *Green v Cobham* [2002] STC 820, three BVI persons were trustees of the residuary estate of a testator who had died resident and domiciled in the BVI. They decided to give one third of the trust fund to six UK residents, and because three of them were under age, those three shares were on 12 November 1990 appointed on accumulation and maintenance trusts. Separate trustees were appointed for these funds, three of whom were UK professionals and four of whom were UK non-professionals.

For CGT purposes the appointments and the rest of the Will Trust were a single settlement whose residence was determined by looking at all ten trustees (see para 37.3). At the time of the appointment the professional trustee rule (para 37.5) meant this composite body was non-resident for CGT purposes, but that changed when on 31 December 1990 one of the professionals retired. The trustees had been aware of this prospective retirement when they made the appointment.

The result of the retirement was that the whole Will Trust became exposed to CGT. The trustees had taken extensive tax advice in connection with the proposed appointment but their attention had not been called to the CGT implications. In these circumstances the trustees applied to the English Court for a declaration that one of the appointments was void, and this application was acceded to by Parker J.

He summarised his reasoning as follows:

> 'I therefore conclude that this is a clear case for the application of the *Hastings-Bass* principle. In my judgement there is no real room for doubt on the evidence that had the then trustees of the Will Trust had regard to the possible capital gains tax consequences of the proposed appointment, they would not – and I stress would not – have gone ahead with it. What other course they might have taken is, I accept, not entirely clear. However, what is entirely clear, in my judgement, is that had the trustees directed their minds, as they should have done, to considerations of capital gains tax, they would not under any circumstances have made an appointment which gave rise to any significant risk that the Will Trust might thereafter become a United Kingdom resident trust for capital gains tax purposes. In this connection, I referred earlier to the substantial accrued capital gains shown in FIL's accounts for the year to 31 July 1989'.

Flip-flop scheme

52.6 In *Abacus Trust Co (Isle of Man) Ltd v NSPCC* [2001] 3 ITELR 846, Isle of Man Trustees had been advised to implement a flip-flop scheme of the kind countered by TCGA 1992, Sch 4B (see para 62.1). The intention was to avoid a charge on the settlor under TCGA 1992, s 86 on the maturity of certain loan notes on 15 July 1998, and also the ensuing beneficiary charge under TCGA 1992, s 87.

Pursuant to the scheme, the creation of the new settlements, the borrowing by the original settlement, the advance to the new settlements, and the exclusion of the settlor and all defined persons under the original settlement, had been effected by 5 April 1998. However, it had also been proposed that after effecting the scheme the residual value in the original settlement would be appointed to one of the remaining beneficiaries, the NSPCC. This appointment was a tidying-up exercise not necessary to the scheme. In error (and contrary to Counsel's advice) the deed effecting this was executed on 3 April 1998 and had the effect of triggering the gain on the loan notes at a time when the settlement was still within s 86 and when even if it was not, the gain would, as the law then stood, have gone into the s 87 pool carried into the new settlement.

In these circumstances the trustees applied to the English Court to have the appointment declared void. Patten J made the declaration requested, his reasoning being encapsulated in the following passage:

> 'The financial consequences for the beneficiaries of any intended exercise of a fiduciary power cannot be assessed without reference to their fiscal implications. The two seem to me inseparable. Therefore if the effect of an intended appointment is likely to be to expose the fund or its beneficiaries to a significant charge to tax that is something which the trustees have an obligation to consider when deciding whether it is proper to proceed with the appointment. Once relevance is established then a failure to take those matters into account must vitiate the exercise of the power unless (as in *Hastings-Bass* itself) it is clear that on a proper consideration of all relevant matters the decision would still have been the same.'

Trustee borrowing

52.7 In *Re Green GLG Trust* [2003] 5 ITELR 590, the Royal Court in Jersey had to consider appointments made by Jersey trustees after the enactment of TCGA 1992, Sch 4B which potentially triggered a charge under the trustee borrowing rules (see Chapter 62). The settlement was a life interest trust created on 29 February 2000. On 18 September 2000 it borrowed funds to make investments envisaged when the trust was set up, and distributions were made to the settlor on 18 September itself and on 5 and 9 April 2001. The potential impact of Sch 4B on these transactions was quite unknown to the trustees until the trustees received an HMRC questionnaire in February 2002.

The Royal Court, having been referred to the English cases discussed above, had no difficulty in holding the appointments void on the grounds that the trustees would not have made them had their attention been drawn to Sch 4B. The Royal Court trenchantly defended the *Hastings-Bass* principle stating that it is 'but a manifestation of the general principle that a trustee must act in good faith, responsibly and reasonably.' The Court went on to state:

> 'We consider that the *Hastings-Bass* principle is entirely consistent with precedent and principle. The Trusts (Jersey) Law 1984 draws substantially on general principles of English trust law and we see nothing in the decisions that we have described which is inconsistent with Jersey law. On the contrary they seem entirely consistent and accordingly we hold that, what is described as the *Hastings-Bass* principle, is equally a principle of Jersey law.'

In *Barclays Private Bank and Trust (Cayman) Limited v Chamberlain* (unreported, 5 May 2005) the trustees of a BVI trust administered in the Cayman Islands held investments through a Guernsey protected cell company. The reason for holding the investment in this way was to avoid gains being assessed on the settlor under a combination of TCGA 1992, ss 13 and 86 (see para 60.11). Unfortunately the trustees funded their cell by loan having raised the money lent by borrowing from a company they controlled. TCGA 1992, Sch 4B thus meant they achieved the very result they had sought to avoid, namely assessment of the settlor to CGT under TCGA 1992, s 86. These events took place in 2000 shortly after Sch 4B was enacted, and the trustees were wholly unaware of its provisions. The Grand Court in the Cayman Islands was satisfied that the trustees would not have acted as they did had they been advised as to Sch 4B and therefore declared the loan to the protected cell company void ab initio.

Accumulation and maintenance trusts

52.8 *Breadner v Granville-Grossman* [2000] 1 ITELR 200 is the one tax case where to date the Court declined to apply *Hastings-Bass*. Here a UK resident and domiciled settlor had on 27 December 1973 created a UK discretionary trust. The introduction in 1974 of Capital Transfer Tax ('CTT'), now Inheritance Tax, caused the trustees to appoint the trust fund on accumulation and maintenance trusts. This appointment was made on 29 March 1976, just in time to qualify for the then maximum transitional relief from CTT. The appointment was in favour of the children of the settlor or his brother now living or born or adopted before the Closing Date. The Closing Date was one day before the eldest of the living children attained 25, ie 2 August 1989. This class of beneficiaries took equal shares but the class could be altered by appointment made before the Closing Date, ie at the latest on 1 August 1989.

Shortly before the Closing Date, on 28 February 1989, the settlement was exported and Isle of Man trustees appointed. These trustees were requested by the settlor to appoint the entire trust fund in favour of the settlor's son, but the appointment was not made until 2 August 1989. The trustees discovered their mistake in 1992, and from then until 1998 administered the settlement as if the appointment had not been made. In 1998, however, they and the son applied to the English High Court to put matters right.

One of their arguments was that the 1976 appointment was invalid under *Hastings Bass*, with the result that in 1989 the trust fund was still subject to the original discretionary trusts, including an overriding power of appointment. This power was not subject to the 1 August 1989 deadline and could thus be said to have been validly exercised on 2 August 1989. The basis for the invalidity claim was:

(a) future-born adopted children were not beneficiaries under the original 1973 settlement;

(b) had an adoption taken place after 1976, the share purportedly appointed to him in 1976 would have remained subject to the original discretionary trusts;
(c) on a very technical view this prevented the 1976 appointment qualifying as an accumulation and maintenance trust;
(d) had the trustees appreciated this they would not have made the appointment;
(e) the *Hastings-Bass* principle therefore applied.

Park J, however, declined to apply the principle. His main reason was the application to the Court was just too late:

> 'It would be astonishing, and to my mind unacceptable, for the emerging *Hastings-Bass* principle to be capable of being invoked in an attempt to upset some action by the trustee, which may have been taken decades ago (as in this case) and on the basis of which many intervening decisions had been taken.'

The principal argument put before the Court was that even assuming the 1976 appointment was valid, the trustees did not, as a body, consider whether to make the appointment until the day on which it was made, i e 2 August 1989. Accordingly, the trustees argued:

(1) they were in breach of the duty they were undoubtedly under which was to consider whether or not to exercise the power of appointment within the time prescribed;
(2) had they in fact discharged that duty they would on the facts have made the appointment within time;
(3) the *Hastings-Bass* principle should be extended to cover what trustees should have done but did not do.

Park J, however, declined to extend the principle in this way. He summarised his reasons as follows:

> 'In my judgement, however, there is a very big difference between, on the one hand, the courts declaring something which the trustees have done to be void, and, on the other hand, the courts holding that a trust takes effect as if the trustees had done something which they never did at all. It is a big step from *Hastings-Bass*, not a small one, and I am not willing to take it, especially when I would be changing the beneficial interests and depriving the cousins of what I consider to be their property, however unpalatable it may be to the trustees that it is the cousins' property. I also believe that such indications as are to be found in the authorities are that the court may undo something which the trustees have done, but will stop short of doing something which the trustees might have done but did not do.'

Offshore trusts: other errors

US tax

52.9 In *A v Rothschild Trust Cayman Limited* [2004–05] CILR 485, the primary beneficiary and settlor of various settlements was contemplating becoming US resident. US advice was that the settlement assets would be deemed to be his for US tax purposes, but that this result could be avoided by resettlement. The trustees therefore effected resettlements. It later turned out that this was precisely the wrong thing to do. The feared adverse US tax consequences were triggered by the resettlements, but would have been avoided by retaining the original settlements with minor amendments. The Grand Court in the Cayman Islands held that the trustees were under a duty to consider the tax consequences of the proposed resettlements, but failed to properly discharge this duty because the advice they received was incorrect. The Court was satisfied the trustees would not have effected the resettlements had they received correct tax advice and declared them void ab initio. A distribution made under the resettlements fell to be repaid.

Erroneous appointment

52.10 In *Abacus Trust Co (Isle of Man) Ltd v Barr* [2003] EWHC 114 (Ch), [2003] 5 ITELR 602, the settlor had on 13 April 1992 formed an Isle of Man settlement under which he took an initial interest in possession. He was advised in the UK by Coopers and Lybrand and the trustee was their associated Isle of Man trustee company. Shortly after creating the settlement the settlor told a UK partner of Coopers and Lybrand that he wished 40% of the trust fund to be appointed on discretionary trusts for the benefit of his sons. The UK partner advised the trustee of the settlor's wishes and instructed the trustee's lawyers to draft the appointment, but in so doing erroneously represented the settlor as desiring 60% to be held on discretionary trusts. The trustee duly executed an appointment in this form on 22 April 1992.

The settlor discovered the mistake in August 1992 but did nothing. £200,000 in income and £200,000 in capital were distributed to the sons under the appointment. In November 2001 the trustee was advised that the appointment was open to challenge under the *Hastings-Bass* principle and proceedings were brought in the English High Court.

In dealing with the application Lightman J made three points.

(1) A mistake made by the trustee does not need to be fundamental to bring the principle into play. All that is required is that the relevant consideration would have affected the trustee's decision, in the sense that no appointment or a different appointment would have been made.
(2) It is not every mistake which brings the rule into play. It must be a mistake of the trustee. Thus if the settlor had himself misrepresented his intentions, the trustee would still have discharged its duty once it had considered those intentions.
(3) On the facts of the case the UK partner was agent of the trustee. As such his failure to represent the settlor's true wishes was that of the trustee.

This third point enabled Lightman J to conclude that the *Hastings-Bass* principle applied. He put the matter thus:

> 'In short, in the context of the relationships between the parties, it is I think plain that the fault in failing to consider the true wishes of the settlor was that of the trustee, its advisers and agents. The fiduciary duty of the trustee required the trustee to ascertain the wishes of the settlor, in particular since he was the life tenant whose interest in the trust fund was to be overridden and since it was his wishes that the appointment was intended to give effect to.'

UK trusts: tax errors

52.11 Two recent applications of the *Hastings-Bass* principle have involved tax errors by UK trustees, errors that could in other contexts have been made by offshore trustees.

Burrell v Burrell

52.12 In *Burrell v Burrell* [2005] EWHC 245 (Ch), [2005] 7 ITELR 622 private trading company shares and quoted investments were held on accumulation and maintenance trusts for the son of the settlor, giving him a life interest at 18. Shortly after he attained 18, a large dividend from the trading company was in prospect, and it was felt undesirable for him to have this. Accordingly the trustees terminated his life interest, appointing the quoted investments on accumulation and maintenance trusts and the private company shares on discretionary trusts.

The rationale of this appointment was that, as the law then stood, it would result in a potentially exempt transfer for IHT purposes as respects the quoted investments, for that is what happened when an interest in possession was terminated in favour of accumulation and maintenance trusts (cf IHTA 1984, s 3A and Chapter 44). The private company shares were not eligible for PET treatment as they were appointed on discretionary trusts, but the trustees were led by their advisers to believe business property relief was available. In this they were mistaken, as that relief requires two years' ownership by the transferor, the son's life interest being equated with ownership and as such failing this test as it had only subsisted since he attained 18 (cf IHTA 1984, ss 49 and 106).

On the mistake being discovered the trustees applied to have the appointment of the trading company shares set aside. Mann J had no difficulty in acceding to this application stating (at para 24) that 'the trustees failed to take a highly relevant consideration into account, and had they taken it into account they clearly would not have acted as they did'. Mann J also held that the discretionary appointment could be severed from the accumulation and maintenance appointment, thereby allowing the latter to stand.

Sieff v Fox

52.13 In *Sieff v Fox* [2005] EWHC 1312 (Ch), [2005] 3 All ER 693, chattels and other assets were held on discretionary trusts in favour of a wide class of the settlor's male descendants. A 10-yearly charge under the IHT discretionary trust regime (IHTA 1984, s 64) occurred on 23 August 2001, and the trustees and their advisors were anxious to avoid being caught by future charges. To that end, chattels and a reversionary lease were on 8 November 2001 appointed to the principal beneficiary absolutely subject to him surviving until 21 November 2001. On 20 November 2001, he assigned this contingent entitlement to an accumulation and maintenance trust he had previously created, the sole member of the class at that time being his infant daughter. On 21 November 2001, the accumulation and maintenance trustees therefore became absolutely entitled as against the discretionary trustees, and the chattels and reversionary lease became held on the accumulation and maintenance trusts.

This exercise did not occasion an IHT exit charge, as the vesting in the accumulation and maintenance trust took place within three months of the 10-yearly anniversary (IHTA 1984, s 65(4)). For CGT purposes, the absolute entitlement of the accumulation and maintenance trustees meant there was a disposal, but the trustees and their advisors believed this could be held over under TCGA 1992, s 260. In this they were mistaken, as that section only applies where the disposal is a chargeable transfer for IHT purposes, (s 260 (2)(a)). This was not the position by reason of the exercise having been effected within three months of the anniversary. It also became clear after the event that the holding of the chattels in a settlement created by the principal beneficiary would give rise to difficulties under the gift with reservation rules, as they were kept in the house where he lived (cf Chapter 47).

Faced with these points, the trustees applied to have the appointment set aside. Lloyd LJ, sitting in the High Court, held that the gift with reservation point was not within the *Hastings-Bass* principle, as it was relevant not to the decision by the trustees to make the appointment, but to the decision by the principal beneficiary to settle his contingent entitlement. But Lloyd LJ was satisfied that the trustees were under a duty to consider the CGT implications of the appointment, and that they had failed to do so properly because they had been given incorrect advice. Had the trustees been given correct advice and known that the appointment would give rise to a CGT charge on the non-exempt chattels, they would not have made it. On this basis he set aside.

The present position

52.14 Apart from *Hastings-Bass* itself all decisions involving private trusts have been at first instance. It therefore remains to be seen what attitude appellate courts take, whether onshore or offshore. In that context reservations expressed, in a non-judicial capacity, by Sir Robert Walker (as he then was) are to be noted (*Private Client Business* [2002] 226). Equally Lloyd LJ's general observations on the principle may be cited (*Sieff v Fox* (supra) at para 82):

> 'It seems to me, however, that on authority, the main ways at present open to the court to control the application of the principle are: (a) to insist on a stringent application of the tests as they have been laid down, (b) to take a reasonable and not over-exigent view of what it is that the trustees ought to have taken into account, and (c) to adopt a critical approach to contentions that the trustees would have acted differently if they had realised the true position, perhaps especially so in cases (unlike the present) where it is in the interests of all who are before the court that the appointment should be set aside. As Park J said in *Breadner*'s case ([2000] 4 All ER 705 at 722, [2001] Ch 523 at 543 (para 61)):
>
> "It cannot be right that whenever trustees do something which they later regret and think that they ought not to have done, they can say that they never did it in the first place".'

Void or voidable

52.15 A critical issue is whether application of the principle results in the trustee action complained of being void or voidable. In many of the cases, the word void is used but in *Abacus v Barr* Lightman J concluded the correct analysis is that the decision is voidable, expressing himself as follows:

> 'But if the trustees have exercised the discretion conferred upon them, but in doing so have failed to take into account a relevant consideration, or have taken into account an irrelevant consideration, it cannot in my view fairly or sensibly be held that they made no decision. It may be held that they made a flawed decision which is open to challenge, but that they made a decision is beyond question.'

The effect of the decision being voidable as distinct from void is that the Court has a discretion as to whether the action challenged should in fact be avoided. In deciding whether to avoid the action, the Court can take account of the time which has elapsed before relief is sought and the issue of acquiescence. In *Abacus v Barr*, Lightman J left this decision for a further hearing and expressed the hope that the parties might themselves agree a compromise to put to the Court. It is plain from his comments that any avoidance could be on terms.

The void or voidable issue was also considered in *Sieff v Fox*. It was not necessary to the decision, but Lloyd LJ expressed doubt over Lightman J's analysis. He referred to an earlier case, *Re Abrahams's Will Trusts, Capaln v Abrahams* [1967] 2 AII ER 1175 in which an appointment had been set aside as void. He concluded that while Lightman J's analysis is attractive it 'required further consideration in the light of earlier authority'.

Breach of duty by the trustees

52.16 As noted above, in *Abacus v Barr*, Lightman J held that the principle only comes into play if the mistake results from a breach of duty by the trustees or their agents. In *Sieff v Fox*, however Lloyd LJ disagreed, pointing out that this qualification is not found in any of the earlier cases.

Would or might

52.17 Also as noted above, the formulation of the *Hastings-Bass* principle requires it to be established the trustees *would* have acted differently. In *Sieff v Fox*, Lloyd LJ pointed out that 'might' is only appropriate in pension cases, where the contractual nexus means the beneficiaries are entitled to require the trustees to act (see [2005] EWHC 1312 (Ch), [2005] 3 AII ER 693 at para 77).

Application to tax

52.18 Both *Hastings-Bass* itself and most of the recent cases have revolved around tax. In these circumstances it may be suggested that it would be difficult to see a higher court deciding that failure to correctly appreciate the tax consequences of an action is not a valid ground for declaring it void or voidable. The trenchant comments of the Royal Court in the *Green* case are particularly to be noted. In *Burrell v Burrell* Mann J stated (at para 19):

> '[*Green v Cobham*] stands as clear authority (if authority be required) for the proposition that trustees must consider the fiscal consequences of their acts, and that a failure to do so is capable of leading to the application of the *Hastings-Bass* principle if it is clear they would not have acted as they did if they had appreciated the true fiscal position.'

Assuming these cases are not overruled in higher courts, the principle is of great value and potentially an antidote to tax legislation such as TCGA Sch 4B which is so badly drafted it is difficult for even the best advised offshore trustees to avoid its traps. The *Hastings-Bass* principle offers, at least in some cases, a solution to the problems thereby posed.

HMRC practice

52.19 In *Tax Bulletin 83* (June 2006) HMRC have given their view of the *Hastings-Bass* principle. Although HMRC have not hitherto participated in any of the decided cases, they will consider doing so in the future if large amounts of tax are at stake and there would otherwise be no party arguing against the application of the principle. They indicate that while in their view the principle might apply in tax cases if no advice is taken, it should not apply just because the tax advice turns out to be wrong or because it has been wrongly implemented. It is also their view that, if the principle does apply, the transaction concerned is voidable rather than void.

It will be interesting to see whether HMRC participate in cases before the courts in offshore jurisdictions and, if so, with what results. Their somewhat restrictive view of the principle goes against the various passages from first-instance judgements cited above.

Chapter 53

Shadow directors

53.1 Whether an offshore company is directly owned or owned in a trust, the issue arises of whether there is anybody who can be said to be a shadow director. This issue is relevant because of the code for taxing benefits in kind described in Chapter 69. On the face of it the benefits in kind code has nothing whatever to do with offshore companies save in the unlikely event that a UK resident is an actual employee or director. In fact this is not so, for ITEPA 2003, s 67 gives the term 'director' an extended meaning for the purposes of the code.

Extended definition of director

53.2 Who is caught by the definition in s 67 turns on how the company is managed. If the company is managed by a director or board of directors, the term 'director' not surprisingly includes any actual director. Should the company be managed by a person similar to a director or by a body similar to a board, the term includes that person or any member of the body concerned. Where the company is managed by the members, the terms includes any member. Last and most important the term 'director' includes any person 'in accordance with whose directions or instructions' any of the persons listed above 'are accustomed to act'.

Strictly, only the last of these categories may be a shadow director in the true sense, but in practice the term may be used to describe everybody in the above list who is not an actual director. There is an exclusion for professional advisers (s 67(2)).

For a long time the better view was that the definition in s 67 did not bring any shadow director who was not an actual employee into the benefits in kind code. The basis for this view was that the code applies to employees and employment and, while s 67 treats certain non-directors as directors, it does not also deem them to have an employment. This view was, however, rejected by the House of Lords in *R v Allen* [2001] UKHL 45, [2001] STC 1537 on the grounds that it was the intention of Parliament in enacting what is now s 67 that accommodation and benefits in kind received by a shadow director should be taxed in the same way as those received by a director. Accordingly the position now is that if a person falls within the definition of shadow director in s 67 he is caught by the code.

Who is a shadow director?

53.3 Ensuring a person is not a shadow director is rendered difficult by the Court of Appeal decision in *Secretary of State for Trade and Industry v Deverell* [2001] Ch 340. This is not a tax case but turned on the company law definition of shadow director in the Company Directors Disqualification Act 1986, s 22(5). This defines a shadow director as follows:

> 'a person in accordance with whose directions or instructions the directors of the company are accustomed to act.'

This definition is essentially in the same terms as the final limb of s 67, and like s 67 it excludes professional advisers.

In *Deverell*, the trial judge had asserted two important limitations to the definition, as follows:

> '... advice on its own will not do. Only if such advice is so given and so accepted as to amount to a direction or instruction (coupled with a pattern of the board being accustomed to act on it) is it relevant'

> 'Directions or instructions are both words with a mandatory effect. Coupled with the word "accustomed" they ... contemplate a situation where the board has cast itself in a subservient role to the "shadow", i.e. it does what it is told or to borrow an expression from trust law it "surrenders its discretion" to the shadow. Being accustomed to follow what somebody says does not of itself make what is said a direction/instruction ... what the court has to find, whether on direct evidence or inference is that the board does what [the shadow] tells it and exercises no (or at least no substantial) independent judgement.'

These limitations were based on obita dicta in earlier cases and widely regarded as correct by advisers. However, they were rejected by the Court of Appeal who in substance accepted the Secretary of State's formulation as follows:

> 'It is suggested that the definition is concerned to identify those with real influence in the corporate affairs of the company whatever the label given to the communications from the shadow to the board. Thus, it is argued, all that is required is that what is said by the shadow to the board is not by way of professional advice but is usually followed over a wide enough area and for long enough. In other words frequent non-professional advice usually acted on is sufficient.'

The Court also held that the shadow director's influence did not have to be over the whole field of the company's activities. Instead it adopted the words of an Australian judge (Finn J) in *Australia Securities Commission v AS Nominees Ltd* (1995) 133 ALR 1:

> 'The reference in the section to a person in accordance with whose directions or instructions the directors are "accustomed to act" does not in my opinion require that there be directions or instructions embracing all matters involving the board. Rather it only requires that, as and when the directors are directed or instructed, they are accustomed to act as the section requires.'

The Court in *Deverell* held that the two individuals under attack were shadow directors. The facts were complex and are not altogether easy to follow in the reported case. However, the following words effectively summarise the factual basis for the decision:

> '[The judge's findings] make it plain that Mr Deverell was concerned at the most senior level and with most aspects of the direction of the company's affairs. This could only be achieved by an ostensible consultant if those who were directors acted upon his directions or instructions conveyed by words or conduct. The judge held in terms that Mr Deverell "bossed everyone around from the directors downwards". It is immaterial that, as the judge observed, he was the sort of man who would boss anyone around. The facts, as found, show that he bossed the directors around and, because what he achieved was within the province of the directors, the directors were accustomed to submit to his requirements.'

Implications of Deverell

53.4 Prior to *Deverell*, most advisers in an offshore context approached the question of whether a person was a shadow director on the lines taken by the trial judge. In other words, danger was avoided provided the board gave genuine consideration to matters put before it, and the alleged shadow gave what could fairly be said to be advice. This approach may well not be valid and the position may well be that if the board of an offshore company consistently comply with a non-board member's wishes, that individual is at risk of being categorised as a shadow director, save insofar as his advice is given in a professional capacity.

Prior to *Deverell*, the view generally taken was that an offshore company was unlikely to have a shadow director resident in the UK unless the involvement of the alleged shadow was such that the company was in any event resident in the UK under the central management and control test. This follows from the fact that genuine consideration by the board negatives residence in the UK (para 38.21) and was thought to negative shadow directorship. Comparison between *Deverell* and the cases on company residence referred to in Chapter 38 indicate this is no longer so, for it is clear that regularly followed advice may make a person a shadow director under *Deverell*.

Also prior to *Deverell* a commonly-held view was that an individual was much more likely to be a shadow director if he directly owned the company as distinct from being settlor of or beneficiary under a trust which owned it. The rationale of this view was first that a controlling shareholder is legally able to remove the board and so in practice can give instructions and second that in any event the shareholder could count as a shadow director as being a member managing the company. These points are still good in relation to directly owned companies and, especially after *Deverell* make it difficult for a controlling shareholder in an offshore company who is not a director to avoid being a shadow director.

But what may have changed as a result of *Deverell* is the position where the offshore company is owned by an offshore trust. Here the trustees are entitled to take account of the wishes of the settlor, and may after due consideration follow them. So too even after the settlor is dead the trustees may at the behest of the settlor be entitled to and in fact follow the wishes of someone designated by him, normally a beneficiary or the protector. Of itself the fact that the trustees follow the wishes of such a person does not make him a shadow director of the company. But three factors may lead to a contrary conclusion. The first is that the person's wishes may be communicated directly to the directors of the company. Second, the trustees may so conduct themselves that they are effectively members managing the company, with the result that the settlor or other person becomes shadow director because of wishes he communicates to them. Third and last, the same individuals acting on behalf of the trustee in relation to the trust may also be directors of the company. In such a case it may be unclear to whom the settlor is in reality addressing his wishes or advice.

Trust structures: practical steps

53.5 For the reasons just given the practical impact of *Deverell* on trust structures is that where trustees regularly take account of and follow the wishes of the settlor or a protector or beneficiary, such person may be at risk of being characterised as a shadow director of any underlying company. What can be done?

First and obvious, the parties can so conduct themselves as to avoid the settlor or other person being a shadow director. But as the discussion above has indicated, such a strategy may not be certain of success if the parties in fact want to give effect to the wishes of the settlor or other person insofar as is possible.

Second, and perhaps less obvious, if the alleged shadow director is a beneficiary it may not matter that he is caught under the benefits in kind code. This is because, as beneficiary, he is likely to be taxable on any benefit, whether because it is income or because it is caught by TA 1988, s 740 or by TCGA 1992, s 87 or Sch 4C. However, in many cases such a solution will not be attractive, partly because the benefit in kind code has different computational rules, and partly because a benefit within the code will not always be income or caught by ss 740 and 87. Examples of the latter are benefits in kind to a non-domiciled beneficiary where either the beneficiary is the settlor or the structure has no income (cf Chapters 56, 63 and 64).

Third, where possible advantage should be taken of the territorial limits of the benefits code described in para 69.18. In appropriate cases it may be possible to ensure that a non-resident member of the family performs the role of shadow.

In many cases none of these solutions is practical in which case only a fourth is left. This is to ensure that the alleged shadow director does not in fact benefit from the company. In many cases this may be easy to achieve. The biggest difficulty is undoubtedly where the benefit is living accommodation, and here possible solutions are described in relation to non-domiciliaries in Chapter 21.

Part C

Anti-avoidance

Section I

Transfers

Chapter 54

Transfer of assets abroad

Introduction

54.1 Chapter III of Part XVII of TA 1988 is entitled 'Transfers of Assets Abroad'. The eight sections in that chapter (ss 739–746) have long been regarded as a most powerful weapon in countering offshore avoidance. In fact, the language of the sections is obscure and unrelated to modern offshore structures. For that reason, much of their power to HMRC lies in the uncertainty they create and the quite disproportionate liabilities which can follow from their application. But in decided cases these very features have rebounded against HMRC, for on more than one occasion the courts have recoiled from the wide construction HMRC have been arguing for (see for example *Vestey v IRC* [1980] AC 1148).

Chapter III contains two charging sections, namely s 739 which taxes offshore income on an arising basis, and s 740 which taxes benefits received by UK residents. Section 739 was the original charging section, being first enacted in 1936 (FA 1936, s 18). For many years it applied to anybody who had power to enjoy the income of an offshore structure, or received a capital sum from it (*Congreve and Congreve v IRC* [1946] 2 All ER 170, HL). But in the landmark decision of *Vestey v IRC* [1980] AC 1148, the House of Lords overruled its own earlier decision and decided s 739 was restricted to transferors (see further para 55.24). As a result what is now s 740 was enacted as FA 1981, s 45 to tax benefits received by non-transferors.

Both ss 739 and 740 are subject to a motive or purpose defence (TA 1988, ss 741 and 741A). This has been a feature of the code since it was first enacted and has always been a significant restraint on the use HMRC can make of it (see Chapter 58).

In 1996 the then government instituted a working party of HMRC officials and practitioners to review the legislation. This group reported at the end of 1997 but its work did not result in any change in the law. However, HMRC published key areas of their established practice as RI 201 in *Tax Bulletin* 40 pp 651–653 (April 1999) and the motive defence was recast as TA 1988, s 741A in 2006 (FA 2006, Sch 7).

It is becoming increasingly clear that the code is to some extent curtailed by the fundamental freedoms in the EU Treaty. Reference should be made to Chapter 49 for discussion of this difficult subject.

Preconditions for liability

54.2 The basic preconditions for liability under ss 739 and 740 are the same. They are set out in ss 739(1) and 740(1)(a)) as follows:

(1) Income is payable to a person resident or domiciled outside the UK.
(2) It has become so payable by virtue or in consequence of a transfer of assets, either alone or in conjunction with associated operations.

These common conditions form the subject matter of this chapter. The further requirements which must be met before liability can arise under s 739 or (as the case may be) s 740 are considered in Chapters 55 and 56 respectively. The overarching motive defence is then explained in Chapter 58.

Transfer of assets

54.3 The term 'transfer' is not defined. However 'assets' are defined as including property or rights of any kind, and, in relation to rights, 'transfer' includes the creation of those rights (s 742(9)(b)).

Normally it is self-evident whether a transaction is a transfer. However the following examples may be noted:

(1) In *Vestey's Executors v IRC* [1949] 31 TC 1, the taxpayers had created a lease of foreign properties they owned under which the lessees were bound to pay the rents to trustees resident outside the UK. Here the right to rent was 'rights' and the lease was the creation of those rights and thus the transfer.
(2) In *IRC v Brackett* [1986] STC 521, the taxpayer entered into a contract of employment with an offshore company. Hoffmann J decided that the contract of employment conferred 'rights' on the company and thus was the creation of those rights and so a transfer of assets.
(3) In *IRC v Willoughby* [1997] STC 995, a transfer of assets took place on the transfer of cash by the taxpayer to the life office in consideration of the issue to him of a personal portfolio policy (see [1995] STC 143, 153 and also para 5.6).

When an offshore settlement is created, rights are created, namely the rights of the beneficiaries. However, of itself the creation of an offshore settlement does not render income payable to the offshore trustees; that results from the transfer to the trustees of the cash or assets settled.

Whatever form the transfer takes, the recipient need not be resident or domiciled outside the UK when it is made. Thus it has been held that s 739 can apply if the original transfer is made to a resident company provided the company subsequently migrates (*Congreve and Congreve v IRC* [1948] 1 All ER 948). So too the creation of a resident settlement which subsequently becomes non-resident is caught.

The view is sometimes expressed that the code does not apply if the assets transferred are already abroad when the transfer is made. The code is headed 'Transfer of Assets Abroad' and ss 739(1) and 740(1)(a) predicate income *becoming* payable to non-residents. Semantically it is difficult for assets to be transferred abroad if they are already abroad, and for income to become payable to non-residents if it is already so payable. However, common sense indicates that such an interpretation is unlikely to be right, and a Special Commissioner has so held in relation to s 739 (*IRC v Willoughby* [1995] STC 143, 161).

It is unclear whether if an individual's assets pass by will or intestacy to an offshore entity, he has made a transfer. The case of *Bambridge v IRC* [1955] 3 All ER 812 decided that a will could be an associated operation (see below), but the issue of whether the will and/or the death was a transfer was not decided.

Associated operations

54.4 An operation is an associated operation if it is an operation of any kind. It must be effected in relation to any of the following (TA 1988, s 742(1)):

(1) the assets transferred;
(2) assets representing those assets, whether directly or indirectly;
(3) income arising from the assets transferred or assets representing them;
(4) assets directly or indirectly representing accumulations of income.

Associated operations can bring a transfer into the code even if it is not otherwise caught. Thus, in *Congreve and Congreve v IRC* [1948] 1 All ER 948, the original transfer did not offend, for the transferee company was then registered and resident in the UK. But the company was subsequently exported and this was held to be an operation associated with the transfer, thereby enabling s 739 to be invoked. Similarly, where an original transfer to a UK company was not caught, the subsequent sales of investments by that company to its Canadian subsidiary brought s 739 into operation (*Corbett's Executrices v IRC* [1943] 2 All ER 218).

Timing issues

54.5 Originally the legislation did not specify any time at which an operation must occur if it is to be associated. But since 5 December 2005 it has been expressly provided that the operation can be effected before, after, or at the same time as the transfer (s 742(1) as amended by FA 2006 Sch 7 para 6(3)). In its reference to operations before the transfer, this amendment reflects what had previously been HMRC's view (*Tax Bulletin 40* (April 1999) p 652).

The legislation does not specify how much earlier than the transfer an associated operation can be, or any period after the transfer beyond which it cannot be associated. As a matter of construction, there are thus no limits as to how far back, or how far forward, the hunt for associated operations must be conducted.

One occurrence which has not been regarded as an associated operation is death (*Bambridge v IRC* [1955] 3 All ER 812). But since it was held that making a will was an associated operation, exclusion of death is of little practical significance. An interesting issue is whether there would be an associated operation if the deceased died intestate. Dicta of Jenkins LJ in Bambridge suggest not.

Personnel issues

54.6 The legislation expressly says that an operation effected by any person can be associated. The term is not restricted to operations effected by the transferor.

This is illustrated by *Corbett's Executrices v IRC* [1943] 2 All ER 218, where the taxpayer and others had transferred investments to a UK company in 1933. Subsequently that company incorporated a Canadian company and transferred some of the investments to it. The latter transfer was an operation associated with the original transfer to the UK company. So too the accumulation of income by a transferee company and the management of the transferred assets have been held to be operations associated with original transfer to the company (*IRC v Herdman* [1967] 45 TC 394). The activities of a partnership in which the transferee was partner have also been held to be associated with the transfer of the partnership share to the transferee (*Latilla v IRC* [1943] AC 377, [1943] 1 All ER 265).

These various cases on associated operations effected by persons other than the transferor have all been cases where it is a fair inference that the operation was instigated by or associated with the transferor. It has not in terms been decided whether an operation effected many years later without any reference to the transferor is associated. As a matter of strict construction there is no reason why not, although this does have the bizarre result that a transferor protected by the motive defence can loose the protection of that defence even if he has no part in the operations putting that defence in jeopardy (see further Chapter 58).

Omissions

54.7 The concept of associated operations figures also in the IHT legislation (IHTA 1984, s 268). The IHT definition expressly provides that operation includes omission. There is no equivalent provision in the transfer of assets code and as a result it may be argued omissions are not included (cf *Nichols v IRC* [1973] STC 497, 5050 per Walton J).

Other assets

54.8 It is important to stress that to be associated, operations must be effected in relation to the assets transferred, the income from those assets, or assets representing the same. If operations are effected in relation to assets falling outside these categories, they are not associated.. Thus in *Carvill v IRC* [2000] STC (SCD) 143, the taxpayer controlled a UK company. He and the minority shareholders transferred their shares to a Bermudan company in 1982 in consideration of an issue of shares. Subsequently the taxpayer bought the shares of one of the minority shareholders and then the Bermudan company bought in the shares of the remaining minority shareholders. A Special Commissioner decided these subsequent operations were not associated with the taxpayer's transfer of his shares to Bermuda as they did not relate to the shares he had transferred. For the same reason, various tax-driven employment arrangements entered into by the taxpayer with the Bermudan company were not associated operations either.

In this connection it is worth drawing a further contrast with the IHT definition. The first limb of that definition corresponds to s 742(1) (see IHTA 1984, s 268(1)(a)). But the second limb, in s 268(1)(b), is not replicated in the transfer of assets code. This is the limb catching an operation effected with reference to another operation, or with a view to enabling or facilitating the other operation.

Representation of assets

54.9 Decided cases give little guidance on when assets 'represent' the assets transferred or the income generated by such assets. However assets, income, or accumulations of income transferred to a company are deemed to be represented by the shares in or obligations of the company (s 742(9)(e)). As a result an operation is associated if it is effected in relation to such shares or obligations. This rule catches cases where offshore trustees transfer the assets transferred to them to an offshore holding company in return for shares or a shareholder loan, and then effect transactions in relation to such shares or loan. The same rule applies to the obligations of any non-corporate person.

Guidance as to the general meaning of representation is given, albeit in another context, in *West v Trennery* [2005] UKHL 5, [2005] STC 214 (see para 59.4). Here the trustees of one settlement had raised money by mortgaging the trust assets, and then advanced the cash to another settlement. In the House of Lords, Lord Millett observed that the cash directly represented the proceeds of the mortgage. Had the trustees invested the cash, the ensuing investments would have indirectly represented the proceeds. Lord Millett further envisaged that the investments in the second settlement would continue to indirectly represent the proceeds so long as that settlement existed.

Where the transferee sells the assets transferred and uses the proceeds to buy other assets it is unclear whether only operations effected with reference to the 'representing' assets – ie the assets owned by the transferee – are associated, or whether operations effected on the original assets are associated as well, despite the fact these have ceased to be owned by the transferor. A further question is whether, if 'representing' assets are sold, it is necessary to continue to look at operations effected in relation to them, or whether the focus is solely on the new 'representing' assets. Common sense would indicate that, where assets have come to be represented by other assets, it is only operations effected in relation to the latter which are relevant. Were this not so, operations effected by complete strangers would count as associated, with irrational implications as respects the motive defence (see Chapter 58).

But if this is right, the position where the transferee sells assets into a company in return for shares or loan has to be considered. Here the shares or loan plainly represent the original assets, a position which would be clear even without the express provision noted above. But if so does this then mean operations effected with reference to the assets in the company cannot be associated? As a matter of common sense it is difficult to see this being the position where those assets are the original assets transferred. But what if they are themselves 'representing' assets, and what if cash is simply transferred to the company, so that strictly the asset held by the company, ie a right against the company's bank, is different from that previously held by the transferee (ie a right against the transferee's bank).

Income payable

54.10 It is fundamental to ss 739 and 740 that the income be payable to a person resident or domiciled out of the UK. The person to whom the income is so payable need not be or include the original transferee (*Corbett's Executrices v IRC* [1943] 2 All ER 218). But the income must become payable to the non-resident or non-domiciliary by virtue or in consequence either of the transfer alone or of the transfer in conjunction with associated operations.

It is sufficient if the entity to whom the income is payable is domiciled outside the UK, even if it is resident there (cf *Gasque v IRC* [1940] 2 KB 80, 23 TC 210). All foreign registered companies are deemed to be resident outside the UK (TA 1988, s 742(8)). As a result ss 739 and 740 still apply even if HMRC establish that an offshore company which the taxpayer contends was non-resident is in fact UK resident under the central management and control test (*R v Dimsey* [2001] STC 1520).

An amendment made in 2006 provides that the income can be payable to the person resident or domiciled outside the UK by virtue or in consequence of the transfer alone, one or more associated operations alone, or a combination of the transfer and associated operations (TA 1988, s 742(1A), (1B)). It is unclear how far this altered pre-existing law.

Trusts

54.11 There is no doubt that s 739 applies if income is payable to non-resident discretionary trustees. This is so even if the proper law of the settlement is that of one of the constituent countries of the UK (*Vestey v IRC* [1980] AC 1148, [1979] 3 All ER 976).

The position is less clear with fixed-interest trusts on account of the general principle that the trust income is treated as that of the life tenant (see para 12.2). In *IRC v McGuckian* [1997] STC 908 the taxpayer had created an offshore trust of which his wife was life tenant. The offshore trustee then sold the right to a dividend for a substantial capital sum. The assignment fell to be disregarded under the *Ramsay* principle, and the House of Lords held that this meant that the dividend was income payable to the trustee for the purposes of s 739. The point that it was the life tenant's income if the sale was disregarded was not discussed. But it may be suggested the outcome was nonetheless correct because ss 739 and 740 look at who the income is payable to, not who it ultimately belongs to.

At one time uncertainty arose with mixed-residence trusts, in that income could not properly be said to be payable to persons resident outside the UK if one or more of them was resident in the UK (cf *Dawson v IRC* [1990] 1 AC 1, [1989] STC 473). Now, however, this difficulty no longer exists, for all trustees of a mixed residence trust are deemed to be UK resident unless the settlor was non-resident and domiciled when he put funds in the settlement (see further Chapter 37).

Chapter 55

Section 739

Introduction

55.1 The basic precondition for the application of s 739 has been discussed in the previous chapter, namely that there must be a transfer of assets, by virtue or in consequence of which, either alone or in conjunction with associated operations, income becomes payable to a non-resident or non-domiciled entity. Section 739 imposes a tax charge if one of two further conditions is met:

(a) the taxpayer has what is called 'power to enjoy' the income, or
(b) the taxpayer receives or is entitled to receive any capital sum.

In the case of power to enjoy, the power to enjoy must exist by virtue or in consequence of the transfer, either alone or in conjunction with associated operations (s 739(2)). In the case of a capital sum, the payment must be in some way connected with the transfer or an associated operation (s 739(3)).

Section 739 does not in terms say it applies only to the person who effected the original transfer. However, both charging sections refer to 'such an individual'. This refers back to sub s (1) which states that s 739 has effect 'for the purpose of preventing the avoiding by individuals … of liability to income tax by means of transfers of assets …'. In *Vestey v IRC* [1980] AC 1148 the House of Lords held that this reference means s 739 is restricted to the individual who made the transfer. This aspect of s 739, and its possible extension to quasi transferors, is discussed further in para 55.24 below.

As already indicated in Chapter 54, s 739 is subject to the motive or purpose defence described in Chapter 58, and may, to some extent, be qualified by the fundamental freedoms discussed in Chapters 48 and 49.

Power to enjoy

55.2 An individual is deemed to have power to enjoy income in five situations specified in paras (a)–(e) of TA 1988, s 742(2).

These definitions are so wide that it is difficult to conceive of actual enjoyment which is not also deemed enjoyment. Furthermore, the normal rules of construction have to be waived in two respects (s 742(3)). First, attention is directed to the substantial result of the transfer and any associated operations; and second, benefits which may accrue to the taxpayer have to be taken into account, even if he has no right in law or equity to them.

In the majority of cases the sole question worth asking in relation to power to enjoy is whether the taxpayer is an actual or potential beneficiary or has non-fiduciary powers of control. If the answer is affirmative, the taxpayer almost certainly has 'power to enjoy'; if negative, he probably does not.

Para (a)

55.3 The first situation in which a taxpayer has power to enjoy is where the income concerned is in fact so dealt with as to be calculated to enure for the benefit of the taxpayer. The application of this paragraph has been held to be a question of fact. In *Vestey's Executors v IRC* [1949] 1 All ER 1108 at 1116 Lord Simonds said the paragraph required precise findings of fact and in *Vestey v IRC (No 2)* [1978] STC 567 at 579 Walton J considered that 'calculated' meant 'reckoned' or 'estimated' rather than 'likely'.

IRC v Botnar [1999] STC 711 is the leading case on para (a). Here the taxpayer had created a Liechtenstein settlement under which the only named beneficiaries were persons in the legal profession connected with the protector. The taxpayer was named as an excluded person and as such clause 23 of the settlement prevented him from taking 'any benefit in accordance with the terms of this Settlement'. Clause 3 of the settlement included wide overriding powers including power, by clause 3(c), to transfer the trust fund to another trust, freed and discharged from the trusts of the original settlement, and notwithstanding that persons who were not beneficiaries of the original settlement might be beneficiaries of the transferee settlement. Clause 3(c) did not contain any express provision preventing the taxpayer from benefiting under any such transferee settlement. A memorandum made when the original settlement was created indicated that it was envisaged that the power in clause 3(c) could at some stage be exercised to transfer the trust fund to a new trust, whose trustees would in due course add the taxpayer as a beneficiary. There was also evidence that leading English counsel had advised that this would be a proper course to take. During the years 1974–1990, no income accrued to the trustees but well in excess of £100m was received by underlying holding companies in dividends from a UK company run by the taxpayer.

The Court of Appeal held that the retention of the income by the holding companies amounted to dealing with the income and that the Commissioners were entitled to find, as they had, that it had been so dealt with as to be calculated to enure at some point in time for the benefit of the taxpayer, as para (a) requires. However, a more fundamental point arose because it was accepted by HMRC that para (a) could only be invoked if the trustees' purpose in so dealing with the income was proper – in other words if their intention to transfer the trust fund to a new trust from which the taxpayer could benefit was proper. Two members of the Court of Appeal held that as a matter of construction it was and the third held that while as a matter of construction it was not, the scheme could still have been effected lawfully, for the settlement gave the trustees power to take and act on the opinion of suitably qualified counsel.

IRC v Botnar is an important decision, not least because it confirms that if there is any possibility of benefit being lawfully conferred on the taxpayer, s 739 is likely to be in point. An interesting point is the acceptance by HMRC that para (a) does not apply if income is dealt with unlawfully or in breach of trust.

A question raised by para (a) is whether it extends to income accumulated and beneficially owned by a natural person. This question would arise if the taxpayer had given the assets to a natural person on the understanding, albeit not the obligation, that the donee would deal with them as the taxpayer directed. Such arrangements may be vulnerable, if in reality the income will at some stage be paid over to the taxpayer. Similarly, devices to route payments out of trusts or companies through natural persons to the taxpayer could be caught, for, as noted, potential benefits can be taken into account, even if the taxpayer has no legal entitlement to them (s 742(3)).

Para (b)

55.4 Paragraph (b) operates where the income increases the value to the taxpayer of assets held by him or for his benefit. It catches the classic operation at which s 739 was originally aimed: sale of income-producing assets to a foreign company in consideration of the issue of shares or debentures. It extends to situations where the purchase price is simply left outstanding or is secured by promissory notes. Here para (b) applies because the income increases the company's assets, thereby enhancing the security, and hence the value of the loan notes (*Howard de Walden v IRC* [1942] 1 KB 389, [1942] 1 All ER 287; *Ramsden v IRC* (1957) 37 TC 619; *IRC v Brackett* [1986] STC 521).

Since para (b) refers to assets held for benefit of the taxpayer, its ambit includes cases where he has settled shares in the transferee company and retains a life interest under the settlement. It probably also extends to settlements of shares where the taxpayer is only a discretionary beneficiary, for then it can be said that he may benefit from any enhancement in the value of the shares (cf s 742(3)).

Para (c)

55.5 Paragraph (c) applies if the taxpayer in fact receives a benefit, or is entitled to receive one. The benefit must come from either the income or monies available because of the effect of associated operations on the income. The term 'benefit' includes any payment (s 742(9)(c)), so there is an overlap with s 739(3), which, as described below (para 55.8) deems the income of the transferee to be that of the transferor if he receives or is entitled to receive a capital sum.

The application of para (c) to companies overlaps with para (b). But one instance where the former would apply and the latter not, would be where the taxpayer has divested himself of the company's shares and the company was empowered to (and did) make a donation to the taxpayer.

Paragraph (c) catches benefits conferred by trustees in breach of trust. Thus in *IRC v Botnar* [1999] STC 711, trustees had funded the acquisition of a flat for the settlor, who was not a beneficiary. It was accepted that the funding had been a misapplication, but nonetheless the settlor's use of the flat was an actual benefit within para (c).

Paragraph (c) has been held to apply in certain rather surprising contexts. Thus in *IRC v Brackett* [1986] STC 521, a taxpayer was held to receive benefits where an offshore company (i) bought properties from the taxpayer in an illiquid market; (ii) provided money for repairs; and (iii) paid a salary to the taxpayer and provided for his moral obligations.

Para (d)

55.6 Paragraph (d) applies if the taxpayer may become entitled to beneficial enjoyment of the income concerned, and the events which will cause him to become so entitled are the exercise of one or more powers. It does not matter in whom the powers are vested, or that consent may be required to their exercise. This paragraph is directed at fiduciary powers (*IRC v Botnar* [1999] STC 711, 729). Accordingly it is principally applicable where income is payable to trustees. It catches the classic device of the revocable settlement, and also settlements where trustees have power to appoint absolute or income interests back to the settlor.

The powers must be so as to confer entitlement to income. Discretionary powers to pay or apply income to the taxpayer after it has arisen are not caught. Thus in *Vestey v IRC* [1980] AC 1148, [1979] 3 All ER 976, potential discretionary income beneficiaries were ignored. Whether a power to appoint accumulations of income is caught was discussed but not resolved in that case.

In *IRC v Botnar* [1999] STC 711 the income had been paid to and retained by offshore companies. The taxpayer was excluded from the settlement which owned those companies, but as noted above, he could have been added as a beneficiary of a settlement to which the trust fund had previously been transferred. The Court of Appeal held on these facts that the reference to the successive exercise of powers would embrace the creation of such a new settlement by the original trustees and the advances of the trust fund to it.

A point which also arose in *Botnar* was whether paragraph (d) is only in point if when the taxpayer becomes entitled to it the income must still belong to the transferee. In *Botnar*, the income had arisen to the offshore companies and yet before the taxpayer could have had any beneficial enjoyment the money would have had to be extracted from the companies by the original trustees and advanced to a new settlement. The Court of Appeal held that in such circumstances paragraph (d) was still in point, it not being necessary for the income still to belong to the transferee when it would be enjoyed.

Para (e)

55.7 This paragraph applies where the taxpayer is able in any manner to control the application of the income. HMRC successfully invoked this paragraph where the transferee was a split-level company in which the taxpayer had retained the voting shares (*Lee v IRC* (1941) 24 TC 207).

HMRC have been less successful with trusts. Situations where a taxpayer is a protector, or where he can hire and fire trustees or otherwise direct how the trust income is dealt with, might seem vulnerable. But the paragraph has not been so applied (*Vestey's Executors v IRC* [1949] 1 All ER 1108, 31 TC 1 and *IRC v Schroder* [1983] STC 480). Apparently, control within para (e) does not extend to fiduciary powers vested in the taxpayer as trustee or protector of a settlement.

Capital sums

55.8 Section 739 also applies if the transferor or his spouse either receives or is entitled to receive a capital sum (s 739(3)). The payment of the sum must be connected with the transfer or an associated operation, and the transferor must be resident in the UK at the time of receipt or entitlement. Otherwise the payment or entitlement can be made or occur either before or after the transfer.

The term 'capital sum' includes the making of a loan to the transferor or the repayment to him of a loan he has made. Otherwise the term 'capital sum' includes any capital sum not paid for full consideration in money or money's worth. A sum is treated as paid to the taxpayer if it is paid to a third party at his direction, or as the result of an assignment by him of his right to receive it (s 739(4) and (5)). The terms 'sum' and 'paid' are not further defined and it would therefore appear that the transfer of non-monetary assets in specie is not caught.

The capital sum need not be paid by the transferee, or, in the case of a loan owed to him, owed by the transferee. All that is necessary is that the payment to the transferor, or his entitlement to repayment, must be in some way connected with the transfer or an associated operation. The breadth of its language means s 739(3) needs to be watched with care when offshore structures are set up.

The courts have tended to construe this head of charge restrictively. Where the purchase price of assets is left outstanding, the debt is not a loan and thus the eventual payment by the transferee to the transferor is not caught. However, it should be noted that the existence of the debt gives the taxpayer power to enjoy within s 742(2)(b) (*Ramsden v IRC* (1957) 37 TC 619). It has been held that a short-term loan to reduce the transferee's pre-existing indebtedness to a bank was not caught on the grounds that it was not connected with either the transfer or with any associated operation (*Fynn v IRC* [1958] 1 All ER 270, 37 TC 629).

The quantum of the taxpayer's liability

Power to enjoy

55.9 Under s 739(2), the taxpayer is liable if by virtue or in consequence of the transfer and associated operations he has power to enjoy any income of a non-resident or non-domiciled person. If he is so liable, all that income is to be treated as his for all tax purposes, regardless of the size of the actual or potential benefit he does or could enjoy. This was established in *Howard de Walden v IRC* [1942] 1 KB 389, 25 TC 121, where all the transferee's assets had come from the taxpayer.

The question which the court left open in *Howard de Walden* was what the taxpayer's position would be if he had provided some only of the transferee's assets; if, for example, he had exchanged assets for shares in a pre-existing foreign investment company. In *Congreve v IRC* [1948] 1 All ER 948, the court held, obiter, that all the income would be taxed as the transferee's if he had the requisite power to enjoy. It now appears this is not the law, for it is quite clear that in *Vestey v IRC* [1980] AC 1148, [1979] 3 All ER 976 the House of Lords regarded a taxpayer as assessable only on income from assets he had himself transferred. This is accepted by HMRC (*Tax Bulletin* 40 (April 1999) p 651). It was followed by a Special Commissioner in *Carvill v IRC* [2000] STC (SCD) 143, 169.

It is plain from the wording of s 739(2) that liability only arises if the taxpayer has power to enjoy in the tax year concerned. He is not caught merely because he had such power in a previous year.

Capital sum

55.10 As regards capital sums, it is clear that the charge is on the transferee's income which has become his by virtue of the transfer and associated operations. Receipt of a single small capital sum can accordingly cause the transferor to be taxed on the entirety of the income concerned (*Vestey v IRC* [1980] AC 1148, [1979] 3 All ER 976). But the charge is restricted to income derived from assets the taxpayer himself transferred.

It is to be stressed that once the transferor has received or been entitled to receive a capital sum within s 739(3), liability under s 739 remains forever even if in subsequent years the transferor does not and cannot benefit. In many respects this is a trap. An exception is made if the s 739(3) charge was occasioned by a loan to the taxpayer and that loan has been repaid for then liability under s 739(3) ceases in the tax year following repayment (s 739(6)).

The draconian nature of s 739(3) can be appreciated from two examples. In the first, the settlor under a settlor-interested settlement receives a capital distribution in cash and is then excluded. Despite the exclusion, s 739(3) continues to deem the income of the trust to be the settlor's. In the second example, an individual is owed money by a company he owns. He settles the shares in the company on offshore trusts, under which he is wholly excluded, and shortly before making the settlement causes the company to repay the loan. Here the repayment may cause the trust income to be taxed as his until he dies.

This construction of s 739(3) may cause surprise. However, its correctness is supported by the exception made where the capital sum is a loan to the taxpayer which has been repaid. It is also supported by *Vestey v IRC*, where both Walton J and the House of Lords proceeded on the basis that receipt of a capital sum would render both current and all future income of the transferee assessable on the recipient (see [1977] STC 414, 427–9 and [1980] STC 10, 17 and 27).

The mere fact that the settlor and his spouse are discretionary beneficiaries does not bring s 739(3) into play for, as a matter of trust law, a discretionary beneficiary is not entitled to anything. But once either of them receives a capital distribution s 739(3) is in point. Section 739(3) would not be in point merely because the settlor or his spouse is life-tenant, for then their entitlement is to income.

Trading profits

55.11 It is often argued that s 739 does not extend to trading profits, on the grounds that what a trading transferee receives are gross receipts rather than income payable to him. Such arguments cannot be supported (*Latilla v IRC* [1943] AC 377, 25 TC 107; *Chetwode v IRC* [1977] 1 All ER 638, [1977] STC 64; *IRC v Brackett* [1986] STC 521). In many cases, however, trading profits are protected from s 739 by the motive defence. HMRC allow trading profits to be offset by past trading losses, but only insofar as losses and profits accrue to the same company (*Tax Bulletin* 40 (April 1999) p 652).

Purchased companies

55.12 It may be that the transferee following a s 739 transfer uses some or all of the assets transferred to purchase shares in an existing company. This point arose in *Vestey v IRC* [1980] AC 1148, where the trustees had purchased a pre-existing Jersey insurance company. Walton J held that the income of the insurance company was not assessable under s 739 on the grounds that it did not arise by virtue of the transfer or any operation associated with the transfer ([1977] STC 414, 438; [1978] STC 567, 584). This point was conceded by HMRC in the House of Lords, although it is clear the position would have been different if and insofar as the trustees had subscribed for shares in the insurance company (see especially [1980] STC 10, 30 per Viscount Dilhorne). As a result it may be concluded that income in a purchased company is not within s 739.

Actual benefit

55.13 Section 743(5) imposes a special rule where the transferor has power to enjoy by virtue of s 742(2)(c), and that sub-paragraph applies by reason of the transferor having received an actual benefit provided out of the income. It charges the full amount or value of the benefit to income tax in the year of receipt, save insofar as the transferor has already been taxed on the income from which it is derived. In *IRC v Botnar* [1999] STC 711, the Court of Appeal decided that where para (c) applies solely by reason of actual receipt of benefit, s 743(5) restricts the charge to the amount or value of the benefit. This decision, it should be noted, will only be of advantage to the transferor where the benefit is not a capital sum within s 739(3), for if it is, the latter subsection will, as noted above, attach to all the transferee's income.

The Court of Appeal in *IRC v Botnar* did not have to consider how the benefit should be valued, but the Special Commissioner did ([1998] STC 38). The benefit in question consisted of the rent-free occupation of a flat under licence and the Special Commissioner held that the value of the benefit for each of the two years in question was the rent the taxpayer would have had to pay on an arm's length letting.

The charge to tax

55.14 Income deemed to be the transferor's is deemed to be his for all purposes of the income tax legislation and tax is charged accordingly (TA 1988, ss 739 and 743(1)).

A curious provision has been inserted into s 743 by ITTOIA 2005 as s 743(1ZA). This provides that, in charging tax under s 739, foreign and UK dividend income is treated as savings income to which TA 1988, s 1A applies by virtue of s 1A(2)(b). Section 1A(2)(b) embraces only UK dividends and similar income, so on the face of it s 743(1ZA) appears to be deeming foreign dividends to be UK dividends. Can this really be right, given that the implication is that foreign dividends within s 739 would then attract the tax credit?

Whatever the case it seems clear that higher-rate tax on dividends caught by s 739 is the dividend rate. There is no reason why s 739 deemed income is not within TA 1988, s 1B as well as actual income.

Dividend income subject to s 739 should be entered in Boxes 6.3A and 6.4A of the Foreign Pages of the self-assessment return, and other kinds of income in Boxes 6.3 and 6.4 (Notes on Foreign p FN10). Details of the assets transferred and the offshore structure should be given in Box 6.39.

Deductions

55.15 TA 1988, s 743(2) allows the taxpayer the same deductions and reliefs as if the income had been his, but no more. Accordingly the management expenses of a transferee investment company are not allowed (*Chetwode v IRC* [1977] STC 64).

An important issue is whether, in computing s 739 liability, the transferor should be allowed deductions for items incurred by the transferee and deductible against general income, for example trading losses and interest payments. The logic of s 739 deeming the transferee's income to be that of the transferor suggests that he should, the transferee's deemed s 739 income being the transferee's total income as computed for UK tax purposes. Dicta in *Carvill v IRC* [2000] STC (SCD) 143, 169, however, indicate this is not the correct analysis, each item of the transferee's income being separately attributed to the transferor with no credit for general deductions. This approach is also that adopted by HMRC, in that they do not allow the transferor to credit the transferee's trading losses against the transferee's other income (*Tax Bulletin 40* (April 1999) p 652).

There seems to be no reason why the transferor's actual deductions and reliefs should not be set against his deemed s 739 income. The wording of s 743(2) suggests that this can be done and such is consistent with the deeming tenor of s 739.

Income already taxed

55.16 Section 739 can apply even if the income is subject to UK tax in the hands of the transferee (*R v Dimsey* [2001] STC 1520, HL). The main situations where the income is so subject is if it is UK source income or if the transferee is resident in the UK without being domiciled there. In practice this latter situation comes about with foreign registered companies resident in the UK, which are deemed to be non resident for s 739 purposes (s 742(8)).

One provision addresses this issue, namely s 743(1), which provides that income tax is not charged at the basic, lower, or dividend rates under s 739 to the extent that it has already born income tax at such rates by deduction or otherwise. This provision does not refer to corporation tax such as is paid by a foreign registered company resident in the UK, but in *R v Dimsey* Lord Scott suggested it should be construed as extending to corporate profits ([2001] STC 1520, 1533).

In *R v Dimsey* (at p 1530), HMRC assured the House of Lords that in taxing the transferor, credit would always be given for any UK tax that had been borne by the transferee, and vice versa. In the Court of Appeal, Laws LJ suggested that if HMRC proceeded otherwise in any particular case, the High Court might be invited to prohibit it as an abuse of power ([1999] STC 846, 867).

In practice, the transferor should claim credit for any corporation tax born by a transferee company on the income. The claim is made by including the corporation tax in Box 6.9 of Foreign Pages of the return and giving details of the company and how the credit is claimed in Box 6.39 (Notes on Foreign Pages pp FN10 AND FN11).

Double tax treaties

55.17 Non-resident entities potentially caught by s 739 are frequently resident in jurisdictions with which the UK has concluded a double tax treaty.

Normally the treaty exempts certain categories of income accruing to the non-resident from UK tax and the issue which arises is whether such exemption confers protection from s 739. Dicta in the Court of Appeal in *Bricom Holdings v IRC* [1997] STC 1179 at 1195 suggest it does, for s 739 simply deems the transferee's income to be that of the transferor. In *IRC v Willoughby*, however, the Special Commissioner took a different view ([1995] STC 143 at 168–169). In that case, the income in question accrued to a Manx enterprise, and as such formed part of the commercial profits of the enterprise exempted from UK tax by Article 3(2) of the Double Taxation Relief (Taxes on Income) (Isle of Man) Order 1955. The Special Commissioner decided that this exemption applied only to the actual person to whom the profits accrued, not to a person whose income they might be deemed to be under s 739.

Deemed income

55.18 Income taxable under s 739 includes offshore income gains under the offshore fund legislation (TA 1988, s 762(5); see para 71.25) and deep discount (ITTOIA 2005, s 459). It also includes sums which would be treated as income under the accrued interest scheme if the offshore entity was UK resident (TA 1988, s 742(4)). The accrued interest scheme applies when securities are sold and its effect is to treat the accrued interest element in the sale proceeds as income (TA 1988, ss 713–714). It applies to foreign corporate and governmental bonds as well to UK bonds and so is material whenever an offshore entity holds fixed interest investments (cf TA 1988, s 710(2) and (12)).

Multiple structures

55.19 It is common for offshore trusts to hold assets through one or more holding companies. On one view, the s 739 liability can be doubled up, as where the company receives income and then distributes the income as dividend to the trust. In practice HMRC are widely believed to avoid such double charging, although such practice has not been formalised in any published statement. In fact, it may be argued the practice accords with law, for the effect of s 739 is to deem income to be that of the transferor for all the purposes of the Income Tax Acts. Accordingly the payment of a dividend by a company to a settlor-interested trust which owns it is effectively deemed to be a payment by the transferor to himself.

A problem does occur if the company does not pay a dividend but is liquidated or wound up. In that event any gain attributed to the settlor under TCGA 1992, s 86 (Chapter 60), is not reduced by the income taxed under s 739.

Overlap with settlement code

55.20 In law, income arising to a settlor-interested offshore trust is taxable both under s 739 and under the income tax settlement code (ITTOIA 2005, s 624, see Chapter 59). In practice HMRC do not regard themselves as entitled to tax the settlor twice (*Tax Bulletin* 40 (April 1999) p 652). Normally the settlement code is invoked rather than s 739. It appears that this practice is also applied where the income arises to an underlying company, but only if it is paid up immediately to the trust.

Territorial limits

Non-residents

55.21 The charging provisions in s 739, sub ss (2) and (3), both refer to 'such an individual'. This in turn refers back to s 739(1), which itself refers to 'individuals ordinarily resident in the United Kingdom'. As a result liability under s 739(2) does not arise unless the transferor is ordinarily resident in the tax year in which he has power to enjoy. Liability under s 739(3) does not arise unless he is ordinarily resident when he receives the capital sum.

As noted in para 55.8, receipt of a capital sum can mean the transferee's income is assessable as that of the transferor for ever after. However, it is clear there are two limitations on this:

(1) For the reason just given s 739(3) does not apply unless the transferor is ordinarily resident in the tax year in which he receives the capital sum.
(2) If in a subsequent year he loses ordinary residence, s 739(3) would still deem the income to be his, but he would escape tax on the foreign source income under general principles. FA 1995, s 128 would restrict tax on UK dividend and income to tax withheld except (perhaps) interest accruing directly to an offshore trust (see s 128(5) and para 34.14).

Non-domiciliaries

55.22 Until 1981, non-domiciled transferors were potentially liable in respect of foreign-source income under s 739 for the section predicates that the income is received in the UK (*Congreve v IRC* [1946] 2 All ER 170, 30 TC 163, 190, per Wrottesley J). But a relaxation was introduced in 1981 and as a result a non-domiciliary is not chargeable to tax in respect of any income which would not, by reason of his foreign domicile, have been chargeable if it had in fact been his income.

This relief, conferred by s 743(3) imports the remittance basis and certainly precludes foreign income from being charged in the year it arises, if it is not remitted in that year. What is less clear is whether a charge arises in a subsequent year if it is remitted then. A strict view is that it does not for income tax is an annual tax and there is no provision analogous to ITTOIA 2005, s 648(5) imposing tax in the event of remittance in a subsequent year (cf para 59.27). But in the present era of purposive construction it is likely that a court would regard the overriding purpose of s 739 as being to look through the transfer and see what the position would have been had it not been made and the income still been the actual income of the transferor. On this basis the better view must be that liability arises in the event of remittance in a subsequent year.

But even if that is right, the question arises of remittance by whom. The statutory fiction that the income is the transferor's is, it may be suggested, wide enough to cover remittance by the transferee or other person to whom the income in fact accrued and remittance by the transferor is plainly caught as well. Remittance by other parties should not be, on the grounds that such persons are in the position of donees (see Chapter 42). But any such person would, if he received income direct from the person to whom it accrued, very likely be taxable under ITTOIA 2005, ss 683 or 687 or TA 1988, s 740.

There is no provision preventing cessation of source from applying to s 739 (see para 40.7). Accordingly remittance of income in a tax year after that in which the source has ceased should be tax free.

Section 743(3) does not in terms cover the charge on benefits received under s 743(5) (see para 55.13). However that charge only arises if the benefit is provided out of income or assets which represent the income. The benefit is therefore inter alia income which is deemed to be transferor's by virtue of s 739, and therefore any charge under s 743(5) is in respect of such income and as such covered by s 743(3). Accordingly, a benefit under s 743(5) received by a non-domiciled transferor should not be taxable unless received or brought to the UK.

As noted in para 40.20, the accrued interest scheme does not apply to foreign securities held by non-domiciliaries. Section 742(5) deems the accrued income to be income of the transferee for the purposes of s 739. When read with s 743(3) it is reasonably clear that accrued interest is not taxable under s 739 if the transferor is non-domiciled. Any other conclusion would put a non-domiciled transferor in a worse position than if he had not made the transfer at all.

Subsequent receipts

55.23 Relief is given where the taxpayer subsequently receives income taxed under s 739. This relief applies if (a) the transferor has been charged to tax on income which has been deemed to be his under s 739 and (b) it is subsequently received by him. If this occurs the income received is deemed not to form part of his income again for income tax purposes (TA 1988, s 743(4)).

Strictly, this relief applies only if the transferor has actually been charged under s 739 rather than being merely chargeable. In theory this rule could cause hardship in cases where s 739 is invoked only after some part of the relevant income has been paid to the transferor as income, for, strictly, such income would be chargeable both at that time and under s 739. In practice HMRC are not thought to take this point. A more serious issue is that relief is not conferred from any tax save income tax. Accordingly, if income is payable to a non-resident company in which the taxpayer holds shares directly, and that company is liquidated, the transferor is liable to CGT in respect of the shares, and the gain will reflect all the income already taxed as his under s 739. Such a charge is avoided, and s 743(4) applies, if the accrued income is paid out as dividend, for then it is income in the hands of the transferor.

The relief for subsequent receipts applies notwithstanding the fact that the receipt is a new source of income, for if the receipt was not a new source, there would be no separate entity to which the income was originally payable, and thus no s 739 charge at all. Accordingly, the relief exempts distributions from a transferee company or trust. As noted in para 55.19, it should also exempt distributions which have had to go through both a company and a trust, although in practice there may be evidential difficulties in identifying the company income charged under s 739 with the payments eventually made from the trust.

The transferor

55.24 The landmark case of *Vestey v IRC* [1980] AC 1148 established that s 739 only applies if the taxpayer himself was transferor in relation to the original transfer and he or his spouse has power to enjoy or receive a capital sum. Obviously a person counts as a transferor if he effects the original transfer. But the *Vestey* case left open a number of questions concerning what is meant by the term 'transferor'.

Multiple transferors

55.25 In *Vestey*, Lord Wilberforce helpfully observed that no difficulty arose with multiple transferors, and in *IRC v Pratt* [1982] STC 756 Walton J explored the matter further. Here a private company had effected the offending transfer and HMRC sought to treat as transferors three directors who together only owned a minority of the shares. Walton J was clearly of the view that if more than one person transferred assets to an offshore entity each would be liable under s 739 on an appropriate proportion of the income and this is accepted by HMRC in practice (*Tax Bulletin* 40 (April 1999) p 651). The same is the position if there is a single transfer and each transferor owns an identifiable part of the asset transferred, as where they are tenants in common.

Where HMRC may be in difficulty is if it is impossible to separate out what each multiple transferor has transferred. Such is the position if two transferors are joint tenants in equity of the asset transferred or if they are the beneficiaries of a discretionary trust who together direct the trustees to make the transfer. The implications of Walton J's remarks is that assessment under s 739 would not be possible. But it may be doubted whether HMRC would accept this.

Quasi transferors

55.26 The problem of quasi transferors stems from a subsidiary ratio in the case overruled in *Vestey, Congreve v IRC* [1946] 2 All ER 170, 30 TC 163. The central dramatis personae of *Congreve* were the taxpayer, her father, and a successful trading company the father had built up and ran. Initially, in 1928, the father transferred 60% of the shares in the trading company to a Canadian holding company and in 1932 he transferred all the shares in that company to the taxpayer. The next stage, also in 1932, was the interposition of a second holding company between the original holding company and the trading company shares. The original holding company was then liquidated, leaving the second holding company directly owned by the taxpayer.

At the same time as these events were taking place, both the taxpayer and the trading company transferred foreign portfolio investments they held to further Canadian holding companies. The final transaction in this series, which was the first of only two at issue in *Congreve*, was the sale by the taxpayer's father of another 28% of the trading company to the second holding company, raising its holding from 60% to 88%, or 93% if an earlier direct transfer by the taxpayer is included.

The result of all these transactions was that foreign income which would otherwise have accrued to the taxpayer and the trading company, and the dividends paid by the trading company, were payable free of income tax to assorted holding companies abroad. The taxpayer had power to enjoy this income because the consideration for the transfers consisted mainly of debentures repayable on demand.

The Commissioners accepted that everything done in relation to the transactions was brought about by the taxpayer's father, the taxpayer merely signing as she had been instructed. The issue was whether the taxpayer could escape liability under s 739 in respect of the trading company dividends or its transferred portfolio investments, on the grounds that the investments were transferred by the trading company, and the shares in the trading company by the original holding company and the taxpayer's father.

Lawrence J considered that s 739 extended to transfers effected by an agent of the taxpayer or by her wholly-owned company, and this brought the transfer by the original holding company into the section. But he held that the father's transfer was not caught with the result that the dividends attributable to the 28% of the shares transferred by him to the second holding company escaped. He appears also to have considered that the trading company's transfer escaped, for at the time of the transfer the taxpayer only controlled 65% of the company.

In the Court of Appeal and the House of Lords, all the difficulties were brushed aside, for, in the ratio overruled by *Vestey*, it was held that the taxpayer was liable under s 739 regardless of whether she had been the original transferor. But in the Court of Appeal, Cohen LJ formulated a subsidiary ratio, to the effect that even if s 739 were restricted to the original transferor, it applied if he or she had procured the transfer. For these purposes Lawrence J's identification of wholly-owned companies with the taxpayer was rejected, but on the facts, the Court of Appeal held that the taxpayer had, through her father as agent, procured all the transfers concerned.

Close reading of the speeches in *Vestey* makes it clear that only the principal ratio of *Congreve* was in terms overruled. The survival or otherwise of Cohen LJ's subsidiary ratio is a matter of difficulty, for while Lords Dilhorne and Keith affirmed it, the other three law lords did not as such endorse it. Instead Lord Wilberforce merely contemplated, as an aside, that s 739 'may be' extended to persons 'associated' with the transfer. The better view must be that Lord Wilberforce's aside, in conjunction with the affirmation by Lords Dilhorne and Keith, does preserve the subsidiary ratio and such was accepted by Walton J in *IRC v Pratt* [1982] STC 756. Accordingly the issue is what exactly Cohen LJ meant in the subsidiary ratio. Undoubtedly the best, perhaps the only, guide to this is to look at the father's role in *Congreve*. Effectively he was the person who devised and set up the schemes, and accordingly it is such persons, the promoters, who are best regarded as quasi transferors.

Such a conclusion is confirmed by *IRC v Pratt* [1982] STC 756, for here Walton J accepted the proposition that the subsidiary ratio could render a person who procured the transfer taxable under s 739. Indeed the term 'quasi transferor' comes from *Pratt*. However, Walton J rejected the proposition that the three directors who were minority shareholders were quasi transferors. He held that the subsidiary ratio applied only to persons who procured the transfer, and that procurement could only take place if the alleged transferor had the power to procure. In a company context this means he has to have control of the company, as in *Congreve* itself.

Walton J's approach in *Pratt* indicates a person cannot be a quasi-transferor if the party who in fact effected the transfer is an individual and the alleged quasi-transferor merely used persuasion. In *Carvill v IRC* [2000] STC (SCD) 143, 163, a Special Commissioner accepted this in principle. However, he contemplated there might be exceptional cases where the alleged quasi-transferor's influence over the actual transferor is so strong as to make him a quasi-transferor.

HMRC, in addressing the issue of quasi transferors, follow the decided cases. Their view, following Lord Wilberforce's words in *Vestey*, is that s 739 can potentially apply to someone who was associated with the transfer, and that such would include a person who procured the transfer (*Tax Bulletin* 40 (April 1999) p 651).

Non-resident transferor

55.27 Income arising before 26 November 1996 was not caught by s 739 unless the transferor was ordinarily resident in the UK at the time he made the original transfer (*IRC v Willoughby* [1997] STC 995). Now s 739 applies provided the transferor is ordinarily resident in the year in which the income arises (s 739(1A)).

HMRC indicated (IR Press Release, 18 December 1997) that they would apply *IRC v Willoughby* to income arising before 26 November 1996 if:

(a) it was not subject to an assessment which had become final; or
(b) any such assessment became final after 16 December 1994; or
(c) the assessment related to a personal portfolio bond.

Spouses and civil partners

55.28 Section 742(9)(a) states that, for the purposes of ss 739–741, references to an individual are deemed to include his spouse. Since 5 December 2005 such deeming has extended also to civil partners (Tax and Civil Partnership Regulations 2005 (SI 2005/3229) reg 97).

Lord Nolan's speech in *IRC v Willoughby* [1997] STC 995 indicates that s 742(9)(a) renders the spouse or civil partner of the transferor to be assessable under s 739 as well as the transferor himself (see p 999f). It is implicit in *Tax Bulletin 40* (April 1999) that such was then also HMRC's view. In that article, HMRC address the position if the transferor spouse is not UK domiciled and the other spouse is. In such case, HMRC said their practice is not to asses the other spouse on income which, in relation to the transferor spouse, is protected by the remittance basis by virtue of s 743(3).

It may be suggested this is an odd reading of s 742(9)(a) and one at variance with *Vestey v IRC* [1980] STC 10. In *Vestey* the whole emphasis is on the transferor alone being the person targeted. The anomaly would be particularly obvious if the spouse putatively caught was not married to the settlor at the time of the transfer and so could not, on any view, be said to be associated with it. Equally anomalous would be the position of the non-transferor spouse after the transferor's death.

The correct construction of s 742(9)(a) is, it may be suggested, that if the spouse or civil partner has power to enjoy or receive a capital sum, s 739 is in point even if the transferor spouse is wholly excluded from benefit. Lord Nolan's comment in *Willoughby* could be explained as being not necessary to the decision in that case. Section 742(9)(a) would thus be equivalent to the provisions in the settlement code treating a settlement as settlor-interested if the settlor's spouse does or could benefit.

Recent HMRC comments in *Tax Bulletin 80* (December 2005) indicate that the above analysis may in fact be accepted by them. Those comments, made in the context of the Civil Partnership Regulations, appear to indicate that a spouse is only caught by s 739 if she is 'involved' in the transfer or associated operations. That may well be right, but if so it follows because she is a quasi-transferor in her own right (see para 55.26), and not because of s 742(9)(a).

If this is the correct analysis, a difficult question, in relation to power to enjoy, is whether s 739 is in point even if the person to whom the settlor is currently married or in civil partnership is excluded, but benefit could be conferred on some future spouse or civil partner. In other words, does the reasoning in *IRC v Tennant* (1942) 24 TC 215 and *Unmarried Settlor v IRC* [2003] STC (SCD) 274 extend to s 739. The impact of those cases is explained in para 60.8 and, while the point is not wholly certain, the better view must be that they could extend to s 739. Their reasoning is, it may be suggested, particularly apposite in relation to s 742(2)(d) (see para 55.6 above).

On the basis that this is right, a settlement which excludes the transferor and his current spouse or civil partner is still within s 739 unless future spouses or civil partners are also excluded. In relation to spouses this is achieved by any well-drawn settlor exclusion clause, and in any new settlement such can and should be extended to civil partners. But existing settlements do not refer to civil partners and so, as a matter of strict construction, it may be that all settlements previously thought to be outside s 739 came within s 739 on 5 December 2005, the date on which the Tax and Civil Partnership Regulations took effect.

Fortunately HMRC have indicated they will not take this point, at least in relation to settlements in existence on 23 November 2005. The relevant correspondence is summarised in para 60.9. But as stated in para 60.9, and despite the correspondence, all trustees would be well advised to extend any existing spouse exclusion to civil partners in all cases where they have power to do so.

Compliance

55.29 HMRC expect taxpayers to draw HMRC's attention to the implications of s 739 when submitting details of transactions to which it may potentially apply (*Tax Bulletin* 40 (April 1999) p 652). As noted above, income taxable under s 739 should be detailed in Boxes 6.3 and 6.3A of the Foreign Pages of the return and details of the offshore structure given in Box 6.39. Disclosure must be made in box 6.5A if the taxpayer is relying on the motive defence.

Chapter 56

Benefits: section 740

Introduction

56.1 The basic preconditions for the operation of TA 1988, s 740 are set out in s 740(1)(a). They are the same as applies to s 739 and are discussed in Chapter 54. Income must be payable to a person resident or domiciled outside the UK by virtue or in consequence of a transfer of assets, either alone or in conjunction with associated operations.

Before liability under s 740 can arise five further conditions must be met:

(1) The motive or purpose defence described in Chapter 58 must not apply (TA 1988 s 741).
(2) The taxpayer must receive a benefit provided out of assets which are available for the purpose by virtue or in consequence of the transfer or of any associated operations. This condition is set out in s 740(1)(b).
(3) There must be relevant income. This is defined in s 740(3) and is discussed in Chapter 57.
(4) The taxpayer must be ordinarily resident in the UK in the tax year in which he receives the benefit.
(5) The taxpayer must not be taxable under s 739 by reference to the transfer.

Where these various conditions are all satisfied the amount or value of the benefit is taxable as the income of the recipient to the extent of the relevant income. It is taxed in the year of receipt if it equals or is less than the relevant income of the current or prior years. Insofar as it exceeds the relevant income it is carried forward and taxed as and when there is relevant income in a future tax year (TA 1988, s 740(2)).

The transfer

56.2 The transfer of assets which brings s 740 into play is that discussed in Chapter 54, namely the transfer which, either alone or in conjunction with associated operations, causes the income to become payable to the non-resident. An important point to note about s 740 is that this transfer can be effected by anyone, for in contrast to s 739, s 740 is not concerned with the taxation of transferors. There is no reason why the transferor cannot be a company or even, it may be suggested, the trustees of a trust.

Transfer or associated operation

56.3 In view of the broad definitions of 'transfer' and 'associated operation' discussed in Chapter 54, it is often unclear whether a transaction is a transfer or whether it is an operation associated with another transaction which is the transfer. To take the typical case of trustees who incorporate a holding company to hold investments, is the income payable to the holding company so payable because of the transfer of assets to the holding company? Or is it so payable because of the transfer of assets to the settlement together with an associated operation represented by the transfer to the holding company?

Such authority as there is is in favour of the former view. In *IRC v Herdman* (1967) 45 TC 394, the House of Lords held that a transfer and associated operations were only together treated as satisfying the preconditions for s 739 where the transfer alone did not satisfy them (see para 54.6). Parity of reasoning suggests that where there is a transfer which on its own causes income to become payable to a non-resident, that is the transfer of assets which brings s 740 into play. If this view is right it is normally a transfer alone which causes the income to become payable to the relevant foreign entity. However, one instance where this would not be so is where the transfer is to a resident trust and the trust then migrates. Migration is not a transfer but it is an associated operation (*Congreve v IRC* [1948] 1 All ER 948).

One transfer or several

56.4 Another issue is whether two or more transactions are a single transfer or several. Typically this arises where an individual makes several transfers to the same transferee, as where a settlor makes a series of gifts to the same settlement. The term 'transfer' is not given any extended definition so as to include a disposition effected by a series of operations and so it may be concluded that a series of transactions is simply a series of separate transfers and thus that in the example postulated each addition to the settlement is a separate transfer. An exception may perhaps be made where there is sufficient linkage in time or otherwise to indicate a composite transaction in the *Ramsay* sense. Otherwise the result is that it is necessary to identify separately each transfer and the income resulting from it or from it and any operations associated with it.

Assets available for the purpose

56.5 As noted above, s 740(1)(b) requires the benefit to be provided out of assets available for the purpose. There is no case law or statutory elaboration on what is meant by 'available for the purpose'. However s 740(1)(b) itself says that availability must be by reason of the transfer or of any associated operation.

The transfer referred to in s 740(1)(b) is the transfer discussed in Chapter 54, namely the transfer which, either alone or in conjunction with associated operations, causes the income to become payable to the non-resident. This conclusion follows because 'transfer' in s 740(1)(b) is prefaced by the definite article. But are the associated operations referred to merely such operations as, together with that transfer, rendered the income payable to the non-resident, or are they any operations which (a) fall within the definition of associated operations, and (b) render the assets out of which the benefit is provided available for the purpose?

Although as a matter of language there is something to be said for the former view it is difficult to see a court adopting it and, the wider view is more consistent with the general tenor of s 740. But even if that is right, assets available for the purpose must still ultimately be derived from the original transfer, for, as noted at para 54.4, a transaction only comes within the definition of associated operation if effected in relation to the assets transferred or income derived from those assets or assets representing such assets or income.

The point may be illustrated by postulating an offshore settlement created in, say, 1995, on which the settlor settled an income producing portfolio of investments. Some years later in, say, 2001, he settled a parcel of real estate which has never produced income. As noted above, the portfolio is one transfer and the real estate another. If, still having produced no income, the real estate is vested in a beneficiary it may be concluded that no liability under s 740 arises, for the benefit provided is not provided out of assets resulting from the transfer of the income producing portfolio or any operation associated therewith.

A related issue arises where trustees transfer some or all of the assets transferred to them to a holding company. Assuming, as per the discussion above, that the transfer of assets to the holding company is the transfer rather than an operation associated with the transfer of assets to the settlement, the issue arises of whether benefits provided out of the trust are provided out of assets made available by the transfer to the company. The answer is that they certainly are insofar as funded by a distribution from the company to the trust or, it may be suggested, by the sale proceeds of the company. This follows because the distribution or sale would be associated operations as being operations effected in relation to the company's income or assets or assets representing them (cf para 54.9).

The position is more complicated if the benefit from the trust is funded out of other assets in the trust. However, as explained in para 54.5, an operation prior to the transfer can be associated and so if all the assets in the trust were transferred to it in a single transaction, the whole transaction could reasonably be regarded as associated with the transfer to the company. If so, any benefit provided out of the trust would be provided out of assets available by virtue of an associated operation. The position would be otherwise if the assets retained in the trust were transferred to it by a transaction separate from that relating to the assets later transferred to the company for then the former transfer would not be an operation associated with the transfer to the company.

What is a benefit?

56.6 The term 'benefit' is not defined, save only that it includes a payment of any kind (TA 1988, s 742(9)). It is plain that the term includes a cash advance to the beneficiary or the transfer of an asset in specie. Since it is the amount or value which is taxed, the charge is on the amount if the benefit is in cash and on its value if it is in kind.

Income benefits

56.7 A benefit is only taxable under s 740 if it is not otherwise chargeable to income tax in the hands of the receipient (s 740(2)). This means s 740 does not apply to receipts from an offshore company in the form of a dividend or to income distributions from an offshore trust.

The rule that s 740 only applies if the benefit is not otherwise chargeable to income tax does, it may be suggested, preclude s 740 where a capital benefit from a trust to a minor child of the settlor is taxed as the settlor's income under ITTOIA 2005, s 629 (cf para 59.8). HMRC do not tax the same benefit under s 740 and under ITTOIA 2005, Part 5, Chapter 5 (*Tax Bulletin* 40 (April 1999) p 652).

Double taxation

56.8 It may be that the relevant income taken into account in taxing a benefit has suffered UK or foreign tax as it arose. Indeed the benefit may be paid out of accumulated income which has itself been subject to withholding or other taxes. In these circumstances the question arises whether tax on the benefit may be relieved by double tax relief. The answer is that it cannot, and so the position is reached that if taxed offshore income is accumulated and paid out as capital to a UK resident overall tax may be increased.

This is a harsh rule. A rationale which is sometimes given is that it compensates for the lack of an equivalent to the CGT supplemental charge (see para 63.26). In other words the deferral implicit in offshore trusts is countered by notional interest in the case of CGT and by the absence of double tax relief in the case of s 740 benefits. But even assuming this argument has some general merit, it is harsh when a s 740 benefit is matched with current or future income. If in such a case the income attracts UK or foreign tax on an arising basis, there really is double tax, once on the foreign entity and again on the recipient of the prior benefit. The moral in such cases is to prevent such income from being relevant income by distributing it as it arises (cf para 57.9).

Life interests

56.9 HMRC consider that a benefit does not arise when a life interest is appointed to a beneficiary or when a beneficiary sells a life interest (*Tax Bulletin* 40 (April 1999) p 651).

Benefits to the transferor

56.10 Section 740 only applies if the benefit is received by someone who is not liable to tax under s 739 by reference to the transfer. As such the transferor is excluded from liability under s 740 should he receive a benefit. It is sometimes suggested this exclusion may not extend to a non-domiciled transferor who escapes liability under s 739 because all the income is unremitted foreign income. This concern is almost certainly ill-founded in law for such a transferor is still liable to tax under s 739, and in practice HMRC do not take the point (*Tax Bulletin* 40 (April 1999) p 651).

Free use of property

56.11 Great difficulty is occasioned where a non-resident trust or company allows a UK resident free use of property or make him interest-free demand loans. Such are certainly benefits in the broad sense of the term but it has been far from clear whether they are caught by s 740. HMRC's view has always been that they are (*Tax Bulletin* 40 (April 1999) p 651) but there are arguments against this view.

An initial point is that s 740 requires the benefit to be provided 'out of assets'. In the case of a loan of money, this condition may be met, for the cash is passed from the non-resident to the beneficiary. With a licence to use property the position is different, for the property remains unimpaired in the ownership of the non-resident. Can the licence then be said to be provided 'out of' the property?

In certain trust cases the borrower or licensee has an interest in possession in the money or property when the benefit is conferred. In such a case it is difficult to see what benefit there is, for the beneficiary is merely enjoying the property in specie in lieu of taking the income.

The central issue, however, is whether, assuming the loan or licence is a benefit, it has a value. In the case of a loan or licence for a fixed term it plainly does – the benefit is conferred at the outset and is equal to the value of the right to use the money or asset for the fixed period. But normally the loan or licence is terminable at will, and in such a case it may be argued there is no value.

The compelling argument in favour of this view is that s 740 lacks any rules as to how such rent or interest should be determined. In this it contrasts with other provisions in the UK tax code, which do provide how loans and rent-free benefits should be valued. The prime example is the benefits in kind legislation now in ITEPA 2003 (see Chapter 69). That this is a relevant consideration is confirmed by Vinelott J's judgment in *O'Leary v McKinlay* [1991] STC 42. Here an employer made an interest-free loan to a trust benefiting an employee, which was outside the benefit-in-kind charge on free loans because the recipient was a trust. In the course of his judgment Vinelott J observed that the benefit of an interest-free loan was not an emolument within the general meaning of the term, for the benefit could not be quantified.

Two decisions bear directly on the point. In *IRC v Botnar* [1998] STC 38 the Special Commissioner decided that the value of the benefit for the purposes of TA 1988, s 743(5) was the market rent of the flat (see para 55.13). But this may not be applicable to s 740, because the expansionary words of s 742(3) do not apply to s 740. In *Billingham v Cooper* [2001] STC 1177 the Court of Appeal decided that an interest-free loan was a benefit within the meaning of the capital payment rules in TCGA 1992, s 87 (see para 65.7). The benefit was the trustee's successive acts in not calling in the loan, to be valued retrospectively as equal to the interest which would have been charged had the loan been at a commercial rate. In theory this case may be distinguishable from s 740 because:

(a) Section 87 requires the valuation of 'the benefit conferred' by the capital payment, whereas s 740 speaks merely of 'the amount or value' of the benefit.
(b) Section 87 refers to the 'conferring of any … benefit' whereas s 740 only applies if the benefit is 'provided out of assets'.

HMRC's approach has always been to disregard all the arguments deployed above and treat the rent or interest foregone as a benefit on an annual basis (Notes on Foreign pages p FN12). It has to be said that in practice this approach has to be accepted, unless *Billingham v Cooper* is overruled or the matter is otherwise considered in the House of Lords. The only sensible advice to taxpayers is to make full disclosure to HMRC and pay tax on the basis that HMRC's view is correct.

Receipts resulting from fair bargains

56.12 On the face of it, the fact that s 740 imposes a charge on benefits indicates that a receipt resulting from a fair bargain is not caught. The point is analogous to that arising under ITEPA 2003, s 201 where the word 'benefits' is used. Here it is has been held in relation to the predecessor to s 201 (TA 1988, s 154) that receipts from fair bargains are outside the charge (*Mairs v Haughey* [1992] STC 495; affd [1993] STC 569).

In the context of s 740, a point which could be raised against such conclusion is the inclusion of a payment of any kind in the definition of the term benefit (TA 1988, s 742(9)(c)). Read literally it could be said this means a payment is a payment even if made under a fair bargain. But it may be doubted whether the inclusion of payments has this effect. One reason is that in ITEPA 2003, s 201, the term benefits has been construed as including out-and-out payments and yet despite that held to exclude fair bargains (*Mairs v Haughey*, supra). A second reason is that in other contexts, payable has been construed as referring to an out-and-out parting rather than a payment for value. Lord Simmons so held in *Lord Vestey's Executors v IRC* (1949) 31 TC 1, 83 in relation to predecessor legislation to ITTOIA 2005, s 625 (see para 59.7).

Sale of a company

56.13 Assuming the above is right, an individual does not receive a benefit when he sells an asset. This is so even if the asset is shares in a non-resident company, all or part of the value of which represents retained profits. A further factor which points to the same conclusion in such cases is that a benefit is only taxable under s 740 if provided out of assets available for the purpose by reason of the transfer (s 740(1)(b)). In the case of a sale any payment is provided out of the purchaser's assets, not out of what is bought.

Liquidation of a company

56.14 The analysis of a liquidation distribution is more difficult. On the one hand the shareholder does not receive any benefit in the normal sense of the term for the liquidation distribution is simply payment to the shareholders of what already belongs to them (*IRC v Laird Group* [2003] STC 1349, 1358). On the other, the distribution is provided out of the assets of the company and can hardly be said to result from a fair bargain. It may be the argument is stronger that the distribution is a s 740 benefit where it is cash than where it is in specie.

Exercise of fiduciary powers

56.15 Most settlements confer on the trustees wide powers to appoint or create new trusts. Sometimes these may be exercised so as to leave the assets in the original settlement and sometimes so as to advance or transfer the assets to a new or different settlement (*Roome v Edwards* [1981] STC 96; *Bond v Pickford* [1983] STC 517; *Swires v Renton* [1991] STC 490; SP 7/84). The appointment or advance may relate to all the assets in the original settlement or just some of them and in some cases, one part of the trust fund may be subject to one appointment or advance and other parts to others. Whatever is done issues arise under s 740 if the benefit and the income are made out of different settlements or funds.

Relevant income prior to exercise

56.16 The most common situation is where income is accumulated prior to the exercise of the fiduciary power and a capital distribution is made thereafter. In this situation, s 740 plainly catches the distribution. The analysis is that the transfer by virtue of which the income arises is the transfer to the settlement. The distribution out of the appointed or advanced fund is out of assets available for the purpose for those assets are so available by virtue of the appointment or advance which is an associated operation. The previously accumulated income is relevant income because it is still able to be used to benefit the beneficiary in receipt of the benefit.

There are, however, two situations where this result may not follow. The first follows on from that described in para 56.5 above and is where there have been separate transfers to the original trust. If the appointment or advance is solely of the non-income-producing assets, a subsequent distribution from that fund will not be taxable by reference to the income in the original settlement for the reasons given in para 56.5. The second is if, after the appointment or advance, but before the distribution, the beneficiary in receipt of the distribution is excluded from any funds still held on the trusts of the original settlement. If on the facts those funds comprise all the retained income it may cogently be argued it is not relevant income, for it is no longer able to be used to benefit the beneficiary in receipt of the distribution (see further para 57.13). But this argument is self-evidently not available if some or all of the previously retained income is included in the appointed or advanced fund, as would invariably be the case if the appointment or advance was of the whole trust fund.

Benefit prior to exercise

56.17 Another scenario is where a distribution is made from the original settlement at a time when there is no or insufficient relevant income and the appointment or advance takes place before such income arises in the future. The issue then is whether, if income does thereafter arise in the appointed or advanced fund, it can render the earlier benefit taxable.

Such a result should certainly follow if the correct analysis is that the original settlement is the transfer, and the appointment or advance is an associated operation. On this scenario, the benefit is provided out of assets which are available for the purpose by virtue of the transfer, and the income in the appointed or advanced fund is available to benefit the benefited beneficiary by virtue of the transfer and the associated operation.

There is, however, an alternate analysis, which is that the appointment or advance is the transfer (cf para 56.3). In this event, the prior distribution would only be taxable by reference to the income in the advanced or appointed fund if the prior creation of the settlement could be seen as an operation associated with the appointment or advance. Despite the fact that associated operations can occur before the transfer, it is not wholly clear that the settlement would be associated with the appointment or advance (cf para 54.5).

There are two situations where liability under s 740 should certainly be avoided. The first is the situation postulated in para 56.5 where there were two separate transfers to the original settlement, one of income-producing assets and one of non-income-producing assets. If the distribution was from the latter and the advance or appointment is of the former then if the analysis in para 56.5 is right, liability under s 740 is avoided. Second, if the recipient of the distribution is totally excluded from the appointed or advanced fund he should escape liability under s 740, for the income arising in that fund will ipso facto not be able to be used to benefit him and so cannot be relevant income (see para 57.13).

Foreign element

Residence of the recipient

56.18 Provided there is sufficient relevant income, a benefit is taxable if the recipient is ordinarily resident in the UK in the year of assessment in which the benefit is received (TA 1988, s 740(1)). Assuming the recipient is UK domiciled, the benefit is fully taxable even if it is received and kept abroad: thus a benefit is received if offshore trustees allow a beneficiary the use of a holiday home in, say, Spain.

Should the recipient not be ordinarily resident in the tax year when he receives the benefit, it is not taxable. But relevant income is not allocated to it and so remains available for allocation to future benefits conferred on UK residents (see further para 57.10). Should there be no relevant income when the non-resident receives the benefit, the benefit remains tax-free even if the recipient moves to the UK, and relevant income thereafter accrues. This is because liability under s 740 is only triggered if the recipient is UK resident at the time of receipt (s 740(1)(b)).

A point of some difficulty arises where the recipient is ordinarily resident at the time of receipt but there is no relevant income until after he has become non-resident. On a strict reading s 740 does impose a charge in these circumstances.

Residence and domicile of the transferor

56.19 A factor which is immaterial to s 740 is the residence and domicile of the transferor. Section 740 can apply even if he has never been resident and domiciled in the UK, although in such circumstances a beneficiary in receipt of benefits may be able to invoke the motive defence (see Chapter 58). A point to stress in such cases is that the relevant income by reference to which any benefit is taxed includes income which arose before the recipient was resident in the UK. In the case of a settlor-interested trust, all the trust income is relevant income if the settlor is non-resident, as is unremitted foreign-source income if he is resident but non-domiciled. The results are avoided if all such income was distributed as income (cf para 57.9).

Residence of the recipient of the income

56.20 As noted at the beginning of this chapter, s 740 only applies if the transferee is resident or domiciled outside the UK. It follows that should the transferee be a trust which has emigrated only post-emigration income is a relevant income. This is accepted by HMRC (Notes on Foreign pages, p FN11).

A more interesting question is whether a benefit received by a UK resident prior to the emigration of the trust is taxable by reference to the trust's post-emigration income. The answer, it may be suggested, turns on whether the associated operations which determine whether assets are available to provide a benefit must be the same as those which cause the income to become payable to a non-resident. The latter, self-evidently, includes the emigration. As noted in para 56.5, the better view is that the two sets of associated operations need not be the same, and if so, a benefit received before the emigration of the trust is caught.

The converse situation is if the trust immigrates to the UK. Here post-immigration income is not relevant income because it does not arise to a non-resident and as such it cannot render prior untaxed benefits taxable. But post-immigration benefits are taxable unless and until all pre-immigration relevant income has been exhausted. Nothing in s 740 precludes this plainly logical result, which also represents HMRC's view (Notes on Foreign pages, p FN11).

As noted in para 54.10 any company incorporated abroad is deemed to be non-resident for the purposes of s 740 even if in fact resident in the UK under the central management and control test (s 742(8)). This means that both pre-emigration and post-immigration income of such companies is relevant income for the purposes of s 740 and, subject to the motive defence, able to render any benefit taxable. As noted in para 56.8, no credit is in law available in taxing the benefit for any corporation tax born by the company.

Onward gifts

56.21 Since non-residents are not taxable under s 740, it is normally good tax planning for non-resident trustees to make capital distributions to them. In some cases, the non-resident may pass some or all of the money on to another family member who is resident in the UK. The issue which then arises is whether HMRC could argue s 740 imposes liability on the UK resident by reference to income in the trust.

On this issue, the first question is whether the distribution is a valid distribution to the non-resident as a matter of trust law. If the distribution is not validly made to the non-resident, and the UK resident is also a beneficiary under the trust, the correct analysis would probably be that the distribution had been made to him and so was caught by s 740. If in such a case the UK resident is not a beneficiary of the trust, the distribution is likely to be a fraud on the power and should thus be a nullity. This ought to mean the money could be returned to the trust without fiscal consequences.

The test of whether the distribution to the non-resident is a valid distribution to him is likely to be the same in both cases (cf *Re Dick* [1953] 1 All ER 559, CA). It may be suggested it will not be such a valid distribution if:

(a) the gift to the UK resident is a condition of the distribution;
(b) the purpose of the trustees in making the distribution was to benefit the UK resident; or
(c) on receiving the distribution the non-resident was under 'irresistible moral suasion' to make the onward gift.

Assuming it is established that as a matter of trust law the distribution was validly made to the non-resident, it could in theory still be argued that the UK resident is taxable under s 740. All that s 740(1)(b) requires is that the benefit received by an individual be provided out of assets which are available for the purpose by virtue inter alia of associated operations. Read literally, the distribution to the non-resident is an operation associated with the transfer of assets to the trust, and as a result of the distribution the money distributed is available to the non-resident to make the onward gift.

But it may be suggested the wider context of s 740 makes this construction untenable. If the UK resident was taxable under s 740, logically the same principle would apply where a UK resident recipient of the distribution makes an onward gift to another UK resident. In such a case, both the original beneficiary and the onward donee could on this construction be assessed under s 740 or HMRC would have to make a choice between them. In *Vestey v IRC* [1980] STC 10, the House of Lords recoiled from such duplication and discretion and it was one of the reasons which led to the restriction of s 739 to transferors. A similar approach should be taken to s 740, to the effect that it bites only on the individual who as a matter of trust law is the object of the exercise of the trustee's discretion.

It is clear that such risks as these are minimised if the non-resident has a reasonable period of unfettered use of the money. It may also be material if he mixes it with his other assets, and there is no obvious correlation between the amount he gives to the UK resident and the amount received from the trust. If these precautions are taken it is not thought HMRC would have any basis for attack and, although there is no published practice, there are no indications they would in fact do so.

Distribution from UK trusts

56.22 HMRC take the position that if a UK resident trust has received capital from a non-resident trust, a distribution to a UK resident beneficiary counts as a benefit from the non-resident trust (Notes on Foreign pages p FN12). In support of this they contend that indirect receipt must be included.

This latter point is wrong, as, in contrast to relevant income, there is no express reference in s 740 to indirect benefit. However, the basic proposition that benefits routed through UK resident trusts are caught may be right, for the assets in the UK trust are available to provide the benefit by virtue of the associated operation represented by the transfer of assets to that trust from the non-resident trust.

It is perhaps significant that HMRC do not contend that a benefit received from another individual is caught, even if such individual has previously received benefit from the non-resident trust.

Non-domiciliaries

56.23 Section 740(5) confers a form of relief on non-domiciliaries. It states that an individual is not taxable in respect of a 'benefit not received in the UK' by reference to relevant income which is such that if 'he had in fact received it he would not, by reason of his being [foreign] domiciled have been chargeable to income tax in respect of it'. Section 740(5) bristles with uncertainty and it requires one to look both at the benefit and at the income.

Benefit not received in the United Kingdom

56.24 In earlier editions of this book the view expressed was that a benefit counts as received in the UK if brought to the UK by the recipient beneficiary in the year of receipt or any subsequent year. In support of this is the incorporation in s 740(5) of the rules as to deemed remittance in ITTOIA 2005, ss 833 and 834 (see para 40.12) and also the use of the word 'received'. Both these indicate that the concepts of remittance applicable to relevant foreign income are intended to apply to the benefit.

In fact closer examination of s 740(5) suggests this is not the correct construction. It is true that the word 'received' is used in ITTOIA 2005, s 832(1) in that the charge on relevant foreign income is on sums 'received' in the UK. But in s 740(5) 'received' is used in the negative sense in that absence of receipt precludes a charge. Further, the word 'received' is also used in the principal charging provision of s 740: under s 740(1)(b) liability arises if the ordinarily resident individual 'receives a benefit'. When read with s 740(1)(b) the natural construction of s 740(5) is then that 'not received in the United Kingdom' harks back to s 740(1)(b) and is simply directed at whether or not the benefit received by the beneficiary was conferred on him in the UK. The reference to ss 833 and 834 can readily be explained as covering the position where the benefit conferred on the recipient is clearing a pre-existing loan account he has or providing collateral in support of a loan.

Relevant income

56.25 The relevant income which is excluded in charging the benefit is income which would not have been chargeable had the recipient of the benefit received it himself. It is clear from this that one category of income is not excluded, namely UK source income, for UK income received by a non-domiciliary is fully chargeable.

With foreign source income a key point to remember is that s 740(5) does not displace the basic provision in s 740(2)(a) namely that if there is relevant income in the year of receipt, the benefit is deemed to be the recipient's income in that year. All that s 740(5) does is provide that if the benefit is matched with income which would not be chargeable it is itself not chargeable. It follows that the benefit remains income in the same way that the relevant foreign income of a non-domiciled individual is income even if not chargeable because it is not remitted.

It is in the light of this point that a construction must be given to the phrase 'such that if he had received it he would not, by reason of his being so domiciled, have been chargeable to income tax in respect of it'. In all material respects the language is the same as that used in TA 1988, s 743(3), the provision imposing the remittance basis on s 739 (para 55.22). As with s 743(3) one view is that the phrase only catches foreign source income if remitted in the year it arises. The contrary view is that it catches such income whenever it is remitted. As with s 740(3), this latter view is to be preferred. A particular argument in favour of it is that relevant income could arise and be remitted in separate years but both could be before the year of charge, ie the receipt of the benefit.

If the above is right, it may be argued that a benefit matched with unremitted foreign income cannot be charged in a subsequent year by reference to any other income, for, even though not taxed, it has already been deemed to be income and could be charged if the actual income is remitted in the future. This point becomes material if in a subsequent year there is UK income or other foreign income which is remitted. The view expressed in earlier editions of this book was that such income would then render the benefit taxable. But as just noted this ignores the point that the benefit has already been deemed to be income and had the unremitted foreign income allocated to it.

It may be thought that the rules as to duplications s 744 (para 57.12) are inconsistent with this analysis, for they state that no income can be taken into account more than once in charging tax under ss 739 and 740. But it may be suggested that the foreign income allocated to the benefit is taken into account in charging tax. This is so even if tax will not actually be paid unless and until the income in question is remitted.

Assuming all this is right, the receipt of a benefit by a non-domiciliary does achieve a form of washing out of relevant income, in that once foreign income is allocated to the non-domiciliary's benefit it cannot thereafter be allocated to a benefit conferred on another recipient. The only circumstance in which such allocation could be made would be if the two benefits were conferred in such circumstances that s 744 would require the allocation to be on a just and reasonable basis. As noted in para 57.12, it may strongly be argued that such allocation is only required where the benefits are conferred in the same tax year.

Four further points arise with the relevant income. The first is whether a remittance of the income renders the benefit taxable only if effected by the recipient of the benefit as could happen following a prior distribution or transfer of the income to him. Or is a remittance caught if effected by the non-resident transferee or other actual recipient of the income? As with s 739, the better view must be that the latter is correct, on the grounds that the hypothesis that the recipient is in receipt of the income extends also to attributing to him the acts of the transferee.

The second point is whether, assuming a remittance of the relevant income in a future year is caught, such applies also where the remittance is effected by a third party to whom the income has been distributed or transferred. It may be suggested it is not, on the grounds that remittance by a donee would not have triggered liability had the income in fact accrued to the recipient of the benefit (see Chapter 42).

The third point to note is no provision in s 740 excludes cessation of source (see para 40.7). It follows that if the source of the relevant income ceases, remittance of the income in a subsequent tax year should not trigger a tax charge on the benefit.

Fourth and last is that accrued interest is relevant income (TA 1988, s 742(5)). There is no provision preventing this even where the recipient of a benefit matched with such income is non-domiciled.

The position in summary

56.26 Assuming all the above is right, the tax exposure of a non-domiciliary in receipt of a benefit may be summarised as follows:

(1) The benefit is matched with relevant income insofar as there is such in the tax year in which the benefit is conferred.

(2) If the recipient receives the benefit in the UK it is taxable by reference to both UK and non-UK relevant income.

(3) If he receives the benefit outside the UK, it is taxable insofar as the relevant income includes UK source income or foreign source income which in the same or a previous tax year has been remitted either by the person in actual receipt of such income or by the recipient of the benefit.

(4) Insofar as the benefit is matched with unremitted foreign source income, it is taxable in future years if such income is remitted.

(5) Insofar as there is no or insufficient relevant income in the year in which the benefit is received, it is carried forward and deemed to be income in a future year as and when relevant income arises. A tax charge will arise if that income is UK income or remitted foreign source income.

Benefits and capital payments compared

Differences between TA 1988, s 740 and TCGA 1992, s 87 and Sch 4C

56.27 TCGA 1992, s 87 and Sch 4C are analysed in Chapters 63 to 65 and, as is explained below, s 740 on the one hand and Sch 4C or s 87 on the other can potentially apply to the same benefit or payment. The main differences between the two codes may be summarised as follows:

(1) Section 740 applies if there has been a transfer of assets, and s 87 and Sch 4C only if there is a settlement.
(2) Section 740 looks at each non-resident recipient of income separately and potentially applies if the benefit provided to the UK beneficiary is provided out of assets available by reason of the transfer to that non-resident. Section 87 and Sch 4C operate by reference to pools of trust gains which can be derived not merely from the trust making the distribution but from underlying companies or other trusts as well.
(3) Section 740 is subject to a motive test but applies whether or not the transfer involved bounty. Section 87 and Sch 4C are not subject to a motive test. In s 87 (and Sch 4C) the use of the term 'settlement' connotes bounty.
(4) Section 740 can apply to a non-domiciled recipient but s 87 and Sch 4C cannot.
(5) Section 740 does not allow income to be washed out by payments to non-resident recipients. Section 87 (but not Sch 4C) does allow gains to be so washed out.
(6) If tax is charged under s 87 or Sch 4C it can be increased by notional interest. Tax under s 740 cannot be so increased.

Both sections apply regardless of the residence or domicile of the settlor or transferor.

Overlap with CGT

56.28 Despite the differences noted above, a capital distribution from an offshore trust is frequently both a benefit under s 740 and a capital payment under s 87 or Sch 4C. The general rule preventing double tax is that if the payment is taxed under s 740 it is not a capital payment at all, for that term is defined as excluding any payment chargeable to income tax (TCGA 1992, s 97(1); see para 65.3).

There are, however, two important points to note. The first is that if the distribution is made to a non-resident beneficiary it is always a capital payment for the purposes of s 87. This result follows because liability under s 740 arises only if the recipient is ordinarily resident at the time of receipt (see para 56.18) and a distribution to a non-resident is only prevented from being a capital payment if as a matter of trust law it is not income (TCGA

1992, s 97(1)). This qualification in fact normally operates as a relief, for a distribution to a non-resident has gains in the s 87 pool allocated to it but no charge to tax results (see para 63.22).

The second point arises if in the year in which a distribution is made to a UK resident beneficiary there is no or insufficient relevant income. On this scenario it is treated as a capital payment to the extent that in the year of the distribution it is covered by gains in a s 87 or Sch 4C pool and, to the extent it is so treated it cannot thereafter be taxed as a benefit when relevant income arises in the future (TA 1988, s 740(6)). If it is not covered by gains in the year of receipt the surplus is carried forward and is treated as a benefit under s 740 to the extent that relevant income arises in the following year, as a capital payment to the extent that there is no such income but there are trust gains in that year, and carried forward again to the extent that there is neither. This subject is discussed further in Chapter 13.

Should the distribution be received by a UK resident who is non-domiciled and be matched with unremitted foreign source income, it cannot be a capital payment for the purposes of s 87 even if it is not then taxed under s 740. The result follows because s 97(1) refers to any payment which is not chargeable to income tax. A distribution to a non-domiciliary is chargeable, even if the quantum of charge is subject to the application of the remittance basis (see para 56.23). That this is the right construction is indicated by TCGA 1992, s 97(3) which provides for the position where an insufficiency of relevant income means the benefit is carried forward. As just noted, s 97(3) prevents the fact that the benefit may be taxable in a future year from precluding it being a trust gain and thus confirms that 'chargeable' in s 97(1) means chargeable now or in the future.

Offshore income gains

56.29 As explained in para 71.19, a capital payment within s 87 is treated as an offshore income gain if the trust has a pool of offshore income gains. Should the capital payment be to a non-resident, the offshore income gain may become s 740 relevant income. The relationship between s 740 and offshore income gains is explained in para 71.26.

Compliance

56.30 Perhaps more than in any other area in offshore tax planning there is great uncertainty as to the construction of s 740. In completing a self-assessment return a taxpayer is entitled to adopt a favourable construction if reasonably satisfied it is correct. But he should explain to HMRC very clearly the position he has adopted. In *Tax Bulletin* 40 (April 1999) HMRC included the following statement:

> 'It is incumbent on taxpayers or their advisers to draw [HMRC's] attention to the implications of the legislation when submitting details of transactions to which it may potentially apply.'

It should be stressed that a construction which is favourable to the taxpayer may not be one which minimises liability under s 740. This can be the position where the benefit is a distribution from a trust, for as noted above, if the distribution is not taxed under s 740 it may, if the recipient is UK domiciled be subject to CGT. Supplemental tax could mean a higher rate of tax (see paras 63.29 and 64.11).

Chapter 57

Relevant income

Introduction

57.1 Relevant income is the key concept in charging tax under s 740, for without it any benefit received is free of tax. The definition of relevant income is contained in s 740(3) and, although brief, is of some subtlety. This chapter explores some of the technical issues which arise. In many cases these may in practice be ignored in favour of a broad-brush pragmatic approach (cf Chapter 13).

The definition

57.2 The definition in s 740(3) is expressed by reference to the individual in receipt of the s 740 benefit and to each separate year of assessment. In relation to the individual, income of a given year of assessment is relevant income if it meets the following conditions:

(a) it must arise in that year of assessment to the person resident or domiciled outside the UK;
(b) it must be capable of being used, directly or indirectly, for providing a benefit for the individual or enabling a benefit to be provided for him;
(c) the capability to so use it must be by virtue or in consequence of the transfer or associated operations referred to in s 740(1).

It will be apparent from this that it is, strictly, a misnomer to refer to pools of s 740 income. Instead the starting point has to be the individual in receipt of the benefit. Four questions have then to be asked:

(1) Which non-resident entities are capable of generating relevant income?
(2) How is the income (if any) of those entities computed?
(3) What of that income is relevant income?
(4) Has any of that income ceased to be relevant income?

Which non-resident entities are capable of having relevant income?

57.3 As the conditions listed above indicate, a non-resident entity's income is capable of being relevant income if by virtue or in consequence of the transfer and associated operations it can be used to benefit the individual. Section 740(3) specifically refers to the transfer and associated operations referred to in s 740(1) and thus comprehends both associated operations which caused the income to be payable to the non-resident and those causing the assets out of which the benefit is provided to be available for the purpose (cf para 56.5).

An important point is that as in s 740(1)(b), 'transfer' is prefaced by the definite article. This means that income cannot be relevant income unless the ability to use it to benefit the individual is the result of the transfer which, with or without the associated operations, results in the income becoming payable to the non-resident. Thus, in the example cited in para 56.5, the income from the portfolio of investments held in a trust would not be relevant income in relation to a benefit comprising a distribution of non-income producing land.

More than one entity may generate income that is relevant income in relation to a benefit. Thus if a single transfer to a trust is in part invested directly and in part used to fund a holding company, income in both the trust and the company is relevant income in relation to benefit conferred by the trust out of value provided by the company. If, contrary to what is suggested above in paras 56.3 and 56.5, the true analysis is that the funding of the company is not a separate transfer but simply an operation associated with the trust, then all the income in the trust and the company is potentially relevant income in relation to any benefit conferred by the trust.

Similar analyses may be adopted where one trust advances funds to another. Here the income which is relevant income in relation to a distribution by the transferee trust includes income in the transferor trust, as the creation of that trust is a transfer with which the advance is an associated operation (see further para 56.15). Strictly there are separate pots of retained income in both the transferor and the transferee trust: in contrast to the gains pools there is no mechanism for a combined pool.

An important point to note is that income is caught not merely if it can be directly used to enable benefits to be provided for the individual but also if it an be used indirectly. The inclusion of the word 'indirectly' may give HMRC scope to counter schemes for avoiding the s 740 which would otherwise be effective.

Computing the income

57.4 In defining relevant income, s 740(3) refers simply to 'income'. It is to be inferred that the decision in *Chetwode v IRC* [1977] STC 64 applies (para 55.15) and thus that what is meant by income is income computed as per the rules applicable to UK income tax. Strictly this means expenses incurred by the recipient of the income would not be allowed save insofar as allowed under those rules. But in practice, as will be seen below (para 57.8), income paid away in expenses is excluded from relevant income.

In cases where the income of the non-resident includes dividends from a UK company, the issue arises of whether the income should be grossed up by the tax credit. It may be suggested that where a non-resident company receives the income beneficially, grossing up is not required, for the general rule is grossing up does not apply to UK dividends paid to non-resident companies (ITTOIA 2005, s 399(3)). The position is otherwise where the recipient is a trust, for here grossing up for the tax credit is required (ITTOIA 2005, s 399(3)).

Losses

57.5 An issue which sometimes arises is if after applying UK computational rules the non resident has losses, for example trading losses or allowable losses on rental income. In a domestic UK context, a variety of reliefs result from such losses, and the issue which arises is how far they are available in a s 740 context. One point which is reasonably clear is that if a loss is incurred in one company or trust it cannot be set against income in another entity, even though income in both entities could be relevant income in relation to the same benefit. This result follows because s 740(3) refers to the income which arises to 'a' non-resident person, and thus focuses on each separately.

The more difficult question is whether a loss in one entity may be set against general income in the same entity or carried forward against future profits. Setting against general income is an issue which arises with trading losses, and would appear to be precluded in a s 740 context as the relevant relieving section, TA 1988, s 380, is expressed in terms of relieving the person who incurred the loss from income tax. With carry forward the position is different in that HMRC do allow the loss to be carried forward. It is suggested this is correct in law and accords with TA 1988, ss 397A and 385. It should be noted that strictly such carry forward is subject to a claim being made by the entity incurring the loss.

Deemed income

57.6 Certain receipts of a non-resident or a non-domiciled person which are in accounting terms capital are deemed to be income for the purposes of s 740. The most important category of such receipt is income under the accrued interest scheme. That scheme applies to UK and foreign securities – ie to loan stock and other debt instruments, but not to shares (TA 1988, s 710(2)). Almost invariably securities are disposed of between interest payment dates and, should the disposal be with the accrued interest, such interest element is deemed to be income for the purposes of s 740 (TA 1988, ss 713, 714 and 742(5)). The practical result is that it is very difficult to avoid accrued interest and, as such interest is treated as income for the purposes of s 740, it is relevant income.

Other categories of deemed income for the purposes of s 740 are life policy gains and (in certain circumstances) offshore income gains. The former are discussed in para 72.14 and the latter in para 71.26. Deep discount also counts as income for the purposes of s 740 (ITTOIA 2005, s 459).

Pre-1981 income

57.7 Income is not relevant income if it arose before 10 March 1981, the start date of s 740 (s 740(7)).

What income is relevant income?

57.8 Assuming the income of the non-resident entity has been computed and that it is capable of being relevant income, the issue then arises of whether it is in fact relevant income. In other words does all the income computed as per the rules described above ipso facto become and remain relevant income or is some of it left out.

Income of past years of assessment

57.9 In relation to income arising to the non-resident in a year of assessment prior to that in which the benefit is conferred there are three possible constructions of the definition of relevant income in s 740(3):

(1) All income which arises in that year to the non-resident is relevant income if the recipient of the benefit could then have benefited from it.
(2) Income which arises in the year to the non-resident and is capitalised is relevant income if the recipient of the benefit could then have benefited from it.
(3) Income which arises in the year to the non-resident is relevant income if it has been capitalised and in the year in which the actual benefit is conferred it is capable of being used to benefit the recipient of the benefit.

If s 740(3) is read literally there is much to be said for the first construction, for if the recipient of the actual benefit could have benefited when the actual income arose then, as s 740(3) postulates, the income could directly or indirectly have been used to benefit him, regardless of what was in fact done with it. This construction is reinforced by the manner in which s 740(3) is expressed in terms of individual years of assessment and is so expressed in the present tense. However in reality this construction cannot be right for if it were, income distributed as income would be relevant income even if the recipient of such income distribution were the later recipient of the capital benefit. This conclusion is accepted by HMRC in that relevant income is treated as not including such part of the income as has already become the income of a beneficiary or otherwise been spent (*Tax Bulletin* 40 (April 1999) p 651; Notes on Foreign Pages p FN11).

The difference between the second and third constructions may be summarised by saying that under the second a floating pool of relevant income is created which can be diminished only by allocation to a s 740 benefit (or by being taxed under s 739). Once an amount equal to the income is included in the floating pool the fate of the actual income is irrelevant. On the third scenario, by contrast, it is necessary to look at what has actually happened to the income and it is only relevant income if at the time the benefit is conferred it is still available to benefit the recipient of the benefit.

As a matter of construction it is difficult to chose between these two alternatives. On a strict reading the second may be preferred, for, as noted above, s 740(3) looks at each year of assessment separately and in relation to each such year uses the present tense. However on a wider view this construction produces a somewhat perverse result, for it would mean an individual would be taxed by reference to retained income from which he could not benefit at the time the benefit is conferred. The use of the present tense in 'can directly or indirectly be used for providing a benefit for the individual …' can without undue strain be read disjunctively with the earlier use of the present tense and so taken to refer to the time at which the benefit is conferred. For this reason the third construction may on balance be favoured.

It appears from *Tax Bulletin* 40 that HMRC take the same view. Thus they state that relevant income does not include income which has been genuinely paid away to a beneficiary, without restricting such payment to payment as income. It is further stated that once relevant income has arisen 'and continues to be available to provide a benefit' it must be carried forward until extinguished by a benefit (at p 651). In the light of these comments, it may be suggested that in completing tax returns, taxpayers are entitled to proceed on the basis that the third construction is correct.

Current and future income

57.10 As noted in para 56.1, if at the time the benefit is conferred there is no relevant income, it is carried forward and taxed if relevant income arises in the future. Here the construction of s 740(3) is rather simpler, for the time when the income arises is the sole time at which it has to be considered whether income is capable of being used to benefit the recipient of the benefit. As with past income the theoretical issue arises of whether income distributed as income is caught, and for the same reasons as are given in para 57.9 the answer is not. Accordingly the answer is that relevant income of the current or future year is the capitalised or retained income of that year.

There are however two important qualifications. The first stems from the fact that s 740(3) requires relevant income to be capable of use to benefit the recipient of the benefit. It follows that if by the time there is relevant income –

ie by the time income arises and is capitalised – the recipient of the benefit is wholly excluded, the income cannot be relevant income in relation to him. The same, it may be suggested, would apply if he was just excluded from income, but was still able to benefit from original capital.

The second qualification is if the recipient of the benefit has died. It is difficult to see the relevant income as resulting in a tax charge if it arises in a tax year that in which the recipient has died.

When does past income cease to be relevant income?

57.11 TA 1988, s 744 makes provision for express circumstances in which past income ceases to be relevant income. Further circumstances may be implied from the discussion above.

Section 744

57.12 Section 744 provides that no income can be taken into account more than once in charging tax under ss 739 and 740. Section 744(2) then states that the reference to income being taken into account is, in relation to s 740, a reference to the amount of relevant income taken into account in charging the benefit. The rule where there is a choice as to persons in relation to whom income is taken into account is that it is taken into account in relation to them in such proportions as appear just and reasonable (s 744(1)).

The language of s 744 is loose and one obvious lacuna is that it does not even provide that relevant income is allocated to a benefit conferred in one year before it is allocated to a benefit conferred in another. However in *Tax Bulletin* 40 (April 1999), HMRC do say that relevant income must be carried forward year by year until extinguished by a benefit and this suggests income is in practice allocated to the benefits of earlier years first. Such it may be suggested is correct in law as, given the self-assessment system, it is difficult to see anything else being just and reasonable.

One important point to note is that relevant income is never allocated to a benefit conferred on a non-resident or on a person who is not an individual as such persons are not within s 740 at all (see para 56.18).

In relation to s 739, the reference in s 744 to charging tax is defined in s 744(2)(a) as a reference to tax charged under s 739 on the income. The use of the word 'charged' signifies that unremitted foreign income, which escapes charge because of the transferor's foreign domicile, does not count as having been taken into account. Accordingly it can be allocated to s 740 benefits conferred on other beneficiaries. In this there is a contrast with unremitted income allocated to a benefit not received in the UK by a non-domiciled beneficiary, for as noted above the reference in s 744(2)(c) is merely to income taken into account (see para 56.23).

A point which is not covered by s 744 is how the relevant income allocated to a benefit is selected. At its simplest, there may be a single non-resident entity which has generated relevant income but in such case the income may have arisen over several tax years. Which year's income is allocated first – the youngest or the oldest? In more complicated cases, more than one entity may have relevant income. It could be that such income in one of the entities would be relevant income if benefits were conferred on other UK beneficiaries but that the same is not true of the income in the other entity. Or it could be that at some stage the income in one of the entities would cease to be relevant income (as in the case of a company after the company is sold). Section 744 gives no guidance as to how such problems are solved.

This problem is particularly germane where one trust advances funds to another. Here income in both the transferor and the transferee trust may be relevant income in relation to a benefit from the transferee trust. Yet the classes of beneficiary may be different.

Other circumstances: trusts

57.13 Based on the discussion in para 57.9 above, and assuming the third construction there referred to is correct, it is possible to envisage circumstances in which trust income ceases to be relevant income in relation to a particular beneficiary otherwise than by operation of s 744. The following circumstances in particular require consideration:

(1) Distribution of the capitalised income to another beneficiary.
(2) Exclusion of the beneficiary from the fund of capitalised income.
(3) Transfer of the capitalised income to another trust.

If the income retained in the trust is distributed to another resident beneficiary s 744 will apply. But if the other beneficiary is non-resident, it does not as there is no s 740 liability. Nonetheless, the conclusions reached in para 57.9 indicate that in such case the distributed funds would not remain relevant income if the capitalised income had in banking terms at all times been kept in a segregated account. Greater difficulty arises if the capitalised income has not been segregated, so that the distribution to the non-resident in accounting terms is out of accumulated income but in banking terms is undifferentiated. In such a situation is it possible to identify such a distribution with the retained income or at least argue the distribution is pro rata retained income and original capital? Section 740(3) gives no indication of whether such an approach is correct, and the better view of both s 740(3) and HMRC's comments in *Tax Bulletin* 40 must be that a distribution to a non-resident does not diminish relevant income unless the income has been clearly segregated.

Broadly similar considerations apply if the capitalised income is retained in trust but the beneficiary concerned has previously been excluded from it. Such a situation postulates that capitalised income and original capital have been segregated in banking terms and that the beneficiary is excluded from the former but not the latter, the latter then being used to fund the benefit. In this scenario the analysis offered in para 57.9 indicates this would prevent the income being relevant income. But again it is difficult to see this analysis holding up if the capitalised income has been accounted separately but has not been segregated in banking terms.

In relation to a transfer of the accumulated income to another trust, it is clear that the income remains relevant income in relation to a beneficiary if he is an actual or potential beneficiary of the transferee trust, for then, as s 740(3) requires, the capitalised income is still available to benefit him. But the position would be otherwise if he is wholly excluded from the transferee trust and the capitalised income had at all times been segregated in banking terms. The position is then the same as on an appointment within the original trust.

Trust expenses

57.14 Section 740 nowhere states expressly that income used in expenses is not or at least ceases to be relevant income. In reality, the same analysis must apply to at least income expenses as applies to income distributions. Indeed the case is if anything stronger as income used in expenses is not available to the beneficiaries in any form. With capital expenses the position is more difficult and here it may be that the strict analysis is the same as that offered above in relation to distributions of capital.

In practice HMRC have given no indication of seeking to treat sums used in expenses as relevant income. In the Notes to the Foreign Pages (p FN11) it is made clear that income which has been 'spent' is excluded. The comment in *Tax Bulletin* 40 about income continuing to be available having to be carried forward indicates they consider both income and capital expenses should be deducted, for what is paid in expenses is patently not available.

Companies

57.15 On the basis of the previous analysis in this chapter, the income of a company becomes relevant income if it is retained by the company and added to reserves rather than being used in expenses or distributed as it arises. However, it is perfectly open to a company subsequently to distribute past income – i e accumulated profits – and the issue then is whether the reserves so distributed cease to be relevant income. On the basis of the above conclusions the answer is yes. The point may be reinforced by the fact that, absent a liquidation or buy-back, such a distribution is an income receipt of the recipient shareholder. This is in contrast to the position with trusts, where distributions of accumulated income are of capital. It is inherently difficult to see retained income remaining as relevant income if it has in fact been distributed as income and HMRC's comments in *Tax Bulletin* 40 are certainly not inconsistent with this view.

This leads on to a point that commonly arises in practice where an offshore trust owns an offshore company. Does retained income at the level of the company cease to be relevant income if it is paid up as dividend to the trust. If it does not, there is double counting, in that the same item of value received by the company inflates the total of relevant income both in the company and in the trust. Indeed there could be triple counting if there are several levels of company. The correct analysis it may be suggested is that this double or triple counting does not in fact occur. The technical solution is that s 740(3) postulates income arising to a particular person resident or domiciled outside the UK which is capable of being used to benefit the recipient of the benefit. Once the retained income at company level has been distributed up it is no longer so capable, and instead has changed its character into income of the shareholder trust or company, where, if retained, it again becomes relevant income.

Tax Bulletin 40 does not in terms deal with double counting, although the remark about being genuinely paid away supports the above conclusion. In practice HMRC are widely believed not to double count where income is paid up as income to another higher level in an offshore structure.

It is unclear whether such informal practice, or the legal analysis offered above, apply only where the company has segregated the retained income from capital in banking terms, or whether it is sufficient if the treatment is as per the company's accounts. In contrast to trusts it may be argued the latter is correct given the rules applicable to company accounting under most systems of company law. However the contrary is also arguable.

Sale of a company

57.16 A rather different point arises where a company is sold. Assuming the previous analysis in this chapter is correct, retained income in the company must, when the company is sold, cease to be relevant income in relation to the sellers or, if the seller is a trust, in relation to the beneficiaries of the trust. This follows because once the sale has occurred the income is no longer able to be used to benefit them. The question of whether a sale of itself could amount to a s 740 benefit is discussed in para 56.13, and the conclusion reached is that it does not.

Chapter 58

The motive defence

Introduction

58.1 Ever since first enacted, TA 1988, s 739 has been subject to a motive or purpose defence. The onus is on the taxpayer but, if he discharges it, s 739 cannot render the income of the transferee taxable as his. The defence applies also to s 740, with the result that where it applies, benefits are not taxable under that section either.

The motive or purpose defence has always been a most important part of the transfer of assets code. Without it, the income of any overseas company would be taxable as that of its controlling individual UK shareholders under s 739 unless those individuals had played no part in setting up the structure. This would be so even if the overseas company was formed for entirely commercial reasons, for there is no relief for exempt activities comparable to that in the CFC legislation (cf para 67.8).

No doubt for these reasons, the motive defence has survived to the present time. However, on 5 December 2005, significant alterations came into effect, enacted by FA 2006, Sch 7. These alterations do not apply to transactions effected before 5 December 2005, and so an understanding of both the new and the old law is essential.

The old law is contained in TA 1988, s 741, a section which is a model of brevity. Section 741A contains the new law, with ss 741B–741D covering the interaction of old and new law in relation to structures existing on 5 December 2005.

Satisfying the motive test does not, it should be stressed, mean tax is necessarily avoided altogether. Income arising directly to the trustees of a settlement can be assessed under ITTOIA 2005, s 624 if the settlor is a beneficiary, regardless of motive (see para 59.2). So too a capital distribution from a trust may be subject to CGT under TCGA 1992, s 87 or Sch 4C even if the motive test displaces s 740 (see Chapters 63 and 64).

The statutory conditions

58.2 Under both s 741 and s 741A, the taxpayer has to show to the satisfaction of HMRC that one of two conditions is met. There is a right of appeal to the Special Commissioners, but their decision is likely to be final as the question is one of fact.

Under s 741, the conditions are contained in paragraphs (a) and (b). The condition in para (a) is that avoiding liability to taxation was not either the purpose, or one of the purposes, for which either (i) the transfer, or (ii) any associated operation was effected. The condition in para (b) is that the transfer and any associated operations were (i) bona fide commercial transactions, and (ii) not designed for the purposes of avoiding liability to taxation.

Section 741 is essentially re-enacted by sub ss (1)–(3) and (9) of s 741A. The differences are as follows:

(a) Paras (a) and (b) of s 741 become Conditions A and B in s 741A.
(b) Both conditions in s 741A require the taxpayer to show 'that it would not be reasonable to draw the conclusion, from all the circumstances of the case' that Condition A or, as the case may be, Condition B is met.
(c) Both conditions in s 741A are expressed in terms of 'relevant transactions'. However, that term is defined in sub-s (7) as the transfer and any associated operations and so does not reflect a substantive change.
(d) Condition B includes the words 'more than incidentally' as a prefix to 'designed'.
(e) Condition B qualifies the phrase 'commercial transactions' with the word 'genuine' rather than 'bona fide'. More significantly, s 741A expressly deems certain types of transaction not to be commercial (see para 58.15 below).
(f) Section 741A(1) provides that Condition B has to be considered only if Condition A is not satisfied. The logic of this is that Condition A is failed if just one of the purposes was tax avoidance. As just noted, an incidental tax avoidance purposes is permitted in Condition B but that condition, like the old para (b), applies only where the transactions were bona fide or genuinely commercial.

Avoiding liability to taxation

58.3 The key phrase in both the old and the new law is 'avoiding liability to taxation'.

Meaning of taxation

58.4 In s 741, the word 'taxation' is not defined. However, it has been held to include any form of UK tax, including taxes on capital (*Sassoon v IRC* (1943) 25 TC 154). But the term 'taxation' does not extend to foreign taxes, and so foreign tax planning does not jeopardise s 741. This is so even if the foreign tax avoided is as close to home as the Republic of Ireland (*IRC v Herdman* [1969] 1 All ER 495).

Section 741A, in contrast to s 741, does define taxation: it includes any revenue for whose collection HMRC is responsible (s 741A(7)). Revenue is then defined as including taxes, duties, and national insurance contributions. It thus clear that, as under s 741, all forms of UK tax are caught. But, in addition, imposts such as customs duties and NICs, which might not normally be designated taxes, are counted as taxes for these purposes.

In s 741A the definitions of taxation and revenue are inclusive. At first sight this raises the question of whether foreign taxes could count as 'revenue' or 'taxation' within the general meaning of the term. It is, however, unlikely that s 741A would be construed as introducing such a fundamental change so obliquely and HMRC have given no indication that they so construe it.

Meaning of avoidance

58.5 There is House of Lords authority on what is meant by tax avoidance in s 741. The case concerned, *IRC v Willoughby* [1997] STC 995, 1003, distinguishes between tax avoidance and tax mitigation. In the course of argument in the House of Lords, Counsel for HMRC formulated the distinction as follows:

> 'The hallmark of tax avoidance is that the taxpayer reduces his liability to tax without incurring the economic consequences that Parliament intended to be suffered by any taxpayer qualifying for such reduction in his tax liability. The hallmark of tax mitigation, on the other hand, is that the taxpayer takes advantage of a fiscally attractive option afforded to him by the tax legislation, and genuinely suffers the economic consequences that Parliament intended to be suffered by those taking advantage of the option. Where the taxpayer's chosen course is seen upon examination to involve tax avoidance (as opposed to tax mitigation), it follows that tax avoidance must be at least one of the taxpayer's purposes in adopting that course, whether or not the taxpayer has formed the subjective motive of avoiding tax.'

The significance of this formulation is that, in the only reasoned speech, Lord Nolan described it as generally helpful and said he accepted the essence of HMRC's submissions. Later he encapsulated in his own words what is meant by tax avoidance:

> 'Tax avoidance within the meaning on s 741 is a course of action designed to conflict with or defeat the evident intention of Parliament.'

Purpose

58.6 Both s 741 and s 741A focus on the purpose of the transactions or, in the case of paragraph (b) and Condition B, the purpose for which they were designed.

Case law

58.7 The case of *Philippi v IRC* [1971] 47 TC 75 is authority that in determining what the purpose of the transfer was, it is necessary to ascertain what the transferor in fact intended and that in carrying out that process all relevant evidence may be considered. In *Philippi*, the transferor had in 1951 formed an Irish trust and holding company and then in 1952 transferred UK securities to the company. By the time of the Special Commissioners hearing in 1966 the transferor was aged 87 and unable to travel from Switzerland where he then lived.

The Special Commissioners found the defence was not proved. In the Court of Appeal the taxpayer argued that in the absence of the transferor it was not possible to establish what he had intended and that a reasonable inference was that he had not on the facts intended to avoid UK tax. The reason given for this inference was that the transferor was at the time of the transfer living in Ireland. He was therefore outside the UK tax net.

The Court of Appeal rejected those arguments, stating that the transferor's intentions may be inferred not just from the evidence he gives. The evidence of others can be drawn on, for example that of his spouse or his solicitors, as can correspondence or what transpired at meetings. In the circumstances the Commissioners were entitled to find that, by not calling any evidence, the taxpayer had failed to discharge the burden on him. Only then did it address the issue of inference, commenting that objectively there plainly had been UK tax advantages in the transfer of shares to the holding company.

Philippi is authority as respects s 741 for a further point. The taxpayer, who was the transferor's son, had also himself transferred UK securities to the holding company in 1961 at a time when he was UK resident. He was then aged 23 and serving in the army. His evidence was that he made the transfer because his father and mother had told him to do so and that he had no thought of avoiding taxation. The Special Commissioners accepted his evidence and applied s 741 to that transfer. HMRC appealed this point but their argument collapsed during the hearing in the High Court. As a result it was sometimes said that the ignorant or naïve taxpayer had better prospects under s 741 than the astute or well-informed.

Section 741A

58.8 Section 741A expressly amplifies how purpose is to be ascertained. First, as noted above, Conditions A and B require one to look at all the circumstances of the case and then ask what conclusion as to purpose it would be reasonable to draw. Second, s 741A(4) provides that account must be taken of the intentions and purposes of advisers and of those who design or effect any of the transactions.

In one limited sense, s 741A indubitably alters the law for, by requiring that the purpose of those who design transactions must be taken into account, it would in *Philippi* have caught the son's transaction. But otherwise it is difficult to see s 741A(4), and the new language in Conditions A and B, as doing anything more than codify what the Court of Appeal said in that case.

HMRC practice

58.9 HMRC stated in 1999 that if a transaction involves tax avoidance, that must be considered as one of its purposes even if the transferor did not have the subjective intention of avoiding tax (*Tax Bulletin 40* (April 1999) p 651). In so asserting HMRC were relying on the last sentence of the first quotation from *IRC v Willoughby*, cited in para 58.5 above, specifically the words 'whether or not the taxpayer has formed the subjective motive of avoiding tax'. But those words come in Counsel for HMRC's formulation of law and, while the formulation was described by Lord Nolan as generally helpful, it was so described not generally but in relation to what is meant by tax avoidance.

Two Commissioners' decisions bear on this issue. In *Beneficiary v IRC* [1999] STC (SCD) 134, the Special Commissioners distinguished the question of whether a transaction amounts to tax avoidance from its purpose. In their view, Lord Nolan's words were directed at the former question, and the latter requires a subjective test. So too in *Carvill v IRC* [2000] STC (SCD) 143, 148, another Special Commissioner took the view that the relevant words of Lord Nolan were doing no more than summarise the HMRC argument and that there was clear authority that the test is subjective. It follows that on this point the Special Commissioners have twice found HMRC's disregard of the transferor's subjective intention to be wrong.

Perhaps surprisingly, the new s 741A gives no support for HMRC's view. Indeed, in its emphasis on the purpose of designers and advisers, it focuses the law if anything more strongly on what the actual subjective purpose was.

Transfer and associated operations

58.10 It is to be stressed that the motive defence is lost if either the transfer or an associated operation fails the test. In view of the breadth of the term 'associated operation' (para 56.3) this is a significant restriction. The result is that a wholly innocent transfer may be tainted by a subsequent tax-driven operation.

The Herdman limitation

58.11 In relation to s 741, an important limitation was imposed in *IRC v Herdman* [1969] 1 All ER 495, HL. In that case the House of Lords decided that a distinction must be drawn between cases where the transfer alone causes income to be payable to a non-resident entity and gives the transferor power to enjoy, and cases where these conditions are satisfied only with inclusion of associated operations as well. In the latter event, it is necessary to show that neither the transfer nor any of the associated operations was tainted by tax avoidance. But in the former event only the transfer need be free of tax avoidance; it is irrelevant if subsequent operations were undertaken to avoid tax.

It appears that HMRC intended by amendment enacted in 1969 to reverse *IRC v Herdman* (see *Tax Bulletin 40* (April 1999) p 652). There is no doubt that as a matter of construction this intention was not achieved in relation to s 741, and HMRC now accept this. HMRC practice in relation to s 741 is stated in the following terms in *Tax Bulletin 40* (April 1999) p 652:

> '[It] has been [HMRC's] practice in considering whether a defence under Section 741 is available to consider only the transfer and any associated operations which directly establish a power to enjoy the income of the overseas person under any particular sub-head in Section 742(2).'

IRC v Herdman was decided in relation to s 739. HMRC do not consider the principle enshrined in it applies to s 740, but the correctness of this may be doubted. It is, however, unclear whether, if the principle does apply to s 740, it means that only the transfer has to satisfy the motive test if it alone causes income to be payable to the non-resident. The alternative view is that other operations in such a case must satisfy the test if they are taken into account in determining whether assets are available for the purpose of providing benefits as per s 740(1)(b) (cf para 56.5). The former would be more in accordance with the scheme of the legislation but the latter represents the common sense view.

Section 741A

58.12 In s 741A, sub-s (8) does now reverse *Herdman*. It provides that any operation which is associated with the transfer must be taken into account if, as a result of taking it into account, Conditions A or B would be failed. It must be so taken into account even if, apart from sub-s (8), it would not be taken into account.

Sub-s (8) represents perhaps the greatest difference between s 741A and s 741. As noted in para 54.4 above, the term 'associated operation' is extremely wide, comprehending operations in relation to both the assets transferred, assets representing them, and income they generate. The effect of s 741A(8) is that even if the transfer is within the defence, the defence is lost by a tainted associated operation, even if that operation was not planned at the time of the transfer and has played no role in causing income to accrue to the non-resident.

The commercial defence

58.13 Paragraph (b) of s 741, and Condition B of s 741A, focus on whether the transfer and any associated operations were commercial and what they were designed for.

Section 741

58.14 In *Carvill v IRC* [2000] STC (SCD) 143, the Special Commissioner considered a transaction can be described as commercial if it implements or facilitates a business end or if it is in furtherance of commerce (at para 87). He said that the reference to design requires that the main purpose was not the avoidance of taxation (at para 89). In this it is more accommodating to tax avoidance than paragraph (a) for the latter only operates if none of the purposes is tax avoidance.

Section 741A – commercial

58.15 Section 741A has made a linguistic change to the commercial defence, in that the transactions are now required to be genuinely commercial rather than bona fide commercial. If this effects a change at all, it imports objectivity.

Of more significance is that certain transactions are now deemed not to be commercial (s 741A(5)). Thus a transaction is only commercial if it is in the course of a trade or business or with a view to setting up a trade or business. The making and management of investments does not count as trade or business unless the person by whom it is done and the person for whom it is done are independent persons dealing at arm's length (s 741A(6)). Further, a transaction is deemed not to be commercial if either its nature is such that it would not have been entered between independent persons dealing at arm's length or if any of its terms are non arm's length (s 741A(7)).

Section 741A – design

58.16 As noted above, Condition B has also inserted the word 'incidentally' as a qualification to designed. Assuming the construction of paragraph (b) of s 741 in *Carvill* is correct, this too represents a significant change. Instead of it being necessary to show merely that tax avoidance was not the main purpose, s 741A requires it to be shown that tax avoidance was, at most, incidental.

On the basis that the motive or purpose test is subjective (para 58.9 above), it is difficult to envisage cases where a transaction which fails Condition A as having a tax avoidance purpose will pass Condition B by showing that that purpose was merely an incidental part of the design. It may be that the use of the word 'incidental' has its origins in HMRC's view on the subjective/objective issue, in that if Condition A is failed because objectively some tax is avoided, Condition B is not failed if such avoidance was merely an incidental part of the design.

But assuming HMRC are wrong on the subjective/objective point, Condition B will, by virtue of the insertion of 'incidentally', rarely apply where Condition A does not. If so, the restrictions in it on what counts as commercial will prove to be of little practical significance.

Transitional

58.17 TA 1988, ss 741B and 741C provide for the phasing in of s 741A. If the transfer and all associated operations occurred before 5 December 2005, they continue to be tested against s 741 (s 741B(3)). If some occurred before that date and some after, the former are tested against s 741 and the latter against s 741A (s 741C). Only if the transfer is on or after 5 December 2005 are it, and subsequent associated operations, exclusively judged by s 741A.

The result is that a structure within s 741 on 5 December 2005 remains so unless and until an associated operation that breaches s 741A happens. The occurrence of such an associated operation brings two results:

(1) If absent s 741, the structure would have been within s 739, the income becomes assessable as that of the transferor.
(2) If the case is not a s 739 case, any benefit received by a UK resident beneficiary becomes taxable under TA 1988, s 740 (assuming the conditions for that section are otherwise met).

Section 741C expressly provides that where an associated operation causes a structure previously protected by s 741 to breach s 741A, income arising before 5 December 2005 is not taxable under s 739, and benefits enjoyed before that date are not taxed under s 740. This led some commentators to suggest that even where the breach of s 741A occurs many years later the effect would be to bring all income since 5 December 2005 into charge under s 739 and all benefits enjoyed since that date into tax under s 740. HMRC have, however, confirmed to professional bodies this is not how they read s 741C. In 2006–07 and subsequent years, income and benefits are not taxed unless arising or conferred in or after the tax year in which s 741A is breached (s 741C(7)).

An important point to note is that once a breach of s 741A causes benefits to be taxed under s 740, past as well as future relevant income is taken into account, even if such income arose before 5 December 2005. HMRC have confirmed to professional bodies that this is how they read the legislation.

Once an associated operation occurs in relation to an existing structure which fails the s 741A conditions, all income becomes taxable under s 739 and all benefits are caught by s 740. This is so even if the offending associated operation neither generates income nor enables benefits to be conferred. A limited relieving provision applies, but only where s 741 was satisfied because of paragraph (b), i e the commercial limb. In such case an associated operation which breaches Condition B in s 741A causes only such of the income as is reasonably attributable to the offending associated operation to be taxed under s 739 (s 741D). The apportionment is on a just and reasonable basis.

It is to be noted that this provision does not apply to s 740. It is unclear whether it applies only to paragraph (b) cases not also within paragraph (a) of s 741. It is suggested it does not, on the grounds that under s 741 either or both of paragraph (a) or paragraph (b) can be satisfied.

The relieving provision applies also where a structure has been protected by paragraph (b) of s 741 as respects transactions before 5 December and by

Condition B as respects operations thereafter. It also applies to post 5 December transactions protected by Condition B. However, in all such cases, a strict reading would disapply the relief if the post 5 December transactions were also within Condition A with the result that, under the terms of s 741A, Condition B was not in point at all.

Impact of s 741A

58.18 In the light of the analysis above, it may be suggested that the impact of s 741A is in two principal areas.

The first is to narrow down the use that may be made of the motive defence in commercial and corporate contexts. This is largely beyond the scope of this book, although it does impact on the matters discussed in Chapter 25.

The second area is that the extension to all associated operations means that a new type of tainting has been created. It is no longer sufficient for the setting up of a structure to be free of tax avoidance. Instead, the subsequent conduct of the structure has to remain equally free. This follows because the definition of associated operation, discussed in paras 54.4 to 54.9, offers no basis for restricting the term to operations instigated or procured by the transferor or operations close in time to the original transfer.

It has to be said that such an approach does, in a sense, conflict with the reasoning in *Vestey v IRC* [1980] STC 10. The speeches in the House of Lords are in many places expressed in terms of s 739 penalising individuals who remove assets abroad so as to gain tax advantages in the UK. If a transferor is himself innocent of any tax avoidance motive, is it right s 739 should penalise him when the transferee subsequently engages in tax avoidance, particularly if the latter is wholly without his concurrence or even knowledge. It may be that, in the future, a purposive and restrictive construction of the term 'associated operation' would be adopted. But at present there is little basis for supposing this will happen.

Avoidance and mitigation

58.19 The practical result of the changes to the motive defence made by FA 2006 is that the meaning of tax avoidance is the issue which is critical to the availability of the defence. Almost everything a transferee company or trust does is an operation that is likely to count as associated. The real issue is therefore what the purpose of such operation is and whether, if UK tax considerations are among those purposes, such is avoidance or mitigation. The first of these questions is one of fact but the second is one of law, turning on the all-important distinction between avoidance and mitigation. The basic law on the distinction is the passages from *Willoughby* set out in para 58.5 above, but both the facts of *Willoughby* and other cases give further guidance.

Willoughby

58.20 *Willoughby* itself concerned offshore personal portfolio bonds, which are life policies where the return on maturity is linked to a portfolio of investments selected by the policyholder (see para 5.12).

HMRC had always accepted that policies linked to general funds were not caught by s 739. However, in *IRC v Willoughby* they sought to bring personal portfolio bonds within s 739, on the grounds that in substance the position is no different from where the policyholder owns the investments directly. This contention was rejected by the House of Lords, on the simple ground that a policyholder merely has a right in contract against the life office, and not a right in rem against the assets held by the life office to which his policy is linked.

The underlying reasoning which led the House of Lords to apply s 741 was that offshore bonds are a means of saving, with a tax regime specifically provided by Parliament, namely the chargeable event legislation described in Chapter 72. On the facts Professor Willoughby had genuinely incurred the expenditure involved in buying the bonds and had in fact bought them to provide for his retirement. As such the bonds fell within the category of tax mitigation rather than tax avoidance.

An issue raised by both this reasoning and by the passages in Lord Nolan's speech cited above (para 58.5) is that two tests are applied in distinguishing mitigation from avoidance. The first is whether the taxpayer has, in economic terms, genuinely incurred the consequences of what, in tax terms, he has done and the second is whether what he has done conflicts with or defeats the intention of Parliament. In reality these tests should mean the same thing, in that it is a reasonable inference that Parliament intends tax consequences to follow economic reality. But there is clearly a risk that even where the economic reality test is met, HMRC, and perhaps judges, will speculate on whether Parliament had some other intention.

The facts of *Willoughby* ought to discourage such speculation, involving as they did personal portfolio bonds. Such bonds were widely seen as sophisticated avoidance and in 1998 were targeted by some of the most aggressive anti-avoidance legislation ever enacted (see paras 72.11 to 72.19).

Challenge and Ensign Tankers

58.21 The origin of the distinction between avoidance and mitigation lies in two judgments of Lord Templeman, in *IRC v Challenge Corpn Ltd* [1986] STC 548 and *Ensign Tankers (Leasing) Ltd v Stokes* [1992] STC 226.

These were not s 741 cases but they were cited in *Willoughby*. In *Challenge* Lord Templeman defined avoidance as follows:

> 'Income tax is avoided and a tax advantage is derived from an arrangement when the taxpayer reduces his liability to tax without involving him in the loss or expenditure which entitled him to that reduction. The taxpayer engaged in tax avoidance does not reduce his income or suffer a loss or incur expenditure but nevertheless obtains a reduction in his liability to tax as if he had.'

Lord Templeman then gave examples of the following terms:

> 'When a taxpayer executes a covenant and makes a payment under the covenant he reduces his income. If the covenant exceeds six years and satisfies certain other conditions the reduction in income reduces the assessable income of the taxpayer. The tax advantage results from the payment under the covenant.
>
> When a taxpayer makes a settlement, he deprives himself of the capital which is a source of income and thereby reduces his income. If the settlement is irrevocable and satisfies certain other conditions the reduction in income reduces the assessable income of the taxpayer. The tax advantage results from the reduction of income.
>
> Where the taxpayer pays a premium on a qualifying insurance policy, he incurs expenditure. The tax statute entitles the taxpayer to reduction of tax liability. The tax advantage results from the expenditure on the premium.'

In *Ensign Tankers* Lord Templeman further amplified what he regarded as tax mitigation as follows (at p 240):

> 'A taxpayer who carries out a "bed and breakfast" transaction by selling and repurchasing shares establishes a loss for capital gains tax purposes because he has actually suffered the loss at the date of the transaction. In "back to back" transactions the taxpayer is entitled to any reduction in tax which Parliament has attached to each transaction.'

Section 703 cases

58.22 Another angle on what is meant by tax avoidance may be gleaned from cases decided on TA 1988, s 703. Like s 739, that section is subject to a motive defence. Its terms are not identical to those of s 741, in that the taxpayer has to show that the obtaining of tax advantages was not one of the main objects of the transactions under attack and that the transactions were either carried out for bona fide commercial reasons or in the ordinary course of making or managing investments (s 703(1)).

The Courts have held that the existence of a legitimate commercial use for monies extracted from a company is capable of bringing transactions within the defence (*IRC v Brebner* [1967] 2 AC 18; *Clark v IRC* [1978] STC 614). In a much quoted passage in the former case Lord Upjohn said:

> 'My Lords, I would only conclude my speech by saying, when the question of carrying out a genuine commercial transaction, as this was, is reviewed, the fact that there are two ways of carrying it out – one by paying the maximum amount of tax, the other by paying no, or much less, tax – would be quite wrong, as a necessary consequence, to draw the inference that, in adopting the latter course, one of the main objects is, for the purposes of this section, avoidance of tax. No commercial man in his sense is going to carry out a commercial transaction except upon the footing of paying the smallest amount of tax that he can. The question whether in fact one of the main objects was to avoid tax is one for the Special Commissioners to decide upon a consideration of all the relevant evidence before them and the proper inferences to be drawn from that evidence.'

This passage was cited by the Court of Appeal in *IRC v Willoughby* [1995] STC 143 at 183 in the context of s 741. The principle is clearly relevant, particularly where s 741 or s 741A is being relied on to protect commercial structures.

Special Commissioners decisions since Willoughby

58.23 Since *Willoughby*, Special Commissioners have had to consider the distinction between avoidance and mitigation on at least three occasions.

Carvill

58.24 In *Carvill v IRC* [2000] STC (SCD) 143 the Special Commissioner adopted the Parliamentary intention approach (at para 91), referring to tax avoidance as a course of action designed to conflict with or defeat the intention of Parliament. The case, however, turned more on what the taxpayer had intended rather than whether it was avoidance or mitigation.

Beneficiary

58.25 In *Beneficiary v IRC* [1999] STC (SCD) 134, the Special Commissioners cited at length from *Challenge*, including the passages set out above. The case concerned a non-resident Japanese gentleman with a granddaughter resident in the UK, and two transactions in particular arose for consideration.

The first was that, following English advice, the gentleman had transferred sterling from a UK account to Jersey. The express purpose of moving the money was to protect it from IHT. The Commissioners considered such a transfer was no different from switching the UK account to a foreign currency account at the same bank, which would have been protected from IHT by IHTA 1984, s 157 (cf para 30.12). As such, the switch would plainly be tax mitigation, for it simply takes advantage of an express relief. The Commissioners considered the movement of funds to Jersey was no different and similarly protected by s 741.

The second transaction was the creation by the gentleman of a Jersey discretionary settlement in favour of his granddaughter. He had taken some UK tax advice, but the Commissioners found his purpose was to secure the financial independence of his granddaughter and ensure she did not have to rely on her mother. This part of the case turned on what the settlor in fact intended, rather than on the distinction between avoidance and mitigation. The key finding being that UK tax was a matter of indifference to the settlor.

Snell

58.26 *Snell v HMRC* [2006] STC (SCD) 296, does not concern s 741, but revolves around the motive test which, under TCGA 1992, s 137, has to be satisfied in order to secure the relief for share exchanges in TCGA 1992, s 135. Its relevance in the present context is that the meaning of tax avoidance applied by the Special Commissioner was that formulated in *Willoughby*.

The case is an illustration of how a test based on the presumed intention of Parliament could differ from an economic reality test. Thus, on the facts, the taxpayer had genuinely been issued with loan stock and so had satisfied the economic conditions for s 135 relief. But he had intended from the outset to emigrate and so render the gain non-taxable rather than merely deferred. This, the Special Commissioner held, went beyond the intention of Parliament and so rendered the exercise avoidance rather than mitigation.

The future

58.27 In the light of these Commissioners cases it is clear there is much in the distinction between avoidance and mitigation which has still to be worked out. The new s 741A will indubitably enhance litigation rather than diminish it. A point that should in particular be kept in mind is that HMRC resist reliance being placed on *Beneficiary v IRC*, claiming their appeal to the High Court was settled on terms acceptable to them.

HMRC have promised guidance on s 741A inter alia, giving their view of what is and is not tax avoidance. At the time of writing this is still awaited.

Section II

Settlements

Chapter 59

Attribution of income to the settlor

Introduction

59.1 Chapter 5 of ITTOIA 2005, Part 5 contains legislation counteracting the income tax advantages of settlements. Where it applies it deems the income arising under the settlement to be that of the settlor and it applies whether the trust is resident or non-resident. In the 1970s the income of resident discretionary or accumulation and maintenance trusts was taxed at 45% and that of individuals at 83%, so the tax sheltering potential of resident trusts was significant. Now there is no rate differential and as a result it is fair to say the prime impact of Chapter 5 is on non-resident trusts.

Until 1995, the predecessor legislation to what is now Chapter 5 (TA 1988 Part XV) consisted of a whole series of overlapping provisions which had been enacted piecemeal over the previous 60 or 70 years. The 1995 Finance Act recast Part XV, and it is as recast that it is now rewritten as Chapter 5. There are three principal charging sections, dealing respectively with retained interests, children, and capital sums.

There is a wide overlap between Chapter 5 and TA 1988, s 739 in relation to non-resident trusts. HMRC recognise they cannot tax the same income under both, although they sometimes raise alternative assessments to protect their position (*Tax Bulletin* 40 (1997) p 652; see further para 55.20).

Retained interest

59.2 The primary charging section is ITTOIA 2005, s 624. This deems the income arising under the settlement to be that of the settlor if it arises from property in which he has an interest.

The settlor is regarded as having an interest in the settled property if it is or will or may become payable to or applicable for the benefit of him or his spouse in any circumstances whatsoever. This definition, in ITTOIA 2005, s 625, is in substantially the same terms as that in the former TA 1988, s 673. In relation to that definition it was held that the settlor had an interest if under the terms of the trust there was some contingency, however remote, that he could benefit. Thus in *Muir v IRC* (1966) 43 TC 367 the trustees of a settlement of which the settlor was not a beneficiary could apply income in paying premiums on any policy in which any beneficiary might have a beneficial interest. It was held that such a policy might be held in another settlement under which the settlor was a beneficiary and accordingly that he had an interest in the settlement so long as that power remained exercisable.

Another example of where the settlor has an interest in the settlement is where the trusts are non-exhaustive. In such a case there is a resulting trust to the settlor and, however remote the possibility of the prior trusts failing, he has an interest.

Exceptions

59.3 There are some exceptions to s 625. The first is that the settlor does not have an interest in the settlement if a defined person can only benefit in the event of:

(1) the bankruptcy of a beneficiary;
(2) an assignment or charge by a beneficiary of his interest;
(3) in the case of a marriage settlement, the death of both parties to and any children of the marriage; or
(4) the death of a beneficiary under 25 (s 625(2)).

The second exception is that the settlor is not regarded as having an interest in the settlement if:

(a) a person is alive and under 25; and
(b) during that person's life the settlor and his spouse cannot benefit (s 625(3)).

A third group of exceptions concern spouses (s 625(4)). The term 'spouse' does not include a person whom the settlor might marry in the future but is not currently married to (s 625(4)(d)). This disapplies the decision in *IRC v Tennant* (1942) 24 TC 215, the effect of which is explained in para 60.8. The term 'spouse' also excludes a spouse from whom the settlor is separated and any former spouse. It is thus possible for a settlement to allow the settlor's spouse to benefit in the event of his death.

As from 5 December 2005, references to spouses are extended to civil partners (Tax and Civil Partnership Regulations 2005 (SI 2005/3229)). This means that if the settlor is in fact in civil partnership, he is treated as having an interest in the settlement unless the terms of the settlement expressly exclude civil partners in the same way as spouses. However, in contrast to s 739 and CGT, it is not necessary for the terms of the settlement to exclude civil partners if the settlor is not currently in civil partnership (ITTOIA 2005, s 625(4)(d)).

Income is also prevented from being treated as that of the settlor if it arises from property which he has given to his spouse or civil partner outright (ITTOIA 2005, s 626). For this exception to apply the gift must be truly outright and must not be subject to conditions. Nor must it be wholly or substantially a right to income. As will be apparent these limitations meaning this exemption is not material to settlements in the true sense of the term.

Derived property

59.4 The settlor has an interest in the settlement not just if the settled property is applicable for his benefit but also if what is called related property is so applicable. Related property is defined inter alia as income from the settled property and property directly or indirectly representing the proceeds of the settled property (ITTOIA 2005, s 625(5)). The term used for related property in TA 1988 Part XV was derived property (TA 1988, s 660A(10)). There is a comparable definition of derived or related property in TCGA 1992, s 77(8). In *West v Trennery*, [2005] UKHL 5, [2005] STC 214, the House of Lords held that property can be related or derived property even if it is no longer in the subject settlement.

The facts of *West v Trennery* were that two resident settlements in apparently identical terms had been used to effect an old-style flip-flop (cf para 62.2) so as to reduce the rate of CGT on a subsequent disposal from 40% to 25%. The settlements were created on 1 April and 4 April 1995 respectively and both gave the settlor an initial interest in possession. On 4 April 1995 the settlor transferred shares to the first settlement and elected, as he was entitled to do, that the gain be held over. On the same day the trustees borrowed 75% of the value of the shares and transferred this sum to the second settlement. The loan was secured by a mortgage of the shares. On 5 April 1995, a deed was executed by the trustees of the first settlement excluding the settlor as beneficiary. On 13 April 1995, in the new tax year, the trustees of the first settlement sold the shares.

The effect of TCGA 1992, s 77 was that the gain on that sale would have been taxable at 40% as the settlor's if it could have been said that in the tax year 1995–96 the settled property of the first settlement or any derived property was payable or applicable for the benefit of the settlor in any circumstances whatsoever. The primary argument of HMRC, and the only one maintained in the House of Lords, was that on the facts of the case the cash transferred on 4 April 1995 to the second settlement remained derived property in relation to the first settlement.

The decision of the House of Lords was that it did. Lord Millett's analysis was that the mortgage of the shares meant the money borrowed was proceeds of the shares. The money transferred to the second settlement directly represented those proceeds and any investment of the money in the second settlement would have indirectly represented the proceeds. As such the money or investments were derived property. But on Lord Millett's analysis they ceased to be derived property once the first settlement sold the shares, for then the property which they represented had gone.

Independent act of third party

59.5 The settlor does not have an interest in the settlement just because he could benefit by an independent act of a third party. The High Court so decided in *West v Trennery* [2003] STC 580, 601 and its decision on this point was not appealed.

The point arose in the context of the power in the first settlement to transfer funds to another settlement, the power that was in fact used on 4 April 1995 as part of the scheme. It was admitted that once the settlor was excluded the power could not be exercised with a view to conferring benefit on him. But it was at least theoretically possible that it could be used to transfer the trust fund to a transferee settlement which could later add him as a beneficiary or that he could benefit incidentally as a dependant of those who were in fact beneficiaries. In the High Court, HMRC argued these possibilities meant the settlor still had an interest in the original settlement even after 5 April 1995. In so arguing they relied on *IRC v Botnar* [1999] STC 711 where the Court of Appeal had held that similar possibilities meant the settlor was taxable under TA 1988, s 739 (see para 55.3). Peter Smith J, however, rejected the argument, stating that if the settlor could only benefit by the independent act of a third party, s 77 should not apply.

The point of distinction between *Botnar* and *West v Trennery* is that in *Botnar* the evidence was that the trustees and the settlor did intend that the power to transfer funds to another settlement would be used to enable the money subsequently to be passed to the settlor. Further the drafting of the settlement itself contained subtle pointers to this conclusion. In *West v Trennery* and indeed in all normal cases these factors are not present. Unless therefore they are present or a power to transfer is in fact exercised with a view to benefiting the settlor, standard clauses excluding the settlor and his spouse from any benefit under the settlement may be regarded as effective. It is, however, prudent to provide that a transfer to another settlement is only effective if the settlor and his spouse are excluded from any possibility of benefit under that settlement also.

Collateral arrangements

59.6 The rules defining whether the settlor has an interest in settled property do not say that such interest has to arise under the terms of the settlement. It can be under any circumstances whatsoever. In *Muir v IRC* (1966) 43 TC 367 Pennycuick J qualified the apparent breadth of this phrase by saying that it is confined to cases where the income or property will or may become so payable either 'under the trusts of the settlement itself or under some collateral arrangement having legal force'. He held that the former TA 1988, s 673 could not apply simply because there was doubt as to the true construction of the settlement and on one construction the settlement would be void and the income would belong to settlor by way of resulting trust.

However, the inclusion of collateral arrangements having legal force can trigger liability under ITTOIA 2005, s 624 even where the terms of the settlement exclude the settlor. Thus in *Jenkins v IRC* (1944) 26 TC 265, the trustees were expressly empowered to apply income in repaying any loan they had incurred and they borrowed money interest free from the settlor. The Court of Appeal held that in these circumstances the settlement income was applicable for the benefit of the settlor. *Jenkins v IRC* was followed in *IRC v Wachtel* (1970) 46 TC 543, where the settlor made an interest-free deposit with the bank to support a borrowing by the trustees at a nominal rate of interest. Trust income was applied in reducing the borrowing and corresponding reductions were made in the settlor's deposit.

The principle which emerges from these cases is that if the settlor or his spouse enter into some arrangement in favour of the trust, the settlor has an interest if there are circumstances in which they could be recouped out of trust income or capital. Such arises in the case of interest-free loans, or if the settlor or his spouse guarantees some obligation of the trust and has a right to be indemnified out of the trust assets.

Payments and commercial transactions

59.7 It might be thought that the settlor could have an interest if the trustees enter into a commercial transaction with him. For example, a purchase by the trustees from the settlor would render the purchase price payable to him. It is, however, clear that the words 'payable to' connote out and out parting with the trust property (*Lord Vestey's Executors v IRC* (1949) 31 TC 1 at 83, HL). Accordingly, transactions with a settlor only give him an interest in the settlement if they involve some benefit to him. The case of *Lord Vestey's Executors v IRC* is authority for the proposition that a loan on commercial terms to the settlor is not an application for his benefit.

Minor children

59.8 Trust income paid to or for the benefit of a child of the settlor who is under 18 is treated as the income of the settlor (ITTOIA 2005, s 629). Insofar as the settlement was made after 8 March 1999 or funds were introduced after that date, the same applies to income appropriated to the child without being paid to him in such circumstances that the income is treated as his for tax purposes (ITTOIA 2005, s 629(1)(b) and Sch 2, para 133). The term 'child' includes a stepchild (s 629(7)).

These rules cannot be circumvented by accumulating income and distributing it as capital. A capital distribution to a child of the settlor is taxed as the settlor's income save to the extent that it exceeds retained income in the trust which has not been applied towards income expenses or otherwise treated as the income of the settlor (ITTOIA 2005, s 631). This rule only applies, however, if at the time of distribution the child is under 18; once he is over 18 a distribution to him cannot be treated as his parent's income.

In the case of a resident trust, TA 1988, s 687 allows the settlor credit for tax borne by the trust (s 687(1)(b)). Section 687 does not apply to non-resident trusts but ESC A93 by concession allows such treatment, insofar as the trust has UK source income. To claim this treatment the trust must be fully compliant. ESC 93 is in broadly the same terms as ESC B18 (as to which see para 12.7).

Capital sums

59.9 A capital sum paid by the trustees of a settlement to the settlor may fall to be treated as his income under ITTOIA 2005, s 633. However, it only falls to be so treated to the extent of the income available up to the end of the tax year in which the sum is paid. It is carried forward to the extent it exceeds such income.

Capital sum

59.10 The term capital sum means any capital sum paid otherwise then for full consideration and any loan or repayment of a loan (ITTOIA 2005, s 634). A loan to the settlor cannot be carried forward against future available income once the settlor has repaid it (ITTOIA 2005, s 638). A capital sum paid to the settlor by a company connected with the settlement counts as paid to the settlor by the trustees, but only insofar as the trustees have made a loan to or repaid a loan from the company or otherwise made a payment to it on non-commercial terms (ITTOIA 2005, s 641).

Income available

59.11 The income available as at the end of a tax year is defined as the undistributed income arising under the settlement (ITTOIA 2005, s 635). In the year in which the capital sum is paid, the income available also includes undistributed income of previous years.

The income available is not the full amount of the undistributed income. From it is deducted income previously taken into account under s 633 and income which has otherwise been taxed as that of the settlor (s 635(3)). There is also deducted an amount equal to tax at the rate for trusts on the income otherwise available (s 635(3)(d)). This deduction is made even if the income has not borne the tax, as where the income is the foreign-source income of non-resident trustees. The rate for trusts used is the rate as at the time the exercise is being done, ie currently 40%.

The charge to tax

59.12 The charge to tax is on the grossed-up capital sum. But as noted above, if the capital sum exceeds the income available, the excess is carried forward and taxed against the available income (if any) of future years.

The grossing up is at the rate applicable to trusts (ITTOIA 2005, s 640(1)). As with the deduction in computing income available, grossing up occurs regardless of whether the available income has borne tax and is at the current rate applicable to trusts (ie 40%).

In computing the settlor's tax liability, a deduction is taken for tax at the rate applicable to trusts (s 640(2)). The deduction is capped at the tax actually paid by the trustees on the income available (s 640(3)(c)). Income of past years is allocated on a first-in first-out basis (s 640(4)).

The practical result of this in relation to the foreign income of non-resident trustees is that the settlor is taxed at 40% on the grossed-up amount of the capital sum. This is not a greater charge than would be applicable to the income available under s 624, as 40% tax is treated as deducted in computing the available income. It is far from clear whether any credit can be claimed for foreign withholding tax suffered by the income.

Application

59.13 As s 660A catches income wherever the settlor is able to benefit, s 633 is principally in point where the trust makes a loan to the settlor or the trust repays the settlor. Such loans are caught even if fully commercial. There is a wide overlap between s 633 and s 739(3) (see para 55.8), but the latter would not apply where, for example, the s 741 motive defence is in point.

Meaning of settlement

59.14 The term 'settlement' is given an extended definition (ITTOIA 2005, s 620(1)). It is defined as including any of the following:

- disposition;
- trust;
- covenant;
- agreement;
- arrangement;
- transfer of assets.

This definition is of great importance, for it is copied or incorporated referentially into other legislation, for example the CGT capital payments code (see para 63.2). The definition follows that in the pre-1995 legislation and has been the subject of much litigation, most of it concerning the issue of whether transactions which are not settlements in the normal sense of the term fall to be treated as such.

Outright gifts

59.15 The inclusion of dispositions and transfers of assets in the definition means outright gifts are caught (*Thomas v Marshall* (1953) 34 TC 178, HL). So too is the release by a life tenant or other beneficiary of an interest under a settlement (*IRC v Buchanan* (1957) 37 TC 365).

As noted above, an outright and unconditional gift by one spouse to another does not result in the income being taxed as that of the donor under s 624.

Arrangements

59.16 The import of the word 'arrangement' is wide. In *IRC v Mills* [1974] STC 130 the taxpayer was an infant film star. Her father created a company to supply her services and she engaged herself to it for a modest salary. He then settled the shares in the company on trusts benefiting the taxpayer and in due course, lucrative contracts were made by the company for the provision of the taxpayer's services. The House of Lords held all these transactions were an arrangement.

So too in *Butler v Wildin* [1989] STC 22 two brothers used monies in their children's deposit accounts to acquire £1 shares in an off-the-shelf company at par value. They were appointed directors of the company and caused the company to enter into a development project, inter alia carrying out all negotiations themselves, lending money to the company and guaranteeing bank borrowings. Vinelott J held this whole exercise was an arrangement.

A third illustration is provided by cases such as *Copeman v Coleman* (1939) 22 TC 594 and *Young v Pearce* [1996] STC 743. Such cases involve the controlling shareholder of a private company causing the company to create preference shares and issuing them to children or other relatives. The controlling shareholder then causes the company to pay exceptional dividends on those shares, either by paying the dividend solely to those shareholders or because the shares carry exceptional dividend rights. In such cases, the creation and issue of the preference shares is an arrangement.

The bounty test

59.17 An important limitation to the definition is that some element of bounty must be present (*IRC v Plummer* [1979] STC 793). What that element is must be determined on the facts of each case. However, one test which has been adumbrated is whether or not the recipient under the transaction benefits without the assumption by him of any correlative obligation (*Chinn v Collins* [1981] STC 1, 12 per Lord Roskill; *IRC v Levy* [1982] STC 442).

Normally the bounty test comes into issue when HMRC seek to bring a transaction which is not in fact a settlement into the statutory definition. Thus in *Bulmer v IRC* (1966) 44 TC 1 a group of shareholders sold shares at an undervalue to a company controlled by a friendly party. The terms were that in due course the shares would be re-transferred at the same price and in the meantime the dividends would be used to repay loans incurred to purchase further shares. HMRC claimed the arrangement was a settlement but this argument was rejected on the grounds that it was a bona fide commercial transaction.

The current case of *Jones v Garnett* [2006] STC 283 is a further illustration of the bounty principle. In that case a husband and wife had each acquired one of the two issued shares in a newly-formed company. The husband was director and the wife company secretary. The company's income was generated by the husband's work as a consultant, but the wife performed some administrative tasks. The husband drew a modest salary and so in some years did the wife. Otherwise profits were paid up in dividend on the two issued shares. HMRC invoked what is now ITTOIA 2003, s 624 in respect of the dividends paid to the wife, claiming these were income under a bounteous arrangement in her favour. It was accepted that there was no bounty in the initial share acquisition and so the issue was whether the dividends and the husband's work at a modest salary was part of the arrangement. The Court of Appeal held not, inter alia because the company and the husband did not enter into a service contract and there was no prior commitment for the company to pay dividends. As Sir Andrew Morritt put it, the fact that the structure might in the future have lent itself to tax mitigation was irrelevant to the existence of bounty.

At the time of writing the case is under appeal to the House of Lords.

Settlor

59.18 The term 'settlor' is defined as meaning any person by whom the settlement is made (ITTOIA 2005, s 620(2)). A person is deemed to have made a settlement if any of the following conditions is satisfied:

(a) he has made or entered into the settlement, directly or indirectly;
(b) he has provided or undertaken to provide funds directly or indirectly for the purposes of the settlement;
(c) he has made with any other person a reciprocal arrangement for that other person to make or enter into the settlement.

Multiple settlors

59.19 The original legislation initially made no provision where more than one person fell within the definition of settlor in relation to the settlement. In *Lord Herbert v IRC* (1943) 25 TC 93 Macnaghten J held that as a result none could be assessed for there was no machinery for apportionment between them.

As a result rules were enacted providing that in relation to any given settlor the property and income comprised in the settlement are restricted to that originating from him (ITTOIA 2005, ss 644 and 645). The term 'originating' is further defined as meaning property which the settlor concerned himself provided, whether directly or indirectly, together with property representing that property and income derived therefrom.

These rules are not comprehensive in that they do not cover the position where one person provides property directly and another indirectly. That lacuna was noted but not resolved in *IRC v Mills* [1974] STC 130, 137.

Bounty test

59.20 The bounty test qualifies also the definition of settlor and in particular its extension to providers of funds. The authority for this is *IRC v Leiner* (1964) 41 TC, 589, where Plowman J said that 'provided' imports some element of bounty. His judgment was later referred to with approval in the House of Lords (*IRC v Plummer* [1979] STC 793, 80, 814).

Identifying the provider

59.21 In *IRC v Buchanan* (1957) 37 TC 365 and *d'Abreu v IRC* [1978] STC 538, the releasor of the prior interest was held to be settlor despite the fact that the actual settlor of the original settlement was somebody completely different. It has never been decided whether the holder of a prior interest whose consent is required before a fiduciary power is exercised constitutes himself settlor if he gives such consent.

Providers of services

59.22 In *IRC v Mills* the House of Lords held that the infant film star provided the funds, on the grounds that the source of the dividends paid to the trust was money paid for her work and that, but for the arrangements, this money would have been received by her. In *Butler v Wildin* the brothers were held to be settlors in relation to the arrangement, on the basis that by their skill, services, and temporary loans, they had provided the child shareholders with income-producing shares free of either risk or cost. Likewise in *Copeman v Coleman* and *Young v Pearce*, the controlling shareholder was held to be settlor of the arrangement on the grounds that he had provided the necessary funds indirectly.

In *IRC v Mills* the point was raised as to whether a person who provides services as an employee or a professional adviser can be treated as a settlor. However, the position of such persons was distinguished by the House of Lords, on the grounds that it is the provision of funds, not the provision of services, that renders a person settlor. For that reason it may be said that a person is not a settlor if he provides services to a trust or to a company underlying a trust. The Court of Appeal judgement in *Jones v Garnett* [2006] STC 283 supports this analysis insofar as the provision of the services is not part of the original arrangement. However, *Butler v Wildin* [1989] STC 22 is a warning of the dangers in taking this kind of argument too far.

It is clear from HMRC comments in *Tax Bulletin* 64 that they consider that a person who works for a company on non-commercial terms can thereby constitute himself settlor in relation to any dividends it pays. *Tax Bulletin* 16 (para 61.11) indicates they would take the same point in relation to a person who provides services to the trust on a gratuitous basis. The correctness or otherwise of HMRC's approach will not be clear until *Jones v Garnett* (para 59.17 above) has been decided in the House of Lords.

For the purposes of the settlement

59.23 A person is only settlor if he is consciously associated with the settlement in question. In *Fitzwilliam v IRC* [1993] STC 502, as part of a complex and pre-arranged IHT avoidance scheme, will trustees on 14 January 1980 appointed funds on trust to pay the income to the testator's widow until 15 February 1980 and subject thereto upon trust for his daughter absolutely. On 7 February 1980, the daughter settled this reversion upon trust to pay the income to the widow until 15 March 1980 and subject thereto on trust for the daughter absolutely. HMRC contended that the testator was settlor of this latter settlement on the grounds that by virtue of the appointment on 14 January 1980 he provided funds for the purposes or in connection with it.

The House of Lords rejected this argument in the following terms ([1993] STC 502 at 516 per Lord Keith):

> 'The words "for the purpose of or in connection with" connote that there must at least be a conscious association of the provider of the funds with the settlement in question. It is clearly not sufficient that the settled funds should historically have been derived from the provider of them. If it were otherwise anyone who gave funds unconditionally to another which that other later settled would fall to be treated as the settlor or as a settlor of the funds.'

Underlying companies

59.24 Where liability arises under s 624 because the settlor has an interest in the settlement an issue arises of whether the income of a company owned by the settlement can be attributed to the settlor. Until 1989 it was expressly provided that it could be (TA 1988, s 681(3), (4)) but this provision was repealed on abolition of the rules providing for apportionment of the income of close companies.

Following such repeal it has generally been accepted that the income of an underlying company is not income arising under the settlement. The authority cited is *Chamberlain v IRC* (1943) 25 TC 317. Here the taxpayer had transferred assets to a holding company in return for shares and loan stock. The company then created a special class of preference share which were subscribed for at a cost of £10 per settlement by four children's settlements created by the taxpayer. Subsequently the taxpayer caused the company to pay each settlement over £2,000 in dividends.

HMRC argued that the incorporation and structuring of the holding company, together with the actual settlements, were an arrangement and that the property and income comprised in such notional settlement were the property and income of the company. Lord Thankerton, with whom Viscount Simon and Lord Atkin concurred, conceded that the incorporation and operation of the holding company could be part of the arrangement. But then he said that the crucial point was 'what the property comprised in the settlement consists of'. His view that such property was not the assets of the company but merely the assets of each of the four trusts. The formation of the company provided an investment for the trusts but 'such investment was not essential to the continuance of the trusts under the deed of settlement'.

There is clearly one situation in which income in a company owned by a settlement could be caught. This is if the settlor makes a gift direct to the company. As it is established that an outright gift falls within the statutory definition of 'settlement', it is difficult to see how the donor would not have an interest in the gifted property within s 624 if he was a beneficiary under the settlement.

The more normal situation is where the trustees transfer assets to an underlying company in return for shares or a shareholder loan. If such a transfer was envisaged by the settlor when he created the settlement, it may well be part of a single arrangement, particularly as an arrangement can in part be made up of commercial or non-bounteous transactions (*Chinn v Collins* [1981] STC 1, 7 per Lord Wilberforce). But, following *Chamberlain* the true analysis is that investment into the holding company is merely an investment of the assets settled by the settlor and is not essential to the continuation of the settlement. As such the assets in the settlement are the shares in and loans to the company, not the company's assets.

To date HMRC have never given any indication of invoking s 624 in relation to company income in the case of a straightforward trust and company structure. It is noteworthy that in *IRC v Mills*, the company income was not assessed on the taxpayer. Further in the extended *Tax Bulletin* article on TA 1988, ss 739 and 740, comments on the overlap between ss 739 and 624 clearly contemplate that only s 739 can be invoked to attack the income of an underlying company (*Tax Bulletin* 40 (April 1999), p 652).

Foreign element

59.25 Income is treated as income arising under the settlement and so potentially within ITTOIA 2005, Part 5 chapter 5 if it is either:

(1) income chargeable to income tax, whether by deduction or otherwise; or
(2) income which would have been so chargeable if received by a person resident and domiciled in the UK (ITTOIA 2005, s 648).

On the face of it this brings in all income wherever arising. In fact a territorial limit is imposed by s 648(3). This excludes from the term 'income arising under the settlement' income which satisfies the following conditions:

(a) Had the income in fact arisen to the settlor he would not have been chargeable to income tax by deduction or otherwise.

(b) The reason why he would not have been so chargeable is that he is not resident in the UK or not domiciled in the UK.

Non-resident settlors

59.26 The effect of s 648(3) is that if the settlor is not resident in the UK, the foreign income of the settlement is not deemed to be his. Conversely, UK income of the settlement is treated as his. These rules follow whether the settlement is resident or non-resident (*IRC v Kenmare* (1957) 37 TC 383, HL).

One result of this is that if the settlor is non-resident, a non-resident settlement with UK source income may be in a better position if settlor-interested than if not. This is so if the settlement has UK beneficiaries, for here the trustees do not enjoy the limitation of tax on UK dividends and interest to tax withheld (FA 1995, s 128(5); see para 34.14). The settlor by contrast does, and as the income which arises under the settlement is deemed to be his by s 624, the limitation should apply. An exception may arise for UK interest payable gross to non-residents, for here such income would not, as s 648(3) requires, have been charged to tax by deduction had it arisen directly to the non-resident settlor. This exception is not in point in relation to dividends as the mechanism for taxing UK dividends paid to non-residents means tax at the dividend ordinary rate is treated as having been paid at source (ITTOIA 2005, s 399).

Non-domiciled settlors

59.27 In relation to resident but non-domiciled settlors, foreign source income is plainly excluded unless remitted. In contrast to other comparable provisions such as TA 1988, s 743(3) (see para 55.22) s 648 contains an express rule dealing with remittance in a subsequent year. Such income is deemed to arise under the settlement in the year of remittance if the settlor would have been chargeable had he then been actually entitled to it (s 648(5)).

This provision was, when originally enacted in 1995, intended to ensure that the remittance basis operates in the same way as if the income had in fact accrued to the settlor (*Inland Revenue Press Release* 28 March 1998, reproduced [1995] STI pp 549–50). Such is indeed its effect for the following reasons:

(1) Income which arose before the settlor became UK resident is excluded because the settlor would not have been chargeable on its remittance had it in fact been his (cf para 40.6).
(2) The same reasoning applies to income whose source has ceased in a prior tax year (cf para 40.7).
(3) Income which has been given away by the settlor, or distributed by the trustees to another beneficiary, is not caught if that person remits it, for even if it arose in the year of remittance and were then the settlor's, the alienation abroad principle would prevent a tax charge (cf Chapter 42).

What is clear is that remittance by the settlor personally following a distribution to him is caught unless the source of the income has ceased in a prior tax year. So too, it may be suggested, is remittance by the trustees on the grounds that the statutory fiction in s 648(5) is wide enough to treat their acts as those of the settlor.

Accrued interest

59.28 Accrued interest taxable under the accrued interest scheme is treated as income arising under the settlement (TA 1988, s 720(6)). If, therefore, Chapter 5 applies, the accrued interest is included in the income deemed to be the settlor's. But this does not result in a tax charge if the settlor is non-resident, as non-residents are not within the scheme (TA 1988, s 715(1)(f)). Nor does it apply to accrued interest on foreign securities if the settlor is non-domiciled, for non-domiciliaries are not within the scheme as respects foreign securities (TA 1988,s 715(1)(j)). But this last point does not apply to Irish securities as the exemption is expressed with reference to the remittance basis for relevant foreign income.

The settlor's liability

59.29 Income treated as the settlor's under ITTOIA 2005, ss 624 and 629 is treated for all income tax purposes as that of the settlor and the settlor alone, (ITTOIA 2005, s 624(1) and 629(1)). The settlor is chargeable under whichever provision of the UK tax code would have applied had it in fact been his income (ITTOIA 2005, s 619(2)). This means inter alia that the settlor takes the benefit of the dividend rates.

In *Tax Bulletin 84* HMRC suggest that where the trust is settlor-interested, the trustees are liable to pay tax at the rate applicable to trusts, leaving the settlor with a credit for that tax. In an offshore context this would apply to the UK source income of the trust and, if right, would mean further tax would rarely be payable by the settlor, a repayment being more common, for example, if he is not a higher-rate taxpayer. But it may be doubted whether the provision HMRC rely on, s 686(2)(b), bears the construction HMRC place on it, for ITT0IA 2005, ss 624 and 629 deem income to which they apply to be the income of the settlor and the settlor alone. On this basis, the trustees would be liable simply for basic or lower-rate tax, leaving the balance recoverable by HMRC from the settlor directly.

The settlor is entitled to recover any tax he pays under ss 624 or 629 from the trustees (ITTOIA 2005, s 646).

Subsequent distributions

59.30 Should offshore trustees distribute trust income to a UK beneficiary it is not taxed again if it has already been taxed as the settlor's under ITT0IA

2005, s 624 or s 629. Where the recipient is the settlor the distribution is simply deemed not to be income (ITTOIA 2005, s 685A(5)). In the case of other beneficiaries it carries a non-refundable credit equal to tax at the higher rate (ibid s 685A(3)).

These reliefs do not apply where the settlor is non UK domiciled and the trust income is unremitted foreign income. In such case, the income does not count as income arising under the settlement (ITTOIA 2005, s 648(3)) and so is not, as the relevant relieving provisions require, taxed under ITTOIA 2005, s 619.

These reliefs have only applied in express form since 6 April 2006 (FA 2006, Sch 13 para 6(2)). But it emerged during consultation in connection with their introduction that they represent previous HMRC practice.

An interesting question would arise if HMRC assessed the trust income on the settlor under TA 1988, s 739 rather than ITTOIA 2005, s 624. In practice this is unlikely to happen as HMRC invoke s 624 rather than s 739 (cf paras 59.1 and 55.20).

Trusts subject to a life interest

59.31 The provisions described above apply only to discretionary distributions of income (ITTOIA 2005, s 685A(1)(b)).

Where the settlor is life-tenant, the income is in any event his, and the sole effect of ITTOIA 2005, ss 624 and 629 is to attribute to him amounts which would otherwise be deductible as income expenses (cf para 12.2). Should another beneficiary be life-tenant, the fact that the income is treated for all purposes as that of the settlor means it cannot be taxed as that of the life-tenant. But an exception may arise for unremitted foreign income if the settlor is non-domiciled. Arguably such income could never fall to be treated as income arising under the settlement as by belonging to the life-tenant it has already been given away and thus is incapable of being rendered taxable by remittance (cf Chapter 42).

Chapter 60

Attribution of gains to the settlor

Introduction

60.1 From 1981 until 1991 gains arising to a non-resident settlement were not in any circumstances charged to UK CGT as they arose. The sole respect in which they were exposed to UK taxation was under the capital payments code, described in Chapters 63 and 65. In 1990 and early 1991 there was widespread press comment on the tax avoidance possibilities of offshore settlements. This comment led to legislation in the 1991 Finance Act attributing the gains of certain offshore settlements to the settlor. In 1998 embarrassment on the part of a government minister led to an enlargement of the categories of settlement caught by the 1991 legislation.

The legislation is badly thought out and unduly severe. Until 1991, no anti-avoidance legislation had attributed either income or gains of any settlement to the settlor unless he or his spouse were actual or potential beneficiaries or enjoyed a benefit. The 1991 legislation breached this sensible principle, for attribution is possible even if the settlor and his spouse are wholly excluded. In this respect the gains of offshore settlements are more severely taxed than their income, and indeed more severely taxed than income and gains realised in onshore settlements.

The present legislation is TCGA 1992, s 86 and Sch 5. It applies if at any time during the tax year in which the gains arise two principal conditions are satisfied:

(1) The settlor has what is called an interest in the settlement.
(2) The settlement is a qualifying settlement.

It may be that s 86 is disapplied by European law in relation to settlements from which the settlor is excluded. This issue is discussed in paras 49.9 and 49.10.

The settlor

60.2 The gains of a qualifying settlement can only be attributed to the settlor if in the year in which the gains arise he is both resident and domiciled in the UK (TCGA 1992, s 86(1)(c)). Self-evidently they can only be attributed to him if he is alive during the year, and, in a curious relieving provision, they cannot be attributed in the year of his death (TCGA 1992, Sch 5 para 3).

A person is a settlor in relation to a settlement if the settled property consists of or includes property originating from him (ibid, Sch 5 para 6). The term 'originating' is further defined as property provided by the settlor and property representing property so provided. The term 'provided by' figures in the income tax settlement code in ITTOIA 2005, Part 5, Chapter 5 and connotes bounteous provision (see para 59.20). As in the income tax code, the provision can be direct or indirect and reciprocal arrangements are countered.

The settlement

60.3 The term 'settlement' is not given the same extended income tax definition as applies under ITTOIA 2005, Part 5, Chapter 5 (cf para 59.14). Accordingly, s 86 applies only to settlements in the true sense of the term. However, bounty must have been involved in the making of the settlement for, as noted above, a person is only settlor if he has made bounteous provision in some form. It follows that a settlement made to attract and motivate staff is outside s 86 (*Tax Bulletin* 16 (April 1995) p 204; see further para 26.5).

Interest in the settlement

60.4 Gains can only be attributed to the settlor if he has what is called an interest in settlement at some time in the year in which the gains accrue. The settlor is treated as having an interest in the settlement if one of two conditions is satisfied (TCGA 1992, Sch 5 para 2(3)):

(1) property or income in the settlement is or will or may become applicable for the benefit of a defined person or payable to him in any circumstances whatsoever; or
(2) a defined person enjoys a direct or indirect benefit from any property or income in the settlement.

The following individuals are defined persons (ibid, Sch 5 para 2(3)):

(a) the settlor;
(b) the settlor's spouse;
(c) any child of the settlor or of his spouse;
(d) the spouse of any child;
(e) any grandchild of the settlor or of his spouse; and
(f) any spouse of such grandchild.

For these purposes step relationships are treated as natural (ibid, Sch 5 para 2(7)).

Subject to the exceptions described below, the principal effect of the rules is that the settlor has an interest in the settlement if he, his children, his grandchildren or any of their spouses is an actual or potential beneficiary. But it should be remembered that the settlor can have an interest in a settlement even where the class of beneficiaries wholly excludes such persons. Under head (2) above, the settlor has an interest in the settlement in any year in which a defined person receives a benefit.

Exceptions

60.5 There are important exceptions to these rules. One is that the settlor does not have an interest in the settlement if a defined person can only benefit in the event of:

(a) the bankruptcy of a beneficiary;
(b) an assignment or charge by a beneficiary of his interest;
(c) in the case of a marriage settlement, the death of both parties to and any children of the marriage; or
(d) the death of a beneficiary under 25 (TCGA 1992, Sch 5 para 2(4)).

Another exception is that gains are not attributed to the settlor if only one defined person has an interest in the settlement in a year of assessment and that person dies during the year or if two or more persons have interests and they all die during the year (TCGA 1992, Sch 5 paras 4 and 5). Gains are not attributed either if the only defined person with an interest in the settlement is the spouse of the settlor, or the spouse of one of his children or grandchildren, and the marriage ends during the year concerned (ibid, Sch 5 para 4).

A third and very important exception concerns the inclusion of grandchildren and their spouses in the class of defined person. This exception applies if two conditions are satisfied:

(a) the settlement was created before 17 March 1998; and
(b) all individual defined persons apart from grandchildren and their spouses are completely excluded from actual or potential benefit.

Where these conditions are satisfied, the settlor is not treated as having an interest in the settlement unless and until it becomes 'tainted' ie one of four conditions specified in Sch 5 para 2A are met (para 2A(1)). The most important of those conditions is the addition of property to the settlement; all four conditions are discussed in Chapter 61 below.

Effectively, this exception prevents gains from being attributed to the settlor if the settlement was made before 17 March 1998 and it is a grandchildren's settlement from which the settlor, his children and their respective spouses are totally excluded. It should be noted that it is not necessary for them to have been excluded on or before 17 March 1998; provided the tainting conditions have not been breached since then, all that is necessary is that the settlor, his children, and their respective spouses are excluded throughout the tax year in which the gains are realised.

Independent act of third party

60.6 The definition of interest in the settlement does not, in contrast to that in s 660A, include reference to derived property. This means the House of Lords decision in *West v Trennery* [2005] STC 214 is not relevant (as to which see para 59.4).

At first instance in *West v Trennery* Peter Smith J indicated that in deciding whether the settlor had an interest in the settlement for the purposes of TCGA 1992, s 677, no account should be taken of what an independent third-party transferee of the settled property might do. In the context of s 86, the point may be material where all defined persons are excluded from benefit, but the trustees have power to transfer all or part of the trust fund to another settlement. Although it would be prudent to ensure that such a transfer is only permitted if all defined persons are expressly excluded from the transferee settlement, *West v Trennery* indicates this is not essential so long as there is no scheme or intention on the part of the transferor trustees to use the transfer as a means of benefiting any of the defined persons. The point is discussed further at para 59.5.

Collateral arrangements

60.7 Head (1) in the definition at the beginning of para 60.4 above does not in terms require the settled property to be applicable for the benefit of, or payable to, the defined person under the terms of the settlement. The wording is similar to that in its income tax equivalent (ITTOIA 2005, s 625(1)). It has been held in relation to the predecessor to that wording (TA 1988, s 673(2)) that the property or income can be payable or applicable under some collateral arrangement having legal force (*Muir v IRC* [1966] 43 TC 367 at 381 per Pennycuick J). This is discussed further in para 59.5.

Future spouses

60.8 Even if the settlor, his children and grandchildren, and their respective spouses are excluded, the settlor still has an interest in the settlement if the settlement allows benefit to be conferred on a future spouse at a time when such person is a spouse. This is the effect of the decisions in *IRC v Tennant* (1942) 24 TC 215 and *Unmarried Settlor v IRC* [2003] STC (SCD) 274. In the first of these cases the settlor held an overriding power of appointment and in the second the trustees had an unrestricted power to add beneficiaries. In both cases the settlor was unmarried, but had he or she married in the future the power could, as a matter of construction, have been exercised in favour of the future spouse. This, it was held, was sufficient to render the settlement settlor-interested within the meaning of the then provisions attributing the income and gains of the resident settlements to the settlor, namely FA 1938, s 38 and TCGA 1992, s 77.

The present versions of FA 1938, s 38 and TCGA 1992, s 77 remove this point as respects resident settlements. This is because TCGA 1992, s 77(3)(a) and ITTOIA 2005, s 625(4)(d) now exclude from the term 'spouse' any person to whom the settlor is not currently married but may later marry. Unfortunately equivalent exclusions are not found in TCGA 1992, Sch 5. The result is that if attribution of gains under Sch 5 is to be avoided the terms of the settlement must preclude benefit to a future spouse at any time when she is a spouse. Any well drawn exclusion clause should achieve this.

Civil partners

60.9 Regulation 126 of the Tax and Civil Partnership Regulations 2005 (SI 2005/3229) has extended all references in Sch 5 to spouses to include civil partners. This regulation came into force on 5 December 2005 (reg 1(1)).

Its obvious effect is that if, under any settlement, the settlor, his children and grandchildren, and their respective spouses are all excluded, the entry of one of them into civil partnership will bring the settlement into Sch 5 unless, before the entry into civil partnership, the trustees amend the terms of the settlement to exclude civil partners. But as a matter of strict construction the effect of the regulations is wider for the decisions in *IRC v Tennant* and *Unmarried Settlor v IRC* are in point. The effect of those decisions is that unless the terms of the settlement preclude any benefit to a future civil partner at a time when he is civil partner, the settlement is within Sch 5.

Self-evidently no settlement drafted before the Civil Partnership regulations were mooted excludes civil partners for the concept of civil partnership was then alien to English law. The result is that on 5 December 2005 all non-resident settlements in which the settlor did not have an interest for the purposes of TCGA 1992, Sch 5 became ones in which he did.

Rather surprisingly this point is not covered in the Tax Bulletin article on the Tax and Civil Partnership Regulations (*Tax Bulletin 80* (December 2005 p 1252). But in correspondence with STEP dated 23 November 2005, HMRC recognised the correctness of analysis outlined above as a matter of construction. HMRC indicated that in relation to settlements drafted thereafter, civil partners should be expressly excluded in the same way as spouses.

As respects existing settlements HMRC gave an assurance in the letter that 'the introduction of the Civil Partnership Act 2004 will not alone result in a change of status for non-resident settlements that are not regarded as settlor-interested under existing law'. In most cases this should provide the requisite level of comfort, but as HMRC also say, trustees may, where the terms of the settlement so permit, wish to amend its terms by appointment or exclusion to reflect the change in the law.

Whether a private letter to STEP is a satisfactory means of granting what is, in effect, an extra-statutory concession, is open to question.

Qualifying settlement

60.10 When TCGA 1992, s 86 and Sch 5 were first enacted a settlement was only a qualifying settlement if either:

(a) it was made on or after 19 March 1991; or
(b) it was made before that date but one of the four 'tainting' conditions in Sch 5 para 9 had been breached since then. Those conditions are in all material respects the same as those which apply to grandchildren's settlements under para 2A (supra) and are thus as described in Chapter 61.

As a result of the amendments introduced by FA 1998, s 132, all settlements are now qualifying settlements, regardless of when made. There is one transitional exception, namely protected settlements. Under Sch 5 para 9(10A), a settlement is a protected settlement in any tax year if the beneficiaries are confined to children of the settlor who are under 18, unborn children of the settlor, and persons who are not defined persons at all. A child counts as under 18 if he is under 18 at the beginning of the tax year concerned. Future spouses of the settlor or his children are also allowed to be included as beneficiaries.

A protected settlement is not a qualifying settlement provided:

(a) it was created before 19 March 1991,
(b) it was a protected settlement on 6 April 1999, and
(c) none of the five conditions set out in Sch 5 para 9 has been breached since 19 March 1991 (Sch 5 para 9(1B)).

The five conditions are the four described in Chapter 61 which applied to all pre-1991 settlements until 17 March 1998 plus one additional one. This is that the settlement has not ceased to be a protected settlement at any time after 5 April 1999 (Sch 5 para 9(6A)). The main circumstance in which a protected settlement would cease to be a protected settlement is if a child of the settlor attained the age of 18 and was not excluded before the end of the tax year.

On a strict construction of para (10A), a settlement is not protected if the settlor's grandchildren are beneficiaries. In practice, however, HMRC allow the beneficiaries to include grandchildren (*Tax Bulletin* 38 (December 1998) p 620).

Computation of the gains attributed

60.11 Where the conditions for the operation of s 86 are satisfied, a computation is made of the amount on which the trustees would have been chargeable to CGT for the tax year concerned if they were UK resident (TCGA 1992, s 86(1)(e)). Certain rules apply in determining this amount (TCGA 1992, Sch 5 para 1):

(1) It is assumed no annual exemption is available.
(2) The fact that gains would be attributed to the settlor under TCGA 1992, s 77 if the settlement were resident is ignored.
(3) Current year losses are allowed. Losses carried forward from previous

years are also allowed, but only if in the year concerned any gains would have been attributable to the settlor under s 86.

(4) No account may be taken of either losses or gains which accrued before 19 March 1991.

(5) Where the trustees are participators in a non-resident close company, gains in the company may be taken into account as if they had accrued in the settlement if two conditions are satisfied. First, the gains must be such as would be apportioned under TCGA 1992, s 13 if the trustees were resident, and second, the trust's interest in the company must have originated from the settlor. The application of s 13 to non-resident trusts is considered in para 66.24, and, as there noted, tax assessed on the settlor by virtue of s 13 may be credited against any tax due from him in respect of distributions from the company made within the specified period of the s 13 gain accruing.

The charge on the settlor

60.12 The result of the computation described above is that there is either a net gain or a net loss for the year concerned. In either event, the computation at this stage is made without giving regard to taper relief. If there is a net loss it is *not* attributed to the settlor and is only able to be relieved by carry forward against future trust gains as described above.

If there is a net gain, it is included in the net gains on which the settlor is chargeable to tax (TCGA 1992, s 2(5)(aa)). Personal losses of the settlor which cannot be offset by his personal gains may be deducted from this net gain (ibid, s 2(5)(aa)(i) and (6)). Taper relief is then applied on the basis of the actual gains which accrued to the trust, trust losses and the settlor's otherwise unused personal losses being allocated to and thus extinguishing trust gains in the manner which produces the most favourable taper result (ibid, ss 86(1)(e)(ii), 2A(6) and 2(5)(aa)(ii)).

Gains in an underlying company which are attributed to the trust under s 13 are not eligible for taper (see para 66.12), and this lack of taper is preserved on attribution to the settlor for the settlor enjoys only the taper for which the trustees would have qualified. Gains apportioned under s 13 are however eligible for loss relief and so would be relieved first after the settlor's personal losses since this produces the most favourable taper result.

Reimbursement by the trustees

60.13 The settlor has a statutory right to recover any tax he has paid from the trustees (ibid, Sch 5 para 6). HMRC do not regard this right, or any provision in the trust deed recognising it, as causing the trust income to be assessable on him under TA 1988 s 739, ITTOIA 2005, s 624 or as a reserved benefit for IHT purposes (SP 5/92 paras 8–10).

In practice few offshore trusts expressly recognise the right of reimbursement. In many cases the settlor is a beneficiary, and so the trustees can reimburse him in exercise of their fiduciary powers. But where this is not so, it is widely believed that the settlor is in difficulty in enforcing reimbursement. This is because the right to reimbursement is conferred by an English statute, and so, unless the proper law of the settlement is English, it is not part of the trust's governing law. As such it is generally believed that a court outside the UK would have some difficulty in recognising it (see for example *Re T Settlement* [2002] 4 ITELR 820, 822).

A possible solution for the settlor may be to bring proceedings in the English courts and then serve the trustees out of the jurisdiction. Assuming this is possible and that he then obtains judgment, one of two courses is likely to be open to him:

(1) If the trust has English assets he could enforce against those.
(2) If the trust is based in a jurisdiction with which the UK has a convention for the mutual recognition of judgments, he could enforce the judgment against the trustees in their home jurisdiction.

The difficulty with this solution is that it may not be possible to serve the trustees out of the jurisdiction with the result that the initial English proceedings will not effectively be brought. In *Prestwich v Royal Bank of Canada Trust Co (Jersey) Ltd* [1998] 1 ITELR 565 Judge Howarth held that such service was possible as of right under the former RSC Ord 11 r 1(2)(b) or, that failing, that the settlor was entitled to leave under Ord 11 r 1(1)(n). But under the present Civil Procedure Rules, the wording of the equivalent to rule 1(1)(n) is restricted to claims by HMRC (rule 6.20(16)). Rule 1(2)(b) is replicated by the present rule 6.19.1A(2) but it may be questioned whether Judge Howarth's construction is consistent with the Court of Appeal decision in *Re Harrods (Buenos Aires) Ltd (No 2)* [1991] 4 All ER 348.

A second solution is suggested by a Jersey case, *Re T Settlement* [2002] 4 ITELR 820. Here a standard exclusion clause excluded the settlor from all possibility of benefit under the settlement. The Royal Court approved a variation of this clause to permit reimbursement of tax liabilities incurred by the settlor as a result of the operation of the settlement. This variation was approved by all the adult beneficiaries and was sanctioned by the Court under Article 43 of the Trusts (Jersey) Law 1984 on behalf of minor and unborn beneficiaries. Article 43 only applies if the court is satisfied the proposed variation is for the benefit of the beneficiaries concerned. The benefit relied on was the discharge of the beneficiaries' moral obligation to the settlor and increased investment flexibility. Those seeking to follow this case should however note that the facts were exceptionally strong in that the settlor was a lady aged 98 who had transferred all her assets to the settlement for the benefit of her family prior to moving back to the UK.

Should the trustees end up reimbursing the settlor by one means or another, HMRC do not regard such reimbursement as a capital payment within TCGA 1992, s 87 (SP 5/92 paras 8–10).

Sch 5 makes no provision requiring trustees to give the settlor information about gains. Where he is not a beneficiary, issues may arise of whether he is entitled to such information, particularly if the result of such information would be a tax charge on the settlor and a claim against the trust.

The difficulties the settlor may experience in enforcing his indemnity is one of the main reasons for supposing that at some stage the application of s 86 to settlements from which the settlor is excluded may be held to breach European law. This point is discussed in paras 49.9 and 49.10.

Temporary non-residence of the settlor

60.14 If the settlor is non-resident for less than five complete tax years, all gains which would have been attributed to him under s 86 had he not emigrated are treated as accruing to him in the year of his return. This is the same as with gains accruing to him directly (see para 27.7) and is expressly provided for by TCGA 1992, s 10A(2)(b).

TCGA 1992, s 86A addresses a problem this poses. This problem is that until the settlor returns, gains in the trust realised in the intervening years are trust gains within TCGA 1992, s 87 because, as the settlor is then non-resident, s 86 does not apply. Should capital payments be made to resident beneficiaries, they are taxed by reference to the trust gains and yet, when the settlor returns, he is then assessable on those gains under a combination of ss 10A and 86.

Section 86A addresses this problem by defining two sums (sub-s (1)(b)). These are:

(a) The pool of tapered trust gains carried forward for the purposes of s 87 as at the end of the year of the settlor's departure.
(b) Distributions during the intervening years actually charged to CGT as gains accruing to resident beneficiaries under the capital payment rules.

If the distributions at (b) exceed the pool carried forward at (a) there is an 'excess'. Where there is such an excess, gains realised by the trust in the intervening years cannot be assessed on the settlor save insofar as they exceed the excess. Should they exceed the excess, the amount by which they exceed it is by definition a tapered amount. It is assessable on the settlor, but cannot be offset against his personal losses (s 86A(2B)). It then drops out of the pool of trust gains carried forward to the year of return for the purposes of s 87.

The general rule is that a capital distribution to a UK resident beneficiary from an offshore trust is assessable to income tax under TA 1988, s 740 to the extent of relevant income (see para 56.1). Only if relevant income is exhausted is it taxable as a capital payment (see para 56.28 and also Chapter 13). Section 86A does *not* allow capital distributions assessed to income tax under s 740 to be deducted from the gains assessed as the settlor's in the year of return.

Double tax treaties

Dual resident trusts

60.15 Section 86 makes special provision for trusts which are resident in the UK under UK domestic law, but are treated as resident in some other territory under the double tax treaty between that territory and the UK. In such a case, the gains which would be assessable on the settlor if the treaty were not in point are subject to s 86, if the conditions for the application of s 86 are otherwise met (TCGA 1992, s 86(4)(a)).

Trusts exclusively resident in a treaty jurisdiction

60.16 What is not expressly addressed in s 86 is the impact of double tax treaties on trusts which are resident in a treaty jurisdiction without being dual resident, ie trusts which are not resident in the UK under UK domestic law. Here, the role of double tax treaties in potentially preventing the attribution to a UK resident of a gain realised by an entity of a treaty jurisdiction is described in relation to TCGA 1992, s 13 in para 66.19. It appears from the Exchange of Notes relating to the 2003 Protocol to the New Zealand treaty that this point may also arise with s 86.

The application of the point is less clear than with s 13, for s 13 deems the gain itself to accrue to the participator, whereas s 86 deems an amount equal to the trust gains for the year to accrue to the settlor. But this may be a distinction without a difference, as the effective result is to deem the gains to be the settlor's. It may not be a case such as *Bricom Holdings v IRC* [1997] STC 1179 where tax is charged on a conventional or notional sum.

Treaty issues will only arise with s 86 insofar as the trustees are resident in a treaty jurisdiction and the treaty has a capital gains article in the OECD form. Particularly with civil law countries, an issue may arise as to whether the trustees are a person and so capable of being resident at all in the other jurisdiction for the purposes of the treaty. But this point should be disposed of provided the treaty defines 'person' as including any body of persons.

Trustees are inherently less likely to be resident in treaty countries than s 13 companies. Further as described in para 66.22, revised language to the capital gains article has closed the point in relation to the most obvious jurisdictions such as USA, Canada, Australia, New Zealand and Mauritius. The exchange of notes relating to the New Zealand treaty implies that otherwise the point is of concern to the government, although it may be that the focus of government concern was artificial schemes.

Multiple settlors

60.17 Since the definition of settlor includes any person who has provided property it is perfectly possible for a settlement to have more than one settlor. In this event any given settlor only has an interest in the settlement if property originating from him could be used to benefit a person who is a defined person in relation to him, or if such a person receives a benefit from such property (TCGA 1992, Sch 5 para 2(2)). A particular settlor is only chargeable on gains accruing on disposals of property originating from him (s 86(1)(e)). So too he is only credited with losses on property originating from him. Gains in an underlying company are attributed to him if the shares in the company originated from him (Sch 5 para 1(2)).

Corporate settlors and beneficiaries

60.18 Unlike other anti-avoidance legislation, TCGA 1992, s 86 and Sch 5 make express provision for the position where a company is settlor or where one or more companies are beneficiaries.

Corporate settlor

60.19 An individual is taken as providing property, and thus as settlor, in certain cases where a company provides the property (TCGA 1992, Sch 5 para 8(4)). An individual is treated as providing all the property provided by the company if he is the only person who controls it. If two or more persons each control the company separately, each is taken to provide the property in equal shares. If two or more persons only control the company by taking them together, they are each treated as providing an apportioned part of the property, subject to a de minimis limit of 5%. For these purposes provision by a company is taken into account whether the company is resident or non-resident, but the company must be close.

The applicable definition of control is that in TA 1988, s 416, the income tax close company definition. In broad terms an individual has control if he has voting control, if he owns over half the company's shares, or if he is entitled to over half any dividend or distribution in a winding up. In determining whether an individual has such control the rights and powers of his associates are attributed to him. An individual's associates are defined in s 417(3) as:

(a) his relatives, ie his ancestors, descendants, siblings and spouse;
(b) the trustees of any settlement of which he is settlor;
(c) the trustees or personal representatives of any trust or estate under which he is interested in the shares.

The last head in this definition of associates is unclear in its meaning. However, it has been held that a personal representative is himself interested in shares in a deceased's estate and so even if an individual is a personal representative with no entitlement under the will or intestacy, any shares held by the estate are treated as his in determining whether he has control (*Willingale v Islington Green Investment Co* (1972) 48 TC 547, CA). A fixed-interest beneficiary under a trust is certainly interested in shares held by the trust (*R v IRC, ex p New Fields Developments Ltd* [2001] STC 901, 906 per Lord Hoffmann). The better view is that discretionary beneficiaries are as well, for there is no requirement that those interested should have a quantifiable interest (cf *Leedale v Lewis* [1982] STC 835). The effect of this is that a beneficiary controls a company if the trust controls it, or if he and the trust, or he, the trust and members of his family, control it.

If the income tax definition of control stood alone in determining who is settlor, an individual could be settlor in relation to a settlement even if he personally owned no shares in the providing company. The legislation attempts to remove this possibility by providing that a person is not for these purposes treated as controlling a company unless he is himself a participator (TCGA 1992, Sch 5 para 8(8)). Unfortunately this provision does not fully hit its target, for the term participator includes actual shareholders and loan creditors, and anybody having a share or interest in the capital or income of the company (TA 1988, s 417(1)). The word 'interest' in this definition certainly brings in fixed-interest beneficiaries in relation to trust shareholdings, and very possibly discretionary beneficiaries as well (*R v IRC, ex p New Fields Developments Ltd*, supra). The result is that it is still possible for a beneficiary under a settlement to be treated as controlling a company, and thus as a settlor in relation to funds provided by the company, even if he personally owns no shares in it. Fortunately this defect has been recognised by HMRC, and ESC D40 provides that for these purposes a beneficiary under a trust is not treated as a participator solely because of his status as a beneficiary.

Corporate beneficiary

60.20 The term 'defined person' includes any company controlled by any one or more of the individual defined persons listed in para 60.4 above and any other company associated with such a company. The rules for determining whether a company is controlled by one or more individual defined persons are the same as those applicable in determining who is settlor, save that ESC D40 does not apply. As under those rules, the term 'associated' is also defined with reference to the income tax close company legislation (ibid, Sch 5 para 5(9)). Two companies are associated if one controls the other or both are under common control (TA 1988, s 416(1)).

In determining whether a pre-1998 grandchildren's settlement attracts the transitional exemption described in para 60.5, the companies which must be excluded from benefit are restricted to those controlled by the settlor, his spouse, or their children and companies associated with any such company. However, this is of little practical significance, for as described above, under TA 1988, s 417, a person's associates include his descendants.

The practical importance of defined persons including companies is that even if all individual defined persons are excluded, the settlor will still have an interest in the settlement if companies are, or are being capable of being added as, beneficiaries under the settlement and such companies do not exclude those which fall within the definition of defined person. The problem may be more widespread than at first appears, for most powers of addition are expressed in terms of persons and the term 'person' normally includes companies. In English law, such is implied by Interpretation Act 1978, Sch 1.

Can a company be settlor?

60.21 Apart from these rules treating participators as settlors, no rule exists to prevent s 86 or Sch 5 from applying to a corporate settlor, although the only categories of defined person would be the settlor company and controlled or associated companies. As a result, if an open company creates a settlement s 86 could apply to it unless it and connected and associated companies are wholly excluded. The language of the Sch 5 para 8(4) is, it may be suggested, wide enough to prevent any close company from being taxed as settlor. These issues arise particularly with employee benefit trusts (see Chapter 26).

Chapter 61

Tainting

Introduction

61.1 As explained in the previous chapter, when the rules in TCGA 1992, s 86 attributing gains to the settlor were first enacted they did not in general apply to settlements made before 19 March 1991. This was achieved by TCGA 1992, Sch 5 para 9, which provided that a pre-1991 settlement was only qualifying, and thus within s 86, if it fell foul of four specified conditions. Falling foul of one of those conditions became colloquially known as becoming 'tainted'.

These rules now apply in determining whether a protected settlement as described in para 60.10 continues to remain non-qualifying. Almost identical rules to those in para 9 are enacted in Sch 5 para 2A and apply to settlements made before 17 March 1998. They govern whether account can be taken of grandchildren and their spouses in determining whether the settlor has an interest in such a settlement and thus effectively determine whether a pre-1998 grandchildren's settlement remains outside s 86 (see para 60.5).

The original conditions

61.2 As originally enacted, para 9 provided that a settlement made before 19 March 1991 became a qualifying settlement if one of the following conditions had become satisfied since 19 March 1991:

- A Property or income was provided directly or indirectly for the purposes of the settlement otherwise than under a transaction entered into at arm's length.
- B The settlement, having previously been resident, became neither resident nor ordinarily resident in the UK.
- C The terms of the settlement were varied so that a person within para 9(7) became for the first time a person who would or might benefit from the settlement.
- D A person within para 9(7) who was not capable of benefiting from the settlement before 19 March 1991 enjoyed a benefit for the first time.

In conditions (C) and (D), the persons within para 9(7) were as follows:

- (i) any settlor;
- (ii) any spouse of any settlor;
- (iii) any child or stepchild of any settlor;

(iv) any spouse of such child;
(v) any company controlled by all or any of the above, and any company associated with such a company.

An exception to condition (A) was made in the following circumstances:

(1) the settlement's expenses relating to administration and taxation for a year of assessment exceeded its income for that year; and
(2) the added property did not exceed the shortfall.

Protected settlements

61.3 Conditions (A)–(D) above and the exception for expenses now apply in determining whether a protected settlement becomes qualifying. A fifth condition, however, is added, namely the settlement ceasing to be protected.

Grandchildren's settlements

61.4 The conditions relating to pre-1998 grandchildren's settlements follow the original (A)–(D) above save as follows:

(a) The settlement is only tainted if one of the conditions has been breached since 17 March 1998, and that is the relevant date for seeing whether a person was capable of benefiting within condition (D).
(b) The class of persons within para 9(7) who thus cause conditions (C) and (D) to be breached is restricted to grandchildren and their spouses, together with companies (and associated companies) controlled by either grandchildren and their spouses alone or by such persons and other defined persons. Since 5 December 2005, the reference to spouses has included civil partners (SI 2005/3229).

Significance of tainting

61.5 The four conditions, and in particular condition (A), were until 17 March 1998 of immense importance, for almost all offshore settlements made by a UK settlor before 19 March 1991 were within s 86 if one of the conditions was breached. In many cases substantial amounts of tax were at stake. In 1992 HMRC issued one of the longest ever statements of practice, SP 5/92. SP 5/92 was subsequently amplified by articles in *Tax Bulletins* 8 (August 1993) and 16 (April 1995). Unfortunately it raised more problems than it solved, and much of the discussion of tainting revolves around assertions it makes. Because the conditions have been retained in relation to protected settlements and grandchildren's settlements this discussion is of continuing relevance, although its importance is thankfully much reduced.

Added property: the law

61.6 The first condition, condition (A), is only infringed if the added property is 'provided'. The provision can be by anybody, and thus condition (A) is infringed not merely if the settlor makes the addition but if the addition is received from a third party, for example, the trustees of another settlement. The word 'provided' is used in income tax settlor rules discussed in Chapter 59 and in that context it was held that the provision must be bounteous (*IRC v Leiner* (1964) 41 TC 589 at 596) (see paras 59.17 and 59.20). An interest-free loan represents the provision of the property lent (*IRC v Wachtel* (1970) 46 TC 543).

The provision of the property must be for the purposes of the settlement. This is a matter of evidence. Thus in *IRC v Mills* [1974] STC 130 at 135, HL, Viscount Dilhorne said:

> 'Where it is shown that funds have been provided for a settlement, a very strong inference is to be drawn that they were provided for that purpose, an inference which will be rebutted if it is established that they were provided for another purpose. In this case there is not a shred of evidence that the funds were provided for any other purpose.'

Property is provided whether it is provided directly or indirectly. Cases on other statutory provisions give guidance as to the meaning of 'indirectly'. In *Potts' Executors v IRC* (1950) 32 TC 211, the House of Lords held that sums paid to the settlor's creditors were not loans made directly or indirectly to him within the meaning of what is now ITTOIA 2005, s 634 (cf para 59.9). Lord Simmonds stated that 'indirectly' does not cover payment to a third party for his own use or benefit, and Lords Normand and Oaksey observed that indirect payments include only payment to a third party accountable to the settlor. In *Yuill v Wilson* [1979] STC 486 at 494, Buckley LJ said in the Court of Appeal that if A transmits an opportunity to B with the knowledge or assurance or expectation that he will pass it to C, he is providing C with the opportunity indirectly, and the same may apply if he merely persuades B. It may be concluded from these cases that indirect provision within condition (A) requires the third party to be accountable to the settlement or there to be an expectation that the third party will pass any such provision on to the settlement.

If it is right that the term 'provided' connotes bounty, the exception in condition (A) for arm's length transactions may be otiose. The term 'transaction' rather than 'bargain' is used, which means that the exception does apply where the other party to the transaction is connected with the settlement (cf TCGA 1992, s 18(2)). In *Mansworth v Jelley* [2002] STC 1013 Lightman J said that arm's length connotes a transaction between two parties with separate and distinct interests, each of whom has agreed terms with a mind solely to his interest.

In an IHT case, *IRC v Spencer-Nairn* [1991] STC 60, certain factors were identified as potentially pointing to a transaction having been at arm's length, notably professional representation for the parties and evidence of genuine negotiation and marketing. However, none of these factors were in fact present in the case. A sale thought by the parties to be between unconnected parties at a market value had in fact been between connected parties at a massive discount on account of a misunderstanding of the law. It was still held that such a transaction was capable of being at arm's length. The conclusion which may be drawn is that it is highly desirable to have separate representation and genuine negotiation but that this is not necessary if the parties believe that they are transacting at arm's length.

Added property: particular transactions

Outright transactions with the trustees

61.7 Clearly condition (A) is infringed if somebody transfers assets or income to the settlement with bounteous intent. Equally it is not infringed when there is no bounteous intent and the transaction is at full value. In practice, the difficulty which arises is when the settlor or somebody connected with him wants to enter into a transaction with the trustees at full value, but, because of his relationship with the trust, is concerned as to whether HMRC will accept that the transaction is in fact at market value. The problem is particularly acute where the asset is difficult to value, for example, private company shares, or where the asset is likely to see a dramatic increase in value.

In practice, common sense indicates that it ought to be sufficient for the transaction to take place at a genuine third party valuation, for such would negative there being bounteous intent. Prudence would perhaps dictate going slightly further and arranging for each side to instruct professional advisers to conduct a genuine independent negotiation. Given the comments in *Spencer Nairn*, it is difficult to see how HMRC could contend such a transaction was anything other than at arm's length.

For some reason HMRC did not in SP 5/92 confirm that transactions with independent representation are outside condition (A). Instead they provided another route for avoiding condition (A), namely for the contract of sale to include an adjuster clause, ie to provide for an adjustment of price with compensating interest if HMRC do not accept the price as market value (SP 5/92, paras 12–15). This route has the advantage of obviating the necessity for two lots of advisers although it does appear one independent valuation is required. The adjustment can be either up or down or (if appropriate) one way (*Tax Bulletin* 16 (April 1995) p 204).

Loans

61.8 In SP 5/92, para 22, HMRC confirm that a loan to the settlement at a low or nil rate of interest is regarded as a provision of property infringing condition (A). The practical difficulty is determining what rate of interest needs to be charged to avoid this difficulty. Loans are often made to a settlement precisely because bank finance is not available or is prohibitively expensive, and this in turn often reflects a lack of realisable security. However, it would be difficult to regard the loan as bounteous provision provided a normal rate of interest is charged, ie something approximating to bank base rates.

The experience of practitioners is that HMRC do not regard condition (A) as infringed if the official rate of interest is charged, ie the rate fixed for the purposes of taxing loans to employees (see para 69.10). This broadly follows mortgage rates but there is no statutory authority for using it in the present context.

Despite the fact that the practice of allowing a subsequent adjustment is expressed in terms of sales, it is thought that HMRC would accept an adjuster clause.

Guarantees and indemnities

61.9 In SP 5/92, paras 34 and 35, HMRC stated that the giving of a guarantee is a provision of funds and that the giving of an indemnity can be so regarded depending on the facts of the case. One type of indemnity which is not treated as the provision of funds is that given by new trustees to retiring trustees. In practice, HMRC are likely to regard the giving of a guarantee as the provision of funds if the guarantee is given on a sale and it increases the price or it prevents the trust from being exposed to the same degree of risk as other vendors accept (*Tax Bulletin* 16 (April 1995) p 204).

It may be suggested that HMRC are wrong in considering that the mere giving of a guarantee or indemnity represents the provision of funds. No property is provided until the guarantee is called or the indemnity enforced. When a guarantee is called, condition (A) would be infringed unless the contract under which the guarantee was given was at arm's length. With indemnities, however, even enforcement of the indemnity may not infringe condition (A). This, it may be suggested, is the position with indemnities given to trustees against possible breaches of trust, for, when enforced, such indemnities provide funds for the trustees personally rather than for the settlement. The trustee has to make good the loss to the trust fund whether or not he has a guarantee or enforces his indemnity.

Underlying companies

61.10 In SP 5/92, para 16, HMRC stated that provision to a company owned by the settlement can amount to indirect provision of property for the purposes of the settlement. HMRC recognised an exception where funds are left in the company for the company's purposes, for example waived dividends or remuneration. But this exception is only likely to apply where the trust owns a relatively small proportion of the company (*Tax Bulletin* 16 (April 1995) p 204).

It may be suggested that HMRC's view is wrong, on the basis of the case law on the meaning of 'indirect' referred to above. Strictly, property provided to a company should only count as provided indirectly for the purposes of the settlement if the company is going to pass the property to the settlement by way of dividend or otherwise, or if it is accountable to the settlement. It follows that cheap loans from the settlor or other family members to the company should not infringe condition (A), although it is unlikely HMRC would accept this.

Services

61.11 HMRC regard both the gratuitous provision of services and the gratuitous improvement of trust property by a tenant as the provision of property (*Tax Bulletin* 16 (April 1995) p 204). As regards services their view is at variance with *IRC v Mills* [1974] STC 130 at 135, where Viscount Dilhorne distinguished the provision of services from the provision of funds (see further para 59.22).

Receipts from companies

61.12 Should a fixed-interest trust receive an enhanced scrip dividend, it may be unclear whether it is income or capital or whether some compensating payment to the life tenant is required (cf SP 4/94). If the trustees take and follow professional advice, HMRC do not contend there has been any addition if the dividend is treated as capital (*Tax Bulletin* 16 (April 1995) p 205).

When a UK company purchases its own shares, the proceeds are capital in trust law, but income for tax purposes unless the relief in TA 1988, s 219 applies. Should the settlor be a beneficiary, the proceeds will be taxable as his income and he will make an addition unless he claims reimbursement from the trust of the tax he has to pay (*Tax Bulletin* 16 (April 1995) p 205).

Expenses

61.13 The exception for expenses relating to administration and taxation is circumscribed. In SP 5/92, paras 25–32, HMRC made the following comments:

(1) Expenses count for these purposes whether charged to income or capital.
(2) 'Administration' excludes loan interest and the costs of acquiring or selling assets.
(3) 'Taxation' encompasses UK tax, foreign tax, and interest and penalties.
(4) The expenses of an underlying holding company are not included.

(5) The measure of trust income is the total arising to the trustees rather than income which would be subject to UK tax if they were resident.
(6) The expenses relating to administration do not include expenditure in connection with a particular asset if that expenditure can be offset by the income of the asset. In such a case the income from the asset brought into account is the net income.
(7) An addition to meet excess expenses need not be made in the year of the shortfall, but should be made as soon as the relevant figures are available.

Far and away the most significant of these points is the exclusion of the expenses of an underlying holding company. This is particularly serious where the sole trust asset is a UK company held through an intermediate offshore holding company. In such a case the only way to fund the offshore company's expenses may be a dividend from the UK company.

A particular problem arises where the trust is a fixed-interest trust and the trustees incur expenses properly chargeable to capital. If in fact a capital expense is taken out of income and the life tenant does not object, that is a provision of property by him.

Statement of Practice SP 5/92 suggests two ways of overcoming this difficulty. One is where the settlement confers express power on the trustee to decide whether expenses should be debited to capital or income. In such a case, HMRC accept that the debiting of a capital expense to income in exercise of such powers is not the provision of income. The other suggestion is for the trustees to borrow their charges from the income account and restore the money out of capital as and when they have capital funds, together with interest over the period of the loan. The appropriate rate of interest is considered to be that payable on the basic account administered by the Court Office of the Supreme Courts of Justice (*Tax Bulletin* 16 (April 1995) p 204). Borrowing from income and charging interest in this way is inconvenient in practice and will no doubt lead to tiresome computations. But if annual charges are indeed capital, it is what trustees have to do unless they have power to debit capital expenses to income.

Expenses chargeable to capital should include a corporate trustee's annual fee for this is for the benefit of the trust fund as a whole (*Carver v Duncan* [1985] STC 356, HL). In practice, HMRC raise no objection if the annual fee is charged to income if this practice has been consistently followed and no part of the fee relates to duties specifically of a capital nature (*Tax Bulletin* 16 (April 1995) 204).

Condition (C): new beneficiaries

61.14 Condition (C) is infringed where the terms of the settlement are varied so as to make a person within para 9(7) a beneficiary. The persons within para 9(7) are detailed at paras 61.2 and 61.4 above. It may be suggested that it is infringed even if other such persons already are beneficiaries. The use of the word 'varied' signifies condition (C) is only in point where the trust is varied by court order or by all the beneficiaries when sui juris, and this is accepted by HMRC (SP 5/92, para 36). HMRC specifically state that the addition of a beneficiary under a power to add within a specified range of persons does not amount to a variation, and this, it may be suggested, applies even where the power to add is a power to add anyone except, say, the settlor and the trustees for the time being.

Condition (D): ultra vires payments

61.15 This condition is only infringed where a person within para 9(7) enjoys a benefit and would not have been capable of enjoying a benefit under the terms of the settlement as those terms stood on 19 March 1991 (or 17 March 1998 in the case of grandchildren's settlements). As HMRC accept, it thus applies to ultra vires benefits and could catch a case where a person benefits in exercise of the trustees' investment powers.

Where the settlement confers power to add anybody except say the settlor and the trustees to be beneficiaries, this condition will not be in point unless the settlor or the trustees are benefited, for anybody else could have been added as a beneficiary before the relevant date. If the trustees have wide overriding powers to resettle or reappoint the trust fund, it may well be non-beneficiaries can incidentally be benefited by such powers. In this case, too, exercise of the power does not infringe condition (D), for the relevant power could have been used to benefit such persons at any time.

Chapter 62

Trustee borrowing

Introduction

62.1 Finance Act 2000 inserted important rules into the CGT treatment of offshore trusts, namely TCGA 1992, Schs 4B and 4C. These schedules impose a complete or partial disposal of all the trust assets in certain circumstances where the trustees have outstanding borrowing. Schedule 4B is the principal schedule. Sch 4C was recast in 2003 and now includes Sch 4B gains in a floating pool insofar as the gains are not attributed to the settlor on an arising basis under TCGA 1992, s 86. It is discussed in Chapter 64.

HMRC gave some guidance on Sch 4B in *Tax Bulletin* 66 (August 2003). The issue of whether it is compatible with European law is discussed in para 49.12.

Flip-flop schemes

62.2 HMRC press releases at the time of the 2000 Budget stated that Schs 4B and 4C were being introduced to counteract a scheme known as the 'flip-flop' scheme. This scheme avoided both the charge on the settlor under TCGA 1992, s 86 and the liability of beneficiaries on capital payments under TCGA 1992, s 87(see Chapters 60 and 63).

In essence the scheme involved the following steps:

(a) in year 1 the trustees borrowed money against the security of the trust assets and advanced the cash to a new settlement;
(b) in year 2 the trustees of the original settlement realised gains;
(c) distributions to the beneficiaries were made from the new settlement.

In the case of TCGA 1992, s 86, the scheme was thought to work because the settlor and his children and grandchildren and their respective spouses were all excluded from the original settlement before the start of year 2 when the gains were realised (cf para 60.4). In the case of TCGA 1992, s 87, capital distributions from the new trust were thought not to be taxable by reference to gains realised in the old trust in year 2, because capital gains only carry forward from one trust to another if realised in the same year as the transfer between the trusts or an earlier year (TCGA 1992, s 90; cf para 63.26).

But even if the reason for enacting Schs 4B and 4C was as stated in the 2000 Budget press releases their impact is far, far, wider than flip-flop schemes. They undoubtedly impose a deemed disposal in many entirely innocent and unexpected contexts and, even worse, the language of the schedules is riddled with uncertainty. Only some of this has been clarified by HMRC in *Tax Bulletin* 66 (August 2003).

Flip-flop schemes were also used to avoid the charge on the settlor on gains on resident settlor-interested trusts (see para 59.4). In relation to these trusts the scheme has been held in the House of Lords to have failed (*West v Trennery* [2005] STC 214). The reasoning behind this decision turned on the inclusion of 'derived property' in the s 77 definition of when the settlor has an interest in a resident settlement. Equivalent words are not found in s 86 or s 87, and to date no case involving flip-flop schemes and offshore trusts has come before the Special Commissioners.

Preconditions

62.3 Schedule 4B para 1 sets out three conditions for the operation of Sch 4B in relation to non-resident settlements:

(1) The trustees make what is termed a transfer of value.
(2) In the tax year of the transfer the settlement is within TCGA 1992, s 86 or s 87. By this is meant either that any net gains in that year are assessable on the settlor on an arising basis or that if there were trust gains and capital payments in that year, a chargeable gain would be treated as accruing to the beneficiary in receipt of the capital payment (Sch 4B para 3). As will be apparent from Chapters 60 and 63 this language comprehends any trust which is not resident in the UK, regardless of whether it has any connection with the UK.
(3) The transfer of value is linked with trustee borrowing. By linked is meant simply that at the time of the transfer there is what is called outstanding trustee borrowing (Sch 4B para 5(1)). This is the key concept in the schedule and requires consideration first.

Schedule 4B does not include any express definition of settlement. It follows that in Sch 4B the term 'settlement' bears its normal CGT meaning, which is itself the meaning of the term under general law (cf *Roome v Edwards* [1981] STC 96).

Outstanding trustee borrowing

62.4 Determination of whether there is outstanding trustee borrowing requires two questions to be asked:

(a) has there been trustee borrowing?
(b) is it still outstanding?

Trustee borrowing

62.5 Trustees are treated as borrowing if money or any other asset is lent to them, or if an asset is transferred to them on terms that it or another asset must be transferred back to the transferor or another person (para 4). Trustee borrowing thus includes loans in the normal sense of the word and the extension of the term to transfers with the obligation to transfer back is anti-avoidance.

The amount of a loan is the amount or value lent (para 4(2)(a)). The amount of a transfer is the value of the asset received on the transfer, less any consideration received by the transferor (para 4(2)(b)). This latter formulation means no account is taken of the obligation of the trustees to make the retransfer, but does allow a deduction for consideration passing from the trustees when the transfer is made.

It is to be noted that the trustee borrowing can be from anybody. Loans from underlying companies, other trusts, or beneficiaries are caught just as much as commercial borrowing such as bank loans. The language is wide enough to cover drawing down on an informal overdraft as well as structured borrowing.

The transaction does however have to involve money or another asset being lent to the trustees or transferred to them with an obligation to transfer it back. What is meant by 'lent' is not defined and so this term must bear its general meaning. There is authority in connection with TA 1988, s 739 that unpaid purchase money is not of itself a loan (*Ramsden v IRC* (1957) 37 TC 619, 625–6). It may be suggested this is applicable to Sch 4B, for unless the creditor expressly agrees to convert the debt into a loan, the transaction is not one of loan. HMRC appear to accept this, for in *Tax Bulletin* 66 it is said bona fide delay in payment of an invoice does not convert the amount invoiced into trustee borrowing.

Another issue raised by the definition is whether a lease comes within the definition of borrowing. If it did, any lease taken by the trustees would result in trustee borrowing. However, it is unlikely that a lease of land amounts to borrowing, for it does not involve either the landlord's interest in the land being lent to the tenant or it being transferred to him. However, the position may be otherwise with a lease of chattels.

When is trustee borrowing outstanding?

62.6 The basic rule is that borrowing is outstanding until it is repaid. However, borrowing which has been applied for what are called normal trust purposes may be disregarded (Sch 4B para 5(2)). Normal trust purposes do not mean any legitimate purpose of the trustees but instead only expenditure falling within three tightly defined heads. These are as follows (Sch 4B para 6):

(a) payments in respect of ordinary trust assets. This does not connote any proper expenditure on any legitimate asset but instead it too is closely defined (see below);

(b) discharging a pre-existing loan applied for normal trust purposes (Sch 4B para 6(3));
(c) bona fide current expenses incurred by the trustees in administering the settlement or any of the settled property (Sch 4B para 6(4)). This is discussed in para 62.8 below.

Ordinary trust assets

62.7 The following, and only the following, are ordinary trust assets (Sch 4B para 7):

(a) shares or securities, securities bearing the standard CGT definition in TCGA 1992, s 132;
(b) tangible property, whether movable or immovable;
(c) property used in a business carried on by the trustees or by a beneficiary who has an interest in possession in the property;
(d) rights in or interests over such tangible or business property.

Interests in mutual funds are not specifically referred to in the definition of ordinary trust assets. However, shares in open-ended investment companies are shares within the general meaning of the term. Units in unit trusts also count as shares, for TCGA applies generally on the basis that unit trusts are companies and units are shares (TCGA 1992, s 99).

Expenditure on ordinary trust assets does not qualify as normal trust purposes unless the asset is held by the trustees immediately after the transfer of value. If the asset is not so held, for example, if it has been sold, the expenditure can only qualify if (para 8):

(a) the asset is then represented by one or more other ordinary trust assets; or
(b) the asset was destroyed or became of negligible value so that TCGA 1992, s 24 applied.

A further point is that expenditure on such assets does not count unless it is on arm's length terms or is less than what would have been paid at arm's length. It must also constitute allowable expenditure within TCGA 1992, s 38 on the disposal of the asset (Sch 4B para 6(2)). Expenditure which is disallowed for CGT purposes solely because it is an income tax deduction counts, however.

This definition of ordinary trust assets if fraught with problems. The first is that not all assets are included, specifically intangibles. Obvious exclusions are insurance policies, intellectual property and futures contracts (*Tax Bulletin* 66, para B6). But potentially more serious is simple debts. A debt is an asset of the creditor for CGT purposes (TCGA 1992, s 21(1)(a)) and perhaps the most common category of simple debt is a bank deposit. The practical result is that trustees who borrow money and pay it into the bank are not making an application for normal trust purposes.

This leads on to a second problem, namely when must the expenditure on ordinary trust assets occur. Must it occur when the borrowing is incurred, as a direct application of the proceeds, or are the proceeds allowed to be represented by another asset first. To take a specific example, can the trustees put borrowed money in the bank, thereby acquiring a debt, and then spend it on ordinary trust assets, or must the money move directly from the lender to the assets. Common sense indicates that the borrowing need not be spent on ordinary trust assets when incurred. This issue is not clarified by *Tax Bulletin* 66 although it is said that putting money in the bank is not regarded as a transfer of value (para 62.10 below). The fact that the issue arises at all shows how ill thought-out Sch 4B is.

A third problem is that particular items of expenditure on ordinary trust assets may not qualify. Thus under TCGA 1992, s 38, enhancement expenditure has to be reflected in the state or nature of the asset at the time of the disposal. Much expenditure, for example, routine maintenance or improvements subsequently obviated, is not so reflected. However such expenditure may still qualify as normal trust purposes under Sch 4B, for in HMRC's view Sch 4B merely requires it to be reflected in the state or nature of the asset at the time it is incurred (*Tax Bulletin* 66, para B5).

Fourth, the fact that simple debts are not ordinary trust assets means any simple loan or capital contribution to any company owned by the trustees is not normal trust purposes. The only way such expenditure can count is if the trustees subscribe for shares or securities in the company. As House of Lords decision have affirmed, the term security means something akin to loan stock and should involve an appropriate document (cf *Aberdeen Construction Group Ltd v IRC* [1978] STC 127; *WT Ramsay Ltd v IRC* [1981] STC 174).

Fifth and last is the requirement that the asset must be held by the trustees immediately after the transfer of value. As noted above this is displaced if the asset has been destroyed or if immediately after the transfer of value one or more ordinary trust assets 'directly or indirectly represent' it. Direct and indirect representation is not defined but on any view should cover the position where the ordinary trust asset is shares and the new asset is shares or debentures acquired on a reconstruction or take-over. Less clear is the position where the original ordinary trust asset is sold and the proceeds applied in the purchase of a new ordinary trust asset. But here it may be suggested that even if the new asset does not represent the old asset it is itself an application of the proceeds of the borrowing providing its purchase price is demonstrably funded out of the proceeds of sale of the old asset.

The prime significance of the requirement that the ordinary trust asset or assets representing it be held immediately after the transfer is that the exemption for ordinary trust assets is not in point if the ordinary trust asset is itself the subject of the transfer.

Schedule 4B provides that if there has been a part disposal of the original ordinary trust asset, the part retained and any asset which represents the part disposed of may be looked at in combination to see if the ordinary trust asset condition is met (Sch 4B, para 8(2)). In HMRC's view this has significance in relation to leases, as described below (para 62.12).

Bona fide current expenses

62.8 Sch 4B para 6(4) requires the expenses to be current, bona fide, and incurred in administering the settlement or the trust property. There is no restriction to income expenses and HMRC accept that capital expenditure is included and instance capital taxes and costs incurred in reorganising the settlement (*Tax Bulletin* 66, para B5). The term does not however cover the mere making of a reserve in respect of future expenditure. In relation to real property para 6(4) allows borrowing used to fund repairs to count as normal trust purposes and the same applies to payments made under the terms of a lease into a common sinking fund (*Tax Bulletin* 66, para B5).

Somewhat more controversially HMRC doubt whether current expenses extends to borrowing taken out to pay off old unpaid debts. This may be right, but the correct analysis is surely that if such expenditure is no longer current it is only so by having become a loan from the creditor. If the original expenditure was bona fide current expenses, borrowing to pay off this loan is borrowing applied in paying off a loan incurred for normal trust purposes and so relieved under para 6(3).

The expenditure must be incurred by the trustees in administering the settlement or on the settled property. This plainly excludes expenditure incurred in administering any underlying holding company. It is for consideration as to whether it excludes the one-off annual fees charged by offshore jurisdictions in respect of exempt companies or IBCs. HMRC say that the costs of a nominee company are included and this indicates that in their view the equivalent costs of a company which owns its assets beneficially are not.

Regulations

62.9 As will be apparent the rules defining normal trust purposes are a mess and give every impression of being drafted by people with little knowledge of how trusts operate in practice. The one redeeming feature is that the Treasury has taken power to amend the rules by regulation (Sch 4B para 9). But to date this power has not been exercised.

The transfer of value

62.10 The term 'transfer of value' does not bear the IHT meaning with which practitioners are familiar. Instead trustees are treated as making a transfer of value in any of the following circumstances (Sch 4B para 2):

(1) they transfer an asset to any person either for no consideration or for consideration less than market value;
(2) they lend money or any other asset to a person;
(3) they issue a security or for consideration less than market value.

The term 'asset' includes sterling (para 13(1)) and the term 'transfer' includes any act which constitutes a disposal for CGT purposes (para 13(2)). It is provided in para 13(3) that the term transfer of an asset does not include the transfer of an asset that is created by the part disposal of another asset. The meaning of this exception is far from clear. However, in its reference to creation it echoes the language of TCGA 1992, s 21(2) providing that there is a part disposal of an asset where an interest or right is created over the asset, as on the grant of a lease. On this basis the most logical meaning to give to para 13(3) is that such part disposals are excluded from being transfers for Sch 4B purposes. However, as described below this does not appear to be the meaning HMRC give it.

The definition of transfer of value plainly covers the ostensible target of Sch 4B, namely flip-flop schemes, for those schemes involved the gratuitous transfer of cash to another trust. But as with Sch 4B generally the ambit of the definition is far wider. In particular, it includes any distribution to a beneficiary and it would appear that all distributions are included however small. HMRC have said that in their view the definition does not embrace distributions which are the income of the recipient (*Tax Bulletin* 66, para B1).

In relation to transfers, ie disposals, it is to be stressed that such a transaction is only caught if it is for no consideration or for less than market value.

Loans

62.11 Not surprisingly, there is no arm's length exclusion for loans. As with trustee borrowing (para 62.5) there is no definition of 'lend'.

A number of issues are raised by loans of which the first is that a loan can be made in one instance where the expenditure is for normal trust purposes. This is when the trustees subscribe for a security, and the issue which arises is whether that transaction is a transfer of value, attracting a deemed disposal under Sch 4B, or expenditure for normal trust purposes. Common sense indicates the latter.

A second point is more basic and is at least unless the loan is a subscription for a security, any loan to a beneficiary, another trust, or an underlying company is caught. Informal loans to underlying companies are particularly common in practice, but now if one is made when there is outstanding trustee borrowing the result is a deemed disposal, inter alia of the trust's shares in the company.

Third, as noted above (para 62.7), the technical legal analysis of a bank deposit is that it is a loan by the depositor to the bank. Accordingly, on a literal reading, whenever the trustees place money in the bank they are making a transfer of value. In fact as *Tax Bulletin* 66 (para B7) affirms this cannot be right, for if it were almost every trustee borrowing of cash would immediately be followed by a transfer of value, regardless of what the ultimate use of the borrowed money was intended to be.

Leases

62.12 As noted above in connection with borrowing a question which may be raised is whether the grant of a lease is a transfer by virtue of being a loan of the asset let. Also as noted above, in the case of land it is suggested not, as in normal parlance a lease is quite simply not a loan of the land. The position may however be otherwise with leases of chattels.

Assuming a lease of land is not a transfer by virtue of being a loan, the issue then raised is whether it is a transfer by virtue of being a disposal. Above it is suggested para 13(3) of Sch 4B means it is not. But even if this is wrong a lease should not be a transfer of value unless on uncommercial terms. This is because on a commercial lease the rent and/or premium is full consideration. Despite these points, however, in *Tax Bulletin* 66 HMRC contend that the grant of a commercial lease by trustees is a transfer of the land. It appears the basis of this view is that a disposal is only prevented from being a transfer if the trustees receive consideration equal to the value of the asset, the relevant asset on the grant of a lease being the land rather than just the lease.

On the basis that the grant of a commercial lease is a transfer, HMRC escape the consequences of it triggering a Sch 4B disposal if the trustees incurred borrowing to buy the land. They do so by saying there are two assets, namely the reversion and the lease, and that the lease is represented by the rental stream. As such they say the ordinary trust asset exception applies on the basis of a combination of the freehold as being part of the original trust asset and the right to rent as representing the rest (see *Tax Bulletin* 66 para B8). All this is probably nonsense, but as in the cases to which it applies it produces what is plainly the right result, nobody is likely to complain.

However what is left unresolved is the position on the grant of a commercial lease should the trustees have outstanding borrowing incurred otherwise than to buy the land. The implication of what HMRC say is that the grant of the lease is a transfer of value triggering a Sch 4B disposal. Assuming such is indeed HMRC's position, it is surely nonsense, both because the lease is for full consideration and because of the para 13(3) point noted above.

Also unresolved is the position on the grant of a non commercial lease, or indeed on the grant of a licence if the latter can correctly be characterised as a part disposal for CGT purposes. Here the full consideration point is not in issue, but the argument that the lease/licence is not a transfer on account of para 13(3) is still at large.

The deemed disposal

62.13 The transfer of value occasions a deemed disposal under Sch 4B if the trustee borrowing is outstanding at the material time. The term 'material time' is defined by reference to the transfer of value as follows (Sch 4B para 2(2)):

(1) if the transfer of value is a loan or security, when the trustees make the loan or issue the security;

(2) if the transfer of value is the transfer of an asset when the transfer is 'effectively completed'.

The term 'effectively completed' means the point at which the transferee becomes for practical purposes unconditionally entitled to the whole of the subject matter of the transfer (para 2(2)).

The deemed disposal is of all the chargeable assets which are retained in the trust immediately after the material time. Either there is a complete disposal of all those assets, or each asset suffers a proportionate disposal. For these purposes the term 'chargeable asset' means any asset on which a gain would be chargeable (para 10(3)). The term thus includes foreign currency but excludes, for example, sterling and qualifying corporate bonds. The deemed disposal is deemed to be on arm's length terms at market value (para 10(2)).

The deemed disposal is of the whole of each retained chargeable asset if the value transferred is more than the effective value of the retained chargeable assets and more than the outstanding trustee borrowing (para 11(4)). In other cases, a proportion of each asset is deemed to be disposed of. The proportion is determined by a fraction of which the denominator is the effective value of the retained chargeable assets and the numerator is the lesser of the value transferred and the amount of the outstanding trustee borrowing (para 11(2), (3)).

For these purposes the effective value of a chargeable asset is its value net of any trustee borrowing attributable to it (para 11(5)). Trustee borrowing is attributable to an asset if either (Sch 4B para 12):

(a) the asset itself was borrowed and has not been applied for normal trust purposes. This will normally be in point where the asset borrowed was foreign currency;
(b) the proceeds of the trustee borrowing were applied in acquiring or enhancing the value of the asset, or another asset which it represents. This only applies to the extent that the borrowing is still outstanding at the material time.

The value of the transfer

62.14 Schedule 4B includes express rules determining the amount of the transfer. In the case of a loan the amount is equal to the amount lent (para 2(3)). The amount represented by a security is the value of the security less any amount received by the trustees for it (para 2(5)). HMRC are understood to consider that the amount received excludes the promise to pay of the other party to the security and in the context of Sch 4B this is surely right.

In the case of a transfer, the basic rule is that the amount of the transfer is equal to the value of the cash or other asset transferred (para 2(4)). But if the trustees receive consideration for the transfer, the amount of the transfer is reduced by such consideration unless any part of the value of the asset is attributable to trustee borrowing (para 2(4)).

Linkage with trustee borrowing

62.15 A point to stress is that the deemed disposal is triggered regardless of whether the transfer of value is funded by or in any way related to the trustee borrowing. All that is necessary is that at the material time there is trustee borrowing which is outstanding. Further even if the borrowing has ceased to be outstanding because the proceeds have been expended on an ordinary trust asset, if that asset is comprised in the transfer of value, the borrowing reverts to being outstanding in relation to that and subsequent transfers of value. As noted above, this is because expenditure on an ordinary trust asset is not an application for normal trust purposes unless the asset or an asset representing it is in the trust immediately after the material time (see para 62.7).

Proportion of the chargeable assets deemed to be disposed of

62.16 As should be apparent from the above, if the transfer of value is small, only a small proportion of each chargeable asset is deemed to be disposed of. This is because the value of the transfer is the numerator of the fraction referred to above unless it is more than the outstanding trustee borrowing. This point means that on a series of small capital distributions only modest proportions of each chargeable asset are disposed of. But even if the ensuing gains are small there may still be formidable computation and compliance costs.

In one scenario, the proportion of the chargeable assets disposed of will be greater than might be expected. This will be the position where the value of any such asset is attributable to trustee borrowing for then that part of the value is excluded in determining the denominator in the above fraction. Accordingly proportion disposed of is correspondingly greater. Thus in an extreme case where the sole retained asset was borrowed by the trustees by way of outstanding trustee borrowing (eg foreign currency or an insurance product), the whole of that asset would be deemed to be disposed of regardless of how small the transfer of value is.

Following a Sch 4B disposal, the base cost of the trust assets on future disposals is uplifted. If under Sch 4B only a proportion of each asset is disposed of, the asset has a blended base cost going forward (*Tax Bulletin* 66, para B10).

Exclusion of trustee borrowing on future transfers

62.17 Once trustee borrowing has been taken into account in relation to one transfer of value it ceases to be outstanding for the future (Sch 4B para 5(2)(b)(ii)). The amount which so drops out is the amount of the value transferred or, if less, the total borrowing then outstanding (Sch 4B para 5(3)).

The charge to tax

62.18 The effect of the deemed disposal if the trust is within s 86 is that the net gain or loss is brought into account in determining whether for the year as a whole the trust has net gains. If it has such net gains, they are attributed to the settlor. Where s 86 does not apply, the gain goes into the Sch 4C pool and may be attributed to capital payments received by resident and domiciled beneficiaries. Sch 4C applies in place of the normal capital payment rules in TCGA 1992, s 87 and is discussed in Chapter 64.

Should the trust hold material interests in non-qualifying funds, those interests are subject to the deemed disposal, for a disposal takes place under the offshore fund legislation when it takes place for CGT purposes (TA 1988, s 757(2); see para 71.10). However that legislation then provides that the capital gain for CGT purposes is net of the offshore income gain (TA 1988, s 763). As a result Sch 4B gains on non-qualifying funds fall to be dealt with under the offshore fund legislation. This means, in the case of an offshore settlement, they go into the pool of offshore income gains or, in certain cases, are income for the purposes of ss 739 and 740 (see para 71.24). What does not happen is taxation on an arising basis under s 86 or inclusion in the Sch 4C pool.

Should the Sch 4B disposal result in an interest in a non-qualifying fund being disposed of at a loss, the loss is not brought into account in charging offshore income gains (cf para 71.13). It follows it is available for offsetting gains on the Sch 4B disposal brought into account under s 86 or Sch 4C.

Immigrating settlements

62.19 It was noted above (para 62.3) that Sch 4B applies to one category of resident settlement, namely settlor-interested settlements whose gains are assessed on the settlor under TCGA 1992, s 77. It also applies to certain resident settlements which are not settlor-interested, namely settlements which have previously been non-resident. This result follows because Sch 4B applies to settlements within s 87 (para 1(1)) and being within s 87 is defined as including cases where chargeable gains would be treated as accruing to beneficiaries under s 89(2) if there were trust gains and capital payments in the year concerned (para 3(4)). Section 89(2) is the provision which carries the s 87 pool forward when a settlement immigrates to the UK (see para 63.19).

Read literally, the hypotheses in Sch 4B para 3(4) mean that any settlement which has immigrated is within Sch 4B if the conditions for the application of the Schedule are otherwise met. This is so even if there is no brought-forward s 87 pool or it has all previously been allocated to capital payments. Since the effect of Sch 4B, if it applies, is simply to impose a deemed disposal, the resident trustees suffer such a disposal and if there is a gain pay tax thereon at the rate for trusts. However it appears that the gain could be doubly taxed for, as is described in para 64.13, it falls also to be included in the Sch 4C pool.

Practical steps

62.20 It cannot be stressed too highly that a Sch 4B transfer is an outcome to be avoided. This is for two reasons:

(1) If the settlement is within s 86 there is an immediate tax charge on the settlor.
(2) In all cases a Sch 4C pool is created. This is so whether or not the Sch 4B transfer results in a gain or loss and whether or not any gain is within s 86. As is described in Chapter 64, the pool includes the Sch 4B gain if the latter is not taxed under s 86. It also includes any prior and current year gains in the s 87 pool. These gains cannot be washed out by payments to non-residents or non-domiciliaries and can be allocated to beneficiaries of any relevant settlement.

The best way of avoiding a Sch 4B transfer is to ensure there is no trustee borrowing or, if there is, to clear it. On the whole, trustees ought to be able to recognise when they are incurring or have incurred trustee borrowing but the following points should be noted:

(1) It should always be remembered that upstream loans from an underlying company, or loans from the settlor, any beneficiary or another trust are borrowing.
(2) Borrowing to invest is borrowing and only ceases to be outstanding so long as the investment falls within the definition of ordinary trust asset and is retained.
(3) Any strategy for managing investment portfolios which could involve margin dealing or other short-term loans may be borrowing.
(4) As described above, outstanding invoices are unlikely to be borrowing, but the position of old invoices needs to be watched.

The injunction to avoid borrowing applies just as much to settlements where the settlor or the beneficiaries are non-domiciled or non-resident as where they are all resident and domiciled. This is because the creation of a Sch 4C pool prevents s 87 gains from being washed out to non-residents and non-domiciliaries. Indeed the practical problems posed by Schs 4B and 4C may be greater for settlements with little UK connection for the trustees may have no awareness of whether a Sch 4B transfer has occurred and if one has, no understanding of the consequences.

One point which may be made is that borrowing in an underlying holding company does not count as trustee borrowing. Accordingly, if the trust is borrowing for investment such may safely be done in a company. However, the money must not then be lent up to the trust. The reality is that the company may have to make the investment, a course which may have drawbacks, as described in Chapter 9.

A perhaps obvious point is that regardless of what they think the borrowing position is, trustees should make a careful check before making any loan (even to a wholly owned company) or distribution. If in fact there is borrowing such loan or distribution will automatically trigger a Sch 4B transfer.

For those who have triggered what appears to be a Sch 4B liability, two final thoughts may be offered. One is to consider whether the charge could be obviated by European law (see para 49.12). The other is to make reference to *Re Green GLG Trust* [2003] 5 ITELR 590. Here the Royal Court in Jersey was persuaded to apply the *Hastings-Bass* principle and avoid distributions made in complete ignorance of the potential impact of Sch 4B (see para 52.7). The case has recently been followed in the Cayman Islands, and is an indication that the *Hastings-Bass* principle will, at least in some cases, provide a remedy for inadvertent triggering of a Sch 4B transfer.

Chapter 63

Section 87

Introduction

63.1 Section 87 of TCGA 1992 pools gains realised by any non-resident trust. Because the trustees are non-resident, the gains are not charged on the trustees but are allocated to beneficiaries who receive capital payments. The s 87 pool excludes any gains allocated to the settlor on an arising basis under TCGA 1992, s 86 (see para 63.13 below).

Should the trustees make a transfer of value linked with trustee borrowing within the meaning of TCGA 1992, Sch 4B, the s 87 pool as at the end of the tax year of the transfer is carried into the new Sch 4C pool (see Chapter 64). Gains realised by the trust in subsequent tax years make up a new s 87 pool (see para 64.5).

This chapter deals with what gains go into the s 87 pool and how they are allocated to capital payments. What is meant by a capital payment, and the circumstances in which it is treated as received from the trustees, is considered in Chapter 65.

The pool

63.2 A section 87 pool comes into existence in the first tax year in which the trustees of the settlement realise net chargeable gains. The pool is added to when the trustees realise gains in subsequent tax years and diminished by capital payments. It may also be added to by transfers from other trusts or diminished by transfers to other trusts (see para 63.26).

The legislation does not refer to pools of gains as such. Instead it refers to 'the trust gains for the year' which are simply the net trust gains realised in the current tax year plus unallocated gains brought forward from prior years (s 87(2)).

The s 87 pool is the computation of the gains realised by a given settlement. In contrast to TCGA 1992, s 86, 'settlement' bears not its normal CGT meaning but is given the income tax anti avoidance definitions described in Chapter 59 (TCGA 1992, 97(7)). The term settlement for the purposes of s 87 pools thus includes in particular any arrangement.

It is difficult to gauge the significance of this extended definition. However it could be used to attribute a single s 87 pool to two or more settlements in the CGT sense if they together amount to an arrangement within the extended income tax definition. In appropriate cases this could match a s 87 pool with a capital payment even though in a CGT sense the payment and the pool are attributable to separate settlements.

The term 'settlor' was, until 5 April 2006, also defined by reference to the income tax legislation, but now bears its general CGT definition, discussed in para 37.9 (FA 2006, Sch 12 para 15(1)). Another change taking effect from 6 April 2006 is that if a settlement within the extended definition does not have trustees, the trustee is deemed to be any person in whom the settled property or its management is vested (TCGA 1992, s 97(7A)).

Computing trust gains

63.3 The starting point of the computation of trust gains is computing the gains for each tax year in which s 87 applies to the settlement. The first tax year for which this exercise should be undertaken is the first tax year of the settlement, ie the year in which it was created. But in the case of settlements made before 6 April 1981 the start date is 6 April 1981 (s 87(10)). If the settlement was made by a non-domiciliary before 17 March 1998 the start date is 17 March 1998 (see para 63.14 below).

Section 87 requires the computation to be of the amount on which the trustees would have been chargeable to CGT under TCCA 1992, s 2(2) had they been UK resident. In other words what is required is a straightforward CGT computation on a year-by-year basis. There are, however, a few points worth noting about this exercise.

Taper relief

63.4 Taper relief applies in computing the gains at trust level, its effect being that it is only tapered gains which are included in the pool (cf TCGA 1992, s 87(6A)).

Losses

63.5 The general CGT rule whereby losses accruing to a non-resident are disallowed is disapplied (TCGA 1992, s 97(6)) with the result that trust losses are allowed. Thus current year losses may be deducted in full as may be prior year losses insofar as unrelieved by prior year gains. Again as per normal rules, losses are deducted before taper relief, and, where the available losses are less than the gains of the year, losses are set against those gains qualifying for the least favourable taper treatment (TCGA 1992, s 2A(6)).

Annual exemption

63.6 Section 87 pools are computed without any annual exemption as that operates on the amount otherwise chargeable under TCGA 1992, s 2 (TCGA 1992, s 3(5)).

Rebasing on death

63.7 One important relief which is available is the automatic rebasing which applies on death. This is in point should the trust be subject to an interest in possession and the life-tenant die (TCGA 1992, s 72(1)). The relief applies even if the life-tenant is the settlor. As respects deaths after 22 March 2006 it is only available if the interest in possession is one of those equated with ownership of the underlying assets (see TCGA 1992, s 72(1A) and Chapter 44).

Absolute entitlement

63.8 The s 87 pool includes the gains accruing when a person becomes absolutely entitled to trust property (TCGA 1992, s 71). But a holdover relief election is competent if the person absolutely entitled is UK resident and the circumstances for relief specified in TCGA 1992, ss 165 or 260 are met. Care needs to be taken in making a holdover election in that on the one hand it avoids increasing the s 87 pool of trust gains but on the other takes the held-over gain into the UK tax net. A holdover election will not normally make sense if the s 87 pool, with the gain on absolute entitlement included, is greater than the value of the assets to which he is becoming so entitled.

Gains in an underlying company

63.9 Under TCGA 1992, s 13(10) gains apportionable under s 13 can be apportioned to non-resident trustees who are participators in the company concerned. Section 13 is discussed in Chapter 66 and the result of s 13(10) is that if the trust holds its investments through a holding company, the latter's gains may count as trust gains (see para 66.25).

Should the trust or any underlying company be a participator in a UK company, gains realised in a foreign company owned by the UK company may be apportioned to the trust and included in trust gains. This is the position where such gains are treaty protected and is the result of TCGA 1992, s 79B (see para 66.27).

The inclusion of the corporate gains in trust gains only happens if 10% or more of the corporate gain is apportioned to the trust and any connected person (see para 66.13). It can result in a doubling up of trust gains, for it means the trust gains include both the gains realised by the company on its investments and any gains realised by the trustees when the company is sold or liquidated. The credit which is otherwise available under s 13(7) on a sale or liquidation of the company does not apply to non-resident trusts, for the trustees do not themselves pay the s 13 tax. So too the credit relief for distributions made within three or more years of the gain being realised will rarely if ever apply. This subject is discussed further in para 66.25.

As described in para 66.8, the general rule is that losses in s 13 companies are not apportionable and do not offset the gains in the company. The one exception is that s 13 losses can be apportioned on a current year basis and set against (and set only against) s 13 gains apportioned to the trustees in the same tax year. The practical result is that in a trust and company structure there may be significant unrelieved loses.

A point also to remember is that s 13 gains are indexed rather than tapered. This means the trust's pool included some tapered gains (its own) and some indexed gains (the s 13 gains).

Offshore income gains

63.10 Offshore income gains are excluded from the computation as these are subject to special rules (see Chapter 71). But should the disposal of an interest in a non-distributor fund generate a loss, that loss is allowable for CGT purposes and so reduces current-year or future gains going into the s 87 pool (see para 71.13).

Special rules in computation

63.11 Although in general the computation is at it would be if the trust was UK resident there are one or two special rules.

Transfers between trusts

63.12 Transfers between trusts cause gains to come into or move out of the pool. This subject is discussed in para 63.26 below.

Gains attributed to the settlor

63.13 The s 87 pool excludes any gain of the trustees which is attributed to the settlor under s 86. Thus gains realised during the settlor's lifetime are likely not to fall into the s 87 pool, but this is not so if the settlor is non-resident or non-domiciled. Further s 86 does not catch gains realised in the year in which the settlor dies (see para 60.2) and so those gains also go into the s 87 pool.

Where the settlor is alive and has always been UK resident and domiciled it is tempting to conclude there will be no s 87 pool until the tax year of his death. In fact this may not be so if the settlement was made before 19 March 1991. Gains realised before 17 March 1998 were normally outside s 86 (see Chapter 61). Such gains therefore went into the s 87 pool and, unless allocated to capital payments, still remain there.

Non-domiciled or non-resident settlor

63.14 Until 17 March 1998 gains realised by a trust were not included in a s 87 pool unless the settlor was resident and domiciled in the UK either when the settlement was made or when the gains accrued. FA 1998, s 130 changed the law and removed this territorial limit to s 87, but for all trusts which previously qualified for such treatment the s 87 pool does not include gains realised before 17 March 1998 and nor are losses accruing before then able to be brought forward (FA 1998, s 130(4)).

Sch 4B gains

63.15 As already noted the effect of a Sch 4B transfer is to extinguish the s 87 pool existing as at the end of the tax year concerned and transfer it to the Sch 4C pool. Gains in the new s 87 pool which springs up thereafter are computed on the basis that the Sch 4B transfer has wholly or, as the case may be, partially rebased the trust assets (see para 62.16).

Allocation to capital payments

63.16 Should the trustees make one or more capital payments in the tax year when the s 87 pool first comes into existence, the pool is set against those payments and, if it is less than the payments, eliminated. The same applies insofar as the trustees have made capital payments in any prior year and those payments have not themselves been set against and extinguished an earlier s 87 pool.

Assuming that in the first year of the s 87 pool it is not eliminated by prior-year or current-year capital payments it is carried forward. If the trustees realise further gains in future years these are added to the pool. If on the other hand they make capital payments such reduce the pool or, if greater than the pool, eliminate it.

If in any tax year, the brought forward and current-year capital payments are less than the brought forward and current year gains in the pool, only gains equal to those in the pool are allocated to the payments. If the payments have been to more than one beneficiary, the pool is allocated pro rata, and the balance of the payments carried forward (s 87(5)).

As explained in para 65.3, a payment to a UK resident only counts as a capital payment for these purposes and so reduces the s 87 pool if it is not charged to income tax. Thus a payment which is matched with relevant income and charged under s 740 or is taxed as an offshore income gain is not set against the s 87 pool.

Trust emigration

63.17 Should the trust be one which has emigrated from the UK, a capital payment made while the trust was UK-resident can have gains in the s 87 pool set against it. But this is only the position if the capital payment was made in anticipation of (a) the trust becoming non-resident, and (b) a disposal then being made (TCGA 1992, s 89(1)). If these conditions are not met, a capital payment made prior to emigration cannot be taxed by reference to any s 87 pool coming into existence after the trust has migrated.

Should the trust be one whose settlor was non-resident or non-domiciled when he made the settlement, capital payments made before 17 March 1998 may be disregarded. But if he became both UK-resident and UK-domiciled between making the settlement and 17 March 1998, the only payments which may be disregarded are those which were (a) made before he became UK-resident and domiciled, and (b) were not made in anticipation of his change in domicile (TCGA 1992, s 89 referring to ibid, s 87(1) as originally enacted).

Sch 4C pools

63.18 If the settlement is a relevant settlement for the purposes of Sch 4C in the tax year in which a capital payment is made, the payment is allocated to the Sch 4C pool and the s 87 pool on a first in, first out basis. If gains of the same tax year are in both the Sch 4C and the s 87 pool, the former are allocated first (see para 64.10). So too if a capital payment is brought forward because of an insufficiency of gains in the Sch 4C or s 87 pools, in any given year it is set against a Sch 4C pool coming into existence in that year before a s 87 pool so coming into existence.

A point to stress is that unlike s 87, s 740, or even offshore income gains, a Sch 4C pool can be allocated to a capital payment even if the pool belongs to a completely different settlement. All that is necessary is that the settlement making the payment is a relevant settlement in relation to the settlement with the Sch 4C pool. In some cases this may make it difficult for a given set of trustees to be certain a capital payment by them diminishes their s 87 pool rather than that of a Sch 4C pool of another settlement of which they know nothing (see further para 64.9).

Repatriation of the settlement

63.19 Should the settlement become UK-resident any s 87 pool outstanding at the end of the last tax year of non-residence is carried forward into the resident period (TCGA 1992, s 89(2)). Thereafter this pool cannot be increased (unless the trust again emigrates) but the gains in it are allocated to capital payments made in the resident period. Once the aggregate payments so made exceed the s 87 pool it is eliminated.

Allocation to the settlor

63.20 Should a capital payment be made to the settlor, gains in the pool are allocated to it in the same way as payments to any other beneficiary. A charge under s 87 will result should the settlor then be resident and domiciled in the UK. This point should normally only arise if the trust is settlor-interested, although it should be noted that ultra vires payments can be taxed as capital payments (see para 65.5). It might be thought that if the trust is settlor-interested there is no s 87 pool, as all trust gains will be attributed to the settlor on an arising basis under s 86. But as noted above (para 63.13), many pre-1991 settlor-interested settlements have a s 87 pool and the same applies to settlor-interested settlements where the settlor has previously been non-resident or non-domiciled.

The charge to tax

Resident and domiciled individuals

63.21 Should gains in the s 87 pool be allocated to a capital payment made to a beneficiary who is resident and domiciled in the UK such gains are treated as the beneficiary's personal gains (TCGA 1992, s 87(4)). They are taxed at his marginal rate of tax and his annual exemption is available. In appropriate cases, the tax charge is increased by a supplemental tax representing notional interest (see para 63.29).

As taper relief is applied at trust level, the gains are not eligible for taper relief in the hands of the beneficiary (s 87(6A)) and nor may they be set against his personal losses (TCGA 1992, s 2(5)). The removal of relief against personal losses occurred when taper relief was introduced in 1998 and was not restored by the changes made in 2002 (as to which see para 60.12).

Non-resident or non-domiciled beneficiaries

63.22 In contrast to Sch 4C pools, gains in a 87 pool can be allocated to capital payments made to non-resident or non-domiciled beneficiaries. However such beneficiaries are not charged to tax. In the case of non-residents this follows from the general territorial limits of CGT (TCGA 1992, s 2(2)) and in the case of non-domiciliaries it is expressly provided for (s 87(7)). A point to stress is that in contrast to other types of gain accruing to non-domiciliaries, a s 87 gain is exempt whether or not brought to the UK.

There is one situation in which a capital payment to a non-resident or non-domiciled beneficiary is chargeable. This arises if there are no or insufficient gains in the s 87 pool when it is made and, by the time the trust does realise such gains, the beneficiary has become resident and domiciled in the UK. This result follows because residence and domicile is looked at at the time of allocation and not (if different) at the time of the capital payment.

Temporary non-residence

63.23 As described in para 27.7 an individual remains in charge to CGT if he is non-resident for less than five complete tax years (TCGA 1992, s 10A). In such a case gains accruing during this absence are assessed in the year of return. This applies to capital payments made to him during his absence as much as to gains resulting from actual disposals, for capital payments to which trust gains are allocated are deemed to be chargeable gains. Prior to 16 March 2005 it could be argued that a beneficiary was protected from this charge if during his absence he resides in a country with which the UK had concluded a treaty giving that country sole rights over capital gains. HMRC, however, did not accept this and changes made in 2005 have put the matter beyond doubt (see para 27.7).

Charitable beneficiaries

63.24 Gains in a s 87 pool may be allocated to a capital payment to a charity and here also are exempt if the general conditions for charitable relief are met (see TCGA 1992 s 256 and para 65.5).

Capricious allocation

63.25 It is a cardinal feature of s 87 that once a capital payment is made it is treated in full as gain save insofar as it exceeds the s 87 pool. This is so even if the s 87 pool is modest in size by comparison with the overall value of the trust fund. There is no concept by which only a proportion of a capital payment is taxed as gain, the proportion being the proportion the pool bears to the trust fund as a whole.

No doubt when s 87 was first introduced this feature was designed to benefit HMRC by ensuring the s 87 pools were taxed sooner rather than later. But if so it ignored the fact that the pool could be allocated to non-taxable beneficiaries, namely non-residents, non-domiciliaries and charities. Like many ungenerous anti-avoidance rules, it has probably lost HMRC more tax than it has gained.

The impact of this point is enhanced when it is remembered that a capital distribution is not taxed as a s 740 benefit if made to a non-resident individual (see para 56.18). This means that gains in a s 87 pool are allocated to it (and so washed out) even if there is available relevant income.

Transfers between settlements

Gains

63.26 A special rule applies where the trustees of one settlement transfer the settled property to another settlement. In such case the s 87 pool of the transferee settlement is increased by what are called the outstanding trust gains of the transferor settlement (TCGA 1992, s 90). Where the transferor trustees transfer only a proportion of the settled property to the transferee settlement, the latter's s 87 pool is increased by a proportionate part of the outstanding trust gains. The legislation does not in terms say that a corresponding reduction is made in the s 87 pool of the transferor settlement but this must follow by necessary implication and the contrary has never been argued.

These rules apply both where the transferee settlement is non resident and where it is UK-resident. In the latter event, the gains transferred go into its s 87 pool inherited from its period of non-residence or, if there is no such pool, constitute a new one.

The outstanding trust gains of the transferor settlement are defined as the s 87 pool of the transferor settlement as at the end of the tax year of the transfer (s 90(2)). In other words they are net of any gains in the pool allocated to capital payments in that year.

Trust gains are not transferred between settlements in accordance with these rules if the transfer is a Sch 4B transfer linked with trustee borrowing. In such case, the s 87 pool of the transferor settlement goes into the Sch 4C pool thereby created (see para 64.5).

Capital payments

63.27 No corresponding provision to s 90 applies to capital payments. Accordingly if the transferor trust has unallocated capital payments, such remain in the transferor trust. Obviously the transfer may of itself generate s 87 gains to offset the payments; such is the position if the assets transferred have latent gains. But where this is not so, for example if the asset transferred is cash, the surplus capital payments are left behind. Accordingly gains realised in the transferee settlement are not taxed until the trustees of that settlement make capital payments.

A further and related point is that capital payments from the transferee trust are not carried back to the transferor trust. They can be set only against gains in the s 87 pool in the transferee settlement, including gains transferred to it from the transferor setlement under s 90.

Sub-trusts and separate settlements

63.28 It is common for trustees to appoint sub-trusts for different groups of beneficiaries. In some cases the various sub-trusts may be operated entirely separately, in accordance with the wishes of the different groups of beneficiaries.

Section 87 pools pose problems for such trusts. Essentially the problems are two-fold:

(1) Gains in the s 87 pool at the time the separate funds are appointed are not allocated to the funds pro rata but remain a single pool, allocated to capital payments in date order regardless of the fund from which such are made.
(2) Gains realised after the appointment of the sub-funds also go into the global s 87 pool, regardless of which fund the gain is realised in. In an extreme case, this can mean a capital gain in one fund is allocated in full to a capital payment from another.

Sometimes this capriciousness can work in favour of the beneficiaries, as where the beneficiaries in receipt of the capital payments to which gains are allocated are non-resident or non-domiciled. In other cases the reverse is true, particularly where, for example, the beneficiaries of the fund realising the gain are non-resident or non-domiciled, and the beneficiaries of the fund making the capital payment are not.

The conventional solution to this problem is for the trustees to appoint not sub-trusts or sub-funds but to create entirely new settlements for the various groups of beneficiaries. If this is done, the rules in TCGA 1992, s 90 described above come into play and the s 87 pool of the original settlement is split proportionately. Further each successor settlement has its own pool allocated only to capital payments it makes.

This solution is not however without difficulties:

(1) It is not effective if the original settlement has outstanding trustee borrowing, for then the transfer to the new trusts creates a Sch 4C pool able to be allocated to any of the new settlements (see Chapter 64).
(2) Insofar as any of the assets are showing latent gains, such are triggered, thereby increasing the s 87 pools.
(3) It is necessary to be certain that the new settlements really are separate settlements.

This last point is of some interest. For CGT purposes generally, funds pass out of one settlement and into another if the trusts of the new settlement are exhaustive with no possibility of the funds reverting to the old one (see *Roome v Edwards* [1981] STC 96; *Bond v Pickford* [1983] STC 517; *Swires v Renton* [1991] STC 490; and SP 7/84). But for s 87 purposes the definition of settlement is, as noted above (para 63.2), not the CGT definition but the income tax anti-avoidance definition (as to which see para 59.14). Two notes of warning may be sounded.

The first arises out of the case of *Elibeck v Rawling* [1980] STC 192. Here in the Court of Appeal Buckley LJ regarded funds transferred from one settlement to another as still subject to the trusts of the original settlement, the trusts of the transferee settlement being treated as if they were written out in the original settlement. *Elibeck v Rawling* was a circular avoidance scheme, but Buckley LJ's reasoning was approved in the House of Lords (*Ramsay (WT) Ltd v IRC* [1981] STC 174).

The second point is that under the income tax definition the term 'settlement' includes any arrangement. In *Chinn v Collins* [1981] STC 1 a contingent appointment followed by the sale and vesting of the interest appointed was seen as a single arrangement, the bounty given by the settlor when he first made the settlement. It is possible to see a similar argument being mounted if the transfer to the new settlement and the realisation of gains or the making of capital payments are all part of a pre-planned scheme. The result could be that the transferor and the transferee settlements would be a single arrangement, and thus settlement, with the result that gains in one would be able to be allocated to capital payments from another.

It is difficult to quantify the extent of these risks. However, they are clearly less if the transferee settlement is a long-standing separate settlement rather than one created specifically for the purpose of effecting the transfer. The House of Lords decision in *West v Trennery* [2005] UKHL 5, [2005] STC 214 does not, it may be suggested bear on these problems. This is because it turned on the definition of property comprised in the settlement for the purposes of TCGA 1992, s 77. This definition finds no equivalent in s 87.

In theory, the sub-fund legislation in TCGA 1992, Sch 4ZA could be used as an alternate to creating new settlements. That legislation is not restricted to onshore settlements. But the conditions for its use are so restrictive that it will rarely be in point. The biggest difficulty is that an election cannot be made if the sub-funds have any beneficiary in common (Sch 4ZA paras 8 and 9).

Notional interest

63.29 The tax charged on capital payments charged under s 87 may in certain circumstances be increased by supplemental tax representing notional interest. The rules are laid down in TCGA 1992, ss 91–95. The most important point to realise is that these rules cannot come into operation unless CGT is charged in respect of the payment, and only impose notional interest on whatever tax is in fact charged. Sections 91–95 do not therefore extend the basic territorial scope of the capital payment rules, so capital payments are free of both CGT and the supplemental tax if the recipient beneficiary is non-resident or non-domiciled.

It may be that in certain instances the inflation of the tax by notional interest will be held to breach European law (see para 49.11)

Matching

63.30 The supplemental tax can only be charged if a capital payment is matched with a qualifying amount of the settlement for the last but one or an earlier year of assessment (TCGA 1992, s 91(1)(c)). For years up to and including 1989–90 there was no qualifying amount (FA 1991, Sch 17 para 2 passim). In 1990–91 the qualifying amount was the s 87 pool for that year, less capital payments made to beneficiaries during the year (FA 1991, Sch 17 para 2(2); TCGA 1992, s 92(2)). For 1991–92 and subsequent years the qualifying amount is the amount computed for the year under TCGA 1992, s 87(2), ie the net gains realised by the trustees in that year, excluding any trust gains carried forward from previous years (TCGA 1992, s 92(1), (2); FA 1991, Sch 17 para 2(3)). Where a non-resident settlement became resident before 1990–91, the qualifying amount was the trust gains outstanding at the end of 1990–91 (FA 1991, Sch 17 para 2(4), (5); TCGA 1992, s 92(2)).

The basic rule is that capital payments are matched with qualifying amounts on a first-in first-out basis, ie earlier payments are matched with earlier amounts (TCGA 1992, s 92(4)(a)). Thus a capital payment can never be matched with a qualifying amount of 1991–92 or a subsequent year until the entire qualifying amount of 1990–91 is exhausted. If a payment cannot be matched with a past amount (because there is none) it is carried forward (TCGA 1992, s 92(4)(b)). Where the capital payments in a year exceed the trust gains, the part of each payment treated as a chargeable gain is matched before any part of any payment not so treated (TCGA 1992, s 92(5)).

Supplemental tax

63.31 The supplemental tax does not apply unless the capital payment is matched with the qualifying amount for the last but one year of assessment or an earlier year (TCGA 1992, s 91(1)). If the recipient beneficiary is taxable on the payment under s 87, the CGT otherwise due is increased by an amount equal to interest at 10% on the tax (TCGA 1992, s 91(2), (3)). The tax is computed on the basis that the capital payment is the first slice of the beneficiary's gains for the year (*Tax Bulletin* 16 (April 1995) p 205).

This notional interest runs for the chargeable period. That period ends on 30 November following the year of assessment in which the payment is made. It begins six years earlier or (if later) on 1 December following the year of assessment in which the qualifying amount matched with the capital payment accrued (TCGA 1992, s 91(4), (5)). The rate of interest may be varied by the Treasury but the total supplemental tax cannot exceed the CGT otherwise chargeable (TCGA 1992, s 91(2), (6)). At current rates of interest the maximum supplemental tax on a higher-rate taxpayer is 24%, which gives total tax of 64%.

Where a capital payment is matched with the qualifying amounts of two or more years of assessment, each earlier than that preceding the making of the capital payment, the capital payment is treated as being as many payments as there are qualifying amounts (TCGA 1992, s 93(1), (2)). The CGT is divided up and attributed to the notional payments on a just and reasonable basis and the supplemental tax computed accordingly. Where part of a capital payment is matched with the qualifying amount or amounts of the last but one or an earlier year of assessment and part is not, the capital payment is divided up and the supplemental tax is only added to tax on the part or parts of the payment matched with the last but one or earlier years of assessment (TCGA 1992, s 93(1), (3)). Necessary apportionments are also directed where a capital payment is matched with part only of a qualifying amount, i e where it is less (TCGA 1992, s 93(4)).

Transfer between settlements

63.32 Special rules apply where the trustees of one settlement advance or appoint all or part of the settled property into or on the trusts of another settlement (TCGA 1992, s 94). If all the settled property is so treated, any unmatched qualifying amounts of the transferor settlement are treated as qualifying amounts of the recipient settlement. They are treated as qualifying amounts of the recipient settlement for the same year as they were in fact qualifying amounts of the transferor settlement. The recipient settlement is assumed to have existed and been non-resident in the years concerned if not in fact so. If part only of the settled property is advanced or appointed, any unmatched qualifying amounts are apportioned between the two settlements. It would appear that capital payments made from the recipient settlement have to be first matched with the recipient settlement's own qualifying amounts prior to the year of the transfer (if any), and then with those inherited from the transferor settlement (TCGA 1992, s 95).

Chapter 64

Schedule 4C pools

Introduction

64.1 Schedule 4C of TCGA 1992 comes into operation where as a result of the rules in TCGA 1992, Sch 4B described in the previous chapter trustees make a transfer of value linked with trustee borrowing. This may be referred to as the Sch 4B transfer and any gains then realised as Sch 4B gains. The function of Sch 4C is to create a pool of gains, the Sch 4C pool, which comprises both gains triggered on the Sch 4B transfer and also any s 87 pool in the settlement at the end of the tax year of the Sch 4B transfer. Sch 4C then allocates this pool to beneficiaries in receipt of capital payments.

Sch 4C was first enacted when the rules as to the trustee borrowing were introduced in 2000. The initial enactment of those rules introduced s 90(5)(a) in its original form which inadvertently provided a mechanism, the new style flip-flop scheme, for avoiding the s 87 charge. Section 90(5)(a) provided that on a transfer between settlements (see para 63.26) gains in the s 87 pool of the transferor settlement did not pass into the transferee settlement in accordance with TCGA 1992, s 90 to the extent that the transfer was linked with trustee borrowing. Accordingly the incurring of a large borrowing in the transferor settlement prior to the transfer enabled the s 87 pool to be left behind, thereby rendering distributions from the transferee settlement tax-free.

In 2003 the government saw fit to block this scheme. It did so not by admitting that the 2000 legislation was flawed (as it was) but by radical amendment to Sch 4C. This amendment not merely blocked the scheme but introduced other significant changes as well.

This chapter describes the law as it exists following the amendment of Sch 4C by FA 2003. The basic concept is that the Sch 4C pool of gains is a floating pool which can be allocated to any resident and domiciled beneficiary who receives a capital payment either from the settlement which effected the Sch 4B transfer or from any other settlement which has directly or indirectly received funds from it. The commencement date of Sch 4C is 21 March 2000, but limited transitional provisions, described at para 64.14 limit its impact as respects events prior to 9 April 2003.

As with s 87, the term settlement bears its extended income tax anti-avoidance meaning, discussed in para 63.2 (TCGA 1992, s 97(7)). The comments in para 63.2 on the term 'settlor' and 'trustees' are also in point in relation to Sch 4C.

When is a Sch 4C pool created?

64.2 A Sch 4C pool comes into existence whenever the trustees of a settlement make a Sch 4B transfer (Sch 4C para 1(1)). A point to stress is that the Sch 4C pool is created even if no gain results from the transfer or if any such gain is attributed to the settlor on an arising basis under s 86 (Sch 4C para 1(5)). Sometimes the transfer of value may be very small, as on a modest capital distribution, and the ensuing Sch 4B gain will be modest or non-existent. But all such cases have the draconian result of bringing a Sch 4C pool into existence.

What gains are in the Sch 4C pool?

64.3 The gains which are included in the Sch 4C pool are the Sch 4B gains and the outstanding s 87 gains.

Sch 4B trust gains

64.4 The Sch 4B gains are the gains realised on the Sch 4B transfer which brought the pool into existence (Sch 4C para 4). However such gains are excluded insofar as they are attributed to the settlor under s 86 (para 6) and they may also be reduced by any brought forward or current year losses. However it is not all losses which are allowed in this way. It is only losses realised on other Sch 4B transfers effected by the trustees (para 7). Such Sch 4B losses can only be offset against Sch 4B gains and, if in any year the Sch 4B losses exceed the Sch 4B gains the surplus is carried forward.

Should the trustees make another Sch 4B transfer in the same tax year as the original one, any ensuing Sch 4B gain is added to the pool, reduced by any applicable Sch 4B loss (Sch 4C para 7B(2)). The same applies to further Sch 4B transfers in subsequent tax years if the Sch 4C pool is then still outstanding – in other words if part at least has not been allocated to beneficiaries (para 7B(3)). If all the gains in the original pool have been so allocated before the beginning of the tax year in which the further transfer occurs, the latter causes a new Sch 4C pool to come into existence in that year.

An important point to note is that it is only Sch 4B gains realised by the settlement that made the original Sch 4B transfer which go into pool. Gains accruing on transfers made by relevant settlements (para 64.8 below) are not so included.

Outstanding s 87 gains

64.5 The outstanding s 87 gains are those gains in the s 87 pool of the settlement which made the Sch 4B transfer which have not been allocated to capital payments before the end of the tax year in which the Sch 4B transfer is made (Sch 4C para 7A). However it is not all capital payments so made which cause gains to be disregarded. Gains are only allocated to capital payments made in the year of the transfer if the recipient beneficiary is chargeable to tax for that year. The term 'chargeable to tax' means the recipient beneficiary must be both resident and domiciled in the UK (Sch 4C para 8(4)).

Gains realised in a subsequent tax year by the settlement which made the Sch 4B transfer are not included in the Sch 4C pool. They therefore are dealt with under ordinary s 87 rules and form a new s 87 pool. However should the settlement make a subsequent Sch 4B transfer these gains are sucked into Sch 4C, into the original pool if it then still exists and otherwise into a new pool (Sch 4C para 7B(3)).

The outstanding s 87 gains do not include offshore income gains (see para 63.10).

Transfers between settlements

64.6 Should the settlement making the Sch 4B transfer receive an advance from another settlement in the year of the transfer, the general rule under TCGA 1992, s 90(1) applies (para 63.26), namely that all or a proportion of the outstanding trust gains of the advancing settlement's s 87 pool passes into the s 87 pool, and thus into the Sch 4B pool, of the settlement making the Sch 4B transfer (Sch 4C para 7A(2)). The term 'outstanding trust gains' is defined in s 90(2) as the trust gains of the settlement making the advance less capital payments made by it in that year. This definition is however disapplied for the purposes of Sch 4C by para 7A(2), for item (ii) of that sub-paragraph refers to the amount by which the s 87 gains would be increased but for s 90(2). The result is that 'outstanding trust gains' is not defined for the purposes of Sch 4C and so it is unclear whether capital payments made in the year of the advance by the advancing settlement are deducted in computing the recipient's s 87 gains going into the Sch 4C pool. Logic suggests they should be for otherwise gains allocated to any such capital payment would fall to be taxed both by reference to the payment by the advancing settlement and in the recipient's Sch 4C pool. If this is right the deduction should extend to capital payments from the advancing settlement to non-residents or non-domiciliaries, for no provision in Sch 4C para 7A prevents this.

Should the settlement making the Sch 4B transfer itself advance funds to another settlement in the year of the Sch 4B transfer, that advance is a Sch 4B transfer if at the time of the advance there is outstanding trustee borrowing (see para 62.10). However it is at least theoretically possible for the transfer to another settlement to be made in the same tax year as the Sch 4B transfer but before the trustee borrowing to which the transfer is linked is incurred. In this situation it is not linked with trustee borrowing and the general rule under s 90(1) is, as noted above, that all or a proportion of the settlement's s 87 pool as at the end of the tax year is added to the recipient's pool. Sch 4C makes no provision as to whether the s 87 gains added to the Sch 4C pool created by the subsequent transfer are net of those going across to the recipient settlement under the earlier advance. But it may be suggested that the gains so added are net, since otherwise the gains going across would potentially be taxed twice once in the Sch 4C pool and again in the s 87 pool of the recipient settlement of the earlier advance.

Allocation of gains

64.7 Gains in a Sch 4C pool are allocated to beneficiaries who receive, or have received, a capital payment from any settlement which falls within the definition of relevant settlement (Sch 4C para 8). As with s 87, the gains allocated to a particular recipient cannot exceed the payment he receives and in the case of multiple payments in the same tax year, the gains are allocated pro rata. The Sch 4C pool is carried forward from one tax year to the next insofar as not exhausted.

The meaning of the term 'capital payment' is the same as for s 87 and is explained in the next chapter. A capital payment does not have gains in the Sch 4C pool allocated to it if the recipient is not chargeable to tax (Sch 4C para 8(3)). Chargeable tax has the meaning given above, namely that the recipient must be resident and domiciled in the UK (para 8(4)).

Relevant settlement

64.8 The term 'relevant settlement' comprises the following (Sch 4C para 8A):

(a) The settlement which made the Sch 4B transfer, or transferor settlement as it is called.
(b) The transferee settlement. This term is defined as any settlement whose settled property directly or indirectly represents the proceeds of the transfer of value (Sch 4C para 14(2)). Self-evidently there is only a transferee settlement where the transfer of value is to another settlement.
(c) Any other settlement to which a settlement which is a relevant settlement makes a Sch 4B transfer of value or a transfer covered by the rules in s 90 as to transfers between settlements (as to which see para 63.26).
(d) Any settlement that is a relevant settlement in relation to any other pool of which the transferor settlement is a relevant settlement at the time of the Sch 4B transfer.

Head (c) in this definition is menacing. It appears it can create an indefinite chain, in that even if a settlement is only itself a relevant settlement by reference to this head, any Sch 4B or s 90 transfer it makes results in the recipient becoming a relevant settlement. It may be noted that a settlement which becomes a relevant settlement under this head or as a transferee settlement may be resident or non-resident. This result is expressly provided for by Sch 4C para 10(1) and in any event follows because s 90 applies to transfers to both resident and non-resident settlements (see para 63.26). So too any settlement brought in under head (d) can be resident or non-resident.

As will be apparent, the effect of the definition is that the category of relevant settlements can constantly grow, for once a settlement has become a relevant settlement in relation to a particular Sch 4C pool, any settlement to which it makes a transfer becomes a relevant settlement.

There are two limitations on the potential growth in the number of relevant settlements. One is that a transfer can only cause a fresh settlement to become a relevant settlement if at the time of the transfer the transferor settlement is a relevant settlement: this is indicated by the use of the present tense in para 8A(3). It inter alia means that transfers between settlements prior to the Sch 4B transfer can be ignored. The second is that the whole apparatus of relevant settlements in relation to a particular Sch 4C pool falls away once distributions have been made to a sufficient level to ensure that pool no longer exists.

A critical point about the definition of relevant settlement is that a transfer between settlements can cause a settlement to become a relevant settlement and so exposed to the Sch 4C pool of a settlement with which it has no connection. Such would happen if Settlement A made a Sch 4B transfer and by that transfer or by later advance, advances part of the trust fund to Settlement B, which a few years later itself advances part of the trust fund to Settlement C. In such a case all the gains in the Sch 4C pool of trust A at the time of the transfer from trust B to trust C could be allocated to the beneficiaries of trust C.

Available capital payments

64.9 This basic rule is that Sch 4C trust gains are allocated to any capital payment made by any relevant settlement to a beneficiary who is resident and domiciled in the UK. A capital payment may have gains allocated to it whether made before or after the Sch 4B transfer and whether before or after the settlement making the payment became a relevant settlement (Sch 4C para 8(1)).

The following capital payments cannot have gains allocated to them:

(1) Capital payments made before 21 March 2000 (Sch 4C para 9(3)(a)).
(2) Capital payments made before the start of the tax year preceding that in which the Sch 4B transfer is made (para 9(3)(b)).
(3) A capital payment to which gains have been allocated in an earlier tax year under Sch 4C or s 87 (para 9(2)).
(4) A capital payment made from a resident settlement if it was made before the Sch 4B transfer and not in anticipation of the transfer (Sch 4C para 10(2)).

These exceptions apart all capital payments made from any settlement which is or becomes a relevant settlement can have Sch 4C gains allocated. A point to stress concerns the position of settlements which become relevant settlements by virtue of a Sch 4B or s 90 transfer after the original Sch 4B transfer. Once such a settlement becomes a relevant settlement, any prior capital payment made by the settlement can have Sch 4C gains allocated to it provided only that (i) the payment was made after 21 March 2000, (ii) it was made after the beginning of the tax year prior to the Sch 4B transfer, and (iii) has not in a prior tax year had gains allocated to it under s 87.

The practical and potentially unfortunate results of all this may be illustrated by the following example. A beneficiary of one settlement, say C, in good faith receives a capital payment which is tax-free as there is no s 87 pool in settlement C. The same year another settlement, A, makes a Sch 4B transfer and a Sch 4C pool of less than the capital payment from settlement C is created. A few years later it makes a transfer to another settlement B, and a few years after that settlement B makes a transfer to settlement C. At this time settlement C still has no s 87 pool and settlement A's Sch 4C pool still exists. Accordingly under the rules described above, the gains in the Sch 4C pool are allocated to the settlement C beneficiary and he is taxable. However neither he nor the trustees of settlement A know this as they are not in direct contact and shortly afterwards settlement A makes a capital distribution to one of its beneficiaries. The Sch 4C gains are, in the minds of the beneficiary and the trustees of settlement A, allocated to that payment and returns made accordingly. The result is that tax is charged on the wrong person. It is for conjecture whether, if that person later discovers the true position, he would have an error or mistake claim, and whether, assuming that claim was upheld, HMRC could make a discovery assessment on the beneficiary of settlement C given he had at all times acted in good faith. The language of TMA 1970, s 29(6) suggests they could.

Quite apart from this kind of situation, the rules give scope for planning or mischief making. Suppose trust A has a Sch 4C pool, and trust B has unallocated capital payments to UK residents. Could trust A make an s 90 advance to trust B to wash out the Sch 4C pool. Would the advance count as an addition if the trustees of trust B declined to accept it? Such declining might be easy if the advance was small, but what would be the position if it was large and in the interests of the beneficiaries of trust B as a whole? In some cases the advance might be in the interests of all concerned, for example if the prior capital payment had been to a single beneficiary and he has losses or is insolvent.

Another point to stress is that the rules apply even if the capital payment is made from a UK settlement which has never been offshore. The only requirement is that it become a relevant settlement. As described above, the payment may be ignored if made before the Sch 4B transfer but not, it should be noted, if made between then and the UK settlement becoming a relevant settlement.

Which gains are allocated?

64.10 Given the comprehensive and all-embracing nature of the rules, it will frequently be the case that gains in both a Sch 4C pool and a s 87 pool can be allocated to a capital payment, and sometimes there may be more than one Sch 4C pool. The latter will be the case where the settlement making the distribution is a relevant settlement in relation to more than one Sch 4C pool.

The basic allocation rule applies just within a single Sch 4C pool. In such case, gains are allocated on a first in first out basis (Sch 4C para 8B). For these purposes any gain realised on the Sch 4B transfer is treated as accruing at the time of transfer and a s 87 gain included in the pool as an outstanding s 87 gain is treated as accruing when in fact realised. The practical result of this is that a capital payment from a relevant settlement is matched against the s 87 pool of the original Sch 4B transferor settlement until such of the gains in the latter as accrued in years prior to the transfer have been exhausted. Given the points made above and the breadth of the definition of relevant settlement, there could be the most extraordinary transfer of old gains between settlements.

The secondary allocation rule applies where a capital payment could have gains from both a Sch 4C pool and a s 87 pool allocated to it. In such case, first in first out applies across the board, but if for a year there are both Sch 4C and s 87 gains the former are allocated first. The legislation is silent as to the position where gains could be allocated from more than one Sch 4C pool, an indication perhaps that the draftsman did not fully appreciate that a settlement could be a relevant settlement in relation to more than one Sch 4C pool.

Notional interest

64.11 As with s 87 (see para 63.29) the tax charge on a capital payment may be increased by notional interest (Sch 4C para 13). This interest is at the same rate as applies under s 87, i e 10%, and runs for a period which ends on 30 November in the tax year following that in which the capital payment is made. The period begins six years earlier, or, if later, 1 December in the tax year following the year of the gain. This has the same meaning as in the allocation rules – i e the year of the transfer if the payment is matched with a Sch 4B gain, and the year the gain was realised if the payment is matched with a gain in the old s 87 pool.

It is to be noted that interest cannot run after the capital payment is made. This is a small mercy for beneficiaries of settlements which become relevant settlements and thereby cause prior capital payments to be taxed. It means that even if there is a longer delay between the capital payment and the settlement become a relevant settlement, the interest clock has stopped running at the time of the capital payment.

Temporary emigration

64.12 As noted above, the Sch 4C pool gains are not allocated to a beneficiary who is non-resident, and the general rule is that this is so even if he is non-resident less than five complete tax years.

However a special rule applies if, in the absence of Sch 4C, Sch 4B or s 87 gains would under s 87 rules have been treated as accruing to the beneficiary in the year of return (see para 63.23) by reason of a capital payment made to him during his absence. In such case, the excess of the capital payment over the gains in the settlement's s 87 pool allocated to it in the year of return is taxed by reference to the Sch 4C pool (Sch 4C para 12A).

Where the settlor is non-resident for less than five complete tax years, the Sch 4B gains included in the gains treated as accruing to him in the year of return are net of any such gains allocated to capital payments in the intervening years (Sch 4C para 12).

Resident settlements

64.13 As described in para 62.19, a Sch 4B transfer may be made by a resident settlement if it has previously been non resident. The better view is that such a settlement remains exposed to Sch 4B even if all the s 87 pool carried into the resident period has been allocated to capital payments or indeed even if there was no such pool.

As described in para 62.19, the effect of Sch 4B on such a settlement is that a Sch 4B transfer results in a tax charge on the trustees since they are UK resident. However in Sch 4C no account is taken of this and so the following results occur:

(1) The gain realised on the Sch 4B transfer goes into a Sch 4C pool and so is potentially chargeable again when a capital payment is made.
(2) The Sch 4C pool also includes any outstanding s 87 pool of the settlement.

The potential for double taxation was avoided by Sch 4C as originally enacted as it applied only to settlements within s 87 – ie non-resident settlements (Sch 4C para 1(1) as originally enacted). In its present form Sch 4C expressly contemplates both non-resident settlements, ie s 87 settlements, and those which have immigrated, ie s 89(2) settlements (para 7A passim). The potential for double taxation appears to be a draftsman's oversight.

Commencement

64.14 Although Sch 4C in its present form results from FA 2003, the basic rule is that it applies in any case where the Sch 4B transfer was made on or after the original introduction date of Sch 4B, namely 21 March 2000 (FA 2003, s 163(4)(a)). Where the Sch 4B transfer was made before the 2003 amendments were announced (9 April 2003), the pool is treated as having come into existence on 8 April 2003.

Under Sch 4C in its original form, there was no inclusion in the Sch 4C pool of the s 87 pool as at the end of the tax year of the Sch 4B transfer. This position is recognised in a limited sense where the Sch 4B transfer took place before 8 April 2003. In such cases the s 87 gains which go into the Sch 4C pool are not the s 87 pool as at the end of the year of the Sch 4B transfer but the s 87 pool as at 8 April 2003 (FA 2003, s 163(4)(b)). It follows that the s 87 pool has to be computed as at that date under s 87 rules, including inter alia the rule that distributions to non-residents or non-domiciliaries reduce the pool. The pool as so computed then goes into the Sch 4C pool, the mechanics being that a notional year of assessment ends on 8 April 2003. That mechanism means that a Sch 4B transfer on 6, 7 or 8 April 2004 will have carried into the Sch 4C pool the s 87 pool as at 8 April 2003, rather than that pool as at 5 April 2004.

A further transitional provision prevents the s 87 pool which passes into the Sch 4C pool as at 8 April 2003 from being allocated to capital payments made from the Sch 4C pool before 9 April 2003 (s 163(4)(e)). Such gains will of course have been allocated under s 87 rules to any payments made from the s 87 pool before that date, the pool going into the Sch 4C pool necessarily being net of such payments.

It is also provided that the Sch 4C rules disregarding capital payments to non-residents or non-domiciliaries do not apply to capital payments made before 9 April 2003 (s 163(4)(d)). This provision applies regardless of the date on which the gains comprised in the Sch 4C pool accrued and so in appropriate cases it may be possible, by careful use of the rules relating to relevant settlements, to wash Sch 4C gains out without tax charge. This could be achieved if the settlement with a Sch 4C pool makes an advance to a settlement which on 8 April 2003 had surplus capital payments to non-residents or non-domiciliaries and such payments were made after the beginning of the tax year before that in which the relevant Sch 4B transfer was made.

A final transitional rule prevents any settlement other than the transferor or the transferee settlement from being a relevant settlement if the actions otherwise making it so took place before 9 April 2003.

Despite these transitional provisions, Sch 4C in its present form has been criticised as retrospective. This is because settlements which made a Sch 4B transfer between 21 March 2000 and 9 April 2003 automatically have their outstanding s 87 trust gains as at 8 April 2003 moved across into the Sch 4C pool. As such the settlement looses the possibility of washing out those gains by subsequent capital payments to non-residents or non-domiciliaries.

This aspect of the 2003 changes also impacts on cases where a new style flip-flop scheme based on the original s 90(5)(a) (see para 64.1) had been effected before 9 April 2003, but the transferee settlement had not by then distributed the funds transferred to it. In such case, the s 87 pool by definition remained with the transferor settlement, whence as at 8 April 2003 it passed into the Sch 4C pool. Nothing in the transitional rules prevents gains in this pool being allocated to distributions after 9 April 2003 from the transferee settlement. It follows that the scheme is nullified save insofar as the transferee settlement had distributed the funds passed to it before 9 April 2003.

Chapter 65

Capital payments

Introduction

65.1 Liability under TCGA 1992, s 87 or Sch 4C arises when a beneficiary receives a capital payment from the trustees (s 87(4); Sch 4C para 8(1)). This chapter considers what is meant by payment, when it is capital, and the circumstances in which it is treated as received by a beneficiary from the trustees. The relevant terms are defined in TCGA 1992 s 97, which applies both to s 87 and to Sch 4C.

Payment

65.2 The term 'payment' is in part a misnomer for it excludes any payment made by the trustees under a transaction entered into at arm's length (s 97(1)(b)). However the term includes the following (s 97(2)):

(a) the transfer of an asset;
(b) the conferring of any other benefit;
(c) any occasion on which settled property become nominee property.

Settled property becomes nominee property when one or more persons become absolutely entitled to it (TCGA 1992, ss 60(1) and 71(1)). Absolute entitlement connotes the ability to direct the trustee as to how to deal with the property subject only to the trustee's lien for costs etc (s 60(2)). Absolute entitlement can either arise by express act of the trustee in appointing property to the beneficiary absolutely or automatically under the terms of the trust, as where the reversion to a life interest vests absolutely on the death of the life tenant.

In general, the various methods by which a payment is made require a positive and voluntary decision by the trustees in that cash or other assets cannot be distributed or benefits conferred without a decision by the trustee to do so. But the position is otherwise with absolute entitlement under the terms of the trust and, while this problem normally arises only with old fashioned fixed-interest trusts, the resultant involuntary capital payment can be most unfortunate (see further para 10.13).

A valuation rule applies where the payment is anything other than an outright payment of money. The amount of the payment is equal to the value of the benefit conferred by it (s 97(4)). This rule applies even where the capital payment is the outright transfer or vesting of an asset in specie and it means that if the value of the benefit conferred differs from the market value of the asset the former is the amount of the capital payment.

Capital

65.3 If the recipient is resident or ordinarily resident in the UK a payment is capital unless it is chargeable as his income (s 97(1)(a)). Should the recipient be non-resident, a payment is capital if it is received otherwise than as income. In other words for UK residents the test is liability to income tax, whereas for non-residents the test is whether as a matter of trust law the distribution is income or capital in the hands of the beneficiary. The trust law distinction between income and capital distributions is discussed in Chapter 12.

In relation to UK residents the exclusion of payments chargeable to income tax means that a capital distribution is not a capital payment if it is taxable as a benefit under TA 1988, s 740 (see Chapter 56) or as an offshore income gain under TA 1988, s 762 (see para 71.19). But as is described in para 56.28 it must in fact be charged to income tax: if it would be chargeable as a s 740 benefit but for the lack of relevant income it is a capital payment insofar as matched with gains in the s 87 or Sch 4C pool in a tax year prior to that in which there is first relevant income (TCGA 1992, s 97(3)).

One curious result of the rules as to whether a payment is capital is that distributions to non-residents are more often capital payments than distributions to residents. This is because the latter are taxed under s 740 if there is relevant income, whereas the former are not. The point is in practice relevant only to s 87 pools, for as noted in para 64.7, capital payments to non-residents are ignored under Sch 4C. The position as respects s 740 and distributions to non-domiciliaries is considered further in para 56.23.

Received

65.4 The word 'received' is given an extended definition. A capital payment is regarded as received by a beneficiary from the trustees in any of the following circumstances (s 97(5)):

(i) he receives it from them directly or indirectly;
(ii) it is directly or indirectly applied by them in payment of any debt of his;
(iii) it is otherwise paid or applied for his benefit;
(iv) it is received by a third party at his direction.

Since it is the position under both s 87 and Sch 4C that capital payments to non-residents are not charged, a question which sometimes occurs is whether liability arises if a non-resident recipient passes the sum received on to a UK resident. In other words can the payment be taxed as if it were received by the

UK resident donee? This issue is discussed in relation to TA 1988, s 740 in para 56.21. It is suggested that for CGT purposes, the UK resident cannot be characterised as the recipient, provided as a matter of trust law the payment is a valid distribution to the non-resident. TCGA 1992, s 97(5) requires the payment to be received from the trustees and, provided the payment is validly made to the non-resident recipient, it is difficult to see how anyone other than him receives it even indirectly from the trustees.

Beneficiary

65.5 Even the term 'beneficiary' has an extended meaning. Should a person who is not a beneficiary receive a capital payment he is deemed to be a beneficiary (TCGA 1992, s 97(8)). This does not however apply where an actual beneficiary can be treated as receiving the payment and nor does it apply so as to treat the trustees of another settlement as a beneficiary (s 97(10)(a)). This latter exclusion is necessary because where one trust distributes or advance capital to another, special rules regulate the transfer of s 87 or Sch 4C gains between the trusts (see paras 63.26 and 64.8).

Should a capital payment be made to a charity which is a beneficiary under the trust it counts as received by a beneficiary, for the charity is as much a beneficiary as any other. In 1998 HMRC accepted that the exemption in TCGA 1992, s 256 would apply (*Tax Bulletin* 36 (August 1998) p 573). Section 256 exempts from CGT any gain which accrues to a charity provided the gain is applicable for and in fact applied for charitable purposes. The effect of the HMRC interpretation is to enable s 87 gains to be allocated to and so washed out by distributions to charity even though not charged. The interpretation was published prior to the enactment of Sch 4C and it is unclear whether it applies to Sch 4C pools also.

Transfers to another settlement

65.6 Difficult issues arise when the trustees transfer all or part of the settled property to another settlement or resettle it. As is explained above, TCGA 1992, s 90 operates unless the transfer is linked with trustee borrowing and provides that all or a proportion of the outstanding trust gains are carried forward to the transferee settlement (para 63.26). Under Sch 4C, the transferee settlement becomes a relevant settlement (para 64.8).

The question which s 90 and Sch 4C do not address is whether the transfer can constitute a capital payment to any beneficiary under the transferee settlement. On one view it cannot, for s 90 and Sch 4C clearly envisage that transfers between settlements will occasion the carry forward of gains rather than a capital payment. Further even if the benefit a beneficiary takes under the transferee settlement were a capital payment the amount would be nil if the beneficiary's interest is discretionary or terminable by the trustees, for then it is valueless.

A contrary argument focuses on the wording of TCGA 1992, ss 97(2) and 97(5)(b). As noted above s 97(2) proves that the term payment includes the conferring of any benefit, and s 97(5)(b) states that a payment is received by the beneficiary if it is paid or applied for his benefit. Reference is then made to the fact that a resettlement or a transfer to a new settlement can be made in exercise of the statutory power of advancement in s 32 of the Trustee Act 1925 or under some similar express power, and the fact that such power only authorises the exercise if it is for the benefit of the particular beneficiary being advanced. In those circumstances it can be said that the resettlement falls squarely within the words of s 97(5)(b) and so is a capital payment to the beneficiary. Further, given that the resettlement is the application for his benefit, the value of his interest under the new settlement is immaterial, for the amount resettled is the amount applied for his benefit and thus the amount resettled is the amount of the capital payment.

HMRC are thought to adopt this analysis both in relation to advances under s 32 and in relation to similar express powers exercisable for the benefit of a specific beneficiary. Whether the analysis is right given the s 90 and Sch 4C regimes for the transfer of trust gains is debatable. If it is right, the capital payment represented by the advance reduces or eliminates the outstanding trust gains carried forward to the new settlement.

In practice, most transfers to a new settlement are effected not in exercise of the statutory power of advancement or some similar power, but in exercise of an express power authorising the trustees to transfer all or part of the trust fund to another trust. Such powers require some at least of the beneficiaries of the transferor trust to be beneficiaries of the transferee trust, but the trustees in exercising the power are benefiting those beneficiaries collectively rather than any particular beneficiary. In these circumstances it is difficult to see the exercise as a payment or application for the benefit of a particular beneficiary within s 97(5)(b), and even if it was it would be such a payment or application for the benefit of all the beneficiaries common to the two settlements. On that scenario the value of the benefit to each, and thus the amount of any capital payment, would be impossible to determine.

HMRC are thought to agree that where the power exercised is a power to benefit beneficiaries generally there is no capital payment and s 90 applies. Obviously there will be cases where it is difficult to tell which side of the line a power falls and here attention to detail is important.

Free use of property

65.7 Trustees frequently allow beneficiaries to borrow from the trust at a low or nil rate of interest. So too, a beneficiary may be given a licence to occupy trust property at a low or nil rent. The question of whether such transactions occasion a capital payment, and if so when and in what amount, have occasioned controversy and difficulty.

Fixed-term loan or licence

65.8 In the case of a fixed term loan or licence, the matter is covered by s 97(4). There is a benefit, conferred when the loan is made or licence granted, and equal to the then value of the loan or licence.

Demand loan or licence

65.9 If demand loans and revocable licences were looked at in the same way as fixed-term loans and licenses, there would be a benefit, but its value would be nil, for at any time after the loan was made or licence granted it could be called in or revoked. On this basis there would be nothing to tax.

In *Billingham v Cooper* [2001] STC 1177, the Court of Appeal decided that this is not the correct approach. The right approach is to focus on the trustees' continuing decision to not call in the loan or revoke the licence. This benefit is valued retrospectively each year according as to how long the loan or licence remains outstanding. If it needs to be determined when the benefit is conferred, time apportionment on a daily basis is the fairest course. This is relevant to the matching exercise necessary to determine if supplementary tax is payable (see para 63.29).

In *Billingham v Cooper*, the trust was a fixed-interest trust where a demand loan had been made to the life-tenant. As a subsidiary argument, the taxpayer contended there was no benefit, for the taxpayer would have been entitled to the interest had it been charged. The Court of Appeal rejected this argument also. One wonders if the taxpayer was worse off through interest not being charged, for had it been charged, the interest would, under the principle in cases such as *Singer v Williams* [1921] 1 AC 41 have been a payment by the taxpayer to himself. It is an interesting question as to whether it would then be taxable.

A subsidiary point in some licence cases arises where occupying beneficiary himself owns a share in the property personally, he and the trustees thus being tenants in common. This was the position in *Carter v Hunt* [2000] STC (SCD) 17, where the taxpayer's share was 20% and the trustees 80%. Here the taxpayer's argument is that there is no benefit and thus no capital payment, for the taxpayer is in occupation by virtue of his rights as co-owner. HMRC's position is that there is a benefit, equal to the percentage of the market value represented by the trustees share. The point was not decided in *Carter v Hunt* and so is still at large.

Valuation

65.10 *Billingham v Cooper* did not determine the amount of the capital payment – ie how the value of the benefit conferred should be determined. In notes to Form 50 FS, HMRC express the view that the benefit in each tax year is the difference between a commercial rate of interest or open market rent on the one hand and the interest or rent actually charged (if any) on the other.

In the case of loans, Form 50 FS confirms that HMRC will in practice accept Official Rate of Interest as a commercial rate. This is the rate prescribed for taxing beneficial loans to employees and is currently 5% (see para 69.10).

In relation to licences HMRC accept that open market rental is a question of fact, depending inter alia on the terms imposed on the occupying beneficiary. In appropriate cases the annual benefit may be low or even nil. Thus in *Carter v Hunt*, the taxpayer was obliged under the terms of the agreement between him and the trustees to insure and repair the property. During the years 1984–85 to 1997–98, the costs of those items exceeded the notional rent and, on the eve of a Commissioners hearing, HMRC conceded there was no benefit and thus no capital payment for any of the years in question.

Payments by and to companies

65.11 TCGA 1992, s 96 lays down express rules dealing with payments involving companies. They apply both to s 87 and to Sch 4C.

Payments by companies

65.12 A payment received from a qualifying company controlled by the trustees counts as received from the trustees (s 96(1)). 'Control' bears its income tax close company definition (TA 1988, s 416), save that no rights or powers of an associate are attributed to a person unless he is himself a participator in the company concerned (TCGA 1992, s 96(10)). A company counts as controlled by the trustees if they control it or if they and the settlor or a person connected with him control it (s 96(7), (8)). A company is a qualifying company if it is close or would be close were it United Kingdom resident (s 96(6)).

Payments to companies

65.13 A payment is also a capital payment if it is received by a non-resident company which would be close if UK resident (s 96(2)). Where such a company is controlled by a single UK resident it counts as received by him. If two or more persons each control the company separately, it counts as received by such of them as are UK resident, divided equally between them if more than one. If it is controlled by two or more persons only if they are taken together, the payment is apportioned among the participators, but excluding any to whom 5% or less would be apportioned (s 96(3)–(5)).

For these purposes control has the same meaning as in the income tax close company provisions (ie TA 1988, s 416), although rights and powers are not attributed to a person unless he is himself a participator (TCGA 1992, s 96(10)). A point overlooked in the legislation is that a beneficiary may count as a participator by virtue of trust holdings in a company (TA 1988, s 417(1)(c); *R v IRC, ex p New Fields Developments Ltd* [2001] STC 901, 906 per Lord Hoffmann). This means, in law, that a capital payment by trustees to an offshore company they own, or between two such companies, could count as a capital payment to the beneficiaries of the trust. The absurdity of this is, however, relieved by concession, in that a beneficiary is not in practice treated as a participator solely by virtue of his status as a beneficiary (ESC D40).

Real difficulties, however, arise if the settlor or a beneficiary own a personal stake in a non-resident company in which the offshore trust, or an intermediate holding company, also own shares. In this event the trustees are associates of the settlor and are likely also to be associates of the beneficiaries either because the beneficiaries are close relatives of the settlor (s 417(3)(b)) or because as beneficiaries they are interested in the shares (s 417(3)(c); see further para 60.19). The result is that if the combined holdings give control, any capital payment made by the trustees to the company or between the companies, may be treated as a capital payment to the settlor or beneficiaries.

In practice, HMRC accept a payment between companies is not a capital payment if it is made under a transaction at arm's length, is subject to income tax, or is a repayment of capital in a winding up (SP 5/92, paras 38–40).

Payments to companies not within s 96

65.14 An interesting issue arises as to whether a payment to the company counts as a capital payment regardless of s 96. The answer is that it does, for s 97(8) operates where any person who is not a beneficiary receives a payment and deems that person to be a beneficiary. Section 97(8) is displaced if the payment is treated as received by an actual beneficiary (s 97(9)) and as a result a company would only be treated as receiving the payment if outside s 96. As the previous discussion has indicated, a resident company is outside s 96, and so also is a non-resident company if controlled by one person alone who is not UK resident or by two or more persons alone each of whom is non-resident.

If this latter point is right, it could offer scope for avoidance, for trustees could simply generate a capital payment by gratuitous transfer to a wholly-owned company. HMRC would have to resile from ESC B40 to treat this as a capital payment to a UK resident beneficiary. Even that would not be open to them if no beneficiary was UK resident who could be regarded as (through the trust) a participator in the company.

Section III

Other Anti-avoidance Legislation

Chapter 66

Corporate gains: section 13

Introduction

66.1 Non-resident close companies are subject to special rules under TCGA 1992, s 13 to prevent their use as devices for avoiding CGT. Section 13 formed part of the original CGT legislation in 1965 and was loosely drawn. It was circumvented by a number of avoidance schemes, and as a result it was tightened up by FA 1996, s 174. The changes made by s 174 applied from 28 November 1995 (FA 1996, s 174(11)). Further amendments were made by both FA 2000 and FA 2001.

In the committee stage debates on the 2001 Finance Bill the Paymaster General said that s 13 as now amended:

> '… is targeted solely on investment gains made by a non-resident, closely controlled company from which UK residents may benefit.'

She went on:

> 'It is difficult to see how a motive test … could be made to work … without rendering ineffective legislation that is tightly drawn and specifically to deal with avoidance.'

As will be apparent from this chapter, this last observation is as incorrect in substance as it is ungrammatical in form.

There are strong grounds to suppose that s 13 infringes European law, at least insofar as any company to which it applies is not a wholly artificial arrangement and is based in a Member State of the European Union or the European Economic Area. This subject is discussed further in Chapter 49.

The apportionment

66.2 Section 13 applies wherever a chargeable gain accrues to a non-resident company which would come within the income tax definition of a close company if it were UK resident (TCGA 1992, ss 13(1) and 288(1)). It requires all or a proportionate part of the gain to be apportioned to two categories of participator, namely:

(a) participators who are resident in the UK (s 13(2));
(b) participators who are non-resident trustees, whether resident in the UK or non-resident (s 13(10); see para 66.24).

Computation

66.3 The chargeable gain apportioned is computed in the same way as it would be if the non-resident company were within charge to corporation tax. This means the computational rules in TCGA 1992 are in point insofar as they are applicable to corporation tax.

The main difference between corporation tax and capital gains tax as applicable to individuals and trusts is that corporate gains are computed with indexation rather than taper. This carries through to s 13, in that s 13 gains are fully indexed but not eligible for taper relief.

Meaning of participator

66.4 The term 'participator' has the same meaning as in the income tax close company legislation (s 13(12)) and thus includes any person having a share or interest in the capital or income of the non-resident company (TA 1988, s 417(1)). It includes loan creditors other than banks (s 417(1)(b) and (9)). The logic of including loan creditors is difficult to follow for, as a general rule, a person who lends money to a company does not benefit from appreciation in its capital assets.

Apportionment to an individual participator is precluded if he is not domiciled in the UK. A beneficiary under a trust cannot be treated as a participator if and to the extent he would otherwise be a participator by virtue of his beneficial interest (TCGA 1992, s 13(14)). A gain apportioned to a UK resident company cannot be apportioned to the participators in that company save in the circumstances described in para 66.23 where the gain is treaty protected and the participator in the UK company is a trust.

A gain apportioned to a UK settlor-interested trust is included in the gains assessed as the settlor's under TCGA 1992, s 77 (ibid s 79(7)).

Amount apportioned

66.5 The proportion of the company's chargeable gain attributed to a person is determined by the extent of his interest as a participator (TCGA 1992, s 13(3)). His interest refers to all the factors by which he is treated as a participator, and its extent involves comparing his interest with those of all the other participators (s 13(13)). An apportionment between his interest and those of the other participators is then made on a just and reasonable basis.

Any appeal as respects the apportionment has to be brought to the Special Commissioners (s 13(15)). A particular point of uncertainty is how the apportionment should be made between holders of shares and holders of loan capital. Is it to be by the value of their respective assets or by the extent to which the value of their asset is increased by the company's gain? HMRC view is that the apportionment should be made to those participators who have the real economic interest in the company and will derive the benefit from the gain (*Capital Gains Manual* para 57262). In the case of an ordinary commercial loan, this excludes loan creditors.

Subsidiaries

66.6 In practice, the participators in a non-resident close company frequently consist of or include another non-resident close company. Where this happens, a proportionate part of any gain accruing to the first company is apportioned to the second company and thence to its participators (TCGA 1992, s 13(9)). This process can be continued through any number of non-resident close companies.

Motive test

66.7 As pointed out by the Paymaster General in the extract cited at the beginning of this chapter, s 13 is not subject to a motive test. The result is that the innocent investor is just as much caught by s 13 as the tax avoider. Under self-assessment the compliance burden on taxpayers with non-controlling holdings in private overseas companies is considerable. Still greater burdens are imposed on trustees in respect of Treaty-protected gains (see para 66.23).

Losses

Company losses

66.8 In contrast to other deeming legislation s 13 apportions each gain realised by the company separately to participators. It does not apportion the company's aggregate net gains of a given tax year. This is a logical approach to take, as participations can change during the tax year. The approach s 13 takes means it is necessary only to look at participations at the time a given gain is realised.

A result of this is that there is no mechanism for taking account of the company's allowable losses. Section 13 recognises this defect, but only to a limited extent. It does allow losses on a disposal to be apportioned to the participators, in the same way that a gain would be if the disposal had resulted in a gain (s 13(8)). But the use the participator may make of the apportioned loss is restricted. He may not set it against his general gains and nor may he carry it forward or back. Instead he may set it only against other gains apportioned to him under s 13 in the same tax year. These gains may be in the same company as realised the loss or in any other non-resident company in which he is participator (s 13(8)). But insofar as the apportioned loss exceeds such current year apportioned gains, it is incapable of relief.

Personal losses

66.9 The restrictive treatment of losses described above does not impact on the treatment of the participator's personal losses (ie his non s 13 losses). These may be set against apportioned s 13 gains insofar as the latter are not offset by s 13 losses.

Exemptions and reliefs

Exempt assets

66.10 Gains on the following assets are excepted from apportionment under s 13:

(1) Assets used for the purposes of a trade carried on by the non-resident company wholly outside the UK (s 13(5)(b)).
(2) Assets used for the non-UK part of a trade carried on by the company partly in and partly outside the UK (ibid).
(3) Assets used in a UK permanent establishment, in respect of which gains are in any event chargeable under TCGA 1992, s 10B (TCGA 1992, s 13(5)(d)).
(4) Currency or a debt representing money in use for the purpose of a trade carried on by the company wholly outside the UK (TCGA 1992, s 13(5)(c)).

If any provisions restrict s 13 in the manner indicated by the Paymaster General in the passages quoted at the beginning of this chapter, it is these. However, if indeed they are meant to restrict s 13 to investment gains they are far from comprehensive. Items (1) and (2) in the above list do not include partially used assets and nor do they cover assets intended for trading but never used or assets out of use at the time of the disposal. Perhaps more importantly the non-trading assets of group holding companies and shares in subsidiaries are absent from the list.

In one respect, items (1) and (2) may offer a tax planning opportunity. They are expressed in the present tense and thus, it may be argued, require solely that the use be exclusive at the time of the disposal. If this is right, a s 13 charge would be avoided if an investment asset is taken into use as a fixed asset of a non-resident company's trade prior to disposal.

Substantial shareholdings

66.11 The relief for substantial shareholdings applies when a company holds 10% or more of another company's share capital (TCGA 1992, Sch 7AC). Any disposals by the owning company out of that holding are exempt from CGT if the various conditions for the relief are met, the most notable of which is that the disponor company must be a trading company or a member of a trading group both for a period before and immediately after the disposal. This relief applies to s 13 for s 13 gains are computed on the same basis as if the company were resident in the UK and subject to corporation tax (para 66.3 above). But the extension of the relief in TCGA 1992, Sch 7AC para 3 is not in point as that extension requires the disponor company to be UK resident.

Taper relief

66.12 Gains apportioned under s 13 are not eligible for taper relief in the hands of the participator (s 13(10A)). This is logical in view of the fact that such gains are fully indexed (see para 66.3 above).

De minimis limit

66.13 A participator is not subject to CGT if the share of the company's gain apportioned to him is 10% or less. However, where part of the gain has also been apportioned to persons connected with him, the combined share apportioned to him and the connected persons must not exceed 10% (s 13(4)). It is regrettable that the limit has not been raised to the same level as the CFC de minimis exemption, namely 25% (cf para 67.21).

For the purposes of this exemption, 'connected' bears its normal CGT meaning (TCGA 1992, s 286). The result is that a participator is free of tax under s 13 if his participation, and those of persons connected with him, attract apportionment of 10% or less of the gain.

Non-resident groups

66.14 Transfers of assets within a non-resident group are governed by the CGT group rules which are specifically applied to non-resident groups (TCGA 1992, s 14(2)). Such transfers are therefore no gain/no loss disposals for the purposes of s 13 (cf *Tax Bulletin* 7 (May 1993) p 74).

'Non-resident group of companies' is defined as:

(1) In the case of a group with no members resident in the United Kingdom, that group (TCGA 1992, s 14(4)(a)(i)).
(2) In the case of a group two or more members of which are not resident in the United Kingdom, the members which are not resident in the United Kingdom (s 14(4)(a)(ii)).

The degrouping provisions in TCGA 1992, s 179 also apply (s 14(3)). This means that the gain which would have been apportioned to the participators on an intergroup transfer is apportioned to the participators should the recipient company leave the group within six years. Under s 179A(4), the gain is treated as accruing to that company at the beginning of the accounting period in which it leaves the group, and so, the apportionment under s 13 is to those who are participators at that time. It is unclear what the position on timing is if the non-resident company has no accounting period, but presumably the fall back provision in s 179(4) would apply, namely that the gain is treated as accruing at the time of the inter group transfer.

Should a member of the group become UK resident, the degrouping charge would apply insofar as the recipient company had made inter group acquisitions within the last six years, for that company would then cease to be a member of the non-resident group. The same result may follow if both it and the transferor group member become UK resident, for they would not thereafter be a group of non-resident companies if viewed alone (cf s 179(2) and *Dunlop v Pardoe* [1999] STC 909).

The group rules in TCGA 1992, s 14 provided the basis for the scheme at issue in *Wood v Holden* [2005] EWHC 547 (Ch), [2005] STC 789 (see para 38.8). They enabled assets to be transferred by a BVI company administered in Geneva to its subsidiary resident in the Netherlands. The case emphasises that s 14 is not in point if the transferee group member is UK resident as then it is not a member of the non-resident group.

Reimbursement

66.15 The shareholders or participators have no statutory right to require the company to reimburse any tax assessed on them. But if in fact the company pays the tax, such is not treated for any tax purpose as a distribution to the participator (TCGA 1992, s 13(11)).

Double charge

66.16 It is inherent in s 13, that the same economic gain may be taxed twice, once when the company realises the gain on disposal of the underlying asset, and subsequently when the profit represented by the gain is distributed to the participator in dividend or realised on the sale or liquidation of the company. In the case of non-resident group structures the gain could be taxed more than twice, as where a gain is realised by a subsidiary, the subsidiary is sold or liquidated, and the parent is then sold or liquidated.

Section 13 does not address this problem in any satisfactory manner. Instead it gives two limited reliefs, one for distributions and one a deduction of tax from gain.

Distribution relief

66.17 The distribution relief applies only if the following conditions are satisfied (s 13(5A)):

(a) a person pays tax in respect of the apportioned company gain under s 13;
(b) the company does not reimburse the participator;
(c) the company distributes an amount in respect of the gain by dividend or in liquidation; and
(d) the distribution takes place within a specified period of the gain accruing.

Where these conditions are satisfied the person who paid the s 13 tax may deduct that tax from any CGT or income tax chargeable on him in respect of the distribution. The distribution is treated for these purposes as the top slice of his income (TCGA 1992, s 13(7A)).

The specified period begins on the date when the gain is realised and ends on the fourth anniversary of that date or, if earlier, three years after the end of the accounting period in which that date falls (s 13(5B)).

There are many reasons why this relief is of limited value:

(a) It only applies if the second tax charge occurs on a distribution and not, for example, if it is triggered on a sale of the participation.
(b) It is limited in time, in that the second tax charge must be triggered within the specified period of between three and four years.
(c) It is limited in scope, in that the second tax charge must be incurred by the same person as is liable for the s 13 charge. Thus it does not apply if he has given away his participation in the meantime and it is only of limited application in respect of non-resident trusts (see para 66.25).
(d) The relief is of no use if either the s 13 gain or the second tax charge is relieved by some relief such as loss relief.

The legislation is unclear as to the position where the company pays a dividend funded out of many receipts, of which the disposal generating the gain is just one. On one view, the dividend would fall to be treated as gain only in the same proportion as the gain comprises of the total funds from which the distribution is made. But it may be suggested that, with disclosure, a s 13 participator would be reasonable in taking the position that a dividend from a mixed fund is, for the purposes of these rules, gain insofar as the fund contains gains. The whole problem is avoided if the company carries the proceeds of disposals generating a gain directly to a separate account, and pays the dividend from that account.

Tax deducted from gain

66.18 This relief applies without time limit (s 13(7)). It allows any CGT paid by the participator on the apportioned gain as a deduction in computing any gain when he disposes of whatever interest caused him to be a participator. This relief is not available insofar as the company reimburses the tax. This relief is capable of applying within the specified period under s 13(5A), and indeed is the only relief from double charge available where the participator sells his interest in the company. Strictly s 13(7) relief only applies if the s 13 tax has been paid, but in practice HMRC do not insist on this (Capital Gains Manual para 57362).

This relief too is far from comprehensive:

(e) It is a deduction of tax from gain, not of tax from tax.

(f) It applies only on the disposal of the participation. It does not operate if the participator receives an income dividend (which is quite unrelieved unless within the time limits for distribution relief).

(g) As described below (para 66.25) it is of no application to non resident trusts, for it applies only if the person realising the gain is the same as the person who paid the s 13 tax.

Double tax treaties

66.19 In contrast to the CFC legislation s 13 is in no way confined to companies resident in offshore jurisdictions. It applies regardless of where the company resides so long as it is not resident in the UK. The only relief from its rigours in such cases is therefore double tax relief.

Credit relief

66.20 As a matter of practice, HMRC allow a participator to credit an appropriate proportion of any overseas tax borne by the company against the UK CGT. Alternatively, he may deduct the overseas tax from the apportioned gain (SP D23).

Exemption relief

66.21 The capital gains article in the OECD model treaty provides that gains are taxable only in the contracting state of which the alienator is resident. Exceptions are made for immovable property and permanent establishment assets in the other contracting state. As s 13 operates by deeming the actual gain realised by the non-resident company to accrue to the participators, it follows a charge cannot be made under s 13 if:

(a) the UK has concluded a treaty with the state where the company is resident;

(b) that treaty contains a capital gains article in the same or similar form to the OECD model;

(c) the asset concerned is not one of those excluded by the article from the general rule giving the country of residence of the alienator sole taxing rights.

The correctness of this proposition is established by *Bricom Holdings v IRC* [1997] STC 1179 where Millett LJ pointed out that exempt income (and thus gains) does not lose treaty protection because it is deemed domestically to be that of another person. The correctness of this was accepted by HMRC in *Wood v Holden* (see para 38.8).

Treaty renegotiation

66.22 In recent years the government have taken account of this point in negotiating treaties. The wording now used in treaties to which the UK is a party contains an override to the capital gains article, reserving the right of the UK to levy tax in respect of gains on persons resident in the UK in the tax year in which the gain is realised. An Exchange of Notes to the 2003 Protocol to the New Zealand treaty points out that this inter alia counters the avoidance of tax by participators in non-resident close companies.

Among countries whose treaties contain this new wording are the United States, Canada, Mauritius, Australia and New Zealand.

Trustee participators

66.23 Even where a treaty does preclude s 13 such does not apply insofar as the trustees are participators. TCGA 1992, s 79B expressly prevents trustee shareholders from enjoying exemption under the treaty.

Section 79B also contains a less rational rule. This operates where a UK close company is a participator in the non-resident company and a double tax treaty prevents gains apportioned to the UK company from being charged under s 13. Here TCGA 1992, s 79B(3) operates insofar as the participators in the UK company are or include trustees. It provides that s 13 has effect as if the UK company were not UK resident. This means the gain in the actual non-resident company can be apportioned through the UK company to the trustees. It is then able to be charged, for s 79B(2) prevents the double tax treaty from relieving it. It is further provided (in s 79B(3)(a)) that if the participators in the UK close company are or include another UK close company that company also is deemed to be non-resident, and so on. The effect is that the treaty-protected gain can be apportioned through any number of UK close companies and, if at the end of the chain there are trustee shareholders, they are charged on the treaty gain.

Section 79B is an unsatisfactory piece of legislation which must be watched. Although there may be cases where trustees deliberately cause non-resident companies to reside in treaty jurisdictions so as to avoid CGT, there are also cases where trustees own companies in treaty jurisdictions for genuine trading or investment reasons. In such cases it is wrong for trustee participators to be penalised by anti-avoidance legislation of this sort but the fact is that they are.

Equally irrational is the way in which s 79B targets trustee shareholders rather than individual or company participators. In particular, this means that trustees holding only a minority interest in a company could be penalised if controlling individual or corporate shareholders cause an offshore company to move to a treaty jurisdiction, although the controlling shareholders will not themselves be within s 79B.

The irrationality of s 79B is enhanced now that the rate of tax borne by trusts on capital gains is 40%. It follows that the tax on the apportioned gain is invariably higher than it would be if the gain was simply apportioned to the UK company. The perverse result is therefore that gains apportioned from offshore jurisdictions are more lightly taxed than gains apportioned from some treaty jurisdictions.

SP D23 has not been abrogated or qualified in connection with s 79B. It follows that trustees caught by s 79B should claim credit for the appropriate part of any foreign tax born by the non-resident company on the apportioned gain. Alternatively it should be argued that s 79B is disapplied by European law (see Chapter 49).

Non-resident trusts

66.24 As noted at the beginning of this chapter, gains in a non-resident close company are also apportionable to any participator which is a non-resident trust (TCGA 1992, s 13(10)). The apportionment does not, of course, result in the trustees being charged to tax for, being non-resident, they are exempt. But if the trust is within TCGA 1992, s 86, any apportioned gains are assessed as the settlor's and, if it is subject to the capital payment rules in TCGA 1992, s 87, the apportioned gains are included in the total of trust gains. These rules are described in Chapters 60 and 63.

Application of reliefs

66.25 In one respect s 13 bears more heavily on non-resident trusts than on UK resident participators. The deduction of tax from gain under s 13(7) is not available, for that relief applies only if the person disposing of the participation is the same as the person who paid the tax (see para 66.18). That condition is not satisfied with non-resident trusts, for the trustees dispose of the participation and yet tax in respect of the apportioned gain is paid by the settlor in the case of s 86 and by the beneficiary in the case of s 87.

The application of the relief for distributions within the specified period (para 66.17) is a matter of difficulty. The key point to remember is that the person paying the s 13 tax must be the same person as is taxed on the distribution. With this established, it is clear that s 13(5A) does give relief to the settlor if he is assessed under s 86 on the company's gain and then assessed either to income tax or under s 86 on the distribution.

With s 87 the position is much more complicated. As described in para 66.17, the conditions for the relief are:

(a) An amount of tax is paid by a person in pursuance of s 13.
(b) An amount in respect of the gain is distributed within the specified period.
(c) The person who paid the s 13 tax is liable to income tax or CGT in respect of the distribution.

On the basis of these conditions s 13(5A) should apply to s 87 if the company in fact distributes the gain to the trust within the specified period. What must then be shown is that a beneficiary in receipt of a distribution or distributions from the trust is by virtue of the distribution subject to CGT on part of the distribution under s 87 by virtue of the company gain and to CGT under s 87 or income tax under s 740 on another part of the distribution by virtue of the distribution from the company to the trust. If these conditions are met it would seem the latter tax can be offset by the former and, provided the company distribution is within the specified period, it would not seem to matter that the capital payment or benefit from the trust is later.

It is however far from clear that this argument would be upheld as a matter of strict construction of s 13(5A). It is also clear that it would be much more difficult to run if capital distributions are made to several beneficiaries, so that it is not possible to show the same beneficiary bears the s 87 tax attributable to the company gain as bears the s 87 or s 740 tax attributable to the company distribution.

Subsidiaries

66.26 At one time, there was an argument that gains in subsidiaries could not be apportioned to non-resident trusts. If this argument was ever good, it is no longer in point on account of amendments to s 13(10) introduced by FA 1996, s 174.

Double tax treaties

66.27 Prior to the enactment of TCGA 1992, s 79B, there was debate as to whether tax treaties with capital gains articles in the OECD form could prevent gains apportioned to non-resident trustees under s 13 from being charged on the settlor under TCGA 1992, s 86 or constituting trust gains for the purposes of s 87. The better view was that they could not (cf *Bricom Holdings Ltd v IRC* [1997] STC 1179). Section 79B has now put the matter beyond doubt for s 79B(2) is expressed in terms of a charge to tax arising rather than merely referring to tax being charged on the trustees. The phrase 'charge to tax arising' is certainly wide enough to catch liability under s 86, and also, it may be suggested, wide enough to catch tax on a capital payment under s 87 by virtue of the treaty protected gain.

One particular sting in s 79B arises where non-resident trustees are participators in a UK resident close company. Should that company have subsidiaries in jurisdictions whose treaty with the UK has a capital gains article in the OECD form, then, as described in para 66.23,gains realised by those subsidiaries are apportionable through to the non-resident trustees. The same result does not follow as respects subsidiaries in other jurisdictions, so the absurd result is reached that gains in companies offshore are apportioned to the UK company and taxed at a top rate of 30%, but gains in companies in certain treaty jurisdictions are apportioned to the non-resident trust and taxed at 40% if s 86 applies. A more serious objection is that the trustees, settlor and beneficiaries are faced with potentially impossible compliance obligations, particularly if the trust is only a minority participator in the UK company.

Chapter 67

Controlled foreign companies

Introduction

67.1 The UK legislation dealing with controlled foreign companies was first enacted in 1984 and was consolidated in 1988 as TA 1988, ss 747–756 and Schs 24–26. Periodic minor amendments were made over the ensuing years, and in 1998 more radical changes were made to accommodate the legislation within the self-assessment regime (FA 1998, ss 112–113 and Sch 17).

The basic rule is that an apportionment of a foreign company's chargeable profits is made if the foreign company is a controlled foreign company ('CFC') and apportionment is not prevented by six circumstances specified in TA 1988, s 748. In offshore tax planning, most important of these circumstances is that the company is engaged in exempt activities.

The apportionment is made among those with interests in the foreign company. Tax is charged under the CFC legislation insofar as profits are apportioned to a UK company and the percentage of the profits apportioned to that company and persons connected or associated with it is at least 25% (s 747(4)).

HMRC publish an explanation of the legislation in the International Manual. It also includes an extra-statutory clearance procedure. HMRC provide guidance wherever possible unless tax avoidance is involved (International Manual para 201010).

Challenges to the legislation

67.2 A Group Litigation Order was made in the High Court on 30 July 2003 concerning inter alia claims that the CFC legislation breaches the EU Treaty, non-discrimination articles in double tax treaties, or the European Convention on Human Rights (IR Press Release, 11 August 2003, reproduced [2003] STI 1442).

In *Cadbury Schweppes plc v IRC* [2004] STC (SCD) 342 a UK plc had formed indirect subsidiaries within the International Financial Services Centre in Dublin taxable at the rate of 10%. The purpose was to secure that favourable tax treatment. The Special Commissioners referred to the European Court of Justice the question of whether, in relation to subsidiaries established in other Member States, Articles 43, 39, and 56 of the EU Treaty preclude legislation such as the CFC legislation.

The European Court of Justice declined to consider Articles 39 and 36 but held that the CFC legislation was only compatible with Article 43 if confined to wholly artificial arrangements. It referred that question back to the Special Commissioners. *Cadbury Schweppes plc v IRC* is discussed in Chapter 49. As there concluded it is likely that it and other pending ECJ cases will result in significant qualification to the CFC legislation. The present chapter explains the legislation as it currently stands in TA 1988.

What is a controlled foreign company?

67.3 A company is a controlled foreign company ('CFC') if three conditions are satisfied (TA 1988, s 747(1)):

(a) the company must be resident outside the UK;
(b) it must be controlled by persons resident in the UK; and
(c) it must be subject to a lower level of taxation in the territory in which it is resident.

Resident ouside the UK

67.4 The question of whether or not a company is resident in the UK is not dealt with in the CFC legislation. Accordingly, the issue falls to be determined under the principles described in Chapter 38.

Controlled by persons resident in the UK

67.5 Control is defined for the purposes of the CFC legislation in TA 1988, s 755D(1). One or more persons have control of a company if they have power to secure that its affairs are conducted according to their wishes and that power is conferred by the holding of shares, the possession of voting power, or by the articles of association. Control may be either direct or through another company.

The ambit of this definition is greatly extended by subsequent provisions in s 755D which attribute to a person powers and rights held by others. The rules are as follows:

(a) There are attributed to a person any interests, rights or powers held by any person connected with him who is resident in the UK and any interests, powers and rights held by any person who is resident in the UK and connected with the connected person. This chain of connection can go on through any number of resident connected persons.
(b) Interests, powers and rights which are or may be required to be exercised on behalf of a person, under his direction, or for his benefit, may also be attributed to him.

A company is deemed to be controlled by a UK resident person in certain circumstances where he and another party together control the company. The circumstances are first that the UK resident must own 40% or more of the interests, rights and powers by which the two parties together control the company. The second is that the other party must own between 40% and 55% of those interests, rights and powers (TA 1988, ss 747(1A) and 755D(3), (4)).

A special provision, in s 747(1B), applies where a dual resident company holds an interest in the non-resident company. A dual resident company is a company which is resident in both the UK and another country under their respective domestic laws, and is treated as resident in the other country under the applicable double tax treaty. Such a company is deemed to be non-resident for all UK tax purposes (FA 1994, s 249) but the effect of the special provision (s 747(1B)) is that this deeming is disapplied for the purposes of the CFC legislation. Section 747(1B) applies only if the company concerned became dual resident after 31 March 2002 (FA 2002, s 90(2)). Where it applies it means interests owned by a dual resident company are taken into account in determining whether the non-resident company is controlled by UK residents. Section 747(1B) does not, in general, apply where the company became dual resident before 1 April 2002 and has remained so (FA 2002, s 90(2)). But an exception is made in certain cases where such a company becomes the direct or indirect owner of a UK subsidiary after 22 March 2006 (ibid as amended by FA 2006, s 78).

The territory in which the company is resident

67.6 Although the CFC legislation does not lay down rules for deciding whether a company is resident in the UK, it does deal with the residence of a company which is not so resident. The basic test is that the company is regarded as resident in the territory where it is liable to tax by reason of domicile, residence or place of management (TA 1988, s 749(1)).

Of itself, this liability to tax test is unsatisfactory for often it will result in a company being resident in several territories. But when this happens the territory of residence is deemed to be the place of effective management, or, if there is no such place or the management is split between two territories, where the greater amount of the company's assets are situated (TA 1988, s 749(3)). If none of these tests produces a single territory of residence, the UK company or companies holding a majority interest in the foreign company may elect between the territories in question (s 749(3)(d)). Should no such election be made, HMRC are empowered to make a designation on a just and reasonable basis (s 749(3)(e)).

The converse of the liability to tax test producing several territories of residence is that it produces none. Here the company is simply treated as resident in an unspecified territory in which it is ipso facto subject to a lower level of taxation (TA 1988, s 749(5)).

The term 'territory' rather than 'country' is used in determining where the company is resident. The term 'territory' includes jurisdictions which do not have full independent status such as the British Crown Dependencies or Overseas Territories.

Subject to a lower level of taxation

67.7 The lower level of taxation requirement is at the heart of the definition of a CFC. It requires the company's profits to be calculated, and then any local tax has to be ascertained, that is to say tax paid in respect of those profits under the law of the territory where the company is regarded as resident. If the local tax paid is less than three-quarters of the corresponding UK tax on those profits, the company is regarded as subject to a lower level of taxation (s 750(1)).

For these purposes the term 'profits' has the same meaning as for corporation tax purposes. Chargeable gains are excluded (TA 1988, s 747(6)(b)) as are UK dividends, for these are not taken into account in computing profits for corporation tax purposes (TA 1988, s 208). Since the income tax rules apply in computing corporation tax profits, the effect is to require a computation by cases and schedules of the foreign company's income. Accordingly, its profits for the purposes of the CFC legislation are not necessarily as per its local accounts.

The profits, the local tax, and the corresponding UK tax all have to be determined by accounting periods. Very broadly a new accounting period begins when the previous one ends or when the company either first comes under the control of UK residents or first commences business (TA 1988, s 751(1)). The normal corporation tax rules apply to determine when an accounting period ends, in that it ends after 12 months or on an accounting date (s 751(3)). An accounting period also ends if the company ceases to be controlled by UK residents or if it becomes or ceases to be liable to pay tax in any particular territory by reason of its domicile, residence or place of management.

The corresponding UK tax is the amount of UK corporation tax which would be charged on the foreign company's chargeable profits were it resident in the UK (TA 1988, s 750(2)). TA 1988, Sch 24 requires certain assumptions to be made. Thus it is assumed that the company is neither a close company nor a member of a group, with the result that such matters as group income and group relief are not in issue. It is also assumed that the company has made all relevant elections and claimed all relevant reliefs but this assumption may be displaced if the UK company or companies holding a majority interest in the non-resident company so elect (Sch 24 para 4). In general, capital allowances and losses cannot be carried forward from periods before the company's profits were apportionable, but election to the contrary can in certain circumstances be made (Sch 24 paras 9 and 10). A further rule is that the relief for blocked remittances (TA 1988, s 584) is applied, on the basis of unremittability to the country of residence as well as to the UK.

In substance, Sch 24 simply predicates what the company's chargeable profits would be if it were in fact amenable to corporation tax. So far as currency is concerned, the chargeable profits are computed in the currency used for the company's accounts (TA 1988, s 747A). The conversion to sterling is effected at the exchange rate prevailing at the end of the CFC's accounting period (s 747(4B)).

In computing the company's profits the UK transfer pricing rules in TA 1988, Sch 28AA apply. This result follows because a potential tax advantage arises whenever the connected party pricing means that for UK tax purposes profits are smaller than they should be (Sch 28AA para 5).

If on the assumption of UK residence the foreign company would qualify for the small companies rate of corporation tax, the corresponding UK tax is determined on that basis . Double tax relief is allowed in respect of foreign tax paid otherwise than in the territory of residence and a deduction may also be taken for corporation tax borne by a UK permanent establishment and basic-rate income tax deducted at source on UK source income (TA 1988, s 750(3)).

A special rule applies should the company have any income which is subject to local tax but is not brought into chargeable profits. The adjustment is simply that the local tax used in the comparison is reduced by local tax attributable to such income (s 750(1A)). The same applies if a repayment or credit in respect of the company's local tax falls to be given to a person other than the company (s 750(1B)). These rules apply to accounting periods beginning after 1 December 2004.

Some offshore jurisdictions have responded to the CFC legislation by offering what are called designer rate tax provisions. These effectively enable a company to agree with the jurisdiction a rate of tax, which, in practice, is fixed just high enough not to count as a lower level of taxation. But since 6 October 1999 such arrangements have been ineffective as a weapon against the UK CFC legislation, for a company is now deemed subject to a lower level of taxation if the local tax is determined by designer rate tax provisions (TA 1988, s 750A). Designer rate tax provisions are as specified by HMRC in regulations and currently comprise certain provisions in the tax laws of Guernsey, Jersey, the Isle of Man and Gibraltar (Controlled Foreign Companies (Designer Rate Tax Provisions) Regulations 2000 (SI 2000/3158)).

Exempt activities

67.8 Apportionment is precluded if the CFC is engaged in what are called exempt activities (TA 1988, s 748(1)(b)). The exempt activities test is one of the most important features of the CFC legislation.

A CFC is engaged in exempt activities if its main business falls outside certain forbidden fields and it satisfies two conditions as to the way in which the business is conducted (Sch 25 para 6). The latter effectively require the control and running of the business to be situated in the territory where the company is resident, and thus it can be said that the exempt activities exemption is satisfied if the company avoids the forbidden businesses and genuinely operates where it is resident.

Forbidden businesses

67.9 The forbidden businesses fall into three categories (Sch 25 para 6(2)):

(1) investment business;
(2) dealing in goods for delivery to or from the UK or to or from connected or associated persons;
(3) wholesale, distributive, financial or service business if 50% or more of the gross trading receipts are derived from defined categories of forbidden person.

The simplest of these categories is (2), which is clearly aimed at invoicing operations. Goods delivered where the CFC is resident are excluded in deciding what the CFC's main business is (Sch 25 para 10).

Investment business is exhaustively defined as follows (Sch 25 para 9(1)):

(a) the holding of securities or intellectual property;
(b) dealing in securities otherwise than as a broker;
(c) leasing of any description of property or rights;
(d) investing funds which would otherwise be available for investment by or on behalf of the persons controlling the CFC and those who are connected or associated with them.

As already noted, wholesale, distributive, financial or service business is only forbidden if more than 50% of gross trading receipts are received from defined categories of forbidden person. Until 27 November 2002, those categories were persons connected or associated with the company and persons with a 25% assessable interest in the company. For accounting periods beginning on or after that date, the list is expanded and the forbidden persons now also include companies and individuals resident in the UK and companies trading in the UK through a permanent establishment (Sch 25, para 6(2A) as amended by FA 2003, Sch 42).

Wholesale, distributive, financial or service business is defined as the following (Sch 25 para 11):

(a) wholesale dealing in goods;
(b) shipping and air transport;
(c) banking and similar financial business;
(d) administration of trusts;
(e) dealing in securities as broker;
(f) dealing in commodity or financial futures;
(g) insurance;
(h) the provision of any other form of service.

Special rules govern the application of the gross trading receipts test to banking and to insurance (Sch 25 para 11). For certain types of insurance business the forbidden persons do not include UK residents (Sch 25, paras 6(2B), 11A, and 11B).

Manner in which the business is carried on

67.10 As already indicated, a CFC whose business is outside the forbidden fields only carries on exempt activities if it satisfies two further conditions as to the manner in which its business is carried on. These are as follows (Sch 25 para 6(1)):

(1) the company must have a business establishment in the territory in which it is resident;
(2) its business affairs in that territory must be effectively managed there.

The rules which apply in determining where a company is resident are as described above (see para 67.6). If these rules do not produce any territory where the company is resident, the company does not qualify for the exempt activities relief, save that if it has somewhere a place of effective management, then it is deemed for these purposes to be resident there (Sch 25 para 5). Companies managed and liable to tax in Hong Kong or Macao are deemed for the purposes of the relief to be resident there (Sch 25, para 5(3)).

The term 'business establishment' means much the same as permanent establishment in double tax treaties. There must be premises, but these can be a mine or long-term building site as well as the more conventional shop, office or factory. More important, the premises must be reasonably permanent and the company's business in the territory must be conducted from them (Sch 25 para 7).

A company is effectively managed in a territory if it employs sufficient personnel there to conduct its business and if services performed for residents outside the territory are not in fact performed in the UK (Sch 25 para 8). More than any other condition, this provision requires the CFC to have a genuine commercial operation where it resides. Services performed by an entity liable to UK tax are ignored in deciding whether and if so what business is performed in the UK.

Holding companies

67.11 If the tests described above stood alone, holding companies would not qualify for the exempt activities relief. In reality the relief is extended to three types of holding company. They are as follows:

(1) The local holding company. The salient feature of this type of company is that its business must consist of holding shares in trading companies which are its 51% subsidiaries and resident in the same jurisdiction (Sch 25 paras 6(3) and 12).
(2) The ordinary holding company. The requirement for this type of company is that its business consists of holding shares in trading companies, whether resident in the same jurisdiction or elsewhere, or in local holding companies (Sch 25 paras 6(4) and 12). Any local holding company must be a 90% subsidiary but the trading companies need only be 51% subsidiaries.

(3) The superior holding company. The business of this type of company must be owning local holding companies, ordinary holding companies or other superior holding companies (Sch 25 para 12A(1)).

For an ordinary holding company to qualify for exemption, at least 90% of its income must be derived from subsidiaries resident in the same territory as it is resident in, or must be what are called qualifying dividends (Sch 25 paras 12(4) and (42A)). Qualifying dividends are dividends which are not deductible in computing the home country tax of the company paying the dividend (Sch 25 para 12(5B)). An additional requirement for ordinary holding companies is that the holding company's subsidiaries must all be local holding companies or companies which are not holding companies but are either engaged in exempt activities or what are called exempt trading companies. An exempt trading company is any company which satisfies the motive defence (para 67.17), or is not subject to a lower level of taxation, or is resident in an excluded territory (para 67.16).

A superior holding company only qualifies for exemption if, like an ordinary holding company, at least 90% of its income is qualifying dividends or is derived from subsidiaries resident in the same territory as it is resident in (Sch 25 para 12(4A)(c)). In addition the companies from which the income is derived must either be exempt trading companies or companies engaged in exempt activities, the latter being able to include other holding companies (Sch 25 para 12(4B)). A further requirement is that at least 90% of the superior holding company's income must represent what is called qualifying exempt activity income. This is income which is directly or indirectly derived from companies which are not ordinary or superior holding companies but are otherwise exempt trading companies or engaged in exempt activities (Sch 25 para 12A(2)).

As with trading companies, a holding company can only be regarded as engaged in exempt activities if it has a business establishment where it is resident and is effectively managed there.

The superior holding company concept was introduced by FA 1998 and removed a gap in the original legislation whereby a holding company did not count as engaged in exempt activities if it derived significant income from other holding companies which were not local holding companies. The inclusion of superior holding companies means it is possible to have tiers of holding companies providing the various other conditions in the legislation are met.

Other cases where an apportionment cannot be made

67.12 Apart from exempt activities, the cases where an apportionment cannot be made are as follows (TA 1988, s 748):

(a) acceptable distribution policy;
(b) public quotation;

(c) low profits;
(d) residence in an excluded territory;
(e) motive exemption.

Acceptable distribution policy

67.13 A company follows an acceptable distribution policy for an accounting period if dividends paid to UK residents are equal to or exceed 90% of the net chargeable profits (TA 1988, Sch 25 para 2). Net chargeable profits are income profits computed as for UK tax purposes, less any tax actually suffered on those profits (Sch 25 para 3(4A)). The dividend must not be paid out of specified profits and it must be paid within 18 months of the accounting period or such longer period as the Board may allow. TA 1988, s 799 applies with the result that a dividend which is not paid for a specified period is treated as paid for the accounting period most recently ended.

The dividend must be taxable in the UK (Sch 25 para 2(1A)). Thus it must not be exempt under TA 1988, s 208 because the company has previously immigrated to the UK. A dividend does not count if it is received by a UK company as a trading receipt as part of a tax avoidance scheme (ibid).

It should be noted that the requirement is not that dividends exceed 90% of chargeable profits but that that limit is exceeded by dividends paid to UK residents. Accordingly, the prima facie rule is that a company with some non-UK resident shareholders has to pay more than 90% of its profits in dividends for its distribution policy to be acceptable. But this rule is relaxed and apportionment is possible where the company has one of two types of capital structure (TA 1988, Sch 25 para 2(4) and (5)). One type is where all its issued capital is represented by a single class of ordinary shares and the other is where the capital consists of a single class of voting ordinary shares and a single class of non-voting fixed-rate preference shares.

The 90% rule is also relaxed where dividends are paid through a series of foreign companies. A dividend is counted as paid to a UK resident if it is paid to another foreign company and that or another related foreign company pays the dividend on to a UK resident (Sch 25 para 4).

A UK company caught by the CFC legislation may not know when it files its return whether the CFC will make acceptable distributions. In such a case, it is entitled to file the return on the basis of what it thinks is likely to happen (s 754A). An amendment should be filed when the position becomes clear.

Public quotation

67.14 The public quotation exemption requires two conditions to be satisfied (Sch 25 paras 13 and 14). First, at least 35% of the company's shares must be owned by members of the public and be quoted and dealt in on a recognised Stock Exchange. Second, the voting power held by the company's principal members must not exceed 85%.

For these purposes the public is anybody who is connected or associated neither with the company nor a principal member. The principal members of the company are the five largest holders of voting power, or, if some such holders hold less than 5% of the voting power, all the holders of more than 5% of the voting power.

Low profits

67.15 The low profits condition is satisfied in any accounting period if the chargeable profits of the CFC are below £50,000 (TA 1988, s 748(1)(d)). As noted above, chargeable profits exclude capital gains, but otherwise are profits computed as per the assumptions in Sch 24.

Residence in an excluded country

67.16 This exemption is couched in terms of regulations. It applies if the CFC is resident in one of the territories specified in the regulations, and satisfies such other conditions as the regulations may specify. This exemption and the regulations made thereunder have replaced the former extra-statutory white list.

The regulations are the Controlled Foreign Companies (Excluded Countries) Regulations 1998 (SI 1998/3081). There are two lists, one of territories where all companies are excluded and one of territories where companies are excluded save for certain specific exceptions. There is an overriding further requirement which is that even if a company is resident in an excluded territory it does not qualify for exemption if its non-local source income exceeds £50,000 or (if greater) 10% of its commercially quantified income. These terms are defined in the regulations and essentially they prevent a company from being exempt unless its profits are local-source income in the territory where it is resident or in another excepted territory in which it has a permanent establishment.

The exemption is now subject to an overriding motive test (SI 1998/3081, reg 4(A2)). To attract the exemption, the company must not have been involved in a scheme or arrangement of which one of the main purposes is the reduction of UK corporate tax. This applies to accounting periods beginning after 31 March 2005.

The motive exemption

67.17 This exemption applies if two conditions are satisfied in the accounting period under review (TA 1988, s 748(3), Sch 25 paras 16–19). The first is that if any transactions reflected in the accounts of the period achieved a reduction in the UK tax such was not one of their main purposes. The second is that reducing UK tax by diverting profits from the UK was not one of the main purposes of the company's existence.

The motive test was at issue in an extremely complex Commissioners case (*Association of British Travel Agents Ltd v IRC* [2003] STC (SCD) 194). The case emphasises that both conditions specified in s 748(3) have to be met before the exemption applies. The first condition involves looking at the transactions at issue and asking whether, if they diverted tax, such was one of their main purposes. The second condition focuses on the non resident entity and, if it reduces UK tax, focuses on whether tax was one reason for using a non-resident rather than a resident entity. In the ABTA case, the insurance transactions at issue satisfied the first test, but failed the second, as on the facts tax had been a factor behind the setting up of the offshore subsidiary.

Harmful tax competition

67.18 Finance Act 2002 inserted s 748A into the CFC legislation. This section disapplies the exempt activities exemption and also all the other exceptions to apportionment if the CFC is incorporated in or liable to tax in a territory designated by the Treasury. The purpose of s 748A is to give the UK tax authorities a weapon in the OECD fight against harmful tax competition. OECD policy is that if a tax haven is uncooperative, OECD members should take fiscal and other counter-measures. Section 748 enables the Treasury to tighten the CFC regime as respects CFCs incorporated in or liable to tax in a non-compliant territory.

The designation of a territory as caught by s 748A must be by statutory instrument subject to affirmative resolution procedures (s 748A(5)). Different provisions may be made for different territories or different cases (s 748A(4)). As at the time of writing no territory has been designated.

An important point to note is the wide range of companies which can be caught if a territory is designated. Not surprisingly a company is caught if it is liable to tax in the territory. More significant is the extension of the section to companies registered in the offending territory (s 748A(1)(a)). This would catch a company registered in the territory even if it in fact carries on all its business elsewhere. This provision therefore gives the UK Treasury a weapon against jurisdictions which provide extensive company registration services.

A company will also be caught if it carries on business in a designated territory through a permanent establishment (s 748A(1)(c)). However, an exception is made if permanent establishments in designated territories form a minimal part of the CFC's business as whole (s 748A(2)).

The consequences of apportionment

Apportionment by interests

67.19 The questions of whether a company is a CFC, and of whether apportionment is precluded, have to be determined for each of its accounting periods. If in any accounting period the company is a CFC and none of the exemptions described above applies, then the CFC's chargeable profits for that period are apportioned among the persons who had an interest in the company in the accounting period concerned. As might be expected, complicated rules exist to decide who has an interest and how the apportionment is effected.

Four categories of person are deemed to have an interest in a CFC (TA 1988, s 749B(1)). The categories overlap and they are as follows:

(a) holders of share capital and/or voting rights;
(b) persons entitled to participate in distributions;
(c) any person who can directly or indirectly secure that the company's assets are dealt with for his benefit. This does not include persons whose rights are solely contingent on a default by the CFC;
(d) any other person who, alone or with others, has control of the company.

The last of these categories makes clear that a person need not be a direct shareholder to have an interest in the CFC; he need only hold shares in an intermediate company which itself holds shares in the CFC (see para 67.5).

The basic rule governing apportionment among the interest holders presupposes that they, and any intermediate holding companies, hold only ordinary shares. This is the normal situation and where it obtains the apportionment is in proportion to the shareholding (s 752(2)). In cases where this is not the position the apportionment is between interest holders on a just and reasonable basis (s 752(4)).

Particular problems are presented where the same interest in a CFC is held both directly and indirectly, as where there is an intermediate holding company. Here the apportionment is to whichever interest-holder has the relevant interest. Rules are laid down for determining which interest is relevant (TA 1988, s 752A). In broad terms any interest held by a UK company is relevant unless it is itself held through another UK company.

It is not just the chargeable profits of the CFC which have to be apportioned, but also its creditable tax. This term effectively means first the double tax relief to which the CFC would have been entitled if UK resident and second the UK tax the CFC has in fact borne, whether by deduction at source or direct assessment (TA 1988, s 751). The creditable tax so computed is apportioned in the same shares as the chargeable profits.

The charge to tax

67.20 Where chargeable profits are apportioned to a UK resident company, an amount equal to corporation tax on the apportioned profits is charged on the company (TA 1988, s 747(4)). If the CFC's profits are computed in a foreign currency, the amount apportioned is converted to sterling at the rate prevailing at the end of the CFC's accounting period (TA 1988, s 747(4A)). The tax charged is corporation tax at the main rate; the small companies rate cannot apply to apportioned CFC profits (International Manual para 210010). The tax so charged is regarded as tax for the accounting period of the UK company in which the CFC's accounting period ends and is reduced by so much of the CFC's creditable tax as is apportioned to the UK company concerned.

An important exemption requires the ascertainment of the proportion of the CFC's chargeable profits apportioned to any given UK company and persons associated or connected with it. If that proportion is less than 25% of the CFC's profits, no tax is charged on the UK company concerned (s 747(5)). This exemption protects portfolio investment by UK companies, but the inclusion of connected and associated persons diminishes its impact.

An interesting issue arises if the CFC is resident in a country with which the UK has concluded a double tax treaty and the CFC's income includes income over which the treaty gives the other country sole taxing rights. The issue is whether the treaty operates also to preclude a charge under the CFC legislation. In *Bricom Holdings Ltd v IRC* [1997] STC 1179, the Court of Appeal decided the CFC charge was not so precluded.

Dual resident companies

67.21 As noted in para 67.5 above, a company holding an interest in the CFC which becomes dual resident after 1 April 2002 is treated as remaining UK resident for the purposes of the CFC legislation. Chargeable profits may therefore be attributed to it and subjected to corporation tax.

It might be thought that in such a case the very treaty which makes the company dual resident would give protection from corporation tax on the attributed profits. However, this is not so, for the apportioned profits do not in fact accrue to the dual resident company. It might also be thought that the dual resident company could avoid the CFC legislation by causing the CFC to make acceptable distributions for, since the dual resident company is deemed non-resident, these would not be taxable. Such a distribution would not, however, be acceptable, as it would not be taken into account in computing the dual resident company's income for corporation tax purposes (Sch 25 para 2(1A)).

Interaction with s 739

67.22 The CFC legislation prevents a CFC's profits from being assessable on a UK resident individual under TA 1988, s 739 (TA 1988, s 747(4); cf Chapter 55). This relief only applies insofar as a UK company is actually charged on the profits so apportioned.

Reliefs

67.23 Where a UK company has an insufficiency of profits against which to set any relief, it may claim to have its liability to tax on any apportioned CFC profits reduced by tax at the same rate or effective rate on the unutilised reliefs (TA 1988, Sch 26 para 1). The reliefs to which this applies are as follows:

(1) losses relieved against general profits;
(2) charges on income;
(3) expenses of management;
(4) capital allowances available for set-off against general profits;
(5) group relief;
(6) non-trading deficits on loan relationships.

Future dividends

67.24 A measure of relief applies if the CFC pays a dividend out of the apportioned profits (TA 1988, Sch 26 paras 4 and 5). The key concept in this relief is the gross attributed tax, which is simply the tax assessed on the UK corporate shareholders. The relief operates by treating this as tax paid by the CFC in the territory in which it is resident, with the result that it counts as underlying tax for the purposes of double tax relief. If only some of the CFC's shareholders are liable to tax under the CFC legislation, then, unless the dividend is paid out of specified profits, the gross attributed tax is treated as underlying tax borne by their notional share of the CFC's profits.

One problem with relief for underlying tax is that it and any local withholding tax on the dividends may exceed what the UK corporation tax thereon would otherwise be. In this event TA 1988, ss 796 and 797 restrict double tax relief to the amount of such UK tax. Where this happens there is an amount of wasted relief, which the CFC legislation, by increasing underlying tax, compounds. To some extent the CFC legislation recognises this, for it allows partial repayment of any tax charge under the CFC legislation to the extent that the wasted relief less than the withholding tax on the actual dividend (Sch 26 para 4(5)).

Future disposals

67.25 Relief from CGT is allowed where a UK company disposes of shares in a CFC whose chargeable profits have previously been apportioned to it (Sch 26 para 3). In these circumstances, any tax paid by the UK company on its share of the chargeable profits may be deducted in computing the chargeable gain on the disposal of the CFC shares, or, if there is an intermediate holding company, on the disposal of the holding company's shares. An apportionment of the relief is made if some only of the shares concerned are disposed of.

This CGT relief does not apply if the CFC has previously paid a depreciatory dividend out of the apportioned profit or a dividend attracting the underlying tax relief noted above. Equally, once shares have suffered a disposal attracting the CGT relief, they cannot found a claim for underlying tax relief in the hands of the new owner.

Transfer pricing

67.26 As described above (para 67.7), UK transfer pricing rules apply in computing the CFC's chargeable profits. If all the CFC's profits have been apportioned to and taxed on UK companies relief may be claimed in respect of any transfer pricing adjustment. The claim is made by the other party to the transfer pricing adjustment and is competent insofar as that party is subject to UK tax. It allows its profits to be computed on the arm's length price rather than the actual price otherwise used (TA 1988, Sch 28AA paras 6 and 6B; see further Chapter 68).

Compliance and clearance

67.27 A supplementary page to the corporation tax self-assessment return deals with CFCs. Any company which has an interest in a CFC must complete this page unless the CFC is within the Excluded Countries Regulations or the interest of the UK company and persons connected or associated with it is less than 25% (International Manual para 214020). In cases of doubt companies should complete the CFC page or consult HMRC. If it is clear that one of the exemptions applies, the company need merely make an entry to that effect (ibid para 214030). So too if there is doubt as to whether the foreign company is a CFC, but one or more of the exemptions would clearly apply if it was, the UK company can simply submit the CFC page and claim the exemption (ibid, para 214020).

CFC liabilities are governed by all the normal self-assessment rules as to record-keeping, enquiries, and penalties. However, the Board's sanction is required if the Inspector makes an amendment otherwise than with the taxpayer's agreement (TA 1988, s 754B).

Any UK company with an interest in an actual or possible CFC may apply for advance clearance in respect of any aspect of the CFC legislation. Once given the clearance will remain valid so long as the underlying facts remain the same. Details of the scope and procedure to be followed in applying for clearance are given in para 214120 of the International Manual.

Chapter 68

Transfer pricing

Introduction

68.1 Transfer pricing is principally thought of in connection with multinational groups of companies. But in fact it potentially arises wherever parties in common ownership or under common control do business with each other. Often there may be no commercial significance in prices agreed between the parties and so if one has a more favourable tax position than the other, the ability to secure a tax advantage is considerable.

Until 1999 HMRC had two principal weapons to counter transfer-pricing, namely a direction challenging related-party prices under TA 1988, s 770 and, where the other party to a transaction was based in a treaty jurisdiction, the associated enterprises clause in the relevant double tax treaty. In addition, in appropriate cases, certain common law principles could also be deployed (see para 68.21).

In 1998 s 770 was repealed and new rules, contained in TA 1988, Sch 28AA, were introduced. These make transfer-pricing adjustments a mandatory part of the self-assessment procedure. Sch 28AA has had effect for corporation tax purposes as respects accounting periods ending after 1 July 1999 and otherwise for 1999–2000 and subsequent tax years (FA 1988, s 109(5)).

When originally enacted Sch 28AA did not apply if the party disadvantaged by the uncommercial price was resident and taxed in the UK (Sch 28AA para 5(2)–(6) as originally enacted). But in 2004, in response to case law in the European Court (see Chapter 48), this territorial limit on Sch 28AA was removed. At the same time a limited exemption for small and medium-sized enterprises was introduced and the thin capitalisation rules formerly in TA 1988, s 208(2)(da) were brought within Sch 28AA. These changes apply from 1 April 2004 (FA 2004, s 37).

This chapter is concerned with Sch 28AA as it now exists. But it also includes mention of the common law principles referred to above, which remain good law.

A point to stress is that Sch 28AA does not just apply in computing trading profits. As noted below it applies generally in computing income and deductions.

The statutory rule

68.2 The rules in Sch 28AA apply if the following conditions are satisfied (para 1):

(1) Provision has been made or imposed as between any two persons. This provision is referred to as 'the actual provision' and the two persons are referred to as 'the affected persons'.
(2) The actual provision has been made or imposed by means of a transaction or series of transactions.
(3) The actual provision differs from what is called the arm's length provision. This is the provision which would have been made had the affected persons been independent enterprises.
(4) The actual provision confers a potential advantage in relation to UK taxation on one or both of the affected persons. A person so advantaged is referred to as 'the potentially advantaged person'.
(5) One of the affected persons participates in the management control or capital of the other or a common third party so participates in both.

Where these conditions are satisfied, the arm's length provision must be substituted for the actual provision in computing the profits or losses of the potentially advantaged person. The substitution is mandatory, and must be effected by the taxpayer in preparing his self-assessment return.

An actual provision is treated as conferring an advantage in relation to UK taxation if, by comparison with the arm's length provision, the advantaged person's profits are less than they should be or his losses are greater (Sch 28AA para 5). It is expressly provided that 'profits' includes income and 'losses' includes relief for interest (para 14(1)). One exception is made to the inclusion of income, namely that in dealing with a non-resident advantaged person, excluded income may be ignored (para 5(7)). Excluded income is UK source income in respect of which the tax liability of non-residents is restricted to tax deducted at source (see para 34.14). The principal categories are dividends and interest.

The term 'transaction' also has an extended meaning. It includes arrangements, understandings and mutual practices, whether or not legally enforceable (Sch 28AA para 3(1)). The term 'series of transactions' includes any number of transactions entered into under the same arrangement. It is not necessary for either of the affected persons to be party to such an arrangement, nor need there be any transaction in the series to which they are both parties (ibid, para 3(4)).

Common participation

68.3 Common participation in management, control, or capital is the fundamental prerequisite of Sch 28AA. Under para 1(1), the participation may be direct or indirect.

Direct participation

68.4 One person can only be treated as participating in the management, control, or capital of another if the latter person is a body corporate or partnership. The participation is direct if and only if the participant controls the partnership or body corporate concerned (para 4(1)).

Control does not bear its extended close company definition but the narrower meaning given by TA 1988, s 840. This applies to partnerships as well as companies.

Under s 840 a person controls a partnership if he is entitled to more than half its assets or more than half the income (TA 1988, s 840). Hence Sch 28AA can apply to transactions between an individual and a partnership in which his share is greater than half, or between two partnerships in each of which one individual enjoys more than a half share. It also applies to transactions between such partnerships and a company which an individual controls.

A person has control of a company under s 840 if (1) he can secure that its affairs are conducted in accordance with his wishes; and (2) he is able to secure that result by one of two methods. The first method is by the possession of share or voting rights and the second is by powers conferred by the articles (TA 1988, s 840).

Indirect participation

68.5 Indirect participation is a much wider and more menacing concept (ibid, para 4(2)). A person indirectly participates in the management, control, or capital of a company or partnership if either:

(a) he would be a direct participant if a whole series of other rights or powers were attributed to him; or
(b) he is one of a number of what are called major participants in the enterprise of the company or partnership.

Attributed rights and powers

68.6 The rights and powers which may be attributed to a person in determining whether he is an indirect participant are as follows (para 4(3)):

(1) Rights or powers which he is entitled to acquire in the future or will become entitled to acquire.
(2) Rights or powers which are or may be required to be exercised on his behalf, under his direction, or for his benefit.
(3) Rights or powers exercisable by any person with whom he is connected, or by any person connected with such a connected person.

For the purposes of (3) persons are connected with each other if they are relatives or if one is the trustee of a settlement and the other is a settlor or a person connected with him (ibid, para 4(11)). Relatives include children, grandchildren, parents, grandparents, and spouses (para 4(12)).

There are two particularly menacing features of these definitions:

(a) The chain of connection at (3) can go on indefinitely (para 4(6)). Thus if X is the son of Y, Y is the brother of Z, and A is the son of Z, X and A are connected. So too X is connected with any settlement of which A is settlor, and vice versa. Such connections would only cease if Y or Z died.

(b) It is unclear what is meant at (2) by rights which are, or may be, required to be exercised on behalf of a person or for his benefit. In particular does it mean that shares or voting rights held in trust must be attributed to a beneficiary? The argument that it does is that all powers vested in trustees have to be exercised for the benefit of the beneficiaries. The argument that it does not is that such powers have to be exercised for the benefit of the beneficiaries collectively rather than for the benefit of any one of them to the exclusion of the others. HMRC consider the legislation does prevent abuse where trusts are interposed (International Manual para 432060).

Major participants

68.7 To determine whether a person is a major participant it is necessary to show that he and one other person control the company or partnership (TA 1988, Sch 28AA para 4(7)). It must then be established that each of those persons has at least 40% of those interests rights and powers which give them control (ibid, para 4(8)). In carrying out these exercises all rights and powers which can be attributed to a person under the tests referred to above are so attributed.

A difficult point of construction arises with the 40% test. Is it 40% of the combined interests, rights and powers held by the two persons who together control the company or partnership? Or is it 40% of the total of such interests, rights and powers whether held by those two persons or by anybody else? The better view is that this is the correct construction of the legislation as enacted (see International Manual para 432070).

Financing arrangements

68.8 A special rule exists in relation to financing arrangements (TA 1988, Sch 28AA, para 4(4A)). It applies where a person is acting together with others in relation to the arrangements and where it applies it allows the rights and powers of those others to be attributed to him. This attribution may be made in determining whether he has control of the company for whom the arrangements are being made or whether he controls any other company which is an affected person in relation to those arrangements. But a transfer-pricing adjustment is not required by virtue of this provision otherwise than as respects the financing arrangements. Subject to transitional provisions, this rule applies to accounting periods beginning after 3 March 2005 (F(No 2)A 2005, Sch 8, para 4).

The arm's length provision

68.9 Schedule 28AA does not define what it means by arm's length provision. Instead it requires that the schedule be construed so as to secure consistency with the OECD guidelines applicable to the transfer pricing article in Double Tax Treaties which follow the OECD model (Sch 28AA para 2). The OECD guidelines are published in looseleaf form under the title, 'Transfer Pricing Guidelines for Multinational Enterprises and Tax Administrations'. Effectively what Sch 28AA says is that these guidelines must be followed in determining what the arm's length provision should be.

Such a rule is admirable in securing international consistency. The difficulty is that the language of the OECD guidelines is often elusive and academic, with the result that clear rules can be difficult to identify. Nonetheless, when all is said and done, there is one overriding principle. If it is possible to identify similar transactions between unconnected parties, the price at which those transactions are done is the arm's length price. The aim of any transfer pricing exercise must be to identify this price, the comparable uncontrolled price, or CUP, as it is called.

Problems start when it is not possible to find similar transactions from which the CUP can be discerned. Often this is because the related party transaction is not one which independent parties would be likely to enter into, e g one party buying the whole output of the other. When this is the case other methods may be used, notably cost plus, resale minus or some formula for dividing overall profit relative to contribution. But in a sense all these are variants of CUP, for what has to be identified is the kind of margin or division that would be agreed at arm's length. Often two of these secondary methods are used to provide a cross-check.

Small and medium-sized enterprises

68.10 Since 1 April 2004, Sch 28AA has not applied at all if the advantaged party is a small enterprise (para 5B). It does not apply to medium-sized enterprises unless, following notice of enquiry into the enterprise's return, HMRC give a notice (para 5B and 5C).

The meaning of the terms small and medium-sized enterprise are those applicable under European law (para 5D). Currently it is set out in the Annex to the European Commission Recommendation of 6 May 2003 concerning the definitions of micro, small and medium-sized enterprises. A small enterprise is one which employs fewer than 50 persons and whose turnover or assets are less than €10 million. A medium-sized enterprise is one which employs fewer than 250 persons and whose turnover or assets are less than €50 million.

Unfortunately, and perhaps unsurprisingly, this exemption from Sch 28AA is not as far-reaching as appears. One reason is that the Annex to the Commission Recommendation differentiates between what it calls autonomous enterprises, partner enterprises, and linked enterprises. In applying the head-count and financial limits, partner enterprises and linked enterprises are aggregated. It appears this aggregation is intended to be carried into Sch 28AA, as such is reflected in paras 5D(3) and 5D(4) (see also Finance Bill 2004 Explanatory Notes to clauses 30–37, para 33). In broad terms, linked enterprises are enterprises under common control and partner enterprises are enterprises with 25% common ownership. In an international context, this plainly means that in applying Sch 28AA, one has to ask not just whether the UK entity is a small or medium-sized enterprise, but whether all international companies in the same ownership are such an enterprise in the aggregate.

The other reason why this exemption is less attractive than appears is that it does not apply unless the other party to the transaction is resident in the UK or in a treaty jurisdiction (para 5B(4)). If the treaty concerned has a standard non-discrimination article, the exemption applies unless the Treasury have designated the territory concerned as non-qualifying (para 5E(2)). But if the treaty does not have such an article, the exemption does not apply unless the Treasury designate the territory as qualifying (para 5E(3)).

Thin capitalisation

68.11 The term 'thin capitalisation' normally refers to the funding of a company with debt rather than equity. In such cases, the return the shareholders draw may be interest able to be set against profits rather than dividend paid out of post-tax profits. For an offshore investor such a scenario is attractive.

Para 1A of Sch 28AA renders payment of such interest subject to transfer-pricing rules. In determining whether too much interest is being paid by the UK company, account can be taken not merely of whether the rate of interest would have been lower at arm's length, but of whether the loan would have been made either at all or if made, in a lesser amount. The same principles are applied where the offshore owner does not itself make the loan but guarantees some commercial lender who does (para 1B). These rules in paras 1A and 1B are expressed as applying only where both the parties to the transaction are companies.

Double counting

68.12 One problem where a transfer-pricing adjustment is made is that the other party may already have paid tax on the basis of having enjoyed enhanced profits or unduly modest losses or other deductions. Sch 28AA para 6 allows adjustment to be claimed where both parties are within charge to UK tax in respect of the transactions concerned. In addition, balancing payments may be made between the parties without tax cost (para 7A).

Most of this is only likely to be relevant where both parties to the offending transaction are UK based. But this is not necessarily so, for example where the attack on thin capitalisation disallows some of the interest on a loan from a non-resident shareholder. Here the claim for adjustment may extend to a claim that the excess interest is not chargeable as UK source income with the result that deduction at source does not apply (see para 6E and Finance Bill Explanatory Notes to clauses 30–37, para 115).

In most cases where a transfer-pricing adjustment is made, double counting results from the other party to the offending transaction being subject to foreign tax. Of itself UK legislation cannot address such foreign tax. But if the other party to the transaction is in the European Union it may be possible to invoke the EC Convention of 23 July 1990. If a double tax treaty is in point, it should be possible to claim adjustment under the associated enterprises article. The point is unlikely to arise in a pure offshore context, as here the whole object of the exercise is to take extra profit offshore free of any tax.

Compliance

68.13 A critical point about Sch 28AA is that tax computations must be based on arm's length prices insofar as the taxpayer has engaged in connected party transactions. Essentially this involves one of two requirements, namely either:

(1) the taxpayer must be able to show that the connected party transactions were such as would have been had the entities been wholly unconnected; or
(2) insofar as this cannot be shown, an adjustment must be made in the taxpayer's self-assessment return.

An equally important point is that transfer pricing is part of the self-assessment regime. This has two important implications:

(1) If the company's self-assessment return is not correct, interest and penalties may be charged on any understated tax.
(2) The company must create and keep appropriate records to substantiate the entries in its return.

These requirements mean not merely that a taxpayer must be satisfied that his connected party prices are at arm's length, but that he must adduce and keep sufficient evidence to prove this. In the case of a company, Board consideration with suitable documentation is required.

In *Tax Bulletin* 38 (December 1998) HMRC indicated the approach they take. In practice the sort of procedures the taxpayer should adopt are as follows:

(1) identify connected party transactions or groups of such transactions as are within Sch 28AA;

(2) identify how the prices and other terms of the transactions were arrived at;
(3) satisfy himself that the prices accord with arm's length prices, ideally by comparison with comparable transactions with independent parties;
(4) if he is not so satisfied, ensure tax computations reflect an appropriate adjustment;
(5) ensure all the above is properly documented with full reasons.

In the case of a company a good method of achieving the above objectives would be a full report to the Board from a suitably qualified person, followed by properly minuted Board consideration and approval.

Should a return not comply with Sch 28AA it may be adjusted with interest on any enquiry. Should fraud or neglect be involved, the issue of penalties will arise. However, HMRC have confirmed that the onus is on them to show fraud or neglect and that they will not look for penalties where taxpayers have made an honest and reasonable attempt to comply with the legislation (*Tax Bulletin* 38 (December 1998) p 603).

Increasingly HMRC are recognising that in many cases requiring a transfer-pricing adjustment the potential tax loss is not great. Typically this is the position where both parties to the transaction are taxed at broadly similar rates, a scenario now all too common under Sch 28AA. Here HMRC have said the business concerned is not expected to do elaborate research or incur significant costs. So too the likelihood of HMRC enquiry is low (see Revenue Press Release, 'Corporation Tax Reform – the next Steps' 10 December 2003 para 1.27).

Risk assessment

68.14 A transfer-pricing enquiry into an enterprise's fundamental pricing structure for cross-border transactions with associated enterprises is not undertaken without a prior risk assessment. This is because HMRC are aware that a full transfer pricing investigation can be time consuming and expensive both for them and for the taxpayer. Details of the risk assessment procedure are given in *Tax Bulletin* 60 (August 2002). A prior risk assessment is not made in such areas as thin capitalisation, imputed interest on outward loans or guarantee or management fees (ibid, p 943).

Advance pricing agreements

68.15 Finance Act 1999, ss 85–87 enables taxpayers and HMRC to enter into advance pricing agreements in relation to transfer pricing. Such an agreement allows the taxpayer to be sure that, to the extent that the agreement provides, transfer prices will be acceptable to HMRC. HMRC guidance as to the making and operation of advance pricing arrangements ('APAs') is set out in SP 3/99.

Information

68.16 Should HMRC initiate an enquiry into a UK company's transfer pricing, they have their normal powers to require the company to produce documents in the company's power or control (FA 1998, Sch 18, para 27). In *Meditor Capital Management v Feighan* [2004] STC (SCD) 273, the taxpayer company was owned by a Bermudan parent which was itself owned by an offshore trust. The Bermudan company was a fund management company and the taxpayer company provided it with investment management services. As part of a transfer-pricing enquiry, HMRC inter alia demanded from the taxpayer company information about the employees of the Bermudan company and information about its interests in the funds under management. On the facts of the case, a Special Commissioner held that such documents were within the power and control of the taxpayer company.

UK property investment

68.17 Transfer-pricing issues can arise when offshore investors acquire UK property. HMRC gave some guidance in *Tax Bulletin* 46 (April 2000) p 740.

Non-resident landlord scheme

68.18 *Tax Bulletin* 46 confirms that Sch 28AA does apply to non-resident landlords.

Loan finance

68.19 Non-resident landlords normally use loan finance to fund their acquisition of UK investment property as the loan interest is a deduction from the rent. This is so even if the borrowing is abroad and outside the obligation to deduct tax (TA 1988, s 21A(4)).

Even though *Tax Bulletin* 46 was published well before the enactment of the express rules in Sch 28AA as to thin capitalisation, it approaches property financing issues in the same way. Thus it takes the position that interest is non-allowable to the extent that the loan exceeds what a commercial lender would lend. It indicates that normally commercial lenders advance 65–80% of the value of the property.

Tax Bulletin 46 does not confine itself to cases where the offshore connected party lending or guaranteeing the loan is a company. In that sense it expresses itself in terms wider than the express provisions now in paras 1A and 1B (para 68.11 above) and the issue therefore arises of whether it is in fact in point where the offshore party is a trust or an individual. This, no doubt, turns on how far paras 1A and 1B duplicate the general language of Sch 28AA.

A widely-debated issue arises where loan or guarantee finance is in excess of the 65–80% guideline but would have been available commercially albeit at a higher interest rate than that in fact being charged. Here *Tax Bulletin* 46 appears to accept a transfer-pricing adjustment is not required, save where on the facts the commercial interest would have been more than the investment could stand, implying that at arm's length the loan would not have been made at all.

Rent-free residential accommodation

68.20 *Tax Bulletin* 46 also addresses a rather different issue. This is where an offshore company provides rent-free accommodation to a participant individual. On a literal reading of Sch 28AA it could be argued that rent should be imputed to the company as that is what would be charged were the participant and the company at arm's length. In fact it is very doubtful whether Sch 28AA would bear this construction. But whatever the correctness of that, HMRC confirmed in *Tax Bulletin* 46 they would not take the point.

General income tax principles

68.21 Two general income tax principles should be remembered in relation to transfer pricing, namely the 'wholly and exclusively' rule and the rule in *Sharkey v Wernher* [1956] AC 58, [1955] 3 All ER 493. Both are wider in ambit than TA 1988, Sch 28AA in that they do not require any element of common ownership between parties to a transaction. They are narrower in that they only apply in computing trading profits.

The 'wholly and exclusively' rule

68.22 Trading expenditure is not allowed in computing trading profits unless it has been incurred wholly and exclusively for the purposes of the trade. There is no requirement that the expenditure be necessarily incurred, but the expenditure must still be incurred for the purposes of the business and for no other purposes (*Mallalieu v Drummond* [1983] 2 AC 861, [1983] STC 665).

A series of decisions have established that trading expenditure is not disallowed simply because it is excessive. As Lord Reid said in *Ransom v Higgs* [1974] 3 All ER 949 at 958, if a trader is activated by nothing but a commercial motive the Crown cannot say that he paid too much. But where enhanced expenditure is incurred for profit diversion or general tax planning reasons rather than for trading purposes, it is not allowable (*IRC v Europa Oil (NZ) Ltd* [1971] AC 760; *Ransom v Higgs*, supra). The issue, therefore, is not whether trading expenditure is excessive, but why it is excessive.

A difficult point is whether, if expenditure is disallowed, all of it is disallowed or merely that part of it in excess of market value. Dicta in *Ransom v Higgs* suggest that the former may be correct. But the point was not argued in the case, and certainly, on general principles, dual purpose expenditure is non-allowable.

The rule in Sharkey v Wernher

68.23 In *Sharkey v Wernher* [1956] AC 58, [1955] 3 All ER 493, the House of Lords held that a trader who appropriates trading stock to his own use should bring it in as a market value receipt. But the substitution of market value was not restricted to appropriations to personal use. Lord Simmonds expressed it as applying whenever trading stock was parted with so that it was no longer stock in trade, and Lord Radcliffe referred to non-commercial disposals. Accordingly, market value has to be substituted if trading stock is dissipated or given away.

Of greater significance is the subsequent extension of the principle in *Petrotim Securities Ltd v Ayres* [1964] 1 All ER 269, [1964] 1 WLR 190. Here a tax avoidance scheme had been implemented and, as part of that scheme, Petrotim sold trading stock to its parent at one quarter its true value. The Commissioners found that the sale was not made in the course of Petrotim's trade, and this was upheld in the Court of Appeal. The Court of Appeal then decided that the amount at which the disposal should be entered in Petrotim's trading account should be market value.

The principle underlying these decisions is that market value is substituted whenever a non-trading or non-commercial disposal of trading stock occurs. It is a question of fact whether a disposal is capable of falling within these categories but it will normally do so if the undervalue is substantial and the underlying purpose is tax avoidance.

Chapter 69

Benefits in kind

Introduction

69.1 The Income Tax (Earnings and Pensions) Act 2003 treats benefits in kind as employment earnings. Most of the provisions are contained in Part 3 of the Act, but the rules relating to shares are now included in the code dealing with employment related securities (ITEPA 2003, Part 7). Part 3 re-enacts provisions formerly in TA 1988, ss 145–168. It applies to directors and most other employees and operates where the benefit is provided by reason of the employee or director's employment.

At first sight this has little to do with offshore tax planning for UK individuals are rarely employees of offshore entities. However this initial impression is incorrect, for as is explained in Chapter 53 in the benefits code applies to shadow directors and there are instances where a UK individual so conducts himself that he is a shadow director of an offshore company.

The heads of charge under the benefits code are as follows (ITEPA 2003, s 63):

- Expenses payments
- Vouchers and credit tokens
- Living accommodation
- Cars, vans and related benefits
- Loans
- Residual liability

Of these heads, the one normally encountered in the context of offshore tax planning is living accommodation. However note also needs to be taken of the charge on loans and the residual liability.

Some heads of charge, but notably not the living accommodation charge, do not apply if the employee's earnings are less than £8,500 (ITEPA 2003, s 216). This however is of limited significance as it does not apply to directors (and thus by inference to shadow directors) unless the director is a full-time working director with no material interest in the employer company. Further in determining whether earnings are below the £8,500 limit, account is taken of benefits in kind (s 218).

Living accommodation

69.2 Living accommodation is brought within the benefits code by ITEPA 2003, ss 97–113. These sections apply to living accommodation provided for an employee or his family or household by reason of his employment (s 97). Where they apply, the cash equivalent of the benefit is treated as earnings from the employment for the tax year concerned (s 102).

By reason of employment

69.3 Any accommodation provided by the employer is regarded as provided by reason of employment (s 97(2)). This deeming provision is not an exclusive definition, and so if accommodation provided by somebody else is in fact provided by reason of employment it is caught.

The extension of this charge to shadow directors is illustrated by *R v Allen* [2001] STC 1537. Here an offshore company in the direct ownership of the taxpayer provided the family home. The taxpayer was found on the facts to be a shadow and thus the house was provided by reason of his notional employment.

Cash equivalent

69.4 In law there are two separate rules for computing the cash equivalent. The first applies if the cost of providing the accommodation is less than £75,000. In this case, according to ITEPA 2003, the cash equivalent is the annual value of the accommodation (s 103). This is defined as the rent obtainable for the property on a yearly letting with the tenant bearing rates and charges normally borne by the tenant and the landlord repairs and insurance (s 110). The cash equivalent is reduced by any sum made good by the employee (s 105(2)(a)).

The second rule applies if the cost of the accommodation is over £75,000. In this case in law the cash equivalent is the sum of two elements:

(a) The annual value of the accommodation; plus
(b) interest at the official rate on the amount by which the cost of providing accommodation exceeds £75,000 (s 106).

Interest at the official rate is interest at the rate prescribed for taxing beneficial loans and is currently 5% (see para 69.12).

Cost of providing the accommodation

69.5 The cost of providing the accommodation is costs incurred in acquiring or improving the property (s 104). These costs are brought into account if incurred by any person involved in providing the accommodation. This latter term is defined as the person in fact providing the accommodation, the employer, and any person connected with either of those two parties (s 112). 'Connected' bears the standard meaning given in TA 1988, s 839 (ITEPA 2003, s 718).

In one situation the actual cost is displaced by market value. This applies where the property was owned by a person involved in providing the accommodation for more than six years before the employee first went into occupation. In such case the cost of providing the accommodation is its market value when the employee first went into occupation plus improvements thereafter (ITEPA 2003, s 107). This rule does not apply in determining whether the £75,000 threshold is exceeded but only in determining the figure to which interest at the official rate is applied if it is.

Reimbursement

69.6 The cost of providing the accommodation may be reduced by payments made by the employee (s 104). To qualify for this treatment the payment must be made to a person involved in providing the accommodation. It must either be 'reimbursement' of expenditure incurred on the acquisition of or improvements to the property or consideration paid by the employee for the grant of a tenancy of the property. Obviously if payments qualifying for this treatment equal the costs there can be no cash equivalent and, to the extent they are less, they reduce the sum on which the notional interest is computed.

In an offshore context, the exception for reimbursement may prove significant. In most cases the reality is that the shadow of an offshore company does provide the funds for the property purchase, for the company is simply the vehicle for an acquisition the shadow is paying for. Economically therefore he ought to be in the same position as the employee of an arm's length company who reimburses accommodation costs. The issue is whether and in what circumstances what he pays may count as reimbursement.

It may be suggested that if the shadow initially lends the company the cost of the property and then, after the property is acquired, writes the loan off he would be reimbursing the cost. Still more so would be the position if the company borrows from a third party and then, after the acquisition, is put in funds by the shadow to enable it to repay the loan. And if this is right, what in substance is the difference if the shadow provides the money to the company before and with a view to the acquisition. In all these cases it may strongly be argued the spirit of the legislation should treat the shadow as making reimbursement.

The same arguments would apply if a trust owns the company, for, as a person connected with the company, the trust is a person involved in providing the accommodation. The trust could therefore fund the acquisition by the company and then, later, be reimbursed by further settlement by the shadow.

Quantum of charge in practice

69.7 As will be apparent from the above there is potentially a double charge on properties costing in excess of £75,000. This is because the cash equivalent includes both (a) the annual rental value, and (b) notional interest at 5% on the cost over £75,000.

In practice this absurdity is avoided in a more than usually blatant example of untaxing by concession. The position is as follows:

(1) Ever since the inception of the accommodation charge annual value has been treated as meaning not the market rental value but the gross rateable value under the old rating system abolished in 1990 (IR Press Release 19 April 1990). Values under that system were last fixed in 1973 so in practice the annual value is very low. For UK properties which did not then exist an estimate of what the gross rateable value would have been is made based on comparables. It has been confirmed that this treatment continues to apply under ITEPA 2003 (Explanatory Notes to ITEPA 2003 para 404).
(2) The use of gross annual value is recognised as inappropriate for properties outside the UK and here annual value is taken as meaning what it says – ie annual market rental value (Employment Income Manual para 11472). But in such case, by concession, the annual rental value is then the sole measure of cash equivalent – in other words notional interest on the price in excess of £75,000 is not included (ESC A91).

Payment of rent

69.8 As will be apparent from the above, payment of an arm's length rent in practice obviates a charge in respect of foreign property. But in relation to UK property, this is not necessarily the position. It is only so if on the facts, the rent exceeds the quantum of benefit as calculated under the rules described above – in other words in the normal case if it exceeds interest at the official rate on the cost.

Exceptions

69.9 Exceptions are made to the accommodation charge, notably for representative occupation and for accommodation provided by individuals in the normal course of personal relationships (ITEPA 2003, ss 97(2) and 98–101). None are normally relevant in an offshore context.

Subsidised loans

69.10 Subsidised loans are brought within the benefits in kind code by ITEPA 2003, ss 173–191. These sections apply insofar as the loan is an employment related loan and a taxable cheap loan. Where they apply the charge is on the cash equivalent.

Employment related

69.11 A loan can be employment-related if it is made to the employee or a relative of the employee (ITEPA 2003, s 17(1)). Relatives are spouses, siblings, parents, and children (ibid s 174(6)).

Not surprisingly, any loan made by the employer (or shadow employer) is employment related. But in addition, ITEPA 2003, s 174(2) specifies a whole series of other loans which are deemed to be employment-related.

The principal categories of loan so treated are as follows:

(1) The lender is a company which controls or is controlled by the employer.
(2) The lender is a company controlled by a person who also controls the employer.
(3) The lender has a material interest in a UK close company which is either the employer or has control of another company which is the employer.
(4) The lender has a material interest in a company (whether UK or non-UK) which itself controls a UK close company which is the employer.

Control for these purposes means voting control (ITEPA 2003, ss 69 and 719; TA 1988, s 840). The term 'material interest', however, is much wider. It means beneficial ownership of or control over more than 5% of the ordinary share capital of the company (ITEPA 2003, s 68(2)). If the company is a UK close company it also means entitlement to more than 5% of the assets on a winding up (ibid s 68(3)).

In an offshore context, an important issue is how far loans are caught where, on the facts, the beneficiary of an offshore trust is found to be shadow director of an offshore company owned by the trust. In such a case a loan is caught if made by the company. It is not caught if it is made by the trust because the offshore company is not a UK company and so not within the applicable definition of a close company (see ITEPA 2003, Sch 1 Part 2, and TA 1988, ss 832(1) and 414). A loan is, however, caught if made by another company controlled by the trust, even if the borrower was not a shadow director of that company.

A point for offshore trustees to watch is interests in UK close companies. If any such interest is greater than 5%, a loan by the trust to a beneficiary is, on a literal reading of the ITEPA provisions, employment-related if the borrower is an employee of the UK company. This is so even if the reason for making the loan has nothing whatever to do with the employment.

It may be that the definition of employment-related loans should not be given a wide construction of this sort. A purposive construction would restrict the term to loans funded by the employer or made for reasons connected with the employment. However, the point has not been at issue in any decided case and there is no indication that HMRC subscribe to it.

A loan is caught if, when it is made, the employment is prospective (ITEPA 2003, s 174(3)). But where the employment is not in existence or in prospect when the loan is made, subsequent employment is immaterial.

Taxable cheap loan

69.12 The loan is a taxable cheap loan in any tax year if the employee holds the employment during that year and no interest is payable on the loan or the interest is less than the official rate (s 175). The official rate is the rate specified by the Treasury in accordance with FA 1989, s 175 (ITEPA 2003, s 181). Currently it is 5% (Taxes (Interest Rate) Regulations 1989 (SI 1989/1297) reg 5).

Certain loans are excepted from being cheap loans by ITEPA 2003, ss 176–180. The main exceptions are certain loans made in the ordinary course of business, loans at a fixed rate of interest equal to the official rate of interest when made, loans where actual interest would qualify for tax relief, and loans of less than £5,000.

It is not necessary for interest to be paid during the tax year for the loan to avoid being treated as a cheap loan. It must be paid for the year, and so can be paid subsequently. Should the interest be paid after the loan has been taxed as a cheap loan, the tax is repaid (ITEPA 2003, s 191).

The cash equivalent

69.13 Where an employment related loan is a taxable cheap loan, the cash equivalent is interest at the official rate for the tax year concerned, or part of the year during which the loan is outstanding. Where any actual interest is paid, the cash equivalent is reduced by such interest. Should the official rate change during the tax year, the different rates are applied pro rata (ss 182 and 183).

Loan released or written off

69.14 Should the loan be released or written off the amount written off is treated as earnings (s 188). This applies whether the employment still subsists at the time of the write-off or has previously terminated. A charge is not however made if the write off is on or after the death of the employee (s 190).

It is particularly important to keep this charge in mind as it can arise long after the employment or shadow employment has ceased. It can be a particular trap for offshore trustees if the wide literal meaning of employment-related loan discussed above is right, for it would catch any write-off in favour of a beneficiary if when the loan was made that beneficiary had happened to be an employee of a UK company in which the trust had more than a 5% interest.

It is unclear whether the charge applies if at the time of write-off the employee is non resident. ITEPA 2003, s 188(2) provides that if the employment has terminated or become an excluded employment, the write-off charge is made as if the employment had not terminated or become excluded. Excluded employments are those where the employee is not a director and the taxable earnings are less than £8,500 per year (ITEPA 2003, ss 216(1) and 63(4). The term does not include becoming non-resident and so it would appear to follow that if at the time of release the borrower is non-resident or non-domiciled, the territorial limits described in para 69.18 below are in point if the borrower is a director or shadow and remains so. HMRC do not adopt this analysis, but in so doing appear to be basing their views on the legislation as it existed prior to the 2003 rewrite (see Employment Income Manual para 21745 and TA 1988, s 160(3)).

Residual benefits

69.15 Benefits not taxed under the specific heads in ITEPA 2003, Part 3 are caught by a residual charge in ss 201–210. This head of charge extends to benefits or facilities of any kind which are provided to the employee or a member of his family or household by reason of the employment (s 201). As with accommodation anything provided by the employer is deemed to be provided by reason of employment (s 201(3)). Any benefit within the specific heads is excluded from this head of charge, with the result that double taxation is avoided and the measure of charge on such specific benefits is that laid down by the specific head of charge in question (s 202).

The residual charge can catch cash sums if for some reason they are not taxable as earnings in the general sense of the term. Payments resulting from a fair bargain are excluded and the employment must subsist at some point in the tax year in which the benefit is conferred (see ITEPA 2003, s 201(4) and *Wilson v Clayton* [2004] EWHC 898 (Ch), [2004] STC 1022.

Cash equivalent

69.16 Where the residual head of charge applies, the cash equivalent of the benefit is included as earnings. The cash equivalent is normally the expense incurred in or in connection with the benefit, less any sum made good by the employee (ss 203(2), 204, and 205(1)). But where the benefit is the transfer of an asset which has already been used, the then value of the asset is used (s 206). Where the benefit is an asset placed at the disposal of the employee without being transferred to him, the cost of the benefit in any given year is taken as 20% of the value of asset or, if the asset does not belong to the employer, rental or hire charges paid by him (s 205).

R v Allen

69.17 The residual head certainly applies to shadow directors. It was successfully invoked in *R v Allen* [2001] UKHL 45, [2001] STC 1537 in relation to the provision of premium bonds to the shadow and his family, the provision of credit cards for their use, and the payment of school fees (see [1999] STC, 846, 858). This case also demonstrates that in the context of shadow directors, the residual head catches what would otherwise be ordinary earnings if there were an actual employment.

Territorial limits of the benefits code

69.18 The starting point in establishing international limits of the benefits code is that anything treated as earnings under the code constitutes, with actual earnings, the general earnings of the individual (ITEPA 2003, s 7(3), (5)). General earnings are charged to tax insofar as they are taxable earnings (s 9(2), (3)).

The taxable earnings of an individual who is resident, ordinarily resident and domiciled in the UK, are simply the full amount of the general earnings for the tax year concerned – ie actual earnings plus the cash equivalent of benefits (ITEPA 2003, s 15). By contrast the taxable earnings of an individual who is not resident in the UK are the general earnings – ie actual earnings and benefits – in respect of duties performed in the UK (ITEPA 2003, s 27). This preserves the rule under the old Schedule E that the emoluments of non residents were taxed only insofar as paid in respect of UK duties. *R v Allen* [2001] UKHL 45, [2001] STC 1537 affirmed that under the old law that limitation applied also to benefits, and this decision is now expressly recognised in ITEPA 2003.

The practical result is that a non-resident who is a shadow is only taxed on benefits insofar as he can be said to perform duties for the company of which he is a shadow in the UK. The implications of this are discussed in relation to living accommodation in para 21.24.

The taxable earnings of a non-domiciliary resident in the UK are his chargeable overseas earnings remitted to the UK plus the full amount of such of his other general earnings as are not chargeable overseas earnings (ITEPA 2003, ss 21 and 22; para 23.3). Chargeable overseas earnings are defined in the same terms as the former foreign emoluments – ie earnings of the non-domiciliary with a foreign employer in respect of an employment whose duties are performed wholly outside the UK (s 23).

The practical result is that a non-domiciled shadow in receipt of benefits escapes charge under the code if all the duties of his notional employment can be said to be performed abroad and no part of the benefit is remitted to the UK. It may be suggested this would apply if the company of which the non-domiciliary is shadow owns a foreign property and use of that property is the benefit.

A broadly similar analysis applies where an employee is resident but not ordinarily resident in the UK. Here general earnings in respect of UK duties are included in full in taxable earnings, whereas general earnings in respect of foreign duties are chargeable only insofar as remitted (ss 25 and 26). The result of this is that a benefit received abroad is not taxable insofar as it is attributable to actual or notional foreign duties.

Shares

69.19 Shares given to employees or transferred to them at an undervalue are treated as earnings in the general sense of the term if the gift or undervalue is in return for services (*Weight v Salmon* (1935) 19 TC 174). Insofar as this is not so, special anti-avoidance rules apply. Until 2003 these rules formed part of the benefits code (ITEPA 2003, ss 192–197). Now they are included in the rules dealing with employment-related securities (ITEPA 2003, Part 7 Chapter 3C).

The effect of those rules is that the gift or undervalue is treated in the same way as a loan under the benefits code insofar as it is not earnings in the general sense of the term. This means that each year notional interest on the undervalue is treated as earnings, and, when the shares are sold, the full amount of the undervalue is taxed as earnings (ITEPA 2003, s 446U). As with loans, that charge is avoided if the shares are retained until the employee's death. But if tax avoidance is one of the purposes of the arrangements under which the shares are acquired, the notional interest regime does not apply and instead the undervalue or gift is treated as earnings when the shares are acquired (ITEPA 2003, s 446UA).

These rules apply to shares or securities insofar as they are employment-related securities. Shares or securities are employment-related if the right to acquire them is made available by the employer or a person connected with the employer (ITEPA 2003, s 421B(3)). 'Connected' bears its normal tax definition and thus, in the case of a corporate employer, means any person controlling the company (ITEPA 2003, s 718; TA 1988, s 839). 'Control', in this context, does not bear the narrow definition discussed in para 69.11 above in relation to loans but the wide anti-avoidance definition in TA 1988, s 416 (TA 1988, s 839(8)).

In contrast to the benefits code there is no deeming shadow directors to be directors or employees. Unless, therefore, the contrary can be inferred as a matter of general interpretation, shadow directors are not caught.

But even assuming that is right, the rules relating to employment-relating securities need to be watched by offshore trustees wherever a beneficiary is employed by a company connected with the trust. Any distribution of shares or securities to the beneficiary in specie may be caught, even though an equivalent distribution of cash would not be. The fact that connected persons are taken into account in determining whether the trust controls the employing company means the ambit of these rules can be unexpectedly wide. A further point is that the rules apply even if the shares are not those of the employing company.

It could be argued that, as and when the relevant provisions in ITEPA are litigated, some limitation will be placed on the apparent breadth of the term 'employment-related securities', requiring there to be some connection with the employment. But at present there is no authority to this effect. The territorial limits of the charge focus on the moment of acquisition and enable shares or securities to be excluded from the rules if at that time any actual earnings from the employment were not taxable (ITEPA 2003, s 421E(2)).

Chapter 70

Pre-owned assets

Introduction

70.1 Finance Act 2004, Schedule 15 enacted an income tax charge made on certain individuals in respect of pre-owned assets. It came into effect on 6 April 2005 (s 84(2)).

The rationale behind this legislation was summarised as follows at para 4 of the 2004 Budget Press Release 'Tax treatment of pre-owned assets' (REVBN 40):

> 'The Government is aware that various schemes designed to avoid inheritance tax have been marketed in recent years. These use artificial structures to avoid the existing rules gifts made with reservation. As a result, people have been removing assets from their taxable estate but continuing to enjoy all the benefits of ownership. The Government is determined to block this sort of avoidance and announced in the Pre-Budget report that people who benefit from these sorts of schemes would be subject to an income tax charge from April 2005, to reflect their additional taxable capacity from receiving these benefits at low or no cost.'

Although a charge has only been able to be made since 6 April 2005, the arrangements which give rise to it can have been put into place many years previously. The general rule is that only transactions effected before 18 March 1986 are excluded. 18 March 1986 was the date from which the IHT gift with reservation ('GWR') rules took effect (cf para 47.2).

The legislation has been supplemented by regulations, namely the Charge to Income Tax by Reference to Enjoyment of Property Previously Owned Regulations 2005 (SI 2005/724). HMRC has published Guidance on its website. Clarification of many technical points has been given to professional bodies by HMRC under Code of Practice 10 ("COP 10 Questions").

At first sight the pre-owned asset rules have little to do with offshore tax planning as they were enacted to counter domestic UK tax avoidance. But they do potentially impact on non-domiciliary house structures and they also need to be kept in mind in other contexts. These issues are discussed at the end of this chapter following a general survey of the rules.

Basic structure

70.2 Schedule 15 imposes three distinct charges, one on land, one on chattels and one on what are called intangibles but is, in fact, a charge on all kinds of settled property other than land or chattels. Schedule 15 then introduces a series of exceptions and exemptions, including those applicable to non-residents and non-domiciliaries.

This chapter follows the form of the schedule. It is to be stressed that the exceptions and exemptions greatly cut down the ambit of the three charges.

Land

70.3 The charging provision dealing with land imposes a charge in any year of assessment in which the taxpayer occupies the land and either what is called the disposal condition or what is called the contribution condition is met (Sch 15, para 3).

The term 'occupies' is not defined. HMRC construe it as it including not merely residence but also use of the land for storage and occasional use coupled with sole possession of the means of access (Guidance para 4.6). Holiday homes and second homes are thus included.

There is no requirement that occupation be for the entire tax year concerned. However, if occupation is for part only of the year, the charge is based only on the period of occupation (Sch 15, para 4(3)).

The disposal condition

70.4 The disposal condition is satisfied if:

(a) the taxpayer owned an interest in the land at any time after 17 March 1986;
(b) at some time after 17 March 1986 he disposed of that interest or of part of it and;
(c) that disposal was not by an excluded transaction (as to which see para 70.11 below).

The disposal condition is also satisfied if:

(a) the taxpayer owned an interest in other property at any time after 17 March 1986;
(b) at some time after 17 March 1986 he disposed of all or part of that interest otherwise than by an excluded transaction;
(c) the proceeds of a disposal of the other property were applied directly or indirectly by another person in acquiring an interest in the land now occupied by the taxpayer.

The precise ambit of this second method by which the disposal condition can be satisfied is unclear. The Explanatory Notes for the 2004 Finance Bill referred to the taxpayer having previously owned an interest in other property which 'funded' the acquisition of the land. It appears that the condition is met if (a) the taxpayer disposed of an interest in the other property to a third party and (b) that third party then disposed of the other property and used the proceeds to acquire the land occupied by the taxpayer. The condition is not met if the taxpayer gives cash to a third party, and that third party uses the gifted proceeds to buy the land occupied by the taxpayer (COP 10 Questions, answer 31). Such a transaction is precisely covered by the contribution condition described below.

The term 'property' bears its IHT meaning (Sch 15, para 1). The IHT definition is inclusive rather than definitive, but it is provided that the term includes rights and interests of any description (IHTA 1984, s 272). In an IHT context the term plainly comprehends not just tangible property but also intangibles and even money.

The term 'owned' is not defined. Sch 15 is not part of the IHT legislation, so the various instances in IHTA 1984 of deemed beneficial entitlement, most notably interests in possession, are not incorporated. But a question still arises of whether an individual could ever be said to satisfy the disposal condition if the land he occupies was formerly owned by a trust of which he is a beneficiary as distinct from being owned by himself personally. It may be it could be, at least if he held an interest in possession, as there is authority in other contexts indicating beneficiaries and in particular life tenants have interests in settled property (see *R v IRC, ex p Newfields Developments Ltd* [2001] UKHL 27, [2001] STC 901, 906).

The contribution condition

70.5 The contribution condition is satisfied if:

(a) another person acquired an interest in the land now occupied by the taxpayer;
(b) the taxpayer directly or indirectly provided all or any of the consideration given by that other person for the acquisition;
(c) that provision was made after 17 March 1986;
(d) the provision was not by way of an excluded transaction (see para 70.11).

The condition is also satisfied if:

(a) the other person acquired an interest in other property;
(b) the taxpayer directly or indirectly provided all or any of the consideration for that acquisition otherwise then by way of an excluded transaction;
(c) the other person has disposed of that property;
(d) the other person has applied the proceeds of that disposal, directly or indirectly, towards the acquisition of an interest in the land now occupied by the taxpayer.

The Explanatory Notes to the 2004 Finance Bill stated that the contribution condition refers to the taxpayer 'funding' some other person in the acquisition of the occupied property. In fact, although cash contributions are plainly caught, so also are contributions in specie, for example shares which are then sold by the other person to fund the land acquisition.

'Provided' is a key term in the contribution condition in that a provision of some kind by the taxpayer is a prerequisite. In the context of the former TA 1988, Part XV, 'provide' has been held to connote some element of bounty (*IRC v Leiner* (1964) 41 TC 589; *IRC v Plummer* [1979] STC 793; see also para 59.21). As 'provided' is not defined in Sch 15, these authorities may be presumed to be in point although it is unclear how far HMRC accept this (COP 10 Questions, answer 32).

Directly or indirectly

70.6 The term 'directly or indirectly' is important to the contribution condition. It may be suggested that the taxpayer directly provides the consideration given by the other person if he makes a direct gift to that person. Indirect provision would perhaps cover routing through a third party, but here case law in other contexts indicates the third party must be accountable to the other person or that at the very least there must be an expectation he will pass the gift on (see for example *Yuill v Wilson* [1979] STC 486 per Buckley LJ and *Pott's Executors v IRC* [1950] 32 TC 211 and para 61.6).

The term 'directly or indirectly' is also used in another context, in that under both the disposal condition and the contribution condition the application of the proceeds of other property in acquiring the land can be direct or indirect. Here the use of the word 'indirect' raises the issue of whether the proceeds of the other property can first be invested in some other asset, and then the proceeds of sale of that asset be used to buy the land.

What is clear in all these contexts is that a tracing exercise is required. If on the facts the money used to buy an interest in the land occupied by the taxpayer cannot be traced back to him, neither the disposal condition nor the contribution condition is met. This is so even if within the buyer's overall estate is money or value gifted by the taxpayer, provided it can be shown that money or value has not directly or indirectly gone towards acquiring the interest in the land.

Interest

70.7 Although the taxpayer has to be in occupation of the land as a physical entity, the disposal condition and the contribution condition both focus on interests in the land. Thus to trigger the disposal condition the taxpayer has to have disposed of an interest in the land and to trigger the contribution condition the present owner has to have acquired an interest in the land.

Overlap between the disposal condition and the contribution condition

70.8 It is clear that as a matter of construction there is overlap between the disposal condition and the contribution condition. Indeed on one view the only scenario on which there is not an overlap is where the disposal condition is met by the interest in the land occupied having been disposed of by the taxpayer to the third party ie the first head of the disposal condition in para 70.4 above.

HMRC now accept that if what the taxpayer parted with was cash, the contribution condition alone is met, for it is not natural to refer to cash being disposed of (see COP 10 Questions, answer 31). But both conditions are met where the taxpayer gives assets in specie to the third party, and the third party then sells the assets and uses the proceeds to acquire the occupied land or an interest in it.

The charge to tax

70.9 When the conditions in para 3 are met and none of the exemptions described below are in point, the chargeable amount is subject to income tax. The chargeable amount is what is called the appropriate rental value less any payments made by the taxpayer to the owner of the land in pursuance of a legal obligation (para 4(1)). Such payments plainly include rent, a point which means a charge is precluded if the taxpayer pays an arm's length rent.

The starting point in determining the appropriate rental value is the rental value of the occupied land. This is its annual value, ie the amount reasonably obtainable on a yearly tenancy if the landlord repairs and insures (paras 4(3) and 5). A fraction is then applied to that figure to arrive at the appropriate rental value. The denominator is the value of the occupied land as a whole. In the case of the disposal condition, the numerator is the value of the interest in the land previously disposed of by the taxpayer or (as the case may be) such part of the land's value as can reasonably be attributed to the taxpayer's previous disposal of his interest in other property. In the case of the contribution condition the numerator is such part of the value of the land as can reasonably be attributed to the taxpayer's contribution.

The rental value is determined every five years (SI 2005/724 regs 2 and 4). The initial determination looks at the rental value when para 3 first applied, this date being 6 April 2005 where the conditions for the application of para 3 were met before then. Thereafter a revaluation is carried out five years after the start of the first tax year in which para 3 first applied, ie 6 April 2010 where the conditions were met before 6 April 2005. HMRC expect the taxpayer to take all reasonable steps to ascertain rental values, in the same way as if he were letting the property on the open market (Guidance para 2.1).

The rental value is proportionately reduced if the disposal condition is in point and as the taxpayer received consideration in money for the disposal. Such a disposal is referred to as a non-exempt sale and must have been of the whole of the taxpayer's interest in the land. (Sch 15, para 4(4)). Self-evidently the point is only in issue if the disposal was non-commercial, as if was at arm's length it would have been an excluded transaction and Sch 15 is then precluded (see para 70.13).

Chattels

70.10 Schedule 15 para 6 enacts the second charging provision of Sch 15, namely that applicable to chattels. It applies where the taxpayer is in possession of or has the use of a chattel and either the disposal condition or the contribution condition is met. In all material respects these conditions are in the same terms as their equivalents relating to land and para 6 is subject to the same exemptions as land. As with land, where the exemptions are not in point, an amount equal to the chargeable amount is subject to income tax.

The chargeable amount where the use of a chattel triggers a charge is not related to any assumed rental value. Instead the appropriate amount equates to interest on the value of the chattel as at the valuation date, reduced where appropriate by the same fractions as are applied to the rental value of land (para 7(2)). The rate of interest is official rate (SI 2005/724, reg 3), currently 5% (see para 69.12 and Explanatory memorandum to SI 2005/724, reg 2). As with land, actual payments made pursuant to a legal obligation are deducted. But because the appropriate amount is based on a rate of interest, payment of a commercial rent for the use of the chattel does not preclude a charge under this head, although it is likely to do so under the GWR exemption (see para 70.20 below).

Trusts

70.11 Schedule 15 para 8 enacts the third and final charging provision namely that dealing with property other than land or chattels. It is expressed as applying to intangible property but that term is defined as any property which is not land or chattels (Sch 15, para 1). The paragraph is of more limited compass than its equivalents relating to land and chattels as it applies only where the intangibles are comprised in a settlement and either are or represent property settled by the taxpayer after 17 March 1986. Further, to come within the paragraph, the settlement must be one whose income is assessable on the taxpayer under ITTOIA 2005, s 624, ie a settlement in which the settlor has an interest (see Chapter 59). But for these purposes any interest of his spouse may be disregarded (para 9(1)(c)).

This paragraph is subject to the exemptions described in para 70.17 to 70.20 below. In particular it does not apply insofar as the taxpayer is treated as beneficially entitled to the property under the GWR rules.

The quantum of charge where settled property is caught by para 8 is interest at the prescribed rate on such of the settled property as represents the value settled by the taxpayer after 17 March 1986. As with land and chattels, both the rate of interest and the valuation date are prescribed by the regulations, the rate of interest currently being the 5% official rate (SI 2005/724, reg 3).

A bizarre point about the para 8 charge is that the income of the intangibles will already be taxable under s 624 as by definition the taxpayer is within ITTOIA 2005, Part V, Chapter 5 (see Chapter 59). This is acknowledged by para 9 in that the chargeable amount is reduced by any tax in fact paid by the taxpayer under s 624, under its CGT equivalent, TCGA 1992, s 77, or under TA 1988, s 739 or TCGA 1992, s 86 or ITTOIA 2005, s 461. But this relief is a deduction of tax from chargeable amount, not a deduction of tax from tax.

Excluded transactions

70.12 Schedule 15 para 10 explains what is meant by excluded transactions. That concept is relevant to the charges on land and chattels. As there noted a disposal by the taxpayer under the disposal condition or a provision by him under the contribution condition cannot lead to a charge under Sch 15 if it is by way of excluded transaction.

Commercial transactions

70.13 The main category of excluded transaction arises in relation to the disposal condition and embraces what may be termed commercial transactions (para 10(1)(a)). A transaction is excluded if it is:

(a) a disposal of the whole of the taxpayer's interest in the property concerned; and
(b) the transaction is at arm's length with an unconnected person.

There is one qualification to the requirement that the whole of the taxpayer's interest must be disposed of. This is that he can expressly reserve a right over the property. HMRC construe this as allowing a lease to be reserved (Guidance para 1.3.1)

The taxpayer's disposal of his whole interest in the property may also be an excluded transaction even if it is to a party connected with him. However, for this to apply the transaction must be 'such as might be expected to be made at arm's length between persons not connected with each other'. This language implies not merely that the terms of the transaction must be commercial but also that it must be a type of transaction which is commercial.

There are three circumstances in which the disposal by the taxpayer of part of his interest in the property is an excluded transaction (SI 2005/724, reg 5). They are as follows:

(1) The disposal was on arm's length terms to an unconnected person.
(2) It was to a connected person and made before 7 March 2005 on commercial terms.
(3) It was made to a connected person after 7 March 2005 on commercial terms and for a consideration not comprising cash or readily convertible assets.

In the third of these conditions, the term readily convertible asset bears the meaning used in taxing employment income. This third condition is nonsensical as if the consideration is not cash or readily convertible assets the disposal is most unlikely to be commercial.

Spouses

70.14 A transfer by the taxpayer to his spouse or to a settlement in which she has an interest in possession is an excluded transaction under both the disposal condition and the contribution condition (Sch 15, paras 10(1)(b) and (c) and 10(2)(a) and (b)). The same applies to transfers in favour of a former spouse if under a court order. However, a settled gift in favour of a spouse or former spouse ceases to be excluded if the spouse's interest terminates (para 10(3)). A spouse is treated as having an interest in possession even if, as a result of FA 2006, Sch 20, that interest in possession is not equated with beneficial ownership for the purposes of IHT.

IHT exemptions

70.15 A disposal or contribution is an excluded transaction if it comes within IHTA 1984, s 11, the section preventing certain dispositions for the maintenance of the family from being a transfer of value. The same applies to dispositions which are wholly exempt transfers by virtue of either the IHT annual £3,000 exemption or the £250 small gifts relief (IHTA 1984, ss 19 and 20).

Outright gifts of money

70.16 An outright gift of money is an excluded transaction in relation to the contribution condition if it was made at least seven years before the taxpayer first occupied the land or, as the case may be, used the chattel (para 10(2)(c)). This exclusion applies whether the money is sterling or some other currency but does not extend to gifts of other assets even though the donee may have converted them to cash before buying the land or chattels. As a matter of law, the seven years runs from first use or occupation even if such preceded enactment of Sch 15. However in practice HMRC accept that any outright gift of cash made before 6 April 1998 is an excluded transaction (Guidance para 1.3.1).

Exemptions

70.17 All three charging provisions are disapplied if the relevant property is, in relation to the taxpayer, property subject to a reservation. This is provided for by Sch 15 para 11. The rules which determine when property is subject to a reservation are those in FA 1986, ss 102–102C. They are explained in Chapter 47.

Meaning of relevant property

70.18 For this exemption to apply it is the relevant property which has to be GWR property in relation to the taxpayer. In relation to the charge on settled intangibles, the relevant property is simply the property from time to time in the settlement (para 11(9)(b)). But in relation to land and chattels the term relevant property has a rather different meaning (para 11(9)(a)).

If the contribution condition is satisfied the relevant property is the property representing the consideration provided. Reference to paras 3 and 6 shows that in the case of chattels such property is normally the chattel itself whereas in the case of land it is the interest in the land which the recipient of the contribution acquired with the contribution.

If the disposal condition is satisfied, the relevant property is the property disposed of. Reference to para 3 and 6 show that this is the normally the interest in the land or chattel which the taxpayer occupies or uses. But in the case of funded acquisitions it is interest in the other property which the taxpayer disposed of.

Derived property

70.19 Sch 15 para 11 also applies where the property which is GWR property is not the relevant property but derived property. Derived property is simply property which derives its value from the relevant property.

This extension of the relief does not apply where the value of the derived property is substantially less than that of the relevant property. Substantial is not defined but HMRC take it to mean 20% or more (Guidance para 4.7). Where the test is failed all is not lost, as a proportionate reduction is made in the notional rent or interest charged

GWR exemptions

70.20 The para 11 exemption is extended to property which would be GWR property but for certain GWR exemptions (para 11(5)). The exemptions concerned include those for gifts to political parties, charities, employee trusts and the like. In the case of land they also include the exemption for a donor's change of circumstances and the exemption applicable where the gifted property is an undivided share in land occupied by the donor and the donee together (FA 1986, s 102B(4)).

In the case of chattels, the para 11 exemption is extended to cases where the donor pays the donee full consideration (para 11(5)(d)). Such prevents GWR treatment (FA 1986, Sch 20 para 6(1)(a)) and this extension of the

GWR exemption means that, in the case of chattels, payment of an arm's length rent precludes Sch 15 (see para 70.10). With land, the same result is achieved by the quantification rules (see para 70.9).

One GWR exemption which is not covered by the para 11 exemption is that for gifts attracting the spouse exemption. In the case of land and chattels the same result is achieved by the rule treating such gifts as excluded transactions (para 70.14 above). But the excluded transaction concept does not apply to settled intangibles, and so as a result, a trust in which the settlor's spouse is initial life-tenant is caught by Sch 15 if the settlor is also a potential beneficiary and his spouse's life interest is one of those equated with absolute ownership (see Chapter 44).

The 2006 changes to IHT mean that this point is not an issue with settlements created after 22 March 2006 as even if the settlor's spouse is given a life interest it is not equated with absolute ownership and as a result the GWR exemption is not in point (see para 43.14). It does, however, catch settlements created before then insofar as the spouse's life interest subsisted on 22 March 2006 or is a transitional serial interest appointed between then and 5 April 2008 (cf para 44.2).

Cash gifts

70.21 Another respect in which, as a matter of construction, the para 11 exemption for GWR property is defective is that it does not, in general, apply where GWR treatment is precluded by the inability of the GWR rules to trace through cash (as to which see para 47.4). This inability applies only to outright gifts, not to settled gifts. But strictly it means that an outright gift sheltered from GWR treatment by the cash tracing rule is not protected from the Sch 15 charge by para 11. However, it appears from the Guidance that HMRC do not read the legislation in this way (see Guidance para 1.3.2).

There are, in any event, two exceptions as a matter of law:

(1) As described in para 70.16 above, a cash gift is an excluded transaction if made before 6 April 1998 or more than seven years before the taxpayer first occupies or uses the land or chattels acquired with the contribution.
(2) The cash rule is disapplied by para 11 itself in the instances described in para 70.20 where GWR exemptions are prevented from disapplying Sch 15 (para 11(8)).

Property in taxpayer's estate

70.22 Under the terms of para 11(1), all three charging provisions are also disapplied where the relevant property or the derived property are treated for IHT purposes as being in the taxpayer's estate. The principal examples of this are settled property in which the taxpayer has an interest in possession which subsisted on 22 March 2006 or which is a transitional serial interest (as to which see Chapter 44).

It appears that, through inadvertence in parliamentary drafting, this aspect of para 11 has been severely truncated, for FA 2006, s 80 inserted into it new sub-paragraphs (11)–(13). Para 11(11)(b) disapplies the para 11 exemption where the taxpayer has directly or indirectly provided any of the consideration for the acquisition of the relevant property and that property or derived property is subsequently treated for IHT purposes as comprised in his estate. This sub-paragraph applies regardless of when the provision took place, and took effect on 5 December 2005 (s 80(5)). On a strict construction para 11 protection is removed from any interest in possession trust to which it otherwise applies. On this scenario, the only exception is where the charging provisions relating to land and chattels are at issue and the settler gave them to the trust and has had an interest in possession at all times since the gift. However, it is clear from the final paragraph of the Guidance that HMRC sees paras 11(11)–(13) as applying only to reverter to settlor trusts. It is to be hoped this will be confirmed or, better still, addressed by amendment.

Excluded liabilities

70.23 Even assuming the 2006 amendment is not in point, para 11(1) is truncated by another rule. This applies where the value of the taxpayer's estate is reduced by an excluded liability and that liability affects the value of the relevant property or (as the case may be) the derived property. Where it applies, the relevant or derived property is only treated as comprised in the taxpayer's estate to the extent its value exceeds the liability.

A liability is an excluded liability if the creation of the liability was an operation associated with either the transaction whereby the relevant property or the derived property came into the taxpayer's estate or the operation by which the value of the derived property came to be derived from the relevant property. Associated operations for these purposes bear their normal IHT meaning (IHTA 1984, s 268).

In the view of the breadth of the term 'associated operation', the key issue in this rule is when it can be said a liability 'affects' relevant or derived property. Must it be an incumbrance or charge or is something looser connoted?

It is reasonably plain that this provision removes the para 11(1) exemption if an excluded liability exceeds the value of the relevant property. The position is less clear if the liability is less, as para 11 makes no provision for apportionment. Given this gap, one view is that the excluded liability rule has no impact unless the liability exceeds the value of the relevant or derived property. The Guidance indicates (at appendix 1) that HMRC do not subscribe to this view. The Guidance says that in such cases the notional rent or interest is pro rata reduced so that it just reflects the excluded liability element of the value of the relevant or derived property.

Interests in possession retained by the settlor after 22 March 2006

70.24 As explained in para 43.14, an interest in possession retained by the settler under an inter vivos settlement created after 22 March 2006 is not equated with absolute ownership. In such a case para 11 protection is therefore only obtained if the settled property is GWR property in relation to the settlor. On a strict analysis this is not the position where the intangibles charge is at issue, as for GWR purposes what the settlor has given away is the reversion. Even assuming powers over capital mean he has retained a reservation in that, it is not the same as the relevant or derived property, which is defined expressly as the property comprised in the settlement (para 11(9)(b)). On this perhaps over strict analysis, the settled property is not GWR property and so is not protected by para 11. Such a conclusion would certainly follow if the life-tenant settlor was not a discretionary object of capital at all, as then there would be no reservation over what he had given away.

In the event that the above analysis is correct, both intangibles comprised in the settlement are exposed to the pre-owned asset charge. The same point may well apply to land and chattels insofar as the contribution condition is at issue, as here the relevant property is the property representing the contribution (para 11(9)(a)). It is difficult to see the reversion as being this. The point may be precluded in relation to land if what was given away was the land as carve-out does not apply on gifts of land (para 47.7).

Territorial limits

Residency

70.25 A taxpayer is only caught by Sch 15 if he is resident in the UK in the tax year concerned.

Non-domiciliaries

70.26 Schedule 15 does not apply to non-domiciliaries save in respect of property situated in the UK. In broad terms this equates with the IHT excluded property concept. However, there is one important difference. This is that para 12(2) focuses on the asset to which Sch 15 would otherwise apply rather than on the asset held by the donee. Thus in the classic structure of a house or chattels owned by an offshore company the asset to focus on is the house or chattels rather than the shares in the company. The exemption under para 12(2) does not apply if the house or chattels are in the UK.

A further relief is to be found in para 12(3). This states that if a person was at any time domiciled outside the UK, no regard is had to any property which in relation to him is excluded property under IHTA 1984, s 48(3)(a). That is the subsection which makes foreign property excluded property if it is comprised in a settlement settled by an individual who at the time of making the settlement was not UK domiciled (cf para 45.2). Paragraph 11(3) carries this concept into Sch 15.

The IHT rules apply in determining whether an individual is UK domiciled. Thus an individual counts as UK domiciled if he in fact has a UK domicile or if he has an IHT deemed domicile (see Chapter 45).

Benefit in kind

70.27 Should the owner of a house or chattels be a company, a charge could arise both under Sch 15 and under the benefits-in-kind code (described in Chapter 69). In such case the charge under Sch 15 arises only to the extent that the chargeable amount under Sch 15 exceeds the amount treated as earnings (Sch 15 para 19). This provision is in point both where the occupier is an actual director or employee of the company and where HMRC are successful in contending he is a shadow director (cf Chapter 53).

De minimis exemption

70.28 Schedule 15 para 13 confers a de minimis exemption. It requires examination of amounts otherwise chargeable under all three heads of Sch 15 in the tax year concerned. If the aggregate of those amounts if £5,000 or less, a charge is not made. However, the limit of £5,000 is not an exempt band, so once it is reached the full amount is taxable.

Transitional relief

70.29 Schedule 15 para 21 gives further relief in relation to land and chattels. It allows the taxpayer to elect into the IHT GWR rules and thus out of Sch 15. In other words he may elect that the asset concerned or any asset substituted for it is to be treated in relation to him as property subject to a reservation. This notional reservation subsists so long as he occupies the land or (as the case may be) possesses or uses the chattel. The election must be made by 31 January following the first tax year in which the taxpayer would otherwise be chargeable under Sch 15 by reference to the land or chattels. In the case of land or chattels which came within Sch 15 when it came into force on 6 April 2005, 2005–06 is the first year in which the taxpayer is otherwise chargeable. The election is therefore needed by 31 January 2007.

The relief under para 21 is generally thought of as a transitional relief as it enables taxpayers to unscramble arrangements pre-dating Sch 15. But it is available if thereafter a taxpayer comes within Sch 15, provided election is made before 31 January following the end of the first tax year in which he first does so.

There is equivalent transitional relief for settled property (para 22). Once the election is made the settled property is treated as GWR property so long as it is comprised in the settlement and TA 1988, s 660A applies to it.

Impact on offshore tax planning

UK domiciliaries

70.30 There are several contexts where Sch 15 may cause trouble for UK domiciliaries in offshore tax planning.

One is where a settlement of intangibles excludes the settlor but he is left with a reversionary interest. This may bring s 624 into play and yet will not be a gift with reservation (cf para 47.7). As noted in paras 70.22 and 70.24, the same result may follow if he holds a life interest.

A second is where a settlement confers a life interest on the settlor's spouse and that interest arose before 22 March 2006 or is otherwise equated with absolute ownership. As is described in para 70.20, it is not protected by the GWR exemption, and yet the income is taxable as that of the settlor. A charge under Sch 15 may be made insofar as the settled property is intangible.

A third context is where an offshore trust from which the settlor really is excluded, or an underlying company, allows the settlor to use land or chattels abroad. Because the settlor is excluded under the settlement, the gift with reservation rules may not apply. Such an arrangement may well be a technical breach of trust, but in the contexts where those sorts of facts arise such breaches often do not occasion the concern they should. Both the potential breach of trust and the Sch 15 exposure are avoided if a commercial rent is paid.

The final context is if artificial or complex tax planning is being undertaken offshore for foreign reasons. Here it is essential to ensure Sch 15 is not inadvertently infringed.

Non-domiciliaries

70.31 The points made above apply also to non-domiciliaries with equal force. The first two points in the preceding paragraph would, if good, result in a Sch 15 charge if the settlement held UK situs intangibles. But there would be no charge if the intangibles were held in an offshore holding company as, with intangibles, the asset to focus on is the asset held at trust level.

The family arrangements of non-domiciliaries can cause trouble. The gift abroad of a chattel, or of cash or other assets used to buy a chattel, would result in a charge if the chattel was brought to the UK and then kept in the donor's house there (unless in the case of cash the gift was made before

5 April 1998 or more than seven years previously). So too a gift abroad of cash would raise the same problems if it is used to buy a UK house occupied by the donor. Some legal systems do not always clearly identify who owns what, and Sch 15 may pose particular problems for non-domiciliaries from those countries.

Absent funding issues of this sort, the main issue for non-domiciliaries with Sch 15 is UK house structures.

Non-domiciliary UK house structures

70.32 The use of non-resident trusts and companies to hold UK houses occupied by the non-domiciled settlor of the trust or owner of the company is discussed in Chapter 21. Such use is a long way from the mischief FA 2004, Sch 15 was intended to counter, but defective drafting means some such arrangements could be caught. A basic point to stress is that the territorial limits to Sch 15 are not in point as, although the occupier may be non-domiciled, the house being occupied is in the UK. However, and this again is a basic point, should the occupier be non-resident Sch 15 does not have to be considered at all.

As the discussion in Chapter 23 makes clear, there are three main kinds of house structures to consider

(1) The house is an asset of a trust settled by the occupier.
(2) The house is an asset of a company whose shares are owned by a trust settled by the occupier.
(3) The house is an asset of a company formed by the occupier whose shares are owned by him personally.

In some of these cases, the structure is all equity, i e the house was wholly paid for out of funds provided or settled by the occupier and any company was wholly funded by share capital. But often there is borrowing. This may be commercial borrowing secured on the house or, in the case of companies, the result of the company being largely capitalised by shareholder loan.

The common sense analysis is that none of these structures are caught by Sch 15. The analysis is as follows:

(a) Where the house is a trust asset, either the settlor has an interest in possession in it or he is a discretionary beneficiary. As such the GWR or interest in possession exemptions in para 11 apply (see para 70.17).
(b) Where the house is held in a company the shares in and the loans to the company are derived property with the result that once again the GWR or interest in possession exemptions are in point.

Unfortunately, as the previous discussion will have made clear, the defective drafting of Sch 15 raises a number of issues with this analysis.

Definition of relevant property

70.33 The first problem arises from the fact that under para 11, the exemptions apply only if the 'relevant property' meets the condition specified. In relation to the contribution condition the relevant property is, as noted in para 70.18, the property directly or indirectly representing the contribution (para 11(9)(a)) and this can without difficulty be read as referring to the trust or company's interest in the house. However, in relation to the disposal condition, the relevant property is the property disposed of, ie in the context of a house structure, the cash or other property the occupier originally settled in trust or paid into the company. This, self evidently, does not satisfy either the beneficial interest or the GWR exemption, as it has been used to pay for the house. Accordingly the position is reached that if the disposal condition applies to house structures, those exemptions are not in point.

The answer to this is, it may be suggested as follows:

(a) for the reasons given in para 70.8 above, if cash was settled, the contribution condition alone is met.

(b) Also for those reasons, if assets were settled in specie both conditions are met. But it is a fair reading of Sch 15 that if in relation to *either* of the conditions the property occupied is the relevant property for the purposes of para 11, the beneficial interest and the GWR exemptions are met. It is, however, unclear if HMRC accept this (see COP 10 Questions, answer 31).

Definition of derived property

70.34 The next area of difficulty concerns houses owned by companies. Here as noted in para 70.19 the exemptions are disapplied if the value of the derived property is substantially less than that of the property occupied. In the case of a company capitalised largely by shareholder loan, the first issue is whether the value of the loan is derived from the occupied property at all, given that the loan is an obligation of the company, and the second is that on any view the shares alone are (because of the loan) worth much less than the property.

The answer to these points is that as a matter of common sense the value of the loan is derived from the property and that again as a matter of common sense, one looks at the shares and the loan together in applying the derived property rules. On this scenario, at least in the typical case, the conditions for derived property should be met. HMRC, for some reason, do not accept this analysis (Guidance para 1.3.2). Nonetheless, at least in relation to cases where the non-domiciliary owns the shares and debt personally, any dispute on the point is unlikely to arise. This is because HMRC do not consider the loan falls within the contribution condition and so, in determining the notional rent, it is excluded in determining how much of the rental value of the property is reasonably attributable to consideration provided by the taxpayer (Guidance para 1.2.1). The rationale is that the loan is in the taxpayer's estate for IHT purposes. If good, this rationale should also apply where the shares and loan are settled.

Another scenario where the conditions for derived property may not be met is where the company itself has taken external borrowing. If the borrowing means the shares and any shareholder loan are worth substantially less than the occupied property then prima facie the derived property exemptions do not apply, and a Sch 15 charge is in issue, however bizarre that may seem. Here too, however, HMRC have accepted in other contexts an analysis which, at least on one view, resolves the problem. This is that the relevant property is not the house, but simply its value net of the commercial borrowing (COP 10 Questions, answer 13).

A further point that has been raised in connection with companies stems out of the provision in para 12(3), to the effect that property in trust which is excluded property under IHTA 1984, 48(3)(a) is disregarded in applying Sch 15 (see para 70.25). Read literally this means one disregards the shares and shareholder loan in a company structure and so one is left with no derived property on to which the exemptions in para 11 can fasten. This construction, it may be suggested, is over literal, and HMRC do not subscribe to it (Guidance, example in appendix 1).

Interest in possession trusts

70.35 As described in para 70.22, the effect of para 11(11), which was inserted by FA 2006, s 80, may be to remove para 11 protection from all cases involving trusts where, for IHT purposes, the settler is the occupier and has an interest in possession equated with beneficial ownership. As there indicated it would apply unless the settlor had given the house to the trust or company in specie. It is to be hoped that HMRC will amend the legislation or at least confirm it should be read as per the Guidance as applying only to reverter to settlor trusts.

Another area of difficulty concerns excluded liabilities. As described in para 70.23 this too is in issue where the occupier is the settler and holds an interest in possession in the house equated with beneficial ownership. If in such case the trustees have borrowed to buy the house, on the face of it the borrowing is an excluded liability. On HMRC's analysis (as signified in the Guidance) the equity element in the house is protected from a Sch 15 charge, but the part funded by loan is not, and so the notional rent charged is reduced to a proportion corresponding to the loan element.

This, of course, is an absurd result. It is fairly clear the excluded liability rules were intended to catch what are sometimes called double trust schemes, not genuine outside borrowing. There are two possible analyses which prevent non-domiciliary house structures from being caught. One is to take the position, suggested in para 70.23, that the excluded liability rule does not apply at all unless the value of the liability exceeds the house. The other is to fasten on the fact that it is the contribution condition which is in point, and that strictly under this condition, what represents the funds originally settled is the equity in the house net of borrowing. HMRC accept this analysis (COP 10 Questions, answer 13) and if so the excluded liability point is circumvented.

A final point is that para 11 protection may not be available in cases involving a trust in which the settlor has a life interest even if the life interest is not one of those equated with outright ownership. As is explained in para 70.24, there are technical arguments that neither of the relieving provisions in para 11 are in point in such a case.

Conclusion

70.36 It is difficult to formulate clear advice on the application of Sch 15 to house structures and yet, on or before 31 January 2007, clear advice in relation to existing structures is needed as that is the deadline for filing the first tax returns affected by the Sch 15 charge, namely the return for 2006–06. Given the underlying purpose of the legislation (para 70.1 above), the course recommended is to take the position Sch 15 does not apply, but make full disclosure of the relevant facts. But if this course is taken it is important for the taxpayer to understand HMRC may open an enquiry.

Planning as respects new structures is a rather different issue. This is discussed in Chapter 21.

Chapter 71

Offshore funds

Introduction

71.1 This chapter explains the special rules applicable when interests in non-distributor offshore funds are disposed of. The legislation was originally enacted in 1984 and is now comprised in TA 1988, ss 756AA–764. The effect of the legislation is to treat as income any gain realised on the disposal of an interest in a non-distributor fund.

Offshore funds are of great commercial significance for much investment is structured through them. This chapter focuses on the tax treatment of non-distributor funds as distinct from what a fund has to do to secure distributor status. The latter is a matter for those managing the fund and in the normal case it is clear to the investor from information the fund puts out whether it has distributor status.

In 2002, the government issued a Consultation Document raising the possibility of radical changes to the offshore fund regime. The radical changes foreshadowed have not, however, materialised. Instead limited reforms were introduced by FA 2004, the thrust of which was to enable more funds to attract distributor status and allow sub-funds to be treated separately. These changes are explained in *Tax Bulletin* 73 (October 2004) p 1152.

This chapter explains the law as it exists as a result of FA 2004. Most of the chapter is devoted to the tax treatment of offshore income gains – i e the gains realised when interests in non-distributor funds are disposed of.

Definition of offshore fund

71.2 The first stage in determining whether a gain is subject to the offshore fund regime is to ascertain whether the entity invested in is in fact as an offshore fund. The term bears a specific definition for the purposes of ss 756A–764.

The definition

71.3 The term 'offshore fund' is exclusively and exhaustively defined in s 756A. An offshore fund is a collective investment scheme constituted by:

(a) a company resident outside the UK;

(b) a unit trust scheme whose trustees are non-resident; or
(c) any other arrangements taking effect under foreign law, which 'create rights in the nature of co-ownership (without restricting that expression to its meaning in the law of any part of the United Kingdom)'.

Collective investment scheme

71.4 The term 'collective investment scheme' bears the meaning given in s 235 of the Financial Services and Markets Act 2000.

Under this definition a collective investment scheme is as follows:

(1) It is an arrangement with respect to property of any description.
(2) The purpose or effect of the arrangements is to enable the persons taking part to participate in or receive profits or income.
(3) The profits or income must arise from the acquisition, holding, management, or disposal of the property.
(4) The persons taking part must not have day-to-day control over the management of the property.
(5) Either the property must be pooled or it must be managed as a whole by the operator of the scheme.

This definition does not specify the legal form of the arrangements. The definition is subject to regulation-making powers in that the Treasury can exclude given categories of arrangement from being collective investment schemes. This is not wholly satisfactory from a tax standpoint as it means that in theory at least categories of fund can be taken out of the offshore fund regime for reasons quite unconnected with tax.

The relevant regulations are The Financial Services and Market Act 2000 (Collective Investment Schemes) Order 2001 (SI 2001/1062). This Order does not in fact remove anything from the definition that would normally be regarded as a unit trust or open-ended company. Indeed in one respect it is helpful, for it expressly provides that the only type of body corporate which can constitute a collective investment scheme is an open-ended investment company. That term is not defined in the regulations but its meaning is given in s 236 of the Financial Services and Markets Act 2000. The essence of the definition is the company must hold and manage its property with a view to spreading investment risk. Investors must be able to realise their investment on the basis of the underlying value of the company's funds.

Foreign law arrangements

71.5 Beyond being collective investment schemes, the type of foreign arrangement within the definition is not further specified. Civil law contractual schemes which are not either companies or unit trusts are the main target.

Umbrella funds

71.6 Until 2004, umbrella funds were treated as a single fund for the purposes of the offshore fund legislation. Now the legislation is applied on the basis that each sub-fund is a separate fund, which means some sub-funds can qualify for distributor status while others do not (TA 1988, s 756B). The same applies to funds with more than one class of interest.

This treatment of umbrella funds applies to account periods ending on or after 22 July 2004 (FA 2004, s 145(2)).

In practice

71.7 In practice the taxpayer seeking to clarify whether his investment is an offshore fund can be reasonably certain it is provided it is a unit trust or open-ended investment company enabling the funds to be pooled and allowing investors to redeem their investments at or close to assets value. Indeed in most cases the entity will be described and marketed as a 'fund' or 'mutual fund' regardless of precise legal status.

Material interests

71.8 The next requirement for the legislation to apply is that the investor's interest must be material. The definition of 'material' is allusive and largely duplicates the basic definition of offshore fund. An interest is 'material' if, on acquisition, the taxpayer could reasonably expect to be able to realise its value within seven years (TA 1988, s 759). Realisation of value means realisation of value as a proportion of net assets of the fund.

An interest in a company is not material if (1) the holder of the interest has the right to have the company wound up; and (2) in the winding up he would be entitled to more than half the net assets (TA 1988, s 759(8)). Quoted shares amount to a material interest if they are habitually traded at net asset value, but not if they only occasionally reach net asset value (SP 2/86, para 3).

Non-qualifying offshore funds

71.9 The third requirement for the legislation to apply is that the fund must be non-qualifying or, to use more colloquial language, that it does not have distributor status.

A fund is 'non-qualifying' unless it is certified by HMRC as a distributing fund (TA 1988, s 760). A distributing fund is itself defined and two conditions have to be satisfied.

The first is that the fund must pursue a full distribution policy. This requires the fund to distribute an amount equal to at least 85% of both its income as per its accounts and its UK equivalent profits (TA 1988, Sch 27 para 1(1)). A fund is deemed to pursue a full distribution policy if it has no income at all or if its gross income is 1% or less of the average value of its assets (ibid, para 1(2)). Income of the fund assessable on investors on an arising basis is deemed to have been distributed (cf ibid, para 3 and para 4.2.1).

The second is that the fund must not hold more than 5% of its assets in other offshore funds. Holdings in distributor funds are disregarded for this purposes, but only insofar as such funds do not themselves hold more than 5% of their assets in other distributor or non-distributor funds (see *Tax Bulletin 73* (October 2004) p 1154 and *Tax Bulletin 78* (October 2005) p 1246).

Detailed rules amplify the basic requirements and relax them in specific situations. Certification is a matter for the fund and HMRC's Offshore Funds Centre in Sheffield, in respect of which some guidance is given in the Offshore Funds Guide published on HMRC's website. An investor only becomes concerned with certification if a fund has failed to apply for certification. In that event, he may apply to HMRC who determine its status (TA 1988, Sch 27 para 18).

Whether a fund is a distributing fund has to be determined for each period of account during which the taxpayer holds a material interest in it, and it is only a qualifying fund if it is a distributing fund for each such period, or for each such period after 1 January 1984 if the taxpayer acquired his interest before then (TA 1988, s 757(7)(a)). Periods of account are the periods for which the fund makes up its accounts (TA 1988, s 760(9)), and, if the fund does not make up accounts, it is non-qualifying (TA 1988, Sch 27 para 1(3)).

In the case of an umbrella fund existing prior to the changes made by FA 2004, the tests as to distributor status have to be applied by reference to the fund as a whole for accounting periods ending before 22 July 2004. Thereafter they are applied separately to each sub-fund. It follows that an interest in a sub-fund acquired before then is not qualifying if before then the fund as a whole was not qualifying even if the sub-fund was and is qualifying. The same applies where classes of interest now constitute separate funds.

HMRC maintain a list of funds certified as having distributor status (see Foreign etc pages notes, p FN11). At the time of the 2002 consultation document there were over 600.

The offshore income gain

Disposals

71.10 What is called an offshore income gain accrues when a material interest in a non-qualifying fund is disposed of. For these purposes, 'disposal' bears the same meaning as for CGT purposes, but subject to two important exceptions (TA 1988, s 757). The first exception is that when a person dies he is deemed to dispose of any material interest he then holds (s 757(3)). The same can apply to settled property when the life tenant dies. But this is only in point if the life-tenant's interest is one of those which for IHT purposes is equated with ownership of the underlying assets (see Chapter 44). In such a case the disposal is deemed to take place under general capital gains tax rules (TCGA 1992, s 72).

Second, a disposal is also deemed to occur if the fund is subject to a takeover or reconstruction otherwise relieved from capital gains tax by TCGA 1992, ss 135 and 136. An exception is made if the acquiring entity is itself a non-qualifying offshore fund (s 757(5)). The same rules apply if interests of different classes are exchanged in a reorganisation of the fund (s 762A).

Pooling and identification

71.11 Interests in offshore funds are securities for the purposes of the CGT rules relating to pooling and identification (TCGA 1992, s 104(3)). This result follows because such interests either are or are deemed to be shares (TCGA 1992, s 99). The consequence is that for individuals and trusts, disposals are subject to the CGT identification rules. These require disposals to be identified on a last in first out basis, save that acquisitions within 30 days of a disposal are identified with that disposal (TCGA 1992, s 106A). Corporate investors are also subject to rules of identification, for interests in non-qualifying funds are relevant securities and so not subject to pooling (TCGA 1992, s 108).

The gain

71.12 The offshore income gain is the unindexed gain, computed as for CGT purposes (TA 1988, Sch 28 para 5). Where the taxpayer held the material interest on 1 January 1984, it is treated as acquired at market value then, if this has the result of diminishing what would otherwise be a gain (TA 1988, Sch 28 paras 4 and 5).

Losses

71.13 Should the computation result in a loss rather than an unindexed gain, the loss is not available for set-off against offshore income gains (TA 1988, Sch 28 para 3(5)). For the purposes of the offshore fund legislation such disposal is treated as a no gain/no loss disposal. It follows that the loss is an allowable loss for CGT purposes.

Offshore funds operating equalisation arrangements

71.14 Equalisation arrangements arise where an investor subscribes for an interest in an offshore fund during an income period, and the first dividend he receives includes a capital payment representing income accrued prior to the date of his purchase (TA 1988, s 758). This capital payment is debited to what is called the equalisation account. The converse of the purchaser's position is that of the seller who redeems an interest in the fund during an income period, for then the proceeds he receives include accrued income in capital form.

The legislation contains two main rules relating to equalisation arrangements. First, the income element in any redemption by the fund counts as a distribution, thereby preventing the fund's distributor status from being jeopardised (TA 1988, Sch 27 para 2). Second, if the fund is a distributor fund, this element is treated as an offshore income gain, save insofar as it exceeds the investor's overall gain on the interest he is redeeming (TA 1988, Sch 28 paras 6–8).

The charge to tax

71.15 The basic rule is that an offshore income gain is taxable as income arising at the time of the disposal (TA 1988, s 761(1)). The territorial limits are as follows:

(1) A person is chargeable if in the tax year of the disposal he is resident or ordinarily resident in the UK. This is achieved by applying to offshore income gains the territorial limits to capital gains tax in TCGA 1992, s 2 (TA 1988, s 761(2)).

(2) A non-resident is only chargeable insofar as he is trading in the UK through a branch, agency, or permanent establishment and the offshore income gain arises on a material interest used or held for the purposes of such trade (TA 1988, ss 761(3) and 11(2)(b); TCGA 1992, s 10).

(3) A resident individual who is not domiciled in the UK enjoys the remittance basis (TA 1988, s 761(3)). However, the rules are those applicable to CGT rather than to income tax (cf Chapter 41), which means avoidance techniques such as cessation of source and segregating income from capital do not work. A tax charge is only avoided if the entire proceeds of the sale of the material interest are kept abroad.

Should the offshore income gain accrue to a resident trust, the charge to tax is at the 40% rate for trusts (TA 1988, s 764). This is so regardless of the form of the trust. If the trust is settlor-interested, the gain is assessable as the settlor's under ITTOIA 2005, s 624 (see Chapter 59). This is not expressly provided for but follows from the basic deeming of the gain to be income and is assumed to be so elsewhere in the legislation (see for example s 762(6)). Where a child would be absolutely entitled as against the trustee but for being a minor, the gain is assessed as the settlor's under ITTOIA 2005, s 632.

Avoidance of double charge

71.16 As noted above most disposals of material interests are disposals for CGT purposes. Where this is so, double taxation is avoided by requiring the offshore income gain to be deducted from what is otherwise the consideration for CGT purposes (TA 1988, s 763(2)). This does not apply where the offshore income gain results from an equalisation element in a distributing fund, but here the normal CGT rule should apply of excluding the income element from the CGT computation (TCGA 1992, s 37).

Where an offshore income gain accrues on a takeover or reconstruction of the fund, it forms part of the acquisition cost of the new holding for CGT purposes (s 763(6)). Tax on an offshore income gain arising on death is a deduction in computing the deceased's estate for IHT purposes (IHTA 1984, s 174). This relief does not, however, apply if the gain accrues to a trust on the death of the life tenant.

Non-resident companies

71.17 As non-residents are not charged to tax on offshore income gains, non-resident companies are not taxable if they realise such gains. But the rules for apportioning capital gains in TCGA 1992, s 13 are applied to offshore income gains (TA 1988, s 762(1)). These rules are described in Chapter 66 and they mean that an apportioned part of the offshore income gain can be assessed on any UK participator provided the non-resident company is close and the participator and persons connected with him own more than 10% of the company. If the participator is an individual it is necessary for him to be UK domiciled (see further para 66.4). The application of s 13 also means that the offshore income gain can be apportioned to any offshore trust which is a participator in the company.

There is obvious scope for double taxation if, after the offshore income gain is apportioned to a UK participator, the company pays the gain in dividend or is sold or wound up. The relief described in para 66.17 allowing the deduction of tax from tax where the gain is distributed within the specified period applies, for that relief is expressed in terms of tax generally (TA 1988, s 762(1)(b) passim). The relief in s 13(7) (para 66.18) also applies, ie if the participator disposes of his shares in the company he can deduct from that gain any income tax paid by him on the offshore income gain (TA 1988, s 762(1)(b)).

The rules in TCGA 1992, s 79B apportioning treaty-protected gains to trustee shareholders are not applied to offshore income gains (cf para 66.23).

Non-resident trusts

71.18 It is expressly provided that the rule deeming offshore gains to be income does not apply insofar as the gain is realised by a non-resident trust (s 761(7)). This means ITTOIA 2005, s 624 cannot apply to treat that gain as income of the settlor. It also confirms the trustees are not subject to income tax on the gain.

Capital payments

71.19 The regime adopted for the offshore income gains of offshore trusts is the capital payments regime in TCGA 1992, s 87 (see Chapter 63). In other words the offshore income gains for each tax year, together with those brought forward from previous years, form a pool. This pool is diminished insofar as a capital payment is made to a beneficiary. Such a beneficiary is treated as realising an offshore income gain equal to the payment and this is so regardless of his residence and domicile. But, as under s 87, he is only taxed on the notional offshore income gain if he is both resident and domiciled in the UK. This is the effect of TA 1988, s 762(2) which applies the rules in s 87.

CGT rules apply in determining whether a payment is a capital payment and in computing the pool. Reference should therefore be made to Chapters 63 and 65.

In accordance with the rules described in para 65.3, a capital payment is not treated as an offshore income gain if the existence of relevant income means it is treated as ordinary income under TA 1988, s 740 (see Chapter 56). But subject to that, a capital payment is treated as an offshore income gain to the extent of the pool of offshore income gains. Only if that pool is exhausted may the payment be set against the pool of ordinary capital gains and treated as capital gain (TA 1988, s 762(4)). The surplus capital payment is not carried forward and set against offshore income gains of the following tax year unless it exceeds available ordinary capital gains of the current year and the relevant income of the next year.

Company gains

71.20 As noted above, the rule in TCGA 1992, s 13 attributing gains of non-resident close companies to offshore trusts applies also to offshore income gains. Company offshore income gains are therefore in the pool.

Trustee borrowing

71.21 As described in Chapter 64, where a transfer of value by non-resident trustees is linked with outstanding trustee borrowing in accordance with TCGA 1992, Sch 4B, all or a proportion of the trust assets are deemed to be disposed of for the purposes of TCGA 1992 (Sch 4B para 10(1)). The impact of this on the offshore fund legislation is not expressly stated. But a disposal under that legislation takes place whenever there is a disposal for the purposes of TCGA 1992 (s 757(2)). It may be inferred from this that a deemed disposal under Sch 4B triggers an offshore income gain insofar as the assets disposed of are material interests in offshore funds.

This gain, being an offshore income gain, is dealt with in accordance with the rules for offshore trusts just described. In other words it goes into the pool of offshore income gains or, as described below, is income for the purposes of ss 739 and 740. It does not go into the trust's pool under TCGA 1992, Sch 4C, for that schedule applies only to Sch 4B trust gains (Sch 4C para 1). The Sch 4B trust gains are defined as the gains on which the trustees would have been chargeable under Sch 4B had they been resident (Sch 4C paras 3 and 4). Those gains exclude offshore income gains, for offshore income gains have to be deducted in computing capital gains (s 763(3)).

Also as described in Chapter 64, the Sch 4C pool includes the pool of s 87 gains as at the end of the tax year in which the Sch 4B transfer takes place. This inclusion does not extend to any pool of offshore income gains as the relevant provision (Sch 4C, para 7A(2)) refers to the trust gains within the meaning of s 87(2) simpliciter rather than to trust gains within the meaning of s 87(2) as applied to offshore income gains by s 762(2).

Notional interest

71.22 In contrast to s 87 proper and Sch 4C, the notional interest regime does not apply to the tax on offshore income gains (TA 1988, s 762(2) passim). This means that the rule attributing offshore income gains before capital gains can work against taxpayers, for it delays the attribution of capital gains and thus potentially increases notional interest.

Section 86

71.23 It will be noted that despite the incorporation of CGT concepts in the taxation of offshore income gains, TCGA 1992, s 86, the section attributing gains to the settlor as they arise, is not applied to offshore income gains. Section 86 cannot apply to an offshore income gain under general principles, for it is expressed as applying only to capital gains, and in computing the capital gain, the offshore income gain is deducted.

Transfer of assets

71.24 TA 1988, ss 739 and 740 are also deployed in taxing the offshore income gains of non-residents. These sections are described in Chapters 54 to 57. In large measure they duplicate ss 13 and 87 but unfortunately not all areas of overlap are properly addressed.

Section 739

71.25 Section 739 is applied as if the offshore income gain was income accruing to the person resident or domiciled abroad (TA 1988, s 762(5)). This means that if s 739 otherwise applies to a trust or company, the transferor is assessable on the offshore income gain.

On the face of it this rule duplicates the rules described above. In fact it does not, for s 739 is described as applying only where an offshore income gain is not under those rules treated as having accrued to a person resident in the UK (TA 1988, s 762(6)). As a result s 739 catches offshore income gains only in two situations:

(1) Where a resident non-domiciliary is transferor in relation to a directly owned non-resident company. Here TCGA 1992, s 13 is precluded as it does not apply to non-domiciliaries, so s 739 applies, albeit on the remittance basis.
(2) Where the offshore income gain accrues to a settlor-interested trust (or to a company owned by such a trust) and it is not matched by a capital payment made in that or a previous year to the settlor or some other beneficiary resident in the UK. Here s 739 applies because in the year the offshore income gain is realised it is not treated as accruing to a person resident in the UK.

Three points may be made about this latter charge:

(1) There is scope for double taxation if a capital payment is made in a year subsequent to that in which the offshore income gain is realised. If the payment is to the settlor, the general s 739 rule preventing a charge where income taxed under s 739 is subsequently received may apply (s 743(4)). But if applicable at all, this rule only applies where the recipient is the transferor, so would not prevent the offshore income gain being attributed to a capital payment received by another beneficiary.
(2) Tax is avoided if the capital payment made in the same or a previous year is received by a non-domiciled resident beneficiary. As the recipient is resident, s 739 is precluded despite there being no charge to tax.
(3) If the settlor is non-domiciled but resident in the UK, the effect if s 739 applies is that the offshore income gain is deemed to be his income but is not chargeable unless remitted (para 55.22). A question arises of whether a capital payment made to a resident beneficiary in a tax year after the offshore income gain is realised, but prior to remittance, would prevent a s 739 charge on the remittance. It is suggested the answer is not, for s 739 deems income to be that of the transferor when it arises, albeit not taxed unless remitted. Here too, therefore, there is scope for double taxation, once when the offshore income gain is remitted and once if a capital payment is made to a resident and domiciled beneficiary in a tax year after the offshore income gain is realised. It may be suggested this would apply if the settlor is a beneficiary and it is he who receives the capital payment.

Section 740

71.26 Like s 739, TA 1988, s 740 applies as if the offshore income gain was income accruing to the person resident and domiciled abroad. This means that it is relevant income, able to be matched with benefits received by beneficiaries resident in the UK.

As with s 739, an offshore income gain is not deemed to be the income of an individual for the purposes of s 740 if it is treated as already having accrued to a person resident in the UK (TA 1988, s 762(6)). In relation to s 740 this rule is not elegantly worded, for s 740 deems the benefit received to be income of the resident recipient rather than the income of the non-resident. However, it seems reasonably clear that the rule applies if under TCGA 1992, ss 13 or 87 offshore income gains are treated as having accrued to the recipient.

Assuming that is right the scope of s 740 in relation to offshore income gains is as follows:

(1) In the case of a directly-owned company it would apply to benefits received by a non-domiciled shareholder who is not caught under s 739 as transferor. In accordance with s 740(5), the charge would be on the remittance basis.
(2) If a trust or underlying company has realised offshore income gains, a s 87 charge is avoided if an amount equal to the gains is distributed to non-residents. Thereafter that amount cannot be allocated to future payments for the purposes of s 87. But in this situation, the offshore income gains would be relevant income under TA 1988, s 740 in relation to a subsequent benefit conferred on UK resident beneficiaries for the offshore income gains would not have been treated under s 762 as having accrued to a UK resident.

What is interesting about this last point is that there is a gap. If the initial capital payment is to a resident but non-domiciled beneficiary, the offshore income gains are attributed to the payment but not charged. But here s 740 cannot apply on a subsequent distribution to a resident beneficiary, for, even if not chargeable, the offshore income gains were still treated under s 762 as having accrued to a UK resident.

Otherwise this point is a trap, particularly for non-domiciliaries. Suppose a trust has offshore income gains and the first capital distribution it makes is to a resident non-domiciliary. In that event (and assuming there is no relevant income), the gains are allocated to the payment and no tax charge results. But if in the same or a preceding year a capital distribution is made to a non-resident, gains are allocated to that distribution for the purposes of s 87 but the gains become relevant income. Accordingly, s 740 applies to the distribution to the UK resident, resulting in a tax charge under s 740(5) if the payment is received in the UK or the gain is remitted.

Trust and company structures

71.27 There is scope for triple tax where an offshore income gain accrues to a company owned by a trust. If the trust is settlor-interested, tax may be charged on the settlor as follows:

(1) Under s 739 when the offshore income gain is realised.
(2) Under ITTOIA 2005, s 624 if the gain is distributed as dividend by the company to the trust, or under TCGA 1992, s 86 if the company is wound up. This charge may be precluded by s 13(5A) but only if the distribution is within the specified period of three to four years after the gain is realised.
(3) Under the combined effect of TCGA 1992, s 13, as applied by s 762(1), and s 762(2), if capital is distributed from the trust to the settlor (assuming such distribution is in a tax year following that in which the offshore income gain accrues).

Chapter 72

The chargeable event legislation

72.1 The UK has a special code for taxing life policies, namely ITTOIA 2005, Part 4, Chapter 9 (formerly TA 1988, Pt XIII Chapter II). When first enacted this was principally concerned with onshore policies but amendments made in 1984 countered the peculiar tax-saving potential of offshore policies. The legislation was further amended in 1998 and, so far as offshore policies are concerned, the most important of those changes was the introduction of a special regime for one particular kind of policy, namely personal portfolio bonds. In this chapter the general legislation is considered first, and then the rules targeted specifically at personal portfolio bonds.

The general legislation distinguishes qualifying from non-qualifying policies and treats the former more generously than the latter. However, offshore policies are by definition non-qualifying. This is because a policy issued by a non-UK life office after 17 November 1983 is non-qualifying save insofar as the premiums are paid to a UK permanent establishment (TA 1988, Sch 15 para 24).

Chargeable events

72.2 The legislation taxes offshore policies as and when a chargeable event occurs (ITTOIA 2005, s 462). Chargeable events are defined in ITTOIA 2005, s 484 as follows:

(1) Death giving rise to benefits.
(2) Maturity of the policy.
(3) Complete surrender of the policy.
(4) Assignment of the whole policy for money or money's worth.
(5) Calculation event.

Calculation events

72.3 A calculation event can occur if there is a partial surrender or assignment (ITTOIA 2005, ss 498–514). Such a partial surrender or assignment results in a calculation event if on the carrying out of calculations prescribed in the legislation an excess is generated (ITTOIA 2005, ss 491(4) and 509).

These calculations are effected by insurance year (ITTOIA 2005, s 498(2)). An insurance year starts when the policy is first made and thereafter a new insurance year starts on each anniversary of that date (ITTOIA 2005, s 499). The final year ends with the maturity or complete surrender of the policy and if that event is in the same tax year as what would otherwise be the end of the previous policy year, the latter is extended to the date of the maturity or surrender to form an extended final year.

To determine whether at the end of the insurance year there is an excess, the net total value has to be compared with the net total payments. If the value exceeds the payments there is an excess (ITTOIA 2005, s 507).

The net total value is the value of partial surrenders that have taken place in the insurance year or at any time previously in the life of the policy. Partial assignments are also included but, unless made before 5 April 2001, only if made for money or money's worth. The net total payments are the net total of allowable payments. These are simply 5% of any premium paid for the insurance year in which it was paid plus 5% for each subsequent year up to and including the current year (ITTOIA 2005, s 507). Should the calculation produce an excess, so that there is a calculation event for the policy year, the net total payments and the net total value then brought into account are deducted in carrying out the calculation in future years.

Although the rules for calculating the excess are very complicated, the practical effect is simple. There is no excess if the value of any partial surrender in a year is less than 5% of the premium. Unused five per cents may be carried forward, thereby allowing a greater surrender if none has previously occurred.

A loan made by the life office is deemed to be a partial surrender equal to the amount lent (ITTOIA 2005, ss 500(c) and 501).

Amount of gain

72.4 The measure of liability on a chargeable event is the gain then realised. Computational rules determine the amount of the gain and these differ as between the different kind of chargeable event.

If the event is a calculation event, i e a gain resulting from partial surrender or assignment, the gain is the excess computed under the rules just described. It accrues at the end of the insurance year concerned (ITTOIA 2005, s 509). But this does not apply if during the year there has been a partial assignment for money or money's worth or a partial surrender followed by a gratuitous assignment. In such case any gain accrues at the time of the partial surrender or assignment (ITTOIA 2005, ss 509–514).

On other kinds of chargeable event, the gain accrues when the event occurs. The gain is the difference between the total benefit value of the policy on the one hand and the total of the premiums paid plus two other elements on the other (ITTOIA 2005, s 491). The first of these elements is any repayments of loans which have been treated as partial surrenders and the second is any gains treated as accruing on prior calculation events under the rules just described (ITTOIA 2005 ss 491(2) and 494).

The total benefit value of the policy is, in general, the sum payable. But on death the sum payable is not used and instead the figure is the surrender value immediately prior to death. Also included in the total benefit value are inter alia all previous payments made under the policy on prior partial surrenders and any loans treated as partial surrenders (ITTOIA 2005, ss 492 and 493).

Certain points should be noted about these computational rules:

(1) The gain on death is not computed by reference to the proceeds payable on death. What matters is the surrender value immediately before death.
(2) Although partial surrenders are not taxed if they keep within the cumulative 5% limit, the tax is deferred rather than avoided. This is because a partial surrender constitutes a capital payment and so is added to the proceeds when the policy matures or is surrendered.

Liability to tax

Individuals

72.5 Any gain on the policy is taxed as the income of an individual if immediately before the chargeable event he or a trust created by him owns the policy (ITTOIA 2005, s 465). Since the ownership test is applied immediately before the chargeable event, any gain on the maturity of a policy on the individual's own life is taxed as his if on his death the policy is owned by him or by a trust created by him. In such a case the gain is treated as his income for the year of his death, and, if he dies early in the tax year, may therefore attract tax at a lower rate than if he dies later on.

An individual is not taxed on a policy gain unless he is resident in the UK in the tax year in which the chargeable event occurs (ITTOIA 2005, s 465(1)). The legislation does not make any provision as regards non-domiciliaries and so the remittance basis does not apply. The charge where the policy is held in trust applies whether the trust is resident or non-resident.

An individual may claim top-slicing relief, but only in respect of tax in excess of the lower rate (ITTOIA 2005, ss 531(1) and 535). Should the policy have been vested in trustees, the individual assessed on the gain has a right of reimbursement (ITTOIA 2005, s 538).

Where the chargeable event is occasioned by complete surrender, death or maturity, the individual may claim a loss should the calculation show a loss rather than a gain as a result of gains previously having been brought into account on prior calculation events (ITTOIA 2005, ss 539–541). The relief, known as corresponding deficiency relief, is only against higher-rate tax (see further *Tax Bulletin 82* (April 2006) p 1286).

Companies

72.6 Companies remain subject to the old legislation relating to life policies in TA 1988, Part XIII Chapter II. A policy gain is deemed to form part of the company's income if immediately before the chargeable event, the policy is in the beneficial ownership of the company or is owned in a trusts created by the company (TA 1988, s 547(1)(b)). The income is deemed to be income chargeable under Schedule D Case VI for the accounting period in which the chargeable event occurs.

The charge is not in its terms restricted to resident companies or to corporation tax. No doubt, in the case of a policy issued by a non-resident life office to a non-resident company, a territorial limit would be implied (cf Chapter 30). But there seems nothing to preclude the deemed income being caught by s 739 if an individual who is transferor in relation to the non-resident company is ordinarily resident in the UK (cf Chapter 55).

Resident trusts

72.7 The gain on the policy is chargeable at the rate for trusts, and assessed on the trustees, if the policy is held in trust and the trust is UK resident. This only applies if immediately prior to the chargeable event the individual who created the trust was either dead or non-resident (ITTOIA 2005, s 467). It does not apply to policies held in trust since before 17 March 1998 if the settlor had died before that date and the policy has not since been varied (FA 1998, Sch 14 para 7).

Non-resident trust or institution

72.8 ITTIOA 2005, s 468 applies if immediately before the chargeable event the policy is held in a non-resident trust in circumstances where the settlor is not liable. It also applies if a foreign institution beneficially owns a share in the rights or if the rights are held for the purposes of a foreign institution. In such case, TA 1988, ss 739 and 740 apply on the basis that the gain is income payable to the trustees or institution.

The term 'foreign institution' means a company or other institution resident or domiciled outside the UK (s 468(5)). On the face of it, s 468 draws a distinction between rights owned by the foreign institution beneficially and rights held for its purposes. In the former case s 468 applies only where a share in the rights is so owned, but in the latter case s 468 applies where either a share or all the rights are held (s 468(5)). 'Rights' presumably means rights under the policy. The distinction is not found in the predecessor legislation (TA 1988, s 547) and is curious.

Since the charge is under TA 1988, ss 739 and 740, tax liability only arises insofar as the motive defence is not in point and the trust or institution confers benefit on a UK beneficiary (see Chapter 56). Until 5 December 2005, only TA 1988, s 740 was in point, with the result that policy gains accruing to non-resident trusts and companies were not taxable on the transferor on an arising basis. The loophole was blocked by FA 2006, Sch 7 para 7.

Partial non-residence

72.9 Should the policy-holder not have been UK resident throughout the life of the policy, only a proportionate part of the gain is taxed. This does not apply if at any time during its life, the policy has been held by non-resident trustees or by a foreign institution (ITTOIA 2005, ss 528 and 529). As just noted, the term foreign institution includes non-resident companies.

Multiple ownership

72.10 Rules exist for apportioning the gain where the policy is in multiple ownership (ITTOIA 2005, s 469).

Personal portfolio bonds

72.11 The tax charge on personal portfolio bonds is set out in ITTOIA 2005, ss 515–527. The legislation and regulations use the concept of the insurance year as defined in ITTOIA 2005, s 499, ie the year starting on the making of the contract and each subsequent year starting on the anniversary thereof.

HMRC have issued Guidance Notes giving their view on practical issues.

Definition

72.12 ITTOIA 2005, s 516 defines a personal portfolio bond as one including the following terms:

(i) The benefits under the policy must be determined in whole or in part by reference to the value of some form of property, or by reference to an index.

(ii) The property or index may be selected by or on behalf of the policy-holder or a person connected with him or by a person acting on behalf of either or both of them.

Permitted self-selection

72.13 ITTOIA 2005, ss 517–521 cut down this definition and permit certain types of self-selection.

An index to which policy benefits are linked may be self-selected if it is the RPI or some similar UK or foreign index of it is a published index of share prices listed on a recognised stock exchange.

Investments may be self-selected if they comprise of units in authorised unit trusts, shares in investment trusts or in open-ended investment companies, interests in foreign collective investment schemes, and cash in a bank or building society. This list of permissible investments is of increasing relevance in modern conditions as it embraces hedge funds.

Self-selection of an index or investments does however have to satisfy one other condition. This is that the index or investment is available for all policy-holders of the life office. Alternatively this condition is satisfied if availability is limited to a class of policy-holders provided that class is published by the life office and does not compromise connected persons.

Self-selection

72.14 Even if the exceptions listed above do not apply, it is to be stressed that a policy is not a personal portfolio bond unless the policyholder has the power to select the underlying investments. As noted above, a power of selection vested in a person connected to the policyholder counts as exercisable by the policyholder, as does a power exercisable by a person acting on behalf of the policyholder (reg 4(1)).

The position where the power to select is vested in an investment adviser is a question of some difficulty. Strictly such investment adviser is appointed by and acting on behalf of the Life Office, but the Guidance Notes indicate HMRC will regard him as acting on behalf of the policyholder if on the facts he is merely the policy- holder's conduit or agent (paras 3.17 and 3.18). The Guidance Notes make it clear that broker managed funds are acceptable (para 3.16), as are funds managed by investment advisers chosen from a menu of possible advisers specified by the Life Office.

A point to be stressed is that it is the *ability* to select which is crucial. A policy is thus caught if the policyholder is entitled to self-select but has so far not availed himself of the opportunity.

Timing

72.15 The test of whether a policy is a personal portfolio bond is applied in each policy year. A policy is caught if it is within the definition at the end of the year (ITTOIA 2005, s 515(1)). Variation during the year can therefore avoid the charge.

The gain

72.16 If a policy is a personal portfolio bond, a gain is treated as accruing in each policy year. In the first year the gain is 15% of the premium. In the second year the gain is 15% of the premium plus 15% of the gain charged in the previous year, ie 15% of 115% of the premium (17.25% of the premium). In subsequent years the gain is 15% of the premium plus 15% of the amount of the gain charged in each previous year since the inception of the policy. In each case the amount to which the 15% is applied is reduced by any excess in the prior policy year or any earlier year.

This formula is draconian in its effect, in that the gain is cumulatively rolled up. This is why personal portfolio bonds should now be avoided. In computing the gain in previous years for policies existing at the start of the regime, it is necessary to go back to the inception of the policy rather than simply to the first policy year ending after 6 April 2000, the date when the regime started.

The charge to tax

72.17 The gain is treated as a chargeable event occurring at the end of the policy year. The rules described above in relation to the chargeable event code apply to determine to whom the gain accrues and at what rate it is charged. All such gains are deductible as calculation event gains in computing any gain when the policy matures or is subject to a complete surrender or assignment (ITTOIA 2005, s 491(2)). However, such gains are not deducted in determining whether there is an excess (ITTOIA 2005, s 507(4)).

The practical result of these rules is to give personal portfolio bonds an unacceptable tax cost if held by a resident taxpayer or in an offshore trust with a living, resident settlor. Such bonds held by other offshore trusts or in a foreign company or other institution do not suffer the immediate tax cost, but the relevant income under TA 1988, s 740 is disproportionately inflated.

Transitional

72.18 The definition of personal portfolio bond is narrowed in the case of any policy which was issued before 17 March 1998 and has not been varied since 16 July 1998 so as to increase the benefits or extend the term. In such a case, the policy is not a personal portfolio bond if in addition to the range permitted generally it allows self-selection within quoted shares or securities (Personal Portfolio Bonds (Tax) Regulations 1999 (SI 1999/1029), reg 3). A policy which does not meet even this wider rule could be varied so as to come within it before the end of the first policy year beginning after 6 April 1999. But such a variation was only effective if since the inception of the policy or if later since 6 April 1994, the self-selection has in fact been within the investments thereby permitted.

Immigrants

72.19 Personal portfolio bonds may prove to be a trap if held by an immigrant to the UK particularly as policy gains do not attract the remittance basis. A measure of relief is given in that if a variation would have been effective under the transitional rule just described such may be made at any time during the first policy year after immigration (ESC B53).

Index

[*all references are to paragraph number*]

B

E

I

N

V

W

Y